Men of Mark

Officials of Stafford County Virginia

1664–1991

Jerrilynn Eby

HERITAGE BOOKS
2012

HERITAGE BOOKS
AN IMPRINT OF HERITAGE BOOKS, INC.

Books, CDs, and more—Worldwide

For our listing of thousands of titles see our website
at
www.HeritageBooks.com

Published 2012 by
HERITAGE BOOKS, INC.
Publishing Division
100 Railroad Ave. #104
Westminster, Maryland 21157

Copyright © 2006 Jerrilynn Eby

Other Heritage Books by the author:

Laying the Hoe: A Century of Iron Manufacturing in Stafford County, Virginia

Men of Mark: Officials of Stafford County, Virginia, 1664–1991

Stafford County, Virginia Officials, 1664–1991: Taken from the 1783 Records in the Stafford County Courthouse

They Called Stafford Home: The Development of Stafford County, Virginia, from 1600 until 1865

All rights reserved. No part of this book may be reproduced or transmitted in any form or by any means, electronic or mechanical, including photocopying, recording or by any information storage and retrieval system without written permission from the author, except for the inclusion of brief quotations in a review.

International Standard Book Numbers
Paperbound: 978-0-7884-3841-7
Clothbound: 978-0-7884-9205-1

Table of Contents

Acknowledgments	v
Dedication	vii
Introduction	ix
Chapter 1—Burgesses, Senators, and Delegates	1
Chapter 2—Justices of the Peace	25
Chapter 3—Miscellaneous County Officials	101
Chapter 4—Post Offices and Post Masters of Stafford	219
Chapter 5—Business Licenses	251
Index	288

Illustrations

Stafford County Jail, Built 1783	p.34
Stafford County Clerk's Office, Built 1783	p.35
Concord. Home of Charles Waller (1702-1749), justice of the peace, 1745	p.50
Richland. Home of William Brent, Jr. (1783-1848)	p.67
Somerset. Home of William E. Moncure (1824-1888), justice of the peace, 1864	p.82
Wayside. Home of Thomas C. Waller (1832-1895), county treasurer, 1875	p.182
Map of Stafford County Post Offices	p.221
Cropp Post Office	p.223
James Monroe's Store, which housed one of the Hartwood post offices	p.224
Hemp Post Office and Frank Stewart's Store	p.225
Onville Post Office	p.226
Roseville Post Office	p.227
Ruby Post Office	p.227
Wide Water Railroad Station (sketch from a photo dated 1959)	p.229

Cover: Stafford Courthouse and Clerk's Office built 1783

Acknowledgments

Mr. and Mrs. Parran Abell (Stone family)
Gilbert K. Alford, Jr. (Chapman family)
Holt Anderson (Banks family
John I. Bell, Jr. (Bell family)
Elmer Biles (Chapman family)
Elizabeth Braden
Mrs. Reese Carrington (Edrington family)
William T. Cheatham (Edrington family)
Lonnie Chrisman (Hord family)
William Weedon Cloe (Cloe and Weedon families)
H. John Coakley (Coakley family)
Cynthia Crigler (Hedgman family)
Karen Dale (Mason family)
Harold Davey (Peyton family)
William L. Deyo (Cox family)
Elaine Dunaway (Tolson family)
Phyllis Heflin Farmer (Heflin family)
Richard P. Farrow (Farrow family)
Sharyl Ferrall (Hedgman family)
Sally Lou Fitzhugh (Shelkett family)
Jim Fristoe (Fristoe family)
John Cole Goolrick (Goolrick family)
George L. Gordon, Jr.
Mary Lou Greenlaw (Greenlaw family)
Jan Hall (Threlkeld family)
Wally Haynes (Hore family)
Laura Hazel (Fox family)
Marshall Heflin (Heflin family)
Morgan Heflin (Heflin family)
Carroll H. Hendrickson, Jr. (Mason family)
Dudley Herndon (Herndon family)
Elizabeth Herndon (Coakley family)
Robin T. Hite (Strother family)
Delia S. Hord (Hord family)
Joanne J. Hughes (Peyton family)
Patricia D. Johnson
Pearl S. Johnson (Schooler family)
Dr. Stewart Jones (Post offices)
Mary Cary Kendall
Barbara Kirby
Alaric R. MacGregor, III (MacGregor family)
Myrtle MacGregor (Post offices)
Robert McCormick (Hedgman family)
Lyn Matthiesen (Hansbrough family)

Debra Miller (Heflin family)
Scott Moncure
Thomas M. Moncure
Edward Moore (Williams family)
N. Richard Mountjoy (Mountjoy family)
Mildred Musselman (Shelton family)
Anne B. Musser (Hedgman and Triplett families)
Rosalie Nadler (Whitecotton family)
Rosalene Nielsen (Combs family)
Colleen Norman (Norman family)
Larry Norman (Norman family)
Donald Parker (Triplett family)
Frances B. Parkinson (Alexander family)
Clark Powers (Powers family)
Winter Powers (Powers family)
Charles Price (Post offices and cemeteries)
Jeannie Proctor (Hedgman family)
Mr. and Mrs. Thomas Purkins (Gaddis, Greenlaw, Purkins, and Garrard families)
Gordon C. Ralls, Jr. (Ralls family)
Arlene Reid (Post offices)
Sarah Reveley (Reveley/Croughton family)
Stephen L. Ritchie (Ashby family)
Lorann Robinson (Owsley family)
Donald Rodeman (Ford family)
John and Betty Sanford (Stone family)
Malone Schooler (Schooler family)
Kathy Schultz (Carter family)
Mr. and Mrs. John Scott (Post offices)
William G. Scroggins (Bridwell, Edrington, and Reddish families)
Edward D. Sloane, Jr. (James family)
Nancy Southworth (Stone, Moncure, and Adie families)
Jane Cloe Sthreshley (Cloe, Sthreshley, Stark, and Clift families)
George B. Stone (Stone family)
Pat Stone (Latham, Kendall, and Robertson families)
Glen Strock (Peyton family)
James W. Tackitt (Tackett and Burroughs families)
Jim Terry (Ficklen family)
Jim Threlkeld (Threlkeld family)
John A. Washington (Washington and Alexander families

Dedication

For over 57 years, George Loyall Gordon, Jr. served as Commissioner of the Revenue for Stafford County. He has the distinction of being the longest-standing constitutional officer in Virginia's history. When George first took office in July 1942, Stafford was far different from what it is today. The county was rural and most of the population was involved in farming. The majority of the county roads were still unpaved and there was no such thing as county water and sewer. Many families lived with no electricity or telephones and most had no indoor plumbing. The need for expanded training facilities for the Marines engaged in World War II necessitated the condemnation of some 30,000 acres in the north end of the county. Because of this action, in the fall of 1942 hundreds of Stafford residents were displaced and the county lost one-sixth of its acreage and tax base.

George's father, George, Sr., was the last official county surveyor and young George's early years were spent accompanying and assisting his father with surveying duties. This provided him with an opportunity to walk over much of the county and become familiar with the varied terrain. Later, in the 1930s, George was employed building roads in the north end of the county, again adding to his familiarity with the land.

During the early years of his tenure as commissioner, George traveled from country store to country store, filling out tax forms for local residents and collecting money for real estate and personal property taxes. Even after he stopped visiting the stores, he personally traveled from house to house doing real estate and personal property tax assessments. He continued this practice until recent years when the county's population became too large for him to handle the job alone. Over the years, George has walked or driven over nearly every inch of soil in Stafford County. He utilized these opportunities to talk to residents about their family and farm histories. Long fascinated with the county's unrecorded history, he became the "keeper of the knowledge" for Stafford's heritage. As Commissioner of the Revenue he had frequent need to explore chains of title and tax records pertaining to particular tracts of land. Blessed with what I consider a photographic memory, each document and conversation was recorded and filed away in his brain. For nearly sixty years, people with questions about Stafford made pilgrimages to the commissioner's office and sought an audience with this walking compendium.

When I was finally old enough to get a driver's license, it was decided that I would practice driving George around the county to do his tax assessments. That was one of the most enjoyable summers in my memory and I not only learned to drive, but also visited remote parts of Stafford and heard many stories about the county and the people who lived there. As a budding historian, it was an invaluable experience.

One of the greatest blessings in my life was the opportunity and privilege of growing up in the shadow of this remarkable man. George has always been willing to share his wonderful knowledge, but has had no time to write down what he knows. My interest and ability to research, compile, and explain Stafford's history is largely due to George's willingness to share his knowledge with me. For years I have kept a list of "George Questions" to which he still graciously provides answers. Of equal importance to the factual information he provided over the years, George taught me that the interpretation of history is largely based upon perspective. In other words, he taught me to look beyond the facts and dates and seek to understand the "whys" and "hows" of history. One can never fully appreciate historical events if they are viewed through the eyes of the current generation. We tend to color and evaluate these events with our own attitudes and values, many of which were different or entirely absent from the people who were actually involved in the events we wish to understand. He also taught me never to underestimate the practicality of earlier generations. If something occurred in a particular way (even if the means or outcomes appear foolish today), there was a very logical and practical reason behind it. Anyone can discover names, dates, and events. It is up to the historian to place this factual material within a social, political, and economic context that is both interesting and informative to modern readers.

I can think of no better person to whom to dedicate a book on Stafford County officials. George Gordon has devoted his life to Stafford and her residents. He has made an immeasurable difference in my life, enriching it beyond words and helping me discover and share Stafford's rich heritage.

Introduction

The names on the following lists were gleaned from the surviving records of Stafford County as well as from personal papers in family collections, records held by the Library of Virginia and Virginia Historical Society in Richmond, the Fredericksburg Circuit Court, the Huntington Library in San Marino, California, the House of Burgesses and General Court minutes, newspaper articles, and the National Archives. This is an attempt to gather the names of those responsible for the day-to-day functioning of Stafford County and the lists include all government offices for which there was a title. Some of these were elected positions and others were appointments made either by the Governor or by county justices. Known vestries of Overwharton Parish prior to the American Revolution are also included as that body was largely responsible for the social and moral welfare of their parishioners. After the Revolution, these duties passed to the county government.

Because Stafford is a burned record county, gaps in the records are obvious in these lists. The years 1715-1749 and 1794-1829 are particularly sparse as records for those years (and others) were destroyed by courthouse fires and by Union vandals during the War Between the States. Occasionally, a deed from one of the lost books will appear in a private collection from which justices' and clerks' names can be gleaned.

Wherever possible, an attempt has been made to include for each person listed birth and death dates, parents' names and dates, spouses' names and dates, land and personal property tax information, census data, business interests, biographical information, and anecdotal material. Despite all efforts, however, the author was unable to find any supporting material for some of those listed.

The information in this book has been divided into five chapters or lists: Burgesses, Senators, and Delegates; Justices of the Peace; Miscellaneous County Officials; Post Office and Postmasters of Stafford County; Business Licenses. Job descriptions at the beginning of each chapter provide a brief evolutionary narrative of each job from its beginning in colonial Virginia until the present or until the job was no longer necessary and eliminated.

The author hopes that this material will be of interest to those seeking information about ancestors who lived in Stafford and who made important contributions to the county. A great many individuals shared the burden of maintaining the wheels and cogs of county government—from the burgesses who received remuneration for their services to the justices who were responsible for the daily functioning of the county (and did so on a largely volunteer basis), to the overseers of the roads who made valiant efforts to maintain a transportation system in the county. The chapter on post offices provides the names of all known post offices and their postmasters. The locations of these post offices have been marked on a map. The names of the postmasters have been footnoted with biographical material where available. Finally, the names of those receiving business, liquor, or ordinary licenses are listed along with information pertaining to the businesses they kept.

Chapter One
Burgesses, Senators, and Delegates

**The General Assembly and the
House of Burgesses**

When representatives from colonial Virginia's boroughs met in Jamestown in 1619, they were beginning an experiment in self-government that would change the world. What would later become known as the General Assembly was the first democratically elected legislative body to convene in the New World. No other colony had anything like it. There were originally twenty-two burgesses elected from nine plantations and three "cities" that boasted nothing more urban than a small village. How the first burgesses were selected is unknown. Thereafter, they were elected annually. Although the burgesses began meeting in 1619, they were not recognized by the Crown until 1628 and, at least in the beginning, had little authority to make or enforce legislation.

During the first five years of settlement in Virginia, local government was not a problem since all authority and population was concentrated at Jamestown. The population quickly spread until by the mid-18th century the characteristic Virginia plantation dominated the colony. Due largely to economics and geography, there were no dense concentrations of population in 17th century Virginia and large areas of unsettled land remained. Tobacco was the chief crop and planters realized the need for large acreages since continuous cultivation without fertilizer soon exhausted the land. The farmer needed new acres to clear as older fields declined in yield. This wasteful agricultural system resulted in a population thinly spread over a large area.

The population continued to increase and spread and in 1634 the Assembly divided the colony into eight shires (soon to become counties) and county government was born. In 1659, five years before Stafford made its first appearance in colonial records, there were seventeen counties. In 1700 there were twenty and, by the mid-18th century, there were fifty counties in the colony.

The annual coming together of the General Assembly provided the chief opportunity for Virginians to make themselves heard. During these sessions, officials from all parts of the colony met to deliberate in the Assembly, tried causes arising in the court, and socialized in Jamestown's taverns. Members of the Assembly marched ceremoniously through the streets of the tiny town in their finest garb and people came from miles around to watch the excitement. For the English living in the frightening and dangerous wilderness, the continuance of traditional English pomp and ceremony was critical and was one of their few ties to the civilization of their homeland.

In the General Assembly's earliest years, the elected delegate's voice was diminished by the fact that the royal governor and his appointed council sat and voted in one body with the burgesses. In 1651 the Assembly divided into two houses, following the long-established bicameral system enjoyed in England. The upper house or Governor's Council of State, represented the Crown's interests and included the Royal Governor and his appointed representatives. The lower house, or House of Burgesses, included representatives who were popularly elected from the plantations, hundreds, or cities as previously mentioned, and later from the counties that developed from these earlier governmental divisions.

Members of the House of Burgesses were paid, if at all, by their respective counties. This position, like that of justice of the peace, was considered an honorable one in which the holder received his reward in the prestige of his office. The county could pay its burgesses if it wished. By 1674, however, counties were required to pay the expenses of the burgess and his horse while at Jamestown.

After the Revolution, the General Assembly became the House of Delegates and the Virginia State Senate.

Burgesses of Westmoreland County[1]

1654/55	John Holland and Alexander Baynham (died 1662)
1658	Col. Gerard Fowke (1618-1669)[2]
1659/60	Thomas Fowke (died c.1663)[3]
1660/61	Col. Gerard Fowke and Theodorick Bland[4] (1629-1672)
1662	Nicholas Spencer[5] (1638-1689) and John Washington[6] (1632-1677)
1663	Capt. Lee[7] and Col. Gerard Fowke

---

[1] Westmoreland included all that area that later became Stafford.

[2] Also served as captain of the Virginia forces in 1658. On March 23, 1662 Fowke was disenfranchised by the Virginia House of Burgesses and "forever disqualified from holding any office in Virginia." This seeming harsh punishment was for alleged cruelty to the Indians and for disobedience and attitude of contempt toward the burgesses, governor and council. Despite this, he was sworn to "fill a vacancy" at James City in 1663. He moved to Maryland sometime after April 1664. His wife, Anne Chandler (died after 1673) was the daughter of Job Chandler (died c.1659). Col. Fowke died in Maryland. His daughter, Mary, married George Mason (1660-1716) of Stafford.

Col. Fowke was a Gentleman of the Bed Chamber to Charles I and a colonel in the Royal Army. He came to Virginia with his brother Thomas and cousin George Mason (1628-1686). Gerard was the son of Richard Fowke of Gunston Hall and Briarwood, Staffordshire, England. According to notes made c.1910 by Sarah Travers Lewis Anderson, Gerard Fowke (pronounced Fook) "was of fiery disposition by heredity—transmitting the same to his descendants" (Gordon). Richard Fowke settled in Westmoreland County and established a plantation there he called Gunston Hall after his home in England. His son, Gerard, inherited the property upon his father's death. Gerard eventually moved to Port Tobacco in Charles County, Maryland. He sold Gunston Hall to his cousin, George Mason, and it passed through the Mason family to George Mason (IV) (1725-1792) who built the fine brick home there which still stands today.

Gerard Fowke was a colonel in the Westmoreland County militia in 1660. He was one of six gentlemen appointed by Sir William Berkeley to have erected a new Virginia state house after the burning of Jamestown in 1676 at the hands of Nathaniel Bacon. After moving to Maryland, Gerard served in that Assembly in 1664 and was a justice of Charles County from 1667 until his death.

[3] On June 10, 1654 Thomas Fowke, merchant, patented 3,350 acres "in Westmoreland County upon the south side of the Potomac River upon a head of a branch of Potomac Creek." 1,350 acres of this were granted for the transportation of 27 persons including Gerard and Thomas Fowke.

[4] The son of John Bland (died 1632) and Susanna de Deblere. Theodorick was born in London and arrived in Virginia in 1652 to take over management of his father's Virginia estate which had previously been managed by his brother, Edward Bland (1613-1652). In 1656 he moved to Berkeley Hundred, Charles City County. In 1660 he married Anna Bennett, the daughter of Richard Bennett. Five years later, he purchased Westover from Sir John Pawlett for £170. Theodorick's sons, Theodorick (1662-1700) and Richard (1665-1720), inherited the Westover plantation (later the home of the Byrd family of Virginia). Theodorick, Jr. was surveyor of Charles City County in 1680 and of Stafford County in 1691. He was appointed to lay out the town of Williamsburg in 1699.

[5] The son of Nicholas Spencer, Esq. of Cople, Bedfordshire, England. Nicholas came to Virginia in 1659. On April 27. 1699 Nicholas Spencer and Lt. Col. John Washington (1632-1677) received 5,000 acres "lying upon the freshes of Potomack river in the County of Stafford...and near opposite the Piscatoway Indian town in Mariland." This land was separated on the north from the lands of Capt. Giles Brent by Little Hunting Creek (now Fairfax County). Nicholas also served as a justice of Stafford in 1667.

[6] John was born in England and emigrated to Virginia with his wife and two children in 1658. Shortly after settling in Westmoreland County, his wife died. In 1660 he married Ann Pope. He established a plantation he called Wakefield and was the great grandfather of George Washington.

[7] Probably Capt. John Lee (1643-1673), the eldest son of Col. Richard Lee (1618-1664) and Anne Constable (born 1622). John was educated at Oxford where he studied medicine. From his father he inherited the plantation called Machodoc on the Potomac River in Westmoreland County, three islands in

1675/76   John Appleton[8] (1640-1676) and John West

Burgesses of Stafford County[9]

1665	Col. Henry Meese[10] (died 1682)
1666-69	Col. Henry Meese
1675/76	Thomas Mathews[11] and George Mason[12] (1628-1686)
1676-1679	William Fitzhugh[13] (1651-1701)
1680-82	William Fitzhugh, George Mason,[14] and Martin Scarlet[15] (died 1695)
1683	William Fitzhugh
1684	George Mason and William Fitzhugh
1685/86	Samuel Hayward[16] (1640-1696) and Martin Scarlet
1688	George Mason (1660-1716) and George Brent[17] (1640-c.1700)

---

the Chesapeake Bay, slaves, and livestock. He died unmarried. John also served Stafford as a justice in 1667.

[8] John Appleton married Frances Gerrard, widow of Thomas Speake and Col. Valentine Peyton (1629-1665). She married fourthly Col. John Washington (1632-1677).

[9] Stafford County was first mentioned as a separate entity in the House of Burgesses minutes of October 1666 and the earliest surviving court order entries date from May 27, 1664.

[10] Col. Meese settled at what is known today as Waugh Point (King George County), having received on June 7, 1666 a grant for 2,000 acres in Stafford County. Around 1669 he returned to England on business. His successor in the House is unknown. Henry also served Stafford as County Lieutenant in 1665 and was a vestryman of Overwharton Parish in 1667.

[11] Thomas was the son of Samuel Mathews (died 1659) who was governor of Virginia from 1656-1659.

[12] George Mason immigrated to Virginia from Staffordshire, England and settled on Accokeek Creek on a farm that later became known as Rose Hill. It is believed that he was responsible for the naming the new county "Stafford." George also served as a justice of Stafford during the years 1664, 1666-1668, and possibly other years as well.

[13] William Fitzhugh arrive in Virginia c.1676 and settled in what was then Stafford but is now King George County. He established a plantation on the Potomac River that he called Bedford. Fitzhugh was a planter, politician, and attorney. He served in the House of Burgesses, Queen's Counsel, as Lt. Colonel of the Stafford militia and as a justice for Stafford from at least 1683-1691.

[14] George's name appears only in the minutes of the first session.

[15] Name appears only in the minutes of the second session. Scarlet and Fitzhugh were bitter rivals. The election of 1691 was particularly contentious; both men were candidates and Scarlet prevailed. During the campaign, Scarlet publicly attacked Fitzhugh's character. Incensed, Fitzhugh complained to the Stafford court that according to Scarlet, "that neither Law nor Justice had been adm'r'd in the County since I [Fitzhugh] sat upon the Bench for nothing was Law or Justice but what I said was soe." Fitzhugh reminded the court that he had served on the bench since 1683 and had followed George Mason as presiding justice in 1686. He had always polled his colleagues before assuming to speak for them. As a result of Scarlet's accusations, Fitzhugh refused to sit again as justice until Scarlet was punished. Scarlet, also a justice, replied that he had never intended any personal affront to Fitzhugh. It is uncertain if Fitzhugh ever again took his seat on the bench or if Scarlet was punished for his accusations.

Martin, who lived near what is now Occoquan, also served Stafford as sheriff in 1696.

[16] Samuel arrived in Virginia c.1675 and served as clerk of the court in Stafford from at least 1685-1690. He married Mildred Thornton, the daughter of John Thornton (died 1777) of Spotsylvania and Caroline counties.

[17] George was born in Worcestershire, England and was the son of George Brent and Marianna Peyton. Sometime between 1660 and 1663 he emigrated to Maryland, but by 1670 was settled on Aquia Creek. In 1677 he married Elizabeth Greene (c.1655-1686) of Bermuda. In 1687 he married Mary Sewall Chandler (died 1694).

George was a successful lawyer and tobacco planter, raised livestock, and owned a sawmill and ferry. In 1679 he was surveyor of Stafford and by 1687 was also surveyor of Westmoreland County. By

1691/92[18]	George Mason[19] and Martin Scarlet
1692/93	Martin Scarlet and Capt. Thomas Owsley[20] (1658-1700)
1693	George Mason and William Fitzhugh
1695/96	George Mason and Thomas Owsley
1696	Thomas Owsley (April session)[21]
1696/97	George Mason and John Withers
1698	George Mason and Thomas Owsley
1699	George Mason and Rice Hooe[22] (1660-1726)
1700-02	George Mason and William Fitzhugh[23] (c.1678-1713)

1683 George was a law partner with William Fitzhugh (1651-1701). That same year he was appointed receiver general for the area north of the Rappahannock River. He served as acting attorney general of Virginia from the autumn of 1686 until the spring of 1688 when he was elected to the House of Burgesses. He was allowed to take his seat even though he refused to take the anti-Catholic oath. By 1688 anti-Catholic sentiments ended his political career. George was an agent for the Northern Neck proprietors at least through the fall of 1696. At the time of his death he owned over 15,000 acres in Virginia plus land in Maryland and England.

George was the nephew of Giles Brent (1602-1671) and lived at Woodstock, now part of Aquia Harbour subdivision. He resided near the old Brent cemetery on the east side of Telegraph Road (State Route 637). Later Woodstock houses were built on the site of the present Aquia Harbour Country Club. An attorney, George's name appears frequently in the court records of both Stafford and Prince William counties.

[18] During this session, burgesses designated a site on Potomac Creek as the official port of entry for Stafford and ordered that it be called Marlborough. No tobacco was to be exported nor any goods landed at any place except the designated port.

[19] John Withers (1634-1699) replaced Mason in the second session. He lived on Potomac Creek just upstream from Marlborough. He also served Stafford as clerk of the court from at least 1693 until his death in 1699. He was a justice for the county from at least 1686-1692.

[20] Thomas Owsley was the son of the Rev. John Owsley (1635-1687) and Dorothea Poyntz (1631-1705). He was born at Stoke-Coursey, now Stogursey, Somerset County, England and arrived in Virginia in 1677 at the age of 19 to seek his fortune. By 1680 he had settled on Little Hunting Creek and Pohick Bay in what was then Stafford but is now Fort Belvoir in Fairfax County. Shortly thereafter, he became an agent for Cadwallader Jones trading with the Nanticoke Indians as well as with the Piscataways of Maryland and Virginia.

Owsley amassed a considerable fortune in the trading business but the extensive traveling was not without risk. In 1679 he was taken prisoner by Algerian pirates. The villagers of Glooston in the parish of Leicestershire, England, where his father was rector, paid his ransom and he was released.

Thomas was granted extensive acreage in Stafford (at his death he owned over 2,300 acres) and held numerous public positions in the county including captain in the Stafford militia (1692-93), clerk of the court (1680-c.1700), justice (1692-93 and probably other years as well), and burgess 1693-94, 1695-96, and 1698). In 1699 Owsley was appointed major in the Stafford militia, making him second in command to George Mason (1660-1716).

Thomas married Anne Harris and had numerous children, most of whom remained in the Fairfax, Loudoun, and Prince William County area.

[21] Shortly after his election as burgess, Owsley was appointed sheriff of Stafford. The position of sheriff was far more lucrative than that of burgess and, by law, the same man could not fill both seats simultaneously. Martin Scarlet was elected to fill Owsley's seat in the House, but shortly after his election, Scarlet died.

[22] The Rev. John Waugh (1630-1706) was elected but not permitted to serve because he was a minister and it was thought that his primary duty was to his parishioners. A second election placed Rice Hooe in the seat. Rice also served as a justice of Stafford during the years 1699-1703, 1714, and 1726 and probably other years as well.

[23] William was the son of William Fitzhugh (1651-1701) the immigrant. A lawyer, young William came to Virginia c.1670 and settled at Bedford, then Stafford County, now King George. In 1674 he married Sarah Tucker (1663-after 1701), the daughter of John Tucker of Westmoreland County. William also served as sheriff of Stafford in 1707 and as justice for various years between 1700 and 1707.

1702-05	Rice Hooe and Richard Fossaker[24] (1662-c.1735)
1705/06	George Mason and William Fitzhugh
1710-12	George Mason and John Waugh, Jr.[25] (1661-1716)
1712-14	John Waugh, Jr. and Henry Fitzhugh[26] (1687-1758)
1715	George Mason and George Anderson[27]
1718	George Mason[28] (1690-1735) and George Fitzhugh[29] (c.1690-1722)
1720-26	George Mason and Maj. William Robinson[30]
1726-34	John Fitzhugh[31] (died 1733) and ___ Thornton
1736	John Peyton[32] (1691-1760) and Maj. Benjamin Strother[33] (c.1700-1789)
1738-40	Lt. Col. Henry Fitzhugh[34] (1706-1742)
1742-47	Lt. Col. Henry Fitzhugh[35] and Peter Hedgman[36] (c.1700-1765)

---

[24] This Richard Fossaker was the son of Richard Fossaker (died 1676). He married Mary Withers, the widow of Thomas Hathaway of Stafford, making him the husband of the daughter and only heir of Capt. John Withers (1634-1699). In 1694 Richard claimed by right of escheat 400 acres adjoining the Hope Patent on Aquia Creek.

[25] This was the second son of Parson John Waugh (1630-1706). John, Jr. also served as sheriff of Stafford in 1701 and was appointed by the Hon. Robert Carter (1663-1732), Virginia agent for the Proprietors of the Northern Neck, to act as his sub-agent in Stafford County. John also owned land in Prince William, Fairfax, and Fauquier counties. He resided on Potomac Creek on his father's old Waugh Point estate. John married Martha Vandegasteel, widow of Giles Vandegasteel (16_-1701).

[26] Henry was the son of Col. William Fitzhugh (1651-1701) of Bedford and Sarah Tucker (1663-after 1701), the daughter of John Tucker of Westmoreland County. In 1718 Henry married Susanna Cooke (1693-1749), the daughter of Mordecai Cooke of Gloucester County. They resided at his father's estate, Bedford.

[27] George Anderson also served as a justice of Stafford in 1708 and 1714 and probably other years as well. He was sheriff in 1709/10.

[28] This was George Mason (III) who lived at Chappawamsic. He was the father of George Mason (IV) (1725-1792) who built Gunston Hall in Fairfax County and authored the Virginia Declaration of Rights.

[29] George was the son of Col. William Fitzhugh (c.1678-1713). George married Mary (born 1731), the daughter of George Mason (II) (1660-1716). He inherited 5,975 acres of his father's Stafford estate. Mary (Mason) Fitzhugh later married Benjamin Strother (c.1700-1789).

[30] Probably William Robinson (1678-1742). William was born in Yorkshire, England and resided in Richmond County, Virginia near Leedstown. In 1707 Robinson patented 3,036 acres on the north side of Aquia Creek and in 1723 and 1729 he paid quit rents on 2,276 acres in northern Stafford. This land is now part of the Marine Corps reservation.

[31] John died before the opening of the fourth session. It is unknown which Thornton replaced him.

[32] John Peyton lived at Stony Hill, which is now part of Aquia Harbour subdivision. He was the son of Henry and Anne Peyton. John's first wife was Anne Waye (1731-1750) by whom he had six children. He married secondly Elizabeth (Rowzee) Waller (c.1715-1782), the widow of Charles Waller (1702-1749) of Essex and Stafford counties. Elizabeth outlived John Peyton and married Maj. Benjamin Strother (c.1700-1789).

[33] In 1757 Benjamin served as vestryman of Overwharton Parish. In 1741 he patented 419 acres on the branches of Aquia Creek near modern Coal Landing. He was the son of Capt. William Strother (c.1665-1726) and Margaret Thornton of King George and the brother of William Strother (c.1696-1733). Benjamin married first c.1726 Mary (Mason) Fitzhugh, widow of George Fitzhugh (c.1690-1722) and daughter of George Mason (1660-1716). He married secondly in 1760 Elizabeth (Rowzee) Waller Peyton (c.1715-1782), the widow of Charles Waller (17_-c.1750) and John Peyton (1691-1760). Benjamin was also the brother of Anthony Strother (1710-1765) who married Behethland Storke (1716-1753). She was the elder sister of Catherine (Storke) Washington (born 1723) who married Bailey Washington, Sr. (1731-1807) of Windsor Forest.

[34] Henry was the son of Col. William Fitzhugh (c.1678-1713) of Eagle's Nest and Ann Lee (1683-1732), the daughter of the Hon. Richard Lee (1647-1715). Henry attained the rank of Lt. Colonel in the Stafford militia. He married Lucy (1715-1763), the daughter of the Hon. Robert Carter (1663-1732) of Corotoman in Lancaster County.

[35] Henry died in 1742 and was replaced by James Waugh (c.1705-1750).

1748/49	William Fitzhugh[37] (1721-1798) and Peter Hedgman
1751	William Fitzhugh
1752-56	William Fitzhugh and Peter Hedgman
1757/58	John Peyton and Maj. Benjamin Strother
1759/60	Thomas Ludwell Lee[38] (1730-1778) and Thomson Mason[39] (1733-1785)
1761-65	William Fitzhugh[40] and Thomas Ludwell Lee[41]
1766-71	John Alexander[42] (1735-1775) and Thomson Mason[43]
1772	John Alexander and Yelverton Peyton[44] (1735-1794)
1773/74	John Alexander[45] and Charles Carter[46] (1738-1796)

---

[36] Peter was the son of Nathaniel Hedgman (before 1682-1721) and his wife Catherine (before 1687-after 1708) who bought George Mason's (1628-1686) Accokeek Run property in 1707. Robert "King" Carter (1663-1732) sent Nathaniel from Lancaster County to be overseer on Carter's Stafford plantations. He met with a violent death and earned the disdain of Col. Carter. The latter wrote of his overseer, "I have heard of late he hath been a very great delinquent from my business and lived a loose, rebelling life, which hath brought him to his untimely catastrophe. As for entertaining his son, a wild young land that hath no experience in the world, I can by no means think proper." Peter was trained in the law and was one of the Crown Commissioners for the location of the Northern Neck boundary in 1746. In 1749 Peter was appointed trustee for the new town of Dumfries in Prince William County. He also served Stafford as a justice in 1729, 1733, 1735, 1744, 1745 and probably other years as well. He served as burgess of Prince William from 1732-1740. In 1721 Peter married Margaret Mauzy (1702-1754), the daughter of his Potomac Creek neighbor John Mauzy (c.1675-1718). They had Nathaniel (born 1729), William (1732-1768), George (1734-1760), and John (1741-c.1764).

[37] William was the son of George Fitzhugh (c.1690-1722) and Mary Mason. He married first Martha (Lee) Turberville (1716-1751), widow of Maj. George Turberville (1694-1742) of Westmoreland County and secondly in 1752 Ann (Frisby) Rousby (1727-1793), the daughter of Peregrine Frisby (1688-1738) and widow of John Rousby (1721-1751) of Maryland. William was a close friend of George Washington and, after his second marriage, removed to Maryland.

[38] Thomas much preferred the solitude of remote Stafford County to the busy atmosphere of Westmoreland and made his home at Bell View, land inherited from his father. Bell View was on the south side of Potomac Creek adjoining Belle Plain. Thomas was born at Stratford Hall in Westmoreland County and was the son of Thomas Lee (1690-1750) and Hannah Ludwell (1701-1750). His brothers were Francis Lightfoot (1743-1797) and Richard Henry Lee (1732-1794), signers of the Declaration of Independence, and Philip Ludwell Lee (1726/7-1775). According to a letter written by brother Richard Henry, Thomas died "after sustaining a severe Rheumatic fever for six weeks." At the time of his death, he had just been appointed one of five judges of the General Court. John Adams described him as "the most popular man in Virginia, and the delight of the eyes of every Virginian, but...[he] would not engage in public life." The Lee family, however, saw public service as a duty and Thomas held numerous public offices including justice of Stafford County. He was also a frequent member of the Assembly and its conventions.

[39] Thomson was the son of George Mason (1690-1735) and Ann Thomson (died 1762) of Chappawamsic. Thomson studied law at William and Mary and practiced in Dumfries. His brother, George Mason (1725-1792) authored the Virginia Declaration of Rights and built Gunston Hall in Fairfax County.

[40] The minutes do not indicate that Fitzhugh was present during the 1763 session.

[41] The minutes do not indicate that Mason was present during the November 1762 session.

[42] John was the son of Philip Alexander (1704-1753) and Sarah Hooe. In 1756 he married Lucy Thornton.

[43] The minutes do not indicate that Thomson was present during the 1770 and 1771 sessions.

[44] Yelverton was the son of John Peyton (1691-1760) of Stony Hill. He married Elizabeth Heath and operated Peyton's Ordinary which was probably located in Aquia Harbour behind Aquia Church.

[45] The minutes do not indicate that Alexander was present during the 1774 session.

[46] Known as Charles Carter of Ludlow, he was the son of Charles Carter (1704-1764) of Stanstead and Cleve and his first wife, Mary Walker. Around 1755 Charles, Jr. married Elizabeth Chiswell (1737-1804), the daughter of Col. John Chiswell (c.1715-1766) and Elizabeth Randolph (1715-1776). The minutes do not indicate that Carter was present during the 1774 session.

Charles, Sr. devised to his son the "Ship Tavern Lott, now in the Possession or Occupation of my said Son Charles, by virtue of an Assignment of William Cunningham, and John Knox by under Tenants."

1775   Charles Carter, John Alexander, and Thomas Ludwell Lee[47]

When the House of Burgesses was temporarily dissolved in 1774, members met in the first revolutionary convention of Virginia. There they elected delegates to the First Continental Congress of the Revolutionary War which met in Philadelphia.

First Virginia Convention—Met in Williamsburg August 1-6, 1774. Members adopted an association based on the Fairfax County Resolves forbidding the importation of English slaves or goods after Nov. 1, 1774 and the export of goods to Britain after Aug. 10, 1775. They also chose Virginia's delegation to the First Continental Congress. The Stafford representatives at the First Virginia Convention were John Alexander and Charles Carter.

Second Virginia Convention—Met at St. John's Church, Richmond, Mar. 20-27, 1775. Members chose delegates for the Second Continental Congress and authorized the arming of militias within each county for the defense of the colony. It was at this meeting that Patrick Henry gave his famous "Give Me Liberty or Give Me Death" speech. At the Second Continental Congress the delegates chose George Washington as commander in chief of the American troops. The Stafford representatives at the Second Virginia Convention were John Alexander and Charles Carter.

Third Virginia Convention—Met from July 17 to Aug. 26, 1775. Members provided for the annual election of delegates, established a Committee of Safety to act as an executive body between sessions, ordered the recruitment of two regiments of regular soldiers and sixteen battalions of minutemen, and revived the dormant militia. The Stafford representatives at the Third Convention were Charles Carter and Thomas Ludwell Lee.

Fourth Virginia Convention—Met from Dec. 1, 1775 to Jan. 20, 1776. The Stafford representatives at the Fourth Convention were Charles Carter and Thomas Ludwell Lee.

Fifth Virginia Convention—Met from May 6 to July 5, 1776. The Stafford representatives were William Brent (1733-1782) and Thomas Ludwell Lee.

The Virginia State Constitution was adopted on June 29, 1776 and redesigned the General Assembly to include the House of Delegates and Senate. The House of Delegates was to consist of two representatives from each county who would be chosen annually. The 24 members of the Senate served four-year terms and were elected by districts.

Charles, Jr. also inherited from his father "three Tun Tavern, in the Town of Falmouth" (King George Will Book 1, p. 169).
[47] John Alexander died before the session began and was succeeded by Lee.

General Assembly
House of Delegates

1776	Charles Carter (1738-1796) and William Brent[48] (1733-1782)
1777/78	Charles Carter and William Fitzhugh[49] (1741-1809)
1778	Charles Carter and William Brent
1779	Charles Carter[50] and James Garrard[51] (1749-1822)
1780/81	Bailey Washington[52] and William Fitzhugh
1781/82	Thomas Mountjoy[53] (born 1740)
1782	John Francis Mercer[54] (1759-1821) and Charles Carter

---

[48] William was the son of Capt. William Brent (1710-1742) and his wife Jane. Around 1754 he married Eleanor Carroll (born c.1737) of Maryland. He inherited thousands of acres in Stafford, Prince William, King George, and Westmoreland counties as well as in Maryland. He was noted for his breeding and racing of fine Thoroughbred horses.

In May 1757 William became a justice for Stafford but in October 1765 he resigned to protest the Stamp Act. The resignation was short-lived and he served as a justice until his death. In 1774 he was elected to the Stafford County Committee to enforce the nonimportation associations enacted by the Virginia Revolutionary Conventions and the Continental Congress. In 1776 he was elected one of two delegates to the last Revolutionary Convention. On July 23 of that year a raiding party from the HMS *Roebuck* landed and burned Richland, his fine brick house on the Potomac River. He rebuilt his home and it survives today. William served in the House of Delegates in 1776 and 1778 during which sessions he sat on the powerful Committee of Propositions and Grievances. In 1780 he was elected to the Virginia Senate to represent King George, Stafford, and Westmoreland counties.

[49] This was William Fitzhugh of Chatham, the son of Henry Fitzhugh (1706-1742) of Eagle's Nest and Lucy Carter, the daughter of Robert Carter (1663-1732) of Corotoman. William was known as a man of high character and influence. From 1772-1775 he represented King George County in the House of Burgesses. He was a member of the conventions of March, July, and December 1775 and of 1776; was a member of the King George Committee of Safety 1774-1775; represented Virginia at the Continental Congress 1779-1780. William was known as a breeder of fine Thoroughbred racehorses that he raced in Fredericksburg, Annapolis, and Upper Marlborough. He owned the estates of Eagle's Nest and Somerset in King George, Chatham in Stafford, and Ravensworth in Fairfax County. In 1763 he married Mary Anne "Nancy" (1747-1805), the daughter of Peter Randolph (1717-1767) of Chatsworth, Henrico County.

[50] Carter became sheriff of Stafford and a new election was held on October 13.

[51] James was the son of Col. William Garrard (c.1715-c.1786) and his second wife, Mary Naughty (born c.1721). William owned Garrard's Ordinary which was located on the site of the present Stafford County School Board offices at the intersection of Hope Road (State Route 687) and U. S. Route 1. James resided on Hampstead, his farm on Poplar Road (State Route 616) in Hartwood. During the Revolution, James served as a captain in the Stafford militia (1776-1777). He removed to Kentucky in 1783 and served as the second governor of that state from 1796-1804.

[52] It is uncertain whether this was Bailey Washington Sr. (1731-1807) or his son Bailey (1753-1814), both of whom resided at Windsor Forest. Bailey, Sr. served as a justice for Stafford in 1779 but does not appear to have done so in 1780 or 1781. It is possible, therefore, that the Bailey Washington listed here was Bailey, Sr.

[53] Thomas was the son of Capt. William Mountjoy (1711-1777) of Locust Hill on Potomac Creek and his wife, Phillis Reilly (1717-1771). In 1772 Thomas served with Col. William Garrard (c.1715-c.1786) as inspector of tobacco at Cave's Warehouse on the south side of Potomac Creek, just upstream from Belle Plain.

[54] The son of John Mercer (1704-1768) of Marlborough and his wife, Ann Roy (c.1729-1770). He received his early education at home and graduated from William and Mary in 1775. He began practicing law in Williamsburg in 1781. During the Revolution, John Francis was a quarter master in the militia and a first lieutenant in the 3rd Virginia Regiment. In 1777 he was promoted to captain and was an aide-de-camp to Gen. Charles Lee (1731-1782).

In 1785 he moved to West River in Anne Arundel County, Maryland where he resided at Cedar Park. John represented Maryland at the Federal Convention in Philadelphia, but left before signing the

1783	Charles Carter and Thomson Mason
1784/85	Bailey Washington, Jr.[55] (1753-1814) and William Brent
1785/86	Col. William Garrard (c.1715-1814) and John Francis Mercer
1786/87	Andrew Buchanan[56] (died 1804) and Gustavus Brown Wallace[57] (1751-1802)
1787/88	Bailey Washington, Jr. and William Fitzhugh
1788	Richard Brent[58] (c.1760-1814) and Andrew Buchanan

The Convention of 1788 met in Richmond from June 2-27, 1788 to discuss the new United States Constitution. When it ratified the Constitution on June 26 of that year, Virginia became the tenth state to enter the Union. The Stafford representatives to the Convention of 1788 were George Mason (1725-1792) and Andrew Buchanan.

1789	Andrew Buchanan and George Brent[59] (1760-1804)
1790	Andrew Buchanan and Travers Daniel, Jr.[60] (1763-1813)

Constitution. He served as governor of Maryland from 1801-1803 and died in Philadelphia. He was buried at Cedar Park. John married Sophia Sprigg (born 1766).

[55] The son of Bailey Washington, Sr. and Catherine Storke of Windsor Forest. Bailey married Euphan Wallace (1765-1845), the daughter of James Wallace and Elizabeth Westwood (died 1824). She married secondly Daniel Carroll Brent (1759-1814).

[56] Andrew Buchanan was a Scots merchant of Falmouth and was the likely builder of Clearview. He was one of those named in a lawsuit of 1797 styled "Justices vs Hunter &c" in which the justices of Stafford County sued Adam Hunter, John Strode, Charles Carter, William Fitzhugh, and Andrew Buchanan for £100,000. Adam Hunter was one of the executors of James Hunter's estate. The other four men were standing as security for the executors. The justices claimed that a debt due by judgment of the Fredericksburg Circuit Court had not been paid and those men acting as security had never actually put up their bonds. The record of this case remains on file in Fredericksburg. During the Revolution, Andrew served as a major in the Virginia militia (1776-78).

[57] Gustavus was the son of Dr. Michael Wallace (1719-1767) and Elizabeth Brown (born 1723) of Ellerslie. During the Revolution, Gustavus served as captain of the 3rd Virginia regiment, February 1776. In March 1778 he was promoted to lieutenant colonel of the 15th Virginia. He was taken prisoner at Charleston in May 1780, released, transferred to the 2nd Virginia regiment in February 1781, and served to the close of the war.

Returning from a business trip to Scotland in 1802, Gustavus contracted typhus. As his ship passed the mouth of Potomac Creek, the captain put him off the boat on the shore of Crow's Nest. Servants found him and took him to Fredericksburg where there was a doctor. He died several days later and was buried in the Masonic Cemetery in Fredericksburg.

[58] Richard was the son of Col. William Brent (1733-1782) of Richland. Little is known of his education except that he studied law and read extensively. In 1782 he inherited 1/3 of his father's land, including all his property in King George. Richard resided in Prince William County from 1793-1794. While a delegate for Stafford, he sat on the Committees for Courts of Justice and of Privileges and Elections. During the 1793-94 session, he served on the Committees of Claims, Courts and Justice, and Propositions and Grievances. Sometime between 1803 and 1808 he gave up his law practice and spent his time running his plantations. In 1808 he was elected to the Virginia Senate and represented the counties of Fairfax and Prince William. In 1809 he was elected t the United States Senate and served until his death. He died unmarried. Richard Brent was distinguished for his eloquence.

[59] George Brent was born at Woodstock, the son of Robert Brent (c.1730-1780) and Anne Carroll (1733-1804). George married in 1785 Molly Fitzhugh, the daughter of William Fitzhugh (1725-1791) of Marmion in King George County. George was a lieutenant in the cavalry in the Virginia Line during the Revolution and was present at the siege of Yorktown. He was also a colonel in the Stafford militia. In 1792 50 acres of his Woodstock plantation were taken for the town of Woodstock (also called Aquia), to be laid off in ½ acre lots.

[60] The son of Travers Daniel, Sr. (1741-1824) and Frances Moncure (born 1745), the daughter of the Rev. John Moncure (1710-1764) of Clermont. The Daniel family owned Crow's Nest, a large plantation on the north side of Potomac Creek. Travers, Jr. married Mildred Stone (1772-1837) of Maryland. Travers and

1791	Travers Daniel, Jr. and Robert Mercer[61] (1764-1799)
1792	Travers Daniel, Jr. and Nathaniel Fox[62] (1748-1819)
1793	Travers Daniel, Jr. and William Alexander[63] (1744-1837)
1794	William Alexander and Nathaniel Fox
1795	Andrew Buchanan and Nathaniel Fox
1796	Daniel Carroll Brent[64] (1759-1814) and Nathaniel Fox
1797/98	John Moncure[65] (1772-1822) and Nathaniel Fox
1798/99	John Fox[66] (c.1770-1843) and Nathaniel Fox
1799-1801	Daniel Carroll Brent and Nathaniel Fox[67]
1801-03	John Moncure and Nathaniel Fox
1803-05	Hancock Eustace[68] (1768-1829) and Nathaniel Fox
1805-07	John Moncure and John Taliaferro Brooke (c.1763-1821)
1807/08	Col. Enoch Mason[69] (c.1769-1828) and John T. Brooke

---

Mildred settled on Mt. Pleasant, part of his father's Crow's Nest tract. Like his father, Travers, Jr. was very involved in county affairs, holding numerous public offices.

[61] Robert was the son of John Mercer (1704-1768) of Marlborough. In 1792 Robert married Mildred Ann Byrd Carter (1774-1837), the daughter of Landon Carter (1751-1811) of Cleve, King George County. In February 1799 he commenced the publication of a Republican newspaper, *The Genius of Freedom*. He died on Sept. 11 of that same year.

[62] Nathaniel was born in King William County, the son of Thomas Fox (c.1710-1792) and Philadelphia Claiborne (died before 1765). He married Sarah Newton, the daughter of Maj. William Newton and Elizabeth Kenyon. Nathaniel was commissioned as a first lieutenant in the 6th Virginia Regiment on Feb. 16, 1776 and was promoted to captain on May 30 of that year. He was wounded at the Battle of Brandywine and retired from service as a major on Sept. 30, 1778. In 1782 Nathaniel served as one of the first commissioners of the land tax and in 1784 was deputy sheriff of Stafford. From 1806-1809 he was a justice of the peace for the county. He died in Stafford at the age of 71.

[63] Probably William A. Alexander, the son of Philip Alexander (1704-1753) and Sarah Hooe. William was born in Prince William County. In 1765 he married in Stafford Sigismunda Mary Massey (born 1745) and at about that time built a large mansion on the west side of Dumfries. During the Revolution, he served as a colonel.

[64] Daniel was the son of William Brent (1733-1782) and Eleanor Carroll. He was born at Richland in Stafford and in 1782 married Anne Fenton Lee, the daughter of Thomas Ludwell Lee (1730-1778) and Mary Aylett of Bell View and Berry Hill. Daniel married secondly Mrs. Euphan Wallace Washington, the daughter of James Wallace and Elizabeth Westwood and the widow of Bailey Washington, Jr. (1753-1814).

For many years Daniel was in partnership with his neighbor and dear friend, Col. John Cooke (1755-1828) of West Farm on the Potomac River. The two men operated under the firm names of Brent & Cooke and Cooke & Brent. According to records in the Fredericksburg Circuit Court ("Cooke vs Green"), Daniel and John were engaged as early as 1799 with Benjamin Adie in a distillery business. From 1796 until Brent's death in 1815, they operated one of the sandstone quarries on Aquia Creek. From 1806-1810 they also shared a partnership in the milling business (at Brent's Mill in Wide Water) and kept a store and blacksmith shop there.

[65] John was the son of John Moncure (II) (1747-1784) and was born at Dipple on Chappawamsic Creek. He inherited Clermont from his father and lived much of his life there though he was buried at Dipple (the Dipple graves were moved to Aquia Church in 1942). Around 1770 John married Anne Conway (born c.1750), the daughter of George Conway (died 1754) of Wicomico and his wife Anne Heath (born 1721).

[66] John was the younger half brother of Nathaniel Fox. He married Nancy "Ann" Threlkeld (1772-1828), the daughter of Col. Elijah Threlkeld (1744-1798) of Coal Trips, Aquia Creek.

[67] The 1800 personal property tax records list Nathaniel as owning 7 slaves and 5 horses in Stafford.

[68] Hancock was the son of Isaac Eustace (died 1795) and Agatha Conway (1740-1826). Prior to his death, Isaac divided his Stafford lands between his two sons, Hancock and William. Hancock received that part of the property that included Isaac's home. At some point this property acquired the name of Woodford. In 1789 Hancock married Tabitha Henry (died c.1840), the daughter of the Hon. James Henry (1731-1804) of Fleet's Bay. Hancock also served as a justice in Stafford.

[69] Enoch was the grandson of George Mason (16_-c.1729) of Aquia. He owned some 2,461 acres in Stafford and lived at Clover Hill in the Roseville area of Stafford. His plantation includes what is now

1808/09	John Moncure and Peter Vivian Daniel[70] (1784-1860)
1809/10	Peter V. Daniel and William Brent[71] (1783-1848)
1811/12	William Henry Fitzhugh[72] (1788-1859) and Charles Julian[73] (1774-1837)
1812/13	William H. Fitzhugh and Daniel Carroll Brent[74]
1813-16	William H. Fitzhugh and Hancock Eustace
1816/17	Alexander Fontaine Rose[75] (1780-1831) and Hancock Eustace
1817/18	George Banks[76] (1779-1837) and Benjamin Ficklen[77] (died 1821)
1818/19	John Moncure and Benjamin Ficklen
1819/20	Benjamin Ficklen, Jones Green[78] (1794-1858) and George Waller[79] (1787-before

---

Roseville Plantation subdivision. Enoch held several official positions in the county, including justice. In 1796 he married Lucy Wiley Roy (died c.1835), the daughter of Wiley Roy (1749-1816) and Sarah Fowke (1748-1821) of King George.

[70] Peter was the son of Travers Daniel, Jr. (1763-1813) and Mildred Stone (1772-1837). He was admitted to the Virginia Bar in 1808 and was only 25 years old when he was elected to the General Assembly. In 1812 he was elected to the Privy Council of Virginia where he served until 1835. Six years later he was elected Lieutenant Governor. Peter sat on the bench of the District Court for Eastern Virginia and, in 1841, was appointed to the United States Supreme Court, the fourth Associate Justice from Virginia. He held this position for 18 years. Peter lived in Richmond for much of his life.

[71] William Brent, Jr. was the son of Daniel Carroll Brent (1759-1814) and Anne Fenton Lee and was a grandson of William Brent (1733-1782) and his wife, Eleanor Carroll. In 1810 he married first Winifred Beale Lee (1790-1833), the daughter of Col. Thomas Ludwell Lee (1751-1807) and Frances Carter of Coton, Loudoun County. William married secondly Roxanna Sommers (1798-1882). In addition to holding public office in Stafford, from 1844-1846 William served as Charge d'Affaires to Buenos Aires. William, Jr. was the last Brent to live at Richland.

[72] William was the son of Thomas Fitzhugh (1760-1820) of Boscobel. When William came of age, his father gave him the old Mason plantation, Chappawamsic, where William made his home for many years. He was very involved in Stafford affairs and served as a justice for the county from 1842-1844. In 1814 he married Eliza Churchill Darby, the daughter of John Darby and Lucy Harrison Churchill. William served as company captain in the War of 1812.

[73] Charles was the son of John Julian (c.1738-c.1787) and Margaret Isabelle Lounds of Scotland. He was born in Fredericksburg and in 1797 married Jane Moor (1777-1851), the daughter of Edward Moor (died c.1806) and Ellen McDonald. He died in Franklin County, Kentucky.

[74] In 1812 Daniel paid taxes on Richland (3,184 acres) and 47 slaves.

[75] Alexander was a French Huguenot descendant and was born in Amherst County, Virginia. He spent much of his early life in New York where many of the Rose family had settled. In 1814 he purchased Hampstead where he lived with his wife, Sarah Rose Fontaine (1796-1863), the daughter of William and Ann (Morris) Fontaine. Alexander was a highly successful attorney and owned extensive acreage in Stafford, Nelson, Fauquier, Hanover, and Albemarle counties as well as in Fredericksburg and in the new state of Kentucky. He was also a merchant in Fredericksburg where he was in business with Presley Thornton (1730-1812).

[76] George was the son of Gerard Banks (1725-1787) and Frances Bruce of Greenbank in lower Stafford County. He was also a great great grandson of Adam Banks (died before 1690), the immigrant. Adam first appeared in the local records in 1674 when he received a deed from William Heabeard for land "in the forest of Pasbitanzy" between the Potomac and Rappahannock rivers (Greenbank). Though George was the youngest son, he inherited Greenbank from his father. He married Jemima Anne Overton (1789-1863).

[77] Benjamin was the son of Anthony Strother Ficklen (died 1844). In 1787 he married Susannah Foushee. Benjamin's obituary appeared in the Oct. 15, 1821 issue of *The Compiler*, a Richmond newspaper.

[78] Jones Green was disqualified because he refused to take the oath required by the anti-dueling act. He was succeeded by George Waller.

Jones was the son of Capt. James Green and Betsy Jones and the grandson of Robert Green who emigrated from Ireland in 1710. In 1821 Jones married Susanna Elizabeth Margaret Scott (1800-1844) in Fredericksburg. For part of his life, Jones lived at Greenock, Culpeper County, this home being named after his father-in-law's estate in Scotland. Around 1819 he moved to Falmouth where he purchased several lots. He was the president of Fauquier White Sulphur Springs Company in Fauquier County.

[79] The son of William Waller (1740-1817) of Concord. Little is known of him.

	1856)
1820/21	George Waller and Alexander F. Rose
1821/22	George Waller and John Mason[80] (1764-1824)
1822-24	Walter Raleigh Daniel[81] (1783-1818) and John Mason
1824/25	Walter R. Daniel and George Mason Cooke[82] (1792-1866)
1825-27	Thomas Gaskins Moncure[83] (1799-1836) and George M. Cooke
1827/28	Richard Cassius Lee Moncure[84] (1805-1882) and George M. Cooke
1828/29	George M. Cooke, R. C. L. Moncure, and William Ford[85] (1788-1834)
1829/30	George M. Cooke and Thomas G. Moncure
1830-32	Thomas G. Moncure
1832/33	Walker Peyton Conway[86] (1805-1884)
1833/34	John Rose Fitzhugh[87] (c.1795-after 1860)
1834-37	John Moncure[88] (1793-1876)
1838	James Waller Ford[89] (1791-1865)
1839-41	Dr. Alexander Fitzhugh[90] (1786-1847)
1841/42	James W. Ford

[80] John was the son of George Mason (1725-1792) of Gunston Hall. He married Anna Maria Murray.

[81] Walter was the son of Travers Daniel, Sr. (1741-1824) and Frances Moncure (born 1745) of Crow's Nest. He married Elizabeth Lewis, the daughter of Dr. Richmond Lewis (1774-1831) of Bel-Air, Spotsylvania County. In 1813 and 1814 Walter served as sergeant of Capt. Fitzhugh's Company, 45th Virginia Regiment. Walter was buried at Bel-Air.

[82] George was the son of Col. John Cooke (1755-1819) of West Farm and Mary Thomson Mason (born 1762). He had business interests with his father in farming, timbering, and fishing as well as in one of the sandstone quarries on Aquia Creek. In 1818/19 George built Chelsea, a fine frame home in the Wide Water area of Stafford. He suffered from financial difficulties, tried his hand at gold mining in Goochland County, and finally returned to Stafford where he lived at Woodford.

[83] Thomas was the son of John Moncure (1772-1822) and Alice Peachy Gaskins (1774-1860). He married first in 1823 Clarissa Bernard Hooe (1800-1829) and secondly Mary Bell Haxall. He was also a vestryman of Aquia Church.

[84] Richard was the son of John Moncure (1772-1822). He was born at Clermont on Chappawamsic Creek. In 1825 Richard married Mary Butler Washington Conway (born 1807), the daughter of John Moncure Conway (1779-1864) and Catherine Storke Peyton (1786-1865). R. C. L. bought Glencairne on the west side of U. S. Route 1 just to the north of Falmouth. He made major improvements to the house and raised high quality cattle there. For some 40 years he was a vestryman of St. George's Parish, Fredericksburg. From 1852-1864 he served as presiding judge of the Virginia Court of Appeals.

[85] R. C. L. Moncure was disqualified after he accepted the office of attorney to the superior court. William Ford succeeded. William was the son of James Ford (died 1794) and Elizabeth Taylor. In 1817 he married Elizabeth Allen Hore (1791-1822), the daughter of Elias Hore (1749-1832) and Theodosia Waller (1753-1829).

[86] Walker was the son of John Moncure Conway (1779-1864) and Catherine Storke Peyton (1786-1865). He married Margaret Eleanor Daniel (1807-1891), the daughter of Dr. John Moncure Daniel (1769-1813). For many years Walker served as presiding justice in the Stafford Court.

[87] The son of Thomas Fitzhugh (1760-1820) of Boscobel and Anne Rose (born 1763).

[88] The son of John Moncure (III) (1772-1822) and Alice Peachy Gaskins (1774-1860), the daughter of Col. Thomas Gaskins and Hannah Hull of Northumberland County. John was born at Clermont and died at Woodbourne, part of the old Accokeek Iron Furnace tract. He married first in 1818 Esther Vowles (1795-1833), the daughter of Col. Henry Vowles (Vowells) (1752-c.1803) of Falmouth. He married secondly in 1834 Frances Daniel (1797-1871), the daughter of Travers Daniel, Jr. (1763-1812) and Mildred Stone (1772-1837). In 1833 John founded the Fredericksburg and Falmouth Marine and Fire Insurance Company. He was a presidential elector for Virginia in 1837 voting for Van Buren. He served in John Catesby Edrington's Company, 45th Virginia Regiment during the War of 1812.

[89] Probably the son of James Ford (1768-1863) and Elizabeth Taylor. The 1860 Stafford census lists James with $20,000 in personal property.

[90] The son of Thomas Fitzhugh (1760-1820) of Boscobel. Alexander was born at Boscobel and in 1815 married Eliza Gibbs Clare of Clarke County.

1842-45	John Grayson Hedgman[91] (1782-c.1845)
1845/46	John LeRoy Chinn[92] (1795-1854)
1846/47	Edmund C. Fitzhugh[93] (died 1883)
1847-49	R. C. L. Moncure
1849-51	Charles Francis Suttle[94] (born 1807)
1852-54	William Hand Brown[95] (died 1852)
1855-60	John Seddon[96] (1826-1863)

The Convention of 1861 met in Richmond from Feb. 13, to Dec. 6, 1861. Members adopted the Ordinance of Secession of Apr. 17, 1861 and joined the newly formed Confederate States of America. Two representatives from Stafford attended this convention, though only one name is known, Edward Waller[97] (1805-1883).

1861/62	Dr. John Henry Moncure Daniel[98] (born 1813)

---

[91] John was the son of John Hedgman (1758-1796) and Catherine Grayson (1760-1795). He married his cousin, Hannah Ball (Daniel) Brown (born 1780), the daughter of Travers Daniel, Sr. (1741-1824) and the widow of Raleigh Travers Brown, Jr. He was a veteran of the War of 1812.

[92] John was the son of Joseph Chinn (1768-1803) and Elizabeth Griffin (born 1773) and was born in Lancaster County. He married Lucy Leland.

[93] Edmund was the son of Dr. Alexander Fitzhugh (1786-1847) and Eliza Gibbs Clare. Edmund married first Cora Bowie of Maryland and secondly his first cousin, Nannie Grayson. Edmund moved to California in 1849 where he served as a judge in the Washington Territory. He returned to Virginia in 1862 and was appointed an officer on the staff of Gen. George E. Pickett. Edmund survived the war and returned to California where he died.

[94] Charles Suttle was a merchant in Alexandria, though he lived for some years in Stafford County. Charles is perhaps best remembered as being the owner of Anthony Burns (1834-1862), the fugitive slave whose arrest in Boston inflamed the city and strengthened the abolitionist movement.

As a young man Anthony was sent to work in Richmond, for which Suttle was to be paid. In February 1854 Anthony managed to escape Richmond on board a ship on which he had a friend. He was carried north to Boston where, shortly after his arrival, he was arrested on a charge of theft. On May 27, 1854 the court determined that the Fugitive Slave Law required Anthony's return to his owner, Charles Suttle. Burns' arrest and the judge's decision so angered residents of Boston that there were riots in the streets. After Anthony returned to Virginia, Suttle sold him. This new master, in turn, sold him to a group in Boston who set him free.

Anthony was converted to the Baptist faith while a youth, probably at Chappawamsic Baptist Church, and was a "slave preacher." After gaining his freedom, he studied theology at Oberlin College and, for a short time in 1860, was pastor of a Baptist church in Indianapolis. Anti-Black sentiment there soon forced him to leave. He moved to Canada where he preached at Zion Baptist Church in St. Catherine's. Anthony Burns died in Canada.

[95] Now representing Stafford and King George counties. In 1852 William died of consumption in Washington. He was buried in the Fredericksburg Cemetery.

[96] John Seddon lived at Snowden, a plantation located a few miles east of Fredericksburg on the Rappahannock River. He was the son of Thomas Seddon, Jr. (1779-1831) and Susan Pearson Alexander (died 1845) and the grandson of Thomas Seddon (1696-1779), the immigrant. In 1848 John married Mary Alexander Little, the daughter of John P. Little of Fredericksburg. A Presbyterian, John took great interest in the girls' orphanage in Fredericksburg at Smithsonia. Each Christmas he provided the girls with a sumptuous turkey dinner. John's brother, James Alexander Seddon (1815-1880) was Secretary of War for the Confederacy.

[97] Edward was the grandson of William Waller (1740-1817) and Elizabeth Allen (1746-1768) of Concord. In 1836 he purchased Grafton from John Rowzee Peyton (1754-1798) of Stony Hill. Edward also owned and operated the freestone quarry at Rock Rimmon on Aquia Creek.

[98] The son of Dr. John Moncure Daniel (1769-1813), he was born on the same day his father died. He married Fenton Brooke (born c.1828), the eldest daughter of Samuel Selden Brooke (1800-1861) and Angelina Edrington (born c.1809) of Millvale. In 1837 John graduated with a degree in medicine from the University of Pennsylvania.

1863-65   Dr. John H. Daniel (first session) and Frederick Campbell Stewart Hunter[99] (c.1879-1929) (second session)

During the War Between the States, there were two governments operating within Virginia. One, which met in Richmond, had declared allegiance to the Confederate States of America. A second governing body met first in Wheeling and then in Alexandria. Stafford was not represented at the Wheeling Conventions of 1861, 1862, or the General Assemblies at Alexandria (December 1863-February 1864; December 1864-March 1865; or June 19-23, 1865).

1865-68   William Hooe Hansbrough[100] (c.1803-1875)
1869   John Conyers Shelton[101] (c.1803-1883)
1871-73   John Benjamin T. Suttle[102] (c.1844-1884)
1874/75   Gustavus Brown Wallace[103] (1810-1882)
1875-79   George Vowles Moncure[104] (1826-1901)

---

[99] F. C. S. Hunter was a native of King George County. He was the son of F. C. S. Hunter and Rose (Turner) Hunter and served as clerk of the court for King George. He also owned the King George Motor Company.

[100] The son of Peter Hansbrough (1796-1843) and Frances Anne Hooe, the daughter of William Hooe of Pine Hill, King George. William was born at his father's estate in Culpeper and married his first cousin, Maria L. Hansbrough Hooe. He also served as a justice of Stafford County 1860-61 and 1864-67.

[101] John represented only Stafford County. The 1871 land tax records list John as owning two tracts of 215 and 5 acres on the Rappahannock River and two tracts of 42 and 42 ½ acres on Horsepen Run ($5.00 building assessment). John was the son of John Shelton, Jr. (1774-1818) and Lethe Conyers (1780-c.1867).

[102] John was the son of John H. Suttle (c.1807-1884), an attorney in Stafford County.

[103] Gustavus was the son of John Wallace (1761-1829) of Liberty Hall and Elizabeth Hooe (c.1766-1850). He married Emily Travers Daniel, the daughter of Travers Daniel, Jr. (1763-1812) and Mildred Stone (1772-1837). Through his marriage with Emily Gustavus became owner of Crow's Nest. Their son, Gustavus M. Wallace, served in the Virginia State Senate from 1897-1906.

Gustavus was badly injured in an accident at his home, Ellerslie. The newspaper notice stated that he had sleepwalked one night and stepped out of a second story window. He fell to the ground and sustained a compound fracture of one leg just above the ankle joint as well as some possible internal injuries. "Mr. Wallace suffered great agony until the broken limb was amputated by Dr. Martin. Mr. Wallace is in the 67th year of his age, but it is hoped his vigorous constitution and temperate habits will enable him to survive his injuries...there is serious apprehension that the accident will result fatally" (*Virginia Star*, Sept. 8, 1877). Gustavus lived for several years after his accident.

[104] George was the son of John Moncure (IV) (1793-1876) of Woodbourne on Accokeek Run. One of Stafford's leading citizens of the 19th century, George was born at Somerset and resided at Chelsea, both of these farms in Wide Water. In 1849 he married Mary Conway Ashby (1830-1897), the daughter of Col. Turner (1789-1834) and Dorothea (Green) Ashby (1789-1865) of Rosebank, Fauquier County. Mary was the sister of Gen. Turner Ashby (1828-1862). George also served as clerk of the court in Stafford in 1864 and 1870 and he frequently appears in the Stafford records as an administrator of estates. His reputation for honesty and integrity was well known in the county. Known also for his meticulous record keeping, George usually maintained two copies of every official document that he produced. Many of the records on file in the courthouse were destroyed during the War Between the States and George's personal copies, many of which survive, provide some of the only information available for that time period.

The Rev. Jaquelin Marshall Meredith (1833-1920), rector of Aquia Church, wrote an obituary for his friend and said of him,

> A member and register and treasure of [the Aquia Church] vestry from 1852 to 1882. Baptized an adult by Rev. Henry Wall, D. D., in 1856, he became the earnest spiritual and active leader in the lay church work. By his personal friendship, his letters and entreaty, he secured the services of Rev. Jaquelin M. Meredith, in November, 1864, as rector at the time when Aquia Church (one of the oldest and largest of the Virginia Colonial Churches), was declared by Bishop Jones as past reclaiming; when its windows were gone, its walls defaced, its marble chancel floors torn up and broken; when the

1879-84	Duff McDuff Green[105] (c.1832-1885)
1885-87	Edward Seymour Ruggles[106] (1843-1919)
1887/88	Dr. Thaddeus Constantine Montague (1838-1898)
1889-94	John Enoch Mason[107] (1854-1910)
1895/96	William J. Rogers
1897/98	T. Weldon Berry[108] (died 1906)
1899/1900	Henry T. Garnett[109] (c.1851-1933)

Episcopal communicants at Aquia and in the county, except members of St. George's Church, Fredericksburg, were only seven, when but three out of 12 of the vestry were communicants, this noble Christian almost fed the Rector's family for twelve months, and gave such help to the noble bank of lay workers (male and female), to the Rector, that when Bishop Johns came to confirm a large class of 83 at Aquia in 1866, he expressed delight and surprise to see the dear old Church and Parish putting on new garments of faith and love for the Lord Jesus Christ. George V. Moncure was foremost among those lay workers, forming the society called "Inner and Outer Circles," that from 1866 to 1873 formed the Company of Believers that visited the sick, comforted the afflicted, relieved the needy, taught the various Sunday schools at Clifton, Aquia, Rockhill, Dumfries, Armstrong's Arbor, and Stafford's store. This lay help, thus well organized, enabled the Rector to carry the membership at Aquia from 7 in 1865 to 90 in 1870 (*Fredericksburg Star*, Oct. 9, 1901).

[105] Duff was the son of Duff Green (1792-1854), a wealthy Falmouth industrialist and his wife Eliza Ann Payne (1806-1876). Duff, Jr. represented Stafford and King George counties.

[106] Edward was born in Wichita, Texas while his Father, Gen. Daniel Ruggles (1810-1897) was stationed there. His mother was Richardetta Barnes Mason Hooe (c.1819-1902), the daughter of Alexander Seymour Hooe (1777-1835) of Friedland, King George County. Edward graduated from the Naval Academy at Annapolis but resigned his commission in the U. S. Navy to join the Confederate Navy. He was captured during the War Between the States and was imprisoned at Johnston's Island. In a subsequent exchange of prisoners, Edward returned to the Confederacy and transferred to the army where he saw action at Elkhorn, Shiloh, Farmington, Memphis, Raymond, Baton Rouge, Chickamauga, Atlanta, Franklin, and numerous other smaller battles. He was severely wounded at Shiloh but recovered and resumed his duties. According to his obituary, "Maj. Ruggles was perhaps the last living man connected in any way with the tragedy of Lincoln, having assisted in rowing Booth across the river and landing him at Port Royal when he was attempting to escape. In this Maj. Ruggles was assisted by his brother, Mortimer Ruggles, and his cousin, Fellow Bainbridge. Mortimer Ruggles and Bainbridge were afterwards arrested for their part in Booth's escape and acquitted" (*Free Lance*, Mar. 4, 1919). Edward always maintained that he didn't know what Booth had done until they were halfway across the river. He also claimed that had he known, he would have secreted Booth away to the safety of the mountains rather than letting him flee on foot at Port Royal. It was Edward Ruggles who was asked to identify the body of John Wilkes Booth. Capt. Dougherty, the officer in charge of the manhunt, asked Edward if the body was that of Booth. Maj. Ruggles replied that he didn't know the man's name but that it was certainly the man he had rowed across the river. The obituary continued, "Maj. Ruggles always declared that Booth's face was covered with powder marks and in answer to the question whether Booth had shot himself, Capt. Dougherty replied that he had."

Edward led a fascinating and varied life. After the war, he became the second officer on a steamship sailing "from New York around the Horn of the West Coast of South America" and was late engaged in the cattle business in the West. He eventually returned to King George to take up farming. He served not only as a legislator, but also as King George supervisor and a member of the Board of Visitors at the University of Virginia.

[107] John was born at Edge Hill, Albemarle County, the son of Charles Mason of Alto, King George County and Maria Jefferson Carr Randolph. John was educated at Bethel Military Academy in Fauquier, Dale Academy in Madison County, and the University of Virginia where he studied law. In 1878 he graduated from the law school of Columbia University in Washington, DC. He practiced law in King George and served as Commonwealth's Attorney there for three terms. In 1885 he married Kate Kearney Henry.

[108] T. Weldon Berry was a native of Criglersville, Madison County.

1901-05	Marion King Lowry[110] (c.1854-1939)
1906-11	Richard Cassius Lee Moncure, Jr.[111] (1831-1917)
1912	Whitfield Dunaway Peyton[112] (born 1870)
1914	James Otto Heflin[113] (c.1887-1969)
1916	Marion K. Lowry
1918-21	Thomas Lomax Hunter[114] (1875-1948)

---

[109] Henry lived at Spy Hill in King George County. He served for some years as Clerk of the House and was chairman of the Democratic party in King George. He married Belle Brown (died 1936) (*Free Lance-Star*, Nov. 16, 1933).

[110] Marion was born at Brooke where he was a member of St. Andrew's Chapel Methodist Church. He served four terms in the Assembly and was appointed in 1905 as collector for the internal revenue for the Second District. He held this position until 1915 when he took up the real estate business. An article about Marion appeared in the local newspaper:

> Mr. M. K. Lowry deserves credit for supplying a long felt want at Brooke in establishing his steam gristmill at that point. The grist ground there are highly spoken of by the patrons (*Fredericksburg Star*, Feb. 6, 1892).

Another article also mentions Marion Lowry's Mill:

> There are but two water grist mills in the county, one on Aquia, the other on Potomac Run, both owned by Lyman Kellogg, Esq. Both of these mills have a good reputation for turning out good grists. There are also two steam mills, one in Falmouth, owned by Mr. James Bloxton, the other at Brooke, owned by Mr. M. K. Lowry. Although hither to there has been some prejudice against grists made at steam mills, both of these mills have considerable reputation among their patrons for good grists. As these two gentlemen are pioneers in this country in that line, they should be sustained by the country people [Editor's note] "Our correspondent overlooked Mr. Roach's mill just across the Rappahannock from this city" (*Fredericksburg Star*, June 22, 1892).

Marion was known as a pioneer of the "good roads" movement in Virginia. In 1901 he introduced a bill in the House of Delegates proposing a survey of the Old Stage Road from Washington to Richmond which was completed in 1927. While in the General Assembly, he also supported the pension bill for aged Confederate soldiers.

In 1939 Marion K. Lowry died in Richmond at the Hotel Murphy where he had lived since 1900. He was buried at Hollywood Cemetery in that city.

[111] Richard was the son of R.C.L. Moncure (1805-1882) and Mary Butler Washington Conway (born 1807). In 1851 he married Virginia A. Buchanan (1881-1938). According to his obituary, R. C. L. was a "brave Confederate soldier" (*Free Lance*, Aug. 7, 1917). He died of blood poisoning following the amputation of one of his toes.

[112] Whitfield was the eldest son of Capt. Simeon C. Peyton (1829-1905) of Stafford. He was born in and received his early education in Stafford County and at age 17 entered Bethel Military Academy. He graduated in his third year as a first lieutenant and entered Richmond College but, due to poor eyesight, was forced to give up before graduating. His eyes gradually improved and he studied law through a correspondence course and, after two years, took up reading the texts at the University of Virginia Law School. In 1901 he passed the Superior Court examination and was admitted to the bar. Whit spent much of his adult life in business in Richmond. Around 1904 he returned to Stafford and purchased a farm.

[113] James was the son of William Nelson Heflin and Virginia Jane Lewis Billingsley. He was a resident of Colonial Beach and for many years worked as an attorney in Hopewell (*Free Lance-Star*, July 19, 1969).

[114] Thomas was born at Belle Grove, Port Conway, King George County. He was educated by private tutors and studied at William and Mary and Georgetown University. His own version of his education was that he was educated "mainly in the Great University of Books." His obituary described him as a "poet, lawyer, and Virginia's best known newspaper columnist" (*Free Lance-Star*, June 21, 1948). He was the author of a widely read column, "As it Appears to the Cavalier" which had been published in the *Times-*

1918-21	John R. Henderson, Jr.[115] (1885-1948)
1924-27	Charles Armistead Sinclair[116] (c.1881-1974)
1928-31	Daniel McCarty Chichester[117] (1896-1986)
1932-36	George William Herring[118] (1877-1966)
1936-39	Frank Peyton Moncure (1889-1969)
1940-44	Edgar R. Conner[119] (c.1878-1960)
1944-59	Frank P. Moncure
1960-63	Stanley A. Owens
1964-69	George Chancellor Rawlings, Jr.[120]
1970/71	Benjamin Woodbridge, Jr.
1972/73	Robert R. Gwathmey
1978-81	Lewis P. Fickett, Jr.
	D. Wayne O'Bryan
1982-87	Thomas M. Moncure, Jr.
	W. Tayloe Murphy, Jr.
1988-90	William J. Howell
	W. Tayloe Murphy, Jr.

Dispatch since 1929. Prior to his writing for the newspapers, he had had two volumes of poetry published and was named poet laureate of Virginia by the 1948 General Assembly.

According to his obituary, "Thomas liked to boast that he never spent more time than was necessary in cities. He spent practically his entire adult life in the country, practicing farming and 'lawyering.' He deplored the rapid pace of modern living and preferred the quiet and solitude of his farm." He actively campaigned against prohibition, claiming it was in infringement upon individual rights.

Thomas died of a heart ailment at Mary Washington Hospital in Fredericksburg. His funeral was conducted from his home, Waverly, near King George Courthouse.

[115] John was born at Lyons Farm, New Jersey. He settled in Stafford soon after World War I and lived for a number of years at Tump Farm. He later owned an automobile dealership in Fredericksburg.

[116] A lifelong resident of Manassas, from 1928-1964 Charles served as treasurer of Prince William County. He was twice mayor of Manassas and was president and chairman of the board of Peoples National Bank of Manassas (*Free Lance-Star*, June 11, 1974). Charles represented Stafford and Prince William counties.

[117] Daniel was the son of the Hon. Richard Henry Lee Chichester (1870-1930) and Virginia Belle Wallace (1871-1961). His father was a former judge of the 15th Judicial Circuit Court and a member of the Virginia Supreme Court of Appeals. Daniel graduated from Virginia Tech in 1919 and began his involvement in politics the following year. He bred prize-winning Guernsey cattle on his farm, Glencairne and, during the late 1930s, he served three times as president of the Virginia State Dairymen's Association. In 1938 he became a partner in what is now Chichester-Graves Insurance Agency. He was also a vestryman of Aquia Episcopal Church for 30 years and served as senior warden from 1955 to 1970.

[118] George was a native of Orange County and was the son of Franklin Towles Herring and Ammorious Butler. From 1898-1912 he was in the mercantile business in Wide Water in partnership with Alfred Joseph Pyke (1865-1938). In 1900 he married Pearl N. Norvelle (died 1953) and served as clerk of the circuit court of Stafford from 1912-1918. He was an organizer of the Bank of Quantico and, after leaving Stafford, resided at Featherstone Farm in Woodbridge. George was owner and operator of Wallace and Herring Lumber Company in Alexandria in partnership with Gustavus Brown Wallace (1876-1955). He was president of the Independence Mutual Fire Insurance Company of Alexandria, a member of the Fredericksburg Presbyterian Church and Masonic Lodge No. 4. After selling Featherstone, he moved to the George Washington Inn on Caroline Street in Fredericksburg where he lived for about 13 years before moving to the Manassas Nursing Home. He was buried in the Graham Cemetery in Orange County.

[119] Edgar was a dairyman from Manassas. He also dealt in real estate, home building, and was a bank director in Manassas. He was a charter member of the Maryland-Virginia Dairymen's Association and built the first opera house in Manassas. This building featured the first electric lights in the area and hosted a Confederate reunion including John S. Mosley. During his term in the legislature, he was instrumental in obtaining funds to reconstruct Manassas Battlefield Park (*Free Lance Star*, Feb. 25, 1960).

[120] Represented Spotsylvania, Stafford, and Fredericksburg.

Virginia State Senate

1776-78	Thomas Ludwell Lee
1778	Thomas Ludwell Lee and Thomas Jett[121] (died 1785)
1779	Thomas Jett and Francis Lightfoot Lee[122] (1734-1797)
1780/81	William Brent (1733-1782)
1781-85	William Fitzhugh (1741-1809)
1785-88	Thomas Lee[123] (1758-1805)
1789	Charles Carter (1738-1796)
1790-93	Alexander Campbell[124] (died 1796) and John James Maund[125] (died 1802)
1797-1801	Daniel McCarty, Jr.[126] (173_-1795)
1801-09	John Pratt Hungerford[127] (1761-1833)
1809-16	John Campbell
1817-21	John Taliaferro[128] (1768-1852)
1821-25	Alexander Fontaine Rose (1780-1831)
1825-29	St. Leger Landon Carter[129] (1785-1850)
1829-31	Joseph William Chinn[130] (1798-1840)

---

[121] Thomas Jett succeeded Lee who died. Thomas lived at Walnut Hill in King George County and was a signer of the Leedstown Resolutions in 1776. He served King George as sheriff and justice for many years. Thomas married Elizabeth Storke Washington, widow of Henry Washington (c.1720-1745).

[122] Francis was the son of Thomas Lee (1690-1750) and Hannah Ludwell (1701-1750) and was a signer of the Declaration of Independence. He married Rebecca Tayloe (c.1748-1797).

[123] Thomas was the son of Richard Henry Lee (1733-1794) and Anne Aylett (c.1736-1768). Thomas married first Elizabeth Ashton Alexander (born 1760). His second wife was Mildred Washington (born 1788), the daughter of John Augustine Washington (1735-1787) and Hannah Bushrod.

[124] Alexander was born in Westmoreland County, the son of the Rev. Archibald Campbell (born c.1754) and Hannah McCoy. Around 1785 he graduated from William and Mary and practiced law in Richmond. He often worked with John Marshall and Patrick Henry and served as U. S. attorney for the eastern district of Virginia. He committed suicide.

[125] John James Maund married Harriet Lucy Carter (born 1768), the daughter of Robert Carter III (1728-1804) of Nomini Hall and Frances A. Tasker (died 1787).

[126] Daniel was the only son of Daniel McCarty (died 1744) and his second wife, Elizabeth, widow of Col. Nicholas Smith (1666-1734). Daniel, Jr. lived at Longwood in Westmoreland County and married as his first wife Mary Mercer (1740-1764), the daughter of John Mercer (1704-1768) of Marlborough.

[127] John was born near Leedstown, Westmoreland County. He served as an officer in the Revolution and held the rank of Brigadier General during the War of 1812. He served in the House of Delegates from 1797-1801, in the Virginia State Senate from 1801-1809, and as a Republican in the 12th Congress from Mar. 4 to Dec. 2, 1811 when he was succeeded by John Taliaferro who contested the election. Hungerford was elected to the 13th and 14th congresses. He died at Twiford, Westmoreland County and was buried in Leedstown.

[128] John was born at Hays, King George County and practiced law in Fredericksburg. He was elected to the 7th U. S. Congress and successfully contested the election of John P. Hungerford to the 12th congress. John Taliaferro was elected to the 18th-21st congresses and elected as a Whig to the 24th-27th congresses. He was chairman of the Committee on Revolutionary Pensions and was Librarian of the U. S. Treasury Department from 1850 until his death. He was buried on his farm Hagley.

[129] This was the second son of Landon Carter (1751-1811) of Cleve, King George County, and Eliza (Carter) Thornton, his wife. Upon the death of his father, St. Leger became the owner of Cleve and resided there until his death. He was noted for his poetry. St. Leger married his cousin, Eliza Ludwell Lee, the daughter of Thomas Ludwell Lee, Jr. (1751-1807). When she died, St. Leger had her buried on the portion of Cleve called Canning. His will requested that he be buried next to her, but the graves were never marked. To this day their exact resting places remain a mystery. Like his mother, St. Leger freed his slaves upon his death.

[130] Joseph was born in Lancaster County, Virginia, the son of Joseph Chinn (1768-1803) and Elizabeth Griffin. In 1819 he graduated from Union College in Schenectady, New York. He was admitted to the bar

1831/32	William Basye and Joseph Chinn[131]
1832-38	William Basye
1838-45	Robert Wormley Carter[132] (1792-1861)
1845-49	James M. Smith
1849-52	Joseph Harvey
1852/53	Charles Mason[133] (1810-1888)
1853/54	Basil Brawner[134] (c.1799-1893) and Charles Mason
1855-62	James Monroe Taliaferro[135] (1809-1893)
1863/64	James M. Taliaferro (first session) and Edward Thornton Tayloe[136] (1803-1875) (second session)
1864/65	Edward T. Tayloe
1865-69	John Hancock Lee (1805-1873)
1869-77	Charles Herndon[137] (1822-1883)
1877-81	Henry William Murray (1826-1881)
1881-85	James Leavett Powell[138] (1834-1914)

---

in 1821 and practiced law in Lancaster County. He was elected as a Jacksonian to the 22nd and 23rd congresses serving from 1831-1835. After leaving congress, he moved to Richmond where he resumed his law practice. Joseph married Mary Ann Smith of Northampton County. He died in Richmond and was buried at Wilna, his farm on the outskirts of Richmond.

[131] Basye succeeded Chinn who resigned.

[132] Known as Robert Carter of Sabine Hall, he was the son of Landon Carter (1757-1820) of Sabine Hall and Catherine Griffin Tayloe (1761-1798) of Mt. Airy. Robert married Elizabeth M. Tayloe (died 1832). Robert inherited the old Carter seat called Parke or Parke Quarter in Stafford County.

[133] Now representing Stafford, King George, and Prince William counties. Charles was born in Stafford, the son of Col. Enoch Mason (c.1769-1828), and was for many years a merchant in Fredericksburg. He left the Stafford/Fredericksburg region for a few years and operated a business in New Orleans before returning home. He was a farmer in King George County and a leader in the Democratic Party. Charles was buried at St. John's Episcopal Church in King George.

[134] Col. Basil Brawner was a native of Prince William County and, at the time of his death, was the oldest resident of Alexandria. Brawner was elected to finish the term of Charles Mason who resigned.

[135] James was born at Oakland in King George County, the son of James Garnett Taliaferro (born c.1772) and Wilhelmina Wishart (born 1772). He was educated at West Point and was a classmate of Robert E. Lee and Joseph E. Johnston. James married first Valeria O'Brien, secondly Marion Landon Grymes (1815-1859). His third wife was Anne E. Coleman (1834-1892), the daughter of his Stafford neighbor, John W. Coleman (1788-1857).

James lived at Loch Lomond in Stafford County near Mt. Olive Church. In 1843 he paid taxes on 3 slaves, 3 horses, 1 gold watch, and 1 wood clock (Hore, Account book).

James died in Washington and was buried at Bethlehem Cemetery in Alexandria. According to his obituary, James was "the youngest of a brilliant family, his brothers having figured in the war history of the country prominently. His oldest brother, John Wishart Taliaferro, was with John Paul Jones on the *Bonne Homme Richard*" (*Free Lance*, Jan. 6, 1893).

[136] Edward was the son of John Tayloe (III) (1772-1828) and Anne Ogle (1772-1855). He was born in Washington. At the age of 16 he entered Howard University and graduated in 1823. In 1828 Gen. William Henry Harrison was appointed Minister to Columbia and made Edward Tayloe his Secretary of Legation. A year later Edward retired to King George County where he built a new home, Powhatan. In 1830 he married his cousin, Mary Ogle (1807-1862) of Belair.

[137] Now representing Spotsylvania, Stafford, and Louisa counties. Charles was an attorney and a member of the Fredericksburg City Council when it first met after the fall of the Confederacy. In 1858 he married Lucy Woodford Gordon (born 1837) of Prospect Hill, the daughter of Basil Gordon (1808-1891) and Lucy Penn Taylor (born c.1830) and the grand daughter of Samuel Gordon (1759-1843) and Susanna Fitzhugh Knox (1775-1869). Charles was also a land speculator, buying up tremendous acreage in Stafford before and during the War Between the States. He lived in Fredericksburg on the northeast corner of the intersection of Prince Edward and Hanover streets.

1885-89	William E. Bibb (c.1845-1910)
1889-97	William Alexander Little, Jr.[139] (c.1866-1944)
1897-1906	Dr. Gustavus Michael Wallace[140] (1849-1937)
1906-12	Frederick Wilmer Sims[141] (1862-1925)
1912-16	Richard Cassius Lee Moncure, Jr.
1916-23	Charles O'Conor Goolrick[142] (c.1877-1960)
1924-35	William Worth Smith, Jr.[143] (1887-1940)
1936-40	S. Bernard Coleman[144] (c.1902-1974)
1940-44	Herman H. Walton[145] (c.1876-1945)
1944-55	Benjamin T. Pitts[146] (c.1889-1964)

---

[138] James was a highly respected citizen of Spotsylvania County. He served as Commonwealth's Attorney for Spotsylvania. During the War Between the States, he fought for the Confederate cause in the 9th Virginia Cavalry.

[139] The son of William A. Little (born c.1819), an attorney from Philadelphia who married one of the Fitzhugh girls of Boscobel. Little ended up owning Boscobel and used it as a country house. William, Jr. graduated at the head of his class and received his law degree from the University of Virginia. He practiced law in Fredericksburg in partnership with his father and for many years was known as one of the ablest lawyers in Virginia. He served several terms as Commonwealths Attorney for Fredericksburg.

Sadly, William had a serious drinking problem. He had married in Fredericksburg, but his wife divorced him. Around 1900 he moved to Washington where he practiced law. Just prior to his death William was arrested for being a habitual drunkard. While in jail he became ill and was taken to the Washington Asylum Hospital where he died (*Free Lance*, Nov. 8, 1910).

[140] This was the son of Gustavus Brown Wallace (1810-1882) of Liberty Hall and Emily Travers Daniel. G. M. Wallace was educated at the University of Virginia and graduated with an M. D. from the University of Maryland. In 1872 he married Dora Ashby Green (1854-1937).

[141] Frederick was born in Louisa County, the son of Dr. Frederick H. Sims and Maria Louise Kimbrough. He was educated at the University of Virginia and was admitted to the bar in 1885. He was elected judge of the Louisa County Court in 1891 and entered the state senate in 1905. He became a member of the Virginia Supreme Court of Appeals in 1924. In 1888 Frederick married Lucy Payne Winston, the daughter of William A. and Lucy P. Winston of Louisa. He ended his own life with a shotgun in the Jefferson Hotel in Richmond. For several weeks prior to his death he had suffered from a nervous breakdown. When his wife took a letter downstairs to mail, he shot himself to death.

[142] O'Conor was the son of Judge John Tackett Goolrick (born 1844) of Fredericksburg and Frances White, a great grand daughter of George Mason (1725-1792) of Gunston Hall. He was the grandson of Peter Goolrick who came to Virginia from Sligo, Ireland c.1794.

O'Conor helped pass legislation establishing what would become Mary Washington College and Goolrick Hall gymnasium is named in his honor. He was one of the sponsors of the "machinery act" granting women the right to vote in Virginia pending adoption of the Nineteenth Amendment. O'Conor served as Fredericksburg City Attorney for 28 years, as mayor of Fredericksburg, and as president of the Virginia Bar Association. He was a member of the University of Virginia Board of Visitors when Mary Washington College was a part of that university.

[143] Now representing Spotsylvania, Louisa, Orange, and Stafford counties and the town of Fredericksburg. William was the son of William Worth Smith, Sr. (died 1924) and Lucinda Lewis (born 1848).

[144] The son of Richelieu Coleman, Bernard was born at Alta Vista in Spotsylvania. For many years he lived at Breezewood Farm and spent his later years in Fredericksburg. Initially, Bernard was an electrical engineer, but in 1925 decided to seek a law degree. He received his degree from the University of Virginia and began his law practice in Fredericksburg in 1928. In March 1939 he resigned from the State Senate to become Commonwealths Attorney for Spotsylvania. He also served as judge of the 39th Judicial Circuit Court (*Free Lance-Star*, Nov. 6, 1974).

[145] H. H. Walton was a Louisa County businessman and president of Walton Lumber Company and Walton and Wood, a farm machinery and automobile dealership. He was also a director of the Peoples National Bank of Charlottesville. He married Elizabeth Trice (*Free Lance-Star*, Sept. 28, 1954).

[146] Born in Fredericksburg, Benjamin was the son of Carolinus and Victoria Pitts. He received little formal education, his schooling ending with the eighth grade. In 1909 he saw a business opportunity in a failed movie theater. He saved $75, borrowed another $50 from his brother, and assumed operation of the theater.

1956-65   Blake Tyler Newton[147] (c.1890-1977)
1966-71   John F. Galleher
1972-77   Paul W. Manns[148]
1978-2003   John H. Chichester

Eventually, he controlled 37 theaters and drive-ins and became a major landowner in Fredericksburg. In 1939 he was named to the State Port Authority and served five terms with this office. He was five times president of the local Chamber of Commerce and a director of the Farmers and Merchants Bank in Fredericksburg. Benjamin sought to give back to his community and established a foundation that gave thousands of dollars in scholarships to deserving high school seniors (*Free Lance-Star*, July 22, 1964).

[147] Representing King George, Lancaster, Northumberland, Prince William, Richmond, Stafford, and Westmoreland counties. Blake was born at Linden, Hague, Westmoreland County. He received his bachelors and masters degrees from the College of William and Mary and was president of the Northern Neck Bar Association. From 1913-1954 he served as Superintendent of Schools, first for Westmoreland, then for Richmond County. From 1946-1957 he was president of the state board of education.

[148] Representing Caroline, Essex, King George, Lancaster, Northumberland, Richmond, Spotsylvania, Stafford, and Westmoreland counties and the city of Fredericksburg.

Sources:
Abercrombie, Janice L. and Slatter, Richard. *Virginia Revolutionary Publick Claims.* Athens, GA: Iberian Publishing Co., 1992.
Alcock, John P. *Five Generations of the Family of Burr Harrison of Virginia, 1650-1800.* Bowie, MD: Heritage Books, 1991.
Boddie, John B. *Virginia Historical Genealogies.* Baltimore, MD: Genealogical Publishing Co., 1990.
Brent, Chester H. *The Descendants of Coll. Giles Brent, Capt. George Brent, and Robert Brent, Gentlemen, Immigrants to Maryland and Virginia.* Rutland, VT: Tuttle Publishing Co., 1946.
Bruce, Philip A. *Institutional History of Virginia in the 17th Century.* NY: G. P. Putnam and Sons, 1910.
Compiler, Oct. 15, 1821, obituary of Benjamin Ficklen
Copeland, Pamela C. and MacMaster, Richard K. *The Five George Masons: Patriots and Planters of Virginia and Maryland.* Charlottesville, VA: University Press of Virginia, 1975.
Crowe, Maude. *Descendants from First Families of Virginia and Maryland: a Family History and Genealogy Covering 350 Years, 1620-1970.* Self-published, 1978.
Dorman, John F. *Claiborne of Virginia: Descendants of Colonel William Claiborne, the First Eight Generations.* Baltimore, MD: Gateway Press, 1995.
Dowdey, Clifford. *The Virginia Dynasties.* NY: Bonanza Books, 1969.
Everman, Henry E. *Governor James Garrard.* Bourbon Press, KY: Cooper's Run Press, 1981.
Flournoy, H. W. *Calendar of Virginia State Papers and Manuscripts from January 1, 1808 to December 31, 1835.* NY: Kraus Reprint Corp., 1968.
Fredericksburg Circuit Court Records:
  "Cooke vs Green", SC/H/1830?51-006
Fredericksburg Ledger, May 2, 1873, obituary of William H. Brown
Fredericksburg Star, Feb. 6, 1892, account of Lowry's mill
---, Oct. 9, 1901, obituary of George V. Moncure
Free Lance, Jan. 6, 1893, obituary of James M. Taliaferro
---, Nov. 8, 1910, obituary of William A. Little, Jr.
---, Aug. 7, 1917, obituary of R.C.L. Moncure, Jr.
---, Mar. 4, 1919, obituary of Edward S. Ruggles
---, Feb. 10, 1925, obituary of Frederick W. Sims
Free Lance-Star, Feb. 1, 1929, obituary of F. C. S. Hunter
---, Nov. 16, 1933, obituary of Henry T. Garnett
---, June 21, 1948, obituary of Thomas L. Hunter
---, Sept. 28, 1954, obituary of Herman H. Walton
---, Feb. 25, 1960, obituary of Edgar R. Conner
---, July 22, 1964, obituary of Benjamin T. Pitts
---, July 19, 1969, obituary of James O. Heflin
---, July 11, 1974, obituary of Charles A. Sinclair
---, Nov. 6, 1974, obituary of S. Bernard Coleman
---, Apr. 30, 1977, obituary of Blake T. Newton
---, Jan. 29, 1986, obituary of Daniel M. Chichester
Gordon, George L., Jr. Papers. Private collection.
Gray, Gertrude E. *Virginia Northern Neck Land Grants.* Baltimore, MD: Genealogical Publishing Co., 1993.
Hageman, James A. *The Heritage of Virginia.* Norfolk, VA: Donning Company Publishers, 1986.
Hall, Wilmer L., ed. *Executive Journals of the Council of Colonial Virginia.* Richmond, VA: Virginia State Library, 1967.
Hayden, Horace E. *Virginia Genealogies: a Genealogy of the Glassell Family of Scotland and Virginia.* Baltimore, MD: Genealogical Publishing Co., 1979.
Heitman, Francis B. *Historical Register of Officers of the Continental Army During the War of the Revolution.* Baltimore, MD: Clearfield, 1997.
Hore, Elias A. W. "Account Book, 1843." MSS5: 3H 7817: 1, Virginia Historical Society, Richmond, Virginia.

King, George H. S. *The Register of Overwharton Parish, Stafford County, Virginia, 1723-1758*. Easley, SC: Southern Historical Press, Inc., 1986.

King George County Deeds and Wills:
    WB 1-169—June 7, 1764—will of Charles Carter

Lee, Edmond J. *Lee of Virginia, 1642-1892: Biographical and Genealogical Sketches of the Descendants of Col. Richard Lee*. Baltimore, MD: Genealogical Publishing Co., 1983.

Leonard, Cynthia M. *The General Assembly of Virginia: July 30, 1619 - Jan. 11, 1978: a Bicentennial Register of Members*. Richmond, VA: Virginia State Library, 1978.

Macrae, Emily. "The Wallace Family." *William and Mary Quarterly Historical Magazine*, vol. 13, (1905), pp. 177-182.

Mapp, Alf J., Jr. *The Virginia Experiment: the Old Dominion's Role in the Making of America (1607-1781)*. Richmond, VA: Dietz Press, Inc., 1957.

McIlwaine, H. R. *Minutes of the Council and General Court of Colonial Virginia*. Richmond, VA: Virginia State Library, 1924.

Morton, Richard L. *Colonial Virginia: the Tidewater Period, 1607-1710*, vol. 1, Spartanburg, SC: The Reprint Co., 1973.

---. *Colonial Virginia: Westward Expansion and Prelude to Revolution, 1710-1763*, vol.2, Chapel Hill, NC: University of North Carolina Press, 1960.

Nagel, Paul C. *The Lees of Virginia: Seven Generations of an American Family*. NY: Oxford University Press, 1990.

National Society of the DAR Centennial Administration. *DAR Patriot Index, Centennial Edition*. Washington, DC: NSDAR, 1994.

Nicklin, John B. "Benjamin Strother (c.1700-1765) and his Wives." *Tyler's Quarterly Historical and Genealogical Magazine*, vol. 19, (1938), pp. 224-227.

Nugent, Nell M. *Cavaliers and Pioneers: Abstracts of Virginia Land Patents and Grants*, vol. 1-3, Richmond, VA: Virginia State Library, 1979.

Pierce, Alycon T. *Selected Final Pension Payment Vouchers, 1818-1864*. Athens, GA: Iberian Publishing Co., 1996.

Proceedings of the Council of Maryland, 1681-1685/6. Maryland Historical Society, Annapolis, MD.

Rose, Christine. *Ancestors and Descendants of Rev. Robert Rose and Rev. Charles Rose of Colonial Virginia and Wester Alves, Morayshire, Scotland*. San Jose, CA, 1985.

Quitt, Martin H. *The Virginia House of Burgesses, 1660-1706: the Social, Educational, and Economic Basis of Political Power* (dissertation). St. Louis, Missouri: Washington University, 1970.

Scribner, Robert L., ed. *Revolutionary Virginia: the Road to Independence*, vol. 1, Charlottesville, VA: University Press of Virginia, 1973.

"Virginia Council Journals, 1726-1753." *Virginia Magazine of History and Biography*, vol. 34, (1926), pp.345-357.

Virginia Star, Sept. 8, 1877, Gustavus B. Wallace injured in accident

Vogt, John and Kethley, T. William. *Stafford County, Virginia Tithables: Quit Rents, Personal Property Taxes and Related Lists and Petitions, 1723-1790*. Athens, GA: Iberian Publishing Co., 1990.

Wayland, John W. *The Washingtons and Their Homes*. Staunton, VA: McClure Printing Co., 1944.

Wulfeck, Dorothy F. *Marriages of Some Virginia Residents, 1607-1800*. Baltimore, MD: Genealogical Publishing Co., 1986.

Chapter 2
Justices of the Peace

In establishing a system of government for the new counties, the Assembly provided for one governing body, the county court, which not only administered justice, but also provided for all local administration not entrusted to the smaller unit called the parish. The original court was held at Jamestown and consisted of the governor and his appointed council sitting as a court and, as late as 1618, they were hearing all cases in the colony, both civil and criminal. In that year, Governor George Yeardley ordered that courts be held in "convenient" places. These bodies were to sit monthly and they soon became the characteristic feature of local Virginia government and endured, essentially unchanged, for nearly three centuries until they were abolished by the Constitution of 1902.

First known as commissioners, justices of the peace were appointed by the governor. All controversies and complaints regarding them were reported to the governor and council. In 1665 the Assembly provided for the recommendation of justices by the courts themselves as a prelude to the governor's appointment. Virginia justices followed the English custom of being honorable, unpaid positions though a revision of the law in 1661 included a proviso that an unsuccessful litigant was to pay the court 30 pounds of tobacco which was passed on to the justices as a small fee.

During the 17th century, any member of the council could sit on the county court with the justices and assist them with their duties. As the council was agent for the Crown, this provided a means of keeping up with the affairs of the colony on a "grass roots" level. That policy changed during the 18th century; members of the council were not allowed to sit in county courts and the governor was also expressly forbidden by royal instructions to execute the office of justice by himself or by deputy.

The purpose of the justices was to extend and make apparent the authority of the colonial government in Jamestown and later in Williamsburg. Many justices were also vestrymen whose duties in that important office touched the conduct of their parishioners. Many, also, were elected to the House of Burgesses, thus linking together local and general affairs. By the Act of 1662 the justices were to be "of the most able, honest, and judicious persons of the county." It is important to realize that while these men were usually considered to be the cost upstanding citizens of their communities, most had little or no legal training.

Meetings of the county courts were at first held monthly. In 1642 the Assembly set the number of meetings at six per year, though a majority of the court could vote to hold extra sessions if necessary. A fixed court day was assigned for each county and the times of the meeting were also specified as from 7:00 to 10:00 a.m. Some evening meetings were occasionally held, also.

The position of justice of the peach tended, by custom only, to become hereditary. This was a natural consequence of the social structure that developed as a result of a century and a half of land acquisition in Virginia. Personal favoritism on the part of the governor also played a small part in the appointment of county officials. Politics and human nature during the 17th and 18th centuries were no different from politics and human nature in the present. In Stafford a shortage of literate and qualified men necessitated the practice of assuming more than one public office simultaneously and also contributed to the practice of passing public office from father to son.

The number of justices in each county varied not with the size of the county, but based upon the will of the appointing authority or the ability to get qualified persons to serve. Courts typically included five to eight members. That number grew rapidly over the years until 1647 when the Assembly passed an act condemning the multitude of commissioners in each county and ordering that the number be limited to eight, including the sheriff, "being at present the eight first in each commission, unless some knowne defect too neere relation to some other of the commission shall render them incapable. And be itt further enacted that the sheriffes place shall after this year be confirred on the first in commission, and so devolve to every commissioner in course."

Despite this act, Governor William Berkeley continued to freely appoint commissioners, many of whom were family or friends. As the counties grew, however, the necessity for prompt and convenient administration of justice necessitated the appointment of an adequate number of justices to do the job. The Act of 1710 virtually repeated in 1748, fixed the number of justices at eight or more, four of whom were required to hold court "according to the ancient custom and usage heretofore in that behalf practised."

From amongst their number, one senior justice was selected to preside. The presiding justice announced rulings and decisions made by the court which, as in the General Court, were reached by a majority vote of the justices present.

The number of justices serving in Stafford varied wildly over the years. While the public records providing names of justices are extremely limited, it appears that there were approximately seven justices in 1664. By 1692 that number had increased to at least 21 and, according to a list on file with the Library of Virginia, there were 35 justices in 1768. In 1796 Valentine Peyton (1756-1815), clerk of the court for Stafford, wrote to the governor warning him of the lack of justices in that county. He reported that the number of active justices was down to nine or ten, most of whom never attended court. Peyton waned that if the governor didn't make some new appointments, there would be no court at all in Stafford.

The early monthly courts presided over by the commanders of the plantations were designed to administer justice in outlying settlements that could not conveniently wait upon the quarter courts held by the governor and council in Jamestown. The jurisdiction of these monthly courts was comparatively narrow. The importance of the justices and of the county courts expanded for several reasons: the creation of counties having definite boundaries, the change from commissioners to justices, the increase in the number of such officials, the increase in the number of counties, and population growth.

The scope of the county courts was defined in 1710 as extending to all cases in common law and chancery, except those involving outlawry, which were to be tried by the General Court. The duties of the courts during the 18th century included supervising physicians and regulating their fees and the prices of drugs; giving the test oath to all suspected papists and keeping a list of those who refused to take the oath; deciding what weapons to allow Catholics to possess; supervising the treatment of indentured servants; providing for the condemnation of land (usually for the building of mill dams); licensing ordinaries and ferries, and enforcing laws against vagrants. Beyond the monitoring of Catholics, the courts were also responsible for fixing the rates for blacksmiths who repaired arms for the militia; executing tariff laws, inspecting the books of the county surveyors; paying the bounties on wolves; inspecting leather for quality; seeing that tar barrels were inspected and marked; encouraging the raising of hemp by paying a bounty to planters who grew it; recording bills of sale for cattle; keeping copies of ships' manifests; ascertaining the qualifications of attorneys desiring to practice in the county; preventing interracial marriages; and suppressing unlawful meetings.

In the 20 years preceding the Revolution, most county courts consisted of four or more justices. They had jurisdiction in all causes in the county related to common law or chancery except:

- Those criminal cases wherein the judgment, upon conviction, should be for the loss of life or member
- Prosecution of cases of outlawry against person or persons
- All causes involving less than 25 shillings sterling or 200 pounds of tobacco

Cases falling into the first two exceptions were handled by the General Court in Williamsburg. To that court appeal could be taken from a county court except in suits at common law or chancery in which the debt or damages, exclusive of costs, should not exceed £10 or 2,000 pounds of tobacco unless the title or bounds of property were in question. The third class of exceptional causes could be determined by a single justice. He was charged with keeping the peach generally and could cause a traitor, felon, pirate, rioter, breaker of the peace, or other criminal offender to be arrested and brought before him or any other justice of the county court.

After 1767 the powers of the county justices were expanded with regards to cases involving incorrigible and runaway slaves. An act of 1765 referred to the trouble and expense caused by the transporting to the governor from different parts of the colony slaves accused of serious crimes. In order to reduce these expenses, the act ordered that justices "try, condemn and execute or otherwise punish or acquit" all slaves committing capital crimes in their county. They were authorized to try the offender without a jury and to award punishment. While this was, no doubt, more cost effective, it was certainly not to the advantage of the defendant.

The county court was the primary administrative body, outside of the governor and council, during the colonial period. The justices were expected to list tithables, lay the county levy, record land transactions, bind out poor children to trades, and combine the functions of orphans, probate, and claims courts. It is especially remarkable that this myriad of duties was performed by unpaid lay justices who might or might not have had a book of law to guide them. As ministers of justice, they executed writs of certiorari, took surety of the peace, and other similar duties. As judicial officers, they acted as judges, issued warrants for capturing felons and, while in session, had jurisdiction in all matters of common law or in chancery expect criminal matters concerning life and limb. They granted certificates of oath for many purposes, and especially to merchants swearing as to invoices of imported goods. Customs officials required these certificates before granting permission to unload a ship.

Initially, juries were comprised of whoever happened to be in court when a jury was needed. Later, jurymen were chosen from among the qualified residents in the county and summoned by the sheriff. A law of 1642 gave the right of trial by jury in criminal cases and required the jury "to keep from food and releife till they have agreed upon their verdict." No doubt, justice was swift.

Court day was always a day of interest and excitement for the people of Virginia and, to a large degree, it paralleled market day in England. Court day brought forth people of all classes. The farmer came to exchange his produce for the goods of the merchant, to settle his taxes with the sheriff, and to hear discussions of topics of current interest. The aristocratic planter came to mingle with his less prestigious neighbors and to carry out his business with the court. Men of all social classes mingled in the taverns, catching up on news and sharing ideas. Candidates for public office then, as now, were always present to shake hands and impress the voters. On the green just outside the courthouse, local bullies paired off in sparring matches. A circle of observers surrounded the fighters, bets were placed, and no one interfered with the proceedings until one of the participants admitted defeat. There were no weapons beyond what God had provided each man and the entertainment afforded by such matches added excitement to the day.

Court day remained largely unchanged for nearly 300 years. The Convention of 1849, however, rang a death knell for this much beloved social institution. From that point on, justices were chosen by popular election rather than be governor's appointment. The county court finally passed out of existence under the Constitution of 1869 though a court by the same name continued until the Constitution of 1904. After 1869 the old county court ceased to be held by justices of the peace and was in every one of the 100 counties presided over by a poorly paid judge "learned in the law."

Courthouses of Stafford

On May 27, 1664 the first session of the court met in the newly formed county of Stafford. The records don't tell the location of their meeting but it was likely in a private home. On Dec. 9, 1665 the court ordered Capt. John Alexander (died 1677) to contract for erecting a courthouse somewhere on the south side of Potomac Creek. The building was used not only as a courthouse but as a church as well, probably only until Potomac Church was completed. This building seems to have burned because by 1690 the court was meeting in the home of Thomas Elzey.

On Nov. 14, 1690 contractors Sampson Darrell (born c.1660) and Ambrose Bayley were ordered to build a new courthouse on the north side of Potomac Creek and in June 1691 Capt. George Mason (II) (1660-1716) and Theodorick Bland (1662-1700) ran lines to show Darrell and Bayley where to place the building. The move to the north side of the creek corresponded to increased activity in a small settlement on Marlborough Point. Mason, then sheriff, brought over the old stocks from the other side of the creek for the "punishment of Drunkards, Riotous & Tumultuous Persons, swears Etc." By December 1691 the justices were meeting in this new building, though it burned around 1718. By this time, activity around Marlborough had waned and it was decided that the next courthouse should be built closer to the center of population which was, at that point, on the south side of the creek. The site of this third courthouse was just upstream from Belle Plain and very close to Cave's Warehouses. This building burned in 1730 or 1731 and the justices ordered that it be rebuilt on the same site. These early courthouses were probably constructed of wood, lighted with candles, and heated with fireplaces, making them fire hazards under the best of conditions.

It may be assumed that this fourth building also burned because in 1752 Nathaniel Harrison (1713-1791) and Hugh Adie were "to be paid for work on a new court house which some evil disposed person...feloniously burned" before it was completed.

As the years passed, Stafford's population increased and shifted inland away from Potomac Creek. No longer was the Belle Plain site convenient for people needing to do business with the county court. The atrocious road conditions also made it impossible for many of the justices to attend court, some sessions being canceled entirely for lack of justices. At the last meeting of the court on this site, only nine of the thirty justices were present. The justices appointed a commission to find the center of the county and determine a suitable location for a new courthouse. They selected the site of the present courthouse and the justices began meeting in William Garrard's ordinary near on or the site of the present-day school board offices. In March 1780 William Fitzhugh (1741-1809) and William Garrard (c.1715-c.1786) deeded to the county land upon which to build the courthouse. Three years later, the new judicial complex was completed and consisted of a courthouse, jail, and clerk's office.

Debate raged among residents who opposed the tax increase imposed to pay for the new buildings and those who simply could not get to the old site. In an effort to cut costs, sandstone used for the jail was acquired for a minimal amount, it being considered "spawl stone" or waste material from the Aquia Creek quarries. At the June term, 1818, the court ordered Cary Selden (1783-1842), Hancock Eustace (1768-1829), Rowzee Peyton (c.1748-1867), and William H. Fitzhugh (1788-1859) "or any three of them...to contract for, and superintend the building of an addition to the Jail of this county for an additional Jail of two rooms" (*Virginia Herald*, Sept. 26, 1818). Despite the effort to improve the jail, it remained of poor construction and notoriously easy from which to escape.

This complex was still standing when Union forces occupied the area in 1862-63. A Union chaplain described the courthouse as "a tumble-down and filthy building, and jail which stands in the middle of the road, is a miserable two-story affair built of rough stone. The lower story is occupied by hogs, and the upper is reached by stairs from the outside. With but one exception, the few surrounding dwellings are of somewhat similar appearance, and like the soil, are worn out...one of the ugliest appearing places one could ask to see." The sad appearance of the area, brought on by age and poverty, was only to worsen as the War Between the States intensified and Stafford County was occupied by hostile and destructive forces.

The War Between the States
Viewed Through the Courthouse Door

Stafford County was nearly destroyed during the War Between the States. Gen. Irvin McDowell landed troops at Aquia Creek on Apr. 18, 1862 and the last Union troops left Stafford in June 1863. Prior to the Battle of Fredericksburg, Federal troops were camped on the grounds around the courthouse, jail, and clerk's office. Failing to make adequate plans for the care of the county's records, officials fled the area as Union forces poured in. Left on site were deed books, court records, furniture, and other county possessions including the court's Bible and seal dating from the colonial period. Union soldiers saw these items as the "spoils of war" and freely vandalized and stole anything within their reach. The minutes of the county court dating from January 1861 through mid-1869 survive and provide some insight into the events of this tragic period. The following entries from those court records shed light on the effects of 14 months of Union occupation.

January 16, 1861
"Ordered that all the Justices of the County be summoned to our next County Court to take into consideration the propriety of making an appropriation for the purpose of arming one volunteer company of the County to act as police in said County and defending the same in cast it be necessary and for such other things as may then be thought proper."

June 19, 1861
"Ordered that W[alker] P[eyton] Conway and G[ustavus] B. Wallace be appointed to uniform a company to be raised by James E. Waller and report to this Court at its July term."

"The Court doth allow Thomas Waller two hundred dollars to be levied at the July Court next for the purpose of defraying expenses of uniform of his Cavalry Company."

July ___, 1861
"The Court appoints N[athaniel] W[aller] Ford in District No. 4 and John Irvine in District No. 2 to act in conjunction with Commissioners appointed at last Court to attend to the wants of families of Volunteers."

August 21, 1861
Thomas H. Hewitt was appointed in District No. 1 "to act in conjunction with Commissioners already appointed to attend to the wants of families of Volunteers."

March 19, 1862
"The Court having maturely considered the propriety of removing the records books and papers of the County to some safer point (and having advised with the Attorney for the Commonwealth and others) are of the opinion that the said records &c. shall not be removed under any contingency from said office and further are of the opinion that the Clerk of this Court ought not to be considered in any wise responsible for said records &c. should he think proper to leave said County on the approach of the enemy."

"Ordered that the Sheriff of the County of Stafford enroll as soon as practicable all able bodied male free negroes between the ages of eighteen and fifty, and report to Court."

The Court met at Chatham (the Lacy house) in 1864 and 1865.

October 19, 1864
"Upon motion of John H. Suttle, Esq. the following resolution being an application for the exemption of certain citizens of Stafford county from Military duty was adopted— Whereas the County of Stafford has been greatly wasted and destroyed by the public enemy and her Citizens from their position being unable to provide supplies unless they produce them from the soil and a very large proportion of the effective labour of the County being now in the Confederate service and another large proportion of said labour with the means of subsistence having been carried off by the enemy thereby reducing the inhabitants to a very reduced means of living and whereas there is now progressing in the County a most sweeping and undiscriminating Conscription taking the heads of families and others whose services are indispensable to supply the means of life to their families and the families of others, who are now in the Confederate service—Resolved that the facts be communicated to the Governor of this Commonwealth and the Hon. Sect. War with the request that such persons only should be taken who can be spared for the public service—and Judge R. C. L. Moncure, H. B. Barnes, and John H. Suttle were appointed to present the same to the executive and Secretary of War."

That same day the justices expressed yet another concern about the conscription. The minutes read,

"Whereas this court is satisfied that there are no more Justices of the Peace in this County than are absolutely necessary to preserve the Peace and perform the duties of the said Office in their County there being only ten Justices now in the County whereas the proper number for said County is sixteen—and the said Court is desirous if it shall be necessary that the certificate of the Governor of Virginia be obtained to protect said Justices from annoyance by the Conscript Officers of the Confederate States." This entry then lists the ten justices remaining in the county along with their ages and notes that three more were presently in the Confederate service.

"At a meeting of the county Court of Stafford at its regular term held on this 19th day of October 1864 at the Lacy House...The first business before the Court was the appointment of a Clerk...and the said Court having decided to go into the election of Clerk (The state of the County being such as to render an Election by the people impossible) George V. Moncure was unanimously elected to the said Office and duly qualified."

November 16, 1864
"Ordered that the Justices of this County be summoned to consider the question of making provision for the indigent families of the soldiers from this County in the Confederate service and of providing for the indigent in said County and that the justices furnish a list of said indigent in their respective districts at the next term."

January 18, 1865
"William T. Patton is appointed agent to purchase or impress the necessary support of the indigent families of soldiers and sailors under the Act of 31st Oct. 1863."

March 15, 1865
"The first business was the appointment of an agent for this County to receive its quota of the funds apportioned by an Act of Assembly of Virginia passed February 1865 for the purpose of affording relief to the indigent families of soldiers. Whereupon Charles Herndon was unanimously appointed as agent."

"The county of Stafford has been from the earliest period of the War subjected to the continuous ravages of the enemy and to protracted occupation and depredations by large armies of the enemy and smaller bodies of Confederate Troops. It is not necessary fully to relate the details of these as they are committed with the well known military campaigns. Gen. McDowell with a large army occupied the County for months. Subsequently, Gen. Burnside occupied the County with his army for any months—twas during this occupancy that the bombardment of Fredericksburg took place from the heights of Stafford. Subsequently to this Gen. Hooker with another large army occupied the County. During these occupations miles and miles of the County were striped [sic] of everything—and general devastation and ruin spread over the whole County, woods fences and habitations were burnt and many of its inhabitants had to seek refuge in other parts of the Commonwealth. There has not been food enough made in the County for two or three years past to approximate the wants of the people of the County to provide subsistence. These difficulties are increasing as most of the adult whit male inhabitants are in the army and the enemy has carried off nearly all the slaves. Great destitution exits [sic] among the families of the soldiers and increasing in a painful degree. The Court has not the means of drawing on the taxable resources of the County to provide adequate funds to relieve this destitution. For long periods during the war the enemy have occupied this County and prevented the Court from holding its regular sessions and the ____ locality of the County subjects it to constant liability to such occupation, and even not the Court holds its sessions not at the Court House, but at another point in the County. These facts entitled this Court in vies of both the letter and spirit of the recent act aforesaid, to claim in behalf of the families aforesaid a participation in its benefits. The Court after close examination of satisfactory sources of information doth certify that one thousand soldiers have in this County been mustered into the military service of the Confederate States during the existing war and the Court doth appoint Charles Herndon as a suitable person to be recommended to said Commissioners as an agent for the County to receive in its behalf, its quota of the funds appropriated by said Act."

"The Court doth request the Representative in Congress from this District, the Hon: D. C. Degarnett to use every effort to have the County of Stafford exempted from Taxation for the year 1864."

May 15, 1865
"It is ordered by the Court that a committee of three judicious citizens of the County be appointed from each Magisterial District, whose duty it shall be to ascertain and supply the pressing wants of the families of such citizens of said County as have enlisted in the

service of their Country during the present war, and who have left their families needy and dependent, that all supplies required for said purpose shall be furnished by said committees respectively at fair cash prices and that they report the same with proper vouchers to the next levy Court of this County when said Bills with interest will be duly levied for by said Court---and said committees are further requested to ascertain and report to the said court what amount they may estimate to be necessary in their respective districts to be levied for to supply such support and maintenance in the future, or what plan in their judgment shall be adopted in the premises in order best to accomplish the object desired. The following citizens are appointed under said order to wit: In Dist. No. 1 William Pollock, William H. Hansbrough and W[alker] P[eyton] Conway. Dist. No. 2 John C. Shelton, Thomas J. Skinker, G[ustavus] B[rown] Wallace, District No. 3 C[harles] A[ddison] Tackett, William T. Patton, James Tolson. Dist. No. 4 William E. Moncure, Samuel S. Brooke, Albert Clift."

September 20, 1865
"Ordered that N[athaniel] W[aller] Ford, Benjamin West, and John H. Suttle be appointed commissioners to repair the Clerk's Office and to purchase the necessary record books for the County and Circuit Courts and they are authorized to borrow the necessary funds upon the credit of the County for such purpose, and they are also directed to consider and report to the Court what repairs are necessary to the Court House and Jail and the probable expense of such repairs."

"Ordered that the United States Telegraph Company be granted the right of way through the County of Stafford along the Old Stage road from Fredericksburg to Alexandria and shall then be permitted to put up Telegraph post and wire—providing they do not in any way obstruct the public road the Court reserves to itself any right of ___ that they may possess."

"The Clerk of this Court is authorized to keep his Office at his dwelling house until the Clerks Office is repaired."

November 16, 1865
"Ordered that the Clerk of this Court record on the minute book the proceeding of the Court held at Falmouth and the Lacy house in the years 1864 and 1865."

December 20, 1865
The Court met again in the courthouse. Present---Nathaniel Waller Ford, Gustavus B. Wallace, John Lowry, and Duff Green.

March 21, 1866
"Ordered that E[lias] A. W. Hore, John H. Suttle, and N. W. Ford be appointed commissioners to contract and have repaired and put in proper order the Court House, Clerk's Office, Jail and Public Lot and that they be authorized to borrow the necessary funds upon the credit of the County for that purpose."

July 18, 1866
"Ordered that the sheriff use proper means to get all the books belonging to the Clerk's Office and especially the book which is known to be in Maryland."

November 21, 1866
"The Court now without a seal, the same having been lost or destroyed during the late war it is ordered that the Governor be requested to provide a seal for the Court to be deposited with the Clerk thereof according to the Code of 1860 ch. 161 and that a copy of this order be forthwith sent by the Clerk to the Governor."

October 16, 1867
Strother Harding and Robert G. Hickerson were appointed "to examine and report upon expenditures upon the Court House, Jail and Clerks Office."

John H. Suttle was appointed "to purchase the furniture necessary for the Court House and Clerks office."

September 16, 1868
"It appearing to the Court that one of the Record Books of Stafford County is now in the hands of some party in the State of Maryland and it being very important for the interests of all the citizens of the County that said Book shall be recovered and restored to the Clerk's Office of said County—It is ordered by the Court that John H. Suttle esq. Comm's. Attorney for said County be and he is hereby appointed the agent of this Court with directions to take all necessary steps to procure and return said Book and to report the expenses incured [sic] by him in this service which will be duly certified and paid out of the County levy."

January 20, 1869
"B. H. Strother esq. of Washington City DC having kindly secured and returned to this office two Record Books which wear [sic] taken off during the last war."

June Term, 1869
"It is ordered that Travers D. Moncure be authorized to proceed to the State of Maryland and recover the record books of this Court in said State."

The damage done to the courthouse and the county records was extensive. Soldiers destroyed, vandalized, or stole most of the contents in the clerk's office and courthouse. Even the 18th century county seal was stolen. An article appearing in a local newspaper and titled "An Ancient Relic" explains the theft of the seal. It read:

Probate Clerk E. M. Young, of Silver City, New Mexico, who is on a visit to his father in this city, has in his possession a rare relic of Colonial days, It is the seal of Stafford Court, Virginia, in the days of George II, and was taken from the old Court House in March, 1862 when Gen. Daniel E. Sickles, with 2,000 men, crossed over from Liverpool Point. It fell into the possession of Capt. Wm. H. Hugo, Company C, 70th New York volunteers, who was in the advance and took possession of the old Court House.

The seal is round in shape, of iron, and is one and a half inches in diameter, four and three fourth inches in circumference, one and a half inches high and weighs about a pound. It represents the King sitting on this throne with two female figures on either side, representing "Justice" and "Right," holding with one hand a crown over the king's head, "Justice" holding in the other hand a pair of balances and "Right" a sprig of evergreen, with a fowl at her feet. Underneath them is this inscription, "We will not sell, deny, or delay justice or right." Over the King's head is the inscription, "Geo. II. R.," and around the seal the words, "The Seal of Stafford Court in Virginia."
(*Fredericksburg Star*, July 1, 1891)

At the same time the old English Bible belonging to the court was taken, and while the troops were crossing Aquia Creek it was dropped into the water and lost.

Probably Mr. Young will restore this ancient relic to the County Court of Stafford, where it will no doubt be zealously preserved and greatly appreciated.

George II ascended the throne of England in 1728 and died in 1760. Hallam says his reign was the most prosperous period that England had ever known.

This was the result not alone from the acquisition of new territory but also from the conquests of new fields of thought effected by Pope, Samuel Johnson, Fielding, Smollet, Reynolds, Hogarth and many others.

Apparently, Edgar M. Young did not return the old county seal while on this visit. He spent many more years in New Mexico, eventually returning to Fredericksburg where he died. His obituary read:

MR. E. M. YOUNG, SR. Passes Away After Long Illness—Funeral Thursday at 3 P. M.

Mr. Edgar M. Young, Sr., died at the home of this sister, Miss Mattie Young, Tuesday night after an illness of two years, aged 60 years. He suffered a third stroke of paralysis of the throat Saturday night which caused his death.

The deceased was born in this city in 1849, being a son of the late John James Young. He was educated here and went after the war to the Greenbrier White Sulphur Springs, engaged in business there and married Miss Mary Constance Calwell by whom he had three children—E. M. Young, Jr., Mrs. Wm. Bernard, and B. C. Young.

Later his store at the White Sulphur was burned and he came back here and lived, with A. B. Botts & Co., dry goods merchants, for several years. After the death of his wife, he went to Silver City, New Mexico, where he married Miss Mary Cobb, of St. Joseph, Mo., by whom he had one daughter, Mrs. John McKalaway Thompson of Silver City, New Mexico.

Mr. Young lived in Silver City 25 years, where he was postmaster and clerk of court. After the death of his second wife his health failed and about two years ago he came to his old home here, where he died.

He was a member of Lodge No. 4, in which he was made a Mason many years ago, and was also an Elk.

Funeral services will be held from St. George's church Thursday at 3 p. m., conducted by Rev. R. J. McBryde.

Pallbearers—Active: Messrs. Clarence R. Howard, H[ouston] K. Sweetzer, W[illiam] S[nowden] Hitt, W[illiam] H. Richards, Jr., W[ilfred] S[mith] Embrey, K[eating] N[elson] Goolrick. Honorary: Messrs. Geo. B. Pearson, Dr. Geo. H. Chewning, A[lbert] B[urnley] Botts, Dr. M. M. Lewis, M. J. Gately, St. Geo. R. Fitzhugh, Thom. W. Franklin, A. Randolph Howard, Dr. A[ndrew] C. Doggett.
(*Free Lance*, Apr. 1, 1909)

Forty years later, Stafford's old records were still turning up. In a newspaper notice was published announcing:

Editor of The Times:
Sir,--Permit me through your columns to call the attention of the proper authorities to the fact that certain records of Stafford county, Va., are now in the State Library at Albany, N. Y.

These records were probably brought North during the war by some Federal soldier, and subsequently at an auction were bought by the librarian of the Albany Library.

I am quite sure that a request for them from either the Governor of Virginia or the judge of Stafford county, would secure their return to Stafford county, to which they must be valuable, and in whose custody they should certainly be.

Very truly Yours,
W. Dudley Powers
No. 281, Fourth Avenue, New York

(*Daily Star*, July 15, 1902)

Stafford County Jail, Built 1783

Stafford County Clerk's Office, Built 1783

Sources:

Barton, R. T., ed. *Virginia Colonial Decisions: the Reports of Sir John Randolph and by Edward Barradall of the Decisions of the General Court of Virginia, 1728-1741*. Boston: Boston Book Co., 1909.

Bruce, Philip Alexander. *Institutional History of Virginia in the Seventeenth Century*. NY: G. P. Putnam and Sons, 1910.

Coppage, A. Maxim and Tackitt, James W. *Stafford Co., Virginia, 1800-1850*. Concord, CA, 1982.

Daily Star, July 15, 1902, "Stafford Papers in New York."

Fredericksburg Star, July 1, 1891, "An Ancient Relic."

Free Lance, Apr. 1, 1909, obituary of Edgar M. Young, Sr.

Hagemann, James A. *The Heritage of Virginia*. Norfolk, VA: Donning Company Publishers, 1986.

Mapp, Alf J., Jr. *The Virginia Experiment: the Old Dominion's Role in the Making of America (1607-1781*. Richmond, VA: Dietz Press, Inc., 1957.

McIlwaine, H. R. "Justices of the Peace of Colonial Virginia, 1757-1775." *Bulletin of the Virginia State Library*. Richmond, VA: Virginia State Library, 1922.

"Mr. E. M. Young, Sr." *Fredericksburg Free Lance*, Apr. 1, 1909.

Porter, Albert Ogden. *Colonial Government in Virginia, a Legislative History, 1607-1904*. NY: Columbia University Press, 1947.

"Public Officers in Virginia, 1680." *The Virginia Magazine of History and Biography*, vol. 4, #3, January, 1894, NY: Kraus Reprint Corp., 1968, pp. 225-252.

Rouse, Parke, Jr. *Virginia: the English Heritage in America*. NY: Hastings House Publishers, 1966.

Stafford County Court Minute Book, 1852-1867. Stafford Courthouse, Virginia.

Virginia Herald, Sept. 26, 1818, improvements to be made to Stafford jail

Justices of the Peace

1664[149]

Richard Fossaker[150] (died 1676)
Capt. John Alexander[152] (died 1677)
Roger Perfitt[154]
George Mason[156] (1628-1686)

Lt. Col. Robert Williams[151]
Richard Heabeard[153] (died c.1720)
Hugh Dowding[155]
John Lord

1665

Col. John Dodman (born c.1613)
Richard Heabeard
Richard Fossaker
Edward Sanders[158]
Hugh Dowding

Roger Perfitt
Capt. John Alexander
Col. Henry Meese[157] (died 1682)
Robert Osborne

1666

Col. John Dodman
Robert Osborne
Richard Heabeard
Capt. John Alexander

Hugh Dowding
Lt. Col. Henry Meese
Maj. George Mason
Richard Fossaker

---

[149] According to Westmoreland County court records, these eight men "took the oaths of allegiance, supremacy and of the Justice of the peace for the County of Stafford before Lt. Colonel William Hardich, Maj. John Washington, Mr. Daniel Hutt, Mr. John Whiston, justices of the peace for the County of Westmoreland, being impowered thereunto by the Governor 5 April 1664" (Dorman, Westmoreland, 56).
[150] Richard Fossaker owned land adjoining Gerrard Masters' and William Waller's Concord and the Hope Patent.
[151] Around 1660 Col. Williams married Frances (Baldwin) Townsend, widow of Richard Townsend (born c.1606).
[152] Capt. Alexander settled in Virginia before 1653. He patented land in Westmoreland County, now King George that included what later became known as Caledon. Over the years, he acquired a tremendous amount of acreage in Westmoreland, including land on the north side of Potomac Creek near Marlborough Point.
[153] Richard patented land near Passapatanzy Creek (now King George County).
[154] Roger patented land in what is now King George County.
[155] Hugh patented land in what is now Fairfax County, but was then Stafford.
[156] This was the first George Mason to settle in the New World, arriving in Virginia c.1652. His ancestral home was in Staffordshire, England and it is believed that it was Mason who suggested the name "Stafford" for the new county divided from Westmoreland. In 1664, the same year in which Stafford first appeared in the records as a separate county, Mason purchased 650 acres of land on Potomac Creek from Valentine Peyton (1629-1665) where he built a home. Over the years, Mason bought several adjoining tracts, increasing the size of his farm to 1,150 acres. The house site is located on the hill at the intersection of Brooke Road (State Route 608) and Marlborough Point Road (State Route 621). It was his great grandson, George Mason IV (1725-1792) who built Gunston Hall in Fairfax County and wrote the Virginia Declaration of Rights. George married Mary French.
[157] One of the very early settlers on Potomac Creek, Col. Meese lived on what is now Waugh Point in King George County and was a member of His Majesty's Council. In 1680 he set sail for England, leaving his wife in Stafford. He had made several trips home during the time he lived in Virginia and probably intended to return from his last visit; however, he died in England in 1682. His Potomac Creek plantation became the property of Parson John Waugh (1630-1706) and was for many years the glebe of Overwharton Parish.
[158] In 1662 Sanders patented 2,900 acres "in the forest between the Counties of Lancaster and N'umberland."

1667
Lt. Col. Henry Meese
Col. Nicholas Spencer (1638-1689)
Maj. George Mason
Capt. John Alexander

Col. Peter Ashton[159]
Maj. Isaac Allerton[160] (c.1627:30-1702)
Capt. John Lee[161] (1643-1673)
Richard Heabeard

1668
Col. John Dodman
Robert Townsend[162] (1640-1675)
Maj. George Mason

Richard Heabeard
Lt. Col. Henry Meese
Robert Howson[163] (died before 1697)

1680
Maj. Andrew Gilson[164] (c.1628-c.1698)
Thomas Gregg[166] (died 1699)

James Ashton[165] (died 1686)

1683
Col. William Fitzhugh[167] (1651-1701)

1684
William Fitzhugh

1685
William Fitzhugh

Samuel Hayward[168] (died 1696)

---

[159] In 1665 Ashton patented 2,550 acres on Machodoc Creek, now King George County.

[160] Isaac was born in Plymouth, Massachusetts, the only son of Isaac Allerton (died 1659), a tailor and merchant. His mother was Fear Brewster (died c.1635). Around 1644 young Isaac moved to New Haven and graduated from Harvard in 1650. Around 1660 he moved to Virginia and settled on land inherited from his father. He married the widow Elizabeth Willoughby Overzee Colclough around 1662. Isaac acquired over 5,000 acres on the Rappahannock and in 1662 became a justice for Westmoreland County. In 1680 he was named escheator for one or more counties in the Rappahannock River valley.

[161] John was the eldest son of Col. Richard Lee (1618-1664) and Anne Constable (born 1622) of York County. He was educated at Oxford and studied medicine. John served as sheriff of Westmoreland County in 1672 and was burgess of that county in 1673.

[162] Robert was the son of Richard Townsend (born c.1606). He lived in the lower part of Stafford that later became part of King George. From his father he inherited lands in York County and his Stafford land was inherited through his mother. In 1665 Robert married Mary Langhorne (died c.1694).

[163] Howson was a Welsh sea captain who patented land on Upper Machodoc in present day Westmoreland County and on Great Hunting Creek near Anacostia, part of which became the city of Alexandria.

[164] Andrew was a justice for Lancaster County. He was also one of the fist justices named for Rappahannock County and later lived in Stafford. In 1664 he married Behethland Bernard (1635-1720).

[165] James was the brother of Col. Peter Ashton. He was born in Kirby Underwood, County Lincoln, England and came to Virginia after 1671.

[166] In 1661, with Gerard Fowke (1618-1669), William Horton, and Richard Granger, Thomas Gregg (also spelled Grigg) patented 2,000 acres in Westmoreland County upon the branches of Upper Machodoc for the transport of 40 persons. On Mar. 18, 1662 he patented 400 acres, also in Westmoreland (later Stafford and now King George), on Passapatanzy Creek adjoining John and William Heabeard and Henry Meese. Thomas married Lucy Heabeard (died c.1730), sister of John Heabeard (died 1690).

[167] This was William Fitzhugh the immigrant. He resided at Eagle's Nest, Stafford County, now King George.

[168] Samuel was the son of Nicholas Hayward, a London grocer and merchant who acted as agent for Col. Nathaniel Pope of Westmoreland County. On Mar. 18, 1662 Samuel patented 200 acres in Westmoreland County "on the head of Choetanck."

1686

George Mason
William Buckner[169] (died 1716)
Mathew Thompson[171]
Dr. William Banks[172] (died c.1687)
Capt. John Withers[174] (1634-1699)

Samuel Hayward
Edward Thomason[170]
Col. William Fitzhugh
Malachy Peale[173] (16_-1698)

1687

Samuel Hayward
Dr. William Banks
George Mason
Col. William Fitzhugh

Edward Thomason
John Withers
William Buckner
Mathew Thomason

---

[169] William was a merchant in York County. He owned land in York and Stafford counties and held offices in both counties. In 1692 William was one of the Surveyors General for Virginia. He died in Yorktown.

[170] On Nov. 20, 1678 Edward Thomason and Robert Hall patented 104 acres on the west side of Aquia Creek and the south side of Austin Run "Beginning at the Bridge going over Austin's Run to their own Landing." That same day they also received 12 acres "with a small point of marsh adjoining, in Ocquia Creek, easterly from their dwelling house" for the transport of James Clifton (c.1640-c.1714). Edward married Lucy Heabeard (born 1656) and died in Loudoun County.

[171] Mathew owned land on Chappawamsic Creek on the northeast side of Francis Hammersley and may have included what later became George Mason's Chappawamsic Farm and John Moncure's Clermont.

[172] An inventory of Dr. Banks' estate was recorded in Stafford County on Mar. 12, 1687/8.

[173] In 1694 Peale patented 1,000 acres "in the freshes of Potowmack Creek in Stafford County." This land later became known as Marlborough Point.

[174] John was the son of William Wither (probably died 1684) of Arkholme in Melling, Lancashire, England. William was listed in local records as a yeoman, or small farmer. Late in the summer of 1655 John, his wife, and younger brother, William (c.1636-1698), arrived in Virginia. John was 21 years old at the time and his brother was not quite of age. John patented 150 acres in Westmoreland County on Potomac Creek for the transport of three persons. Later, both men took up more land along the creek so that they owned adjoining tracts. They died within a year of each other. Both left wills recorded in the Stafford County court, but these were subsequently destroyed either in one of the courthouse fires or by Union vandals during the War Between the States.

John married three times, first in England to Ann Withers. The name of his second wife is unknown. This third wife was Frances (Townsend) Dade who survived him and later married Col. Rice Hooe (1660-1726).

In 1662/3 John was appointed constable of Potomac Parish and served as a vestryman of Potomac Church. He was one of the men appointed to lay out the town of Marlborough on Nov. 11, 1691 which was the site of the old courthouse until it burned in 1717. He was elected to the House of Burgesses in April 1692 but resigned to become clerk of the court, an office he held until his death.

On Nov. 11, 1692 John appeared in court complaining against John Story, cooper. Withers had contracted with story to have the latter "build or set him up Three tonne of Cyder Cask." Story built the casks and Withers filled them "expecting that they had been good and firm according to agreement but the most part of them proved unsound and leaky and did leak out the quantity of three or four hundred gallons of Cyder whereby the plt doth in fact say he is damnified and damage hath received to the value five thousands pounds of Tobacco." The jury found in favor of Withers and order John Story to pay the damages.

According to Stafford court records, on Nov. 13, 1691 John Withers was granted a license to keep a ferry on Potomac Creek which sailed "from the town of Port Point for this County onto the Valley next or Lunsfords Hills." For his services, Withers was to be paid 4,000 pounds of tobacco collected from the public levy. A later entry dated Dec. 28, 1691 clarified the destination of the Potomac Creek ferry stating, "It is therefore ordered that the valley inserted in the order for keeping the Ferry is intended and meant to be the valley above Lunsford hill toward Mr. John Waughs house." This indicates that the ferry traveled from Marlborough Point across Potomac Creek to the vicinity of Waugh Point.

1688
Francis Hammersley[175]
George Mason
William Buckner
Mathew Thompson
Malachy Peale

Col. William Fitzhugh
John Withers
Edward Thomason
Samuel Hayward

1689
Col. William Fitzhugh
Samuel Hayward
Capt. George Mason
Mathew Thompson

John Withers
William Buckner
Edward Thomason

1690
Col. William Fitzhugh
James Ashton
Mathew Thompson
Samuel Hayward

Edward Thomason
Capt. George Mason[176] (1660-1716)
William Buckner
Capt. John Withers

1691[177]
Martin Scarlett (died 1695)

Dr. Edward Maddox[178] (16_-1694)

---

[175] Hammersley patented 1,795 acres between Aquia and Chappawamsic creeks adjoining Mathew Thompson, Richard Cary (1621-after 1660), Giles Brent (1602-1671), and George Brent (1640-c.1700). He married Giles Brent's widow and lived at Giles' old home, Retirement, somewhere on Brent's Point in modern Wide Water. In 1690 Hammersley had a mill in Stafford (perhaps the Brent's mill that stood near the intersection of Wide Water Road (State Route 611) and Decatur Road (State Route 635) and was destroyed by fire c.1901). Hammersley's association with the Brents suggests that he may have been Catholic and may explain why there are so few surviving public records pertaining to him.
  On Oct. 9, 1691 Giles Brent, Jr. selected Hammersley as his guardian. Upon attaining the age of 14, minors were allowed to name their guardians.
[176] The son of George Mason I and Mary French. He was born at his father's Accokeek plantation.
[177] There is an amusing entry in the court records dated Oct. 6, 1691 which states, "Forasmuch as several disorders misrules and Riots committed during the sitting of this Worshipful Court and the Court taking into consideration the Fatal consequences of such unhappy malignant and Tumultuous proceedings as well against the peach of their Majesties as all their Liege Subjects doe accordingly order Therefore tis ordered that no person of what degree condition of Quality whatsoever shall sell any sort of Liquor whatever to any manner of person or persons whatsoever upon a court day whilst their Majesties Justices of the peace are Sitting without first Leave being prayed for and granted by the Court" (Stafford county Court Records, 1691-1692, p.167).
  1691 was a turbulent year for the justices. Three men were appointed as justices but refused to serve. William Buckner said "that he refused to take the oaths appointed instead of the oaths of Allegiance and Supremacy alledging that whereas he had formerly taken the said Oaths of Allegiance and Supremacy to King James the second in the County cannot now in his conscience think himself fairly discharged from the said Oaths in the life of King James and therefore humbly desires to be Excused from his being obliged to take the said Oaths until hereafter he may in his conscience be better satisfied concerning the same." Thomas Gregg, Sr. also refused to serve as did Capt. John Washington who refused to take the "oaths appointed instead of the oaths of Allegiance and Supremacy and the oath of a justice of the peace for this County" though he claimed "that he was not yet a liver in this County and did therefore think himself incapable of doing such service."
[178] Dr. Maddox married the widow of George Mason I (1629-1686). His only child, Amy, married Thomas Derrick without her father's approval. As a result of this, Dr. Maddox left his 450-500-acre plantation to Overwharton Parish for use as a glebe. This property was on the south side of Potomac Creek and on Muddy Creek (the present dividing line between Stafford and King George counties and not far from John Waugh's seat. Overwharton sporadically used the Maddox plantation as a glebe until after the death of the Rev. Robert Buchan in 1804. By the time of Buchan's death, most glebe lands in Virginia had been sold.

Edward Thomason
Mathew Thompson
Malachy Peale

Col. William Fitzhugh
Capt. George Mason
Capt. John Withers

1692
Capt. Malachy Peale[179]
Capt. John Withers
Robert Alexander[180] (c.1634-c.1704)
Capt. Thomas Owsley (1658-1700)
Capt. Richard Fossaker[182] (1662-c.1735)
Lt. Sampson Darrell[183] (born c.1660)
Lt. Joseph Sumner[184] (1641-1734)
Lt. David Strahan
Joell Stribling
Philip Buckner[186] (1639-1700)

Edward Thomason
Nathaniel Thompson
Capt. George Mason
John Harvey[181] (died 1700)
Lt. Thomas Gregg
Lt. Charles Ellis (c.1650-1708)
Lt. John West
William Downing[185]
Dr. Edward Maddox
Martin Scarlett

1693
Capt. Malachy Peale
Mathew Thompson
Thomas Owsley
Robert Alexander
Martin Scarlett
Edward Thomason

Capt. George Mason
Richard Fossaker
Philip Buckner
John Harvey
Dr. Edward Maddox

1698
Burr Harrison[187] (1637-1706)

1699
Burr Harrison
George Mason
Richard Fossaker
William Williams[188]

Giles Vandegasteel (16_-1701)
Mathew Thompson
Philip Buckner
John Washington[189] (1671-1718:21)

Dr. Maddox's descendants brought suit in court claiming that the property was no longer being used as a glebe as stipulated in his will, recovered it, and sold it for their own benefit.
[179] Peale's property between Potomac and Aquia creeks was known as Peale's or Potomac Neck long before it became known as Marlborough. He became presiding justice of the Stafford Court in 1692.
[180] Robert was the son of John Alexander (died 1677). He was born in England and came to Virginia c.1653 with his mother and father. In 1664 Robert patented 500 acres on a branch of the Upper Machodick dam for the transport of 10 persons. He married first Priscilla Ashton and secondly Frances Fitzhugh(?).
[181] On Mar. 9, 1691 John Harvey was summoned to court to answer charges "for offering and attempting to Ravish Elizabeth Trumbell." The outcome is unknown, but he continued as a justice until at least 1699.
[182] The son of Richard Fossaker (died 1676). He married the daughter and executrix of Capt. John Withers (1634-1699) and his grandson, John Fossaker, was living in Stafford in 1756.
[183] Sampson Darrell patented land on Dogue's Run in what is now Fairfax County.
[184] Joseph was the son of John Sumner (1618-1670) who was born in London and died in Nansemond County.
[185] In 1668 William Downing patented 1,570 acres in Northumberland County on Wicomico Creek for the transport of 18 persons including two William Downings (father and son?).
[186] Philip was baptized in Oxford, England and arrived in Virginia around 1669. He first settled in Gloucester County, but by 1692 was a resident of Stafford.
[187] Burr was the eldest son of Cuthbert Harrison. Burr immigrated to America and settled on Chappawamsic Creek in what later became Stafford. In 1699 he was dispatched by the House of Burgesses as an embassy to the Piscataway Indians. Burr married first in 1695 or 1696 Lettis (Green) Smith (died 1699), the widow of Edward Smith. He married secondly Mary Mansbridge, the widow of William Mansbridge (died 1697).

Robert Colston
Robert Alexander
Joseph Sumner
Edward Hart (died 1703)

1700
Rice Hooe
George Mason
John Washington
William Williams

1701
Richard Foote[192] (1666-1725)
Robert Alexander
Col. Rice Hooe
Capt. Richard Fossaker
Capt. Joseph Sumner
William Bunbury (born c.1670)
John Harvey
Robert Colston

John Harvey
Rice Hooe[190] (1660-1726)
John Waugh, Jr. (1661-1716)
Thomas Gregg

Thomas Gilson[191] (1665-1707)
Joseph Sumner
Richard Fossaker
Mathew Thompson

Col. George Mason
Mathew Thompson
Edward Hart
John Washington
John Waugh, Jr.
John West
Philip Buckner
Capt. Charles Ellis

---

[188] In 1688 Parson John Waugh married Mary Hathaway (born 1679), daughter of Thomas Hathaway of Aquia, deceased, to Mr. Williams. This would have been a common enough occurrence except that at the time of her marriage, Mary was only nine years old. In a suit filed in 1691 the justices ruled that upon attaining the age of 12, Mary could "publickly disclaim the said marriage and protest against it, then it is the Judgment of this court the aforesd marriage...is utterly null and void as if the same had never been had or made." On Dec. 28, 1691 "he very day by the mercy of God that I am twelve years old," Mary declared her freedom citing "infancy and impuberty as well as force and fraud" at the time of her marriage to William Williams. She further claimed "that by no means I can entertain a thought of ever receiving him for a spouse or husband...and soe I bid the said Mr. Williams heartilie farewell and wish him a very good fortune" (Stafford Order Book 196).

In 1693 Mary chose Mr. Richard Fossaker as her guardian as he had married her mother, Mary (Withers) Hathaway, daughter of Capt. John Withers (1634-1699). Capt. Withers was Mary's maternal grandfather and one of the justices hearing the case against William Williams. He and Mathew Thompson dissented from the majority opinion, declaring that they were "of the opinion that the said Mary Hathaway is the wife of the said William Williams not only [now] but aloee when she shall arrive at the age of twelve years...it appearing to them that she was married by the said Mr. John Waugh, Clerk, as aforesd, and that by consent of her guardian."

[189] John lived in the Chotank area of what is now King George County. He was the son of Lawrence Washington (1635-c.1676), the younger immigrant brother. John was a first cousin of George Washington's grandfather who had been guardian of that man's three orphans, including George's father, Augustine (1694-1743). John married Mary Townsend.

[190] Rice originally established himself in Henrico County. He seems to have settled in Stafford as a result of legal difficulties in Henrico. On several occasions he was charged with abuse of his servants (both slave and indentured) and was facing trial there when he left.

[191] Thomas was the son of Andrew Gilson (1628-c.1698) who was sheriff of Rappahannock County in 1660 and justice of that county in 1656 and 1664. Andrew married c.1664 Behethland (1635-1720), the daughter of Capt. Thomas Bernard (died c.1651) and the widow of Capt. Francis Dade (1621-1663). Thomas Gilson married Elizabeth Newton (died 1763), the daughter of John Newton, Sr. who owned Little Falls, a plantation on the Rappahannock River in Stafford.

[192] Richard was selected, along with Nathaniel Pope of Westmoreland County, to proclaim the Queen. This was a ceremony conducted at public occasions such as the annual fair at Marlborough and consisted of volleys of cannon and rifle salutes, followed by a proclamation by Pope. In November 1702 the Stafford Court ordered that Foote be paid "860 pounds for powder" used in the ceremony.

Richard was the son of Richard Foote (1632-c.1697) and Hester Hayward (born 1640), the daughter of Nicholas Hayward (died 1697). Richard, Jr. was born in London.

Richard Colt

Thomas Gregg

1702
Col. George Mason
Mathew Thompson
Capt. Philip Alexander[193] (c.1664-1705)
Capt. Charles Ellis
John Waugh, Jr.
William Bunbury[195] (born c.1670)
Capt. Richard Fossaker
Edward Hart
John Washington

Capt. Joseph Sumner
Lt. Col. Rice Hooe
Robert Alexander
Capt. Thomas Clifton[194] (born 1660)
Richard Foote
Thomas Gregg
Capt. John West
Thomas Gilson

1703
Col. George Mason
Lt. Col. Rice Hooe
Capt. Richard Fossaker

Capt. Joseph Sumner
Richard Foote
Capt. Charles Ellis

1704
William Bunbury

Capt. Richard Fossaker

1705
William Bunbury
Capt. Richard Fossaker

Joseph Sumner

1706
Richard Fossaker
Capt. Charles Ellis
Thomas Gregg

William Fitzhugh[196] (c.1678-1713)
John Anderson
Edward Mountjoy[197] (c.1660-1712)

1707
William Bunbury
Edward Mountjoy

Joseph Sumner, Jr.
Richard Fossaker

1708
Richard Fossaker
Richard Foote

Mathew Thompson
George Anderson[198]

---

[193] Philip was the son of John Alexander (died 1677) and was probably born in Stafford. Around 1695 Philip married Sarah Ashton (born c.1675), the daughter of Capt. John Ashton (died 1677) and Grace Frizer. John died intestate in Stafford. Sarah married secondly Capt. Thomas Clifton (born 1660), the son of James Clifton (c.1640-1714) and Anne Brent. Thomas was also a justice of Stafford.

[194] Thomas was the son of James Clifton (c.1640-1714) and Anne Brent. James and Anne received from Margaret Brent (c.1600-1671) a tract of land on the Potomac River which is today known as Clifton. This property adjoins Richland to the south and Dipple, now part of Quantico Marine Corps Base on its north

[195] William was born in Virginia and married Frances Mason (born 1688).

[196] This was William Fitzhugh of Eagle's Nest. A very wealthy man, he inherited from his father 18,723 acres in Stafford County. He married Ann Lee (1683-1732), the daughter of Richard Lee (1647-1715).

[197] Edward was one of four Mountjoy brothers to immigrate to Virginia during the late 17th century. In 1703 he patented 940 acres on Accokeek Creek that became known as Locust Hill (Eby, They 217). Sometime prior to 1687, Edward married Elizabeth Monroe, widow of Maj. Andrew Monroe (c.1630-c.1668) of Monroe Creek, Northumberland and Westmoreland counties. He married secondly c.1710 Mary Crosby (16_-1756), the daughter of George Crosby of Stafford.

[198] In 1694 George received a patent for 2,466 acres on Little Hunting Creek. He married Mary Matthews, the daughter of John Matthews, an early resident of the Potomac Creek area.

1714

George Mason
John Washington
Dade Massey[199] (1679-1735)
George Anderson
John Mauzy[200] (c.1675-1718)
Henry Fitzhugh[202] (1686-1758)
Rawleigh Travers[203] (16_-1722)

Rice Hooe
Joseph Sumner
John West
John Waugh
James Jameson[201] (died 1736)
Thomas Lunn

1715

George Anderson

1726

Rice Hooe
Henry Fitzhugh
Thomas Hopper
Townsend Dade[206] (c.1688-1761)

Dade Massey
William Storke[204] (1690-1746)
Thomas Harrison[205] (1665-1746)
Maj. John Fitzhugh[207] (died 1733)

---

[199] Dade was born in St. Paul's Parish, the son of Robert Massey (1655-1689) and Mary Dade (1661-c.1694). Dade married Elizabeth Ellis (born c.1680), the daughter of Charles Ellis (c.1650-1708) of Stafford.

[200] John Mauzy was the son of Michael Mauze. John came to America c.1700. It is believed that he married his first wife in England, a daughter of Dr. William Conyers, a London physician. John and his Conyers wife appeared in Virginia at about the same time as Henry Conyers, who is believed to be the Conyers girl's brother. John Mauzy married secondly Mary (Crosby) Mountjoy (16_-1756), the widow of Capt. Edward Mountjoy (c.1660-1712) and the daughter of George Crosby of Stafford.
    John Mauzy's daughter, Margaret (1702-1754) married Maj. Peter Hedgman (c.1700-1765), the son of Nathaniel Hedgman (before 1682-1721), formerly of Lancaster County. In 1704 Nathaniel acquired Rose Hill, the old plantation and burial place of George Mason I. Nathaniel had been sent to Stafford by Robert "King" Carter to manage his property there. According to a letter later written by Carter, Nathaniel became drunk and was killed in a violent accident. Peter Hedgman applied to Carter for work, but the latter believed that Peter was probably no more dependable than his father and refused to hire him. Peter, however, inherited the Rose Hill property and served Stafford for many years as a vestryman, justice, militia officer, and burgess.

[201] Possibly James Jameson who emigrated 1680-83 from Scotland and settled first in St. Paul's Parish, then in what would later become Prince William County.

[202] Henry was the son of William Fitzhugh (c.1678-1713) who was very active in the affairs of Stafford. Henry was the scholar of the family. At age 11 he was sent to school in Bristol and, at age 14, to Westminster School. He matriculated from Christ Church, Oxford in 1722. Later, he served Stafford as a tobacco inspector, justice, and burgess and was known as "Blind Henry" because of his poor vision. In 1717 Henry married Susannah Cooke (1693-1749), the daughter of Mordecai Cooke and Frances Whiting. He and his wife are buried in St. Paul's Churchyard in King George County.

[203] In 1700 and 1701 Rawleigh Travers of Crow's Nest was paid 5,000 pounds of tobacco for operating the ferry over Potomac Creek. In 1703 the license for this ferry was granted to the Rev. John Waugh.

[204] In 1667 William received 600 acres in Stafford between the Potomac and Rappahannock rivers. The south side of his property adjoined that of John Washington and the north side was bounded by the lands of Capt. Ashton and John Alexander. In 1714 William married Elizabeth Hart, the daughter of Edward Hart (died 1703) and Mary Field.

[205] Thomas was the son of Burr Harrison (c.1668-c.1715). Thomas lived on Chappawamsic Creek and served as a justice of Prince William after that county was divided from Stafford in 1731.

[206] Townsend was the son of Francis Dade (c.1659-1698) and Frances Townsend (died 1726). Townsend also served as county lieutenant of Stafford in 1725 and sheriff in 1730. He married first c.1714 Elizabeth Alexander (1698-1736), the daughter of Philip (c.1664-1705) and Sarah (Ashton) Alexander (born c.1675). In 1745 he married secondly Rose Grigsby (c.1700-1785).

French Mason[208] (1695-1748)
Charles Broadwater[210] (died 1733)
Anthony Thornton[212] (1695-1757)
Maj. Robert Alexander[214] (c.1688-1735)

Abraham Farrow[209] (c.1670-1731)
John Linton[211]
Rice Hooe, Jr.[213] (born c.1692)

1729
Dade Massey
Townsend Dade
French Mason
Charles Broadwater
Henry Fitzhugh
Capt. Elias Hore (1700-1730)
John Washington[217] (c.1697-1742)

Thomas Harrison
John Fitzhugh
Abraham Farrow
Anthony Thornton
Dennis McCarty[215] (1704-1742)
Thomas Grigsby[216] (c.1680:95-1745)
William Triplett[218] (died 1749)

---

[207] John Fitzhugh was the son of Col. William Fitzhugh (1651-1701) and Sarah Tucker (1663-after 1701). John inherited from his father 2,273 acres in Stafford. Around 1719 he married Anna Barbara, the daughter of Daniel McCarty.

[208] The son of Col. George Mason (1660-1716) and Mary Fowke. In 1748 French married Mary Nicholson. He owned the official tobacco warehouses at the mouth of Pohick Creek and a mill on the south side. He resided in what would later become Fairfax County.

[209] When Abraham Farrow died, his estate included some 2,400 acres of land in what is now Prince William County. He was listed as a millwright in a legislative petition to Williamsburg dated Jan. 20, 1704. Around or before 1691 Richard Gibson (died before June 1701), a Stafford County attorney, built a grist mill on Quantico Creek, probably a short distance above Interstate 95. It appears that Abraham was the millwright responsible for the construction of this mill. By 1704 Farrow and Richmond County attorney, Joshua Davis, jointly owned the mill; in 1709 Abraham bought out his partner's interest for 5,000 pounds of tobacco. When Abraham died in 1731, he devised his Quantico Mill to his youngest son, also named Abraham (died c.1743).

[210] Charles patented land on Accotinct Run and Great Hunting Creek and on Pimmit's Run in northern Virginia. He also owned 217 acres on Difficult Run known as Wolf Trap Branch.

[211] John was the son of Anthony Linton and Mary Page, the daughter of William Page who died in Stafford in 1716. John Linton married Winifred, the daughter of Col. Peter Presley of Northumberland County. He patented land on Broad and Difficult runs.

[212] Anthony was the son of Francis Thornton (1651-c.1726).

[213] This was the son of Rice Hooe (1660-1726) and probably his first wife, Mary (Dade) Massey. Around 1724 Rice, Jr. married Catherine Taliaferro (died 1731), the daughter of Richard (died c.1677) and Sarah Taliaferro of Richmond County. Rice, Jr. married secondly Tabitha Harrison.

[214] The son of Robert Alexander (c.1634-1704) and Priscilla Ashton. Sometime prior to 1709 young Robert married Anne Fowke (1690-1739), the daughter of Gerard Fowke (1662-1735) of Charles County, Maryland and his second wife, Sarah Burdett. The Stafford County quit rent rolls list Robert, Jr. as owning 4,675 acres in the county. He also served as a major in the Stafford militia.

[215] Dennis was the son of Capt. Daniel McCarty (died 1724) of Cople Parish, Westmoreland County who was twice burgess for that county as well as Speaker of the House of Burgesses. Dennis' mother was Elizabeth (Pope) Payne (born 1667), the daughter of Humphrey Pope. Daniel willed his Stafford land to Dennis who married in 1724 Sarah Ball (born 1705), the daughter of Col. William Ball (1674-1740) and Hannah Beale (c.1674-before 1744). Dennis and Sarah made their home in what is now the Mount Vernon area of Fairfax County. He was a member of Pohick Church in Truro Parish and, in 1731 when Prince William was divided from Stafford, became a justice for the new county. By this change in county boundaries, Dennis' Stafford land fell into Prince William and, later still, into Fairfax, though he mentioned in his will 1,000 acres in Stafford County lying on Aquia Run. Dennis represented Prince William County in the House of Burgesses from 1728-1736.

[216] Thomas Grigsby was the son of John Grigsby (1624-1730) and Jane Prosser. Thomas married Rose Newton (c.1700-1785).

[217] John was the son of John Washington (1668-1721) of Chotank and Mary Townsend. He inherited his father's Chotank plantation and in 1721 married Mary Massey, the daughter of Dade Massey. John died in King George County.

William Lynton[219]
Francis Aubrey[220] (c.1685-1741)
                                    Maj. Peter Hedgman (c.1700-1765)

1730
John Gregg[221] (1706-c.1736)

1731
John Lee[222] (c.1709-1789)   Capt. William Brent[223] (1710-1742)

---

[218] William was the son of William Triplett, Sr. of King George. In 1740 he was living in St. Mark's Parish, Orange County, later Culpeper County, and was vestryman of that parish in 1741. He later moved to Prince William County. On Sept. 29, 1747 George Brent (c.1703-1789) sold William 500 acres on the southwest side of Quantico Creek where he was living at the time of his death. This land is now part of the Marine Corps reservation and William was buried on this property. He married Elizabeth Hedgman, the daughter of Nathaniel Hedgman, Jr. (born 1729) of Stafford.

[219] William Lynton (Linton) married Johanna Lewis, the daughter of Edward Lewis of Richmond County.

[220] Francis was the youngest son of John Aubrey (c.1623-c.1692) and the nephew of Henry Aubrey (died c.1694) of Essex County who mentioned him in his will. In 1717 Francis established a plantation near Pohick and from that time until 1731 speculated in land in what later became Loudoun County. He also owned land on Broad and Cub runs and Catoctin and Goose creeks. In 1731 he served as tobacco inspector at Dumfries. The following year he was named to the same position at Pohick. Francis also served as a justice in Prince William County after its formation in 1731. He married Frances Tanner.

[221] Probably the son of James Gregg (died c.1724) and Jane Owsley.

[222] John was the son of Capt. Hancock Lee (1653-1709) and Mary Kendall of Northumberland County. Hancock also owned extensive tracts in Stafford, including 570 acres on Horsepen Run near the Rappahannock River and 1,750 acres on Chappawamsic Run adjoining the land of Thomas Harrison (1665-1746). John inherited his father's Chappawamsic tract, but it is unclear if he lived on the property. John was probably unmarried as he willed this land to his nephew, also named John Lee. He died at this nephew's home in Orange County.

[223] William was the son of William Brent (c.1677-1709) and Sarah Gibbons (c.1692-1733). Capt. Brent married c.1730 Jane (surname unknown), probably from Maryland. He inherited land in Maryland that had originally been granted to Giles Brent (1602-1672). The land passed to Giles Brent, Jr. (1652-1679), who died intestate, and finally came to William. Unspecified legal wrangling in Maryland forced William into the courts to defend his title, but he died before a final decision was made. William's administrator, Peter Hedgman, petitioned the House of Burgesses on Sept. 15, 1744:

> That William Brent, late of the County of Stafford, dec'd., having a Title to great estate in Lands in the Province of Maryland, did commence a Suit for the said Lands in the said Province, and recovered the same there; upon which the Parties concerned appeal'd to England and several Persons in Great Britain advanced large Sums of Money to enable the said Brent to carry on the said Appeal. And soon after the Recovery of the Estate of the said Lands, he return'd to Virginia and died, leaving your Petitioner his Executor; and that the lands and real Estate of the said Deceased are now vested in his eldest son, William Brent, to whom your Petitioner is Guardian; and that his Debts, particularly those in England are left unpaid, and that his personal Estate is exhausted in paying his other Debts; and praying, that he may be enabled to apply the Rents and Profits that arise from those Lands, to the Discharge of his Debts."
> (McIlwaine, Journals, 1742, p. 93)

A bit more research revealed that Brent's Maryland lands were occupied by Benjamin Tasker (1690-1768) ironmaster and owner of Baltimore Iron Works. It was Tasker who had brought suit against Brent. When the court found in favor of Brent, Tasker appealed to England. William was forced to go to England, "where being entirely destitute of money, John Philpot and John Buchanan, merchants, in London, upon the credit of his title to the last mentioned lands, did advance the sum of £300 sterling, to enable him to defend the said appeal, which was determined in his favour."

Robert Massey
James Carter[225] (1684-1743)
Henry Fitzhugh

Henry Washington[224] (1694-1748)
James Markham[226]
Townsend Dade

1732
Philip Alexander

Henry Fitzhugh, Jr.

1733
Anthony Thornton
Hugh French[228] (17_-1740)
Swan Jones[229] (1703-1736)
Peter Hedgman

Chandler Fowke[227] (1692-1745)
William Brent
Robert Massey

1734
Henry Washington
Thomas Harrison

Hugh French

1735
Henry Fitzhugh
Peter Hedgman

William Brent

1736
Capt. Philip Alexander[230] (1704-1753)

Chandler Fowke

1737
Henry Washington
Townsend Dade

John Lee
William Harrison[231] (1703-1745)

At the time of his death, William owned land in Stafford and Prince William counties as well as in Maryland.

[224] Henry was the son of John Washington (1663-1698). He grew up on Westmoreland County but inherited land on Machodoc Creek to which he removed. Henry also served as sheriff of Stafford and was a captain in the county militia.

[225] James was the son of Thomas Carter of Lancaster County and his wife Katharine Dale. In 1724 James married Mary Brent, the daughter of Hugh Brent of Lancaster, and moved to Stafford where they resided on Palace Green.

[226] On Aug. 27, 1728 James received a patent for 1,034 acres on Aquia Run adjoining George Crosby and James Wood.

[227] Capt. Chandler Fowke of Gunston Hall, Stafford County, now Fairfax, was the son of Col. Gerard Fowke (1662-1734) and Sarah Burdett (c.1665-1747). Chandler married Mary Fossaker (c.1700-1783), the daughter of Col. Richard Fossaker.

[228] Hugh married Betty Brittingham, the daughter of Nathaniel Brittingham, and lived on the north side of Potomac Creek.

[229] Swan Jones was the son of Maurice Jones (c.1659-c.1733) and Judith Swan (c.1680-1742). He was a resident of Northumberland and Stafford counties and, while living in Stafford, resided on the north run of Chappawamsic Creek. He died in Northumberland County.

[230] Philip was the son of Philip Alexander (c.1664-1705). In 1726 he married Sarah Hooe (c.1707-1758), the daughter of Rice Hooe (1660-1726) and Frances Townsend. Sometime during the 1740s, Philip left his home in Stafford and moved to what is now Alexandria. He made his home here for some years. He died at Salisbury in King George and was buried there.

[231] William was the son of Thomas Harrison (1665-1746) of Chappawamsic. The Harrison land along Chappawamsic Creek occupied both sides of the creek and included modern Locust Shade Park in Prince William County. In 1732 William married Isabella (Triplett) Hore, the widow of Capt. Elias Hore (1700-1730) and the daughter of Capt. William Triplett (1650-1725) and Isabella Miller. William was a justice in Prince William in 1731 and vestryman of Overwharton in 1746.

1738
James Hooe[232]
Richard Foote[233] (1704-1774)
William Harrison
Mott Doniphan[235] (died c.1776)

Richard Bernard (1705-1753)
Townsend Washington[234] (1705-1743)
John Waugh
Capt. John Hooe[236] (1702-1766)

1740
Mott Doniphan

Philip Alexander

1741
John Peyton (1691-1760)

Peter Daniel[237] (1706-1777)

1742
Peter Daniel
Chandler Fowke

Peter Hedgman
Capt. John Grant[238] (16_-1749)

1743
John Peyton
Mott Doniphan
Townsend Washington
James Scott

Philip Alexander
Peter Daniel
William Fitzhugh[239] (1725-1791)
Capt. John Grant

1744
John Hooe
Peter Daniel
Philip Alexander
Richard Bernard
John Peyton

Mott Doniphan
Peter Hedgman
Henry Washington
Richard Foote

---

[232] James was the son of Howson Hooe (1696-1733) and Mary Dade.
[233] Richard was the son of Richard Foote (1666-1725). In 1726 he married Katherine Fossaker.
[234] Townsend was the youngest son of John Washington (1671-1718:21) and Mary Townsend. He married Elizabeth Lund and lived on her inherited property at the head of Chotank Creek on the estate called Green Hill. This property was later called Panorama and was home to the Lomax family.
[235] Mott was the second son of Alexander Doniphan (1653-1717) of Richmond County and his second wife, Margaret Mott. He married Rosanna, the daughter of Capt. George and Mary (Mathews) Anderson of Stafford.
[236] John was the eldest child of Col. Rice Hooe (1660-1726) and this third wife, Frances Townsend. He is usually referred to as "Capt. John Hooe of Hooe's Ferry." John also served as sheriff of Stafford in 1739. In 1726 he married Anne Alexander (born 1712), the daughter of Robert Alexander (c.1688-1735) and Anne Fowke (1690-1739).
[237] Peter was the son of James and Margaret (Vivian) Daniel (died 1727) of Middlesex County. He moved to Stafford as a young man and in 1736 married Sarah Travers (171_-1788), the daughter of Rawleigh Travers (died c.1722) and Hannah Ball (c.1683-1748). Hannah was the daughter of Col. Joseph Ball (1649-1711) of Lancaster County.

Peter was a zealous advocate of American freedom and was the first justice to sign Stafford's 1765 protest against the Stamp Act. He was presiding justice of the Stafford court for many years as well as a member of Stafford's Committee of Safety in 1774.
[238] John married first in 1727 Hester Foote and secondly Margaret (Watts) Strother, the widow of William Strother (1696-1733).
[239] William Fitzhugh of Marmion. He married first Ursula, the daughter of Col. William Beverley of Essex County. He married secondly Hannah (?).

1745
Henry Fitzhugh
Charles Waller[241] (1702-1749)
Townsend Dade[243] (1707-1781)
John Lee
Robert Massey
Capt. John Hooe
Richard Foote
John Peyton
William Fitzhugh, Sr.[245] (1721-1798)
Nathaniel Chapman[247] (1709-1760)

William Walker[240] (born 1710:25)
Maj. Benjamin Strother[242] (c.1712-1789)
Peter Hedgman[244]
Henry Washington
Philip Alexander
Richard Bernard
Mott Doniphan
Peter Daniel
Capt. James Waugh[246] (c.1705-1750)
Capt. William Harrison

1746
James Waugh
Townsend Dade

Peter Daniel
Richard Bernard

1747
Philip Alexander
John Peyton
Henry Washington
Richard Bernard

Mott Doniphan
James Waugh
Charles Waller

---

[240] Probably the son of Thomas Walker (died c.1726) and Lydia Hardwich of Westmoreland County. In 1741 William and his wife Sarah bought land in Prince William County, later Fauquier, and by 1766 they were in Bute County, North Carolina.
   There was another William Walker (died 1750) who resided in Stafford and married Elizabeth Monk. This William's son, also named William, was the intended architect of Aquia Church but died in Williamsburg while finishing another building project. One of the William Walkers served as a tax collector in 1781, accepting payment in hemp or tobacco (Auditor of Public Accounts).

[241] Charles was the brother of Edward Waller (1706-1753). These two brothers came to Virginia from Essex and built Concord on Aquia Creek (see illustration).
   Charles Waller operated a sawmill and may have been in the boat building business as well. In 1749 he sold 7,013 feet of pine planks to Kingsbury Iron Furnace in Maryland and 596 feet of oak planks to Accokeek Furnace in Stafford. The following year Accokeek paid him £30.12.6 "for a New flat with oars masts anchors & cable" (Eby, Laying, Ledger).

[242] Benjamin was the son of Capt. William Strother (c.1665-1726) and Margaret Thornton of King George. Benjamin was the brother of William Strother (c.1696-1733). Maj. Strother married first c.1726 Mary (Mason) Fitzhugh, the widow of George Fitzhugh (c.1690-1722) and the daughter of Col. George Mason (1660-1716).

[243] Townsend was the son of Robert Dade (1684-1714). He married Parthenia (Alexander) Massey (1709-after 1776) and died in Fairfax County.

[244] In 1749 Peter was named one of the trustees for the town of Dumfries in Prince William County.

[245] William was the son of George Fitzhugh (c.1690-1722) and Mary Mason. He was a member of the House of Burgesses 1748 and 1751. Around 1755, after his second marriage, he removed from Stafford to Maryland.

[246] James was the son of John Waugh (1661-1716) and Martha Vandegasteel and the grandson of Parson John Waugh (1630-1706). In 1740 James married Betty (Brittingham) French, the daughter of Nathaniel Brittingham and the widow of Hugh French, Jr. James was a vestryman for Overwharton Parish when replacement of the old wooden chapel at the Aquia Church site was first considered. He was also a member of the House of Burgesses at this same time and was, no doubt, influential in having the petitions of "sundry inhabitants" of Stafford, including their spokesman Maj. Lawrence Washington (c.1716-1752), rejected.

[247] Nathaniel was the son of Jonathan Chapman (died before 1749) of Four Mile Run in Fairfax. Nathaniel was manager of Maryland's Principio Iron Company that for 25 years made its headquarters at Accokeek Furnace. In 1732 Nathaniel married his cousin, Constantia Pearson (1712-1788), the daughter of Capt. Simon Pearson (died 1733) of Stafford.

CONCORD. Home of Charles Waller, justice of the peace, 1745.

1748
John Mercer[248] (1704-1768)
John Peyton
Samuel Hopkins
Mott Doniphan

Philip Alexander
John Buckner[249]
James Waugh
Richard Bernard

1749
Peter Daniel
John Peyton
Mott Doniphan

Henry Fitzhugh, Jr.[250] (1723-1783)
Richard Foote
James Waugh

1750
Mott Doniphan
Col. Francis Thornton[251] (died 1784)

Richard Foote
Gerrard Fowke[252]

---

[248] John Mercer immigrated to America in 1720 from Dublin, Ireland, settling first in Maryland, then in Virginia. He soon became a prominent entrepreneur, attorney, and landowner. He was the son of John and Grace (Fenton) Mercer of Dublin. John arrived in Stafford around 1725 and almost single-handedly rebuilt the failed town of Marlborough. On the site he built houses, a racetrack, distillery, warehouses, and a windmill for grinding grain. Until very recent times, Marlborough Point was commonly referred to as "Windmill Point." Here, also, were the courthouse, jail, several ordinaries, a ferry across Potomac Creek to what is now King George County, and another ferry across the Potomac River to Maryland (on which Mercer transported his race horses to Maryland tracks).

In 1725 Mercer married Catherine Mason (1707-1750). He practiced law in Prince William and Stafford counties but was eventually banned from the courts in Prince William for too freely speaking his mind. His nephew was George Mason (1725-1792) who, after his father's accidental death, was largely raised and educated by Mercer. Though George Mason never received any university training, a broad education received in his uncle's extensive personal law library enabled him to later compose the Virginia Declaration of Rights.

[249] John was the son of William Buckner (died 1716), justice of the peace for York County in 1694 and Surveyor General of the Virginia colony.

[250] This was Henry Fitzhugh of Bedford. In 1746 he married Sarah Battaile of Caroline County.

[251] This was probably the Francis Thornton of Society Hill in King George County who married in 1747 Sarah Fitzhugh. From about 1752 until his death, Col. Thornton was prominent in horse racing in Virginia

Travers Cooke[253] (1730-1759)
Thomas Fitzhugh[255] (1725-1768)
Capt. Philip Alexander
John Peyton

John Washington, Sr.[254] (c.1716-1751:52)
Wharton Ransdall[256]
Peter Daniel
Henry Fitzhugh, Jr.

1751
John Peyton

Peter Daniel

1752
John Mercer
Richard Bernard
John Peyton
William Fitzhugh
Col. Francis Thornton
Gerard Fowke
John Moncure[258] (1710-1764)

Capt. Philip Alexander
Mott Doniphan
Peter Daniel
Henry Fitzhugh, Jr.
Thomas Fitzhugh
William Fitzhugh, Jr.[257]
Capt. Anthony Seal[259]

1753
John Mercer
Thomas Fitzhugh
John Peyton
Col. Francis Thornton

Peter Daniel
Mott Doniphan
Henry Fitzhugh
John Stuart[260] (1728-1787)

1754
Henry Fitzhugh
John Peyton

Peter Daniel
John Stuart

---

and Maryland. He was known as "a gentleman of great respectability and proverbial for his great knowledge of pedigrees" (*American Turf Register*, vol. VI, p. 57).

[252] Possibly Gerard Fowke (c.1718-1781), the son of Capt. Chandler Fowke (1692-1745) of Gunston Hall. In 1745 Gerard married Elizabeth Dinwiddie (died 1781). He died in Fauquier County.

[253] Travers was the only son of the Irish Immigrant John Cooke (died 1733) and Elizabeth Travers. In 1754 Travers married Mary Doniphan (1737-1781), the daughter of Mott Doniphan (died c.1776). The only child of Travers and Mary Cooke who survived infancy was Col. John Cooke (1755-1819). In 1784 he married Mary Thomson Mason (born 1762). Mary (Doniphan) Cooke married secondly Col. William Bronaugh (1730-1800).

[254] John was the only son of Nathaniel Washington (c.1689-1718) and Mary (Dade?) and the grandson of John Washington (1663-1698). He married Margaret Storke who survived him and later married Andrew Monroe.

[255] Thomas was the son of Henry Fitzhugh (1686-1758) and Susanna Cooke (1693-1749). He married first in 1746 Catherine Booth (died 1748) of Gloucester County. He married secondly in 1750 Sarah Stuart (1731-1783), the daughter of the Rev. David Stuart (c.1692-1749). Thomas built Boscobel near Potomac Creek. This is now the site of Boscobel Farms subdivision.

[256] In 1759 Ransdall was appointed one of the justices of the Fauquier court. Prior to this, he served as a justice in Prince William County.

[257] It isn't certain which William Fitzhugh this was.

[258] John was elected but not allowed to serve because he was a minister. The General Court felt that Rev. Moncure had enough to do in looking after his parish and would not have time to also serve as a justice.

[259] Anthony resided in Prince William and married Anne Bristow.

[260] John was the son of the Rev. David Stuart (c.1692-1749) and Jane Gibbons (c.1700-1750) of Fair Haven, King George. He married Frances Alexander (1728-after 1777).

1755

Mott Doniphan
John Stuart
John Mercer
John Peyton
Bailey Washington, Sr.[263] (1731-1807)
Col. Samuel Selden[265] (1725-1790)
William Bronaugh[266] (1730-1800)
John Wright[267] (1735-1791)

Gerard Fowke
John Stith[261] (1724-1773)
Col. John Washington[262] (1730-1782)
Henry Fitzhugh
Gowry Waugh[264] (1734-1783)
Peter Daniel
Col. Henry Fitzhugh

1756

John Mercer
Peter Daniel

John Peyton
Mott Doniphan

---

[261] John was the son of Lt. Col. Drury Stith (born c.1695) of Brunswick County and Elizabeth Buckner, the daughter of Maj. William Buckner (died 1716) of Yorktown. John died unmarried. His sister, Elizabeth Stith (born 1754), married Henry Fitzhugh (1747-1815) of Bellair, very near Boscobel on Potomac Run.

[262] This was Col. John Washington of Hylton near Chotank Church. He was the son of Henry Washington (1694-1748) and Mary Bailey. John married first Betty Massey and secondly Catherine Washington, his third cousin. She was the daughter of John Washington (c.1697-1742) and Mary Massey. John was a contemporary and friend of his cousin, George Washington. Col. Washington also served as sheriff of Stafford in 1767. He died of consumption.

[263] Bailey was the son of Henry Washington (1694-1748). From his father Bailey inherited land on Aquia Run which became known as Windsor Forest. This farm was on the east side of Onville Road (State Route 641) and is now part of the Quantico Marine Corps reservation. In 1749 Bailey married Catherine Storke (born 1723), the daughter of William and Elizabeth (Hart) Storke of St. Paul's Parish.

[264] Gowry was the son of Joseph Waugh (died 1747) and Million Travers (died 1748) and the great grandson of Parson John Waugh (1630-1706). Gowry erected a handsome dwelling house at Belle Plain and seems to have attained the greatest wealth of any of the colonial Waughs. In 1783, the year in which he died, he paid taxes in Stafford on 39 slaves, 19 horses, and 57 cattle, 429 acres in Stafford and 1,100 acres in King George. He married Letitia Turberville, the daughter of Maj. George Turberville (1694-1742) of Westmoreland County.

[265] Samuel resided at Salvington (Eby, They 212) on the south side of Potomac Creek. He was the son of Joseph Selden (1680-1720) of Buckroe, Elizabeth City, and Mary Cary (1704-1775). He was the grandson of Samuel Selden the immigrant who settled on this property in 1699. Family tradition holds that it was Joseph Selden who built the fine brick home on this plantation. The 1782 land tax records list this tract as consisting of some 1,700 acres. A descendant of James McClure Scott (1811-1893), who resided at Salvington prior to the War Between the States, described it as a brick home with large rooms and a front porch made of stone. From the porch, one looked east down a bend in the Potomac River, between Marlborough and Maryland (Scott Memoirs). Union soldiers burned the house to the ground during the winter of 1862/63 and used the bricks to make chimneys for their winter quarters.

In June 1771 Samuel was appointed second lieutenant in the 1st Virginia Regiment. In June 1779 he was promoted to captain lieutenant. He was taken prisoner at Charleston in May 1780 and exchanged in November of that year. He was wounded in June 1781 but served to the close of the war.

Col. Selden married first in 1751 Mary Thomson Mason (1731-1758), the daughter of George Mason III (1690-1735). He married secondly Sarah Ann Mason Mercer (born 1738), the daughter of John Mercer (1704-1768) of Marlborough.

[266] William was the son of Col. Jeremiah Bronaugh (1702-1749) and Simpha Rosa Enfield Mason (1703-1762), the sister of George Mason III (1690-1735). William signed the Westmoreland County protest against the Stamp Act in 1764. In 1760 he married Mrs. Margaret Murdock, secondly in 176_ Mrs. Mary (Doniphan) Cooke (1737-1781), and thirdly in 1783 Rebecca Craine. He died in Loudoun County.

[267] John was the son of William Wright (c.1700-1789). In 1755 he married Rosamond Grant (1733-1799), the daughter of Capt. John Grant (c.1704-1762) and Margaret Bronaugh (c.1698-1756). At the time of his death, John Wright was inspector of tobacco in Spotsylvania County.

1757
John Mercer[268]
William Fitzhugh (1725-1791)
William Brent[269] (1733-1782)
John Peyton

Francis Thornton
Peter Daniel
Thomas Ludwell Lee (1730-1778)

1758
John Mercer[270]
Thomas Ludwell Lee
John Peyton
Mott Doniphan

Peter Daniel
William Brent
Henry Fitzhugh (1723-1783)
Gowry Waugh

1759
John Mercer
Mott Doniphan
Henry Fitzhugh
John Peyton
William Brent

Rev. John Moncure (1710-1764)
Peter Daniel
John Washington
John Fitzhugh[271] (1727-1809)

1760
John Mercer
William Bronaugh
Peter Daniel

John Fitzhugh
Col. Henry Fitzhugh
John Wright[272] (1735-1791)

1761
John Stuart
William Brent
Col. Henry Fitzhugh

John Washington
John Mercer
Peter Daniel

1762
Thomas Ludwell Lee
Peter Daniel
John Stuart
John Mercer

John Washington
William Bronaugh
Mott Doniphan

---

[268] In May 1757 Thomas Ludwell Lee replaced Mercer against whom Francis Thornton and William Fitzhugh complained to the General Court that, in a particular case, Mercer only heard witnesses for the plaintiff as the defendant hade not summoned anyone to invalidate the testimony. The General Court found in favor of Thornton and Fitzhugh and Lee was appointed head of the Stafford court. Mercer, Peter Daniel, and William Fitzhugh (who had moved to Maryland) were removed from the bench.

[269] The son of Capt. William Brent (1710-1742). William lived at his family home, Richland, on the Potomac River in Wide Water.

[270] In 1758 Mercer was reinstated to his former position as head of the court. Peter Daniel was also officially restored to his seat.

[271] The son of Henry Fitzhugh (1686-1758) of Bedford and Susanna Cooke (1693-1749). In 1746 John married Alice, the daughter of Rowland Thornton of Crowes in King George. His obituary read, "Died: On Thursday morning, at his seat in Stafford County, John Fitzhugh, Esquire. Though near the commencement of his 83rd year when he died, he had never been confined a single day by sickness and though a gentleman of affluence and family, he never sued nor was sued in his life" (*Virginia Herald*, May 13, 1809). He lived at Bellair, later owned by the Daffan family, which adjoined Boscobel, the home of his brother, Thomas Fitzhugh (1725-1768). Like his father, John was afflicted with poor vision and was blind from about the age of 45.

[272] John was the son of William Wright (c.1700-1789). In 1755 he married Rosamond Grant (1733-1799), the daughter of Capt. John Grant (c.1704-1762) and Margaret Bronaugh (c.1698-1756). At the time of his death, John Wright was inspector of tobacco in Spotsylvania County.

1763
John Mercer
Peter Daniel

Robert Washington[273] (1729-1800)

1764
Thomas Ludwell Lee

Peter Daniel

1765[274]
Travers Daniel, Sr.[275] (1741-1824)
Gowry Waugh
William Bronaugh
John Mercer
Samuel Selden
Robert Washington

Peter Daniel
John Alexander
William Brent
Thomas Ludwell Lee
Thomas Fitzhugh

1766
Thomson Mason[276] (1733-1785)
John Alexander[277] (1735-1775)
Richard Hooe
Charles Stuart[279]

Travers Daniel
Robert Washington
Lawrence Washington[278] (1728-c.1813)
Samuel Washington[280] (1734-1781)

---

[273] Robert was the son of Townsend Washington (1705-1743) and Elizabeth Lund (c.1708-1778). He owned Chotank and Green Hill in King George County and married Alice Strother (born c.1710) in 1756.

[274] The justices appointed to the Stafford court in 1765 refused to serve. On Oct. 5, 1765 these justices wrote a letter to Lt. Gov. Francis Fauquier saying that they had, since the outset of their commission "faithfully, diligently, and with a safe conscience discharged our duty at our own expense without one farthing salary, allowance or fee of any nature…which we should, and very willingly, would have continued to do as formerly, if that unconstitutional Act of Parliament, imposing the stamp duty had not prevented us—being fully satisfied in our consciences that we should incur the guilt of perjury by acting as justices any longer than till that Act is to take place, and therefore we will not in any case whatsoever (except meeting at the November Court in order that such new Commission may be sworn to) act as Justices after that day. Our County Seal is his late Majesty sitting on his throne, with justice and mercy supporting his crown over his head and this invaluable Chapter of Magna Carta…we are firmly persuaded both we and all other his most dutiful and loyal subjects in America…will not only be protected in all their liberties and properties which they have the must undoubted right to claim but meet even in indulgences and proper encouragements in their most universal Poverty (occasioned by their taxing themselves for years to come towards supporting the late Glorious war far above their abilities" (Reese, Papers, vol. 3, pp. 1281-1282).

[275] Travers was the son of Peter Daniel (1706-1788) and Sarah Travers Pierson (died 1788), the daughter of Rawleigh and Hannah (Ball) Travers and the widow of Capt. Christopher Pierson. Travers lived at Crow's Nest for much of the year though his summer residence was a home he called Tranquility on the western side of Crow's Nest.

[276] Thomson was the son of George Mason III (1690-1735) and Ann Thomson (1699-1762). He married Mary King Barnes (1740-1771).

[277] John was the son of Philip Alexander (1704-1753) and Sarah Hooe. In 1756 he married Lucy Thornton, the daughter of William Thornton and Mary Taliaferro (died 1770).

[278] Lawrence Washington of Chotank was the son of Capt. John Washington (c.1697-1742). In 1751 he married Elizabeth Dade (1734-after 1796).

[279] In 1752 Charles Stuart married Frances Washington (born 1731), the daughter of Capt. John Washington (c.1697-1742) of Chotank and his wife Mary Massey.

[280] Samuel was George Washington's brother. He married first c.1754 Jane Champe (died c.1755); secondly c.1756 Mildred Thornton (1741-c.1762); thirdly c.1762 Louisa Chapman (1743-c.1763), the daughter of Nathaniel Chapman (1709-1760) and Constantia Pearson (c.1712-1791). Louisa died in childbirth and was buried in the Washington vault in Westmoreland County. Samuel married his fourth

William Fitzhugh, Jr.
William Adie[282] (1729-1797)
John Mercer
Peter Daniel
Francis Thornton
John Stuart
John Washington
Samuel Selden
William Brent
John Whiting

1767
Thomas Ludwell Lee
Henry Fitzhugh
Thomas Fitzhugh
Bailey Washington, Sr.
Samuel Selden
William Brent
Thomson Mason (removed)
Robert Washington
Samuel Washington (removed)
John Brown[284]
John James
Yelverton Peyton[285] (1735-1794)
Charles Alexander[287] (1737-1806)
John Gibson
Townsend Dade
John Bronaugh[290] (1743-1777)

William Edrington[281] (c.1741-1794)
John James[283] (c.1732-1794)
Thomas Ludwell Lee
Henry Fitzhugh
Thomas Fitzhugh
John Stith (1724-1773)
Bailey Washington, Sr.
Gowry Waugh
William Bronaugh
John Foster

Peter Daniel
Francis Thornton
William Fitzhugh
John Washington
Gowry Waugh
William Bronaugh
Travers Daniel
Lawrence Washington
William Fitzhugh, Jr. (removed)
William Edrington
William Adie
Gerrard Hooe[286] (1733-1785)
Andrew Grant[288]
John Chambers
William Hooe[289] (1743-c.1777)

---

wife, Anne Steptoe (1737-1777) in 1764. He married fifthly c.1778 Susannah Ferrin (1753-1783). After leaving Stafford, Samuel resided at Harewood in Jefferson County, West Virginia.
[281] The son of William Edrington (c.1712-c.1796) and Elizabeth "Betty" Helm (c.1722-after 1797). William, Jr. married Mrs. Jemima Smith Porter (died 1816). William and Jemima removed to Fairfield County, South Carolina where they died.
[282] According to the Adie family Bible, a copy of which is in the collection of Mrs. Nancy Southworth, William Adie married in 1754 Elizabeth Parrender (born 1729) of Maryland. William was employed as a carpenter at Accokeek Iron Furnace in Stafford as was his father. This elder William Adie was probably the same man whose name appeared on a Principio Company payroll ledger of c.1724-25. The younger William lived at Bloomington, a farm on the south side of Wide Water Road (State Route 611) and presently bounded on the east by Rectory Road. Bloomington appeared on a 1792 re-survey of 17th century patents in the area. According to Travers Daniel, the county surveyor, the small square tract was originally patented by Charles Wells and then conveyed to Adie.
[283] John James was the son of George James (c.1702-1753) and Mary Wheeler, the daughter of John Wheeler (1684-1746). In 1763 John married Anne Strother (born c.1710).
[284] In 1751 John Brown married Hannah Cooke.
[285] Yelverton also served as sheriff of Stafford in 1776. He married Elizabeth Heath (born c.1740), the daughter of Samuel Heath and Anne Johnston Gerard.
[286] Gerrard was the son of Capt. John Hooe (1702-1766) and Anne Alexander (1712-c.1776). He inherited his father's Barnesfield plantation where he resided until his death. In 1761 Gerrard married Sarah Barnes (1742-1805), the daughter of Richard Barnes and Penelope Manly of Richmond County.
[287] Charles was the son of John Alexander (1711-1764).
[288] In 1770 Andrew married Mary Matthews.
[289] William was the youngest son of Howson Hooe, Sr. (died 1777:81).
[290] John was the son of Jeremiah Bronaugh (1702-1749) and Simpha Rosa Enfield (Mason) Dinwiddie (1703-1762). He married Mary Anne Carter (born 1747), the daughter of Joseph Carter (1690-1764) and

1772 (Removed from Stafford County after appointment)
William Bronaugh
Thomson Mason
Samuel Washington
Charles Alexander

1772 (Active justices)
Thomas Ludwell Lee
Francis Thornton
John Washington
Gowry Waugh
John Alexander
John Brown
Yelverton Peyton
William Hooe
Henry Fitzhugh
John Stuart
Samuel Selden
William Brent
Robert Washington
John James
Townsend Dade
Charles Carter[291] (1738-1796)

1773
Thomas Ludwell Lee
John Stuart
Samuel Selden
William Brent
John Brown
Townsend Dade
Charles Carter
William Fitzhugh (1725-1791)
Yelverton Peyton
Francis Thornton
John Washington
Gowry Waugh
Robert Washington
John James
William Hooe
John Alexander
Bailey Washington, Sr.

1774
John Washington
Richard Fowke[292]
William Mountjoy[294] (1737-1820)
John James
Yelverton Peyton
William Garrard[296] (c.1715-c.1786)
Thomas Mountjoy[297] (1739-c.1818)
Townsend Dade
Dr. William Gibbons Stuart[293] (1749-1796)
Travers Daniel
Samuel Selden
Col. Robert Stith[295]
William Brent

Margaret Mason (died 1751) of Lancaster County. John was the brother of William Bronaugh (1730-1b who served as a justice of Stafford from at least 1760-1772).

[291] Charles was the son of Charles Carter (1707-1764) of Stanstead (the present site of Servicetown Truck Stop) on U. S. Route 17 and the grandson of Robert "King" Carter (1663-1732) of Corotoman.

[292] Richard was the son of Capt. Chandler Fowke and Mary Fossaker of Pasipatanzy (King George County) and later of Gunston Hall (Fairfax County). In 1760 he married Anne Bunbury (born 1741), the daughter of Thomas and Sarah Bunbury. Richard served and died in the Revolutionary War.

[293] William married Mary Fitzhugh.

[294] The son of Capt. William Mountjoy (1711-1777) of Locust Hill near Brooke and his wife Phillis Reilly (1717-1771), the daughter of Thomas and Elizabeth Reilly of St. Paul's Parish. The younger William inherited his father's Locust Hill property.

[295] Robert lived at Windsor in what is now King George County. In 1773 he married Mary Townsend Washington, the daughter of Lawrence Washington (1728-c.1813) and Elizabeth Dade (1734-after 1796).

[296] William owned Garrard's Ordinary just north of the present Stafford Courthouse and on or near the site of the school board offices. The court met here from 1779-1783 when a new courthouse was built on the present courthouse site. During the Revolution, he was a colonel in the Stafford County militia. William Garrard's son, James Garrard (1749-1822) moved to Kentucky after the Revolution and became that state's second governor.

[297] Thomas was the son of William Mountjoy (1711-1777). In 1767 he married Ann Withers (born 1748), the daughter of Keene Withers (1728-1756) and Elizabeth Cave. Thomas inherited from his father 200 acres on Accokeek Creek near Locust Hill. During the Revolution, he served in the militia. Thomas also

1775
William Brent
Henry Fitzhugh

Townsend Dade
Samuel Selden

1776
Yelverton Peyton
William Hooe

Townsend Dade

1777
William Fitzhugh[298] (1741-1809)

Col. William Garrard

1779
Bailey Washington, Sr.
John James
John Pollard
Robert Brent[300] (1730-1780)
Col. James Garrard (1749-1822)

Charles Carter
Col. William Garrard
Harris Hooe[299] (1736-1824)
Thomas Mountjoy

1780
John Fleet[301] (1724-1792)
Henry Lawson
Harris Hooe
Col. William Garrard
John James
Col. James Garrard

Thomas Lawson[302] (died 1793)
John Pollard
William Hewitt[303] (c.1740-1795)
Thomas Fitzhugh
Yelverton Peyton[304]
William Alexander[305]

---

held numerous official offices including tobacco inspector at Cave's Warehouse 1772-73 and 1777; coroner 1783-84; churchwarden 1785; sheriff 1787. In 1815 his grandson, Thomas Mountjoy Morton (1787-1859), took him to Kentucky where he died.

[298] This was William Fitzhugh, the builder of Chatham and the son of Henry (1706-1742) of Eagle's Nest and Lucy Carter. He married Ann Randolph (1747-1805) of Henrico County. In addition to Chatham, William owned Eagle's Nest and Somerset in King George and Ravensworth in Fairfax County.

[299] The third son of Howson Hooe, Sr. (1696-1773) and Anne Frances Harris. He was born in Prince William County.

[300] Robert was the son of George Brent (1703-1778) of Woodstock and Catherine Trimmingham (died 1751). Around 1755 Robert married Ann Carroll (1733-1804), the daughter of Daniel Carroll of Marlborough, Maryland. Robert's early education was at a school in Maryland taught by Jesuits. He later attended the College of St. Omer in the Netherlands.

[301] John was the son of William Fleet and Sarah Ann (Jones) of Lancaster County. In 1746 he married Mary Edwards.

[302] In 1761 Lawson was appointed one of the trustees for the town of Dumfries. He also worked as manager of the Occoquan and Neabsco iron furnaces.

[303] In 1786 John Brown and John Cooke brought suit against William Hewitt in a pleas of trespass for £200 damages. According to the deposition of John Thomson Mason dated Nov. 10, 1789, in the winter of 1783 or 1784 William Hewitt went to the house of John Brown asking to rent the boat *Royal Ann* belonging to Brown and Cooke. Brown didn't want to send the boat out for fear of the winter weather. William insisted that he needed the boat because "he had caught a great many fish, which he could get no market for, and which he must loose unless he could get this Boat to carry them to Alexandria." Brown finally agreed saying that the usual rent was $1 per day for the hire of the boat, but since the weather was "cold and precarious," Hewitt could have it for a half dollar per day. William agreed to the deal and transported his fish, but by April 1793 he had not yet returned the boat and Brown and Cooke were seeking to either have it returned or paid for. Unfortunately, no decision was included in the records ("Brown and Cook vs Hewitt," DC/L/1786/387-60).

[304] In May 1783 Yelverton submitted a claim to the Stafford Court for forage, billeting 45 soldiers, firewood, forage for one night for 11 horses, victuals, etc. procured from him by the Continental Army.

1781

John Murray[306]	Daniel Triplett[307] (1753-1818)
Col. William Phillips (c.1744-1797)	John Rowzee Peyton[308] (1754-1798)
William Alexander	William Eustace[309] (1729-1800)
Samuel Selden[310]	Gowry Waugh
William Brent	John Brown[311] (died c.1804)
John James	Charles Carter
Arthur Morson[312] (1734-1798)	Col. William Garrard
John Pollard	Daniel Payne[313] (1728-1796)

---

[305] Possibly William Pearson Alexander (1758-1804), the son of John Alexander (1711-1763) and Susannah Pearson (born 1717). Around 1780 William married Sarah Bruce Casson of Stafford and resided near Falmouth.

[306] John Murray, tobacco factor or agent, sailed from Glasgow to Virginia prior to 1770. He settled in the Aquia area.

[307] The son of Francis Triplett (1680-1772) of King George and the grandson of Capt. William Triplett (1650-1725), the immigrant. Francis may have been the "Francis Triplett, Mariner" who in 1720 was living in Washington Parish, Westmoreland County, now King George. Francis was constable of King George in 1748.

Daniel, who was a merchant in Falmouth, married Elizabeth Richards (1755-1826), the daughter of John Richards (1734-1785) and granddaughter of William Brice Richards who emigrated from Drysdale, England. Daniel Triplett's name appears on the list of soldiers of Capt. William Edmond's company on Sept. 25, 1761 who were recruited from Fauquier County. He was also listed in the 1787 Stafford County personal property tax records as owning a 4-wheeled stage wagon. He owned land in the vicinity of Hartwood Baptist Meeting House (behind Hartwood Elementary School off State Route 754) as his property line was mentioned in a 1780 deed between Arthur Morson and Lazarus Maddox. Daniel and Elizabeth both died in Norfolk, Virginia.

John Richards, Daniel's father-in-law, was a substantial landowner in King and Queen County. In 1775 Richards purchased 300 acres from John Dixon (c.1740-1791) of Falmouth, the tract including the Belmont property and what is now Ingleside subdivision. Sometime prior to 1800, Richards constructed a canal on his property to power the four mills in Falmouth, three on the river and one on the canal itself. The first mill here was known as Contest Mill and was built near the canal dam in the early 1790s.

[308] John was the son of John Peyton (1691-1760) of Stony Hill and his second wife, Elizabeth (Rowzee) Waller (c.1715-1782).

[309] William was the son of Isaac Eustace (died 1795) and Agatha Conway (1740-1826). He served as a captain during the Revolution and married Ann Gaskins. William died in Fauquier County.

[310] In April 1782 Samuel Selden submitted a claim to the Stafford court for 25,000 pounds of hay (£50), 86 ½ pounds of bacon (£3.4.10), 7 beeves, 87 pounds of beef, 14 bushels of Indian meal (£14.17.6), 6,000 pounds of beef (£25), and 1,000 pounds of hay (£2) procured from him by the Continental Army.

[311] John was probably a merchant. He was in business with John W. Bronaugh (c.1773-1834) and John Cooke (1755-1819). In November 1802 John was called to court because "on the tenth day of May in the year 1802 [he] Knowingly Willfully and Wittingly suffered the game of Billiards to be played in his house, and in a House in his use & Occupation situate in the County of Stafford." Brown stated that "in December 1801 he rented out the house in which the billiards table was erected to one Henry Woodrow…and this affiant has never been in the possession of the house from the time he rented it to the said Woodrow, the affiant himself being only a tenant for one year of the said House, the House being the property of John Bronaugh who's Guardian John Cooke rented it to this affiant" ("Commonwealth vs Brown").

[312] Arthur Morson of Greenock, County Renfrew, Scotland, sailed for Virginia on February 14, 1751 on the *Greenock Snow* and arrived in the Rappahannock River on June 6. A merchant in Falmouth, he served as a justice for King George in 1766 and 1770 as his home, Hartwood, was then in that county. Morson married Marion Andrew (c.1724-1808) at Hartwood.

[313] Daniel Payne was born at Red House, then King George County, now Westmoreland. He never married and died at Falmouth.

Daniel assisted his father, John Payne (c.1693-1750) with his mercantile business in Leedstown. Later, he removed to Dumfries where he employed himself as a merchant. During this time, he served as a

Gerrard Banks[314] (1725-1787)
William Fitzhugh
John Moncure
Raleigh Travers Brown[315] (1753-1803)
Thomas Fitzhugh[316] (1760-1803)
John Cooke[317] (1755-1819)

Harris Hooe
Thomas Mountjoy
Henry Washington
William Hewitt
Col. James Garrard

1782
John James
William Hewitt

Thomas Mountjoy
Harris Hooe

1783
Col. James Garrard
Gerrard Banks
John Rowzee Peyton
Harris Hooe

William Alexander
Col. William Phillips
Bailey Washington, Jr.[318] (1753-1814)

1784
Arthur Morson
Col. James Garrard
Charles Carter
Townsend Dade
Bailey Washington, Jr.
Col. William Garrard
Harris Hooe
Thomas Mountjoy

Gerrard Banks
William Alexander
Robert Washington
Robert Stith
John Brown
John Pollard
William Fitzhugh
William Hewitt

---

banker for about 350 residents of the Dumfries area, many of whom were members of the Dumfries Jockey Club. In 1764 Daniel served as sheriff of Prince William and was a justice for that county in 1768.

In 1771, with a starting investment of £5,000, Charles Yates (c.1728-1809) of Fredericksburg, Daniel Payne of Dumfries, and Edward Moor of Falmouth formed a partnership of Payne, Moor, and Company, merchants of Falmouth. Their store was in the large brick building now known as Lightner's Store. Daniel was the principal manager of the firm which, prior to the Revolution, carried on a lucrative foreign trade. At the outset of the war, Moor moved as a as an epidemic of smallpox swept the Falmouth region. Payne remained and took over sole management of the firm's affairs. Yates was occupied with his other business in Fredericksburg. At the close of the war, the partnership was dissolved and Daniel continued in business on his own.

In 1777 Payne, Arthur Morson, James Buchanan, William Love, and Edward Moor were named trustees for Falmouth, Daniel serving as treasurer.

Daniel died at his residence above one of his Falmouth warehouses. He was buried in the family cemetery at Cedar Hill, three miles from Leedstown.

[314] Gerrard was the son of Adam Banks (1700-1755) and Rosanna Bryan (died after 1784). Around 1750 he married Frances Bruce (1735-1818). Gerrard represented Stafford in the Virginia House of Delegates during the 1817-1818 session, was sheriff 1785-1786, and coroner 1783-1784. He died at his estate, Green Bank, on the south side of the Warrenton Road (U. S. Route 17), part of which is now occupied by the GEICO Insurance Company.

[315] Raleigh married his cousin Million Waugh (c.1763-1799), the daughter of Joseph Waugh (c.1736-1763) and Mary Bronaugh (died 1799). Raleigh and Million resided at Windsor, very near Crow's Nest.

[316] The son of Thomas Fitzhugh (1725-1768) and Sarah Stuart (1731-1783) of Boscobel. Thomas married Anne Rose (born 1763), the daughter of Col. John Rose.

[317] John lived at West Farm that adjoined Clifton and Dipple in upper Wide Water on the Potomac River. He was involved in the quarry business on Aquia Creek and, in partnership with Daniel Carroll Brent (1759-1814) operated a store in Brent's Mill.

[318] Bailey was the son of Bailey Washington, Sr. (1731-1807) and Catherine Storke (born 1723). Bailey, Jr. was the brother of Col. William Washington (1752-1810) who distinguished himself at the Battle of Cowpens.

Thomas Fitzhugh
Col. William Phillips
William Alexander

Daniel Triplett
John R. Peyton

1785
Col. William Garrard
Thomas Mountjoy
John Brown
Arthur Morson
Gerrard Banks
William Fitzhugh
Thomas Fitzhugh
Col. William Phillips

John R. Peyton
Bailey Washington, Sr.
Charles Carter
John Pollard
Harris Hooe
William Hewitt
Daniel Triplett
William Alexander

1786
Arthur Morson
Daniel Triplett

William Alexander
William Hewitt

1787 (Refused to act after they were appointed and were removed from office)
Bailey Washington, Sr.
William Fitzhugh

John Brown
Thomas Fitzhugh

1787
William Phillips
Bailey Washington, Jr.

John R. Peyton

1788[319]
Robert Baylor Morton[320] (1761-1807)
Henry Vowles[321] (1752-c.1803)
Alexander Morson[322] (1759-1822)

Daniel Carroll Brent (1759-1814)
Joseph Smith
George Brent[323] (1760-1804)

---

[319] The Council did not appoint James Withers a Justice "because he is now an acting inspector of the said county [or] John Mountjoy because he is now an acting under sheriff" (Reese, George, 233).

[320] Robert was the son of George Morton (1717-c.1765) of King George and Lucy Baylor, the daughter of Robert and Frances Baylor. He inherited land in Orange County from his father. In 1786 Robert married Mary Mountjoy (1769-1804) in Maryland.

[321] Henry was the son of Thomas Vowells who married in 1747 in St. Mary's County, Maryland Susannah Chunn. Thomas and Susannah eventually settled in Fauquier County. Henry was born in St. Mary's and served in the Revolution. Shortly after the Revolution, he married Mary Frazier, the daughter of George Frazier (died c.1765) and his wife Esther.

By his marriage Henry acquired two lots in Fredericksburg on William Street between Caroline and Sophia streets, now the site of the Ben Franklin Store. At the outbreak of the war, this large brick house was owned by Mary Frazier, then a minor. It was taken over by Revolutionary troops for use as a barracks and hospital. This occupation lasted throughout the Revolution, during which time the floors, window sashes, and other wooden parts of the structure were torn out and used to fuel fires. After the war, Henry repaired the house, completing the restorations in 1783. Experts at the time assessed the damages at £500. Henry petitioned for payment of damages and for rent during the war years. The U. S. Congress determined that this was a state matter. He then submitted his claim to the state which rejected it.

During the Revolution, Henry was appointed adjutant of the 7th Virginia regiment in December 1776. In January 1778 he was promoted to brigade major of William Woodford's brigade. He resigned in May 1779, but later served as a captain lieutenant of another Virginia regiment.

[322] Alexander was the son of Arthur Morson (1735-1798) and Marion Andrew (c.1724-1808). In 1818 he married Ann Casson Alexander (1781-1833), the daughter of William Pearson Alexander (1758-1804) of Snowden. Alexander Morson resided at Hollywood in the southeastern part of Stafford.

[323] George lived at Woodstock, the ancestral home of the George Brent family in Virginia. The Woodstock plantation is now part of Aquia Harbour subdivision.

William Taylor   Kellis Hord[324] (c.1744-1815)
Travers Daniel, Jr. (1763-1813)

1789
Peter Daniel[325] (1706-1777)   Travers Daniel
Thomas Ludwell Lee, Jr. (1751-1807)

1790
Henry Vowles[326] (1752-c.1803)   Alexander Morson
Joseph Smith   Thomas Mountjoy
Robert B. Morton   Daniel C. Brent
Travers Daniel, Jr.[327]   Arthur Morson[328]
Kellis Hord   Thomas Ludwell Lee, Jr.
William Smith   William Taylor
Alexander Vowles   George Brent

Over the years, there were several houses on Woodstock. The earliest, built during the second half of the 17th century, stood next to the Catholic cemetery on the south side of Telegraph Road (State Route 637) behind the Crucifix. The hearth from this dwelling was recently excavated by archeologists. During the early 1930s, George L. Gordon, past Commissioner of the Revenue, worked on the county roads and helped haul gravel from this site for road construction. The gravel pit was very close to the old house site, the foundations of which was still clearly visible at that time. After the crews had completed the road, they bulldozed the area around the house site to smooth it. Lost in this procedure was the stone foundation measuring approximately 20' by 40' and the old stone-lined well.

At some point, the Brents decided to build a new house on higher ground. The selected site was the high hill overlooking the town of Aquia. This is now the site of the Aquia Harbour Country Club.

In 1795 George Brent married Molly Fitzhugh, the daughter of Col. William Fitzhugh (1725-1791) of Marmion. George's son, Robert Carroll Brent (died 1837), was the last Brent to live at Woodstock.

[324] The son of Peter Hord (born c.1715) of Stafford and the grandson of John Hord (died 1747) the immigrant who settled in Caroline County in 1685. John Hord was engaged in the rebellion of the Duke of Monmouth against King James II, and came to America after the Duke's defeat. He was the son of Alan Hord of Ewell, England. In Caroline County, John acquired a tract of land on the Rappahannock River that he named Shady Grove, about eight miles below Port Royal. The house was still standing as late as 1898 when it was photographed. Little is known of his grandson, Kellis, who married his first cousin, Mary "Molly" Hord (born 1744), the daughter of Thomas and Jane (Miller) Hord.

[325] Peter was the son of James Daniel (c.1680-1727) of Middlesex County. Peter settled first in Northumberland County and later in Stafford. In 1736 he married Sarah (Travers) Pierson (died 1788), the daughter of Rawleigh and Hannah (Ball) Travers and widow of Capt. Christopher Pierson. Peter was presiding justice in the Stafford court at the time of his death.

[326] Henry owned a tavern in Falmouth on Butler Road (State Route 664) across from the old Falmouth Post Office. Built around 1785, this building was a large frame two-story structure with a huge brick chimney on each end. During the brick making process, Henry had his initials set in the chimneys using glazed bricks. This was the only licensed tavern in the area from 1789-1792 when five licenses were issued. Unlike many buildings of the period which had outside kitchens, servants in Vowles' Tavern used the large stone fireplace in the basement for cooking. In 1793 Henry advertised the sale of his tavern. No purchaser was forthcoming and it was advertised again two years later, boasting of "fertile garden and productive billiard table." The 1800 personal property tax records list Vowles as owning 12 slaves and 4 horses.

In the 1820s Murray Forbes converted this building to a residence for his sister, Delia Forbes Smith (1780-1841), the widow of George Alexander Smith (1775-1822). The structure sat abandoned for much of the author's early life, but was purchased in 1976 by Richard and Barbara Westebbe, dismantled, and moved to Holly Corner Road (State Route 655). The initials "HV" are still clearly visible in the chimney.

[327] The 1800 land tax records list Travers as owning 2,166 acres in 3 parcels.

[328] In 1800 Arthur Morson's estate paid personal property taxes on 16 slaves, 11 horses, 1 coach, and a 4-wheeled chariot.

1791
Daniel Triplett[329]
William Alexander
Bailey Washington
Henry Vowles, JR.

Thomas Mountjoy
William Phillips
Joseph Smith
Travers Daniel, Jr.

1792
Thomas Mountjoy
Robert B. Morton
William Hewitt
Travers Daniel, Jr.
Bailey Washington, Jr.
Joseph Smith

William Alexander
Henry Vowles
George Brent
William Phillips
Kellis Hord
Daniel C. Brent

1793
Capt. Hancock Eustace[330] (1768-1829)
William Hewitt
Daniel C. Brent
Joseph Smith
Bailey Washington, Jr.

Thomas Mountjoy
William Alexander
Henry Vowles
George Brent

1795
William Alexander

1796
Samuel Heath Peyton[331] (c.1770-1832)
Kellis Hord
Hancock Eustace
Travers Daniel, Jr.

Gerrard Banks[332]
George Brent
William Alexander
John Taliaferro (1768-1852)

1797
Thomas Mountjoy[333]
Robert Howson Hooe[334] (1748-1834)

Kellis Hord
Alexander Morson

---

[329] In 1800 Daniel paid personal property taxes on 19 slaves and 6 horses.

[330] Hancock was the son of Isaac Eustace (died c.1795) and Agatha Conway (1740-1826). Isaac made his fortune in the shipping business and purchased a large tract in northern Stafford that became known as Woodford. In 1792 he deeded one half of the tract (525 acres) to his son, Hancock. This half included his father's mansion house. In 1789 Hancock married Tabitha Henry (died c.1840). He served as presiding justice of Stafford County for many years.

[331] Samuel was the son of Yelverton Peyton (1735-1794) who operated Peyton's Ordinary in the village of Aquia. His sister, Elizabeth, married John Peyton Harrison (c.1748-1807) who owned the Floury tract to the north of the church (now Aquia Town Center). Samuel was listed in the tax records as residing at Pleasant Retreat (location unknown) in Stafford. He married Ann Samuel. During the War of 1812, Samuel served as lieutenant colonel of the 45th Virginia Militia.
During the War of 1812, Samuel served as lieutenant colonel of the 45th Regiment organized in Stafford County. He commenced his service on June 23, 1807. Regiments were called out sporadically during this period; most of Stafford's militia companies being called out by the General Order of July 16, 1813 at which time they were stationed at Potomac Church. They were called out again in July 1814 when a few mustered with the Spotsylvania and Caroline militias.

[332] This could have been one of several Gerard Banks who were living at this time. The most likely candidate was Gerard (c.1759-1816), the son of Gerard Banks (c.1725-1787) and Frances Bruce (1735-1818) of Greenbank. The younger Gerard lived for some years in Culpeper and represented that county in the House of Delegates 1787-1788 and 1797-1798. He died and was buried in Alexandria.

[333] In 1800 Thomas paid taxes on 10 slaves and 8 horses.

William Alexander
Henry Vowles
Col. Enoch Mason[335] (c.1769-1828)
James Primm (1754-1820)

Daniel C. Brent
George Brent
Samuel H. Peyton
Benjamin Ficklen (1737-c.1806)

1798
Hancock Eustace
Henry Vowles
Samuel H. Peyton

John Moncure[336] (1772-1822)
George Brent
Col. Enoch Mason

1799
Thomas Mountjoy
George Brent
Col. Enoch Mason

Henry Vowles
Hancock Eustace

1800
William Alexander
Henry Vowles

Alexander Morson

1801
John Rowzee Harrison
Hancock Eustace
Kellis Hord[337]
Alexander Morson
John Peyton Harrison[339] (c.1748-1807)

John Moncure
Samuel H. Peyton
John Nicholas
William Richards[338] (1765-after 1803)

1802
Kellis Hord

Samuel H. Peyton

1803
Hancock Eustace
John P. Harrison

George Brent

1804
Thomas Mountjoy
Enoch Mason
Hancock Eustace

William Richards
Samuel H. Peyton

1806-1809
Thomas Mountjoy

Alexander Morson

---

[334] In 1800 Robert paid personal property taxes on 9 slaves, 6 horses, a coach, and a 2-wheeled chariot.
[335] Enoch was the great grandson of George Mason of Aquia (16_-c.1729). Enoch was a successful attorney who amassed some 2,461 acres upon which he built a fine home that he called Clover Hill. The house site was located 4.9 miles west of the courthouse on Mountain View Road (State Route 627). In 1796 Enoch married Lucy Wiley Roy (died c.1835), a descendant of Col. George Mason (1628-1686) of Accokeek Creek.
[336] In 1800 John paid taxes on 10 slaves, 5 horses, and a 4-wheeled phaeton or stage.
[337] In 1800 Kellis paid taxes on 6 slaves and 4 horses.
[338] William was the son of John Richards (1734-1785) and Susannah Coleman (died 1778), the daughter of Robert Spilsby Coleman (died 1761). William married Ann, the daughter of John and Ann Blackwell. Following the Revolution, William was actively involved in the Falmouth milling industry. He inherited his father's plantation, Richards' Hill just above Falmouth and made his home there. This property was later re-named Ingleside.
[339] John was appointed ensign in the 2nd Virginia regiment in September 1775. He was made first lieutenant in May 1776 and captain in May 1777. He retired from service in February 1781.

Kellis Hord
Hancock Eustace
James Primm[340] (1754-1820)
Robert H. Hooe
Enoch Mason
Thomas Fristoe[343] (1767-1815)
Joel Mason[344] (died 1813)
Robert Lewis[346] (1769-1829)
John Taliaferro Brooke[348] (1761-1821)

Travers Daniel, Sr.
John Moncure
Benjamin Ficklen[341] (1737-c.1806)
Samuel H. Peyton
Capt. William Brown Wallace[342] (1757-1833)
Nathaniel Fox (1748-1819)
Nicholas Voss[345]
Dr. John Moncure Daniel[347] (1769-1813)
Thomas Seddon[349] (1779-1831)

---

[340] James was the son of John de la Pryme (1715-1780) and Margaret Welch (1709-1770). During the Revolution, he served in the Virginia militia and died in Washington, Maryland.

[341] Benjamin was the seventh and youngest son of William (c.1695-1756) and Sarah Ficklen. He was born in King George County but died in Stafford where his estate was administered. In 1768 Benjamin married Margaret Grant. He later married a sister of Robert Crutcher (died 1829). The Ficklin/Ficklen family were well-to-do businessmen and mill owners in Falmouth during its heyday in the late 18th and early 19th centuries. In 1800 Benjamin paid personal property taxes on 9 slaves and 5 horses.

[342] William was the son of Dr. Michael Wallace (1719-1767) and Elizabeth Brown (born 1723) of Ellerslie, Stafford County. In 1787 he married Barbara Fox (1766-1833). Both succumbed to cholera in Lawrenceburg, Kentucky.

[343] Thomas was the son of the Rev. Daniel Fristoe (1739-1774), minister of Chappawamsic Baptist Church, and his wife Mary Barker (1735-1759). Thomas served in the War of 1812 as a captain and commanded a company of infantry in Peyton's 45th Virginia Regiment. War records indicate that he served from July 16, 1813 to Sept. 2, 1814. In Columbia, Missouri there is a chapter of the U. S. Daughters of 1812 named the Thomas Fristoe Chapter.

Thomas married Lydia Wells, the daughter of Carty Wells of Stafford County, later Shelby County, Kentucky. The Fristoe family was long established on Chappawamsic Run in upper Stafford.

[344] Joel was the brother of Col. Enoch Mason (c.1769-1828) of Clover Hill. He married Sarah Bourne (c.1771-1835), the daughter of George Bourne.

[345] In 1794 Nicholas married Mary Spotswood, the daughter of T. Spotswood.

[346] Robert was the son of Fielding Lewis (1725-1781) and Betty Washington (1733-1797) of Kenmore. Robert became one of his uncle George Washington's private secretaries. After leaving that position, he returned to Fredericksburg, served briefly as a justice in Stafford, then as mayor of Fredericksburg, a position he held from 1820-1828. Robert married Judith Brown (born c.1770). His obituary stated that he died "after a lingering illness" (*Virginia Herald*, Jan. 21, 1829).

[347] Dr. Daniel was the son of Travers Daniel, Sr. (1741-1824) and Frances Moncure (born 1745). He studied medicine in Scotland and was a surgeon during the War of 1812.

[348] The son of Richard Brooke (died 1792) and the grandson of Robert Brooke who came to Virginia in 1710. Robert was a surveyor by profession and, in 1716, accompanied Alexander Spotswood and the Knights of the Golden Horseshoe on their expedition west. During the Revolution, John T. Brooke and his three brothers served in the continental army. His eldest brother, Robert (1751-1799), served as governor of Virginia from 1794-1796. In 1798 Robert was elected Attorney General of Virginia. It was Robert Brooke who built beautiful Federal Hill in Fredericksburg. John's twin, Judge Francis Taliaferro Brooke (c.1761-1851), was a member of the Virginia Supreme Court of Appeals for 40 years, was elected to the Virginia State Senate in 1800 and, in 1804, was made Speaker of the Senate. Another brother, Dr. Lawrence Brooke (c.1758-1803), served as a surgeon aboard John Paul Jones' *Bonhomme Richard* during its historic battle with the British warship, *Serapis*. After the war, Dr. Brooke returned to Fredericksburg where he practiced medicine.

John T. Brooke practiced law in Fredericksburg and was a partner with James Madison from 1786-1790. After the Revolution, he received 2,666 acres for active duty service. Later in life, he virtually abandoned his law practice to concentrate on real estate speculation and the operation of his Stafford plantation, Millvale. He actively acquired property in Fredericksburg, was the first president of the Farmers Bank of Fredericksburg, and dabbled in politics, representing Stafford in the House of Delegates from 1805-1808. In 1812 he was presidential elector for his old friend, James Madison. John and his brother, Francis were both charter members of the Virginia Society of the Cincinnati which held its first meeting in the Town Hall of Fredericksburg in 1783. This organization is the oldest hereditary military

George Lane[350] (died c.1823)
Maj. Benjamin Tolson[351] (c.1763-1836)
Charles Julien[353]
Isaac Newton[355] (c.1745-1838)
Robert Crutcher[356] (died 1829)
Thomas W. Cowne[358]

George Brooks
William Brent[352] (1783-1848)
Zachariah Vowles[354] (died 1825)
Daniel C. Brent
Maj. William Henry Fitzhugh[357] (1788-1859)
Thomas Seddon

---

society in North America. Founded in 1783 in the Newburgh-Fishkill area of New York, the society's objectives were to perpetuate the ideals of the Revolution, to maintain friendships formed among officers, and to extend help "towards those officers and their families who, unfortunately may be under the necessity of receiving it." George Washington was the first president general of the society. Membership was restricted to commissioned officers of the continental line forces of the United States and France who had served for at least 36 months during the Revolution. Membership passed from father to eldest son. The society is still active today.

In 1793 John married Anne Mason Mercer Selden (1770-1812), the daughter of Samuel Selden (1725-1790) of Salvington and his second wife, Sarah Ann Mason (Mercer) (born 1738). Sarah was the daughter of John Mercer (1704-1768) of Marlborough.

[349] Thomas was the son of John Seddon of Stafford. Early in his life Thomas was a merchant in Falmouth. Later, he moved to Fredericksburg where he became the cashier of the Farmers Bank of Virginia. He was a major landowner in Stafford with various parcels from one end of the county to the other. Most of his property, however, was concentrated on Potomac Run along the U. S. Route 1 corridor. His resident plantation, called Oakland, stretched from Glencairne northward to include the Crane's Corner area as well as much of the land around the site of Potomac SMC Mulch Company. His obituary stated that he was "remarkable for great strength and rapidity of mind; clear-sighted and penetrating in affairs of business; he was eminently gifted with useful talents." He died as a result of "a protracted fever." (*Virginia Herald*, Aug. 17, 1831)

Thomas and his wife Susan R. Seddon had seven children.

[350] Before moving to Stafford, George and his wife Mary D. Lane were residents of Prince William County. Upon settling in Stafford, they lived on Rock Hill Farm which George bought from Benjamin Ficklen and Robert Crutcher around 1812. This property is now part of the Quantico Marine Corps Base.

[351] Benjamin was the son of George Tolson (1726-1785) of Stafford. In 1817 he purchased Bellfair Mills on Chappawamsic Run and operated this large commercial mill until his death. Little is known of his personal life, but he amassed a considerable fortune and owned land on Chappawamsic and Beaverdam runs. During the War of 1812, Benjamin served in the 45th Regiment formed in Stafford County, beginning his service on June 23, 1807.

[352] William was the son of Daniel Carroll Brent (1759-1814). He married first in 1810 Winifred (Lee) Beale (1790-1833), the daughter of Thomas Ludwell Lee, Jr. (died 1807) of Loudoun County. He married secondly Roxanna Sommers (1798-1882).

[353] Charles Julien married Jane Moor (1777-1851), the daughter of Edward Moor (died c.1806) of Falmouth.

[354] Zachariah was the son of Thomas Vowells and Susannah Chunn of St. Mary's, Maryland and, later, Fauquier County. Zachariah died intestate and unmarried.

[355] Isaac was the son of Maj. William Newton (c.1712-1789) and his second wife, Elizabeth Kenyon. From his father he inherited that part of Little Falls plantation on the Rappahannock River that included the house, mill, and quarry. He served in the War of 1812.

[356] Robert was the son of Hugh Crutcher (died 1779) of Culpeper County and Frances Coleman and the grandson of Thomas Crutcher, Sr. (1695-1786). In 1809 Robert married in Stafford Tarissa Hamble Phillips (born 1783), the daughter of Col. William (1744-1797) and Elizabeth (Fowke) Phillips (died c.1830) of Traveler's Rest, Stafford County.

[357] Known as William H. Fitzhugh of "Chappawamsic." Around 1804 his father Thomas Fitzhugh (1760-1820) of Boscobel purchased Chappawamsic, the old George Mason home and established young William there when he returned from Princeton College. William lived at Chappawamsic for many years before moving to Falmouth where he died. In 1852 he sold the farm to James Ashby (1827-1861).

On Dec. 26, 1811 William was staying at a hotel in Richmond when it caught fire. He saved himself by jumping from his window to the street below. He served as a major during the War of 1812 and in 1814 married Eliza Churchill Darby.

1810
Maj. William H. Fitzhugh
William B. Wallace[360]
Robert Lewis
John Moncure[361]
Benjamin Tolson[363]
Thomas Fristoe
Alexander Morson[366]
Robert Crutcher

Robert H. Hooe[359]
Thomas Seddon
Zachariah Vowles
George Lane[362]
Hancock Eustace[364]
Isaac Newton[365]
Joel Mason[367]
Thomas W. Cowne

1811
Hancock Eustace
Robert Crutcher
Joel Mason
George Lane
William B. Wallace

Benjamin Ficklen
Kellis Hord
John Moncure
Samuel H. Peyton
Robert Lewis

1812
Thomas Mountjoy
George Lane
Benjamin Ficklen[368]
Zachariah Vowles
Thomas W. Cowne
Robert Crutcher
John Moncure[369]
William Brent, Jr. (1783-1848)
Kellis Hord

John T. Brooke
Samuel H. Peyton
Robert H. Hooe
William B. Wallace
Enoch Mason
Hancock Eustace
Maj. William H. Fitzhugh
Thomas Fristoe

---

[358] Thomas operated a school in Falmouth and offered courses such as reading, spelling, penmanship, grammar, geography, history, arithmetic, bookkeeping, and Latin. Tuition was $20 per student (*Virginia Herald*, Dec. 11, 1816).
   In 1809 Thomas married Martha Hewitt Buchanan (died 1818), the daughter of Maj. Andrew Buchanan (died 1804). Thomas married secondly in 1820 Susan Latham of Fauquier County.
[359] According to the 1810 Stafford census, Robert owned 47 slaves.
[360] According to the 1810 Stafford census, William owned 13 slaves.
[361] According to the 1810 Stafford census, John owned 18 slaves.
[362] According to the 1810 Stafford census, George owned 15 slaves.
[363] In 1812 Benjamin paid taxes on 9 slaves. He also owned Bellfair Mills, a large commercial merchant mill on Chappawamsic Run.
[364] According to the 1810 Stafford census, Hancock owned 34 slaves.
[365] According to the 1810 Stafford census, Isaac owned 25 slaves.
[366] According to the 1810 Stafford census, Alexander owned 47 slaves.
[367] In 1812 Joel paid taxes on 6 slaves.
[368] In 1812 Benjamin paid personal property taxes on 15 slaves and 1,117 acres at the head of Aquia Run.
[369] In 1812 John paid taxes on 16 slaves and his 1,400-acre Somerset farm (Eby, They 57).

RICHLAND - The home of William Brent, Jr. (1783-1848). The original Brent house was constructed of brick and was burned by Lord Dunmore's troops in 1776. The frame house illustrated here was built on the site shortly after the Revolution.

1813
Robert H. Hooe
Thomas W. Cowne
Thomas Fristoe
George Lane
Benjamin Ficklen

Zachariah Vowles
Maj. William H. Fitzhugh
Robert Crutcher
John Moncure

1814
William Brent, Jr.

1815
Hancock Eustace
Dr. Alexander Fitzhugh[370] (1786-1847)

George Lane

1816
Capt. William B. Wallace
Walter R. Daniel[371] (1783-1818)

Samuel H. Skinker

1817
Thomas W. Cowne
Col. Enoch Mason
Zachariah Vowles

Robert Crutcher
Hancock Eustace
Benjamin Tolson

1818
Walter Raleigh Daniel

John Grayson Hedgman[372] (1782-c.1845)

---

[370] Alexander was born at Boscobel, the son of Thomas Fitzhugh (1760-1820) and the brother of Maj. William H. Fitzhugh. Dr. Fitzhugh was listed in the 1830 Stafford census as owning 39 slaves. From 1838-1840 he represented Stafford County in the Virginia House of Delegates. In 1815 Alexander married Eliza Gibbs Clare of Clarke County, Virginia and lived in Falmouth.
[371] Walter was the son of Travers Daniel, Sr. and Frances Moncure. He married Elizabeth Lewis, the daughter of Col. Zachary Lewis (1731-1803). Walter served in the War of 1812.

Thomas Gaskins Moncure (1799-1836) Benjamin Tolson
Nathaniel P. Williams[373]

1819
John G. Hedgman Benjamin Tolson
Rowzee Peyton[374] (1789-1867)

1820
Nathaniel P. Williams Zachariah Vowles
Benjamin Tolson

1821
Rowzee Peyton Col. Enoch Mason
John Moncure Samuel H. Peyton
Zachariah Vowles Murray Forbes
Thomas Seddon

1822
Rowzee Peyton Dr. Alexander Fitzhugh
William Brent, Jr. William Fitzhugh
Walter R. Daniel Nathaniel P. Williams
Robert Crutcher

1823
Samuel Hampson Skinker[375] (1785-1856) Zachariah Vowles
Rowzee Peyton John G. Hedgman

1824
William H. Fitzhugh Murray Forbes[376] (1782-1863)
John G. Hedgman William Brent, Jr.

---

[372] John was the son of John Hedgman (1758-1796) and Catherine Grayson (1760-1795) of Prince William County. John G. Hedgman married his cousin Hannah Ball Daniel Brown (born 1780), the daughter of Travers Daniel, Sr. (1741-1824), and the widow of Rawleigh Travers Brown.

[373] Nathaniel was the son of Pearson Williams (c.1743-c.1824) of Stafford County. Based upon a court notice involving settlement of the estate of Joseph Harrison Combs, Nathaniel married Mary Combs, probably the daughter of the above Joseph Combs.

[374] Rowzee was the son of John Rowzee Peyton (1754-1798) of Stony Hill and Anne Hooe (1754-1833). Rowzee married first c.1818 Eliza Strother Galleher (1791-1822). In 1826 he married as his second wife Eliza Murray (1791-1878). During the War of 1812, Rowzee served as a captain in John Catesby Edrington's (1775-1820) company where he worked as clerk and adjutant. He was a vestryman of Aquia Church 1815-1824. After his second marriage, he removed to Geneva, New York. The 1830 census listed Rowzee as owner of 26 slaves.

[375] Samuel was the son of William Skinker and Mary (Sells) Powlett (c.1745-1798) and the grandson of Thomas Skinker (born 1729). Sometime prior to 1776, Thomas purchased 1,021 acres from Charles Carter (1738-1796). Part of this tract became known as Oakley and was inherited by Samuel H. Skinker. The fine old frame house, located on the west side of Poplar Road (State Route 616) and in the corner created by the intersection of this road and Shackelford's Well Road (State Route 754), collapsed in 2003.

Samuel married Margaret Wilson Julian (died 1863), the only daughter of Dr. John Julian of Fredericksburg. He devised Oakley to his daughters, Louise and Lucy and to his son, John Howard Skinker (1814-1867). Samuel was a veteran of the War of 1812.

[376] The son of Dr. David Forbes (1751-1789) and Margaret Sterling (1754-1806), the daughter of the last Laird of Herbertshire. Murray was born in Dumfries, Prince William County. In 1815 he married Sallie Innes Thornton (1776-1807), the widow of Col. Francis Thornton (1767-1836). Murray was listed in the 1830 census as owning 11 slaves and served in the War of 1812.

1825
William Richards Gordon[377] (1780-1855)
William J. Roberts[379]
William Churchill Beale[380] (1791-1850)
Maj. William H. Fitzhugh
Zachariah Vowles
Nathaniel P. Williams
William Hewitt
Col. Enoch Mason
Rowzee Peyton
Thomas Seddon

Thomas B. Adams[378] (died 1836)
Dr. Alexander Fitzhugh
Murray Forbes
Walter R. Daniel
George Banks[381] (1779-1837)
Robert H. Hooe
Robert Crutcher
Samuel H. Peyton
John G. Hedgman

1826
William C. Beale
Zachariah Vowles
William Gordon
Col. Enoch Mason

Dr. Alexander Fitzhugh
Reubin Triplett Thom[382] (1782-1868)
Samuel H. Peyton
Walter R. Daniel

1827
Col. Enoch Mason
Dr. Alexander Fitzhugh
Samuel H. Skinker

Rowzee Peyton
William C. Beale
Alexander Fontaine Rose[383] (1780-1831)

---

[377] In 1813 William and his wife Mary A. M. Gordon bought a tract of land from Falmouth businessman, Benjamin Ficklen (died 1821). This became known as Rosedale and stood on the north side of Mountain View Road (State Route 627) and the east side of the intersection of Mountain View and Rock Hill Church Road (State Route 644).

[378] Thomas was formerly of Fredericksburg but died in Copia County, Mississippi (*Virginia Herald*, Dec. 14, 1836).

[379] In 1817 William married Martha Lomax in Fredericksburg.

[380] William was the son of William Beale and Hannah Gordon of Fauquier County. His first wife was Susan Vowles. In 1834 he married secondly in Fredericksburg Jane Briggs Howison (1815-1882). The couple spent their first five years of marriage in the Conway House in Falmouth before moving to Fredericksburg.

In 1825 Beale purchased from James Vass (c.1769-1837), Scottish merchant and miller of Falmouth, a half interest in the Thistle Flour Mill that Vass had built next to the Rappahannock River in 1812. This was the most technologically advanced of the flour mills in Falmouth and was described in a newspaper advertisement as "a large and commodious mill...to which is annexed every description of machinery eligible, convenient, useful, or essential to the complete and perfect operation of the said mill" (*Virginia Herald*, Sept. 16, 1812). A policy with the Mutual Assurance Society estimated the mill's value at $20,000. Sometime before 1836 Beale bought out the other half interest owned by John and Wright Southgate. After Beale's death in 1850, Duff Green (1792-1854), Falmouth industrialist, bought the Thistle Mill and renamed it the Eagle Mill. William served in the War of 1812.

[381] George was the son of Gerard Banks (1725-1787) and Frances Bruce (1735-1818) of Greenbank, Stafford County. In 1806 George married Jemima Ann Overton (1789-1863).

[382] Reubin was the son of Alexander Thom of Invernesshire, Scotland and Elizabeth Triplett of Culpeper. In April 1857 he was elected president of the Aqueduct Company of Fredericksburg and worked as director of the Farmers Bank of Virginia. For 52 years he served as a vestryman of St. George's Church in Fredericksburg. He also served for 45 years as senior warden of that church. He married Eleanor Reat (1786-1869).

[383] Alexander lived at Hampstead on the west side of Poplar Road (State Route 616) and immediately south of Poplar Grove. In 1816 he married Sarah Rose Fontaine (1796-1863), the daughter of William and Ann (Morris) Fontaine. Alexander represented Stafford County in the Virginia House of Delegates from 1816-1817 and from 1820-1821. The 1830 census listed Alexander as owning 26 slaves.

On Oct. 16, 1827 a local newspaper published an article titled "Anti-Jackson Meeting" which reported on "a meeting of the citizens of the county of Stafford, opposed to the election of General Andrew

Hancock Eustace	Samuel H. Peyton
Walter R. Daniel	Nathaniel P. Williams
Robert H. Hooe	Robert Crutcher
William H. Fitzhugh	John G. Hedgman
William Brent	William Washington Peyton[384] (1799-1847)

1828

John G. Hedgman	Robert H. Hooe
William W. Peyton	

1829

Robert H. Hooe	John G. Hedgman
Col. Enoch Mason	William H. Fitzhugh

1830

Duff Green[385] (1792-1854)	John Moncure

Jackson to the presidency of the United States, and friends to the present administration, held pursuant to notice in the newspapers, in the court-house of said county, on Monday, the 8th day of October, 1827" (*Political Arena*, Oct. 16, 1827). At this meeting Alexander F. Rose, Esq. "was called to the chair" and John Moncure Conway (1779-1864) appointed secretary. A committee consisting of some of Stafford's leading citizens including Col. Enoch Mason, Gen. George Mason Cooke (1792-1866), William C. Beale, Robert H. Hooe, William Ford (1788-1834), and Hancock Eustace were appointed to prepare a report and resolutions. Their goal was to prevent the election of a man they felt was "wholly unqualified for the station."

[384] William was the son of Dr. Valentine Peyton (1756-1815) and Mary Butler Washington (1760-1822). He married Mary/Lucy Mason (1801-1838), the daughter of Col. Enoch Mason and Lucy Wiley Roy of Clover Hill, Stafford County. Around 1840 William removed to Mississippi and died on his cotton plantation near Jackson.

[385] A Scotsman from Culpeper County, Duff Green moved to Falmouth early in the 19th century. By 1818 he had begun buying property in the town, one of his early purchases being a lot near the modern bridge that crosses over the Rappahannock River. In 1824 he married Eliza Ann Payne (1806-1876), the daughter of Capt. William Payne (1755-1837) of Fauquier County and his second wife, Marion Andrew Morson (c.1724-1808). Around 1826 Duff moved to Belmont, later the home of the prominent Ficklen family. He later purchased a farm just north of Falmouth (the present site of Stafford Senior High School) that he called Ridgeway.

By 1850 Duff owned a merchant flour mill, a cotton mill, a wood carding mill, and two retail stores, one in Falmouth and one in Fredericksburg. He was very involved in life in and around Falmouth. Among other activities, he commanded the town militia company and, during the 1830s, was inspector of flour for the port of Falmouth. He was a director of the Farmers Bank of Fredericksburg, worked on the committee to build the Mary Washington Monument. Duff was a director of the Baltimore and Rappahannock Steam Packet Company and was an active member of St. George's Episcopal Church in Fredericksburg. He owned the Falmouth Hotel which burned in 1835 along with several nearby buildings that also belonged to him. In 1837 he built the Elm Factory on lot #3 in Falmouth. This was a 3 ½-story brick building with a slate roof. Its mechanical workings were powered by a steam engine and produced primarily yarn and osnaburg, a coarse cotton fabric. As a result of the war, economic conditions in Virginia changed drastically. The Elm Factory continued to operate sporadically during the second half of the 19th century though the Falmouth port had long silted in, the national economy had faltered, and business in Falmouth had all but ceased. Newspaper articles indicate that the mill was open in January 1877, but had closed by August of that year. By April 1880 an unnamed gentleman from Massachusetts had leased it for five years and was preparing to put the machinery in order to once again manufacture cotton and yarns (*Fredericksburg Star*, Apr. 7, 1880). The last mention of the mill came a few days later when the paper claimed that the mill would soon be open (*Fredericksburg Star*, Apr. 18, 1880). Sometime shortly thereafter, the mill was closed and abandoned.

In 1850 Duff purchased the Eagle Flour Mill from William C. Beale's estate. He operated this commercial merchant mill in partnership with George B. Scott (c.1821-1881), Fredericksburg businessman.

John G. Hedgman
Benjamin Tolson
William W. Peyton
Dr. Robert Osborne Grayson[387] (1789-1841)
Nathaniel P. Williams
Dr. John M. Daniel[389] (1800-c.1845)
William Brent, Jr.

Rowzee Peyton
William H. Fitzhugh[386]
Samuel H. Peyton
Charles Tackett[388] (c.1780-1834)
Dr. Alexander Fitzhugh
Alexander F. Rose
William Hewitt

1831
Thomas Towson[390] (1779-1861)
Walker P. Conway[392] (1805-1884)
Enoch Mason, Jr.[394] (born c.1797)
John Rose Fitzhugh[395] (1795-after 1860)

Samuel Selden Brooke[391] (1800-1861)
Anthony Strother Ficklen[393] (died 1844)
Alexander F. Rose
Nathaniel P. Williams

Duff died in 1854 at the age of 62 and was buried in the family cemetery at Ridgeway. The graveyard is located beneath the water tower. Eliza died in 1876 at the age of 71 and was also buried at Ridgeway. The 1830 census listed Duff as owner of 21 slaves.

[386] The 1830 census listed William as owner of 45 slaves.

[387] Robert was the son of Benjamin Grayson (1763-1829) and Ann Bronaugh (born 176_). He married first Susan Margaret Peyton (1787-1824) and secondly Sarah Mason Cooke (1791-1861), the daughter of Col. John Cooke (1755-1828) and Mary Thomson Mason (born 1762).

[388] Charles was the son of William Tackett, Jr. (c.1751-after 1830) of Prince William County and his wife Frances Reno (c.1750-1796:99). In addition to operating Tackett's Mill, Charles was also a hotel keeper and schoolmaster. He married Ann Nancy Barber. The 1830 census listed Charles as owner of 19 slaves.

[389] Dr. Daniel was the son of Dr. John Moncure Daniel (1769-1813) who was born at Crow's Nest. This elder John married first Maria Niven, the daughter of a Spanish merchant of Cadiz who had a home in Glasgow, Scotland where he was studying medicine. She died in Dumfries, Virginia in 1792. In 1793 he married Margaret Eleanor Stone (1771-1809), the daughter of the Honorable Thomas Stone (1743-1787) and Margaret Brown of Maryland. He married thirdly Maria Vowles.

John, Jr. married first around 1823 Eliza Mitchell (died c.1835), the daughter of William Mitchell of Stafford. He married secondly Euphemia Tolson (1805-1844), the daughter of James E. Tolson (1795-1865) and Anne E. Hickerson (1827-1897).

[390] The son of John Towson (c.1746-1832) and Penelope Buck (c.1753-1794) of Baltimore County, Maryland. Thomas was a wealthy businessman and landowner in Stafford. He owned the busy landing and docks at Coal Landing and lived at Rockdale on the north side of Courthouse Road (State Route 630). His primary occupations were quarrying and land speculation. The 1871 land tax records list Thomas as owning tracts of 42, 236, 101, 7, and 50 acres near Austin Run, 137 acres near the courthouse, 146 ¼ acres on Aquia Creek, 197 acres on Rocky Run (this was Rockdale, his residence), and 33 acres on the Aquia Road (Garrisonville Road—State Route 610). Thomas married Eleanor Norman (1782-1848) of Edge Hill whose family were also involved in the Aquia stone quarries. He married secondly Lucy P. Stone (c.1806-c.1876).

[391] Samuel was the son of John Taliaferro Brooke (c.1763-1821) of Millvale. He married Elizabeth Young and moved to Roanoke where he was clerk of the court.

[392] For many years Walker was one of Stafford's most influential citizens, serving as presiding justice in the county for some 30 years. Prior to the War Between the States, Walker was president of the Virginia Bank in Fredericksburg, his partner being Warren Slaughter (c.1821-1866). During the war, he moved to Richmond and continued in the banking business until war's end. After Slaughter's death in 1866, Walker organized and was senior member of a new banking house, Conway, Gordon, and Garnett. He married Margaret Eleanor Daniel (1807-1891) of Stafford.

[393] Anthony was the son of Charles Ficklen (died c.1816) and Mary (Strother?) of Fauquier County. He was listed in the Stafford census of 1810. Anthony married in Fauquier but died childless.

[394] The son of Col. Enoch Mason of Clover Hill. Enoch, Jr. married Mary Elizabeth Mason, the grand daughter of George Mason (1725-1792) of Gunston Hall. He 1830 census listed Enoch as owner of 16 slaves.

[395] John was the son of Thomas Fitzhugh, Jr. of Boscobel and Anne Rose (born 1763). Little else is known of him.

Dr. John M. Daniel
Benjamin Tolson
Rowzee Peyton
William Hewitt
William W. Peyton

Thomas G. Moncure
John G. Hedgman
John Moncure
Charles Tackett

1832

Samuel H. Peyton
Dr. Alexander Fitzhugh
William W. Peyton
William Hewitt
Walker P. Conway
Robert O. Grayson
Dr. John M. Daniel
John Moncure
Duff Green
Benjamin Tolson

George Banks
Charles Tackett
Isaac Newton
Thomas Towson
John R. Fitzhugh
Samuel S. Brooke
John G. Hedgman
Enoch Mason, Jr.
Robert H. Hooe

1833

Thomas Towson
Duff Green
William W. Peyton
James Briggs[396] (1787-1845)
Samuel S. Brooke
John Moncure
Dr. John M. Daniel
Thomas Norman[398] (c.1790-1846)
William Hewitt
Alexander P. Williams[399] (died c.1839)
Alexander Morson[400] (1759-1822)

Walker P. Conway
Dr. Alexander Fitzhugh
George Mason Cooke (1792-1866)
Thomas Hill[397] (c.1781-c.1870)
John G. Hedgman
Enoch Mason, Jr.
Robert H. Hooe
Benjamin Tolson
William Brent, Jr.
Robert O. Grayson

1834

Walker P. Conway
George M. Cooke
John G. Hedgman
Samuel S. Brooke
William W. Peyton
Dr. John M. Daniel
William Hewitt
John R. Fitzhugh

Samuel H. Skinker
Robert H. Hooe
Enoch Mason, Jr.
Thomas Towson
Thomas Hill
Charles Tackett
Duff Green
William H. Fitzhugh

---

[396] James McDonald Briggs was the son of David Briggs (1730-1813), a Scots merchant in Falmouth and Jean McDonald (c.1750-1810), the daughter of the Rev. Neal McDonald of Brunswick Parish. James inherited his father's plantation, Stony Hill, which stood on the north side of Stony Hill Road (State Route 662). The old house survived well into the 20th century but, after being abandoned for many years, was destroyed by fire. The old Briggs cemetery, located about 50 yards north of the house, remains.

[397] Thomas Hill inherited Oak Grove from his father Leonard Hill (died c.1814). This farm was originally granted to Augustine Washington (1694-1743) and remained in the Hill family from 1784-1875. Leonard Hill had been overseer at Landon Carter's (1757-1820) Parke Quarter.

[398] The Norman family resided at Edge Hill and operated at least one of the Aquia Creek sandstone quarries. Thomas also served as commissioner of the revenue from 1838-1840.

[399] In 1815 Alexander ran a school in Stafford.

[400] Alexander was the son of Arthur Morson (1734-1798), a Scots merchant who emigrated from Scotland to Falmouth where he operated a lucrative mercantile business. Arthur built Hartwood (Eby, They 351) on the south side of the Warrenton Road (U. S. Route 17). Alexander was also a Falmouth merchant, but he built and resided at Hollywood (Eby, They 256). He married Anne Casson Alexander (1781-1833).

1835
Walker P. Conway
John G. Hedgman
James Briggs
James Morton[401] (died 1859)
William W. Peyton
Robert O. Grayson
Thomas Norman
George M. Cooke
Dr. John M. Daniel
John Jameson[402] (1763-1842)
Isaac Newton

Robert H. Hooe
Samuel S. Brooke
William H. Fitzhugh
Samuel H. Skinker
Thomas Towson
Duff Green
Thomas Hill
Benjamin Tolson
John R. Fitzhugh
George Banks
Alexander Morson

1836
Walker P. Conway
William Hewitt
Thomas Hill
John G. Hedgman
James Morton

Thomas Towson
Samuel S. Brooke
James Briggs
Thomas Norman

1837
Walker P. Conway
Robert H. Hooe
John R. Fitzhugh
William Hewitt

Duff Green
Dr. Alexander Fitzhugh
John G. Hedgman
Thomas Hill

1838
John G. Hedgman
James Briggs
James Morton
Samuel S. Brooke
William W. Peyton
Robert H. Hooe

Samuel H. Skinker
Walker P. Conway
Duff Green
Thomas Hill
John Jameson
Dr. Alexander Fitzhugh

---

[401] James Morton was the son of Richard Morton (1771-1812) and Margaret Ursula Waller (1771-1821) and grandson of Ursula (Brightwell) Morton of Maryland. After the death of her husband and just after the Revolution, Ursula came to Stafford from Maryland. According to her grand daughter, Mrs. Annie (Morton) Dix (c.1842-1922), Ursula didn't plan on staying in Stafford, but one of her children became ill while in the vicinity of the courthouse. She liked the people here and bought a home on part of the old Waller farm, Spring Hill (now Vestavia Woods subdivision on Courthouse Road (State Route 630). Here she remained until her death. According to Mrs. Dix, Ursula had three children, Ann, Mary, and Richard. Ann married George Hedgman and had three sons, Peter Daniel Grayson Hedgman (c.1800-after 1885), George F. S. Hedgman, and John Hedgman. Richard married Margaret Ursula Waller, the daughter of William Waller (1740-1817) of Concord and his second wife (and cousin), Margaret Waller (1744-177_) of Spring Hill. Richard and Margaret had 11 children, including James Morton, the justice of the peace. James married Lucy Horton (c.1818-1898) and had 11 children. His sister, Mary, married Joel James Jameson (1801-after 1861) of Stafford.

James was a land speculator, buying and selling numerous parcels within the county. He owned much of the property on the east side of U. S. Route 1 between Aquia and Potomac creeks. Following his death, his estate had to be settled by the court. Some of these records are on file in the Fredericksburg Circuit Court.

James devised to his son, Thomas, his "mill and mill seat." His will also mentioned his children William, James (1851-1902), Elizabeth, Allen Waller, Nancy, Margaret (Morton) Martin, Maria, John, and George (Stafford Deed Book AA, p. 334).

[402] John was the son of David D. Jameson (1725:30-1794) of Prince William County.

Alexander Morson
Thomas Norman
George W. Stone[404]

Dr. John M. Daniel
Dr. Alexander Hamilton Mason[403] (1807-1858)

1839
John G. Hedgman
Edward Waller[405] (1805-1883)
Walker P. Conway
Robert H. Hooe
Dr. John Henry Daniel[406] (born 1813)
William Hewitt
John R. Fitzhugh
Dr. Alexander Fitzhugh

Thomas Norman
Duff Green
Dr. Alexander H. Mason
Samuel H. Skinker
George W. Stone
James Briggs
Samuel S. Brooke

1840
John G. Hedgman
Edward Waller
Samuel S. Brooke
Dr. John H. Daniel
Dr. Alexander Fitzhugh
George W. Stone
William Barber[407] (1787-1881)
Thomas Hill
Travers Daniel Moncure[408] (1811-1886)

Thomas Norman
William Hewitt
Dr. Alexander H. Mason
Walker P. Conway
James Briggs
John Jameson
Samuel H. Skinker
James Morton
Duff Green

---

[403] The son of Col. Enoch Mason (c.1769-1828) of Clover Hill. Alexander received his medical training at the University of Virginia and was listed in 1831 as an alumnus of that institution. That same year he married Jane Allen Smith (died 1812), the daughter of Augustine Jaquelin Smith of West Grove, Fairfax County.
    The 1871 land tax records list Alexander as owning 130 acres near Falmouth known as Dogtown. While the exact location of Dogtown is unknown, judging from the tax records, it was somewhere along Warrenton Road (U. S. Route 17), in the vicinity of Hunter's Iron Works.

[404] On May 12, 1834 George petitioned the Stafford court to "erect a mill and mill dam on his own land in this county." The sheriff was ordered to impanel a jury of 12 men to determine what effect this would have on the land above and below the mill and "what damage it will be to the several proprietors, and whether the mansion house of any such proprietor, or the offices, curtilage or gardens thereunto immediately belonging, or orchards will be overflowed; to enquire whether and in what degree, fish of passage and ordinary navigation, will be obstructed; whether by any and by what means, such obstruction may be prevented; and whether in their opinion the health of the neighbours will be annoyed by the stagnation of the waters." On Dec. 8 of that year George was granted "leave to build the said mill and dam" on Rocky Pen Run (Stafford Circuit Court Minute Book, 1830-1835, p. 370).

[405] In 1835 Waller purchased the Grafton property on the north side of Garrisonville Road (State Route 610) from the Harrison family. Edward was the son of Edward Waller (1768-1818) and Elizabeth Chadwell of Concord on Aquia Creek. He was involved in the sandstone quarries on Aquia Creek. The 1871 land tax records list Edward as owner of the 647 ½-acre Shelbourne tract on Aquia Run ($1,200 in building values), the 190-acre Short tract on Aquia Run, 130 acres of the old Woodstock tract, and the 170-acre Rock Rimmon tract that included the sandstone quarry. The 1860 census lists Edward with real estate valued at $15,000 and $55,000 in personal property.

[406] The son of Dr. John Moncure Daniel (1769-1813). John married Fenton Brooke (born c.1828), the eldest daughter of Samuel S. Brooke of Mill Vale and his wife Angelina Edrington (born c.1809). He graduated from the University of Pennsylvania in 1837 with a degree in medicine. The elder Dr. Daniel died on the same day that this son was born.

[407] William Barber was one of Stafford's most prominent 19th century citizens, yet little is known of him or his family. He lived at Wyoming, his farm in the north end of the county. This property was condemned in 1942 for the expansion of Quantico Marine Corps Base.

1841

John G. Hedgman	Walker P. Conway
Dr. Alexander H. Mason	Duff Green
James Briggs	Thomas Hill
Dr. John H. Daniel	Samuel H. Skinker
Robert H. Hooe	Dr. Alexander Fitzhugh
William Barber	John Jameson
Robert Kendall (c.1787-1860)	Samuel S. Brooke
James Morton	Dr. Valentine Yelverton Conway[409] (1803-1881)
George W. Stone	Burkett Pratt Bowen[410] (c.1802-1852)

1842

John G. Hedgman	Walker P. Conway
Dr. Alexander H. Mason	Robert H. Hooe
William Hewitt	Maj. William H. Fitzhugh
Travers D. Moncure	William Barber
John Jameson	Dr. Alexander Fitzhugh
Dr. John H. Daniel	Samuel H. Skinker
James Briggs	Thomas Hill
Edward Waller	Thomas Towson
Robert Kendall	George W. Stone

1843

Dr. John M. Daniel	William Hewitt
Samuel S. Brooke	Walker P. Conway
Dr. John H. Daniel	Dr. Alexander H. Mason
Dr. Alexander Fitzhugh	Robert Kendall
George W. Stone	Maj. William H. Fitzhugh
Thomas Norman	Travers D. Moncure
Thomas Hill	Robert H. Hooe
Samuel H. Skinker	John R. Fitzhugh
William Barber	Thomas Towson
James Morton	

1844

James Morton	Dr. Alexander Fitzhugh
Dr. Alexander H. Mason	Thomas Hill
Robert Kendall	Walker P. Conway
Thomas Towson	Edward Waller
William Hand Browne[411] (died 1852)	Burkett P. Bowen
James R. Benson[412] (1814-c.1890)	Samuel H. Skinker
Dr. John H. Daniel	John G. Hedgman

---

[408] Travers was the son of John Moncure (III) (1772-1822). He was born at Clermont and died at Oakwood in Stafford. In 1838 he married Susan B. Carter.

[409] Valentine was the son of John Moncure Conway (1779-1864) and Catherine Storke Peyton (1786-1865). In 1824 Valentine married his first cousin, Mary Catherine Washington Henry (1806-1890), the daughter of Edward Hugh Henry and Elizabeth Washington Peyton and the great grand daughter of Patrick Henry. They resided at Cabin Hill in Stafford and Dr. Conway provided medical care to Stafford residents for many years.

[410] Burkett was the son of John Pratt Bowen (died c.1838) and Elizabeth Curtis. Burkett resided at the Glebe on Muddy Creek, a 400-acre plantation he inherited from his father.

[411] William married Letitia Wishart. In 1829 he served as a midshipman.

[412] James was the son of William Willis Lewis Benson (died 1815) and Eleanor Bullard (1786-1846). In 1814 he married Susan R. Benson and died in Montgomery, Alabama.

Samuel S. Brooke
Travers D. Moncure

1845
James Morton
Walker P. Conway
Edward Waller
Thomas Hill
William Barber
Dr. John H. Daniel

1846
James Morton
Dr. Lawrence Berry Rose[414] (1821-1887)
Thomas Hill
Walker P. Conway
Burkett P. Bowen
Dr. Hawkins Stone[415] (1816-1903)

John LeRoy Chinn[413] (1795-1854)
Maj. William H. Fitzhugh

Samuel S. Brooke
Dr. Alexander H. Mason
Travers D. Moncure
Robert Kendall
John R. Fitzhugh

Samuel H. Skinker
Dr. Alexander Fitzhugh
Dr. Alexander H. Mason
Robert Kendall
William H. Browne
John Warren Slaughter[416] (c.1821-1866)

---

[413] John owned the old Drummond's Race Field near Chatham and Little Whim. His heirs sold the property to Alexander K. Phillips (1805-1892) who, just prior to the War Between the States, built a fine brick home there. Union soldiers using the house during the Battle of Fredericksburg set fire to it and burned it to the ground, though it is not clear if this was a deliberate or accidental act.

In 1843 John paid taxes on 15 slaves, 6 horses, 1 carriage, 1 metal clock, 1 gold watch, 1 piano, silver plate, 1 carriole (a light covered horse-drawn cart with room for one person), and two tracts of 100 and 350 acres respectively (Hore, Account book).

[414] The son of Capt. Alexander Fontaine Rose (1780-1831) and Sarah Fontaine Rose (1796-1863) of Hampstead. He was educated at the College of William and Mary and received his medical training at the University of Pennsylvania, the first medical institution in the country. He commenced his medical practice in Stafford, then moved to Falmouth where he resided during the War Between the States. After the war, he moved to Fredericksburg. In Lawrence's first election for mayor of Fredericksburg, he lost to Wiley Roy Mason by about 30 votes. Wiley resigned the office a few days afterwards and Dr. Rose was elected without opposition. He served several terms as mayor (*Virginia Star*, Apr. 14, 1877). Dr. Rose married Eliza S. Wellford (1827-1899), the daughter of John S. and Jannet Henderson Wellford. He died in Fredericksburg of a heart ailment.

[415] Hawkins was born in Stafford on June 16, 1816. He was a descendant of Thomas Stone (1743-1787) of Charles County, Maryland who represented Maryland in the Continental Congress and signed the Declaration of Independence. Hawkins' ancestors moved to Stafford from Maryland in 1779 and established a plantation on Aquia Run. This plantation, known as Mt. Olive, is now part of the Quantico Marine Corps reservation. In 1843 Hawkins graduated from medical school in Philadelphia and returned to Stafford where he practiced medicine for the next sixty years. Around 1850 he married Hannah Ann Waller (1823-1896). The couple had four children, all of whom predeceased their father.

Family tradition holds that Hawkins was an outspoken opponent of the Union occupation. Shortly after their arrival in Stafford, Union soldiers arrested Hawkins and sent him to a prison camp. Because he was not only the sole medical provider in his north Stafford community, but also ran the local grist mill, Union authorities were forced to send him home in order to prevent further hardships for the women, children, and elderly who remained in the area.

Another family tradition holds that Hawkins owned the first automobile in Stafford. The doctor's prominent position and need for transportation certainly makes this a possibility, although no documentation has yet been found to prove the story.

Dr. Stone's farm is now the site of the Home Depot and Giant Food stores on Garrisonville Road (State Route 610). His mill, located near the modern dam at Smith's Reservoir, was built c.1812 by his father, Richard Stone (died before 1857). Doc Stone Road (State Route 659) began merely as a dirt trail leading from Garrisonville Road back to the mill and creek.

William Barber
William Brent, Jr.
Dr. John H. Daniel

Edward Waller
Thomas Norman
Travers D. Moncure

1847

James Morton
Dr. Hawkins Stone
Walker P. Conway
Dr. Alexander H. Mason
John W. Slaughter
William Barber
Edward Waller
Jefferson Spindle[418] (c.1804-1861)
Thomas Hill
Dr. Lawrence B. Rose
William H. Browne
James R. Benson

Thomas Towson
William Irvine[417] (c.1781-1859)
John L. Chinn
William Brent, Jr.
Dr. Alexander Fitzhugh
Travers D. Moncure
Dr. John H. Daniel
John A. Swetnam (1792-1854)
Robert Kendall
Burkett P. Bowen
John R. Fitzhugh

The 1871 land tax records list Hawkins with 197-acre home in Garrisonville, 160 acres with a store in Garrisonville (exact location unknown), a second store on 30 acres in Garrisonville, and 85 acres on Beaverdam Run.

Dr. Stone developed a melanoma on his face and neck and died of this awful cancer. His wife and children had all predeceased him and, as the cancer progressed, he became unable to care for himself. A niece, Mary "Mamie" Catherine Edmunds (c.1844-c.1927), moved in with Hawkins and care for him through his last months. He finally died on Jan. 20, 1903 and was buried in the family plot on the farm. When the shopping center was built in 1999-2000, the Stone family graves were moved to Ebenezer Church cemetery on Onville Road (State Route 641). His obituary described him as "one of Stafford's most remarkable citizens" (*Free Lance*, Jan. 27, 1903).

[416] Born in Culpeper, John was the son of William and Harriet Slaughter. He was Walker P. Conway's business partner and was involved in cotton manufacturing in Falmouth. Sometime prior to 1844, Conway and Slaughter converted the old flourmill at Rappahannock Forge to a cotton mill that they called the Falmouth Cotton Factory. This mill employed about 20 men and 30 women, but ceased operations as a result of the War Between the States. John married Sally Moore Braxton (born c.1828), the daughter of Carter M. and Elizabeth H. Braxton.

An inventory of his real estate made following his death and used in a court case, "Slaughter vs Slaughter" (Fredericksburg, 1867) revealed that John owned his residence, Hazel Hill Farm (value $10,000), a 1/6 interest in an unnamed iron furnace ($5,000), a 1/3 interest in the Vaucluse Gold Mine ($3,000), a house and lot on Leigh Street in Richmond, a ½ interest in a Chancellorsville farm ($4,000), a farm in Powhatan ($3,000), and a house on George Street in Fredericksburg ($5,250). Slaughter was buried in Fredericksburg.

In October 1865 Warren Slaughter, Walker P. Conway, and George W. Garnett (died 1876) formed a banking partnership under the firm name of Conway, Slaughter and Garnett. After Slaughter's death, William K. Gordon (1799-1886) was admitted to the partnership and the firm name was changed to Conway, Gordon and Company. Previously, these three men had been officers of the old Virginia Bank in Fredericksburg. This business evolved into the Conway, Gordon & Garnett National Bank.

[417] William resided on Hartwood, the old Morson plantation on the south side of Warrenton Road (U. S. Route 17). He married Sinah "Sarah" Davis Conyers (c.1798-1883), the daughter of his neighbor, John Conyers (c.1754-1819). In 1872 William was appointed one of the commissioners of the Free Bridge between Fredericksburg and Stafford County.

[418] Jefferson was the son of William Spindle (1774-1836) and Elizabeth Alsop. He married Maria A. Tackett (c.1810-1883), the daughter of Charles Tackett, Sr. (c.1780-1834) and his wife, Ann Barber. Jefferson assisted his father-in-law with the Mill Farm Seminary, a school he had started in 1818 at Tackett's Mill. The two organizers of this school were Tackett and his father-in-law, William Barber (c.1789-1881). Jefferson also served as postmaster of the Tackett's Mill Post Office from 1841-1846. In 1846 he purchased the old Washington plantation, Windsor Forest from Charles Prosser Moncure (born 1819). Here he established his own school.

1848

James Morton	Edward Waller
Dr. Hawkins Stone	Walker P. Conway
Dr. Lawrence B. Rose	Dr. John H. Daniel
Thomas Towson	William Irvine
William Brent, Jr.	Dr. Alexander H. Mason
John W. Slaughter	Jefferson Spindle
William Barber	Thomas Hill
Robert Kendall	Travers D. Moncure
John A. Swetnam	

1849

James Morton	Dr. Alexander H. Mason
John L. Chinn	

1850

James Morton	Thomas Towson
Walker P. Conway	Travers D. Moncure

1851

Walker P. Conway	Dr. Alexander H. Mason
William Barber	

1852

William H. Browne	Edward Waller
Walker P. Conway	John L. Chinn
John J. Withers[419] (1819-1861)	John Howard Skinker[420] (1814-1867)

1853

Arthur Fielding Clift[421] (c.1815-1888)	John Maurice O'Bannon[422] (1800-1870)
William Slaughter	John L. Chinn
John Seddon[423] (1826-1863)	Joshua Reamy[424] (1792-1857)

---

[419] John married Eliza J. Withers.

[420] John was the son of Samuel Hampson Skinker (1785-1856) and Margaret Wilson Julian. Samuel devised his Stafford plantation, Oakley, to son John Howard and unmarried daughters Louisa Virginia Knox Skinker (died 1886) and Lucy E. Scott Skinker (1807-1896). Early in his life, John studied law, medicine, and divinity, though he never practiced the latter two. He served as a justice in Stafford and as an editor of a newspaper in Warrenton. During the War Between the States, John was the only one in the Skinker family to take the side of the Union and, thereby, was an outcast amongst his kinsmen. During the war, he served as a lieutenant colonel under Gen. Patrick. After the war, he practiced law in Washington. John died unmarried.

[421] Arthur married Marian M. Alexander, the daughter of Fielding Alexander (died 1847) and Minnie Schooler. In 1869 Arthur's only daughter, Frances Marian, married Marias Sthreshley (1847-1931).

[422] John M. O'Bannon was born in Rappahannock County and moved to Stafford where he resided near Falmouth. In 1830 he married Harriet Ann Corbin (1813-1891), the daughter of Jameson Corbin (born c.1790) of Falmouth. In December 1837 John purchased Carlton from the Rev. Cumberland George. John is probably buried in the family cemetery at Carlton, but no stone remains to mark his resting place. The 1850 census listed him as a merchant, but he also leased slaves for loading and unloading ships at Falmouth. His son, Henry Clay O'Bannon (1843-1916), served as a justice of Stafford from at least 1871-1877. The 1871 land tax records list John O'Bannon's estate as including 298 acres on the Rappahannock, 1.5 acres near Falmouth, 274 acres on the Rappahannock ($400 in buildings), 331 acres near Falmouth ($500 in buildings), and 119 ½ acres on Aquia Run.

[423] John lived at Snowden on the Rappahannock River east of Fredericksburg. He purchased the property in 1847 from the Morson family. During the War Between the States, Union troops sailing up the

Benjamin C. Wamsley[425] (c.1814-1886)   William Botts[426] (1820-1868)

1854
Walker P. Conway
Benjamin C. Wamsley
William F. Moore[428] (c.1812-1864)
Arthur F. Clift
James Morton
John J. Withers
William Botts

James W. Stone[427] (c.1805-1857)
Joshua Reamy
John M. O'Bannon
John H. Skinker
Edward Waller
William H. Browne

1855
John J. Withers
Benjamin Clark
Arthur F. Clift
Edward Waller
Samuel S. Brooke
James Morton
William Botts

Benjamin C. Wamsley
John M. O'Bannon
Walker P. Conway
James W. Stone
William F. Moore
Joshua Reamy

1856
John H. Skinker
Charles Carter Wellford[429] (1802-1870)
John J. Withers
Edward Waller
William Botts
Joshua Reamy

John Beale
F. S. Myer
Walker P. Conway
Arthur F. Clift
William H. Browne
Samuel S. Brooke

Rappahannock mistakenly believed Snowden to be the home of John's brother, James A. Seddon (1815-1880), Secretary of War for the Confederacy. The soldiers ordered the family out of the house, then opened fire, burning the elegant brick house to the ground as the family watched helplessly.
[424] Joshua was descended from the immigrant Jacob Remy (c.1630-1721), a French Huguenot who settled in Cople Parish in Westmoreland County. Joshua Reamy (1792-1857) was known as Capt. Reamy and was the son of Berryman Reamy (c.1770-1850) and the grandson of Joshua Reamy (c.1747-1820). Young Joshua served as a captain in the Virginia militia until his death. In 1814 he married Meriah Neale. He married secondly in 1818 Frances Morris by whom he had sons, Thomas Benton Reamy (1836-1910), justice of Stafford County, and William Daingerfield Reamy (1852-1939), treasurer of Stafford.
  In 1846 Joshua purchased the old Landon Carter plantation, Parke Farm. In his will, he ordered that Parke be divided between his children. The portion on the southwest side of Potomac Run, approximately 500 acres, was to go to his wife for her lifetime. At her death, that parcel passed to daughter Charlotte T. Reamy and son William. The portion on the northeast side of the run, approximately 400 acres, passed to son Thomas.
[425] In 1871 Benjamin paid taxes on 264 acres on Cannon Run. This land is now part of the Quantico Marine Corps reservation. Benjamin married Eliza F. Shelkett (c.1827-1879), the daughter of John and Nancy Shelkett.
[426] The Botts family had long owned land on Chappawamsic Run in the upper part of the county (now part of Quantico). The 1871 land tax records list William Botts' estate as including 450½ acres on Chappawamsic.
[427] James was the son of Charles W. Stone (died 1842).
[428] William died in Stafford of consumption.
[429] Charles was the son of Dr. Robert Wellford (1753-1823) and Catherine Yates Thornton (1760-1831), the daughter of the Rev. Robert Yates of Gloucester County. Charles married Mary Katherine Stiff.
  In June 1865 Fredericksburg was still occupied by Federal troops. According to a newspaper report, Charles was assaulted and beaten in front of his residence in Fredericksburg "by some soldiers belonging to a battery stationed near the city." His son Thomas came to his aid and was also beaten severely (*Fredericksburg Ledger*, June 7, 1865).

John Seddon
Robert G. Hickerson[430] (1829-1898)
William Carter[431] (1807-1874)
Edmund F. Rose
Strother Harding[432] (c.1812-c.1853)
John G. Rowe

William F. Moore
Benjamin C. Wamsley
John M. O'Bannon
James W. Stone
James Morton

1857
James Morton
Arthur F. Clift
Walker P. Conway
Joshua Reamy
John H. Skinker
Henry Laurens Brooke[434] (1808-1874)

John J. Withers
Strother Harding
Robert G. Hickerson
John Seddon
James W. Stone[433]

1858
Strother Harding
John H. Skinker
John J. Withers
Henry L. Brooke
Gustavus Brown Wallace[436] (1810-1882)

Fielding Barton Stone[435] (born c.1827)
Edward Waller
John M. O'Bannon
Robert G. Hickerson
William H. Browne

---

[430] According to Robert's obituary, the deceased, together with James P. Simpson, W. B. Jones, William Snellings, and Edward Sterns, were appointed commissioners to view the road between Belle Plain and James' Hill and to ascertain the cost of reopening it. After completing their survey, the group met at the home of Simeon C. Peyton (c.1829-1905) for dinner. After their meal, the men retired to the parlor for cigars and port. Robert dropped dead with an apparent heart attack. He was buried at Auburn, his home in the upper part of the county.
   In April 1863 Robert enlisted as a sergeant with the 9th Virginia Cavalry. He was later appointed quartermaster sergeant. Robert married Mary E. Combs, the widow of Bolivar C. Combs (1831-1862).

[431] William Carter purchased the old Fristoe's Mill and lived at Tranquility, the Fristoe home place. William, James Tolson, and John Clark (1804-1882) were co-owners of Bellfair Mills, a large commercial merchant mill on Chappawamsic Run.

[432] Strother was listed in the 1850 Stafford census as a merchant. The 1871 land tax records list him as owner of 283 acres on Aquia Run.

[433] James died in office. He was replaced by Fielding Barton Stone (born c.1827).

[434] Henry, an attorney, was the son of John Taliaferro Brooke (c.1763-1821) and Ann Cary Selden. Early in his law career, Henry settled in Richmond. There he accumulated some debts and sold his home to settle them. Around 1854 he moved his family to "New Salvington" on Potomac Creek. This tract had been divided from his mother's ancestral home, Salvington (Brooke 7).
   In 1859 Henry moved to Ashland and was replaced as a Stafford justice by James Monteith (c.1813-c.1859). Henry's son, St. George Tucker Brooke (1844-1914) described his father as "exceedingly handsome. His face indicated intellect and refinement. He was perhaps five feet nine inches high with a strong stoutly built frame...His eyes were dark grey, full and very expressive...His taste in dress was perfect and he was fastidiously neat" (Brooke 6).
   Henry married Sarah Virginia Tucker (born 1815), the daughter of Henry St. George Tucker (1780-1848).

[435] Fielding was the son of William Hawkins Stone (c.1809-c.1851) and his wife Mildred (born c.1829). In 1858 Fielding married Ann Schooler (born c.1831), the daughter of Thomas E. (born c.1787) and Mary Schooler (born c.1795).

[436] The son of John Wallace (1761-1829) and Elizabeth Hooe (c.1766-1850) and the grandson of Dr. Michael Wallace (1719-1867) of Ellerslie. In 1832 Gustavus married Emily Travers Daniel, the daughter of Travers Daniel, Jr. (1763-1812) and Mildred Stone (1772-1837). Sometime prior to her death, Mildred Daniel purchased from the heirs of her son, Moncure Daniel, Crow's Nest, the old Daniel plantation on Potomac Creek. Mildred willed Crow's Nest to Emily and Gustavus and they resided there until they were forced to flee an invasion of Union troops during the War Between the States. Before leaving, the soldiers

James Morton
Edmund F. Rose
John Seddon

Arthur F. Clift
Walker P. Conway
William Carter

1859
John J. Withers
Robert G. Hickerson
Strother Harding
John M. O'Bannon
William H. Browne[439]
Edmund F. Rose
Gustavus B. Wallace
William Carter

John H. Skinker
Walker P. Conway
James Monteith[437] (c.1813-c.1859)
James Morton[438]
Edward Waller
John Seddon
Fielding B. Stone
Fielding Lawrence Clift[440] (born c.1808)

1860
Robert G. Hickerson
Walker P. Conway
Fielding B. Stone
James Monteith
Edward Waller[441]
Gustavus B. Wallace
Edmund F. Rose
William Edwin Moncure[442] (1824-1888)
Powhatan Moncure[444] (1830-1908)

Strother Harding
John H. Skinker
John Seddon
John M. O'Bannon
William Carter
Arthur F. Clift
John J. Withers
Dr. James Thomas Cropp[443] (1829-1865)
William Hooe Hansbrough[445] (c.1803-1875)

---

stole what they wanted then burned the house to the ground. In 1872 Gustavus was appointed one of the commissioners of the Free Bridge between Fredericksburg and Stafford County.

[437] The Monteith family of Stafford descended from Sir Thomas Monteith (1694-1747) of Scotland who arrived in Virginia during the 18th century and settled near Belle Plains.

[438] This notation appeared in the court records of Apr. 18, 1859: "The Court being informed of the recent death of James Morton, Esq. for a quarter of a century a justice of this Court and considering it proper to take some suitable notice of the sad event; do resolve that in the death of James Morton, this County has lost an upright Magistrate—Society one of its honored members and his family, a husband father and Master who discharged with exemplary fidelity all the duties imposed by these delicate and responsible relations."

[439] William tendered his resignation from the court on Feb. 15, 1859.

[440] The son of Fielding Clift (c.1774-1856) and Elizabeth "Sallie" Elkins.

[441] Unanimously elected presiding justice.

[442] William was the son of John Moncure (IV) (1793-1876) and his first wife, Esther Vowles (1795-1833). In 1853 he married Georgianna Cary Bankhead (1830-1890) of Spring Grove, Caroline County, the daughter of Dr. William Bankhead (1795-1873) of Port Royal and his wife Dorothea Minor (1805-1868). William was a vestryman of Overwharton Parish and resided at Somerset in the Wide Water area (see illustration). This farm is now a part of the Quantico Marine Corps reservation.

[443] James was the son of John Cropp and Rosie Thomas. In 1857 James married Elizabeth J. Wharton, the daughter of John Wharton. During the War Between the States, he served as a surgeon in the 37th Virginia Regiment. James was buried in the family plot on the former Sherman farm on Skyline Drive (State Route 615).

[444] Powhatan lived at Ravenswood, part of which has been used for the airport interchange on U. S. Route 1 and at the adjoining Oakenwold. He married Dorothea Ashby (1838-1911), the daughter of Col. Turner Ashby (1789-1834) and the sister of Gen. Turner Ashby (1828-1862) of Fauquier County.

During the painful years following the War Between the States, there was a good deal of excitement about a deposit of coal found on Powhatan's property, but it proved to be a small deposit of poor quality.

In 1872 Powhatan was appointed one of the commissioners of the Free Bridge between Fredericksburg and Stafford County.

SOMERSET: Home of William E. Moncure, justice of the peace, 1864.

1861
John H. Skinker
Fielding B. Stone
James Monteith
Edward Waller
Robert G. Hickerson
Edmund F. Rose
William E. Moncure

Dr. James T. Cropp
John R. Evans[446] (c.1799-1873)
Arthur F. Clift
Strother Harding
Powhatan Moncure
William H. Hansbrough

1862
George W. Conway[447] (1818-1879)
Dr. James T. Cropp
Fielding B. Stone
Strother Harding
Edward Waller
Powhatan Moncure

John H. Skinker
Gustavus B. Wallace
Arthur F. Clift
Edmund F. Rose
Robert G. Hickerson

1864
Gustavus B. Wallace
Arthur F. Clift
James Monteith
George W. Conway
Strother Harding

Fielding B. Stone
Edmund F. Rose
William H. Hansbrough
William E. Moncure
Edward Waller

---

[445] William was the son of Peter Hansbrough (1796-1843) and Frances Anne Hooe, the daughter of William Hooe of King George. William also represented Stafford in the Virginia House of Delegates from 1865-1869. After the close of the War Between the States, William assisted with the distribution of state funds to ease the conditions of citizens left destitute by the conflict.
[446] John was born in Maryland.
[447] Probably George Washington Conway, the son of John Moncure Conway (1779-1864). The 1871 land tax records list George as owning 286 ½ acres on Chappawamsic Run.

1865
Powhatan Moncure
William E. Carter[449] (c.1825-after 1873)
Fielding B. Stone
James McDonald Briggs, Jr.[451] (1822-1900)
Benjamin S. West[452] (c.1829-1905)
Monroe Kelly[453] (c.1818-1892)
John Lowry (c.1808-after 1870)

Duff McDuff Green[448] (c.1832-1885)
Nathaniel Waller Ford[450] (1820-1880)
Edmund F. Rose
Strother Harding
James Monteith
Gustavus B. Wallace
William H. Hansbrough

---

[448] The son of Duff Green (1792-1854) and Eliza Ann Payne (1806-1876).

[449] William was the son of Loyal and Elizabeth Carter. A carpenter by trade, in 1860 he married Margaret E. Shelton (born c.1842), the daughter of Richard Mason Shelton (c.1819-1892) and his wife Eliza.

[450] Nathaniel lived on the old George Brent plantation, Woodstock. He was the son of Capt. William Ford (1788-1834) and Elizabeth Allen Hore (1791-1822), the daughter of Elias Hore (1748-1852) and Theodosia Waller (1753-1829). Nathaniel married Margaret Ursula Waller (1821-1901) of Bloomington. She was the daughter of James Waller (17_-1824) and Ann Adie (1792-1870). The 1871 land tax records list Nathaniel as owner of the 500-acre Woodstock plantation ($2,000 in buildings), and the 365-acre Providence tract ($500 in buildings) 7 miles northeast of the courthouse.

His obituary read:
> Truly, 'in the midst of life we are in death.' Ere, this can be published, the sad news of the death of N. W. Ford, Esq. of Stafford County, has spread throughout the community, in the 61st year of his age. God has summoned him before the Throne of Mercy. Fully prepared for the call of the messenger of death, it was well said by Dr. Murdaugh, upon the occasion of Litany, 'from the battle and murder, and from sudden death, Good Lord deliver us' was not applicable to him. From a sickness of the past summer he had apparently fully recovered. On Sunday last he attended a church in this neighborhood, on Monday rode to Richmond; on Tuesday to Circuit Court at Stafford Courthouse; on Wednesday and Thursday was busy at home about his farming operations. Eating his supper Thursday night, he read until about 9 o'clock, and then retired, uttering no complaint. About 1 a.m. he got up, and while standing near his bed, bell upon it, face downwards, speechless; six hours afterwards he had ceased to breathe, an apoplectic attack the doctor said. Nat Ford was a deservedly prominent man in his county; his natural abilities were of a high order; and he possessed a strong vigorous intellect with an unerring instinct, he separated right from wrong. Clinging with great tenacity to the former, he at all times and places, unsparingly denounced the tattler. The universal sorrow at his death, and the large number of all classes and color that followed the remains to their final resting place, attest the respect and confidence and affection of his fellow citizens. In all the public and private relations of a long life, whether as President of the Agricultural Society of his neighborhood, or as Justice of the peace, or as a successful and enlightened farmer, Mr. Ford always maintained an unstained record for honesty of purpose and integrity of character. Stafford will miss Nat. Ford because in his death, she has lost one of her most useful citizens, one of her most patriotic sons" (*Virginia Star*, Apr. 14, 1880).

In 1872 Nathaniel was appointed one of the commissioners of the Free Bridge between Fredericksburg and Stafford County.

[451] The son of James McDonald Briggs, Sr. (1787-1845) of Stony Hill and Charlotte Ashmore Keith (1782-1866), the daughter of Isham Keith and Charlotte Ashmore of Fauquier. In 1845 he married Louisa Ann Smith of Fauquier County but inherited and lived at his father's Stony Hill plantation in Stafford. During the War Between the States, James was a captain in the Virginia militia. In 1872 he was appointed one of the commissioners of the Free Bridge between Fredericksburg and Stafford County. James was buried at Briggs Station, Clarke County, Virginia.

[452] During the War Between the States, Benjamin served in the 9th Virginia Cavalry, Company A, Stafford Rangers.

[453] In 1866 Monroe served as president of the Board of Trustees of the Corporation of Falmouth. He was also a school teacher.

John Conyers Shelton[454] (c.1803-1883)
Lyman Kellogg[456] (1813-1897)

Capt. Robert Brooke Alexander[455] (c.1811-1878)

1866
Nathaniel W. Ford
Strother Harding
Lyman Kellogg
Duff Green
Fielding B. Stone
Monroe Kelly
Edmund F. Rose
James M. Briggs

Benjamin S. West
Powhatan Moncure
James Monteith
William E. Carter
John Lowry
Gustavus B. Wallace
William H. Hansbrough
John C. Shelton

1867
Duff Green
Fielding B. Stone
Benjamin S. West
James M. Briggs
Lyman Kellogg
William H. Hansbrough
Horace Broadman Hewitt[457] (1816-1882)

Lewis McKenzie
Monroe Kelly
Strother Harding
William E. Carter
Nathaniel W. Ford
James Monteith
Powhatan Moncure[458]

1868
Lewis McKenzie
William E. Carter
James M. Briggs
Lyman Kellogg
William H. Hansbrough
Benjamin S. West
John Lowry
Fielding B. Stone

Strother Harding
Edmund F. Rose
Nathaniel W. Ford
John C. Shelton
Gustavus B. Wallace
Duff Green
Robert B. Alexander
James Monteith

---

[454] The unmarried son of John Shelton, Jr. (1774-1818) and Lethe Conyers (1780-c.1867) and the grandson of John Shelton, Sr. (1740-1805) and Susanna Hord (1742-1799).

[455] The son of Philip Thornton Alexander (1783-1817) and Lucy Brooke (born c.1783). Robert married Julia Anton Kale (1833-1887). He was a painter and journalist and in 1850 was living with the family of another painter, Alexander A. Muse. Prior to the War Between the States, Robert became owner and editor of the *Democratic Reporter*. Robert and Julia later resided on Caroline Street in Fredericksburg. He was a member of Lodge 63 of the Masons and was buried in the Masonic Cemetery in that town.

[456] Lyman was the son of Ezekiel Kellogg (died 1828) and Luna Clark (born 1778). The 1850 Stafford census records his place of birth as Canada though his parents also lived in Heartland, Connecticut and Southwick, Massachusetts. Lyman settled in Stafford c.1838 and in 1850 married Frances A. Waller (1815-1887), the daughter of Sylvanus Waller of Fauquier.

In Stafford Lyman owned and operated Kellogg's Mill on Potomac Run. By 1871 his mill, built on a 15-acre lot, was assessed at only $400. The remains of the foundation of his mill survive on the south side of the bridge over Abel Reservoir. In 1872 Lyman was appointed one of the commissioners of the Free Bridge between Fredericksburg and Stafford County.

[457] According to the 1850 Stafford census, Horace was born in Connecticut. He was the son of Jonas Hewitt and was a resident of Falmouth. The 1871 land tax records list him as owner of 152 acres on Poplar Road (State Route 616). In 1841 he married Jane Smith (1823-1871). Following the War Between the States, Horace submitted a claim to the Southern Claims Commission asking to be reimbursed for $2,710.19 worth of quartermaster stores taken from him by the Union army. He was granted $1,440.

[458] According to the court minutes of Jan. 19, 1867, the justices ordered an election to choose a magistrate to replace Powhatan Moncure, the seat "made vacant by removal." Edward M. Henry was elected as a replacement.

1869

Lyman Kellogg
William E. Carter
James A. Anderson (c.1832-c.1869)
Horace B. Hewitt[460]
Isaac Silver[462] (c.1808-1901)
James L. Lowry (1817-1889)

Fielding B. Stone
John R. Evans
Joseph Golatt[459] (c.1816-1879)
George Garnett Glascock[461] (1807-1879)
Charles W. Tankersley[463] (born c.1840)

1870

Aquia	William E. Carter (3 years)
	Nathaniel W. Ford (3 years)
	Thomas T. Gaskins[464] (born c.1837) (2 years)
	Arthur F. Clift (2 years)
	James L. Lowry (1 year)
	John R. Evans (1 year)
Falmouth	James A. Daffan[465] (c.1820-1890)
	Duff Green
	Thomas W. Franklin[466] (c.1844-1928)
Hartwood	Henry Clay O'Bannon[467] (1843-1916) (3 years)
	Henry A. Embrey[468] (c.1805-after 1871) (2 years)
	Paul Hull[469] (1808-1892) (1 year)

---

[459] The 1871 land tax records list Joseph as owner of 365 ½ acres on Aquia Run, 8 miles west of the courthouse. He died of typhoid fever.

[460] Horace was born in Connecticut, the son of Jonas Hewitt.

[461] The 1871 land tax records list George as owner of 385 ½ acres on Chappawamsic Creek ($2,000 in buildings). He married Agatha Ann (born 1814), the daughter of Edwin Conway Moncure (178_-1816) and Eleanor Edrington.

[462] Isaac was born in New Jersey and came to this part of Virginia just prior to the War Between the States. After the war, Isaac submitted a claim for $1,190 worth of quartermaster stores taken from his property by the Union army. He was granted $1,065.
Isaac's obituary read:
> Mr. Isaac Silver, the oldest citizen of Stafford county, died suddenly Wednesday, aged 93 years. The deceased was a very active man up to a few days before his death, and was fond of driving spirited horses. He was a prosperous farmer and during the war of 1861 and '65 was conspicuous for his fidelity to the cause of the Union. He is survived by several children and a large number of grandchildren. Funeral services were held from Zion Tabernacle church, which the deceased built years ago, Thursday at 2 p.m.. Rev. Mr. Landstreet, of the Northern Methodist Church, officiating, the interment was made in the churchyard (*Free Lance*, Dec. 28, 1901).

[463] Charles was the son of Henry Tankersley and Catherine Mackey. He was born in Caroline County and in 1866 married Bettie Humphries (born c.1849), the daughter of Julia J. Humphries.

[464] Thomas was the son of Henry Lee Gaskins (1813-1846) and Mary E. Towson (c.1818-c.1874), the daughter of Thomas Towson (1780-1861). The 1871 land tax records list Thomas as owner of 269 acres on Austin Run and 170 acres on Aquia Road (modern Garrisonville Road—State Route 610). According to the 1870 Stafford census, Thomas owned a sawmill.

[465] James was the son of William Daffan (c.1777-1855) and his first wife, Nancy (born c.1795). The Daffan family resided on the north end of the old Fitzhugh tract, Bellair.

[466] Thomas was the son of Thomas E. and S. M. Franklin and was born in Lancaster County, Pennsylvania. He was a resident of Virginia for over 50 years, first taking up residence in Stafford, then moving to Fredericksburg c.1921. In 1877 he married Gissie Ashton (born c.1848), the daughter of Dr. Horace D. (1821-1894) and M. T. Ashton of King George. He was a member of St. George's Episcopal Church (*Free Lance*, May 17, 1928).

[467] The son of John Maurice O'Bannon (1800-1870) and Harriet Ann Corbin (1813-1891) of Carlton on the hill above Falmouth. Henry married Pattie Ann Payne.

[468] Henry married Mary E. English (c.1836-1865).

Horace B. Hewitt (Radical)

1871
Aquia
William E. Carter
Nathaniel W. Ford
Thomas T. Gaskins
Arthur F. Clift
Hartwood
Henry C. O'Bannon
Henry A. Embrey
Rock Hill
Charles James French[470] (1835-1920)
Lyman Kellogg
Benjamin S. West

1873
Aquia
William E. Carter
John R. Evans
Hartwood
James M. Briggs
Henry C. O'Bannon
Rock Hill
Lyman Kellogg
Charles J. French
George Milton Weedon[471] (1840-1902)

1877
Aquia
Edward Waller
Nathaniel W. Ford
James L. Lowry
Falmouth
John M. Luck[472] (1827-1888)
Randolph Coalter Fitzhugh[473] (1832-1902)

---

[469] Paul was born in Northumberland County, but lived much of his life in Stafford. The 1871 land tax records list Paul has having a life estate in the 122 ¾-acre Hull Cottage tract on Potomac Run ($800 in building values). Paul died on Jan. 8, 1892 and his wife, Sarah "Sally" Elizabeth Moncure (1809-1892) died on Jan. 18.

[470] The son of James French (1803-1865) and Sarah A. Curtis (1812-1872) of Poplar Grove. Charles died unmarried.

[471] The second and youngest son of George and Julia (Trone) Weedon. George Milton was born at Cole Hill. He married first in 1863 Virginia Clark, the daughter of the Rev. John Clark of Prince William who preached at Chappawamsic Baptist Church. He married secondly in 1885 Amy A. Tolson (born 1849), the daughter of James E. Tolson (1795-1865).

On June 23, 1861, just two months after the outbreak of the War Between the States, George and his brother, Marshall B. Weedon, went to Fairfax Courthouse where they enlisted for one year in the Prince William Cavalry under the command of Capt. William E. Thornton. From November to December 1861 George served as a courier at Gen. Louis T. Wigfall's headquarters. On Mar. 7, 1862 he re-enlisted with Capt. Thornton for two more years, for which he was paid the customary $50. He served as a scout for Gen. Williams C. Wickham from January through April 1864. On Sept. 29, 1864 at the Battle of Waynesboro, his horse was shot out from under him. After the war, George settled in Stafford where he became the first superintendent of schools. In 1914 he was posthumously awarded the Southern Cross of Honor by the United Daughters of the Confederacy.

Beginning about 1870 George was engaged in the mercantile business at Belfair Mills which he continued until 1885 when Gen. Fitzhugh Lee was elected governor of Virginia. Lee appointed Weedon superintendent of schools for Stafford as a reward for his distinguished services during the war. He was re-appointed for four consecutive terms.

[472] In 1853 John married Mary A. Rowe (1824-1902), the daughter of the Rev. George Rowe and Lucy Leitch.

[473] The son of Maj. William H. Fitzhugh (1788-1859) and Eliza Churchill Darby of Chappawamsic Farm, the old George Mason home on Chappawamsic Creek. Randolph attended VMI and was a civil engineer in

	George G. Lightner[474] (1839-1898)
Hartwood	John Peden[475] (1820-1892)
	John E. Coakley (c.1810-1881)
	Henry C. O'Bannon
Rock Hill	Benjamin S. West
	Thomas Benton Reamy[476] (1836-1910)
	Joseph C. Wine[477] (c.1832-1909)
1879	
Aquia	Nathaniel W. Ford
	Alexander Hamilton Mountjoy[478] (c.1826-c.1902)
	James L. Lowry
Falmouth	John M. Luck
	Randolph C. Fitzhugh
	Thomas W. Franklin
Hartwood	John Peden
	Daniel Webster S. Knight[479] (c.1824-1909)
	John E. Coakley
Rock Hill	George M. Weedon
	Joseph C. Wine
	Robert G. Hickerson
1881	
Aquia	Alexander H. Mountjoy
	William M. Norman[480] (c.1838-1918)
	James L. Lowry
Falmouth	Randolph C. Fitzhugh

Fredericksburg. He was also a magistrate, teacher, and farmer in Stafford. Randolph served as a vestryman of St. George's Parish, Fredericksburg and was the brother of St. George R. Fitzhugh (1842-1925). He died at Mary Washington Hospital.

[474] The son of George W. Lightner (c.1805-1886) and Mary L. Coakley (born c.1817) and the brother of Harry G. Lightner. According to the 1850 Stafford census, George W. Lightner was a painter and had been born in Maryland. In 1859 young George married Eliza T. Cox (born c.1835), the daughter of Delia B. Cox (born c.1800). George also served as postmaster of Falmouth from 1881-1885 and in 1889. He was a member of the original board of bridge commissioners and manager and treasurer of the bridge until about one year before his death. He was succeeded in this position by John Isemonger French (1847-1906) (*Free Lance*, Dec. 15, 1898).

[475] John was the son of David and Ann Peden of Baltimore County, Maryland. He was a millwright by profession and lived on Warrenton Road (U. S. Route 17), just north of Falmouth. He married Louisa E. Curtis (1829-1915), the daughter of Fielding Curtis (1793-1844) and Anne C. Leach. Following the War Between the States, John submitted a claim to the Southern Claims Commission asking to be reimbursed for $1,970.87 worth of fuel taken from him by the Union army. He was granted $987.50. John was one of the original commissioners appointed to oversee the building of a bridge across the Rappahannock River (*Free Lance*, Aug. 2, 1892). He was buried in the Confederate Cemetery in Fredericksburg.

[476] In 1871 Thomas owned 420 acres of the old Parke plantation ($420 in building values). He married Harriet "Hallie" Margaret Curtis (1840-1917), the daughter of Francis Curtis (1806-1891).

[477] In 1870 Joseph owned 82 acres in the Woodcutting near Ramoth Baptist Church.

[478] Alexander was the son of Thornton Mountjoy (1794:7-1881) and Mary Payne (1794-1856). During the War Between the States, he served in the 9th Virginia Cavalry as a private. He was wounded and discharged on July 31, 1864. Around 1850 he married Mary Frances Herndon (1826-1910).

[479] Daniel was the son of Bailey Knight (c.1787-1862) and Elizabeth Kendall (c.1794-c.1828). In 1878 he was appointed to fill the unexpired term of Henry C. O'Bannon who removed from the county.

[480] During the War Between the States, William served in the 9th Virginia Cavalry. In April 1862 he was held in Falmouth as a prisoner of war. The 1870 Stafford census records that William worked at a sawmill. He was an invalid for the last 40 years of his life.

	Thomas W. Franklin
	___ Monteith
Hartwood	John E. Coakley
	Daniel W. S. Knight
	Fielding B. Stone
Rock Hill	George M. Weedon
	___ Barber
	Benjamin C. Wamsley

1885

Aquia	Richard Hughlett Bryan[481] (1820-1908)
	Alexander H. Mountjoy
	William M. Norman
Falmouth	Lee Wallace[482] (c.1856-1935)
	Randolph C. Fitzhugh
	Thomas W. Franklin
Hartwood	Robert A. Johnson
	William Frank Dodd[483] (c.1840-1909)
	John Peden
Rock Hill	George M. Weedon
	Thomas B. Reamy
	Joseph C. Wine[484] (c.1832-1909)

1887

Aquia	Charles F. Norman (c.1834-c.1900)
	John W. Garrison (born c.1852)
	Benjamin G. Hedgman[485] (born c.1836)
Falmouth	Thomas W. Franklin
	Randolph C. Fitzhugh
	Lawrence Martin
Hartwood	William F. Dodd
	Fielding B. Stone
	Thomas F. Graves
Rock Hill	Strother Harding (born c.1853)
	Robert F. Lunsford (c.1832-1903)

---

[481] Richard was born in Chesapeake City, Cecil County, Maryland. He was the son of Joseph and Susan Bryan. Richard graduated from Dickinson College, Carlisle Pennsylvania. After graduation, he taught school in Green County, Alabama for two years, and then returned to Chesapeake City where he was engaged in the grain commission business under the firm name of Joseph Bryan and Son. In November 1858 he moved to Stafford, settling on Ingleside, a farm about ½ mile above Falmouth. He married Eliza Cropper (died 1890) of Accomack County.

In May 1869 Richard was appointed clerk of the court of Stafford, serving about one year. He was Commissioner of Accounts for the Stafford court for 35 years and a justice of the peace for about that same period. His children were Joseph K. Bryan (died 1948), former Deputy Treasurer; Charles Avery Bryan (1849-1918), clerk of the Circuit Court of Stafford; Richard H. Bryan, Jr. of Washington; Walter W. Bryan of Wilmington, Delaware, and Annie L. Bullock of Philadelphia (*Free Lance*, Feb. 8, 1908).

[482] Lee was the son of Gustavus Brown Wallace and his second wife Margaret Elizabeth McFarland (died 1864). For some 40 years he taught school in Stafford and was a resident of White Oak. He never married, but lived with Lucien Newton whom he raised from infancy. He was buried at Bethel Church in White Oak.

[483] William was the son of Humphrey (c.1815-1895) and B. A. Dodd. He was a schoolteacher and in 1866 married Columbia N. Gray (born c.1844), the daughter of William and E. A. Gray.

[484] Joseph lived near Crest (Mountain View). He was a blacksmith most of his live and was buried in the family cemetery.

[485] Benjamin was the son of Peter D. G. Hedgman (c.1800-after 1885).

John W. Cooper

1889
Aquia
    Richard H. Bryan
    Charles F. Norman (c.1834-c.1900)
    Richard Ashby Moncure[486] (1864-1923)
Falmouth
    Thomas W. Franklin
    Lee Wallace
    Patrick Martin (c.1822-1895)
Hartwood
    William F. Graves[487] (c.1835-1895)
    John E. Beale[488] (1852-1936)
    Thomas Graves (born c.1832)
Rock Hill
    William Brooke Robey[489] (1839-1907)
    Robert F. Lunsford[490] (c.1832-1903)
    Charles H. Edmondson

1891
Aquia
    James Morton, Jr.[491] (1851-1902)
    Richard A. Moncure
    Alexander H. Mountjoy
Falmouth
    Randolph C. Fitzhugh
    Thomas W. Franklin (c.1845-1928)
    Dr. Gouveneur Thomas Greenlaw[492] (born c.1860)

---

[486] Richard was the son of George Vowles Moncure (1826-1901) and Mary Ashby (1830-1897).

[487] William was a merchant and postmaster of Hartwood. A Confederate soldier, he served in Company C of the 30th Virginia Regiment. He died of pneumonia.

[488] The son of William L. and Hannah J. Beale. He was born in Pennsylvania and in 1874 married N. A. Lunsford (born c.1851), the daughter of James Leon and Margaret Lunsford. John was a resident of Glendie and was buried at Antioch Methodist Church (*Free Lance-Star*, Aug. 10, 1936).

[489] William was born at Hopewell, Spotsylvania County, the son of Henry Richard Robey and his first wife, Clarissa T. Brooke (died 1843). During the War Between the States, he served with the 9th Virginia Cavalry. In 1866 William married Mary H. Peake (died 1874), the daughter of James B. and Louisa Peake.

[490] The son of William (born c.1785) and Willie Lunsford (born c.1795). In 1861 he married Aphia F. Swetnam (born c.1844), the daughter of John A. (1792-1854) and Sarah Swetnam (born c.1811).

[491] James was the son of James Morton, Sr. (died 1859). He made his living as a merchant and in 1878 married Mattie H. Jones, the daughter of S. H. and M. C. Jones of Prince William County.

    His business, known as Morton & Payne, consisted of a store at Brooke Station. On the old tavern site he erected "a neat two story frame building which he intends opening as a hotel." He also planned on "putting up a stable just opposite, thereby supplying two wants which have been long felt, as well as adding greatly to the appearance of the place" (*Virginia Star*, Oct. 20, 1877).

[492] The son of William Price Underwood Greenlaw (1834-1869) and Sarah Virginia Braxton Purkins (1838-1903). Gouveneur lived at Hollywood, a large 18th century brick home in the southwestern corner of the county. Hollywood burned in June 1890 and Gouveneur moved his family to Washington, DC where his father owned a great deal of real estate. His Fredericksburg drugstore was also moved north and was called Greenlaw Medicine Company. A delightful article about the business appeared in the June 10, 1892 issue of the *Fredericksburg Ledger*:

    Greenlaw's Remedies. The headquarters of Dr. G. T. Greenlaw's Celebrated Liniment, have been transferred to No. 417, 4 ½ street, S. W. Washington city.

    We are pleased to learn that the remedies prepared by Dr. Greenlaw are becoming as popular in Washington as they are in this section where they have stood the test of several years' trial.

    Some remarkable cures have been made by Greenlaw's remedies and they have been awarded certificates of merit and praise by a number of Fredericksburgers and by may people in the surrounding counties who have used them.

Rock Hill	Robert F. Lunsford (c.1832-1903)
	William Brooke Robey
	Turner William Herndon[493] (1862-1939)
1893	
Aquia	James B. Burton[494] (born c.1857)
	Richard A. Moncure
	Richard H. Bryan
Falmouth	Thomas W. Franklin
	Randolph C. Fitzhugh
	Lee Wallace
Hartwood	John Moncure Hull[495] (1835-1908)
	William Frank Dodd[496]
	Fielding B. Stone
Rock Hill	Robert F. Lunsford
	John A. Ryan[497] (c.1839-1918)
	Turner W. Herndon
1895	
Aquia	James B. Burton
	John W. Garrison[498]
	Richard H. Bryan
Falmouth	Randolph C. Fitzhugh
	Thomas W. Franklin
	Lee Wallace

While the Doctor's remedies are growing in popularity, we hope for the sake of the comfort and convenience of the proprietor, he will not grow to any larger dimensions.

Another wonderful article about Greenlaw appeared in the June 25, 1895 issue of the *Daily Star*:
The Comorn correspondent of the *Dispatch* says:
Dr. G. T. Greenlaw, of Washington, D. C., visited his country home in Stafford last week, and also paid a brief visit to friends here. He is the famous "big man," but having reduced on account of warm weather, he only weighs 390 pounds now—some ten or twelve pounds less than his "winter weight." Dr. Greenlaw wears a beautiful gold medal, inscribed: 'Dr. G. T. Greenlaw, 100 yards dash, River view, September 4, 1893.'
Dr. Greenlaw is a native of Stafford county, Virginia, and is quite a young man, notwithstanding his 400 pounds avoirdupois. His grandparents, who died in Stafford some years ago, weighted 700 pounds—the grandfather 400, and the grandmother 300 pounds. His mother, at present in Washington, weighs a fraction under 300 pounds, and is active and handsome.

[493] The son of William Herndon (1824-1904) and Isabella (Atchison) Berry (1832-1897). In 1887 Turner married Annie Frances Weedon (born 1867), the daughter of George Milton Weedon (1840-1902) and Virginia Clark. Annie and Turner were residing in Fredericksburg in 1917.

[494] James was the son of Marshall Burton (born c.1817). In 1879 he married M. W. West (born c.1858), the daughter of James and A. West.

[495] John was the son of Paul Hull and Sarah "Sally" Elizabeth Moncure (1809-1892). He married Anna Jane Moncure (born 1835), the daughter of the Hon. Richard C. L. Moncure (1805-1882) and Mary Butler Washington Conway (1807-1895) of Glencairne.

[496] William lived near Tackett's Mill. He dropped dead while walking in the Congress Hall Hotel in Washington (*Free Lance*, Jan. 7, 1909).

[497] John was a resident of Toluca, Stafford County but was born in Spotsylvania County. He served four years in Confederate service with Jackson's Stonewall Brigade and was present at the surrender at Appomattox. (*Free Lance*, Nov. 28, 1918).

[498] John was the son of Elzey and Sarah Garrison. In 1875 he married Mary Garrison (born c.1858), the daughter of W. L. and Riddy Garrison.

Hartwood	Charles A. Truslow[499] (1860-1947)
	Fielding B. Stone
	William F. Dodd
Rock Hill	William B. Robey
	John A. Ryan
	Robert F. Lunsford

1897
Falmouth	John "Jack" Leland Gouldin[500] (1859-1923)
	Lee Wallace
	Thomas W. Franklin

1899
Aquia	Richard H. Bryan
	John W. Garrison
	John William Payne[501] (c.1858-1927)
Falmouth	Lee Wallace
	Randolph C. Fitzhugh
	Thomas W. Franklin
Hartwood	Daniel W. S. Knight
	William F. Dodd
	Fielding B. Stone
Rock Hill	John W. Wamsley[502] (born c.1845)
	George F. Moore[503] (born c.1847)
	William B. Robey

1901
Aquia	James Norton
	John A. Evans (1832-1921)
	Richard H. Bryan
Falmouth	H. Samuel Stephens (c.1858-1902)
	Randolph C. Fitzhugh
	Lee Wallace
Hartwood	William F. Dodd
	Daniel W. S. Knight
Rock Hill	William B. Robey
	George F. Moore
	Frederick Mason Mountjoy[504] (1855-1924)

---

[499] Charles was the son of Charles and Frances Truslow and was a farmer and merchant. He was the door keeper for every session of the General Assembly held between 1910 and 1946. In 1887 Charles married Callie E. Gallahan (born c.1860). He was a member of Hull's Memorial Church and the local Masonic Lodge (*Free Lance-Star*, Sept. 6, 1947).

[500] John was the son of J. F. and Victoria Gouldin. He was born in Caroline County and married in 1894 Julia Lane Gray (1871-1944), the daughter of Robert Atchison Gray (1830-1915) and Adalaide Gettys Hayman (1830-1921). John lived at Albion on Rt. 3 east of Fredericksburg but was buried at Eastwood.

[501] For nearly 20 years John was also the deputy treasurer under William D. Reamy. He lived near Brooke, was a member of Andrew Chapel, and married Susie Winkler (1860-1935).

[502] John was the son of Benjamin C. (c.1814-1886) and Eliza F. Wamsley (born c.1827). In 1882 he married Mary Virginia (Massie) Hickerson (born 1853).

[503] George was the son of Henry (born c.1822) and Tabias Moore. In 1870 he married Delila A. Limerick (born c.1847), the daughter of Landon Limerick (c.1813-after 1880).

[504] The son of Alexander H. Mountjoy (1826-c.1902) and Mary Frances Herndon (1826-1910). In 1894 he married Lucy Ellen Bridwell (c.1857-1935).

1903
Aquia   John W. Payne
                           Richard H. Bryan
                           William M. Norman
Falmouth   ___ Pollard
                           Lee Wallace
                           Robert Hayman Gray, Jr.[505] (1873-1958)
Hartwood   William F. Dodd
                           Daniel W. S. Knight
                           Joseph Blackwell Smith[506] (born c.1881)
Rock Hill   John A. Ryan
                           ___ Armstrong
                           William B. Robey

1907
Aquia   John W. Payne
                           Frederick Mason Mountjoy
                           ___ Monroe
Falmouth   Robert H. Gray
                           Lee Wallace
Hartwood   William F. Dodd
                           Daniel W. S. Knight
Rock Hill   John A. Ryan
                           George F. Moore
                           Henry T. Garrison[507] (born c.1842)

1911
Aquia   F. Mason Mountjoy
                           ___ Monroe
                           J. A. Payne
Falmouth   Lee Wallace
                           ___ Young
                           Robert H. Gray
Hartwood   Joseph B. Smith
                           ___ Ballard
                           Thomas Jefferson Spicer[508] (born 1872)
Rock Hill   Andrew Briggs[509] (c.1861-1927)

---

[505] Robert was the son of Robert A. Gray (1830-1915) and his wife Adelaide (1830-1921). For some 25 years he presided in Stafford's Juvenile and Domestic Relations Court and was a member of the county school board. He never married and resided at Eastwood, the old Gray home that was once part of Traveler's Rest. Eastwood is on the west side of Caisson Road (State Route 603). Robert was crushed to death when he attempted to take down a huge apple tree on his farm (*Free Lance-Star*, Feb. 15, 1958).

[506] Joseph was the son of William D. (born c.1848) and Martha (Grinnan) Smith (born c.1848). In 1900 he married Lizzie Dye (born c.1882), the daughter of Aldridge and Mary Dye.

[507] Henry was the son of Robert Garrison (c.1808-c.1852), a merchant in the upper end of the county. During the War Between the States, he served with the 9th Virginia Cavalry.

[508] Thomas was born in Culpeper County, the son of Mallory Howard Spicer (1840-1906) and Sarah Jane Smith (1846-1886). In 1917 Thomas married Mabel Clara (Curtis) Graves (died 1918), the daughter of Frederick Euston Curtis (1860-1921) and Annie Anderson (1858-1897).

[509] Andrew resided in Roseville and was connected with the W. H. Peden Lumber Company. In 1883 Andrew married Martha "Mattie" Ella Herndon (born c.1862), the daughter of Ludwell (1823-1908) and Rosanna Rebecca Herndon (c.1828-1903). He died of stomach cancer.

For many years there was confusion over the spelling of Andrew's surname. The land tax records reflect this, alternating for many years between "Briggs" and "Bridges." Elias A. W. Hore noted in his account book, "Andrew Briggs (alias Bridges)" (Hore, Account book).

Henry T. Garrison
John A. Ryan

1915
Aquia John W. Payne
Andrew Jackson Woodard (1878-1959)
Falmouth Robert H. Gray
William T. Berry[510] (c.1871-1942)
Lee Wallace
Hartwood William L. Embrey[511] (born c.1870)
Joseph B. Smith
Thomas J. Spicer
Rock Hill Andrew Briggs
Robert L. Bridwell (1887-1972)
Wade Hampton Moore[512] (1878-1952)

1919
Aquia John W. Payne
F. Mason Mountjoy[513]
Welford Clinton Atchison[514] (1848-1924)
Falmouth Lee Wallace
John Bullock
Robert H. Gray
Hartwood Wellford B. Armstrong[515] (born c.1865)
Thomas J. Spicer
Rock Hill Andrew Briggs
Robert Lee Templeman[516] (1860-1928)

1923
Aquia John W. Payne
Warren Goodloe Sneed[517] (1895-1961)
Richard Arthur Botts[518] (1898-1981)
Falmouth Lee Wallace
Charles Wesley Newton[519] (1897-1944)
Rev. Ernest E. Fisher[520] (c.1880-1969)

---

[510] In 1883 William married Mary A. Payne of Stafford.
[511] William was the son of William and Lina Embrey. In 1895 he married Elizabeth Bettis (born c.1873), the daughter of Thomas and Georgeanna Bettis.
[512] Wade was the son of George F. Moore (born c.1847) and owned a general store on the southeastern corner of Shelton Shop Road (State Route 648) and Mountain View Road (State Route 627). This intersection is still referred to by locals as "Moore's Corner." After he sold his store, he moved across the road and sold fertilizer and other supplies from a small metal building. He was buried at Chestnut Grove Cemetery in Herndon, Virginia.
[513] In 1894 Frederick married L. E. Bridwell (born c.1857), the daughter of Charles W. (born c.1834) and Pauline Bridwell.
[514] Welford lived near Mount and married Lydia C. Minnick (1852-1925).
[515] In 1888 Wellford married A. C. Blackburn (born c.1866).
[516] Robert was the son of James Benjamin Templeman (c.1822-1892) and Nancy Louise Holmes (1830-1900). He lived near Ruby.
[517] Lived on Bell's Hill Road (State Route 631) in the present-day Cloe house.
[518] Richard was the son of Clinton Alexander Botts (1861-1925) and Cynthia Burton Cooper (c.1866-1957).
[519] Charles was the son of Hugh Newton (1785-1964) and his cousin, Mary (Newton) Newton (1878-1967). In 1920 Charles married Fannie Estelle Rowe in Stafford.
[520] Ernest was an ordained Baptist minister and came to Stafford in 1922. He was highly involved in the court system, serving as a federal commissioner for the U. S. courts, as an associate judge for Stafford, and

Rock Hill	Robert Lee Templeman (1860-1928)
	Andrew Briggs
	Charles W. Bridwell[521] (c.1867-1953)

1927
Aquia	Charles Pierson Gilchrist[522] (1891-1951)
	John Alaster MacGregor[523] (1869-1953)
	Edward W. Theinert
Falmouth	Robert H. Gray
	Lee Wallace
	Ernest E. Fisher
Rock Hill	R. L. Templeman
	Stafford Tilden Heflin[524] (1875-1938)

1931
Aquia	Lewis G. Stewart (1895-1963)
	Powhatan Gallahan (1890-1935)
	Max M. Murray (c.1890-1938)
Falmouth	Robert H. Gray
	Ernest E. Fisher
	Lee Wallace
Hartwood	Harry Selah Brown[525] (c.1884-1967)
	Charles A. Burgess[526] (c.1880-1951)

1935
Aquia	Lewis G. Stewart
Falmouth	Ernest E. Fisher
	Aubrey R. Sullivan[527] (died 1970)
	James Oscar Lee[528] (c.1894-1952)
Hartwood	Charles A. Burgess

---

was also the county's juvenile court judge. According to his obituary, "For a long time he had sat in a courtroom at Cambridge and King streets near the old Falmouth bridge" (*Free Lance-Star*, June 16, 1969).

[521] Charles was the son of Charles W. Bridwell (born c.1824) and Pauline Herndon (born c.1837). In 1895 he married Virginia Cooper (born c.1870), the daughter of George R. (1832-1892) and Betty Cooper. He was a merchant in Stafford.

[522] Charles was a native of South Carolina and a retired Marine Corps Major. He served in World War I and married Ellen Moncure (1897-1971).

[523] John was the son of John Ridout MacGregor (1829-1900) and Mary Eliza MacGregor (born 1831). John married Bessie Knight (1879-1959), the daughter of Capt. Wesley Knight (1846-1937).

[524] Tilden was the son of William Henry Heflin (1840-1911) and Delia Ann Armstrong (1845-1930). He was a carpenter by profession and lived near Cropp. In 1902 he married his first wife, Louisa Dora Beach. He married secondly in 1912 Ocie Lephia "Letha" Dye (1882-1971).

[525] Harry was a native of New York City. In 1909 he opened one of Fredericksburg's first movie theaters. An accomplished musician, he played the piano while the movies were being shown. In 1927 he founded Brown's Motel, the first motel between Richmond and Washington. This group of buildings still stands across U. S. Route 1 from Drew Middle School. Harry retired as a foreman of the FMC Avisco plant in Spotsylvania.

[526] Charles was a veteran of the Spanish American War.

[527] Aubrey ran a store at the intersection of Ferry Road (State Route 606) and White Oak Road (State Route 218). There is still a store there today.

[528] James was the son of James O. Lee (1847-1908) and Lucy A. Lee. He was a lifelong resident of Stafford and a member of Bethel Baptist Church.

1939
Aquia   Alfred Henry MacGregor[529] (c.1898-1961)
Falmouth   Ernest E. Fisher

1943
Aquia   Alfred H. MacGregor
Falmouth   Ernest E. Fisher

1947
Aquia   Alfred H. MacGregor
            William Massie[530]
Falmouth   Ernest E. Fisher
Hartwood   William C. Cleverly

1955
Aquia   Alfred H. MacGregor
Falmouth   Ernest E. Fisher
Hartwood   Woodrow Fleming "Flip" Monroe

1959
Aquia   Alfred H. MacGregor
            Irene Vazquez
Falmouth   Ernest E. Fisher
Hartwood   Woodrow F. Monroe

1963
Aquia   Irene Vazquez
            Helen Dennis
Hartwood   Linwood H. Ellington

1967
Aquia   Thomas A. Butler
            Fred Dillon
            Ann H. Riley
            Irene Vazquez
Falmouth   Harrison Berry
Hartwood   Linwood H. Ellington

---

[529] Alfred died in DeLand, Florida.
[530] Operated Massie's Store near the courthouse.

Sources:

Abercrombie, Janice L. and Slatten, Richard. *Virginia Revolutionary Publick Claims*. Athens, GA: Iberian Publishing Co., 1992.

Alcock, John P. *Five Generations of the Family of Burr Harrison of Virginia, 1650-1800*. Bowie, MD: Heritage Books, 1991.

American Turf Register and Sporting Magazine. Vol. VI, p. 57.

Anderson, Sarah T. *Lewises, Meriwethers, and Their Kin*. Richmond, VA: Dietz Press, Inc., 1938.

---. Personal notes for *Lewises, Meriwethers, and Their Kin*, c.1910, from the personal collection of George L. Gordon, Jr.

Auditor of Public Accounts, 1781-1787. Accession # APA 653. Richmond, VA: Library of Virginia.

Benz, Katherine P. *The Tolson Family of Virginia and Missouri, Including Related Lines of Combs, Harrison, Bullitt, Ratcliffe, and Herndon*. Madison, Wisconsin, 1990.

Boddie, John B. *Virginia Historical Genealogies*. Baltimore, MD: Genealogical Publishing Co., 1990.

Bodine, Ronny O. *Thomas Owsley - a Virginia Gentleman*. Privately published.

Brent, Chester H. *Descendants of Coll. Giles Brent, Capt. George Brent and Robert Brent, Gent*. VT: Rutland Publishing Company, 1946.

"British Mercantile Claims, 1775-1803 [May 1801-May 1802]." *The Virginia Genealogist*, vol. 14, #1, (January-March 1970), pp. 169-177.

Brooke, St. George Tucker. "Autobiography of St. George Tucker Brooke, Written for his Children." MSS2 B7906 a1, Virginia Historical Society, Richmond, Virginia.

Brown, Alexander. *The Cabells and Their Kin*. Harrisonburg, VA: C. J. Carrier Co., 1978.

Buckner, Mary Ann, ed. *Early Virginians*. Fredericksburg, VA, 1974.

Butler, Stuart Lee. *A Guide to Virginia Militia Units in the War of 1812*. Athens, GA: Iberian Publishing Co., 1988.

Chapman, Sigismunda M. *A History of the Chapman and Alexander Families*. Richmond, VA: Dietz Press, Inc., 1946.

Copeland, Pamela C. and MacMaster, Richard K. *The Five George Masons: Patriots and Planters of Virginia and Maryland*. Charlottesville, VA; University Press of Virginia, 1975.

Coppage, A. Maxim and Tackitt, James W. *Stafford Co., Virginia, 1800-1850*. Concord, CA, 1982.

Crowe, Maude. *Descendants from First Families of Virginia and Maryland: a Family History and Genealogy Covering 350 Years, 1620-1970*. Self-published, 1978.

Daily Star, June 25, 1895, obituary of Gouveneur Greenlaw

Des Cognets, Louis, Jr. *English Duplicates of Lost Virginia Records*. Baltimore, MD: Genealogical Publishing Co., 1981.

Dobson, David. *Scots on the Chesapeake, 1607-1830*. Baltimore, MD: Genealogical Publishing Co., 1992.

Dorman, John F. *Claiborne of Virginia: Descendants of Colonel William Claiborne, the First Eight Generations*. Baltimore, MD: Gateway Press, 1995.

---. *Westmoreland County, Virginia Records, 1661-1664*. Washington, DC, 1972.

Dowdey, Clifford. *The Virginia Dynasties*. NY: Bonanza Books, 1969.

Eby, Jerrilynn. *Laying the Hoe: a Century of Iron Manufacturing in Stafford County*, Virginia. Westminster, MD: Willow Bend Books, 2003.

---. *They Called Stafford Home: the Development of Stafford County, Virginia, from 1600 until 1865*. Bowie, MD: Heritage Books, 1997.

"The Eustace Family." *William and Mary College Quarterly Historical Magazine*, vol. 11, (1902-1903), NY: Kraus Reprint Co., 1977, pp. 209-210.

Fisher, Therese A. *Marriage Records of the City of Fredericksburg and of Orange, Spotsylvania, and Stafford Counties, Virginia, 1722-1850*. Bowie, MD: Heritage Books, 1990.

---. *Marriage Records of the City of Fredericksburg and the County of Stafford, Virginia, 1851-1900*. Bowie, MD: Heritage Books, 1994.

Fitzpatrick, John C., ed. *The Writings of George Washington, from the Original Manuscript Sources, 1745-1799*. Washington, DC: U. S. Government Printing Office, 1944.

Flournoy, H. W. *Calendar of Virginia State Papers and Manuscripts from January 1, 1808 to December 31, 1835*. NY: Kraus Reprint Corp., 1968.

Foote, A. Edward. *Chotankers: a Family History*. Florence, AL: Thornwood Book Publishers, 1982.

Ford, Worthington C. "The Will of Augustine Washington, Father of George Washington." *Wills of George Washington and his Immediate Ancestors*. Brooklyn, NY: Historical Printing Club, 1891.

Fredericksburg Circuit Court Records:
    "Brown & Cook vs Hewitt" DC/L/1786/387-60
    "Commonwealth vs Brown" DC/R/1803/565-140
    "Justices vs Hunter &c" DC/L/1797/561-21
    "Ficklen vs Tyler als" CR/SC/H/98-18

The Fredericksburg Confederate Cemetery Register. Central Rappahannock Regional Library, Fredericksburg, VA.

Fredericksburg Ledger, June 7, 1865, Charles C. Wellford beaten by Federal troops
---, June 10, 1892, "Greenlaw's Remedies"
Fredericksburg Star, Apr. 7, 1880, notice for Elm Factory
---, Apr. 14, 1880, obituary of Nathaniel Waller Ford
---, Apr. 18 1880, notice for Elm Factory
---, Mar. 25, 1885, Stafford Judges and Registrars
---, July 1, 1891, "An Ancient Relic"
Free Lance, June 23, 1885, obituary of Duff Green
---, June 23, 1891, obituary of Alexander H. Mason
---, Feb. 20, 1894, obituary of Dr. John H. Daniel
---, Feb. 26, 1898, obituary of Robert G. Hickerson
---, Dec. 15, 1898, obituary of George J. Lightner
---, Dec. 28, 1901, obituary of Isaac Silver
---, Jan. 27, 1903, obituary of Dr. Hawkins Stone
---, Feb. 8, 1908, obituary of Richard H. Bryan
---, Jan. 7, 1909, obituary of William F. Dodd
---, Nov. 28, 1919, obituary of John A. Ryan
---, May 17, 1928, obituary of Thomas W. Franklin
Free Lance-Star, Aug. 10, 1936, obituary of John E. Beale
---, Sept. 6, 1947, obituary of Charles A. Truslow
---, Feb. 15, 1958, obituary of Robert H. Gray
---, June 16, 1969, obituary of Ernest E. Fisher

French, David M. *The Brent Family*. Self-published, Alexandria, VA, 1977.

Gray, Gertrude E. *Virginia Northern Neck Land Grants*. Baltimore, MD: Genealogical Publishing Co., 1993.

Hall, Wilmer L., ed. *Executive Journals of the Council of Colonial Virginia*. Richmond, VA: Virginia State Library, 1967.

Harris, Mary K. and Jorgensen, Mary I. *James Stark of Stafford County Virginia and his Descendants*. Fort Worth, TX: Self-published, 1985.

Harrison, Fairfax. *Landmarks of Old Prince William: a Study of Origins in Northern Virginia*. Baltimore, MD: Gateway Press, Inc., 1987.

"Harrison of Northern Virginia." *Genealogies of Virginia Families from The Virginia Magazine of History and Biography*, vol. 3, pp. 671-686.

Hayden, Horace E. *Virginia Genealogies: a Genealogy of the Glassell Family of Scotland and Virginia*. Baltimore, MD: Genealogical Publishing Co., 1979.

Heitman, Francis B. *Historical Register of Officers of the Continental Army During the War of the Revolution, April, 1775 to December, 1783*. Baltimore, MD: Clearfield Publishing Co., 1997.

Helligso, Martha S. *George Mason Including One Line of Descent and Related Lines of Demourvell, Fowke, French, Lee, Neale, Presly, Rodham, Spence, Sturman, Talbott, Thompson, Thoroughgood, and Youell*. Self-published, 1983.

Herndon, Dudley L., Jr. *The Herndons of the American Revolution, Part IV: #82, William Herndon of Prince William County, Virginia and his Descendants*. Baltimore, MD: Gateway Press, Inc., 1992.

Hodge, Robert A., ed. *Fredericksburg Cemetery Company Interment Register, 1844-1961*. Central Rappahannock Regional Library, Fredericksburg, VA, 1989.

Hopkins, William L. *Some Wills from the Burned Counties of Virginia and Other Wills not Listed in Virginia Wills and Administration, 1632-1800.* Richmond, VA, 1987.

Hore, Elias A. W. "Account Book, 1843." MSS5: 3H 7817:1, Virginia Historical Society, Richmond, Virginia.

Hubard, William S. *Descendants of John Newton (1639-1697).* Self-published, Roanoke, Virginia, 2000.

Hudgins, Dennis R., ed. *Cavaliers and Pioneers: Abstracts of Virginia Land Patents and Grants*, vols. 4 and 5, Richmond, VA: Virginia Genealogical Society, 1994.

Jillson, Willard R. *Kentucky Land Grants.* Louisville: Standard Printing Co., 1925.

Johnson, John J. "Duff Green, Falmouth Industrialist." *Fredericksburg Times*, February 1996, pp. 9-14.

---. "The Falmouth Canal and its Mills: in Industrial History." *The Journal of Fredericksburg History*, vol. 2, Fredericksburg, VA: Historic Fredericksburg Foundation, Inc., 1997, pp. 25-43.

Joyner, Peggy S. *Northern Neck Warrants and Surveys, 1710-1780.* Self-published, 1986.

Kennedy, Mary S. *Seldens of Virginia and Allied Families*, vols. 1 and 2. NY: Frank Allaben Genealogical Co., 1911.

King, George H. S. "Memorial to Henry Fox, Gentleman, of 'Huntington,' King William County, Virginia." *Tyler's Quarterly Historical and Genealogical Magazine*, vol. 21, (1940), pp. 217-290.

---. "Notes of the Flourey Tract." Nov. 16, 1976. Central Rappahannock Regional Library, Fredericksburg, VA.

---. *The Register of Overwharton Parish, Stafford County, Virginia, 1723-1758.* SC: Southern Historical Press, 1986.

Krick, Robert K. *30th Virginia Infantry.* Lynchburg, VA: H. E. Howard, Inc., 1983.

Lee, Edmond Jennings. *Lee of Virginia, 1642-1892: Biographical and Genealogical Sketches of the Descendants of Col. Richard Lee.* Baltimore, MD: Genealogical Publishing Co., 1983.

Lee, Ida J. "King William County Personal Property Tax Lists, 1782-1850." *William and Mary College Quarterly Historical Magazine*, series 2, vol. 7, (1927), pp. 114-122.

Lowry, Noreta Weber. *The Lowry/Lowery Family, 1775-1987.* Arcadia, OH. 1987.

Macrae, Emily. "The Wallace Family." *William and Mary Quarterly Historical Magazine*, vol. 13, (1905), pp. 177-182.

Mauzey, Armand J. "The Mauzey-Mauzy Family." *Genealogies of Virginia Families from The Virginia Magazine of History and Biography*, vol. 4, Baltimore, MD: Genealogical Publishing Co., 1981, pp.308-315.

McIlwaine, H.R. *Journals of the House of Burgesses, 1742-1747, 1748-1749.* Richmond, VA: Virginia State Library, 1909.

---. *Minutes of the Council and General Court of Colonial Virginia.* Richmond, VA: Virginia State Library, 1924.

Moncure, Thomas M. and Pynn, Molly A. *The Story of Aquia Church.* Fredericksburg, VA: Cardinal Press, Inc., 2000.

Musselman, Carl P. and Mildred H. *Musselman-Powell and Bowling Families of Stafford and Spotsylvania Counties, Virginia.* Fredericksburg, VA: Bookcrafters, 1993.

Musselman, Homer. *Veterans and Cemeteries of Stafford County, Virginia.* Fredericksburg, VA, 1996.

National Society of the DAR Centennial Administration. *DAR Patriot Index, Centennial Edition.* Washington, DC: NSDAR, 1994.

Nicklin, John B. "Benjamin Strother (c.1700-1765) and his Wives." *Tyler's Quarterly Historical and Genealogical Magazine*, vol. 19, (1938), pp. 224-227.

Nugent, Nell M. *Cavaliers and Pioneers: Abstracts of Virginia Land Patents and Grants*, vols. 1-3, Richmond, VA: Virginia State Library, 1979.

Owsley, Harry B. *Genealogical Facts of the Owsley Family in England and America, from the Time of the Restoration to the Present.* Chicago, IL, 1890.

Payne, Brooke. *The Paynes of Virginia.* Berryville, VA: Virginia Book Company, 1937.

Pierce, Alycon T. *Selected Final Pension Payment Vouchers, 1818-1864.* Athens, GA: Iberian Publishing Co., 1996.

Pippenger, Wesley E. *John Alexander: a Northern Neck Proprietor—His Family, Friends, and Kin.* Baltimore, MD: Gateway Press, 1990.

Political Arena, Oct. 16, 1827, "Anti-Jackson Meeting"

Porter, Albert O. *County Government in Virginia: a Legislative History, 1607-1904.* NY: Columbia University Press, 1947.
"Public Officers in Virginia, 1680." *The Virginia Magazine of History and Biography*, vol. 1, no. 3, (January 1894), pp. 225-252.
Reamy, Morris R. *A History of the Reamy Family of Westmoreland and Stafford Counties in Virginia, 1655-1975.* Self-published.
Recum, Franz Y. *Withers—America or a Collection of Genealogical Data Concerning the History of the Male Line of James Withers (1680/1-1746) of Stafford County, Virginia.* NY, 1949.
Reese, George H. *Journals of the Council of the State of Virginia*, vol. IV. Richmond, VA: Virginia State Library, 1967.
Reese, George, ed. *The Official Papers of Francis Fauquier, Lieutenant Governor of Virginia, 1758-1768*, Charlottesville, VA: University Press of Virginia, 1983.
Reese, Lee F. *The Ashby Book.* San Diego, CA, 1978.
Reps, John W. *Tidewater Towns: City Planning in Colonial Virginia and Maryland.* Williamsburg, VA: Colonial Williamsburg Foundation, 1972.
Rhodes, Howard J. *The Rhodes Family in Virginia: a Genealogy and History.* NY: Greenwich Publishers, 1986.
Robbins, Michael W. *The Principio Company, Iron Making in Colonial Maryland: 1720-1781.* NY: Garland Publishers, 1986.
Robertson, Haywood L. and Owsley, Laurel J. *The Owsley Family: a Partial Genealogical History.* Self-published, 1987.
Rose, Christine. *Ancestors and Descendants of Rev. Robert Rose and Rev. Charles Rose of Colonial Virginia and Wester Alves, Morayshire, Scotland.* San Jose, CA, 1985.
Rouse, Parke, Jr. *Virginia: the English Heritage in America.* NY: Hastings House Publishers, 1966.
Sandberg, Trudy J. and Gott, John K. *Valiant Virginian: the Story of Presley Neville O'Bannon (1776-1850).* Bowie MD: Heritage Books, 1994.
Scott, Bradford Ripley Alden. "Memoirs of the Civil War." Unpublished manuscript.
Scribner, Robert L., ed. *Revolutionary Virginia: the Road to Independence*, vol. 1. Charlottesville, VA: University Press of Virginia, 1973.
Selden, Jefferson S. *Samuel Selden the Immigrant and his Wife Rebecca Yeo Selden.* Self-published, 1981.
Skinker, Thomas K. Samuel Skinker and his Descendants. St. Louis, Missouri, self-published, 1923.
Southern Churchman, Aug. 4, 1848, obituary of John Gray, Esq., p. 115.
Sparacio, Ruth and Sam. *Stafford County, Virginia Deed and Will Abstracts, 1686-1689.* McLean, VA: The Antient Press, 1989.
---. *Stafford County, Virginia Deed and Will Abstracts, 1699-1709.* McLean, VA: The Antient Press, 1987.
---. *Stafford County, Virginia Deed and Will Abstracts, 1722-1728, 1755-1765.* McLean, VA: The Antient Press, 1987.
---. *Stafford County, Virginia Wills, 1729-1748.* McLean, VA: The Antient Press, 1987.
---. *Stafford County, Virginia Deed and Will Abstracts, 1780-1786.* McLean, VA: The Antient Press, 1987.
---. *Stafford County, Virginia Deed and Will Abstracts, 1809-1810.* McLean, VA: The Antient Press, 1992.
---. *Stafford County, Virginia Deed and Will Abstracts, 1810-1813.* McLean, VA: The Antient Press, 1992.
---. *Stafford County, Virginia Deed and Will Abstracts, 1825-1826.* McLean, VA: The Antient Press, 1992.
---. *Stafford County, Virginia Order Book, 1664-1668/1689-1690.* McLean, VA: The Antient Press, 1987.
---. *Stafford County, Virginia Order Book, 1691-1692.* McLean, VA: The Antient Press, 1987.
---. *Stafford County, Virginia Order Book, 1692-1693.* McLean, VA: The Antient Press, 1987.
Spotsylvania County, Virginia Works Progress Administration Historical Inventory. Fredericksburg, VA: Central Rappahannock Regional Library.
Stafford County Circuit Court Minute Book, 1830-1835.
Stafford County Land Tax Records, 1782-1861, 1870-1910, Stafford Courthouse, Virginia.
Stafford County Personal Property Tax Records, Stafford Courthouse, Virginia.

Stafford, George M. *General George Mason Graham of Tyrone Plantation and his People*. New Orleans: Pelican Publishers, 1947.

Stannard, William G. and Newton, Mary. *The Colonial Virginia Register*. Albany, NY: Joel Munsell's Sons, 1902.

Tarter, Brent, ed. "Stafford County Court." *Virginia, the Road to Independence*, vol. 7. Charlottesville, VA: University Press of Virginia, 1983, pp. 722-723.

Tayloe, W. Randolph. *The Tayloes of Virginia and Allied Families*. Self-published, Berryville, VA, 1963.

Templeman, Eleanor L. and Netherton, Nan. *Northern Virginia Heritage*. Middleburg, VA: Self-published, 1966.

Tucker, Norma. *Colonial Virginians and Their Maryland Relatives*. Baltimore, MD: Genealogical Publishing Co., 1915.

Tyler, Lyon G. *Encyclopedia of Virginia Biography*. NY: Lewis Historical Publishing Co., 1915.

Virginia Herald, May 13, 1809, obituary of John Fitzhugh

---, Sept. 16, 1812, ad for sale of Thistle Flour Mill

---, Oct. 13, 1813, obituary of Dr. John M. Daniel

---, Dec. 11, 1816, notice for Thomas H. Cowne's school in Falmouth

---, Jan. 21, 1829, obituary of Robert Lewis

---, Aug. 17, 1831, obituary of Thomas Seddon

---, Dec. 14, 1836, obituary of Thomas B. Adams

Virginia Star, Apr. 14, 1877, obituary of Dr. Lawrence B. Rose

---, Oct. 20, 1877, James Morton, Jr. erected hotel at Brooke

---, Apr. 14, 1880, obituary of Nathaniel W. Ford

"Virginia Troops in the French and Indian Wars." *The Virginia Magazine of History and Biography*, vol. 1, (1894), pp. 278-287.

Vogt, John and Kethley, T. William. *Stafford County, Virginia Tithables: Quit Rents, Personal Property Taxes and Related Lists and Petitions, 1723-1790*. Athens, GA: Iberian Publishing Co., 1990.

Washington, George. *The Diaries of George Washington, 1748-1799*. Cambridge, Mass: Riverside Press, 1925.

Watkins, C. Malcolm. *The Cultural History of Marlborough, Virginia*. Washington, DC: Smithsonian Institution Press, 1968.

Wayland, John W. *The Washingtons and their Homes*. Staunton, VA: McClure Printing Co., 1944.

White, James T. *Points of Interest in the Pohick Cemetery and Churchyard*. Lorton, VA, self-published, n.d.

Winston, Hugh J., Jr. *History of New Hope Methodist Church, Route 605 at 669*. Stafford, VA, self-published, 1962.

Wise, Erbon W. *The Bridwell Family in America*. Alexandria, Louisiana: Louisiana Offset Printers, 1978.

Withers, Robert E. *The Withers Family of the County Lancaster, England, and of Stafford County, Virginia, Establishing the Ancestry of Robert Edwin Withers, III*. Richmond, VA: Dietz Printing Co., 1947.

Wulfeck, Dorothy F. *Marriages of Some Virginia Residents, 1607-1800*. Baltimore, MD: Genealogical Publishing Co., 1986.

Chapter Three
Miscellaneous County Officials

Sheriff

The office of sheriff first appeared in colonial Virginia in 1634 with the creation of counties. Prior to that time, the sheriff's functions were carried out by the provost marshal or by the commander of the plantation or hundred, the government units into which the new Virginia colony was initially divided.

No single public official had as much influence or impact upon his jurisdiction as did the sheriff; similarly, no single public official caused colonial authorities as much trouble as did the sheriff who was frequently accused of abusing his substantial power. The system of appointing sheriffs varied over the years based upon attempts to control their influence. Initially, sheriffs were appointed by the monthly courts and each county was allowed one. Occasionally, the governor used his authority to dispose of an obnoxious member of the House by appointing him sheriff of some distant locality. Later, sheriffs were appointed by the governor and council with the recommendation of the county courts. Eventually, justices filled the position of sheriff on a rotating basis, each serving a term of one year.

The sheriff served a ministerial rather than judicial function in the county and his duties were numerous. He executed orders and sentences of the county court as well as the general court, made arrests, and managed the county jail. It was his duty to proclaim the accession of the king and to announce publicly at the courthouse the annulling of an act of Assembly by the king. He acted as county treasurer and tax collector, collecting the royal quit rents as well as the public, parish, and county levies. The sheriff was also responsible for collecting all fees charged by other county officials for their services. He held the election of burgesses, received grievances and public claims to be presented t the House of Burgesses, summoned grand and petty juries for the county court and general court. Upon the order of the council, he attended the election of the vestry of the parish, administered oaths to voters, presided at vestry elections, and reported to the council the names of newly elected vestrymen. He also acted as an agent of the governor and council in publishing orders and proclamations, and in summoning the officers of the militia. He communicated to the commanders of the militia, naval officers, and customs collectors the orders of the governor and council regarding the capture of pirates. He recorded the departure of ships, assisted the surveyor-general, and transmitted copies of escheated lands. He reported his account of the quit rents to the receiver-general as well as fines imposed by the general court which he had collected. To the county court he reported his collection of the levies and, once a year, accounted with the treasurer of the colony for this revenue.

During the 17th and most of the 18th centuries, there were five taxes to be administered—customs, quit rents, public, county, and parish levies. Customs was administered by the authorities in Jamestown while the rates were set in England. The quit rent was a direct charge on land and its collection was a local matter. Public levies were set by the Assembly. County levies were set by the county court and the parish levies set by the vestry. These last three taxes were collected in each locality by the sheriff.

Basically, a levy was a poll tax charged on each male person, free or bound, who was over the age of 16. These individuals were also known as tithables. Levies formed the chief source of revenue for all areas of government until the needs of the Revolution made a broader-based tax system necessary. According to the court records of Westmoreland County of Oct. 28, 1663, "The Court doth appoint Collonel Valentine Peyton, Sherriffe, to be Collector for the gathering of the Levies abovesd which for 685 persons comes to 181 pounds of tobacco per poll and in case of non payment the Court orders the Sheriffe to distreine to Act of Assembly" (Westmoreland 18).

The chief difficulty with the tithe was determining an exact list of tithables. Initially, the sheriff had the duty of listing all tithables from accounts made by the planters. This was unsatisfactory as the planters rarely submitted an accurate list that would increase their taxes and it was impossible for the sheriff to personally check every household. In 1692 the people of the upper parish refused to give an account (**footnote**). In response, the Stafford court ordered that the constables be responsible for listing tithables individually.

In 1705 the system of having the sheriff report tithables was abandoned. The job was given, instead, to the justices. Each county was to be divided into precincts, one justice assigned to each, and planters were required to submit their lists of tithables in their households to the justice of that precinct. This was a slight improvement over the old system as the local justice was likely to have knowledge of the families living in his precinct.

The administration of elections was a county function in the 17th and 18th centuries as it is now and the sheriff, as the one executive officer in the county, was responsible for them. Prior to an election, the Assembly sent the sheriff a writ of election, which he was required to publish within ten days of receiving. After the election, he made returns to the secretary of the colony. Initially, the place of the election was left to the sheriff's discretion. After 1668 the courthouse was fixed as the polling place for each county.

The position of sheriff was a lucrative one. He received 10% of what he collected for the public, county, and parish levies and the same for collecting the quit rents. He also received compensation in the form of certain fees on all business conducted in the county court, these fees being specified by the Assembly. He received a fee from the secretary, clerk of the court, and surveyors for whom he collected all accounts of their usual fees. He also received a fee from a master to whom he returned a runaway servant. So lucrative was the office of sheriff that, until about 1700, it was a much sought after office. It was claimed, perhaps rightfully so, that many bought the office and held it for longer than was legally allowed.

By 1710 economic factors caused a reduction in the price of tobacco (in which most fees were paid) and it became difficult to get qualified men to accept the position of sheriff. To ensure that each county had a sheriff, a law was passed imposing a fine of 300 pounds of tobacco on anyone who refused to serve when appointed. The fluctuating price of tobacco likely influenced the exorbitant charges demanded by the sheriffs and the cases of fraud and misappropriation of funds which sometimes occurred.

Considering the sheriff's responsibilities, the need for monitoring was obvious. He was not only a poor tax collector and bookkeeper, but frequently dishonest as well. The continuous stream of legislation relating to the behavior of sheriffs did little to curtail their shady activities. Though he was commanded by the Assembly to be honest and efficient, authorities remained concerned about his behavior throughout the colonial period.

The chief trouble with the fee system prevented the sheriff from collecting more than his due; yet a steady stream of legislation throughout the 17th and 18th centuries did little to prevent corruption in this office. In 1644 the sheriff was forbidden from collecting fees or private debts until the public levies had been taken and that same year, the county courts were ordered to prevent extortion of extra fees by the sheriffs (Porter 29). This was, however, nearly impossible to enforce as the sheriff conducted much of his business away from the justices' watchful eyes. In 1671 the Assembly declared that, due to illegal fees imposed by sheriffs, a table of allowable fees should be published by the courts and posted on the courthouse door. This probably had little effect on the sheriff's activities as most of the county residents were unable to read, much less get to the courthouse to study the fee table.

The act of 1660/61 required that the sheriff be required to be a member of the bench. During the years after 1660, the same man might simultaneously hold the offices of clerk, escheator, surveyor, and sheriff of the same county. This combination of offices was so full of responsibility and attended by so much profit, that it was deemed harmful to the public good and by 1676 it was declared illegal to hold multiple offices while sheriff. After that time, the sheriff was not allowed to hold any other public office, he was required to be a native of the county or to have been a resident there for at least three years, and he could not have been convicted of a serious crime.

The opportunities for fraud, the charge most frequently brought against sheriffs, their close association with nearly every phase of local government, and their involvement in the elections of burgesses and vestrymen, created a position of power and influence exceeded only, perhaps, by the justices. Abuses of this power caused the Assembly to pass an act in 1765 forbidding anyone from sitting in the House of Burgesses while holding the office of sheriff or for two years after retiring from that position (Flippin 316). So common were complaints against sheriffs that, almost without exception, every session of the Assembly during the colonial period produced some type of legislation related to the sheriff. According to Albert Porter, though he was implored, ordered, and commanded to be honest and efficient," the Assembly remained troubled by the fraudulent behavior of the sheriffs (Porter 83).

Sheriffs appointed their own deputies or under sheriffs. By law, no under sheriff could serve more than two years in succession without the approval of the county court. It was felt, and rightly so, that serving multiple terms enabled the under sheriffs to gain undue influence and encouraged them to "commit many acts of oppression and injustice" (Porter 72).

There was a slow but steady decline in the value of tobacco during the 18th century which affected all areas of society, including the office of sheriff. By 1732 the sheriff was allowed a salary of 1,000 pounds of tobacco in addition to his fees. He was still responsible for collecting the fees of all other officials. He could seize and sell property, if necessary, to complete his collection and if he failed to make the collections, the other officials could secure a judgment against the sheriff for the amount due them.

During the latter half of the 18th century, the use of coins increased and people could choose to pay their fees and fines in currency or tobacco. Overcharges frequently occurred when calculating the difference between money and tobacco values. In 1769 the Assembly passed an act with the intention of preventing sheriffs from defrauding those who didn't pay their taxes in tobacco. Not all residents were capable of calculating the rate of exchange between currency and tobacco, a situation that invited fraud by an unscrupulous sheriff. This act also ordered the sheriffs to furnish all persons paying them fees or fines with a receipt providing a detailed description of the account and method of payment.

By 1772 pre-Revolutionary disturbances caused severe fluctuations in the value of tobacco, making it all but useless as a medium of exchange. The Assembly provided that official fees could be paid in money at the rate of 12 shillings 6 pence per 100 pounds of tobacco. The confusion and fraud occasioned by the conversion from tobacco to money was definitely to the detriment of the county citizens, most of whom simply had to take the word of the sheriff as to the accuracy of the conversion.

After the Revolution, the sheriff conducted the elections for the House of Delegates. The creation of the new federal government added to his duties as he was also required to conduct the elections for representatives in Congress and for President.

The duties of the sheriff remained virtually unchanged for many years. By 1800 the justices were still rotating through the office of sheriff. The sheriff was eligible to serve two terms, but the second term wasn't compulsory. The state constitution of 1830 didn't change this but it did increase the sheriff's bond to a sum of between $30,000 and $90,000 at the discretion of the court. The sheriff still appointed his own deputies who could be any honest persons acceptable to the court. The sheriff was still paid by fees and much of this money came from keeping prisoners in the jail. In 1794 he was restricted from charging more than 34 cents per day for the maintenance of a prisoner. Although the sheriff received these fees, the actually management of the jail was in the hands of a deputy. An act of 1805 permitted the court to make an annual allowance of $25 to that lower official and permitted him to demand the jail fees of debtors from their creditors every three months.

Deputy sheriffs caused as many problems as did the sheriffs. In 1772 the term of office was limited to two years. Though the sheriffs' terms had long been limited to one or two years, deputies often held their positions for years. This practice often allowed the deputies to indulge in more fraudulent activities than their superiors. Deputies received money and tobacco for levies and often converted it to their own use rather than turning it over to the colony, often to the total ruin of the sheriff who employed them.

The difficulties that plagued the office of sheriff continued until after the close of the War Between the States. In 1869 new new laws removed from the sheriff's domain all fiscal functions. He was again forbidden from holding any other office simultaneously with that of sheriff and was ordered to pay a $20,000 to $50,000 bond as determined by the county judge. At this point, his duties were limited to court and peace functions only, eliminating many of the complaints of fraud and deception.

Clerk of the Court

From the earliest days of Virginia's history, this was one of the most important county offices. The office of the clerk of the court was probably created at the same time as the monthly court as even from the earliest days of the colonial courts, someone was designated to maintain records created by these judicial bodies.

The early clerks were appointed by the governor. After about 1723, however, the clerks were appointed by the secretary of the colony and, later, by the county courts themselves. According to a law of 1792, if the court was divided over the appointment of a new clerk, the sheriff could break the tie (Porter 186). Clerks were similar to justices in that they were frequently members of conspicuous and influential families. Of course, this was often the case, also, because the clerk had to be well educated and only wealthy families could afford formal education for their children. This office was lucrative enough that men of good estates and political importance sought to fill the seat.

The duties of the clerk were not very different in the 17th and 18th centuries than they are today and his primary responsibility was to maintain the court records and the vital statistics for his county. The

Assembly of 1659 ordered that records of births and deaths be kept in each parish and a report of such be made annually to the clerk for a permanent record. When marriage licenses were created in 1660, they were to be signed by the oldest justice and filed with the clerk who was to report all marriages to the court during the September term.

Until the mid-19th century, the clerks played a more critical role in the effective administration of their counties than they do at present. With a bench of lay justices, the clerk was often the only person versed in law connected with the court and his advice surely decided many cases. The clerk was also a semi-permanent official, normally remaining in office for many years. Another source of his influence was that he could always be found. The justices were planters, lived in different parts of the county, and normally only appeared at court when on official duty. The clerk was always at the county seat. The court met every one to two months, but the clerk was on duty every day and could be consulted on a variety of problems when no justice of the peace was available.

The clerk's duties were outlined by rules established in the mid-18th century and remained virtually unchanged for 200 years. Though charged with nearly the financial authority of the sheriffs, for some reason clerks generally didn't cause "the troubles and difficulties which beset the office of sheriff" (Porter 76). The reputation of the old county clerks gave character to the office long after the position was filled by popular election and much of the same class of men were chosen long after the new system was adopted.

Once chosen, clerks tended to remain in office for the remainder of their lives and, in some cases, public opinion seemed to hold that the position was hereditary. It was not uncommon for a son to succeed his father, as was the case in Stafford with Henry Tyler who was followed in office by his son, Thomas G. S. Tyler. The clerk was also allowed to appoint his own deputy.

Clerks were paid by fees charged for the many services they performed and the office was relatively lucrative. Fees due the clerk as a result of criminal trials were paid by the prisoner upon his conviction. In 1732 the fee schedule for clerks was revised and a salary of 1,000 pounds of tobacco was established. By 1736 this was increased to 1,200 pounds.

An act of 1830 fixed a term of seven years for clerks but did not limit the number of terms he could serve. For good reason only the court could remove its clerk from office with a 2/3 vote by the justices though removal was a very rare occurrence.

Coroner

The duties of the coroner were both ministerial and judicial. As a ministerial officer he executed all processes sent to him. In the event that the sheriff was personally interested or involved in a case, the coroner was authorized to act for him. The coroner's primary function was to hold inquisitions over bodies of persons thought to have met violent or unexplained deaths and he could order the constable or other officers to assist him in summoning a jury. From time to time, he also acted as administrator for some estates for which no other executor or administrator could be found.

The position of coroner doesn't appear at all in the 17th century records. During that period, the justices assumed the responsibilities later assigned to coroners. The job of coroner was created sometime early in the 18th century and the man selected to fill that position was normally already serving in some other capacity. He was recommended by the county court, usually from among the justices, and appointed by the governor with the advice of the council. Coroners made an annual report of their activities to the council. They also furnished the auditor with an account of their services performed during the years. After about 1700, there were a total of 54 coroners in Virginia.

In the event of the absence of the coroner, a justice performed the coroner's duties and received the fee. During the first half of the 18th century, the fee for holding an inquest was 13 shillings, 4 pence or 133 pounds of tobacco, at the choice of the coroner, to be paid out of the estate of the deceased. If the deceased left no estate, the county paid the fee. Near the end of the colonial period, coroners were required to provide a bond on £500 in the county court.

In 1792 the laws were revised and the coroner's duties were more clearly outlined. Among his responsibilities the coroner could officiate only in his own county; he was required to take a prescribed oath upon his appointment; he could act as administrator for an estate if there was no one else willing or able to do so; he was authorized to seize and hold the property of persons named as guilty in an inquest until they were apprehended; they were to provide a written report of the inquest to the jury in the event of a trial; the coroner issued the warrant for the arrest of the accused and was fined $100 for failing to produce the individual; he had the authority to act as sheriff when that office was vacant or the sheriff was absent. The coroner was not, however, allowed to collect levies, militia fines, or official fees in the absence of the sheriff. The coroner was a minor county official who, like the sheriff, was paid by fees charged for his services. The office was not very lucrative, however, unless he was fortunate enough to have several unexplained deaths in his district requiring several juries to be summoned.

The coroner became a constitutional officer in 1830, but the system of nomination by the court and appointment by the governor was not changed at that time. In most cases, the coroner continued to be a member of the county court. The term of office was limited only by the personal behavior of the individual holding the office.

Constable

The constable first appeared in the records of colonial Virginia in 1645. He was usually a man of good standing in his county and was appointed by the county court for precincts that were established by the justices. He was basically an assistant to the sheriff and coroner and his duties included serving warrants, summoning witnesses, summoning a coroner's jury, maintaining the stocks and pillory, administering whippings, and serving writs.

The constable served a two-year term, a practice which was continued by the act of 1830 and the court could appoint as many constables as were needed. In 1807 the court was ordered to lay off each county into districts with one constable each. The position of constable was made a constitutional office in 1830 and they were last elected in 1939.

At the June 1834 term, the Stafford Court laid off the county into constable districts. The bounds of District #1 began "at Potomac run where the stage road crosses it—running thence by Stafford Ct. House to near Aquia Church, thence leaving stage road by Garrison's and Strother Hardings to Stafford Springs, thence with County boundaries around to the mouth of Potomac creek, thence with the creek and run to the beginning." District #2 consisted of "the balance of the upper or northern division of the County." District #3 was "all that portion of the county south of Potomac run and east of stage road from Potomac run to Falmouth Bridge over Rappahannock River." Finally, District #4 was "all that portion of the county south of said run and west of said road."

Surveyor

The very foundation of colonial Virginia society was its plantation system based upon grants and patents of land to new and established settlers. Essential to the patent program were the surveyors who trekked through the wilderness laying out the boundaries of new tracts. It was their responsibility to ensure that adjoining patents didn't overlap (though in fact they often did) and that each planter received his due share of land.

County surveyors were appointed by the surveyor-general and approved by the governor and council. They came under the court's supervision as early as 1657 when the county courts were authorized to regulate surveyors and their fees. After 1692, surveyors were allowed to appoint their own deputies. Every April the surveyors delivered to the auditor a list of all surveys made that year with a detailed account of each. The surveyor was an essential, though minor, colonial official who was limited in his duties and took no part in the general administration of the county.

Surveyors were paid fees fixed by law. In 1624 the fee was set at 10 pounds of tobacco per survey which was later increased to 20 pounds. By 1666 surveyors were receiving 40 pounds for every 100 acres surveyed. The person for whom the land was being surveyed was responsible for paying the surveyor. For special surveys ordered by the governor, the surveyor was paid from the quit rents.

By 1783 surveyors were appointed by the governor on the basis of an examination by the professors of the College of William and Mary. Deputy surveyors were appointed by the court on the recommendation of the surveyor. The deputy was also required to pass an examination by two county justices. This seems to be the first instance of a test for technical competence required for public office.

The number of surveyors assigned to each county varied from one to several. It was impossible for the surveyor to know every foot of terrain in his county and he was sometimes guided by a local resident known as a "pilot."

Surveyors faced a number of challenges and dangers in their work. Injuries sustained in the wilderness could easily prove fatal as little or no medical attention was available. In 173_ Thomas Barber, Stafford County surveyor, wrote to John Lee (c.1709-1789) of Northumberland County concerning the surveying of land on Chappawamsic Creek. He said, "I will wait on ye Honour in September I hopes to get My Journey (to ye backwoods) prolonged till ye Danger of ye Snakes is Over" (Joyner 162).

The position of surveyor remained largely unchanged until 1869 when it became an elected office with a term of three years. The last elected surveyor to serve Stafford was George L. Gordon, Sr. (1862-1952) who served in this capacity from 1919 until his death in 1952. By the 1950s the county surveyor had become a technical advisor who was called upon in the event of land disputes and his findings were taken above those of any other surveyor.

Escheator

This was an important position in colonial government as the escheator was responsible for ensuring that land was kept in the hands of productive citizens and not allowed to be abandoned. According to the laws governing land grants and patents, the grantee was required to seat or plant his land within three years of the date of his patent. Failure to do so resulted in the land reverting to the crown or proprietors through a process known as escheating. When a land owned died without heirs, the land also escheated.

Life in early Virginia was short and uncertain; consequently, there was always a quantity of abandoned land available. Anyone desiring this land could petition the general court to claim it, but the decision as to who would receive the new patent ultimately depended upon the governor's favor. Once an abandoned tract was brought to the attention of the escheator's office, the governor issued a warrant to the escheator of the district in which the land was located. The escheator and a jury of twelve men made an inquisition into the ownership of the land in question. A report of the inquisition was returned to the secretary's office where it remained for nine months. If, during that time, no one came forth with a legal claim to the property, a patent was issued to the petitioner selected by the governor from those applying for the land.

There were four escheators in the colony, each serving several counties and each allowed to select one deputy. The escheator was usually appointed by the governor from the membership of the council and was not supposed to hold this office while also serving as surveyor, sheriff, or clerk of the court, though this rule was not always enforced. Not surprisingly, escheators were often charged with irregularities while in office. They were allowed £5 currency or 1,000 pounds of tobacco for every inquest, the fee being paid by the petitioner desiring to claim the escheated land. The petitioner was also required to pay the receiver-general two pounds of tobacco per acre for the land he obtained.

Because of widespread abuse, after 1685 the governor's power over escheats was curtailed. He was not to dispose of any escheated land until a proper inquest was held. He was also required to send to the Board of Trade an account of the matter and await directions from them.

By 1787 there was one escheator per county appointed through a process similar to that used to appoint sheriffs. Today, abandoned property is rare. It will normally be noticed first by the commissioner of the revenue's office because the land taxes will become delinquent. If the commissioner is unable to locate an owner, he/she reports to the escheator. This is usually an attorney appointed by state authorities to deal with abandoned property. The escheator will advertise for an owner and, if no one can be found who cam make legal claim to the land, it is sold, the money going into the state coffers. So little land escheats now that it is unnecessary to have an escheator for each county. Instead, one escheator handles a region composed of several counties.

Tobacco Inspectors

Virginia produced a variety of goods, chiefly pitch, tar, turpentine, plank, hogshead and barrel staves, shingles, wheat, flout, Indian corn, beef, pork, tallow, was, butter, hogs, geese, and turkeys. Without question, however, its most valuable product was tobacco. Various types were brown, but only two varieties were received at the official warehouses, Oronoco and sweet-scented. The latter grew primarily in the lower parts of Virginia up to the Rappahannock and the south side of the Potomac. Farmers in the back country generally planted Oronoco and this was what the merchants most often dealt with. By 1784 Virginia was annually producing and exporting about 50,000 pounds of tobacco, valued at about £5 per hogshead. This was sent to England who sold it to France, Holland, Norway, Hamburg, the Baltic, Guernsey, Jersey, and Ireland for about £9 per hogshead ("Description," pp. 87-93).

The act of 1730 ordered official inspection warehouses to be built 12 to 14 miles from one another on all navigable water. Merchants were assured that the tobacco they bought from these warehouses was of good quality. Planters could sell their tobacco without carrying along a sample and the distance from their plantations to the warehouses was not unreasonable. Before hauling the tobacco to the warehouse, the planter packed it in hogsheads. By an act of Assembly, each hogshead was required to weigh at least 950 pounds; thus, merchants were generally assured that four hogsheads weighed approximately one ton as this was how they were charged freight by the ship captains. Tobacco thus packed was called "crop tobacco."

Once the tobacco arrived at the warehouse, official inspectors graded it and gave the planter crop notes that he could in turn sell to the merchant. Crop notes often passed from hand to hand before the tobacco was actually exported.

As early as 1632 commissioners were appointed by the governor to supervise the tobacco warehouses. The number of warehouses increased rapidly and by 1732 there were 71 warehouses in the colony staffed by 133 inspectors. By 1738 courts in the counties in which public warehouses were located recommended annually four suitable men from whom the governor selected two for each warehouse. These inspectors performed a vital function by maintaining the quality of tobacco being exported from the colony and ensuring its safe storage until such time as it could be shipped.

Once the tobacco was harvested, dried, stripped from the stems, and packed in hogsheads, it was transported to the nearest warehouse for storage until it was either sold or exported. Transportation of the hogsheads was accomplished by running a long pole through the center of the barrel from one end to the other, leaving a handle protruding from each end. This allowed the hogshead to be rolled, the handles being manned either by two laborers or attached to the harness of an ox. Trails known as "rolling roads" were created from outlying plantations to the tobacco warehouses. These trails were just slightly wider than the hogsheads and a few remain marked on modern maps.

Rolling the tobacco for great distances, however, damaged both and tobacco and the hogsheads. The earliest official warehouses were usually located in major ports on rivers with deep-water wharves. Ships could tie up right outside the warehouse and be loaded with the barrels of tobacco, then sail on to other ports. Early on, most of the planters lived right along the rivers and were, therefore, in close proximity to the warehouses. As the population spread, planters opened and planted new land further inland. Planters living at greater distances from the warehouses had a more difficult time transporting their tobacco and wanted warehouses on the nearest navigable creeks. Consequently, by the mid-18th century, the number of "rolling houses" had greatly increased.

Once the tobacco arrived at the warehouse, the planter received from the inspectors a receipt for the amount of tobacco he had brought for storage. Known as "crop notes," these receipts circulated as currency and were used to pay for anything that required more cash than mere pocket change. Crop notes were payable on demand by the inspectors who signed them and were good for one year but no longer.

In order to maintain the value of the currency, it was important to ensure that the leafy product was in good condition. The duties of the tobacco inspector included breaking open and inspecting all hogsheads of tobacco brought to the warehouse for storage, sale, and shipping. The inspectors then weighed the hogsheads and marked each with an official warehouse stamp. They collected a special tax of two shillings on each hogshead received at the warehouse. Because of the opportunities for fraud, an inspector was required to take an oath for faithful performance of his duties and furnish the local court with a bond of £1,000.

In an effort to limit the amount of inferior tobacco, the law required any tobacco not meeting well-defined standards be burned. As a result, planters tried to sell their low quality tobacco secretly rather than have it destroyed. In 1765 the justices were authorized to issue warrants for the search and seizure of unlawful tobacco and impose fines for violating the grading laws (Porter 64). The sheriff and his deputies were ordered to report to the court the export of any unlawful tobacco. This same act also empowered the courts to build and maintain warehouses at the expense of the colony and to audit the accounts of the inspectors. Any two justices could hear complaints against the inspector and could inspect a warehouse at any time.

In the early years of the colony, the salary for the inspectors was low. From 1680-1732 each inspector received £60 per year. After 1732, the salary ranged from £25 to £70 and was specified by the Assembly for each warehouse according to its importance and the quantity of tobacco that was stored there (inspectors in Stafford frequently petitioned for salary increases, though these were rarely granted). After deducting their salaries, rent for the warehouses, and expenses, the inspectors accounted annually with the treasurer who reported to the Assembly. The inspectors also reported to the county court the disposition of all tobacco in their warehouse and made a report to the Commissioners of the Customs of all tobacco inspected, its disposal and, if it was exported, the names of the ships and captains.

Because they controlled the colony's "cash" and were responsible for maintaining the value of the tobacco, the inspectors were in a position of influence and power. In an effort to control that power, which could easily give way to corruption, inspectors were not eligible to serve in the House of Burgesses while holding the office of tobacco inspector nor for two years after resigning that position and could take no part in elections. Corruption in the office became enough of a problem that in 1738 the Assembly passed an act forbidding inspectors from collecting quit rents as well as public, parish, or county levies. The inspectors were also forbidden from accepting any gift or gratuity while in office. They couldn't buy, sell, or exchange any tobacco in their warehouses. By 1742 the justices were given the authority to visit the warehouses to determine that the tobacco inspectors were faithfully performing their duties.

Tobacco inspectors were phased out as the economic importance of tobacco declined after the American Revolution. The last tobacco inspector in Stafford, for which there is any record, was Henry Peyton (1744-1814) who was still running the warehouse at Aquia in 1805. Because so many of the Stafford records of the early 19th century are missing, it is impossible to determine how long after 1805 the Aquia warehouse remained in operation.

Vestry

During the colonial period, the administration of the affairs in each Virginia parish was largely under the control of a local body known as the vestry. From the beginning, a few men were selected to aid the clergyman with his work and the duties assumed by them were patterned closely after English tradition. Each vestry was composed of the foremost men residing in the parish, based upon economics, intelligence, education, and with respect to social position. Many vestrymen were also members of the House of Burgesses, the county court, or the general court.

Members of the vestry were chosen by the inhabitants of the parish and were intended to be the true representatives of the people within their sphere of jurisdiction. As the leading citizens of their parishes, vestrymen were the principle guardians of public morals. They were looked upon as models of that which was the most polished and cultured in their communities. The vestry's jurisdiction extended to the repression of all forms of immorality, care of the indigent, and administration of the affairs of the church. As such, they worked closely with other local officials and played a vital role in the administration of county affairs.

After the meeting of the first Assembly in 1619, appointments of vestrymen seem to have been made by the monthly court and by 1641 the parishes were electing their vestries. The utmost care was taken that only men suited in character, ability, and estate should be named to this important position. Although the vestrymen were elected officials and intended to be accountable to the people, they sometimes abused the power vested in them. Over time, the vestry was given the authority to fill vacancies by voted of their own members without submitting to periodic re-election by parishioners. Gradually, they became self-perpetuating, all but eliminating regular elections.

Largely in control of local affairs, vestries became powerful entities. In June 1676 a law was passed ordering that vestries be chosen in mass at least once every three years. This new law reflected the belief that by requiring all members to face re-election together at definite intervals, their power would be lessened by making the vestrymen more responsive to their parishioners. Of the many grievances presented to the Commissioners after the failed insurrection of 1676, one of the most frequently expressed was the vestry's excess of power and lack of responsibility to the people of the parish.

By the end of the 17th century, vestrymen were elected by popular vote of the freeholders and householders of the parish. The vestry retained the authority to fill a vacancy on their board created by death, resignation, or removal from the parish. This was a practical solution to a common problem as it enabled the vestry to carry on its parochial business without interruption. It was also highly impractical to expect the heads of households to gather for new elections each time there was a vacancy on the vestry.

From an early date, the number of men on the vestry seems to have been restricted to twelve. This number was established as law by an act of 1660. Also included in this act was the requirement that the vestry meet at least twice each year. The minutes of these meetings were often incorporated into the minutes of the county court. Regular meetings of the vestry were often held in the home of one of the members and sometimes in the parish church.

The duties of the vestry were essential to the efficient operation of the county. One of their most important functions was to appoint the clergyman of their parish. They also investigated cases of drunkenness, adultery, and other moral offenses which they were authorized to present, through the church wardens, to the county court for final prosecution. Preliminary hearings before the vestry for cases of grave moral misconduct were not always the rule, but the vestry could, and did at times, act as a grand jury, determining if there was sufficient evidence for an indictment.

In 1658 vestries were empowered to settle, according to their own judgment, all matters relating to their parishes and parishioners, including the apportioning of the levies. These funds, which also included fines imposed as penalties for swearing, were used for the building and repairing of churches and chapels-of-ease, buying and maintaining glebes, paying the salaries of rectors, readers, clerks, and sextons, etc. The vestry usually met in October to lay the levy as by that time the tobacco crop had been harvested, cured, and was ready for export. In order to determine the amount of the levy, a list was made of all parochial expenses, adding to this the expense incurred for collection of the levy and administration. This amount, figured in pounds of tobacco, was then divided by the number of tithables residing in the parish. Tax payers had the right of appeal to the General Assembly if they believed that the levies were oppressive. This occurred in Stafford on at least two occasions--when the vestry decided to build Aquia Church and when the justices decided that they needed a new courthouse.

County residents paid three types of levies, parish, county, and public. The vestry could excuse any parishioner from paying the parish levy on the grounds of disability, age, or some physical defect that prevented his working in the fields. These individuals were often excused from paying the county or public levies as well. Initially, the vestrymen collected the parish levies. Over time, however, collection of these taxes was added to the duties of the sheriff who was already responsible for collecting the public and county levies. There was little more work involved for the sheriff to collect both payments simultaneously and the collection of parish levies placed a burden upon the vestrymen who had to take time away from their plantation duties in order to make the rounds of the county collecting taxes.

Vestries as a government entity began to disappear shortly after the signing of the Declaration of Independence. The Church of England was no longer the only legally permissible denomination and congregations, long dissatisfied with the church's administrative policies, eagerly sought other denominations for spiritual guidance. This phase of church history was known as the Disestablishment and it nearly destroyed what would become known as the Episcopal Church. As members abandoned their old churches, so did financial support for the long-established programs that had become part of the system of colonial government. Authorities at all levels of government struggled to make up for the loss of the established church.

After the Disestablishment, the vestry became a private body. All standing vestries were dissolved and new ones were chosen by members of each church. One of the most important functions of the old vestries had been the care of the poor in each parish. In 1780 the Assembly created a board of five men, elected by the freeholders, who were charged with taking care of the poor. This office became known as the "overseer of the poor" and it was a part of the Virginia government until the Depression and the New Deal abolished it.

The law of 1780 also ordered the county court to lay off districts within the county and provide for the election of three overseers of the poor from each district to serve three-year terms. The overseers were to meet annually and lay a levy on county tithables for the support of the "poor, lame, blind, and other inhabitants of the districts who are not able to support themselves." The primary duties of the overseers included supervising the care of orphans, filing indentures with the clerk for binding out orphans, and providing doctors in cases of illness. In Stafford County poor houses were built in each district providing shelter for the homeless and references to these tracts are found in land records up to the end of the 19th century. One poorhouse, built near Falmouth on the Warrenton Road (U. S. Route 17), became a private residence and was occupied until well into the 20th century.

Churchwardens

The two vestrymen with the most responsibility and authority were the churchwardens who were selected annually in each parish. By 1641 the justices of the county courts appointed the churchwardens. This position was rotated through members of the vestry in order to equally share the burdens of the office.

The duties of the church wardens included presenting to the county court all persons leading profane and ungodly lives such as swearers, blasphemers, violators of the Sabbath, drunkards, fornicators, slanderers, disturbers of the congregation of the church, gossipers, and all masters and mistresses failing to catechize the young and ignorant who were dependent upon them. The wardens were required to return a correct account of all collections made in accordance with the vestry's assessments. Further, they were responsible for disbursing these collections according to the vestry's orders, maintaining church buildings in good repair, purchasing the books necessary for the recording of marriages, births, and deaths, purchasing communion cloths, napkins, and cushions for the pulpit. Finally, the wardens were charged with ensuring that all ceremonies and rites performed in the church conformed to the orders and canons of the Church of England.

As monitors of the moral conduct of their parishioners, the churchwardens presented moral offenders to the county court, often acting as prosecutors. Upon the presentation of the case in court, the justices ordered the accused to appear at the next meeting of the court to defend himself against the charge. The primary purpose of the wardens' prosecution of moral offenders was to spare the county the expense of supporting unwed mothers and their children. When a female servant gave birth to a child fathered by her master, the servant was sold for a period of two years, the money from her sale being paid to the parish. When the child was born to a free English woman of a black father, the woman was ordered to pay £15 sterling within one month after the birth of the child. If she was unable to do this, she was sold to the highest bidder for a period of years. If the mother was a servant, she served out her indenture and was then sold for a period of five additional years.

The churchwardens were also required to bind out fatherless children until they attained the age of 30. This also included all orphans who lacked a means of support. Orphaned children were normally placed with a planter or tradesman where they were expected to remain until they reached the age of 21. Children could be taken from homes where the parents were unable to care for them or from parents who were likely to encourage their offspring along bad courses. The churchwardens were to supervise the care given these children in their foster homes and were required to notify the courts in cases of abuse or neglect.

The churchwardens were also expected to oversee all cases of extreme poverty, from the aged pauper to the youngest orphan. A few counties, including Stafford, established a fund to care for the helpless poor. Almshouses, or poor houses, were built to feed and shelter those who had nothing. Sometimes, the poor person was lodged in the home of a citizen willing to accept him for a small sum. It should be remembered, however, that extreme poverty was rare in colonial Virginia. Food was plentiful and the opportunities for earning a livelihood were numerous. All but the most aged and infirm could do simple tasks such as stripping tobacco leaves and anyone strong enough to lift a hoe could weed corn for a living.

Overseers of the Roads

For three centuries, highway administration was entrusted to local authorities "with such indifferent success that at last the State has taken over all roads and Virginia, finally, has an adequate highway system" (Porter 20). For 300 years, the Assembly engaged in a never-ending battle to make county officials responsible for maintaining decent roads. The first road law was passed in 1631 requiring that "Highways shall be layd out in such convenient plans as are requisite according as the Governor and Counsell, or the commissioners for the monthlie corts shall appoynt, or according as the parishioners of every parish shall agree" (Porter 21). The roads resulting from this act were little more than trails, passable only on horseback or foot and hardly usable by wheeled traffic. These were probably sufficient early on when most travel was by water. The chief need for roads was for getting to church and to the county seat, but in an area so divided by water courses, as is Virginia, ferries were a much more important consideration than were roads.

The Assembly attempted to provide free ferry service but gave up in 1647 and turned the problem over to local authorities. By an act of 1647 the county court was authorized to license ferries, fix the rates, and prescribe service. In 1657 the Assembly passed a law creating the office of surveyor of highways and provided for his appointment by the court with the additional requirement that the courts insure that roads were cleared at least once a year. The creation of this office probably brought about some improvement in transportation, but poor roads continued to be the norm until early in the 20th century.

Road surveyors remained minor county officers for many years. Their jurisdiction varied from a single road to what amounts to a modern road district as determined by the court. The surveyors were authorized to summon every tithable in their area to work on the roads either in person or by substitute. The planter class was exempt from working on the roads, though they had to send two or more servants in their stead.

In addition to maintaining the roads, the surveyors were also responsible for the waterways designated as public highways. It was important to keep them clear of floating logs and snags. In Stafford, not only were the navigable creeks such as Aquia and Potomac a part of this system, but shallow runs such as Rocky Run, a tributary of Aquia Creek, also formed an important part of the road system. Throughout much of the 18th and 19th centuries, Rocky Run with its firm sandstone bottom was used as a major county road leading from the central part of Stafford to Coal Landing. Ruts carved by wagon wheels so many years ago are still visible today in the sandstone creek bed.

In 1705 the Assembly ordered the counties to construct sufficient roads to provide access to the courthouse and other public places as well as a road to the capital at Williamsburg. In 1738 the road surveyors were ordered to post directional signs at all intersections.

In 1742 the courts were authorized to make contracts for building and maintaining roads and bridges. Prior to this time, all road construction had to be paid for at one time from one levy. With this new law, the county could assume debt or extend payment for road construction over several levies.

A more comprehensive road act was passed in 1748 in which the courts were ordered to lay out the roads to the courthouse, ferries, mills, and churches. This act also ordered that the width of the road leading to Williamsburg was to be no less than 30 feet. When a new road was proposed, the court was to appoint three viewers or inspectors to report on the project. This viewer system lasted through the colonial period. This act also provided for the county to be divided into precincts with a road surveyor in each. The number of surveyors varied with the size of the county.

In 1762 a law provided that all mill dams were to be a minimum of 12 feet wide at the top to allow for a road across the creek or run which had been impounded behind the dam. A justice could issue a warrant against any miller who failed to maintain the proper width at the top of his dam or who didn't maintain the road built thereon.

Highway administration was primarily a county function though parishes frequently became involved. The Stafford County court records contain an account of George Brent's struggle to repair the roads. According to Brent, the people in his precinct refused to work on the roads, claiming that they had already been called upon to do roadwork in another precinct. The court ordered the vestry of the upper parish to take over the roads in question (Stafford County Order Book, 1689-1690, p. 102).

Another comprehensive road act was crafted in 1785 which authorized the courts to open new roads or alter old ones on the petition from area inhabitants. Upon receiving such a petition, the court was to appoint three viewers to survey the proposal and report back. The precinct surveyor of the roads was to summon "all male laboring persons, of the age of sixteen or more, except such as are masters of two or more laboring slaves" to work on the new or altered road (Porter 113). It was further ordered that road districts were not to be more than three miles long or three miles wide. According to the law, nearly any male above the age of sixteen could be required to work on the roads, regardless of physical condition. A public outcry resulted in an amendment to the law:

> Exempt from Working Roads—The Legislature, at its last session, amended the road law so as to exempt the following people from working on the roads: Ministers of the Gospel, persons under 16, and over 60 years of age; persons who reside in a town that provides for its poor and keeps its streets in order; and any person who has lost an arm or leg, or is otherwise disabled, to be exempted on certificate of the county court of such disability. Until this amendment was made there was no provision for the relief of disabled persons. It will be observed that those claiming exemption on account of any disability, must obtain a certificate from the County Court (*Fredericksburg Ledger*, Oct. 4, 1872).

This system of maintaining the roads was far from satisfactory, many thoroughfares being all but impassable for much of the year. Various road laws were enacted in an attempt to ensure adequate roads, but none proved satisfactory. On the eve or yet another new road law, an article appeared in a local newspaper:

The Roads
The awful condition of the roads every winter becomes a prominent topic. The present system of keeping the roads in order does not comment itself to us. We believe that a road law, to be effective, should provide for overseers, to be paid a reasonable salary, with the privilege of hiring laborers to work on the roads. The overseers to be elected by the people, and required to give bond and security for a faithful discharge of duties. Good roads are a great blessing, beside they enhance the value of property beyond the amount of assessment that would be required to have them kept in order (*Fredericksburg Star*, Feb. 18, 1885).

The subject of roads was a popular one, articles from various points of view appearing frequently in the local newspapers. Another article, titled "Stafford Roads," was written by an unidentified writer from Brooke who claimed that the conditions described in an earlier article were not exaggerated, in fact, the writer had "not spoken strongly enough. Our roads are almost impassable between this place and your city; for more than half the distance, there is nothing more than a ditch, and not a very good ditch, to travel over. The lower Potomac ford is no longer safe for the man best acquainted with it to cross; yet we are told, by one who travels over a large portion of the county, that this road is good when compared to many" (*Fredericksburg Star*, July 27, 1886). The road referred to here is now Brooke Road (State Route 608) that was for folks living in this part of Stafford the main thoroughfare to Fredericksburg. Of what we know today of Route 1 the writer noted, "Very few now think of travelling portions of the 'Telegraph road' in vehicles of any kind."

The effects of poor roads further isolated Stafford from social and economic progress. The editorialist commented, "Will our county continue to fall behind the times, and refuse to invite purchasers within our borders by careless neglect? The county will remain poor just so long as we are unwilling to be taxed for home improvements. The present defective road system is a disgrace to any civilized country...We may be taxed shortly to pay damages for accidents that must sooner or later occur to the traveller" (*Fredericksburg Star*, July 27, 1886).

By the late 19th century, members of the community who wished to be designated as overseers of the roads submitted bids to the Board of Supervisors. A newspaper notice reported on some of these bids made at the May 23rd meeting stating, "The bids for the roads were so high the Board rejected all filed, except one of Daniel Tolson, for road districts Nos. 20, 21, 22 of Rock Hill District. Here is one of the bids: 'The undersigned will agree, and bind himself under the present road law, to keep in good order the section of road from Berea church to Falmouth, a distance of four miles, for 12 months, for the sum of one thousand dollars, provided, however, the county fathers will furnish one road plow, one scraper, one crow bar, one stone hammer and half-dozen long-handled shovels'" (*Fredericksburg Star*, June 28, 1890). Those who were appointed overseers of the roads were able to supplement their meager farm incomes and it is easy to understand why local residents were so adamantly opposed to the State's assumption of those duties in the 1920s.

Commissioner of the Revenue

The commissioner of the revenue is a relatively new office in Virginia local government and was a product of the more elaborate tax system necessitated by the expenses of the French and Indian War and the Revolution. During this turbulent period, residents were subject to war taxes paid on slaves, tobacco, land, tithables, farm produce, wheeled vehicles, horses, cattle, and business licenses. For the first time in Virginia's history, property owners were taxed on their land. Although they had been paying quit rents since the first grants and patents had been made, that was not really a tax on the land, but a rent paid to the Crown or the Proprietors of the Northern Neck. The new land tax as set by the Assembly was one shilling, three pence on each 100 acres of land as shown on the quit rent rolls plus an additional tax on wheeled vehicles, and a tax of one shilling on each tithable. This tax scheme was in place from 1757-1760, the revenues used to pay for the expenses of the French and Indian War.

With this new system of taxation, the problem of finding and valuing property was more complex than the simple system of colonial administration could manage. The old method of having the justices list property and tithables collapsed and a new set of revenue officers was created in 1777, the commissioner of the revenue.

When this office was first established, the commissioners were to be elected annually by the freeholders and householders of the county. By law there was to be one commissioner for each county except in large counties where the court was authorized to divide the county into two districts, each with its own commissioner. Stafford was one of these larger counties and was divided into two districts, Potomac Creek and Run forming the dividing line. As always, the election was in the hands of the sheriff except that two senior justices were required to sit with the sheriff and have final judgment on the qualifications of both candidates and voters.

The commissioners were to be paid 10 shillings per day and were to oversee the work of assessors who actually made the rounds of the county, listing tithables and taxable property, both real and personal. The assessors were given four to six weeks to visit each person in their district, taking account of all property, setting a value, deciding the amount of tax due, and giving the owner an account thereof. For their efforts, the assessors were paid £30 per year. Once the taxes were determined, it was the duty of the sheriff to collect the money or tobacco.

After 1786, the duties of the commissioners were more clearly outlined. They were to:
♦ maintain tax records
♦ personally call on every person subject to taxation
♦ make lists of all taxable property
♦ send copies of these lists to the clerk, sheriff, solicitor general, and keep one on file
♦ provide the clerk with an annual list of all changes in land ownership

Late in the 19th century, Stafford was divided into four districts—Rock Hill, Aquia, Falmouth/Hartwood, and Leeland. The north-south dividing line remained Potomac Creek. The east-west line was the primary north-south road which was at that time Mountain View Road (State Route 627) northward through Garrisonville, past Tusculum, and on to Bellfair Mills.

Board of Supervisors

This familiar governmental body was established by the Constitution of 1869 which also provided that each county would hold a monthly court headed by a county court judge. The broad powers of the county justices had been sharply curtailed by this time. This re-defined county judge held office for six years and was required to reside in the county in which he presided.

The duties of the board of supervisors as defined by the Constitution of 1869 was similar to those of the earlier bench of magistrates. They were expected to hold meetings as necessary with an annual meeting on the first Monday in December. The board was responsible for auditing county accounts; settling with the treasurer, sheriff, and other officers owing money to the county; checking the accounts of the overseers of the poor; examining the books of the assessors; laying the county levy for the upcoming year; maintaining and insuring county buildings; examining claims and issuing warrants; furnishing supplies to other county officials, and publishing a full account of their proceedings.

For all their work, the supervisors were compensated handsomely; the law of 1869, which created the board, ordered that members be paid $2.00 per day plus 5 cents per mile for travel. They could not collect more than ten days' pay in a single year. The clerk of the court usually served as clerk of the board and, as such, he was to keep the minutes, record all reports made to the board, and preserve and file all accounts.

The primary duty of the board of supervisors remains today much as it was in the 19th century—effectively managing the county budget. A late 19th century newspaper article reported that "claims [expenditures] amounting to $1,700 (including road claims) were allowed and warrants ordered issued therefor." The report continued by stating, "The county finances are in a sound and healthy condition. The levy for 1889 sill just about pay all indebtedness, including an arrearage of about $1,800. The poor house has saved the county this year about $1,000; to-wit: levy of 1887, $1,197.43; 1888, including cost of poor house and other expenses, $4,575.09; 1889 to July 1, 1890, $1,070.19. It is estimated that the new road law will save at least $800 on the next levy. Road expenses for fiscal year ending July 1, 1890, about $2,500. This can be cut down very much next year" (*Fredericksburg Star*, June 28, 1890). To say the least, the county budget has increased dramatically in 110 years.

County Treasurer

The Constitution of 1869 also established the office of county treasurer who took over the fiscal duties of the sheriff, reducing that officer to court and peace functions only.

Attorney for the Commonwealth

This office was established in 1788 by the same act that created the district courts. Because of the volume of cases being tried, the attorney was allowed to have deputies. By 1890 the Commonwealth's Attorney was appointed by the court of each circuit, county, and corporation court and was paid on a fee basis. He was made a constitutional officer in 1830 and was to be elected for a four-year term.

Districts in Stafford

From its formation in 1664, Stafford was divided into an upper and lower parish. Certain officials, such as overseers of the roads and constables, were appointed to serve within these jurisdictions. By 1782 land taxes had replaced the old quit rent system and the 1777 boundary change with King George County had put the county within its present lines. Potomac Run was recognized as the dividing line between District 1 (all that land south of the run) and District 2 (all that land north of the run). As the population increased, it became necessary to divide the county into ever smaller areas in order to keep up with tax collection and voting. By Apr. 22, 1870, the governor had appointed commissioners Nathaniel Waller Ford (1820-1880), Gustavus B. Wallace (1810-1882), Strother Harding, and John M. Homes (c.1818-1850) to divide Stafford into four townships or districts. The divisions made at that time were described as:

District 1—Falmouth Township—beginning at the mouth of Potomac Creek and running with the said Creek to Bankse's Ford. Thence with the east side of the Woodcutting road to the Telegraph road. Thence with the west side of the Telegraph road to the Corporation line of Falmouth. Thence with said line on the north and west to the Rappahannock river. Thence with said river to the King George Line. Thence with the King George line to the beginning.

District 2—Hartwood Township—Beginning at Bankse's Ford on the Potomac run and running up said run to (left blank). Thence to Raleigh Lathams on the Warrenton road, thence with the east side of said road to the Fauquier line. Thence with the said County [line] to the Rappahannock river. Thence with the said river, to the Corporation line of Falmouth or Falmouth township. Thence with said Township to the beginning.

District 3—Rock Hill Township—Beginning at Jonesville on the Potomac run and running on the east side of the Woodcutting road to the fork of the roads near Mrs. Master's. Thence with the west side of the road leading by Mr. Adie's to the Elk run and Aquia road. Thence on the north side of said road to the fork of the road near James B. Garrison's store. Thence on the north side of said road to the Stafford Store road near Ebenezer Church. Thence on the east side of the Stafford Store road to the fork of the road near Tusculum. Thence with the north side of Tusculum road to where it intersects the Brenton road. Thence with the north side of the Brenton road to the Franklin road. Thence with the north side of the Franklin to the Chappawamsic road. Thence with the west side of said Chappawamsic road to Chappawamsic run near the Bellefair Mills. Thence with the west side of the road, down said run to the Prince William line and the Fauquier line to the Warrenton road, corner to Hartwood Township. Thence with said Township to the beginning.

District 4—Aquia Township—Beginning at Jonesville on the Potomac run, corner to Rock Hill Township and running with said Township to the Prince William line. Thence with said County to Potomac river. Thence with said river to the mouth of Potomac Creek. Thence with said creek to the beginning. (Stafford Deed Book 26-A, p. 724)

Sources:
Barton, R. T., ed. *Virginia Colonial Decisions: the Reports of Sir John Randolph and by Edward Barradel of the Decisions of the General Court of Virginia, 1728-1741.* Boston, Massachusetts: Boston Book Company, 1909.
Bruce, Philip A. *Institutional History of Virginia in the Seventeenth Century.* NY: G. P. Putnam and Sons, 1910.
Des Cognets, Louis, Jr. *English Duplicates of Lost Virginia Records.* Baltimore, MD: Genealogical Publishing Company, 1981.
Flippin, Percy S. *The Royal Government in Virginia, 1624-1775.* NY: Columbia University, 1919.
Fredericksburg Ledger, Oct. 4, 1872, "Exempt from Working Roads"
Fredericksburg Star, Feb. 18, 1885, "The Roads"
---, July 27, 1886, article on county roads
---, June 28, 1890, notice for bids for overseers of roads
Hageman, James A. *The Heritage of Virginia.* Norfolk, VA: Donning Company Publishers, 1986.
Johnston, F. *Memorials of Old Virginia Clerks.* Lynchburg, VA: J. P. Bell Co., 1888.
Joyner, Peggy S. *Abstracts of Virginia's Northern Neck Warrants & Surveys*, vol. 3. Self-published, 1986.
Mapp, Alf J., Jr. *The Virginia Experiment: The Old Dominion's Role in the Making of America (1607-1781).* Richmond, VA: Dietz Press, Inc., 1957.
Morton, Richard L. *Colonial Virginia: the Tidewater Period, 1607-1710.* Chapel Hill, NC: University of North Carolina Press, 1960.
Porter, Albert O. *County Government in Virginia: a Legislative History, 1607-1904.* NY: Columbia University Press, 1947.
"Public Officers in Virginia, 1680." *The Virginia Magazine of History and Biography*, vol. 1, no. 3 (January 1894). NY: Kraus Reprint Corp., 1968.
Rouse, Parke, Jr. *The English Heritage in America.* NY: Hastings House Publishers, 1966.
Stafford County Deeds:
    Deed Book 26-A, p. 724, Apr. 22, 1870, establishment of districts within Stafford.
Westmoreland County, Virginia Records, 1661-1664.

County Officials

1664
Sheriff—Col. John Dodman (born c.1613)
Under Sheriffs—John Clark and John Samwaids
Constable—Thomas Gregg[531] (died 1699)
Clerk—Anthony Bridges
Church Wardens—William Green and Vincent Young
Surveyors of the Roads—Oliver Balse, Robert Street, Thomas Dovacke—"from Capt. Alexanders to the extent of the county"
    John Mathies and Michael Hill—"from head of Potomac to Capt. Brents"
    John Axton and Thomas Rowland—"from Parsbitansy to the head of Potomack"

1665
Sheriff—Maj. George Mason (1628-1686)
Under Sheriff—John Clark
Constable—Christopher Lund[532] (died 1674)
Clerk—Samuel Hayward (1640-1696)

---

[531] Thomas Gregg married Lucy Heabeard (died c.1730).
[532] Christopher was a resident of Chotank Parish, Westmoreland County, later King George.

County Lieutenant—Col. Henry Meese[533] (died 1682)

1666
Sheriff—Capt. John Alexander (died 1677)
Under Sheriff—John Clark
Clerk—Samuel Hayward
Church Wardens—John Withers[534] (1634-1699) and Robert Osbourne
Vestry—Capt. John Alexander   Vincent Young
       Richard Fossaker (died 1676)   William Greene
       Richard Heabeard   Thomas Humphrey
       John Heabeard (died 1690)   Thomas Gregg
       William Heabeard[535] (died c.1720)
Surveyor of the Roads—John Mathews[536] and William Harris—"from Paspetanze to Potomack Creek"
    Edward Sanders and William Withers (c.1636-1698)—"from Potomac Creek to Aquia Creek"
    Robert Mosley and William Beach—"from Aquia to Chopawamsic"
Surveyor—Capt. John Alexander

1667
Sheriff—Richard Fossaker[537]
Under Sheriff—John Clark
Vestry—Col. John Dodman   Lt. Col. Henry Meese
       Maj. George Mason   Capt. John Alexander
       Richard Heabeard   Robert Townsend (1640-1675)
       William Heabeard   William Greene
       John Wiser   Thomas Gregg
       Vincent Young   David Anderson
Church Warden—John Withers
Surveyors of the Roads—William Beach—"from the frontiere Westmoreland down to the head and ferry at Acquia"
    Michael Hill and John Massey—"from Acquia to the ferry and head of Potomack Creek"
    William Heabeard—"from Potomack Creek ferry to the court house and to horse bridge
    Christopher Lund—"from the Plantation of Mr. Richard Hope to the ferry at Potomack"

1668
Sheriff—George Mason
Clerk—John Withers

1669
Sheriff—George Mason
Surveyor—William Horton

1670
Sheriff—George Mason

---

[533] On Feb. 14 and 15, 1665 the Stafford Court ordered that Meese "have 1600 pounds of Tobacco out of the next leavey for keeping the ferry until the 20th 9ber [September] next." This would have been the ferry across Potomac Creek.

[534] In 1691 John Withers was granted a license to keep the ferry from Marlborough Point across Potomac Creek "to the Valley next or Lunsford Hills." John also represented Stafford in the House of Burgesses in 1696 and 1697. He served as clerk of the court from 1693 until his death in 1699.

[535] William was the son of John Heabeard (died 1690). He married Margaret Newton, the daughter of Benjamin Newton. Margaret later married John Travers.

[536] According to a patent of 1669, Mathews kept an ordinary on Potomac Creek.

[537] On Feb. 14 and 15, 1665 the Stafford Court ordered that Richard Fossaker "take care to provide that a ferry be kept at Acquia and that he allow not above 2600 pounds of Tobacco for the same."

1672
Surveyor—Samuel Wye

1680
Clerk—Thomas Owsley

1681
Surveyor—George Brent (1640-c.1700)

1682
Sheriff—George Mason

1683
Sheriff—Edward Thomason
Under Sheriff—Patrick Hume

1685
Clerk—Samuel Hayward

1686
Clerk—Samuel Hayward
Deputy Clerk—John Basford

1687
Sheriff—Malachi Peale[538]
Under Sheriff—Joshua Davis[539] (died 1703)
Clerk—Samuel Hayward
Deputy Clerks—John Basford and James Hearse

1688
Sheriff—Malachi Peale
Under Sheriff—Joshua Davis
Clerk—Samuel Hayward
Deputy Clerks—John Basford and James Hearse

1689
Sheriff—Malachi Peale
Under Sheriffs—Robert Colston, Joshua Davis
Constables—William Bunbury—"for the upper parts of the lower parish"
        Jonathan Mottershed—Upper precincts
        Symon Stacey—Potomac Creek precincts
        Jeffrey Wood—Chappawamsic precincts
        William Rustall—"for the Precinct of Pasbitanzy"

---

[538] Malachi arrived in Virginia in 1678, settling first in Elizabeth City where he received a patent of 843 acres. He then moved to Stafford and on Oct. 4, 1694 he patented 1,614 acres on Potomac Creek. By his will he devised the land to Margery and Elizabeth Walker, the daughter of Endimion Walker of Exon in Devon, England. Margaret and Elizabeth failed to pay the quit rents (as Malachi had also failed to do). The patent book reads, "29 Sept. 1705 and 1706 we by our Agent reentered. Grant to Thomas Hooper of Lancaster County for 1,614 acres by paying rent and arrearages from 4 Oct. 1694. ___ day of ___ 170_" (Gray, vol. 1, p. 40).

Malachi also obtained a patent on Oct. 5, 1694 for another 489 acres on Potomac Creek. He never paid rent on this tract either and by will devised this property to Mr. John Pim, merchant of Exon. Mr. Pim also failed to pay the rents. The land was re-patented on Sept. 29, 1705 to Thomas Hooper.

[539] Joshua was a prominent attorney in the Northern Neck, his name appearing in the records of Rappahannock, Stafford, Westmoreland, and Richmond counties.

William Balthrop[540]—"for the Precinct of the lower Parish Vizt of St. Pauls"
Clerk—Samuel Hayward
Deputy Clerk—James Hearse

1690
Sheriff—Malachi Peale[541]
Under Sheriffs—Richard Gibson, William Willford, Vincent Young, George Andrews
Constables—Giles Vandegasteel—upper precincts
　　　　John Higgison—Potomac Creek precincts
　　　　Matthew Gosse—Chappawamsic precincts
　　　　David Anderson—"for the Precinct of Pasbitanzy"
　　　　Edward Platt[542]—"for the Lower Parish"
　　　　Thomas Ellis—"for the Precinct of the lower Parish Vizt of St. Pauls"
Clerk—Samuel Hayward
Collector of Levies and Public Dues—Capt. George Mason
Surveyors of the Roads—Lower parish precincts—Col. William Fitzhugh (1651-1701), John Withers, William Buckner, William Bunbury
　　　　Upper parish precincts—John Waugh[543] (1661-1716), Joseph Newton[544] (c.1639-c.1697), Capt. George Brent, Richard Gibson, Robert Colston

1691
Sheriff—Capt. George Mason (II) (1660-1716)
Under Sheriffs—Robert Colston, William Willford, John Squire
Constables—William Mansbridge (died 1697)—"of upper Parish"
　　　　Jonathan Mottershed—"of upper precincts of upper parish"
　　　　William Wentworth Matheny[545] (1664-1705)—"in the Room and Stead of John Higgison"
Coroner—John Harvey
Surveyor of the Roads—John Waugh

---

[540] William married Mary Christian.

[541] According to the court records of Dec. 10, 1690, "Whereas Capt. Malachi Peale high sheriff of this County did publickly in this Court refuse the collection of the County Levy for this present year he alledging for his reason that the upper Parish of this County had taken the Collection of the parish Levy out of his hands and that Mr. Sampson Darrell the Chief undertaker for the Erecting and building of a new Courthouse for this County did here likewise in Court offer and Tender himself to Levy and Collect the County Claims and Levys" (Stafford Order Book, 1664-1668, p. 122).

[542] In the court minutes of July 9, 1690 William Willford, deputy sheriff, complained against Edward Platt, "one of the Constables of the lower Parish of this County that the said Platt doth in contempt of authority and contrary to an order of this Court neglect and refuse to receive an order of Court for the Impowering of him the said Platt to take the List of Tithables in his precincts and to give in a True and Perfect account of the same."

[543] The second son of Parson John Waugh (1630-1706). The parson died intestate and his land holdings, including 6,350 acres on the headwaters of Potomac Creek, which he had patented in 1691, passed to his eldest son, Joseph (c.1660-1727). The year after his father's death, Joseph divided the Potomac Creek tract into five parcels of approximately 1,200 acres each and put each of his three brothers, John (c.1661-1716), Alexander (166_-1722), and David (168_-1753) into possession of equal fifths of it. John married Martha Vandegasteel, widow of Giles Vandegasteel (16_-1753) of Stafford County.

[544] Joseph Newton was the first of this family to settle in Virginia. He was the eldest son of Thomas Newton of Kingston-upon-Hull, Yorkshire and was a mariner by profession. He immigrated to America after the death of his third wife, settling first in Maryland c.1672 and then in Virginia c.1677. Around 1676 he married in Westmoreland County Rose Gerrard Tucker (born c.1629), the widow of Thomas Gerrard and John Tucker.

[545] The son of Daniel Mathena (1638-1685) and Sarah Wentworth (died 1700). Daniel, who participated in the uprisings against the Catholic government in Maryland, moved from that colony to Stafford in 1681 or 1682. William married Frances Mason and died testate in Stafford.

Surveyor—Theodorick Bland[546] (1662-1700)
Deputy Surveyor—William Buckner

1692
Sheriff—Capt. George Mason
Under Sheriff—George Anderson
Constable—Samuel Kent—"of Upper parish"
        John Peake—"of upper precincts of the upper parish"
Coroner—John Harvey
Surveyor of the Roads—John Waugh—upper precinct
Surveyor—Theodorick Bland
Deputy Surveyors—William Buckner and Richard Pasker

1693
Sheriff—George Mason
Clerk—John Withers[547]
Surveyor—Theodorick Bland

1694
Clerk—John Withers
Surveyors—Theodorick Bland and George Brent

1695
Sheriff—Thomas Owsley
Clerk—John Withers

1696
Sheriff—Martin Scarlet[548] (died 1695)
Clerk—John Withers

1697
Sheriff—Thomas Owsley
Clerk—John Withers

---

[546] The son of Theodorick Bland (1629-1671) the immigrant who settled in Charles City County. Theodorick, Jr. was heir to Westover plantation which he shared with his brother Richard (1665-1720). Theodorick, Jr. was surveyor of Charles City County in 1680 and of Stafford from 1692 until at least 1694. In 1699 he was appointed to lay out the new town of Williamsburg.

[547] On Nov. 13, 1691 John Withers was granted a license to keep the ferry over Potomac Creek. A notation made in the Mar. 11, 1692 court minutes states that Withers "now finding since by many pregnant and sufficient reasons that the same would be very prejudicial and injurious to him he living soe remote and far away from the Ferry and Mr. John Waugh coming into Court and assumed to undertake and keep the Ferry over Potomack Creeke for the ensueing year for the sum of four thousand pounds of tobacco."

Parson Waugh had previously operated the ferry across Potomac Creek as evidenced by the records of Oct. 9, 1686 when payment for his services was ordered by the court then meeting in the little village that would later become Marlborough. An amusing letter from the governor and council referred to the "many great neglects in ye dispatch of messengers sent on his Majesties this his Country's Service occasioned by severall persons keeping Ferries who have refused to Trans[port] such messengers and their horses with ready pay" (Stafford Deed Book D, p. 108). The Council ordered that from hereafter, "no person whatsoever keepinge Ferry or which hereafter shall keep Ferry demand or take pay of any person for Transportacon of himself and horse over any River in this Countrye that shall be sent by his Excellency the Governor to any of ye Councell or others of his Majties." The sheriff was ordered "to make publicacon hereof at ye next Court to be held for [Stafford] County."

[548] Sheriffs served from spring to spring rather than for the calendar year. Scarlet was appointed sheriff of Stafford in the spring of 1695 to serve until the following spring. He died shortly thereafter. It appears that Thomas Owsley may have finished out Scarlett's term.

1698
Clerk—John Withers

1699
Sheriff—George Mason
Clerk—Thomas Owsley
Church Warden—George Mason
Surveyor—Thomas Gregg
Deputy Registrar—Richard Cornwell
Commander of the Militia—Col. George Mason
Major of the Militia—Thomas Owsley
Naval Officer Receiver—Col. Rice Hooe (1660-1726)

1700
Sheriff—Richard Fossaker
Deputy Sheriff—John Trammill
Clerk—Thomas Owsley
Church Warden—George Mason
Surveyor—Nicholas Brent[549] (died 1711)

1701
Sheriff—John Waugh, Jr. (c.1661-1716)
Clerk—Maj. William Fitzhugh[550] (c.1678-1713) of Eagle's Nest
Deputy Clerk—Nathaniel Pope

1702
Sheriff—Charles Ellis
Deputy Sheriff—George Anderson
Clerk—Maj. William Fitzhugh
Surveyor—Thomas Gregg

1703
Sheriff—Dade Massey[551] (1679-1735)
Clerk—Maj. William Fitzhugh
Colonel of the Militia—George Mason
Lt. Colonel of the Militia—Rice Hooe
Surveyor—Thomas Gregg, Jr.

1704
Clerk—Maj. William Fitzhugh
Deputy Clerk—Nathaniel Pope
Surveyor—Thomas Gregg

---

[549] Nicholas was the son of Capt. George Brent (1640-c.1700) and Elizabeth Greene (c.1655-1686). In 1711 Nicholas married Jane, the daughter of Capt. Thomas Mudd of Maryland.
[550] William inherited from his father, Col. William Fitzhugh (1651-1701) the immigrant, 18,723 acres in Stafford and Westmoreland counties. He also served as a burgess for Stafford from at least 1701-1703 and as a justice. He married Ann (1683-1732), the daughter of Richard Lee, Esq. (1647-1714) or Westmoreland County. She married secondly Capt. Daniel McCarty (1679-1724) of Westmoreland who was a burgess, justice, and sheriff of that county and speaker of the assembly from 1715-1720. He was buried at the old Yeocomico Church in Westmoreland.
[551] Dade was the son of Robert Massey (1655-1689) and Mary Gilson. He married Rose Newton (c.1700-1785), the daughter of John Grigsby of Stafford.

1705
Sheriff—George Mason
Clerk—Nathaniel Pope[552] (1669-1719)
Deputy Clerk—Thomas Thorne

1706
Sheriff—George Mason
Clerk—Nathaniel Pope
Deputy Clerk—Henry Parry
Surveyor—Nicholas Brent

1707
Sheriff—Maj. William Fitzhugh
Clerk—Nathaniel Pope
Deputy Clerk—Henry Parry
Surveyor—Thomas Gregg

1708
Sheriff—"none submitted"

1709
Sheriff—George Anderson
Surveyor—Edward Barrow

1710
Sheriff—George Anderson
Surveyor—Thomas Gregg

1711
Sheriff—Joseph Sumner
Deputy Clerk—Henry Parry

1712
Sheriff—Joseph Sumner
Clerk—Nathaniel Pope
Deputy Clerk—Henry Parry
Surveyor—Thomas Hooper

1713
Sheriff—George Mason (1660-1716)
Surveyor—Thomas Hooper

1714
Sheriff—George Mason
Clerk—Thomas Fitzhugh[553] (died 1719)
Coroners—John Waugh and John West
Surveyors—Thomas Gregg and Thomas Hooper

---

[552] Nathaniel married Jane Browne (16_-1752), the daughter of Capt. Originall Browne (1648-1697) of Westmoreland County.
[553] Thomas was the brother of Henry Fitzhugh who was sheriff in 1715 and the son of Col. William Fitzhugh (1651-1701). Thomas married Ann Darrall, widow of William Darrall and the daughter of Col. George Mason (II). He inherited from his father 4,334 acres of land.

Keeper of Weights and Measures—John Waugh
Tobacco Inspectors—John Waugh and Henry Fitzhugh[554] (1686-1758)

1715
Sheriff—James Jameson (died 1736)
Clerk—Thomas Fitzhugh
Surveyors—Thomas Hooper and Edward Barrow

1716
Sheriff—Henry Fitzhugh
Clerk—Thomas Fitzhugh
Surveyor—Edward Barrow

1717
Sheriff—John Washington[555] (1668-1721)
Clerk—Thomas Fitzhugh

1718
Clerk—Thomas Fitzhugh

1719
Sheriff—Thomas Hooper
Clerk—George Mason (1690-1735)

1720
Clerk—George Mason

1721
Sheriff—Thomas Hooper
Clerk—George Mason

1722
Sheriff—French Mason[556] (1695-1748)
Clerk—George Mason
Surveyor—Thomas Hooper

1723
Sheriff—French Mason
Clerk—George Mason
Compiler of Quit Rents—James Carter[557] (1684-1743)
Surveyors—Thomas Hooper and John Savage[558] (died c.1745)

---

[554] The son of Col. William Fitzhugh (1651-1701) the immigrant. Henry inherited from his father 17,598 acres in Stafford. He also represented Stafford in the House of Burgesses in 1736. In 1718 he married Susanna (1693-1749), the daughter of Mordecai Cooke of Gloucester, Virginia.

[555] John was the son of Lawrence Washington (1635-1676) and his second wife, Joyce Fleming. John resided at Chotank and married Mary Townshend in 1686.

[556] The son of George Mason (II) (1660-1716) and Mary, the daughter of Gerard Fowke (II) (1662-1734). French lived on the north side of Pohick Creek on 1,455 acres of land he inherited from his father. He also owned the official warehouse near the mouth of Pohick Creek and the mill on the south side. He married Mary Nicholson.

[557] James lived at Palace Green, just to the north of Aquia Harbour subdivision. He married first in 1715 Hannah Neale (died 1722), the daughter of Daniel Neale. He married secondly in Stafford in 1724 Mary Brent, the daughter of Hugh Brent (II) (1659-1716) of Lancaster County.

[558] John was one of the surveyors chosen in 1736 to ascertain the boundaries of the Northern Neck Proprietary. By mid-October of that year, the party of surveyors and their assistants were deep inside the

1724
Sheriff—Townshend Dade[559] (c.1688-1761)
Clerk—George Mason
Compiler of Quit Rents—James Carter
Surveyors—John Savage and Thomas Barber
County Lieutenant—Townshend Dade

1725
Sheriff—Townshend Dade
Clerk—Catesby Cocke[560] (born 1702)
Surveyors—Thomas Barber and John Savage

1726
Sheriff—William Storke[561] (1690-1726)
Clerk—Catesby Cocke
Coroner—Henry Fitzhugh
County Lieutenant—Robert Carter, Esq.[562] (1704-1732)
Surveyors—Capt. Henry Conyers (16_-1733), James Thomas, John Savage

1727
Sheriff—Anthony Thornton[563] (1695-1757)
Clerk—Catesby Cocke
Surveyor—John Savage and John Warner[564] (c.1680-1742)

1728
Sheriff—Maj. Dennis McCarty[565] (died 1743)
Clerk—Catesby Cocke
Surveyors—John Savage, John Warner, and Thomas Barber

Virginia wilderness and were dangerously short of food. Col. William Byrd wrote that the party was "almost reduced to the hard necessity of cutting up the most useless person among them, Mr. Savage, in order to support and save the lives of the rest" (Brown, Stuart 88).

[559] Townshend married Susan, the daughter of Henry Fitzhugh (1723-1783). He also served as a justice of Stafford in 1729, 1731, 1737, 1745, 1746, and probably other years as well.

[560] Catesby lived at Belmont in what was then Stafford, but later became Fairfax County. He was the first clerk of that county upon its formation.

[561] William was the son of Nehemiah Storke (died 1693) and Behethland Gilson (died 1693). He married Elizabeth Hart, the daughter of Edward Hart (died 1703) and Margaret (Field) Cossom.

[562] The son of Robert Carter (1663-1732) and his second wife, Betty Landon Willis (1684-1719). Robert resided at Nomini Hall and in 1725 married Priscilla Churchill (1705-1757), the daughter of William and Elizabeth Churchill.

[563] Anthony was the son of Francis Thornton (1651-1726) and Alice Savage (1653-1695). On Oct. 12, 1726 he gave bond and was "this day sworn in the office of Sheriff for the next year." Anthony replaced William Storke who died at the beginning of his term. John Fitzhugh (died 1733) and Townshend Dade, the previous sheriff, joined with Anthony to pay the required £1,000 bond.

[564] Probably born in Pennsylvania, John married Margaret ___. Their daughter, Elizabeth "Lettice" Warner (1720:25-1795) married in Stafford Brereton Jones (1716-1795). John was considered the best surveyor in the area and in 1736 was appointed one of a group of surveyors charged with determining the bounds of Lord Fairfax's Northern Neck Proprietary. He was buried outside the old frame chapel on the present site of Aquia Church.

[565] Of Cople Parish, Westmoreland County. In 1724 he married Sarah Ball (born 1705) and served as a justice in Prince William County in 1731. Dennis was buried at Pohick Church in Fairfax County.

1729
Sheriff—Abraham Farrow[566] (c.1670-c.1731)
Clerk—Catesby Cocke
Coroner—Dade Massey
County Lieutenant—Robert Carter, Esq.
Surveyors—John Warner and James Thomas

1730
Sheriff—Townshend Dade
Clerk—Catesby Cocke
Surveyor—John Warner

1731
Sheriff—Thomas Grigsby[567] (1680:95-1745)
Clerk—Catesby Cocke[568] and Thomas Claiborne[569] (1704-1735)
Surveyors—John Warner and John Savage

1732
Sheriff—John Washington
Deputy Sheriff—James Ireland
Constable—Edward Clements[570]
Clerk—Thomas Claiborne

1733
Clerk—Thomas Claiborne

1734
Sheriff—Capt. Philip Alexander[571] (1704-1753)
Clerk—Thomas Claiborne

---

[566] Abraham may have been a millwright. In 1704 he entered a partnership in a mill on Quantico Creek owned by Joshua Davis, a Richmond County attorney. In 1709 Abraham bought out Davis' interest in the mill. He accumulated some 2,400 acres in Stafford, now Prince William.

[567] Probably the son of John Grigsby (1624-1730) and his wife Jane (died c.1756). Thomas married Rose (c.1700-1785), the daughter of Gerrard Newton (c.1677-c.1706).

[568] On Mar. 11, 1731 Catesby Cocke became clerk of the newly formed county of Prince William. He was replaced in Stafford by Thomas Claiborne.

[569] The son of Thomas Claiborne (1681-1732) and Ann Fox (1684-1733) of King William County. Thomas died unmarried. He owned land on Potomac Creek that he had purchased in 1733 from John Mercer (1704-1768).

[570] In 1728 Edward married Elizabeth Fruye.

[571] The son of Philip Alexander (c.1664-1705) and Sarah Ashton (born c.1675), the daughter of Capt. John Ashton (died 1677). By 1746 Philip, Jr. was living in what would later become the city of Alexandria on land he inherited from his father. A petition submitted to the legislature in 1748 proposed building a town in the midst of his estate. He opposed the idea, suggesting instead that the town be established on the head of Great Hunting Creek. It is said that in order to prevent an impasse, Philip was placated by naming the town Alexandria in honor of his family. By July 1749 lots were being sold in the new town. In 1726 Philip married Sarah Hooe (c.1707-1758), the daughter of Col. Rice Hooe (1660-1726) and his third wife, Frances Townsend (1667-1726).

1735
Sheriff—Capt. Chandler Fowke[572] (1692-1745)
Constable—Robert Suddath[573]
Clerk—Thomas Claiborne

1736
Sheriff—John Washington[574] (c.1697-1742)
Clerk—Capt. Henry Tyler[575] (c.1710-1777)
Surveyor—John Warner

1737
Sheriff—Henry Washington[576] (1694-1748)
Clerk—Henry Tyler

1738
Clerk—Henry Tyler
Surveyor—John Warner

1739
Sheriff—Capt. John Hooe[577] (1702-1766)
Clerk—Henry Tyler
Surveyors—John Warner, James Thomas, John Grant[578] (c.1704-1762)

1740
Constable—Robert Sudduth
Clerk—Henry Tyler
Deputy Clerk—James Waugh (c.1705-1750)
Surveyors—John Savage and James Thomas

1741
Sheriff—Richard Foote[579] (1704-1774)
Deputy Sheriff—George Waller[580] (1703-1768)

---

[572] Appears in the records as Chandler Fowke of "Pasipatanzy" in King George and later of Gunston Hall in Stafford, now Fairfax County. Around 1716 he married Mary Fossaker (c.1700-1783), the daughter of Col. Richard Fossaker and Mary Withers.
[573] In 1741 or 1742 Robert married Sarah Walker in Stafford County.
[574] The son of John Washington (1668-1721) of Chotank and Mary Townshend. John, Jr. inherited Chotank and in 1721 married Mary Massey, the daughter of Dade Massey (1679-1735).
[575] Henry Tyler descended from a prominent York County family. He was the son of Francis (c.1688-after 1723) and Rebecca Tyler (born c.1695). In 1738 Henry married in Stafford Alice Strother (c.1719-c.1792), the daughter of William Strother (c.1665-1726) and Margaret Watts. For 41 years his distinctive and beautiful handwriting adorned the records of Stafford County.
[576] Henry was the fourth and youngest surviving son of John Washington (1663-1698) who, in turn, was the youngest son of Col. John Washington (c.1634-1677), the immigrant. Henry grew up in Westmoreland County but inherited land on Machodoc Creek in then Stafford (now King George) and settled there. He served Stafford as a justice, captain in the militia, and succeeded his cousin, John Washington (c.1697-1741/2) as sheriff.
[577] John was the son of Rice Hooe (1660-1726) and Frances (Dade) Townsend (1667-1726). He married Anne Fowke Alexander (1713-c.1776).
[578] John Grant was the son of William Grant (c.1675-c.1734) of Richmond County. He married Margaret Bronaugh (c.1698-1756), the daughter of Jeremiah Bronaugh (1702-1749).
[579] In 1726 Richard married Katherine Fossaker.
[580] George Waller lived at Spring Hill, a large plantation that included what is now Vestavia Woods subdivision on Courthouse Road (State Route 630).

Clerk—Henry Tyler
Surveyor—John Warner

1742
Clerk—Henry Tyler
Tobacco Inspectors:
    Aquia—William Harrison[581] (1703-1745)
    Falmouth—John Grant
    Cave's—Charles Waller[582] (1702-1749) and William Mountjoy[583] (1711-1777)

1743
Sheriff—Richard Bernard[584] (1705-1753)
Clerk—Henry Tyler

1744
Clerk—Henry Tyler
Vestryman—Capt. William Harrison

1745
Sheriff—Mott Doniphan[585] (died c.1776)
Clerk—Henry Tyler
Vestry[586]—John Mercer (1704-1768)   Mott Doniphan
    John Wheeler (1684-1746)   James Withers (1680-1746)
    Capt. William Harrison   Capt. Henry Tyler
    James Scott   William Mountjoy
    Capt. James Waugh

1746
Sheriff—George Waller
Clerk—Henry Tyler

---

[581] William also served as a justice in 1737, 1738, 1741, and probably other years as well. He was the son of Capt. William Harrison and Sarah Halley. In 1732 William married Isabella (Triplett) Hore, the widow of Capt. Elias Hore (1700-1730).

[582] Charles was the son of Charles Waller (1674-1724) of Essex County and Susannah Forrest (1678-1748). He and his brother Edward (born c.1713) inherited land from their father on Aquia Creek where they settled with their mother. This became the plantations of Concord and Spring Hill.

[583] William Mountjoy was the son of Edward Mountjoy (c.1660-1712), the immigrant. William lived at Locust Hill near Brooke and built a stone gristmill that was later known as Brooke's Mill. A patriot, he signed the Leedstown Resolutions.

[584] In 1729 Richard Bernard married Elizabeth (Hart) Storke.

[585] Mott was the second son of Capt. Alexander Doniphan (c.1653-1717) of Richmond County and Margaret Mott. By his marriage to Rosanna Anderson, the daughter of Capt. George Anderson, he acquired much acreage in Stafford County including Coal Trips, a large plantation on Aquia Creek where he made his home.

[586] It was this vestry that first considered replacing the wooden edifice at the Aquia Church site with a large brick church. A great controversy ensued between the vestry, burgesses, and the county residents who did not want to be taxed to pay for what they believed to be an elaborate and unnecessary building project. At this time James Waugh was also a member of the House of Burgesses. He was no doubt influential in having rejected the numerous petitions which "sundry inhabitants" had filed against the vested and proposed church (Eby, They 100).

    James succeeded Col. Henry Fitzhugh (1706-1742) as burgess of Stafford. His election was contested by John Peyton (1691-1760) of Stony Hill. Peyton's complaint against Waugh failed to produce action and in 1746 he withdrew it. Capt. Waugh served in the House of Burgesses from 1744-1746 and was replaced in the fall session of 1748 by William Fitzhugh (1725-1791).

1747
Sheriff—Peter Daniel[587] (1706-1777)
Clerk—Henry Tyler
Church Warden—Capt. John Lee (c.1709-1789)
Surveyor—George Byrne

1749
Sheriff—Benjamin Strother[588] (c.1700-1765)
Clerk—Henry Tyler
Surveyor—John Mauzy (c.1696-1780)

1750
Sheriff—James Waugh
Clerk—Henry Tyler
Tobacco Inspectors:
    Aquia—Taylor Chapman[589] (c.1715-1749) and Edward Waller[590] (1706-1753)
    Falmouth—Thomas Hord[591] (1701-1766)
    Cave's—William Mountjoy and Thomas Monroe[592] (died c.1777)

1751
Sheriff—Philip Alexander (1704-1753)
Clerk—Henry Tyler
Tobacco Inspectors—Falmouth—Thomas Hord
Surveyor—George Waller

1752
Clerk—Henry Tyler
Tobacco Inspectors—Falmouth—Thomas Hord
County Lieutenant—William Fitzhugh[593] (1721-1798)

---

[587] Peter was the son of James Daniel (c.1680-1727) and Margaret Vivian (died 1727) of Middlesex County. In 1736 he married Sarah Travers Pierson (died 1788), the daughter of Rawleigh Travers and Hannah Ball and widow of Capt. Christopher Pierson. Peter settled first in Northumberland County, then Stafford. In 1765 he signed the protest against the Stamp Act. In 1774 he was a member of the Stafford Committee of Safety.

[588] Benjamin was a major in the Stafford County Rangers. On Jan. 8, 1724 he married Mary (Mason) Fitzhugh, the widow of Col. George Fitzhugh (c.1690-1722) and the daughter of George Mason (1660-1716) and Mary Fowke. Benjamin married secondly Elizabeth (Rowzee) Waller (c.1715-1782) of Essex County, the widow of Charles Waller (1702-1749) of Essex and, later, of Stafford. Elizabeth married thirdly John Peyton (1691-1760) of Stony Hill, now Aquia Harbour subdivision.

[589] The son of Jonathan Chapman (died before 1749) and Jane Taylor and the grandson of Nathaniel Chapman (1709-1760) who had been manager of Accokeek Iron Works and owned land in Charles County, Maryland as well as in Stafford, Fauquier, and Fairfax counties. The Stafford land passed down through Jonathan to Taylor and to Taylor's heir, Thomas Chapman (1769-1827). This land, located on Chappawamsic Run, eventually ended up in the hands of the Tolson family and, well before 1848, was known as Bellfair Mills. In 1739 Taylor married Margaret Markham in Stafford.

[590] The son of Charles Waller (1674-1724) of Gloucester and Essex counties. Together with his brother Charles (1702-1749), Edward inherited land on Aquia Creek to which they removed in the 1730s with their mother and built Concord. Edward married Ann Tandy of Essex County.

[591] The son of John Hord (1664-1747) of Caroline County. John was born in Ewell, England and settled in Virginia in 1685. Thomas was born in England, came to Virginia with his parents and later became a resident of King George County. In 1726 he married Jane Miller.

[592] In 1745 Thomas Monroe married Catherine Hore, the daughter of Capt. Elias Hore (1700-1730) and Isabella Triplett. Thomas died in Fairfax County.

Colonel of the Militia—Henry Fitzhugh (1686-1758)

1753
Clerk—Henry Tyler
Surveyor—John Mauzy

1754
Clerk—Henry Tyler
Surveyor—John Mauzy

1755
Clerk—Henry Tyler
Surveyor—John Mauzy

1756
Clerk—Henry Tyler
Vestryman—Benjamin Strother

1757
Sheriff—John Stuart[594] (1728-1787)
Under Sheriff—Withers Conway[595]
Clerk—Henry Tyler
Church Wardens—Peter Daniel and Travers Cooke[596] (1730-1759)
Vestry—Peter Hedgman (c.1700-1765)   John Mercer
       Peter Daniel   John Lee
       Mott Doniphan   Travers Cooke
       Henry Tyler   John Fitzhugh (1727-1809)
       William Mountjoy   John Peyton
       Benjamin Strother   Thomas Fitzhugh (1725-1768)

1758
Sheriff—Bailey Washington, Sr. (1731-1807)
Clerk—Henry Tyler

1759
Clerk—Henry Tyler
Surveyor—George Waller

1760
Sheriff—Samuel Selden[597] (1725-1790)

---

[593] This William Fitzhugh also represented Stafford in the House of Burgesses in 1748 and 1751. Around 1755, after his second marriage, he removed to Maryland where he was appointed to the council there. Despite the fact that he had become blind during the Revolution, William took an active role on the American side as a member of the Maryland convention of 1776 and, later, of the Council of State. William inherited a large tract of land in Stafford and, deciding to sell the property, he had it surveyed. The surveyor discovered that the tract was already seated by Bailey Washington (1731-1807) who had built a large home there he called Windsor Forest.
[594] John was the son of the Rev. David Stuart (c.1692-1749) and Jane Gibbons (c.1700-1750). He was born at Fair Haven, King George and in 1749 married Frances Alexander (1728-after 1777).
[595] Withers was the son of Christopher Conway (born 1684) and Sarah Withers. In 1752 he married Dulcabella Berry, the daughter of Enoch Berry (c.1700-1763) and Dulcabella Bunbury of St. Paul's Parish.
[596] In 1754 Travers married Mary Doniphan, the daughter of Mott Doniphan. He served as a vestryman in Overwharton Parish in 1752. Travers was the father of Col. John Cooke (1755-1819) of West Farm.
[597] Samuel was born in Elizabeth City County, the son of Joseph Selden (1680-1720) and Mary Cary. Samuel signed the Leedstown Resolutions.

Clerk—Henry Tyler

1761
Clerk—Henry Tyler
Surveyors—John Mauzy and Bertrand Ewell[598] (1715-1795)

1762
Clerk—Henry Tyler
Surveyor—John Mauzy

1763
Clerk—Henry Tyler
Tobacco Inspectors—Aquia—Maj. Benjamin Strother
Surveyor—John Mauzy

1764
Clerk—Henry Tyler

1765
Clerk—Henry Tyler

1766
Sheriff—John Stuart
Clerk—Henry Tyler

1767
Sheriff—John Washington[599] (1730-1782)
Clerk—Henry Tyler
Surveyor—Thomas Bullitt[600] (1730-c.1778)

1768
Sheriff—John Brown
Clerk—Henry Tyler

1769
Sheriff—Original Young[601] (born c.1740)
Clerk—Henry Tyler

1770
Clerk—Henry Tyler

---

[598] The brother of Capt. Charles Ewell (1713-after 1747). Bertrand surveyed extensively in Prince William County.
[599] Also served as a justice in 1755, 1759, 1761, 1763, 1766-69, 1772, and probably other years as well. John was the son of Henry Washington (1694-1748) and Mary Bailey of Stafford. In 1759 John married Katherine Washington. He lived at Hylton in what is now King George County.
[600] Thomas, a French and Indian War veteran, was the son of Benjamin Bullitt (1693-1766) and Ann Carter, the daughter of Robert Carter (1663-1732). In 1766 Thomas built an inn at Hot Springs, Virginia, then a remote and hostile wilderness. He realized, however, that people were quickly settling the western "back country" and travelers had need of a place to eat and sleep. In 1773 he led a surveying party from Virginia to the falls of the Ohio River where he laid out a town where Louisville, Kentucky now stands. Thomas married Diana Moore Gwathmey.
    In March 1776 Thomas was appointed Lieutenant Colonel Deputy Adjutant General of the Southern Department. He held the rank of colonel from May 1776 to September 1778.
[601] Original resided on Cedar Run in what is now Fauquier County.

1771
Sheriff—William Edrington[602] (c.1741-1794)
Clerk—Henry Tyler

1772
Clerk—Henry Tyler
Tobacco Inspectors:
    Cave's[603]—Col. William Garrard[604] (c.1715-c.1786) and Thomas Mountjoy[605] (1739-c.1818)

1773
Sheriff—Samuel Washington[606] (1734-1781)
Clerk—Henry Tyler
Tobacco Inspectors:
    Cave's—Col. William Garrard and Thomas Mountjoy
    Aquia—Yelverton Peyton (1735-1794)
Falmouth Trustees—William Love, Edward Moor (died c.1806)

1774
Clerk—Henry Tyler

1775
Clerk—Henry Tyler
Surveyor—Griffin Garland

1776
Sheriff—Yelverton Peyton
Clerk—Henry Tyler

1777
Sheriff—Elijah Threlkeld[607] (1744-1798)
Clerk—Henry Tyler

---

[602] Also served as a justice in 1766, 1768, and probably other years as well.

[603] The minutes of the House of Burgesses for Mar. 12, 1772 include a petition from several persons claiming "that the Water in the Creek, at Cave's Inspection, is so shallow, that a Boat, with four Hogsheads of Tobacco, cannot easily go down it, and it is daily growing worse; and that the Expenses of the said Inspection considerably exceeds the Money it brings into the Treasury; and that the building of a Warehouse, by Virtue of an Order of the County Court of Stafford, at the said Inspection, was lately undertaken by Thomas Mountjoy, one of the Inspectors there, in a private, unfair, and illegal Manner, and for a much larger Sum than the Work is really worth; and therefore praying that the said Inspection may be discontinued" (Journal of the House of Burgesses of Virginia, 1770-1772, pp. 253-254). The burgesses rejected the petition.

[604] Owner of Garrard's Ordinary just north of the courthouse. He also served as a justice for Stafford in 1774, 1779-81, 1784-85 and probably other years as well.

[605] The son of Capt. William Mountjoy (1711-1777). Thomas moved to Kentucky where he died. He also served as a justice for Stafford in 1774, 1779, 1781-82, 1784-85, 1790-93, 1797, 1806-1809 and probably other years as well.

[606] Samuel was a brother of Gen. George Washington. After the Revolution, he removed to Jefferson County, now West Virginia, where he died. Samuel also served as a justice for Stafford in 1766, 1768-69, 1772 and probably other years as well.

[607] Lived on Aquia Creek at Coal Trips. Elijah was the son of Christopher Threlkeld, Jr. (1698-1757) and Susannah Threlkeld whom he married c.1719 in King George. In 1772 Elijah married Mary (Bronaugh) Waugh (died 1799), the daughter of Capt. David Bronaugh of King George and the widow of Joseph Waugh (c.1736-1763).

Tobacco Inspectors:
    Aquia—John Waller[608] (died 1791) and Col. William Garrard, Inspectors
        William Waller[609] (1740-1817), Assistant
    Cave's—Thomas Mountjoy (1739-c.1818) and Edward Raleigh, Inspectors
        Raleigh Travers Brown (1753-1803), Assistant
Surveyor—Travers Daniel, Sr. (1741-1824)

1778
Deputy Sheriff—Maj. Nathaniel Fox[610] (1748-1819)
Clerk—Thomas Gowry Strother Tyler[611] (c.1740-1816)
Tobacco Inspectors:
    Falmouth—Mason Pilcher[612] (died c.1791), Inspector
        Edward Dickenson, Assistant
    Cave's—Raleigh Travers Brown and Alvin Mountjoy[613] (1745-1827), Inspectors
        Jonathan Finnal,[614] Assistant

---

[608] John was the son of Charles Waller (1702-1749) and Elizabeth Rowzee (Strother) (c.1715-1782). John married before 1757 Mary Harrison, the daughter of William Harrison (died before 1757) of Stafford.

[609] The son of Edward Waller (1706-1753) of Essex County and Ann Tandy. Edward and his brother, Charles, built Concord on Aquia Creek. William Waller married first Elizabeth Allen (1746-1768), secondly Margaret Waller (1744-1777), and thirdly Ursula Withers (1752-1818).

[610] Nathaniel was commissioned as a first lieutenant in the 6th Virginia Regiment on Feb. 16, 1776 and was a captain on May 30 of that year. He was wounded at the Battle of Brandywine and retired from service as a major on Sept. 30, 1778. He served in the House of Delegates in 1792 and from 1794-1805. Nathaniel also served as a justice for Stafford County from 1806-1809. He married Sarah Newton.

[611] Thomas G. S. Tyler was the son of the previous clerk, Henry Tyler (c.1710-1777). Like his father, his penmanship was exceptional. Thomas married Ann Fisher Adie (1756-1818), the daughter of William Adie (1729-1797). Thomas and Ann were separated after having a large family of seven children ("Ficklen vs Tyler & als").

Among the Fredericksburg Circuit Court records are several cases regarding Thomas Tyler. According to one case, Thomas "took [the] oath of insolvent debtor 180_," having found the management of his own affairs too taxing and believing them better left in other hands. One of the suits records Thomas' claim that his father-in-law, William Adie, had unfairly deprived him of a tract of land that Tyler had deeded to him in 1782. A deposition by Anne (Adie) Tyler stated that her father "wanting confidence in his son in law Tyler but anxious to provide for their mutual support loaned [Anne] and said Tyler four negroes...Not long after the marriage aforesaid this defendant's husband sold two of the aforesaid negroes without her father's consent." As soon as William learned of this, he took back the other two slaves. In order to repay Adie for the slaves that he had sold, Thomas deeded him a parcel of land on Austin Run. In the suit Thomas claimed that it was not only unfair for William to have kept the land, but also wrong of him to have conveyed it to someone else. Thomas apparently never reimbursed his father-in-law for the slaves and William bequeathed the property to his daughter. In another case, Ficklen vs. Tyler et al, the will of William Adie was annexed in which he left his land (Bloomington) and still to son Benjamin and Tyler's 120 acres to daughter Anne, along with several slaves.

[612] Mason was the son of Moses Pilcher. He was mentioned in the British Mercantile Claims (May 1801-May 1802) as owing £41.18.21 ½ to Fredericksburg Store. The notation in the claim read, "He died about 13 years ago possessed of considerable property but very much in debt. His executrix proceeded to sell and pay immediately after his death, but the estate was found inadequate" (British 169).

[613] Alvin was the son of William Mountjoy (1711-1777). During the Revolution, he served as a first lieutenant under the command of Col. William Washington (1752-1810). He resigned from service in December 1777. In that year he married Mary "Mollie" Edwards (1760-1839), the daughter of Andrew Edwards (1725-1788). By May 1786 Alvin had moved to Bourbon County, Kentucky where he served as sheriff and justice of the peace. He died in Pendleton County, Kentucky.

[614] Jonathan married Magdalin Monteith Doniphan, the daughter of Sir Thomas Monteith (1694-1747) and Phillis Gallop of King George and the widow of Anderson Doniphan. The Finnal cemetery is located in a field just off Bethel Church Road (State Route 600) about .6 mile from White Oak Road (State Route 218).

1779
Sheriff—Charles Carter, Jr.[615] (1738-1796)
Clerk—Thomas G. S. Tyler

1780
Sheriff—Charles Carter
Clerk—Thomas G. S. Tyler
Deputy Clerk—Henry R. Conway
Tobacco Inspectors:
    Dixon's—Joseph Vant (Fant)[616] (c.1738-1812)
Escheator—Charles Carter
Surveyor—Travers Daniel, Sr.

1781
Sheriff—Col. William Garrard
Clerk—Thomas G. S. Tyler
Tobacco Inspectors:
    Falmouth—Mason Pilcher and Edward Dickinson, Inspectors
                  Francis Jett[617] (c.1735-1791), Assistant
Surveyor—Travers Daniel, Sr.

1782
Clerk—Thomas G. S. Tyler
Commissioners of the Land Tax:
    Nathaniel Fox and Edward Cary (Northern District)
    Nathaniel Fox and Elijah Threlkeld (Southern District)

---

[615] Known as "Charles Carter of Ludlow," this was the son of Charles Carter (1707-1764) of Stanstead and Cleve and Mary Walker (died 1742). Around 1755 Charles, Jr. married Elizabeth Chiswell (1737-1804), the daughter of Col. John Chiswell (c.1715-1766) and Elizabeth Randolph (1715-1776).

[616] The name of Joseph's first wife is unknown, but by her he had Betsy (born 1774), Annie (born 1774) who married in 1809 Fielding Ficklen (died 1809), John Penn (born 1776), and George Stanfield (born 1778). Joseph married secondly Hannah Lewis. He was the son of William Fant (born c.1720) and Catherine Stewart.

[617] Francis was born in King George (later Stafford), the son of Peter Jett (c.1717-1784) and Rebecca Bowen, the daughter of Stephen Bowen (died 1749). Francis married Barsheba Porch (c.1738-1817), the daughter of Richard and Mary Porch. The Fredericksburg Circuit Court records include papers relating to the settlement of Francis Jett's estate. After he died at his White Oak home, his will disappeared under questionable circumstances and his heirs took the issue to the Stafford Court. Archibald Rollow (1755-1829), Francis' son-in-law, stated that two to three weeks after Francis' death, he happened to be at the home of his widowed mother-in-law along with his brother-in-law, Thomas Jett, and several others. "After drinking pretty freely and being a little lively with liquor, a paper was handed to him (by whom he doth not recollect) which he was requested to put in the fire." Archibald did as he was asked, "wholly ignorant at that time, of its contents, and without any fraudulent design whatever." Archibald claimed to have no objection to the will himself, but noted that "he can only account for his conduct from the insinuation of the defendant Thomas Jett, who having a legacy of five pounds only, left him by the said will could alone be dissatisfied therewith, and had frequently declared before the will was destroyed that his father was incapable in law of making any will and that consequently his mother (one of the complainants) would be put to her thirds and be deprived of so great an interest as her deceased husband had intended for her" ("Cox vs Jett").

    There is no record of this case in the surviving Stafford records, but it ended up in Fredericksburg on appeal. That judge evidently believed Archibald and proceeded to reconstruct the will. Mrs. Jett was given a life interest in the estate.

1783
Sheriff—Col. William Garrard
Clerk—Thomas G. S. Tyler
Deputy Clerk—James Primm[618] (1754-1820)
Commissioners of the Land Tax:
      William Alexander (c.1736-1810)
      John Hardy[619] (17_-1794)
Coroners—Thomas Mountjoy (1739-c.1818) and Gerrard Banks[620] (1725-1787)
Surveyor—Travers Daniel, Sr.

1784
Sheriff—Mason Pilcher
Deputy Sheriffs—James Primm and Nathaniel Fox
Clerk—Thomas G. S. Tyler
Coroners—Thomas Mountjoy and Gerrard Banks
Commissioners of the Land Tax—John Rowzee Peyton[621] (1754-1799), William Alexander, John Hardy
Surveyor—Travers Daniel, Sr.

1785
Sheriff—Garrard Banks
Clerk—Thomas G. S. Tyler
Coroners—William Phillips (1744-1797) and Daniel Triplett[622] (1735-1799)
Commissioners of the Land Tax—John R. Peyton, William Alexander, John Hardy
Church Wardens—Thomas Mountjoy and John R. Peyton
Vestry—John Mountjoy[623] (1741-1825)   Col. William Garrard

---

[618] James was the son of John Primm and Margaret Welch. In the early 1800s James and friends Mason Harding and Edward Bethel left Stafford for the "Western Country" ("McInteer vs McInteer").

[619] John Hardy married Hannah Ball (Daniel) (Hedgman) (Foote) (1737-1829), the daughter of Peter Daniel (1706-1777) and the widow of George Hedgman (1734-1760) and Gilson Foote (1736-1770).

[620] The son of Adam Banks (1700-1755) and Rosanna Bryan (died after 1784). Gerrard married Frances Bruce, the daughter of Charles Bruce (c.1680-1754) and Elizabeth Pannell and lived at Green Bank on the Rappahannock River.

[621] John lived on the old Peyton plantation Stony Hill. He was the son of John Peyton (1691-1760) and Elizabeth Rowzee (c.1715-1782). John Rowzee graduated from William and Mary College. In 1773 he traveled to Florida where he was captured by the Spanish. They marched him to New Mexico where he was imprisoned. The following year he escaped and set off for Virginia. Enroute, he participated in the Battle of Point Pleasant (1774). From 1776-1783 he served in the Continental Line and in 1777 married Anne Hooe (1754-1833), the daughter of Howson Hooe (died c.1796) of Occoquan.

[622] Daniel was the son of William Triplett (died 1749) and Elizabeth Hedgman, the daughter of Nathaniel Hedgman (before 1682-1721). Daniel Triplett was a merchant by profession. He served as a justice in Stafford from 1784-1785.

[623] John was the son of William Mountjoy (1711-1777). With his father he was a signer of the Leedstown Resolutions. In September 1776 the Continental Army was formed to provide a common defense against the British. Virginia was authorized to create fifteen district battalions, later designated regiments. Each district battalion was ordered to raise companies commanded by local patriots.

    Stafford organized a company of about eighty men under the command of Capt. John Mountjoy. Initially known as the Caroline District Minute Battalion, it was later renamed the 10th Virginia of Foot, 9th Company. This company included men from Caroline, Spotsylvania, and King George as well as from Stafford. Mountjoy's troops fought at the Second New Jersey Campaign (January to June 1777), Brandywine (Sept. 11, 1777), and Monmouth (June 28, 1778). On June 15, 1818 John applied for a pension in Pendleton County, Kentucky.

Moses Phillips[624] (c.1736-1811)　　　　Elijah Threlkeld
Capt. George Burroughs[625]　　　　　　James Withers[626] (died 1791)
Surveyor—Travers Daniel, Sr.

1786
Sheriff—Gerrard Banks
Clerk—Thomas G. S. Tyler
Commissioners of the Revenue:
　　William Alexander (District 1—southern half of county)[627]
　　William Garrard (District 2—northern half of county)
Assistant Commissioners of the Revenue:
　　Elijah Threlkeld and Nathaniel Fox
Escheators:
　　Bailey Washington, Jr. (1753-1814)
　　Thomas Fitzhugh[628] (1760-1820)
　　William Hewitt[629] (1740-1795)
Surveyor—Travers Daniel, Sr.

1787
Sheriff—Thomas Mountjoy
Deputy Sheriff—John Mountjoy
Clerk—Thomas G. S. Tyler
Tobacco Inspectors:
　　Aquia—Thomas Peyton (died 1795)

　　　　In 1772 John married Mary Ann Garrard (1753-1823), the daughter of Col. William Garrard (c.1715-c.1786) and Mary Naughty (born c.1721) and the sister of James Garrard (1749-1822) who became governor of Kentucky. From his father he inherited the mill at Brooke. Around 1794 he removed to Kentucky and served as a justice of the peace in Campbell County.

[624] Moses kept an ordinary on the south side of the present courthouse in the vicinity of Lewis Insurance Agency. The Stafford court granted him licenses to keep the ordinary in 1780 and 1785 (and probably in other years as well). Moses was probably the son of William Phillips who emigrated from Wales to Philadelphia. In Pennsylvania William married ___ Penn, a descendant of William Penn, by whom he had eight children. William eventually moved his family to Spotsylvania where Moses was born. Around 1760 Moses married Sarah Jeffries (born c.1740) of Amherst County, Virginia by whom he had eight children. In the fall of 1789 Moses removed to Mason County, Kentucky. Shortly after arriving there, three of his sons, Moses, Jr. (c.1775-1787), Thomas, and John (born c.1773), were attacked by Indians, the first two being killed and scalped. John managed to escape. Moses, Sr. eventually settled on North Fork and Stone Lick Creek. He died at nearby Pea Ridge (*Weekly Maysville Eagle*).
　　Moses' daughter Susan (1765-1834) married William Byram (1764-1829). William was the son of William Byram and Sarah Gough of Stafford. Daughter Lucy Phillips (c.1752-1836) married c.1781 Peter Byram (c.1760-c.1799), also a son of William and Sarah (Gough) Byram.

[625] Possibly the same George Burroughs who was appointed sergeant of the 2nd Virginia regiment in May 1776. He was a regimental quartermaster in February 1777 and retired from service in September 1778. A George Burroughs also served in the War of 1812.

[626] James was the eldest son of Thomas Withers (1724-1784) and the grandson of James Withers (1680-1746) and Elizabeth Keene. Thomas was born at his father's home on Potomac Creek and died at the home of his son, Joseph Withers (1757-after 1798) in Fauquier.

[627] The dividing line between the northern and southern district was Potomac Creek/Run.

[628] Thomas replaced Bailey Washington who resigned.

[629] Replaced Thomas Fitzhugh who resigned. William was the son of James Hewitt (died 1763) and Susanna Crump (1723-1797) of King George County. He married Catherine Edmonds (1756-1823), the daughter of John Edmonds (1732-1798) of Fauquier County.
　　William resided at Locust Grove in Stafford, which he inherited from his father. In 1815 this tract consisted of 855 acres on White Oak Run. After the War Between the States, the old Hewitt house and 169 acres belonged to Simeon C. Peyton. The property passed to Simeon's son, William T. Peyton.

    Dixon's—William Brown Wallace[630] (1757-1833)
Commissioners of the Revenue:
  William Alexander (District 1)
  William Mountjoy (District 2)
Surveyor—Travers Daniel
Deputy Surveyor—James Leach[631] (died c.1823)

1788
Deputy Sheriff—John Mountjoy
Clerk—John Taylor Ford[632] (died 1824)
Tobacco Inspectors:
  Falmouth—James Withers and William Jett
Commissioners of the Revenue:
  William Alexander (District 1)
  William Mountjoy (District 2)

1789
Sheriff—William Hewitt
Deputy Sheriffs—Robert Howson Hooe (1748-1834) and John Curtis[633] (c.1735-1813)
Constable—George Fant[634] (1745-1839)
Clerk—John T. Ford
Deputy Clerk—William Garrard, Jr.[635]
Commissioners of the Revenue:
  William Alexander (District 1)
  William Mountjoy (District 2)
Captain of the Militia—Mason Pilcher
Overseers of the Roads:

---

[630] In March 1777 William was appointed second lieutenant in Col. William Grayson's regiment. He transferred to Col. Nathaniel Gist's regiment in April 1779 and resigned from service in June of that year. He was later appointed second lieutenant of the 1st Continental Artillery and was taken prisoner at Camden in August 1780. He was paroled at the close of the war.

[631] The spelling of this surname varies between "Leach" and "Leitch." James was probably the son of Benjamin Leitch (died c.1812). He owned part of the Richlands tract between Route 17 and the Rappahannock River near the present site of Richlands Baptist Church.

[632] Johnston says of John T. Ford, [He] was a good and well-informed clerk afterwards became clerk of Fauquier county; thence clerk of the superior court of the United States; and finally second assistant postmaster-general, and died while holding this latter position...Mr. John T. Ford was, when appointed clerk of the old chancery court, clerk of the courts of Stafford county. He was a thorough clerk, of more than ordinary intelligence, and a sound lawyer. He had fine conversational powers, and his office was the daily resort of very many men who afterwards became distinguished, such as Robert C. Stanard, John W. Green, John T. Lomax, Philip Harrison, and the like, who were kindred spirits, and much to the advantage of the junior clerks in the office, who could but listen and be improved by the constant discussions incident to such meetings" (Johnston 122).
  In 1810 John married in Fredericksburg Patsy Gregory (c.1786-1858), the daughter of Walter Gregory.

[633] John was the son of Richard Curtis (born c.1710) and Sarah Jones, the daughter of George Jones and Anne Philpin of King George County. He was a brother of George Curtis, Sr. (1730-c.1806) of Stafford. John married Elizabeth Porch, the daughter of Richard Porch.

[634] George was the son of William Fant (born c.1720) and Catherine Stewart. On Apr. 1, 1777 George enlisted as a private for a period of three years in Capt. Abell Westfall's Company, 8th Virginia Regiment. The name of his first wife in unknown but by her he had sons Armistead, Fielding (1775-1824), Nelson (born 1777), and a daughter known only as M. M. He married secondly in 1785 Elizabeth Lewis Sewell, a widow. George died in Coles County, Illinois

[635] The son of Col. William Garrard (c.1715-c.1786). Little is known of William Jr., but his older brother, Col. James Garrard (1749-1822) became the second governor of Kentucky.

Wilson Hilton—"from Mrs. McDaniel by way of Peytons Mill to Bailey Washingtons gate"
Benjamin Pettit[636] (died 1800:05)—"from Falmouth to Chapman's Ordinary"
Surveyor—Travers Daniel, Sr.

1790
Sheriff—William Hewitt[637]
Deputy Sheriffs—Robert H. Hooe and John Curtis
Constables—John Connor, William Jett, and George Fant[638]
Clerk—John T. Ford
Coroner—William Phillips
Commissioners of the Revenue:
 William Alexander (District 1)
Tobacco Inspectors:
 Falmouth—William Jett and ____ Winlock[639]
 Dixon's—James(?) Withers and ____ Wallace
Captains of the Militia—John Wallace[640] (1761-1829) and George Fant
Overseers of the Roads:
 Elijah Nichols—"leading from near Richard Coopers to a road called Popular [Poplar] road"
 William Poles—"from the Red House to Aquia"
 James Latham—"from James Lane to Drummond's old field"[641]
 Richard Stone[642] (died 1825)—"from Mrs. McDaniel by way of Peytons Mill to Bailey Washingtons gate"
 Philip Callender—"from the Stage Road to James Withers Mill"
 James Faunt [Fant]—"from Falmouth to Chapman's Ordinary"
 William Jones—"from Accakeek Bridge to the Courthouse"
 John Smith—"from Acquia to Chappawamsick"

---

[636] In 1772 Benjamin married Mary Banks and moved to Lincoln County, Kentucky.

[637] William Hewitt's last year of acting as sheriff of Stafford County was 1790/91 during which time he collected the taxes as usual. For whatever reason, he never made an accounting or conveyed these funds to the Commonwealth. When he died in 1795, then sheriff William Phillips attempted to sell part of the estate with the intention of paying the state what was due in taxes. On Feb. 7, 1792 he put up for auction Hewitt's 600-acre farm, Locust Grove, and 12 Negroes, but was unable to complete the sale for lack of bidders. Phillips repeated these sales each year until he died in 1797, never settling the account with the state. The sales were attempted each January or February through 1803, though they were never completed due to want of bidders. In 1808 the Commonwealth brought suit against William's widow Catherine and his heirs. Still the case was not settled. In June 1816 William's land was divided between his heirs, two of whom then sold their portions to other individuals who were unaware that there was a lien on the property. Finally, William Stannard Marshall was made commissioner and ordered to sell what he could. In Feb. 1819 he sold part of Locust Grove and from the proceeds passed $417.38 on to the State ("Hewitt vs Samuel").

[638] On May 10, 1790 George Fant was replaced by John Connor who was replaced on June 14, 1790 by William Jett.

[639] Probably William Winlock.

[640] Wallace was appointed in April 1790 but the appointment was reversed in June of that year. George Fant was appointed in his place. He was the son of Dr. Michael Wallace (1719-1767) and Elizabeth Brown (born 1723). John married Elizabeth Hooe (c.1766-1850).

[641] "Drummond's old field" was also known in the mid-18th century as "Drummond's Race Ground." It was part of Henry Fitzhugh's (1723-1783) property (part of the old Wilkinson patent), which he leased to Andrew Drummond. It later became known as Mulberry Hill and was the home of Alexander Keene Philips (1805-1892), a wealthy Fredericksburg merchant.

[642] Richard Stone lived at Mt. Olive in what is now the Marine Corps reservation. He married Hannah Withers (c.1796-1857).

Elijah Curtis (c.1765-before Feb. 1829)   John James, Jr.
Thomas Seddon (died 1810)   Henry Jones

Surveyor—Travers Daniel, Sr.

1791
Sheriff—Daniel Triplett
Deputy Sheriffs—Elijah Threlkeld, John Mountjoy, Daniel Bell
Constables—William Jett,[643] Enoch Berry Benson,[644] Anthony Marquis[645] (1752-1821)
Clerk—Valentine Peyton[646] (1756-1815)
Deputy Clerk—John Fox[647] (c.1770-1843)
Court Commissioners—George Strother[648] (died 1811), Isaac Newton[649] (c.1745-1838), James Hore
Commissioners of the Revenue:
  William Alexander (District 1)
  William Mountjoy (District 2)
Assessors—George Strother, Isaac Newton, James Hore
Captain of the Militia—Lewis Mason[650] (born 1757)
Tobacco Inspectors:
  Falmouth—William Jett, Edward Dickinson, Mason Pilcher
Overseers of the Roads:
  Elijah Threlkeld[651]—"from lower ford on Accakeek Run to Potomack Church, from the same
      ford to John Mountjoys Mill"
  William Alexander—"from Falmouth to Potomac Run"
  Basil Burroughs—"from Acquia to Chappawamsick"
  Thomas Seddon—"from Potomac run to Ackokeek run"
Surveyor—Travers Daniel, Sr.

1792
Sheriff—Daniel Triplett, William Phillips

---

[643] Resigned and was replaced in November by Berry Benson.

[644] Berry was replaced in August 1792 by Anthony Marquis. He was the son of James Benson (died 1812) and Dulcebella Berry. By 1831 Berry was a resident of Union County, Kentucky.

[645] The spelling of this surname varies between "Marquis" and "Marquess." Anthony married Elizabeth Winlock and lived about ½ mile above the old Berea Post Office. He purchased this farm in 1803 from the estate of James Hunter (1721-1784).

[646] The son of John Peyton (1691-1760) and Elizabeth Rowzee (c.1715-1782) of Stony Hill. During the Revolution, he served as a surgeon. Around 1780 he married Mary Butler Washington (1760-1822), the daughter of Bailey Washington (1731-1807) and Catherine Storke (born 1723).

[647] The younger half brother of Nathaniel Fox (1748-1819). He married Nancy "Ann" Threlkeld (1772-1828), the daughter of Elijah Threlkeld (1744-1798).

[648] The son of Anthony Strother (1710-1765) and his second wife, Mary James. In 1795 George married his cousin, Sarah Kenyon, and lived at Albion on the Rappahannock River.

[649] Isaac was the son of William Newton (1705-1787). Isaac married Peggy Strother and resided at Little Falls on the Rappahannock east of Falmouth (Eby, They 268). This tract had been patented by the immigrant John Newton, Sr. and was in King George County until the boundary change of 1777. Little Falls is about 2 ½ miles east of Fredericksburg on U. S. Route 3. The south side of the farm adjoined the lands of Col. Joseph Ball. From his father Isaac inherited the westernmost 250 acres with the dwelling house. He also inherited the 4-acre freestone quarry on the river and the adjoining 10-acre mill lot. Isaac purchased other parcels of the property from his siblings. An insurance policy issued by the Mutual Assurance Society in 1796 described the house as 46 feet long by 18 feet wide, 1 ½ stories high, built of wood, and covered with wooden shingles.

[650] Lewis was the son of John Mason (1722-c.1796) and Mary Nelson (172_-c.1801), the daughter of Henry Nelson (c.1700-c.1750). He married Mary Bethel (died 1831) and had issue: Nimrod, Bartlett, Nelson, and James.

[651] Resigned and was replaced in November by Henry Southard.

Deputy Sheriff—Col. Enoch Mason[652]
Constables—John Day, William Alexander, William Holliday, Berry Benson, Anthony Marquis
Jailers—John Cropp[653] (died 1830), Robert Cropp,[654] William Brooke
Coroners—Henry Vowles (1752-c.1803) and George Brent[655] (1760-1804)
Clerk—Valentine Peyton
Deputy Clerk—John Fox
Court Commissioners—James Lyon, William Gant, William Alexander,[656] Kellis Hord[657]
Commissioners of the Revenue:
    Kellis Hord (District 1)
    William Mountjoy (District 2)
Assessors—James Lyon and William Gant
Tobacco Inspectors:
    Aquia—Thomas Peyton
Overseers of the Roads:
    William Ball[658] (1768-1815)—"from Potomack run to Ackokeek run"
    Charles Sterne[659] (1756-1818)—"from Stony Bridge to Aquia Road"
    Pearson Williams[660] (c.1743-c.1824)—"from the lower ford on Accakeek run to Potowmack Church"
Surveyor—Travers Daniel, Sr.

1793

Clerk—Valentine Peyton
Deputy Clerk—John Fox
Commissioners of the Revenue:
    Kellis Hord (District 1)
    William Mountjoy (District 2)
Coroners—Henry Vowles and George Brent
Tobacco Inspectors:
    Dixon's—Charles Withers[661] (c.1761-1818)

---

[652] Enoch served in the U. S. Army during the War of 1812.
[653] The son of James Cropp, Jr. (born 1755) and Joyce Hinson. John married Eliza Fallis (born 1798), the daughter of Thomas Fallis and Polly James.
[654] Robert was the son of James Cropp and Susan Thomas.
[655] The son of Robert Brent (1730-1780) and Ann Carroll (1733-1804). George was born at Woodstock. In 1785 he married Molly Fitzhugh, the daughter of William Fitzhugh (1725-1791) of Marmion. She married secondly Henry Woodrow. Robert served as a lieutenant in the Virginia Line during the Revolution and was present at the siege of Yorktown. He was also a colonel in the Stafford militia.
[656] William Alexander resigned and was replaced on May 14, 1792 by Kellis Hord.
[657] Kellis was the son of Peter Hord (c.1715-c.1790). A notation in the list of alienations at the end of the 1792 land tax records states that Peter's will ordered his 620 acres be divided equally between his two sons, Kellis and Peter, Jr.
[658] The son of William Ball (died 1782) and Martha Brumfield. William married Jane Vernon, the widow of Abner Vernon (died 1792), bookkeeper at Rappahannock Forge.
[659] Charles was the son of Francis Sterne (died 1804) and was born in Stafford. Around 1789 he married Susannah Waller (1762-1834), the daughter of John Waller (1732-1753) and Mary Matthews. In October 1792 Charles Sterne resigned his position as overseer of the road and was replaced by James Fant. Charles and his family removed to Pendleton County, Kentucky. During the Revolution, Charles served as a sergeant in the Continental Line.
[660] Pearson was the son of ___ Williams and Polly Combs. During the Revolution, Pearson served as a private in the 3rd Virginia Regiment. He was the father of Nathaniel P., John P., Charles, Walter, and Hannah B. Williams.
[661] Charles was the son of James (1736-c.1818) and Susan Withers (died before 1810). He lived in what later became known as the Chartters Place on Sanford Road (State Route 670). He was buried on the west side of Sanford Road in a clump of trees.

Aquia (?)—James Withers[662] (1736-c.1818)

Overseers of the Roads:
- John Holloway[663] (died c.1831)—"from Poplar Road to the Old Furnace"
- Kenaz Ralls[664] (1763-after 1833)—"Acquia Road beginning at the Marsh Road and running from thence to the borders of Fauquier"
- John Wallace[665] (1761-1829)—"from Chapman's old Ordinary[666] to Joseph Fants gate"
- Joseph Fant—"from Joseph Fants gate to Falmouth"
- James Leach—"from Strothers Mill to Wests Road leading from thence to the Pea Fields"
- Thomas Ludwell Lee[667]—"from Potomac run to the Courthouse"

Surveyor—Travers Daniel. Sr.
Deputy Surveyor—James Leach

1794

Sheriff—Col. William Phillips
Deputy Sheriff—Col. Enoch Mason
Clerk—Valentine Peyton
Deputy Clerk—John Fox
Commissioners of the Revenue:
- Kellis Hord (District 1)
- William Mountjoy (District 2)

1795

Sheriff—James Primm
Clerk—Valentine Peyton
Commissioners of the Revenue:
- Kellis Hord (District 1)
- William Mountjoy (District 2)

1796

Sheriff—Henry Vowles
Deputy Sheriff—Col. Enoch Mason, Samuel H. Peyton[668]
Clerk—Valentine Peyton
Tobacco Inspectors:
- Aquia—Henry Peyton[669] (1744-1814) and Alexander Gaddis[670] (died c.1811)

---

[662] James Withers was the son of John Withers (1713-1794) and Hannah Allen (died 1801), the daughter of William and Margaret Allen of Prince William. In 1757 James married Susan Waller, the daughter of Charles Waller (17_-c.1750). In 1794 he inherited his father's land on Rocky Run.

[663] John's Holloway ancestors were Quakers who came to Stafford to work at Rappahannock Forge. By about 1812 most of the Quakers had moved west but John remained in Stafford where he died. He resided at Milton Christie's old farm on Poplar Road (State Route 616), just southeast of Poplar Grove and owned what later became known as Kellogg's Mill on Potomac Run. The "Old Furnace" referred to here is Accokeek Furnace.

[664] The court records note that Kenaz Ralls "who is displaced," was replaced on Apr. 9, 1793 by Enoch Harding. Kenaz was called out for military service in 1781 by Benjamin Harrison. He served as a substitute in Capt. Warren's company of the Prince William County militia. Kenaz was the son of Edward Ralls (1725-1785) and Mary Rawleigh (died c.1804).

[665] John was the son of Dr. Michael Wallace (1719-1767) and Elizabeth Brown (born 1723). In 1792 he married Elizabeth Hooe (c.1766-1850), the daughter of Howson Hooe (died c.1796) of Prince William County. John served as an officer in the Revolution (*Virginia Herald*, May 6, 1829).

[666] The exact location of Chapman's Ordinary is unknown, but it seems to have been somewhere on the Warrenton Road (U. S. Route 17) in the vicinity of Falmouth.

[667] Lee resigned and was replaced on Apr. 9, 1793 by Charles Bruce (c.1771-1845).

[668] Samuel served in the War of 1812.

[669] Henry was the son of Yelverton Peyton (1735-1794).

Commissioners of the Revenue:
  Kellis Hord (District 1)
  None named for District 2

1797
Sheriff—Daniel Triplett[671] (1753-1818)
Deputy Sheriffs—Henry Vowles, Col. Enoch Mason, Elijah Threlkeld
Clerk—Valentine Peyton
Commissioners of the Revenue:
  Kellis Hord (District 1)
  Capt. George Burroughs[672] (District 2)
Tobacco Inspectors:
  Aquia—Henry Peyton
Deputy Surveyor—James Leach

1798
Sheriff—Hancock Eustace (1768-1829)
Deputy Sheriffs—Col. Enoch Mason and William Mason
Clerk—Valentine Peyton
Commissioners of the Revenue:
  Kellis Hord (District 1)
  Capt. George Burroughs (District 2)
Tobacco Inspectors:
  Aquia—Henry Peyton
Deputy Surveyor—James Leach

1799
Sheriff—Elijah Nichols
Clerk—Valentine Peyton
Commissioners of the Revenue:
  Kellis Hord (District 1)
  Capt. George Burroughs (District 2)
Tobacco Inspectors:
  Aquia—Henry Peyton
Deputy Surveyor—James Leach

1800
Sheriff—John Moncure[673] (1772-1822)
Deputy Sheriffs—James Primm and Robert Crutcher[674] (died 1829)
Clerk—Valentine Peyton[675]
Tobacco Inspectors:
  Aquia—Henry Peyton
Commissioners of the Revenue:
  Kellis Hord (District 1)

---

[670] This was the son of Alexander Gaddis (c.1745-1786), both of whom resided at Palace Green on the border of Wide Water and Aquia Harbour subdivision.
[671] Daniel was the son of Francis Triplett (died c.1767) of King George County. He married in Falmouth Elizabeth Richards, the daughter of John Richards (1734-1785) and Susannah Coleman (died 1778).
[672] George served as a vestryman for Aquia Church in 1816 and possibly other years as well. His daughter, Elizabeth, married Hawkins Stone (1748-1810). George was also a veteran of the War of 1812.
[673] The son of John Moncure (1747-1784) and Anne Conway (born c.1750). John was born at Dipple and in 1792 married Alice Peachy Gaskins (1774-1860).
[674] Robert served as a major during the War of 1812.
[675] The 1800 personal property tax records list Valentine as owning 23 slaves, 10 horses, and a 4-wheeled coach or chariot.

Capt. George Burroughs[676] (District 2)
Presidential Electors—Col. John Cooke (1755-1819), John Taliaferro Brooke (1761-1821), Travers Daniel, Isaac Newton[677] (died 1838), John Moncure (1772-1822)
Deputy Surveyor—James Leach

1801
Sheriff—James Primm
Deputy Sheriff—Robert Crutcher
Clerk—Valentine Peyton
Commissioners of the Revenue:
    Kellis Hord (District 1)
    Capt. George Burroughs (District 2)
Tobacco Inspectors:
    Aquia—Henry Peyton and Alexander Gaddis
Escheator—Col. Enoch Mason

1802
Sheriff—Benjamin Ficklen (1737-c.1806)
Deputy Sheriff—Robert Crutcher
Clerk—Valentine Peyton
Commissioners of the Revenue:
    Kellis Hord (District 1)
    Capt. George Burroughs (District 2)
Tobacco Inspectors:
    Aquia—Henry Peyton and Alexander Gaddis

1803
Sheriff—James Primm
Deputy Sheriffs—Robert Crutcher and Innis Browne[678]
Clerk—Valentine Peyton
Commissioners of the Revenue:
    Kellis Hord (District 1)
    Capt. George Burroughs (District 2)
Tobacco Inspectors:
    Aquia—Henry Peyton and Alexander Gaddis
Coroner—Robert H. Hooe

1804
Clerk—Valentine Peyton
Commissioners of the Revenue:
    Kellis Hord (District 1)
    Capt. George Burroughs (District 2)
Tobacco Inspectors:
    Aquia—Henry Peyton and Alexander Gaddis
Deputy Surveyor—James Leach

1805
Sheriff—Joseph Botts[679] (1748-1814)
Deputy Sheriff—Benjamin Ficklen
Clerk—Valentine Peyton

---

[676] The 1800 personal property tax records list George as owning 9 slaves and 9 horses.
[677] Isaac served in the War of 1812.
[678] Innis married Sarah Botts (1787-c.1826), the daughter of Aaron Botts (1746-1790).
[679] Joseph was the son of Seth Botts (1713-1776) and Sabina Bridwell. He was born in Stafford and married in 1772 in Prince William County Catherine Butler. Joseph died in Montgomery, Kentucky.

Commissioners of the Revenue:
    Kellis Hord (District 1)
    Capt. George Burroughs (District 2)
Tobacco Inspectors:
    Aquia—Henry Peyton and Alexander Gaddis
Escheator—Col. Enoch Mason

1806
Sheriff—Samuel Heath Peyton (c.1770-1832)
Clerk—Valentine Peyton
Commissioners of the Revenue:
    Samuel H. Peyton (District 1)
    Nathaniel Pope Williams[680] (District 2)

1807
Clerk—Valentine Peyton
Commissioners of the Revenue:
    Samuel H. Peyton (District 1)
    Nathaniel P. Williams (District 2)
Deputy Surveyor—James Leach[681]

1808
Sheriff—Samuel H. Peyton
Deputy Sheriff—William Bell[682] (1771-1855)
Clerk—Valentine Peyton

1809
Sheriff—Samuel H. Peyton
Deputy Sheriff—William Bell
Clerk—Valentine Peyton
Clerk of the Superior Court—John Taylor Ford
Commissioners of the Revenue:
    Thomas Fristoe (1767-1815) (District 1)
    Nathaniel P. Williams (District 2)

1810
Sheriff—Col. Enoch Mason
Deputy Sheriff—William Bell
Clerk—John Moncure Conway[683] (1779-1864)
Commissioners of the Revenue:

---

[680] Nathaniel was the son of Pearson Williams (c.1743-c.1824). Other siblings included John P., Walter, and Hannah B. Williams. Nathaniel married Polly Combs, the daughter of Joseph Combs (c.1751-1810) and Margaret Rousseau (born c.1760). He resided in the northern end of the county on land that is now a part of the Marine Corps reservation. Nathaniel served in the War of 1812.

[681] James served in the War of 1812.

[682] William was the son of one of the John Bells of Stafford. He married Elizabeth Ratliff (1775-1847) of Stafford and was very involved in county affairs. He resided in Falmouth where he operated a tavern as early as 1807 and until 1827 or longer. William was the first known tax collector for Falmouth, serving as such in 1811 and 1812. He was also First Inspector of Tobacco at Dixon's Warehouse in Falmouth from at least 1830 until 1834 or 1835. William served as Assistant to the Marshall for the Eastern District of Virginia and, as such, certified the county censuses of 1820, 1830, and 1840. In 1800 he was captain of the Falmouth Company, 2nd Battalion, 45th Regiment, Virginia Militia. William and his family lived in Falmouth until around 1845 when they removed to Montgomery, Alabama.

[683] According to J. Johnston, John M. Conway was "a man of liberal education and an intelligent, faithful clerk, and a highly esteemed citizen." His son, Eustace Conway (1857-1887) was a circuit court judge.

Nathaniel P. Williams (District 1)
Thomas Fristoe[684] (District 2)
Surveyor—Travers Daniel, Sr.

1811
Sheriff—Samuel H. Peyton
Deputy Sheriff—William Bell
Clerk—John M. Conway
Commissioners of the Revenue:
Nathaniel P. Williams (District 1)
Thomas Fristoe (District 2)
Tax Collector—Falmouth—William Bell

1812
Deputy Sheriff—William Bell
Clerk—John M. Conway
Commissioners of the Revenue:
Nathaniel P. Williams (District 1)
Thomas Fristoe (District 2)
Tax Collector—Falmouth—William Bell

1813
Deputy Sheriff—William Bell
Clerk—John M. Conway
Commissioners of the Revenue:
Nathaniel P. Williams (District 1)
Thomas Fristoe (District 2)
Surveyor—Gabriel Long

1814
Deputy Sheriff—William Bell
Clerk—John M. Conway
Deputy Clerk—James Waller Ford (1791-1865)
Commissioners of the Revenue:
Thomas Fristoe (District 1)
Nathaniel P. Williams (District 2)

1815
Deputy Sheriff—William Bell
Clerk—John M. Conway
Deputy Clerks—Pichegru Woolfolk[685] (c.1795-1862) and James W. Ford
Commissioners of the Revenue:
Samuel Hampson Skinker[686] (1785-1856) (District 1)
Nathaniel P. Williams (District 2)
Deputy Surveyor—James Leach

---

[684] Thomas served in the War of 1812. He was adjutant (1813) and company captain (1814) of the 45th Virginia Militia.

[685] Pichergru was born at Holly Hill in Caroline County, the only son of Charles (c.1763-1803) and Frances Woolfolk (1760-1825). He inherited this property at his father's death and was buried there. In 1819 he married Angelina Frances Winston and seems to have resided in Caroline for much of his life. At one time he served as sheriff of that county.

[686] In 1814 Samuel was paymaster of the 45th Virginia Militia.

1816
Deputy Sheriff—William Bell
Clerk—John M. Conway
Deputy Clerk—Pichergru Woolfolk
Commissioners of the Revenue:
    Samuel H. Skinker (District 1)
    Nathaniel P. Williams (District 2)
Surveyor—James Leach

1817
Sheriff—Nathaniel Fox
Deputy Sheriff—William Bell
Clerk—John M. Conway
Deputy Clerk—Henry R. Conway
Commissioners of the Revenue—Benjamin Ficklen (died 1821)
                                     Samuel H. Skinker

1818
Sheriff—Hancock Eustace
Deputy Sheriffs—William Bell and Thomas Hill
Clerk—John M. Conway
Deputy Clerk—Henry R. Conway
Commissioners of the Revenue:
    Samuel H. Peyton (District 1)
    Nathaniel P. Williams (District 2)
Deputy Surveyor—James Leach

1819
Deputy Sheriffs—William Bell and John Moncure (1772-1822)
Constable—N. O'Bryan
Deputy Clerk—Henry R. Conway
Commissioners of the Revenue:
    Samuel H. Peyton (District 1)
    Nathaniel P. Williams (District 2)
Deputy Assessor—Benjamin Ficklen

1820
Sheriff—Hancock Eustace
Deputy Sheriffs—William Bell and John Moncure
Clerk—John M. Conway
Deputy Clerk—Henry R. Conway
Commissioners of the Revenue:
    Samuel H. Peyton (District 1)
    Nathaniel P. Williams (District 2)

1821
Deputy Sheriff—William Bell
Clerk—John M. Conway
Deputy Clerk—Henry R. Conway
Commissioner of the Revenue—Samuel H. Peyton

1822
Sheriff—Alexander Morson[687] (1759-1822)
Deputy Sheriff—William Bell
Clerk—John M. Conway
Deputy Clerks—Henry R. Conway and William F. Phillips[688]
Commissioner of the Revenue—Samuel H. Peyton
Surveyor—Zachariah Cox

1823
Sheriff—Benjamin Tolson[689] (c.1763-1836)
Deputy Sheriff—William Bell
Clerk—John M. Conway
Deputy Clerk—Henry R. Conway
Commissioner of the Revenue—Samuel H. Peyton
Surveyor—Zachariah Cox

1824
Sheriff—Thomas Hill[690] (c.1781-c.1870)
Deputy Sheriff—William Bell
Constable—Joseph D. Withers[691] (born 1803)
Clerk—John M. Conway
Deputy Clerk—Henry R. Conway
Commissioner of the Revenue—Samuel H. Peyton
Surveyor—Alexander P. Williams

1825
Deputy Sheriff—William Bell
Clerk—John M. Conway
Deputy Clerk—Henry R. Conway
Commissioner of the Revenue—Samuel H. Peyton
Surveyor—Alexander P. Williams

1826
Sheriff—Benjamin Tolson
Deputy Sheriffs—William Bell and Robert Beaty[692]
Clerk—John M. Conway
Deputy Clerk—Henry R. Conway

---

[687] Alexander was the son of Arthur Morson (1735-1798), a wealthy Scots merchant with businesses in Falmouth. In 1800 he married in Stafford Ann Casson Alexander (1781-1831) who inherited her family home, Snowden, after the death of her brother in 1804. Alexander resided on Hollywood, a plantation that adjoined his wife's Snowden property (Eby, They 252).
[688] William served in the War of 1812.
[689] Benjamin owned Bellfair Mills and the old Fristoe's Mill in the north end of the county. Bellfair was a commercial mill that ground flour for export as well as for local consumption. Fristoe's was a much smaller mill, though it was fitted with a saw as well as with stones for grinding.
    Benjamin served as a major in the War of 1812.
[690] Probably the son of Leonard Hill (died c.1814), overseer of Landon Carter's (1710-1778) Parke Quarter. Thomas resided at Oak Grove, which adjoined Parke. This property was located to the west of the intersection of Skyline Drive (State Route 615) and Hartwood Road (State Route 612). Thomas served as captain of a cavalry troop during the War of 1812.
[691] Joseph married Eliza Elzira Gatewood (born c.1803), the daughter of John Gatewood (c.1780-1846:51) of Caroline County and Frances Coleman (c.1782-1853).
[692] Robert served in the War of 1812.

Commissioner of the Revenue—Samuel H. Peyton
Surveyors—Alexander P. Williams and Zachariah Cox

1827
Sheriff—George Banks[693] (1779-1837)
Deputy Sheriffs—William Bell, Alexander H. Mason, Thomas Hill, Joseph D. Withers
Clerk—John M. Conway
Deputy Clerk—Henry R. Conway
Commissioner of the Revenue—Samuel H. Peyton
Surveyor—Alexander P. Williams

1828
Sheriff—George Banks
Deputy Sheriffs—William Bell, Alexander H., Mason
Clerk—John M. Conway
Deputy Clerk—Henry R. Conway
Commissioner of the Revenue—Samuel H. Peyton
Treasurer—Murray Forbes
Surveyor—Alexander P. Williams

1829
Sheriff—George Banks
Deputy Sheriffs—William Bell and Joseph D. Withers
Clerk—John M. Conway
Commissioner of the Revenue—Samuel H. Peyton
Surveyor—Alexander P. Williams

1830
Sheriff—Robert Howson Hooe (1748-1834)
Constables—Luke Masters, Thornton Patton[694] (1793-1869), Lewis Jones, Jr., John Hore, Fielding Baker (1799-after 1870)
Clerk—John M. Conway
Deputy Clerk—Henry R. Conway
Commissioner of the Revenue—Samuel H. Peyton
Tobacco Inspectors:
    Dixon's—Thomas Cropper Scott[695] (1791-1857)
School Commissioner—Strother Ficklen,[696] Charles Addison Tackett (1814-1896)

---

[693] George was the son of Gerrard Banks (1725-1787) and Frances Bruce (1735-1818) of Greenbank. This old farm was located on the Rappahannock River northwest of Falmouth and is now the site of the GEICO Insurance Company. The Banks family operated their own gristmill on the property and the farm was the site of a ford used by Union troops during the War Between the States.

[694] Thornton was the son of George Patton (1757-1813) and Sarah Stringfellow (1766-1848). His first wife was Sarah McInteer (died c.1844), the daughter of Alexander McInteer (c.1730-1807) and Sarah Sinclair. Thornton married secondly Sarah A. Perry (born c.1822).

[695] Thomas was the only son of Ann Browne, the wife of Joseph Browne (died 1806). He was a merchant in Falmouth and resided at Clearview. He also owned lots 47 and 48 in Falmouth, which he rented to Thornton Alexander (1790-1842). Thomas married Mary Lucinda, the daughter of Thomas Seddon (1779-1831). The 1830 Stafford census listed Thomas with 18 slaves. In 1843 he paid taxes on 7 slaves, 5 horses, 1 metal clock, 1 "common silver watch," 353 acres in Stafford and 15 lots in Falmouth (Hore, Account book). He owned land in Kentucky as well as in Prince William and Stafford counties (Scott ledger, 1817-1823). Thomas served in the War of 1812.

[696] This was probably Anthony Strother Ficklen (died 1844), the son of Charles Ficklen (died c.1816) and Mary Strother (?) of Fauquier County. Strother lived for some years in Stafford, then returned to Fauquier where he died. He married but left no children. On Sept. 13, 1830 Strother resigned as school commissioner. The court appointed Charles A. Tackett in his stead. Strother served in the War of 1812.

Flour Inspector for Falmouth—William Stringfellow[697] (died 1831)
Surveyor—Alexander P. Williams
Overseers of the Roads:
    James Withers Stone[698] (c.1805-1857)—"of the Road of which William H. Stone was the surveyor"
    Byram Harding[699]—"the road of which Richard Bridwell was overseer"
    Zachariah Bradshaw[700] (c.1785-before 1850)—"from Burnt Ordinary[701] to Edmund Burr's"
    John Catesby Edrington[702] (1800-1879)—"from Aquia to Williamsville in place of Thomas Franklin"[703]
    Nelson Mason[704]—"from Spotted Tavern to the Fauquier Line"
    Thomas Jones—"from Crops tavern to Crops mill"
Other Overseers of the Roads:
    William Norman   John Stewart   William Bell
    Ezra Burr (c.1780-1856)   John Irvine[705] (c.1794-1871)   M.(?) Patterson
    William Augustus Moncure[706] (1803-1862)

1831
Sheriff—Robert H. Hooe
Deputy Sheriffs—Joel James Jameson[707] (1801-after 1861) and William Mitchell
Jailer—Thornton Alexander[708] (1790-1842)
Clerk—John M. Conway
Deputy Clerk—Henry R. Conway

---

[697] The 1830 census lists William as owning 9 slaves. He died in office.

[698] James was the son of Richard Stone (died 1825) and Hannah Withers (c.1774-1857) of Mt. Olive in what is now part of the Marine Corps reservation.

[699] Byram served in the War of 1812.

[700] Zachariah was probably the son of Jeremiah Bradshaw (born c.1753) and Nancy "Dicey" Jeter.

[701] The Burnt Ordinary was in the vicinity of Spotted Tavern on the western side of the county.

[702] John resided at Myrtle Grove on Aquia Creek where he had a store and fishery and probably a sandstone quarry. He was the son of John Catesby Edrington (1775-1820) and Sarah Porter Stone (1769-1816). The younger John married Elizabeth Hawkins Stone (1810-1891), the daughter of Hawkins Stone and Elizabeth Burroughs (dead by 1833). The 1830 Stafford census lists John with 42 slaves. During the War of 1812, John served as a captain in charge of a light infantry company, 45th Regiment, Virginia Militia.

[703] Thomas served in Edrington's Company, 45th Virginia Militia, War of 1812. He lived near the old town of Aquia.

[704] Nelson was the son of Lewis Mason (born 1757) and Mary Bethel (died 1831). He served in the War of 1812. Children of Nelson Mason: Enfield (1796-1836), Jane, Robert, and William.

[705] John was the son of William Irvine (c.1781-1859). He was born in Ireland and died of gangrene in Stafford.

[706] William was the son of John Moncure (1772-1822) and was born at Clermont. In 1828 he married Lucy Ann Gatewood (1807-1895), the daughter of Capt. James Gatewood of Caroline County. William was educated at William and Mary and served in both houses of the Virginia Legislature. In 1857 he was elected Second Auditor and Superintendent of the Literary Fund of Virginia.

[707] Joel was the son of John Jameson (1763-1842) and lived in the north end of the county.

[708] Thornton's parentage is uncertain, though he was undoubtedly related to the Stafford Thornton family. During the War of 1812, Thornton served in the 45th Regiment (Stafford County) of the Virginia Militia. In 1816 he married Frances A. Waller of Stafford (*Virginia Herald*, Mar. 2, 1816). In 1819 Thornton took over Moses Phillips' old ordinary near the courthouse. He maintained an ordinary license from that time until 1831. The following year the license was granted to his wife, Frances. On Sept. 10, 1827 he was commissioned lieutenant colonel in the 45th Regiment of the Virginia Militia. Thornton was a member of the Fredericksburg and Falmouth Masonic lodges from 1816-1826.

    Thornton moved to Natchez, Mississippi c.1837 and became manager of the Steamboat Hotel. Frances died at about this time and he remarried. In 1840 a tornado struck Natchez and nearly destroyed the hotel. His second wife, Almira, was found seriously injured clutching her two dead infants. Thornton died two years later and Almira continued managing the hotel.

Master Commissioner—Robert H. Hooe
Commissioner of the Revenue—Samuel H. Peyton
Tobacco Inspectors:
> Dixon's—William Bell (1st Inspector), Thomas C. Scott (2nd), George Kiger[709] (c.1767-1857) (3rd), Thomas Stringfellow (4th)

Flour Inspector—William Stringfellow[710]
School Commissioners—Charles A. Tackett, Thomas G. Moncure, William Washington Peyton[711] (1799-1847), Samuel Selden Brooke, Samuel H. Skinker,[712] John Gray[713] (1809-1848), John Grayson Hedgman[714] (1782-c.1845), Robert H. Hooe, Col. Enoch Mason (Treasurer)
Overseers of the Poor[715]—James Briggs (died 1843), Thornton Alexander, Walker P. Conway, William H. Fitzhugh, James Morton, John H. S. Potts (died c.1850)
Overseers of the Roads:
> James Beagle—"leading from S[amuel] S[elden] Brookes mill to the road leading from Marlborough to Falmouth passing through the land of said Brooke and others"
> Thomas Dickinson—"from the Brent Town road to the Stafford Springs"
> George Curtis[716] (1767-1844)—"from Peter Rollow's[717] to Abner R. Alcock's[718]"
> Absalom King[719] (c.1791-1853)—"from Falmouth to Edmund Burr's gate on the Mountain road"
> James Morton—"from Thornton Alexander's fence leading to the Hope creek"

Other Overseers of the Roads:
> John M. Bronaugh   Alexander Obyrhim[720]   Richard Stone

---

[709] George Kiger was an apprentice in his uncle Fielding Lucas' tannery. Fielding's tannery burned in 1807 and George established his own tannery in Falmouth in 1809. In 1843 he paid taxes on 5 slaves, 2 horses, 2 carrioles (small covered horse-drawn carts with room for one person), 1 wood clock, 4 lots in Falmouth, and 1 acre in Stafford (Hore, Account book). He was a veteran of the War of 1812.

[710] William served in the War of 1812.

[711] William was the son of Dr. Valentine Peyton (born 1756) and Mary Butler Washington (1760-1822). He married Mary Mason, the daughter of Col. Enoch Mason.

[712] The court minutes of Nov. 15, 1831 note that Samuel was not re-appointed for 1832 due to poor health.

[713] John was the son of John Gray (1769-1848), Scots merchant and owner of Traveler's Rest on the Rappahannock. The Grays owned and operated the old Newton's Mill on which was "fixed one of Davidson's Cotton Gins, with 51 Saws." William Walker ran the mill and Gray advertised that "Cotton will be picked and packed in round bales of 300 lbs. for one eighth Toll" (*Virginia Herald*, Jan. 17, 1827).

[714] John was the son of John Hedgman (1758-1796) and Catherine Grayson (1760-1795). He resided on the south side of Aquia Creek.

[715] The court minutes of Mar. 14, 1831 state, "Ordered that the election of Overseers of the poor for the County of Stafford in District No. 1 be held at the house of Luke Masters on Saturday the 9th day of April next under the superintendence of Charles Tackett and Strother Ficklen--& in District No. 2 at Duff Green's tavern in the Town of Falmouth on the 8th day of April next under the superintendence of Murray Forbes and William C. Beale who will make return according to law."

[716] The son of George Curtis, Sr. (1730:35-c.1806) and Elizabeth Jett, the daughter of Peter Jett and Rebecca Bowen. George, Jr. probably married first c.1792 Mary McIlhaney. He married secondly in 1804 Jemima Payne (died c.1869), the daughter of Francis Payne and Susannah Jett. George and Jemima both died and were buried at their home, Green Meadows, located between Poplar Road (State Route 616) and Stefaniga Road (State Route 648). Part of George's extensive land holdings in this part of the county later became Seven Lakes subdivision and had once been part of the old Carter plantation, Ludlow. George was a veteran of the War of 1812.

[717] Peter Rollow (1801-1873) was the son of Archibald Rollow (1755-1829) and Ann "Nancy" Jett (1757-1830). Peter left Stafford and in 1842 married Permelia Payne in Loudon County, Tennessee. He died in Quitman, Arkansas.

[718] Abner Roane Alcock (died c.1831) was the son of Thomas Alcock (1744-1834) who owned Spotted Tavern and Alcock's Mill.

[719] Absalom was the son of Daniel and Sarah King of Prince William County. He was a cooper by trade and served in the War of 1812.

William Heflin	Luke Masters	William F. Moore
James S. Quisenberry	Henry Jones	Thomas Jones
Samuel Marquis[721] (c.1780-c.1850)	John G. Hedgman	Nelson Mason
William Hawkins Stone[722] (c.1809-c.1851)	Thomas Stone	Triplett Douglas
Capt. William Ford[723] (1788-1834)		

Surveyor—Alexander P. Williams

1832
Sheriff—Robert H. Hooe
Deputy Sheriff—Enoch G. Jameson[724] (born 1810)
Clerk—John M. Conway
Deputy Clerk—Henry R. Conway
Constables[725]—Thornton Curtis, James W. Stone, Luke Masters, Thornton Patton, John Hore, George Honey,[726] Francis Cox[727]
Commissioner of the Revenue—John G. Hedgman
Coroners—Robert H. Hooe and William Barber[728] (1787-1881)
Tobacco Inspectors:
    Dixon's—William Bell, Thomas C. Scott, George Kiger
Flour Inspector—Duff Green (1792-1854)
Master Commissioner—Robert H. Hooe
Overseers of the Poor—William H. Fitzhugh, Thornton Alexander
School Commissioners—Charles Carter Randolph (1788-1863),[729] Alexander P. Williams
Commissioners of Elections:
    Falmouth District—Murray Forbes (1782-1863), Thomas Wallace,[730] George Banks, William Hewitt (died c.1850), William Churchill Beale (1791-1850)
Overseers of the Roads:
    Thomas Franklin (c.1789-c.1850)—"from Aquia run to Benjamin Williams[731] old shop on the stage road"
    Abner Schooler[732]—"from Holloway's Mill[733] road near Thornton Taylors,[734] to Lewis',

---

[720] During the War Between the States, Alexander served with the 47th Virginia Infantry. He was described as being of dark complexion with blue eyes, light hair, and about 5' 10" tall. He deserted his unit and on Dec. 27, 1864 took the oath. He remained in Washington.

[721] The son of Anthony Marquis (1752-1821). Samuel was listed in 1810 and 1820 Spotsylvania censuses.

[722] The son of Barton Speake Stone.

[723] William was the son of James Ford (1768-1863) and Elizabeth Taylor. He married first Deborah Thompson Duncan (died 1813) of Baltimore. He married secondly Elizabeth Allen Hore (1791-1822), the daughter of Elias Hore (1748-1852) and Theodosia Waller (1753-1829).

[724] Enoch was the son of John Jameson (1763-1842) of Stafford. In 1847 Enoch married Mary S. Eakin in Botetourt County, Virginia.

[725] On June 11, 1832 the court ordered that Stafford be but one district with respect to constables. Prior to this time, constables were elected from the various districts into which the county was divided.

[726] George Honey was a veteran of the War of 1812.

[727] Probably John Francis Cox, the son of Presley Cox and Sarah Jett. Francis lived in White Oak near New Hope Church.

[728] William was the son of Edward and L__ Barber of Stafford. He resided on a farm he called Wyoming which was located on the western side of what is now the Marine Corps reservation.

[729] In 1825 Charles married Mary Ann F. Mortimer in Spotsylvania County.

[730] Thomas was a veteran of the War of 1812.

[731] Benjamin was a veteran of the War of 1812.

[732] Abner was the son of Thomas Schooler and Mary Fant of Spotsylvania and served in the War of 1812. He married Margaret Kirk and in 1835 moved his family to Autauga County, Alabama.

[733] This later became known as Kellogg's Mill, which used to stand on the south side of Kellogg's Mill Road (State Route 651) and the east side of Potomac Run, very near the boat landing on Abel Reservoir.

[734] In 1835 Thornton married in Fredericksburg Eleanor Baxter, the daughter of Thornton Baxter. He was a veteran of the War of 1812.

now Harding's mill"

Other Overseers of the Roads:

William A. Moncure	James M. Sthreshley[735]	Harberson Bradshaw (c.1785-1843)
Fountaine H. Lane	Edward Towson[736]	Slighton Smith
John H. Suttle[737]	James Armstrong	Barnett Stewart (1814-1871)
James F. Murray	James Jones	John Strother
James Tolson[738] (1795-1865)	Robert Garrison	William P. Cropp
William Ford	George Curtis	Thomas Stewart
Alexander Payne	William Shelkett[739]	William F. Moore[740] (c.1812-c.1869)
Henry McInteer, Jr.	Lemuel Chadwell	Thomas Harwood[741] (1769-1845)
Rawleigh Travers Cooke Brown[742]	George Fling	
William Pollock[743] (1797-1865)	Robert Kendall (c.1787-1860)	
Armistead A. Armstrong[744] (c.1816-1885)		

Surveyor—Alexander P. Williams

1833

Sheriff—William H. Fitzhugh
Deputy Sheriffs—Joel J. Jameson and Enoch G. Jameson
Constables—Dixon Brown, Fielding Peyton, William Hawkins Stone[745] (c.1809-c.1851), James W. Stone, John Hore
Coroner—Robert H. Hooe
Clerk—John M. Conway
Deputy Clerk—Henry R. Conway
Commissioner of the Revenue—John G. Hedgman
School Commissioners—Robert H. Hooe, John G. Hedgman, Charles Tackett, Samuel S. Brooke, William W. Peyton, John Gray, Alexander P. Williams, Col. Enoch Mason
Tobacco Inspectors:
    Falmouth—William Bell, Thomas C. Scott, George Kiger
Flour Inspector—Duff Green[746]

---

[735] In 1828 James married in Fredericksburg Mary Peyton Bolling Fitzhugh (born 1808).
[736] James Edward Towson (1808-1888), the son of Thomas Towson (1780-1861) of Rockdale.
[737] John married Catherine Tolson, the daughter of Benjamin Tolson (c.1763-1838).
[738] James Edward Tolson was the third son of George Tolson and a grandson of George Tolson (1726-1785). His first wife was a Miss Edrington about whom nothing is known. In 1855 at the age of 55 he married 28 year old Anne E. Hickerson (1827-1897).
[739] In 1822 William married Lucy Waller, the daughter of Sylvanus Waller of Fauquier County. He was a veteran of the War of 1812.
[740] William married Mary, the daughter of Enoch Renno (c.1740-1832).
[741] Thomas was the son of John Harwood (died c.1787) who had been a millwright at Rappahannock Forge. Thomas inherited the family farm, the house on which stood in the vicinity of the Wingate Inn on the south side of Warrenton Road (U. S. Route 17) across from Servicetown Truck Plaza.
[742] The son of Rawleigh T. Brown (1753-1803) and Million Waugh (c.1763-1799). He married his cousin, Hannah Ball Daniel (born 1780).
[743] William Pollock was a Scottish immigrant. He married Jennett R. Gray, the daughter of John Gray (1769-1848), and established himself as a farmer in Stafford. William owned Rumford Farm on King's Highway (U. S. Route 3) east of Fredericksburg. In 1843 William paid taxes on 24 slaves, 13 horses, 1 carriage, 1 wood clock, 2 gold watches, silver plate, and 1,006 acres of land (Hore, Account book). He died of dysentery. Issue: John, Atchison, and Matthew Pollock.
[744] Armistead was the son of James and Catherine Armstrong.
[745] William was the son of Barton Speake Stone.
[746] Duff's official report on flour inspected in Falmouth for the quarter ending Apr. 1, 1833:
    10,195 Bls. Superfine
       379 Fine
       191 X Middlings
        10 Condemned

Overseers of the Poor—William Rousseau Combs[747] (1784-1836) "in the room of Thornton Alexander removed," John H. S. Potts, Walker P. Conway

Overseers of the Roads:
    Franklin Richards[748]—"from Richard's Ferry to the Yellow Chappel"
    James Bryant—"leading from Norman's gate by Brents and Fitzhugh's mill, to where it intersects the road leading to Potomac river near the millrace"
    John C. Edrington—"leading from Aquia to Foxe's point"
    Benjamin Smith—"from W. P. Conway's towards Richards ferry, until it intersects the road leading from said ferry to the Yellow Chappel"
    John Gray (1809-1848)—"from John Gray's little fall mill towards the White Oak Meeting house, of which Charles Bruce[749] was the last overseer"
    George F. G. Hedgman[750]—"from 'the ford' over Accakeek run at Samuel S. Daniels gate to Marlborough"

Other Overseers of the Roads:

William Barber	Jeremiah Carter[751] (c.1810-186_)	Barnett Fritter[752] (1792-1872)
William W. Peyton	Samuel S. Brooke	Lewis Jones
M__ly Knoxville	Thomas Jones of Ludlow	William Kendall
Thomas Timmons	Daniel Wamsley[753]	Thomas Griffis
Fountaine H. Lane	William (?) Sterne	Thomas Jones
John Shelkett[754] (1793-1857)	Walter Hore[755] (1781-1858)	Ambrose Armstrong
William Mitchell	Thornton Mountjoy[756] (1794:47-c.1881)	
Ransom Hickerson[757] (c.1794-1847)		

Surveyor—Alexander P. Williams

---

    120 Half Bls. Superfine
    11,291 Total
(*Virginia Herald*, Apr. 17, 1833)

[747] William was the son of Ennis Combs and Margaret Rousseau (born c.1760). He married Sallie Wickliffe. William was listed in the 1850 Stafford census with 29 slaves.

[748] Probably Benjamin Franklin Richards (1806-after 1879), the son of Capt. James Richards and Winifred Berry Benson (1782-1856). He married Dulcibella C. Benson.

[749] Charles Bruce (c.1771-1845) was the son of Robert Bruce of Caroline County. He resided at Springfield in White Oak.

[750] George was the brother of Peter Daniel Grayson Hedgman (c.1801-after 1885) and John T. Hedgman (c.1804-1857). They were the sons of John Grayson Hedgman (1782-c.1845).

[751] Jeremiah's parentage is somewhat uncertain. He was likely related to the Carters who owned and quarried the Palace Green tract on Aquia Creek. Joseph Carter (died c.1765) had a son Jeremiah to whom he devised 400 acres in the vicinity of Stafford Courthouse. The Jeremiah here is probably a grandson of the earlier Jeremiah by either his son Henry (born 1755) or Joseph (born 1759). Jeremiah married Elizabeth Wamsley (c.1818-1886), the daughter of Benjamin Wamsley, and lived at Eastern View just east of the courthouse.

    Jeremiah was charged with the murder of William Hewitt (died c.1850). On Nov. 1, 1850 a grand jury determined that there was sufficient evidence to send the case to a jury. The outcome of the case is unknown.

[752] Barnett was probably the son of John Fritter (born 1752). He married first Betsy Fant (1774-c.1826) and secondly Mary L. Fant (1792-1861). Barnett was a veteran of the War of 1812.

[753] Daniel was a veteran of the War of 1812.

[754] John Shelkett was a veteran of the War of 1812 and operated a gristmill on the upper end of Aquia Run. He was born in Scotland and married Nancy Stark (1786-1834).

[755] Walter was the son of Elias Hore (1748-1852) and Theodosia Waller (1753-1829). He resided at Edgefield, now part of the Marine Corps reservation and was a veteran of the War of 1812.

[756] Thornton was the son of John Mountjoy (c.1772-c.1844) and Aurelia Reily (died 1844). Around 1818 he married Mary Payne (1794-1856), the daughter of Ezekiel and Susan Payne. Thornton owned property near Chapman's Mill on Chappawamsic Run.

[757] Ransom was the son of Charles Hickerson of Fauquier County. He married Mary Mason Kendall (born 1799), the daughter of George Kendall of Fauquier County.

1834

Sheriff—Dr. Alexander Fitzhugh[758] (1786-1847)
Deputy Sheriffs—Joel J. Jameson, Enoch G. Jameson, Thomas A. S. Doniphan
Constables:
    Thornton Patton (1793-1869) (District 1)
    William Carter (1807-1874) (District 2)
    Fielding Peyton (District 3)
    William H. Stone (District 4)
Clerk—John M. Conway
Deputy Clerk—Henry R. Conway
Commissioner of the Revenue—John G. Hedgman
Master Commissioner—Walker P. Conway
Tobacco Inspectors:
    Dixon's—William Bell, Thomas C. Scott
Overseers of the Poor—William Barton Stone[759] (died 1845), Robert Kendall, Robert H. Hooe, James Briggs
School Commissioners—Robert H. Hooe, Charles C. Randolph,[760] James Briggs, John G. Hedgman, Samuel S. Brooke, Enoch Mason, Jr. (c.1797-c.1835), William W. Peyton, Alexander P. Williams, Charles Tackett, John Gray
Overseers of the Roads:
    Thomas Franklin—"from Aquia to Chapawamsic run"
    James Bryant—"through the farm of William H. Fitzhugh to the Potomac river"
    Burr A. Harrison—"from Scott's landing on the Potomac river to the intersection of the road leading to Brent's Mill"
    William Bryant—"from the White Oak meeting house to Robertson's shop"
    Zachariah Holloway—"leading from the old ford near John Alexander's to the Red House"
    Thompson M. Bloxham—"from the sign post near John T. Hedgman's to the Potomac Church road near Charles A. Harrows"
Other Overseers of the Roads:

William Dickenson	Barnett Fritter	Ransom Hickerson
Fountaine H. Lane	William Heflin	James W. Stone
John R. Queen	Charles Peyton	James H. Garrison
John Latham	Posey Whaling	Eastham Coppage[761]
Samuel S. Brooke	Thomas Chilton[762]	
Thornton Shelton[763] (1805-1851)	William S. Sterne[764] (c.1789-after 1860)	

Surveyor—Alexander P. Williams

---

[758] Alexander was a veteran of the War of 1812.

[759] According to the court minutes of May 12, 1834, there was a tie in the election for this office between William R. Combs and William B. Stone. The court appointed Stone to fill the position. W. B. Stone was the son of Richard Stone (died 1825) and Hannah Withers (c.1774-1857) of Mt. Olive in what is now part of the Quantico Marine Corps base.

[760] James Briggs replaced Charles C. Randolph "removed."

[761] In 1825 Eastham married Marian Curtis (born 1808), the daughter of Richard Curtis (born before 1765). The Coppage family owned part of the very old Richlands tract in the southwestern part of the county.

[762] Thomas was a veteran of the War of 1812.

[763] Thornton was the son of Thomas Shelton (1776-1870) and Elizabeth Stark (born 1777) of Stafford. Thornton moved to Adams County, Ohio and married Elizabeth Leechman.

[764] William lived at Walnut Hill on the west side of Rock Hill Church Road (State Route 644). On June 13, 1865 he advertised the sale of his farm declaring that he had "determined to move to the South. This tract was comprised of about 400 acres and "has on it a first rate mill seat."

1835

Sheriff—Alexander Fitzhugh
Deputy Sheriffs—Joel Jameson, Enoch Jameson, Thomas A. S. Doniphan, Charles F. Suttle, Thomas Hill
Constables:
    Richard Stark[765] (c.1813-1877) (Upper District)
    Joseph W. Honey[766] (1810-1879) (Falmouth District)
    Thomas Monteith[767] (1811-1858)
Clerk—John M. Conway
Deputy Clerk—Henry R. Conway
Commissioner of the Revenue—John G. Hedgman
Flour Inspector—Duff Green
Overseers of the Poor:
    Upper District—William H. Fitzhugh, Robert Kendall, William B. Stone
School Commissioners—Robert H. Hooe, John G. Hedgman, Samuel S. Brooke, James Briggs, John Gray,
    Alexander P. Williams, Enoch Mason,[768] William W. Peyton, Charles Tackett[769]
Overseers of the Roads:
    Thomas Monteith—"beginning on the land of Monteith on the main ridge road from Falmouth to
        King George Court House about ½ mile below White Oak Meeting House and
        running between the farms of Alexander and William Morson to the River Side
        road leading to and from the same places"
    Moses Garrison, Sr.—"from Ebenezer meeting house by Mr. Stone's mill to John Burrough's road"
    Jesse Payne—"from Accakeek run to Potomac Church"
    James Monteith (c.1813-c.1859)—"from Pollards below White Oak Meeting House to the River
        side near James Montieth"
    W. S. Williams—"from Rollows old place to Pudding Hill"[770]
Other Overseers of the Roads:

Henry Gaskins[771] (born c.1843)	James W. Stone	Fielding Peyton
Lemuel Chadwell	John Patton	Luke Anderson
Benjamin Tolson	William Randall	Dr. John M. Daniel
William Smith, Sr.	William H. Fitzhugh	Hugh Cox
Robert Chapman	Silem Frederick Gustavus Phillips[772] (1790-c.1872)	

---

[765] Richard was the son of Joseph Stark and Mary Edwards. Around 1838 he married Eleanor Bell, the daughter of Thomas Bell and Catherine Arrington.
[766] Joseph married Jane A. Harding, the daughter of Mark Harding. In 1881 Jane deposed to the court, "that her said husband is entirely thriftless and wanting in business capacity; that his disposition to waste and squander whatever may come into his possession is proverbial—that he is notoriously insolvent—that as for years past he does nothing & will do nothing towards the support of your petitioner; but that in fact his support & maintenance now & for years has devolved on your petitioner" ("Honey vs Harding").
[767] Monteith was named constable "in place of Fielding Peyton, resigned." He was born in Stafford, the son of Samuel Owens Monteith (born c.1787) and Mildred Fines (born c.1787). Thomas married Anne "Nancy" Limerick/Limbrick.
[768] Enoch Mason was initially appointed treasurer of the school commissioners. The court minutes of Oct. 12, 1835 state, "It appearing to the Court that the Clerk omitted to notice on the minutes of the last term the appointment of William W. Peyton by the Board of School Commissioners as their Treasurer vice Enoch Mason removed from the state."
[769] Charles Tackett died shortly after being named to this board. He was replaced by John Jameson.
[770] Pudding Hill is on the east side of Bethel Church Road (State Route 600) very near the King George County line.
[771] Henry was the son of Armistead Gaskins. In 1888 he married Delilah Brown (born c.1847), the daughter of James and Charity Brown.
[772] Silem was the son of Col. William Phillips (1744-1797) and Elizabeth Fowke (died c.1830) of Traveler's Rest in what is now the Marine Corps reservation. He served in the War of 1812. Silem lived as

Alexander W. Massey (died c.1839) Reubin T. Fritter[773] (c.1795-1874)
Joseph Burwell Ficklen[774] (1800-1874)
Benjamin F. Richards
William Armstrong[775] (born c.1817) Fielding Lawrence Clift (born c.1808)
John A. Starke[776] (c.1794-c.1865) Thomas H. Cushing Daniel (c.1811-1896)
Peter Wiggenton[777] (c.1813-1866)
Surveyors—Alexander P. Williams and Zachariah Cox

1836
Constable—Noah H. Latham[778] (born 1814) (Falmouth District)
Clerk—John M. Conway
Deputy Clerk—Henry R. Conway
Commissioner of the Revenue—John G. Hedgman
Tobacco Inspectors:
    Dixon's—Thomas C. Scott (First Inspector), George Kiger (Second Inspector), James Coones[779] (c.1795-after 1850) (Third Inspector)
School Commissioners—John Jameson, Jefferson Spindle (c.1802-1861), James Briggs, Robert H. Hooe, William W. Peyton,[780] John G. Hedgman, Samuel S. Brooke, John Gray
Trustees of the Town of Woodstock—William H. Fitzhugh, Thomas Towson, Walker P. Conway, Capt. William Barber[781] (c.1791-1881), Samuel S. Brooke
Surveyor—Alexander P. Williams

1837
Clerk—John M. Conway
Deputy Clerk—Henry R. Conway
Commissioner of the Revenue—John G. Hedgman
Surveyor—Alexander P. Williams

---

a bachelor in his father's old house, sharing it with his two sisters. He was probably buried there as the cemetery contains numerous unmarked graves.

[773] Reubin was the son of Enos Fritter. He married Anna E. Litterel (c.1804-1892).

[774] Joseph was born in Culpeper and lived at Belmont in Falmouth. He owned several of the mills in Falmouth as well as property (including Amaret Farm) in Fredericksburg and surrounding counties. At one time he owned some $100,000 in real estate and $300,000 in personal property.
    In 1836 he was the Falmouth/Fredericksburg agent for the Aetna Insurance Company.
    In 1871 Joseph submitted to the Southern Claims Commission a claim for $23,938.07 for damages wrought by Union troops during the War Between the States. His case file, several inches thick, is on file in the National Archives. Only those with a long-standing and documented allegiance to the U. S. government could make claims, a fact that riled many of his neighbors who believed Joseph was actually a secessionist in search of money. Thirteen witnesses were called to testify as to Joseph's position on the issue of secession, seven Confederates, five Unionists, and one undecided. Duff Green, Jr. a secessionist and the most outspoken witness against Ficklen, claimed that prior to the war, he and Joseph had been in agreement about secession. Although Joseph had voted in favor of secession, he claimed that he had done so only to prevent retaliation and to protect his family and property. Testimony was spirited but divided and, in the end, Joseph received $8,200 for damages.

[775] William married Mary Ann Conyers (born c.1821), the daughter of John Conyers (c.1789-c.1844), millwright, and his wife Ann Blackburn (born c.1789), widow of Christopher Blackburn (died c.1819).

[776] John was the son of William Stark (1754-1838) and Mary Kendall (1760-1858). He never married.

[777] Peter owned what became known as Masters' Mill on Aquia Creek.

[778] Noah was the son of Jesse Latham (died 1826) of Fauquier County.

[779] James married Louisa Harwood (c.1807-1885), the daughter of Thomas Harwood (1769-1845).

[780] William was appointed treasurer of the commission.

[781] William was the son of Edward Barber who lived near Deep Run. He married Sarah Roy Mason, the daughter of Col. Enoch Mason (c.1769-1828) of Clover Hill. William lived in the northwest part of the county on a 367-acre farm he called Wyoming. The property was located on Cannon Branch and is now part of the Marine Corps reservation.

1838
Clerk—John M. Conway
Deputy Clerk—Henry R. Conway
Commissioner of the Revenue—John G. Hedgman
Surveyor—Capt. William Barber

1839
Sheriff—John G. Hedgman
Deputy Sheriff—William M. Craig[782] (born c.1792)
Clerk—John M. Conway
Deputy Clerk—Henry R. Conway
Commissioner of the Revenue—Thomas Norman (c.1790-1846)
Surveyor—Capt. William Barber

1840
Sheriff—John G. Hedgman
Deputy Sheriff—William M. Craig
Clerk—John M. Conway
Deputy Clerk—Henry R. Conway
Commissioner of the Revenue—Thomas Norman
Surveyor—William Barber

1841
Constable—James H. Garrison
Clerk—John M. Conway
Deputy Clerk—Henry R. Conway
Commissioner of the Revenue—Travers Daniel Moncure[783] (1811-1886)
Surveyor—William Barber
Deputy Surveyor—Gabriel Long[784]

1842
Clerk—John M. Conway
Deputy Clerk—Henry R. Conway
Commissioner of the Revenue—Travers D. Moncure
Surveyor—William Barber

1843
Sheriff—Duff Green
Deputy Sheriff—Elias A. W. Hore[785] (1821-c.1891)
Clerk—John M. Conway

---

[782] William was the son of Adam Craig and Mary Mallory, the daughter of William Mallory. In 1817 William married Mary Bronaugh Fox (born c.1796), the daughter of John Fox and Nancy Threlkeld.

[783] The son of William Moncure (1774-1832) of Windsor Forest and Sarah Elizabeth Henry. Travers lived at Oakwood, a 150-acre tract on Meadow Branch in Wide Water. His home was near the old Brent's Mill that used Meadow Branch for power.

[784] In 1846 Gabriel was a school commissioner in Spotsylvania County.

[785] The son of Walter Hore (1781-1858) and Margaret E. Combs (c.1784-1859) and the grandson of Elias Hore (1748-1832) and Theodosia Waller (1753-1829). Elias resided at Dipple, the old Scott plantation on Chappawamsic Creek and the Potomac River. There he operated a profitable fishery for many years. A newspaper notice announced the opening of a store there as well, saying, "Our friend, E. A. W. Hore has opened quite a large store at his house, and is doing a thriving business. You know he belongs to the irrepressibles, and, as Tom Latham would say, is a hard man to keep down" (*Virginia Star*, Feb. 21, 1877).

Deputy Clerks—Henry R. Conway and Edgar S. Moore
Coroner—Robert H. Hooe
Commissioner of the Revenue—Travers D. Moncure
Surveyor—William Barber

1844
Sheriff—Thomas Towson[786]
Clerk—John M. Conway
Deputy Clerk—Henry R. Conway
Commissioner of the Revenue—Travers D. Moncure
Surveyor—William Barber

1845
Sheriff—Thomas Towson
Clerk—John M. Conway
Deputy Clerk—Henry R. Conway
Commissioner of the Revenue—Travers D. Moncure
Surveyors—William Barber and Alexander P. Williams
Deputy Surveyor—John Baker

1846
Sheriff—Samuel Selden Brooke
Clerk—John M. Conway
Deputy Clerk—Henry R. Conway
Commissioner of the Revenue—Travers D. Moncure
School Commissioners—Thomas Hill, Thomas Norman, Burkett P. Bowen, James Tolson, Samuel S. Brooke, Robert Kendall, John Swetnam, John Irvine
Surveyor—William Barber

1847
Sheriff—Samuel S. Brooke
Clerk—John M. Conway
Deputy Clerk—Henry R. Conway
Commissioner of the Revenue—Travers D. Moncure
Surveyor—William Barber

1848
Sheriff—Walker P. Conway
Deputy Sheriff—George Washington Conway (1818-1879)
Clerk—John M. Conway
Deputy Clerk—Henry R. Conway
Commissioner of the Revenue—Travers D. Moncure

1849
Sheriff—Walker P. Conway
Clerk—John M. Conway
Deputy Clerk—Henry R. Conway
Commissioner of the Revenue—Travers D. Moncure
Surveyor—William Barber

1850
Sheriff—John Rose Fitzhugh (c.1795-after 1860)

---

[786] Thomas Towson was one of the wealthiest men in 19th century Stafford, his money being made in the stone business. In 1843 he paid taxes on 16 slaves, 13 horses, 1 gig, 1 "patent silver watch," 1 lot in Aquia, and 2,909 acres of land (Hore, Account book).

Deputy Sheriffs—James E. Towson and James E. Lawson, Jr.
Clerk—John M. Conway
Deputy Clerk—Henry R. Conway
Commissioner of the Revenue—Travers D. Moncure
Overseer of the Poor—Roy Herndon (1819-1898)

1851
Sheriff—John R. Fitzhugh
Deputy Sheriffs—James E. Lawson, Jr. and George W. Conway
Commonwealth's Attorney—John Conway Moncure[787] (1827-1916)
Clerk—John M. Conway
Deputy Clerk—Henry R. Conway
Commissioner of the Revenue—Travers D. Moncure

1852
Sheriff—Travers D. Moncure
Deputy Sheriff—George W. Conway
Clerk—Henry Rowzee Conway[788] (1825-1863)
Commonwealth's Attorney—John C. Moncure
Commissioner of the Revenue—James E. Towson
Surveyor—John Marshall Homes[789] (c.1818-1873)

1853
Sheriff—Harris Hill
Deputy Sheriffs—Elias A. W. Hore, Charles F. Suttle
Clerk—Henry R. Conway
Commonwealth's Attorney—John C. Moncure
Commissioner of the Revenue—James E. Towson
Surveyor—John M. Homes

1854
Sheriff—James Monteith (c.1813-before1850)
Deputy Sheriffs—Walter M. Cox[790] (born c.1820) and James E. Lawson, Jr.[791]

---

[787] The son of the Hon. R. C. L. Moncure (1805-1882) of Glencairne and Mary Butler Washington Conway (born 1807). John graduated valedictorian from VMI in 1847. After graduation, he studied law with his father and was admitted to the bar in 1849. In 1850 John married Fannie Dulaney Tomlin and built Mont Anna on the north side of his father's Glencairne farm. This attractive two-story frame house is still standing and occupied. John served as Commonwealth's Attorney for Stafford from 1851-1860 when he removed to Shreveport, Louisiana to practice law. There in 1861 he enlisted in the Confederate Army as a private. He resumed his law practice in Shreveport in 1865 and was elected a member of the Louisiana Legislature for the sessions of 1871-74 and 1879. During the 1873-74 session, he was elected Speaker of the House. In 1874 he was elected state treasurer but was unable to serve due to the reconstruction government. John also served as a justice for the Louisiana Supreme Court. He died tragically as a result of burns from a gas stove.

[788] Henry was the son of John Moncure Conway (1779-1864), former clerk of the court. Henry married Elizabeth Griffin Chinn, the daughter of John Leroy Chinn (1795-1854) of Lancaster County.

[789] In 1857 John married Susan Peters of Fauquier County.

[790] During the War Between the States, Walter served with Company I of the 47th Virginia Infantry. He was described as being 5'10" tall with dark complexion and dark hair and eyes.

[791] The sheriffs and deputy sheriffs were still responsible for collecting the levies and, upon occasion, the court had difficulty in making these tax collectors deposit the funds collected. The minutes of the court for Feb. 13, 1854 state, "the Court doth adjudge that the said James E. Lawson, Jr. deputy sheriff do pay to the Overseers of the Poor the sum of one hundred and seventy seven dollars and three cents, the amount of Poor Levies for the years 1850 and 1851—it being the opinion of the Court that the same is payable by said Deputy and not by the other Deputy George W. Conway."

Constables—Simeon Chancellor Peyton[792] (1829-1905), Thomas A. Withers (c.1814-c.1865), William T. Patton (c.1823-1905), Richard Stark
Clerk—Henry R. Conway
Commonwealth's Attorney—John C. Moncure
Commissioner of the Revenue—James E. Towson
Overseers of the Poor:
    John A. Swetnam[793] (1792-1854)
    William Armstrong (born c.1817)
Overseers of the Roads:
    William B. Stone[794]—"from Waller's Fishery to Aquia"
    William S. Green—"from Falmouth Bridge through Falmouth to the old Brick Kiln in the road to Stafford Court House"
    John J. Leitch[795] (c.1822-1882)—"from Hopewell Church to the old Stage road between Fredericksburg and Potomac Creek"
    John M. O'Bannon—"from Mrs. Fant's to Falmouth (ordered that the road now be styled as 'the road leading from Mrs. Fants or John Peden's) to J. H. Hewitt's corner in the town of Falmouth'"
Other Surveyors of the Roads:
    George W. Conway   Thomas Gollahorn   William Sullivan
    George H. Armstrong (1830-1863)   John E. Green[796]   George V. Moncure
    John R. Perry (born c.1822)   John A. Swetnam   Samuel H. Griffis
    William S. Cloe[797] (1832-1919)   Landon J. Huffman[798] (c.1810-1873)
    Strother Harding (c.1812-c.1853)   Flavius Josephus Ballard[799] (1808-1892)
    Benjamin W. Bridwell (c.1823-1856)   George K. Blackburn[800] (1824-1890)

---

[792] Simeon was the son of Thomas and Sarah Peyton. In 1869 he married Roxanna T. Chinn (1836-1898), the daughter of William and Mary Chinn. One of the local newspapers carried a notice of a fire that destroyed some of his wood—"Heavy loss of Cord Wood - We regret to learn that Mr. Simeon Peyton, of Stafford County, had from eight hundred to a thousand cords of wood destroyed by fire, on Friday last. The wood was cut on Belle Plain farm, in the vicinity of Potomac creek, ready to be forwarded to Washington city market. An old colored man was burning corn-stalks in the vicinity, when the fire was communicated to the cord wood. Mr. Peyton had an insurance of $1000 on the wood, which is better than nothing, but his loss is still heavy" (*Virginia Herald*, Apr. 29, 1872).
    Another newspaper notice stated that Simeon "is prepared to accommodate [the public] at all hours with hacks, buggies or saddle horses, at the shortest notice and on reasonable terms" (*Fredericksburg News*, Dec. 1, 1856).
[793] John died in office and was replaced by William Armstrong.
[794] William was the son of Charles W. Stone (died 1842) and Hannah Stone. He suffered from financial troubles whereupon in 1842 he, James W. Stone (1796-1869), and Richard Stone conveyed land to Elijah Hansbrough.
[795] In 1854 John Leitch married Martha J. S. Russell (c.1826-1885).
[796] John married Parthenia Newton of King George County.
[797] William was the son of Alexander (born c.1800) and Drucilla Cloe (born c.1800). In 1860 he married Hannah Kate Stark (1842-1884), the daughter of Richard Stark (c.1813-1877) and Eleanor Bell (born c.1817) and lived near Bellfair Mills. During the War Between the States, he served with the 9th Virginia Cavalry under Thomas C. Waller and Thomas Towson. At the time of his pension application he was suffering from almost total blindness and other infirmities of old age.
[798] Prior to the War Between the States, Landon was a merchant in Stafford. After the war, he moved to Princess Anne Street in Fredericksburg. He was a member of the Methodist Church and served on the City Council. From 1865 until his death Landon was Collector of city taxes. He also served as a school trustee in the town.
[799] Flavius was the son of James Ballard (1763-1856) of Spotsylvania. His second wife was Aphia Sanford (c.1814-1846), the daughter of Lawrence Sanford (1778-1858) and Aphia Farmer (1784-1864).
[800] George was the son of Christopher Blackburn (died c.1819). Christopher's widow, Ann (born c.1789), married secondly John Conyers (c.1789-c.1844) by whom she had Benjamin Conyers and Mary Ann, who

Alexander H. Mountjoy[801] (1826-c.1902)
Criers of Elections:
    Aquia—Travers D. Moncure
    Coakley's—James McDonald Briggs (1822-1900)
    Falmouth—John William Duncan Ford[802] (c.1801-1876)
    Hartwood—Joseph W. Honey
    Master's Store—Henry Moore (born c.1822)
    Stafford Store—William Tolson (born c.1823)
    White Oak—Isaac Fines (born c.1807)
Surveyor—John M. Homes

1855
Sheriff—James Monteith
Clerk—Henry R. Conway
Coroner—Dr. John H. Daniel
Commonwealth's Attorney—John C. Moncure
Commissioner of the Revenue—James E. Towson
Superintendent of Schools—Samuel S. Brooke
School Commissioners—James E. Tolson[803] (1795-1865), Thomas Hill, Robert Kendall, John Irvine
        John H. Hickerson[804] (c.1818-c.1876), William Hand Browne (died 1852), Edward Waller
Overseer of the Poor—William Armstrong (born c.1817)
Overseers of the Roads:
    Thomas H. Johnson[805] (c.1820-1903)—"from Falmouth and Warrenton Roads one mile above Falmouth to Potomac Run"
    John C. Edrington—"from Fox's Point to Horton's Gate"
    John W. Jones (born c.1821)—"from his own gate to the Marlborough Road"
    John Anthony (born c.1821)—"from the Stage road at Claibourne's Run to Potomac run at John Furneyhoughs"
    James W. Beaty[806] (died 1906)—"from St. George's branch to Concord"
    James McClure Scott[807] (1811-1893)—"from the old stage road leading from Aquia to Dumfries

---

married William Armstrong (born c.1817). George Blackburn married Mary E. Abbott (1824-c.1874), the daughter of John and Mary Abbott. His brother was Alexander W. Blackburn (1817-1871).

[801] Alexander lived near Bellfair Mills and, during the War Between the States, served with the 9th Virginia Cavalry.

[802] John was the son of Capt. William Ford (1788-1834) and his first wife Deborah Thompson Duncan (died 1813) of Baltimore. He died unmarried.

[803] James was the son of Benjamin Tolson (c.1763-1838). He married first a Miss Edrington. She died sometime before 1827 and at age 60 he married Anne E. Hickerson (1827-1897), the daughter of Ransom Hickerson (c.1794-1844).

[804] John was listed in the 1860 Stafford census with real estate valued at $2,300 and $14,500 in personal property.

[805] Thomas served in the 9th Virginia Cavalry, Company A, Stafford Rangers.

[806] James was a native of Jackson, Mississippi. He came to Stafford prior to the War Between the States. During the war, he fought here with the Confederate army. After the war, he married Mollie Hart, the daughter of Robert Hart of Fredericksburg. He later returned to Mississippi where he worked for the Capitol Bank of Jackson.

[807] James was the son of Dr. James Scott and Mildred Thomson and was born in Albemarle County. He was educated at Hampden-Sydney College and married in 1832 Sarah Travers Lewis (1813-1891). For some years the Scotts resided at Bel-Air in Spotsylvania County, a farm which Sarah had inherited from her father, Dr. Richmond Lewis. In 1852 James purchased land in Stafford about two miles from Fredericksburg. Here he built a beautiful frame home that Sarah called Little Whim. This building is still standing on the north side of White Oak Road (State Route 218).

    Shortly before the outbreak of the war, James sold Little Whim and rented Kenmore in Fredericksburg. During this time, he bought Pine Grove the former home of his friend Henry Thompson of

"to the road leading from Aquia to the Potomac River"
Francis "Frank" T. Forbes[808] (c.1825-1904)—"from Spotted Tavern to the Fauquier County line"
Other Overseers of the Roads:
    William Bloxham   Edward Templeman[809]   Robert G. Hickerson[810]
    Robert J.(?) Lee   Henry Payne[811] (c.1837-1862)   Lyman Kellogg[812] (1813-1897)
    George V. Moncure   Samuel H. Griffis (1814-c.1887) John R. Perry
    James Stark[813] (c.1811-1860:70)
Surveyor—John M. Homes

1856
Sheriff—James Monteith
Deputy Sheriff—Walter M. Cox[814] (born c.1820)
Constables—Thomas A. Withers (c.1814-c.1865), John S. Monteith (c.1829-after 1880), William T. Patton, Richard Stark
Clerk—Henry R. Conway
Commonwealth's Attorney—John C. Moncure
Commissioner of the Revenue—James E. Towson
Overseers of the Poor:
    District 1—James H. Ball[815] (c.1831-1907)

Chambersburg, Pennsylvania. James intended on building a home of the property, but the outbreak of the war and the advancing armies of both sides necessitated his return to Bel-Air where he remained for the remainder of his life.
    Prior to the war, James was advised to transfer his money and family to Europe in order to avoid being so near the military struggle. James' reply was, "I have no more right to do so than others and will abide by the fortunes of my State" (Anderson 266). That loyalty caused him to invest his money in Confederate bonds which, at the end of the war, were worthless. By selling much of his land, he was finally able to pay off his debts, but the family were absolutely destitute. "He and his family led a life of privation at 'Bel-air' for the rest of his life" (Anderson 267).
[808] Francis, "Frank," was born in Falmouth. He served four years in the Confederate service during which time he was a captain in the commissary in Richmond. After the war, he spent four years as postmaster of Fredericksburg. In 1851 he married Ann Mercer Chew, the eldest daughter of John James Chew.
[809] Edward resided near Tackett's Mills.
[810] During the War Between the States, Robert served with Company A of the 9th Virginia Cavalry. In April 1863 he was appointed quartermaster sergeant.
[811] During the War Between the States, Henry served with the 47th Virginia Infantry. He was killed in action at Seven Pines in May 1862.
[812] Although the 1850 Stafford census records Lyman's place of birth as Canada, he was the son of Ezekiel Kellogg (died 1828) and Luna Clark (born 1778) of Southwick, Massachusetts. Around 1838 or 1839 Lyman moved from Southwick to Stafford where he settled near Crest. In 1850 he married Frances A. Waller (1815-1887), the daughter of Sylvanus Waller of Fauquier County. Lyman lived just west of modern Abel Reservoir. For many years he operated Kellogg's Mill, the foundation of which remains on the edge of the reservoir. This was a combination grist and sawmill. During the War Between the States, Union soldiers occupied his farm and stole his cattle and crops. At the close of the war, Lyman held some $20,000 in Confederate currency, which was worthless (Hopkins 782).
    Lyman was a steadying influence on his community following the war. Union occupation and the resulting vandalism had so devastated the area that many Stafford residents were unable to support themselves and were forced to leave the county. Following the war, Lyman employed a number of the remaining men in his neighborhood, thereby enabling them to stay in Stafford and feed their families.
[813] James was the son of Joseph Stark (1771-1841) of Stafford and Elizabeth Edwards. He married Mary Carter, the daughter of William Carter (1807-1874) of Stafford.
[814] Walter was the son of Charnock Cox, Jr. and Leah Owens (Monteith) Owens. Leah's first husband was her first cousin, Thomas Owens. Walter's middle name was probably Monteith.
[815] James lived near Monteithville in southeastern Stafford. During the War Between the States, he served with Walker's Battalion and the 9th Virginia Cavalry and was wounded in the head and leg. He was paroled at King George Courthouse in May 1865.

District 2—William Armstrong
District 3—John Shelkett
District 4—Bayliss Davis[816] (c.1808-1857)

Overseers of the Roads:
George Sullivan (born c.1808)—"from Accakeek to Potomac run"
Peter D. G. Hedgman[817] —"from Accakeek run (lower ford) to Marlborough"
James A. Daffan[818] (c.1820-1890)—"from Potomac run to Hopewell Meeting house"
William G. Pollock[819] (1829-1865)—"from Warren's corner to Chatham ferry"
Robert T. Peyton[820] (1823-1871)—"from White Oak Meeting house to Robertson's Black Smith shop"
John Green—"from Stafford Court House to the [Accakeek] bridge"
Abraham Primmer[821] (1811-1896)—"from the corner of Peyton's (formerly) now Roy's fence on the road from Hopewell to Falmouth to the Potomac Creek road at the corner of Mrs. Coalter's fence"

Other Overseers of the Roads:
Albert B. Alsop[822] (1820-1864)
John Anthony (born c.1821)
James B. Templeman[825] (1822-1892)
Thomas Norman Towson[823] (1822-1863)
Harrison Brockenbrough Barnes[824] (born c.1813)
Rodham P. Shelkett[826] (1822-1899)

Surveyor—John M. Homes

1857
Sheriff—James Monteith

---

[816] Bayliss was the son of Thomas Davis.

[817] Following the War Between the States, Peter submitted a claim to the Southern Claims Commission asking to be reimbursed for $20,678 worth of fencing, houses, and other commodities taken from his property by the Union army. His claim was rejected.

[818] James was the son of William Daffan (c.1777-1855) and his first wife Nancy (born c.1795).

[819] During the War Between the States, William served as a captain with Company A of the 47th Virginia Infantry. In December 1864 he was promoted to captain, but was furloughed for chronic diarrhea. He was buried at Traveler's Rest.

[820] Robert was the son of Thomas and Sarah Peyton. In 1853 he married Sarah Ann Catlett. Robert died in Stafford of "intemporate drinking."

[821] A native of Chemung County, New York, Abraham lived at Bellair, one of the old Fitzhugh plantations on Deacon Road (State Route 607) and now known as the Walnut Farm. He was the son of Peter and Pheoba Primmer of New York. Little is known about Abraham's first wife. He married secondly Elizabeth A. "Libby" Carter (1824-1888), the daughter of Johnson Carter (1797-1861). Johnson was also from Chemung County, New York and both men settled in Stafford around 1854. Johnson Carter resided at Bellmead just north of Falmouth and across from Glencairne. Bellair has recently been developed into Leeland Station subdivision.

[822] During the War Between the States, Albert served in Company A of the 9th Virginia Cavalry, enlisting in April 1861. He was captured at New Market, Maryland and died Aug. 1, 1864. He was buried in Hollywood Cemetery in Richmond.

[823] Thomas was the son of Thomas Towson (1779-1861) and Eleanor Norman (1782-1848). In 1843 he married Mary Frances Smith of Fauquier. Thomas operated a sandstone quarry in Stafford and his estate inventory included 1 jackscrew, 1 pair quarry wheels, wedges, sledge hammers, picks, and 1 sawmill and fixtures. The total value of his estate was $1,570.95 (Stafford Deed Book 26A, p. 34).

[824] During the War Between the States, Harrison served with the 47th Virginia Infantry. In 1850 he married Frances L. B. Peyton (born c.1823) and was a merchant in Falmouth (*Fredericksburg News*, Mar. 26, 1850).

[825] James was the son of Edward and Setha Templeman and married Louisa Holmes (1830-1900). He was a member of Rock Hill Baptist Church where he served as clerk. He died of consumption. His obituary appeared in the same issue of the newspaper as did a brief article about the home of Mrs. James B. Templeman (near Rock Hill) being destroyed by fire (*Fredericksburg Star*, Feb. 17, 1892).

[826] Rodham married Virginia Lula Daffan (1833-1875), the daughter of William Daffan (c.1777-1855) and his first wife, Nancy (born c.1795). Rodham died of cancer.

Deputy Sheriff—Walter M. Cox
Jailer—William L. Morgan[827] (c.1805-1873)
Clerk—Henry R. Conway
Commonwealth's Attorney—John C. Moncure
Commissioner of the Revenue—James E. Towson
School Superintendent—Samuel S. Brooke
School Commissioners—James Tolson, William H. Browne, Thomas Hill, Robert Kendall, Edward Waller, John H. Skinker, James W. Stone, Jr.
Overseers of the Poor—William Armstrong, John Shelkett,[828] William Ashby[829] (born c.1814), Baylis Davis,[830] John R. Perry
Surveyor—John M. Homes

1858
Sheriff[831]—James Monteith
Deputy Sheriff—Walter M. Cox
Clerk—Henry R. Conway
Constables:
    District 1—John S. Monteith (c.1829-after 1880)
    District 2—Thomas A. Withers
    District 3—William T. Patton
    District 4—Richard Stark
Commonwealth's Attorney—John C. Moncure
Commissioner of the Revenue—James E. Towson
School Superintendent—Samuel S. Brooke
School Commissioners—Thomas Hill, Robert Kendall, James Tolson, Gustavus B. Wallace, Edward Waller, William H. Browne, John H. Skinker
Overseers of the Roads:
    Luther Rice Daffan[832] (c.1834-1906)—"from Potomac run to Hopewell Meeting house"
    Lewis Hammett[833] (c.1802-1892)—"from Hopewell Meeting house to the road leading from Potomac Creek to Fredericksburg"
    John Newton (born c.1830)—"from the old stage road to James' land through the farm of Henry L. Brooke"
    George Payne (born c.1830)—"from Accakeek to Potomac run"
    Alexander Morson Green[834] (c.1828-1904)—"from Potomac run to Hopewell Meeting house"

---

[827] William was for many years a merchant in King George County. In 1851 he bought Paint Ridge near Accokeek Run and east of Stafford Courthouse. Around 1855 he purchased the old Garrard's Ordinary just north of the courthouse. During the War Between the States, he was engaged in operating a store there. He married Margaret James (born c.1795) of Fredericksburg.

[828] John Shelkett died while in office and William Ashby (born c.1814) was elected to fill the vacancy.

[829] In 1872 William was appointed one of the commissioners of the Free Bridge between Fredericksburg and Stafford County.

[830] Baylis Davis died while in office and John R. Perry was elected to fill the vacancy.

[831] According to the court minutes of Sept. 15, 1858, there was a problem filling the position of sheriff. The minutes read, "Walter M. Cox who was regularly elected Sheriff of this County on the 27th day of May last—having failed to execute a bond and give security according to law and this being the last session of the Court at which the said Cox can legally execute the said bond and give the said security, the Court declares the office of Sheriff vacant—whereupon it is ordered that the Clerk do issue a writ of election for filling the said vacancy—The said election to be held on the 14th day of October next."

[832] Luther was the son of William Daffan (c.1777-1855) and his first wife, Nancy (born c.1795). During the War Between the States, Luther served with the Fredericksburg Artillery. From November 1863 until the end of the war, he was detailed as a hospital nurse in Danville. Luther married Mary Robertson of North Carolina and died at his home at Eley's Ford, Culpeper County.

[833] Lewis' farm was in Hartwood on the corner of Warrenton Road (U. S. Route 17) and Holly Corner Road (State Route 655).

William Brown—"from the sign post near Paul Hulls to the stage road leading from Stafford Court House to Falmouth"

Littleton C. Fleming[835] (born c.1821)—"from the old stage road to James land through the farm of Henry L. Brooke"

Other Overseers of the Roads:

George Herndon[836] (1821-1898)	Charles Turner (born c.1825)	William Bloxton
Joseph C. Wine[837] (c.1832-1909)	William Snellings (born c.1821)	William J. Carter
John T. Groves (c.1833-c.1899)	James Armstrong	Richard Stark
James West (born c.1810)	John M. Brooks (born c.1820)	Thomas H. Johnson
Noah Jones[838] (c.1821-1901)	Benjamin C. Wamsley (c.1814-1886)	Charles Guy
Thomas N. Towson	William Carter (c.1804-1874)	Thomas Towson
Henry Fitzhugh[839] (born c.1820)	Thomas Gollahorn	
William Fleet Cox (1821-1905)	James Bullock (born c.1816)	
James L. Heflin (born c.1827)	George W. Swetnam (born c.1830)	
James B. Garrison (born 1827)	James Horace Lacy[840] (1823-1906)	
James W. Watson[841] (born c.1819)	John J. Knoxville[842] (born c.1825)	

---

[834] Alexander was the son of Duff Green (1792-1854) and brother of James Lane Green (c.1831-1902) of Fredericksburg, Duff Green, Jr. of Stafford, and Charles Jones Green (born c.1840) of Texas. He served in the 9th Virginia Cavalry, Company A, Stafford Rangers and never married.

[835] During the War Between the States, Littleton served in Company A of the 47th Virginia Infantry where he was detailed as a wagon master. He also worked with the Quarter Master department. In 1888 Littleton was leasing and residing at Selwood, the western end of the Crow's Nest tract.

[836] George was the son of John Herndon (c.1794-1882). He was born in Fauquier and died in Laurel, Maryland, but spent most of his life in Stafford.

[837] Joseph lived at Crest and was a blacksmith by trade.

[838] During the War Between the States, Noah served with the 47th Regiment of Virginia Volunteers. He was wounded at Cold Harbor where he was shot through the neck. His wound affected the left side of his body and resulted in permanent disability. Noah died unmarried.

[839] Following the War Between the States, Henry submitted a claim to the Southern Claims Commission asking to be reimbursed for $65,415.50 worth of hogs, sheep, and other commodities taken from him by the Union army. He was granted $21,810.

[840] James was born in Tennessee, the son of a Presbyterian minister, though his lineage included numerous notable Virginians. He graduated from Washington University, now Washington and Lee, with a degree in law, though he practiced his profession only a short time. In 1848 he married Bettie Jones (born 1829) of Ellwood, Spotsylvania County. Maj. Lacy was noted as a speaker, his obituary noting, His was a very high order of intellectual endowment and he had a cultivated mind. Indeed, there was little of the best literature, ancient or modern, that he had not acquired. Thus equipped, and having inherited from his distinguished ancestry the powers to speak, he was an orator of great ability."

A few years after his marriage, the Lacys moved from Ellwood to Chatham where he was engaged in farming. During the subsequent war, this fine old home was known as the Lacy House. When hostilities erupted, he joined the Confederate army and eventually became a major on the staff of Gen. Kirby Smith. After the war, he returned to Chatham, which had been vandalized and abused by its Union occupants.

In 1870 a committee of Fredericksburg citizens visited him at Chatham and asked him to speak at the Baptist church in honor of Gen. Robert E. Lee who had just died. Maj. Lacy accepted the invitation "and on that occasion delivered an address that no one will ever forget who was so fortunate as to hear him (*Free Lance*, Jan. 30, 1906). At about this same time the Ladies' Confederate Memorial Association requested him to present their cause to the people of the South. The United States government passed a law providing funds for the establishment and maintenance of cemeteries for Union soldiers, but specifically denied funding for cemeteries for Confederate dead. Throughout the South groups of women, many of them widows of soldiers, banned together to raise money to create and maintain Confederate cemeteries. At his own expense Horace Lacy traveled to the Southern states and spoke to their legislatures, thereby ensuring that the Confederate cemeteries would always be maintained.

[841] James was the son of John and Nancy Watson of Brooke. In 1868 he married Eliza Brooks (born 1845), the daughter of Thomas and Elizabeth Brooks.

George W. Strother (born c.1806)　　Col. William James Green[843] (1825-1862)
James Sanford Garrison[844] (c.1820-1910)　James Cox (born c.1816)
Surveyor—John M. Homes

1859
Sheriff—Elias A. W. Hore
Deputy Sheriff—Cassius Williams[845] (c.1840-1862)
Jailer—William L. Morgan
Clerk—Henry R. Conway
Commonwealth's Attorney—John C. Moncure
Commissioner of the Revenue—Travers D. Moncure
Superintendent of Schools—Samuel S. Brooke
School Commissioners—Robert Kendall, Thomas Hill, Gustavus B. Wallace, Edward Waller, John H. Skinker, James Monteith, Robert G. Hickerson[846] (c.1829-1898)
Overseers of the Roads:
　　James McClure Scott[847] (1811-1893)—"from the Foot of James' Hill to the stage road through Belleplains in the place of L[ittleton] C. Fleming"
　　Littleton C. Fleming—"from Harris' corn Houses near the creek to the stage road from Fredericksburg at George P. King's corner"
　　George R. Cooper (1832-1892)—"from James Tolson's Black Smith shop to the Prince William line in place of John H[enry] Bridwell [c.1832-1891]"
Other Overseers of the Roads:

Charles W. Brewer[848] (1816-1892)	John Payne	Austin Pollard
John J. Knoxville	Lewis Hammett	John Arnold
Arba Randall Packard[849] (1819-1902)	William Bloxton	George Herndon
Daniel S. Coakley (c.1805-c.1866)	Richard Coleman Powers (born c.1805)	

---

[842] John was the son of Townley and Lucy Knoxville. In 1861 he married J. V. Milstead, the daughter of Samuel Milstead of Stafford.

[843] William was the son of Duff Green (1792-1854). During the War Between the States, he served with the 47th Virginia Infantry. On June 27, 1862 he was killed in action at Gaines' Mill while serving as an aide on Gen. William Dorsey Pender's staff. His brother, Capt. Charles Jones Green (born c.1840) was "desperately wounded" (*Alexandria Gazette*, July 9, 1862).

[844] The 1850 Stafford census lists James as a blacksmith. He was a long-time member of Aquia Church and died in Prince William.

[845] During the War Between the States, Cassius served with the 9th Virginia Cavalry. He was killed in action near Barnesville, Maryland.

[846] The son of Ransom Hickerson and Mary Mason Kendall. He married Mary Virginia Massie (born 1833) and lived at Apple Grove on Aquia Run and Garrisonville Road (State Route 610).

[847] The son of Bradford Ripley Alden Scott and Mary Miller Anderson. He was born in Albemarle County and died at Bel-Air, Spotsylvania. James married Sarah Travers Lewis (1813-1891).
　　At this point James resided at Salvington, the old Selden farm. He also lived at Little Whim and, at the outbreak of the War Between the States, at Pine Grove. The Union army burned Salvington to the ground during the winter of 1862/63 and used the bricks for chimneys for their winter quarters. Little Whim, where his family had first resided upon moving to Stafford from Spotsylvania, became Gen. Burnside's headquarters. The Scotts were forced to flee Pine Grove as the Union army massed for the assault on Fredericksburg. The enemy took over James' carpenter shop in the basement and used it as a battery.

[848] Charles was born in Prince William County but lived much of his life in Falmouth. He died of paralysis (stroke).

[849] In 1872 Arba was appointed one of the commissioners of the Free Bridge between Fredericksburg and Stafford County. He was originally from Massachusetts. In 1887 a newspaper notice announced that he was making superior quality brooms from broom corn grown on his farm. The writer stated, "One of these brooms will be sent to Uncle Sam on inauguration day" (*Virginia Star*, Jan. 31, 1887). Arba and his wife Rebecca (1816-1887) are buried at New Hope Methodist Church on New Hope Church Road (State Route 605).

Raleigh Lewis Cooper[850] (1832-1892)   Simeon Chancellor Peyton[851] (1829-1905)
Roy Herndon[852] (1819-1898)   James M. Hickerson[853] (1831-1871)
Julius L. Lee[854] (c.1822-after 1902)   John H. Schooler[855] (1812-1875)
Robert Lawrence Flatford[856] (1852-1898)   William Norman Blake[857] (c.1804-1892)
James A. Anderson (c.1832-c.1869)   Samuel Gordon Wallace[858] (1831-1897)
Thomas Benton Reamy[859] (1836-1910)   John Peden (1820-1892)
Surveyor—John M. Homes

1860
Sheriff—Elias A. W. Hore
Deputy Sheriff—James Ellen Waller[860] (c.1824-1862)
Constables:
    District 1—John S. Monteith
    District 2—Thomas A. Withers
    District 3—William T. Patton
    District 4—Richard Stark

---

[850] Raleigh was the only child of Richard Cooper (1806-1892). During the War Between the States, Raleigh commanded Cooper's Battery and was twice wounded. He lived near Stafford Store.

[851] The son of Thomas Peyton and Sarah Maddox. Simeon resided in White Oak.

[852] Lee Roy Herndon was the son of John Herndon (c.1794-1882) and Lucinda "Lucy" Combs (c.1796-c.1867). Roy was baptized at Chappawamsic Baptist Church on Sept. 24, 1874. Around 1852 he married Catherine A. Keys (1833-1906). They lived on Brentown Road in the northern end of Stafford that later became part of the Marine Corps reservation.

[853] James was the son of Ransom M. Hickerson (c.1794-1844) and Mary Mason Kendall (c.1798-c.1867). In 1856 James married Mary Virginia Massie (born 1853) and lived at Apple Grove. Mary married secondly John. W. Wamsley.

[854] Julius lived at Monteithville near Bethel Church. During the War Between the States, he served with the 30th Virginia Infantry. In April 1865 he was captured at Five Forks and released from Point Lookout in June 1865.

[855] For many years John was a resident of Stafford. Following the War Between the States, John submitted a claim to the Southern Claims Commission asking to be reimbursed for $5,290 worth of cattle taken from him by the Union army. He was granted $1,450. John was accidentally killed by a streetcar in Richmond while trying to cross the Clay Street line of the Richmond Railway and Electric Company. After being hit, he was pushed down the line for some distance resulting in multiple severe injuries. His obituary stated, "Mr. Schooler was a gallant soldier of Company C, 30th Virginia Regiment, of which Capt. C. Wistar Wallace was commander" (*Free Lance*, July 7, 1896). In 1892 John submitted a Confederate service pension application stating that he had been shot in the back while the service and that the wound had disabled him. The wound, which was actually to his neck and back, occurred at Drewry's Bluff in May 1864. John was also a member of Maury Camp, No. 2, Confederate Veterans. He was the brother of James Wilson Schooler (1824-1916) of Hartwood and the son of Thomas E. Schooler (born c.1787).

[856] Robert was a talented businessman who was involved in a variety of endeavors. According to his obituary, "He conducted a grocery store, ran two saw mills, and was one of the largest shippers of lumber, poplar wood and railroad ties in this section" (*Free Lance*, Sept. 27, 1898). Robert also owned the wharf at Coal Landing, and was the county chairman of the Republican party of Stafford. Robert married Fannie Edmonia Gill (1852-1936), the daughter of Charles E. Gill (c.1818-1890) of Stafford. Robert lived on the present site of North Stafford High School and died of typhoid fever.

[857] William was the son of Robert Norman Blake (c.1804-1892) and his wife Mary Ann (born c.1823). In 1897 William married Kathleen Scaggs (born c.1873), the daughter of George L. and Georgiana Scaggs of Maryland.

[858] Samuel resided at Liberty Hall and was the brother of Casper Wistar Wallace (1834-1907) and Judge Alexander Wellington Wallace (1843-1927). He was buried at Liberty Hall.

[859] Thomas married Harriet "Hallie" Margaret Curtis (1840-1917), the daughter of Francis Curtis (1806-1891).

[860] James was the son of James and Ann Waller (born c. 1798). In 1856 he married Bettie Ann Wickliff (born c.1834), the daughter of Davie and Emilie Wickliff of Fauquier County.

Clerk—Henry R. Conway
Commonwealth's Attorney—John C. Moncure
Commissioner of the Revenue—Travers D. Moncure[861]
Overseers of the Poor:
    District 1—Henry Washington Edwards[862] (1829-1899)
    Unspecified District—William Lee[863]
Superintendent of Schools—Samuel S. Brooke
School Commissioners—William T. Patton,[864] John H. Skinker, Gustavus B. Wallace, Edmund F. Rose, Robert
        G. Hickerson, James Monteith, Edward Waller
Overseers of the Roads:
    Joseph C. Gee[865] (c.1836-c.1897)—"from outer gate at Boscobelle by Mrs. Cox's lane to the stage road
        near Falmouth in the place of William Carter removed from the County"
    Robert Mountjoy[866] (1828-1891)—"from Chappawamsic road to Purcell's mill"
    John W. Brewer—"from Mrs. Waller's corner in Falmouth to A. K. Phillips' Gate"
    Robert A. Gray[867] (1830-1915)—"from King George line to Pollock's Mill (on the river road)"
    Elias A. W. Hore—"from W. Waller's gate to E. A. W. Hore's gate"
    James Heflin ("Manager for J. Horace Lacy at Chatham")—"from Scott's run to Chatham bridge"
Other Overseers of the Roads:
    John R. Goodwin[868] (c.1828-1911)   John J. Withers
    James Ashby[869] (1827-1861)   James I. Eustace[870] (born c.1826)
    Wesley A. Musselman[871] (born c.1835)   George Watson (born c.1830)
    John C. Edrington, Jr. (1800-1879)   Granville Embrey[872] (c.1828-1906)
Surveyor—John M. Homes

---

[861] The court minutes of Nov. 22, 1860 read, "Travers D. Moncure having failed to qualify as Comr of the Revenue for the County of Stafford within the time prescribed by law, it is ordered that an election be held for the election of a Comr for said County on the second Saturday in December next at Stafford Court House." On Dec. 19, 1860 the minutes record that Travers "made the oath prescribed by law and entered into and acknowledged a bond in the penalty of five thousand dollars."

[862] Henry was one of the bridge commissioners and was buried at New Hope Church. He lived at New Boscobel, his farm to the east of the old Fitzhugh farm, Boscobel.

[863] On Aug. 15, 1860 a new election was called to fill this position as William Lee "refuses to qualify."

[864] Appointed by the court to fill the seat of Robert Kendall who died.

[865] During the War Between the States, Joseph was a member of the Fredericksburg Artillery. In April 1864 he was captured at Stafford Courthouse and held as a prisoner of war.

[866] Robert was the son of Thornton Mountjoy (1794:7-c.1881) and Mary Payne (1794-1856). In April 1861 Robert enlisted in the Confederate army but was discharged one year later due to pneumonia. In 1864 he married Mary Mildred Griffis (c.1844-1909), the daughter of Samuel H. Griffis (born 1814) of Stafford.

[867] Robert Atchison Gray was the son of John Bowie Gray (1809-1848) and Jane Moore Cave (1811-1890) of Traveler's Rest. During the War Between the States, Robert served with the 9th Virginia Cavalry. In September 1863 he transferred to Company H of the 4th Virginia Cavalry.

[868] John was the son of William and Mary Goodwin of Prince William County and lived in the Onville area of Stafford. In 1858 he married Margaret E. Bridwell (1842-after 1911), the daughter of Benjamin and Ann Bridwell (born c.1807) of Stafford. John submitted a pension application as a disabled Confederate veteran, having been a member of the 9th Virginia Cavalry under Capt. Thomas C. Waller and Sgt. Hugh Adie. John joined the service at Chappawamsic in 1862 but served only about six months before being captured. Although he was paroled, his imprisonment resulted "disease of the stomach and bladder" that made it nearly impossible for him to get around or work.

[869] James was the son of Col. Turner Ashby (1789-1835) of Fauquier County and Dorothea Farrer Green (1797-1865) and the brother of Gen. Turner Ashby (1826-1862). James married Frances Vowles Moncure (1828-1910), the daughter of John Moncure (1793-1876) of Woodbourne. He was to be in command of the 9th Virginia Cavalry, but died before the unit was formed.

[870] James was the son of John Eustace of Fauquier. In 1859 he married Mrs. S. M. Pritchett (born c.1829), the daughter of Robert and Eliza Kendall of Stafford.

[871] Wesley was the son of Alice Musselman. In 1854 he married Susan E. Bryant (1835-1890).

[872] During the War Between the States, Granville served in Cook's Brigade. He died unmarried.

Flour Inspector—William Head (born c.1812)

1861
Sheriff—Elias A. W. Hore[873]
Deputy Sheriffs—James E. Waller (c.1824-1862) and Cassius Williams
Constables:
    District 1—John L. Monteith (born c.1831)
    District 2—Thomas A. Withers (born c.1814)
    District 3—William T. Patton
    District 4—Richard Stark
Jailer—William L. Morgan
Clerk—Henry R. Conway
Commonwealth's Attorney—John C. Moncure[874]
Commissioner of the Revenue—Travers D. Moncure
Overseers of the Poor:
    John L. Garrison[875] (born c.1814), James E. Schooler[876] (born c.1833), William Armstrong, William Ashby (born c.1814)
Overseers of the Roads:
    James Heflin—"from Mrs. Waller's corner in Falmouth to A. K. Phillips'[877] gate"
    Thomas Lee—"from Potomac Run to Accakeek"
    Abraham Primmer—"from mouth of Cox's Lane to the old Stage Road from Fredericksburg to Potomac Creek"
    John Green—"from Potomac run by Arnold's to Stafford Court House"
    James French[878] (1803-1865)—"from Long branch to a live tree"
Other Overseers of the Roads:

John Hitaffer	James Cox[879]	Duff Green
John Moncure (1793-1876)	James M. Scott	James Leach
William Tolson (born c.1823)	Thomas Gollahorn	William Snellings
Lelwellington E. Pearson (born c.1823)	Johnson Carter (1797-1861)	George Gollahorn
Charles H. Roberson (c.1823-1892)	Hedgman Green (c.1800-1878)	
James W. Armstrong[880] (born c.1839)	Richard E. Monteith[881] (born c.1834)	

---

[873] Elias tendered his resignation from the position of sheriff at the July term of 1861. He was then appointed crier of the circuit and county court of Stafford.
[874] The court minutes of June 19, 1861 read, "John C. Moncure having this day tendered his resignation as Commonwealth's Attorney for this County—The Court doth appoint Charles Herndon, Esq. Attorney for the Commonwealth till the election shall be ordered to supply said vacancy."
[875] The 1850 Stafford census listed John as a millwright.
[876] James was the son of John H. Schooler (1812-1875) of Orchard Field just east of the courthouse. John also owned and operated the Gourds Fishery from his property. James married Lucy E. Hedgman (born c.1834), the daughter of John and Mary Hedgman. James and Lucy lived for many years at Garrard's Ordinary where they operated a store and post office.
[877] Alexander Keene Phillips (1805-1892) was, until the War Between the States, a wealthy Fredericksburg businessman. He lived at Mulberry Hill in Stafford. More commonly known as the Phillips' House, this beautiful (and then brand new) brick home was occupied by Union soldiers during the Battle of Fredericksburg and was burned to the ground.
[878] James French was born at Oak Hill in Loudoun County, the son of William Lewis French (born 1775) and Anna Guy Isemonger (born 1776). In 1830 James married in Washington Sarah A. "Sally" Curtis (1812-1872), the daughter of George Curtis, Jr. (1767-1844) and Jemima Payne (died c.1869). George gave James and Sally Poplar Grove Farm (located on the west side of Poplar Road (State Route 616), which adjoined his own Green Meadows. Poplar Grove had been seated by Quakers who were employed at James Hunter's Rappahannock Forge and who left the area around 1812. Both James and Sally are buried at Poplar Grove.
[879] Probably James Cox (born c.1816), the son of Samuel and Sarah Cox. James was a brother-in-law of William Fleet Cox (1821-1905). He married Ann "Nancy" Newton, the daughter of John Newton and Mildred Curtis.

Cuthbert Byram[882] (born c.1822) James M. Sthreshley[883] (1795-1869)
Harrison J. Skinner[884] (c.1821-1862) Charles Benson Bullard[885] (1815-1873)
Robert Norman Blake[886] (c.1816-1892)

Surveyor—John M. Homes

1862

Sheriff—Elias A. W. Hore
Clerk—Henry R. Conway
Commonwealth's Attorney—John C. Moncure
School Superintendent—Edward Waller
School Commissioners—Gustavus B. Wallace, Edmund F. Rose, James Monteith, Robert G. Hickerson, William T. Patton, John H. Skinker, Samuel Selden Brooke, Jr.[887] (1841-1918)
Surveyor—John M. Homes

1863

Clerk—Henry R. Conway
Surveyor—John M. Homes

1864

Sheriff—Elias A. W. Hore[888]
Constables—Richard Stark, William T. Patton, William Monteith[889] (c.1822-1905), Marshall Payne[890]

---

[880] During the War Between the States, James served with the 30th Virginia Infantry. In November 1862 he was captured on the Rappahannock River and held at Old Capitol Prison until being exchanged in May 1863.

[881] Richard, a carpenter, was the son of James and Elizabeth Monteith (born c.1806). In 1859 he married Georgianna Rowe (born c.1834), the daughter of the Rev. John G. Rowe. During the War Between the States, Richard served with Company A of the 47th Virginia Infantry.

[882] "Cuth" was the son of Cuthbert and Sarah Byram (born c.1785) and lived on property that is now the site of Colonial Forge High School on Courthouse Road (State Route 630). In 1855 he married Jane Musselman (born c.1836), the daughter of Jesse (born c.1794) and Delila Musselman (born c.1808).

[883] The son of Capt. William Sthreshley and Elizabeth Buckner Jones, widow of Thomas Jones of Stafford. In 1828 James married Mary Peyton Bolling Fitzhugh (born 1808), the daughter of John Bolling Stith Fitzhugh (1778-1825) and Frances Tabb (1794-1868).

[884] In late March or early April 1862 Harrison enlisted in Company A of the 47th Virginia Infantry. About six weeks later, he died of measles at Chimborazo Hospital.

[885] Charles was the son of Charles Bullard (1770:80-1850:60) and Martha Herndon. Prior to the War Between the States, Charles B. Bullard was a member of the Virginia Home Guard. In 1838 Charles married Sarah Ann Chancellor (1819-1915) of Chancellorsville. At the outset of the War Between the States, he and his wife resided just east of Chancellorsville. Their home was destroyed during the battle and they moved to Stafford. Charles died of pneumonia. He was a member of Masonic Lodge #4 in Fredericksburg and was first buried in the Masonic cemetery in that town. Later, his body was moved to Gatewood Cemetery in Washington, DC where he and his wife were buried.

[886] Robert was the son of Samuel Blake and was born in Middlesex County but lived most of his life in Stafford. He lived at Woodend adjoining Greenbank and near Berea Church. Robert died in Stafford of paralysis.

[887] Samuel attended VMI for one year and then enrolled at the University of Virginia. In April 1861 he enlisted in the Stafford Guards, Company 1, 30th Virginia Infantry, later the 47th Virginia Infantry. He was promoted to captain in May 1862. Samuel served in most of the major battles including Fredericksburg, Chancellorsville, Wilderness, Spotsylvania, and North Anna. After the war, Samuel returned to Stafford where he tried and failed at the lumber business and farming. He then studied law in Fredericksburg where he practiced until 1882. In 1872 he married Betty Lewis Young of Fredericksburg. In 1882 he removed to Roanoke where he served as clerk of the Circuit Court for 31 years. He died in 1918 of Bright's Disease.

[888] Also served as Crier of Elections for 1864.

[889] At the outset of the War Between the States, William enlisted with the 47th Virginia Infantry. He deserted in June 1862.

(1824-1887)
Clerk—George Vowles Moncure[891] (1826-1901)
Commonwealth's Attorney—Samuel Greenhow Daniel[892] (acting)
Cotton Agent—Nathaniel W. Ford[893]
Surveyor of the Roads:
    Dr. Hugh Morson[894] (1811-1877)—"from the King George line to Lacy's Mill [Chatham Mill]"
Surveyor—John M. Homes

1865
Sheriff—Elias A. W. Hore
Jailer—Elias A. W. Hore
Constables—Richard Stark, William T. Patton, James Wilson Schooler[895] (1824-1916)
Clerk—James E. Towson
Commissioner of Accounts of the Court—John H. Suttle
Commonwealth's Attorney—John H. Suttle
Commissioner of the Revenue—Robert G. Hickerson
Cotton Agent—Duff Green[896]
Salt Agent—Elias A. W. Hore[897]
Committees to Care for Citizens Made Needy by the War:
    District 1—William Pollock, William H. Hansbrough[898] (c.1803-1875), Walker P. Conway
    District 2—John C. Shelton, Thomas Julian Skinker[899] (1819-1900), Gustavus B. Wallace

---

[890] Marshall was born in Fauquier County. He married first in 1847 Harriet A. Curtis (born c.1822). In 1865 he married secondly Mrs. Matilda N. (Whitescarver) Oliver. Marshall served in the Confederate army and died at Bellevue, Fauquier County.

[891] George was the son of John Moncure (IV) (1793-1876) of Woodbourne near Accokeek Run. In 1849 he married Mary Conway Ashby (1830-1897), the sister of Gen. Turner Ashby (1828-1862). George and Mary resided at Chelsea, a 460-acre farm in Wide Water. This tract is now Chelsea Manor subdivision on Wide Water Road (State Route 611).

[892] Samuel was the son of Travers Daniel, Jr. (1763-1812) and Mildred Stone (1772-1837) of Crow's Nest. In 1859 he married Maria Henderson (born c.1837). In 1856 and 1857 he practiced law in Fredericksburg.

[893] The court minutes of 1864 state that Ford "was unanimously appointed by the Court as agent for the purchase and distribution of cotton cloth, cotton yarns, and cotton cards for the County of Stafford." The minutes indicate that he resigned this position on Jan. 18, 1865. John Coakley (died 1874) was appointed in his stead.

[894] In 1849 Dr. Morson married Rosalie V. Lightfoot (1819-1889), the daughter of Philip Lightfoot and Sallie Bernard of Port Royal. He removed to Port Royal c.1869 where he practiced medicine. Hugh was the son of Alexander Morson (1759-1822).

[895] James was born in Stafford and, during the War Between the States, served in the 30th Virginia Regiment. He lived his later years in the Confederate Soldiers Home in Richmond but returned to Fredericksburg each year to enjoy the fair. He did so in 1916, celebrated his 92nd birthday while there, and the following day suffered a massive stroke. He was buried in the Confederate Cemetery in Fredericksburg (*Free Lance*, Nov. 7, 1916).

[896] On Jan. 18, 1865 "the Court reconsidered the appointment of J. Coakley as agent for the purchase and distribution of Cotton for the County of Stafford, as it was under the impression no one in the County of Stafford would accept. But it was ascertained before the Court adjourned that McDuff Green would do so, the Court withdrew the appointment of J. Coakley of Fredericksburg and returned his bond and then unanimously elected McDuff Green Cotton agent."

[897] Elias was instructed by the Court "to buy for the County for full Compliment of Salt to which the County is entitled. The court undertaking to indemnify the said agent all loss by the public enemys depredations or otherwise and to allow the said agent a reasonable compensation for his services after the Same shall have been procured."

[898] William lived at the Glebe on Muddy Creek. He served in the 9th Virginia Cavalry, Company A, Stafford Rangers.

[899] Thomas J. Skinker was the son of Samuel Hampson Skinker (1785-1856) and was born at Wolfmarsh, Clarke County, Virginia. During the War Between the States, he served with the 9th Virginia Cavalry.

District 3—Charles A. Tackett, William T. Patton, James Tolson
District 4—William E. Moncure, Samuel S. Brooke, Jr., Albert Clift[900] (c.1808-1890)

Agents to Distribute the State Funds Received by Charles Herndon:
District 1—William H. Hansbrough
District 2—Fielding Barton Stone[901] (born c.1827)
District 3—Charles A. Tackett
District 4—William E. Moncure

Overseers of the Poor:
John L. Garrison[902] (born c.1814), James E. Schooler, William Armstrong (born c.1817)

Criers of Elections:
Falmouth—Harris Hill[903] (c.1809-1908)

Surveyors of the Roads:
Dr. Hugh Morson—"from the Chatham bridge to Pollock's Mill"
James Pollard—"from Berea Church to Falmouth"
Edwin C. Walker (c.1828-1892)—"from Pollock's mill to the King George County line"
Fielding Alexander Coakley[904] (c.1837-after 1908)—"from Coakley Store to Peden's Gate"
Charles W. Brewer—"from Peden's Gate on the Warrenton road to Falmouth"
Joseph C. Wine (c.1833-1909)—"from Potomac Run to Mrs. Master's"
William Gollahorn (born c.1827)—"the old stage road from Potomac run to the old Brick Kiln"
William Snellings (born c.1821)—"from the corner of Mrs. E[liza] A[nn] Green's farm at the junction of the Court House road to Coakley's Store on Potomac Run"
Richard Henry Stevens—"from Stafford Court House to Accakeek Run"
Alexander Morson Green[905] (c.1828-1904)—"from Accakeek run to Potomac Run"
Fleet Cox—"from King George Line to the White Oak run"
Amos Rowley—"from Ficklen's bridge to the old brick kiln"
John Henceford Garner[906] (c.1811-1886)—"from Walnut tree at James Monroe's[907] to Warrenton road at Hamets"[908]
James MacDonald Briggs (1822-1900)—"from Spotted Tavern to Hartwood"
Ludwell Herndon[909] (1823-1908)—"from Villers shop to long branch"

Thomas was captured in Stafford in May 1863 and was paroled from the Old Capitol Prison in June 1863. His disdain for the North was so intense that after the war, he refused to cross the Potomac River. He married Annie Brown Rose (1848-1900) and lived at Oakley for some years before moving to Middleburg where he died.

[900] In 1872 Albert was appointed one of the commissioners of the Free Bridge between Fredericksburg and Stafford County.

[901] Fielding was the son of William Hawkins Stone (c.1809-c.1851) and his wife Mildred. In 1858 he married Ann K. Schooler (born c.1831), the daughter of Thomas E. (born c.1787) and Mary Stone of Stafford.

[902] John was listed in the 1860 Stafford census as a wheelwright.

[903] Around 1845 Harris Hill married Mary A. Latham (c.1812-c.1860), the daughter of George Latham (c.1780-c.1846) of Spotted Tavern. An 1855 newspaper announced the arrest of Harris Hill for the murder of John Limerick. The notice stated, "Hill is said to be a man of inoffensive disposition, making it probable that he acted in self-defense" (*Virginia Herald*, Jan. 8, 1855).

[904] Fielding was the son of Daniel S. Coakley (1805-c.1866) and made his living as a merchant in Stafford. In July 1861 he enlisted in Company C of the 30th Virginia Infantry. He was transferred to the Surry Light Artillery in April 1864.

[905] Alexander was the son of Duff Green (1792-1854) of Falmouth and the brother of James L. Green of Fredericksburg, Duff Green, Jr. of Stafford, and Charles J. Green of Texas. He never married.

[906] The son of Henceford Garner. John died in Stafford of pneumonia.

[907] James Monroe (c.1789-1867) was involved with the gold mines in the south end of the county. Following the War Between the States, James submitted a claim to the Southern Claims Commission asking to be reimbursed for $1,646.75 worth of supplies taken from him by the Union army. His claim was rejected.

[908] The Hammett farm was on the south side of Route 17 and on the northwest side of the intersection of that road with Holly Corner Road (State Route 655).

Samuel H. Griffis (1814-c.1887)—"from Chappawamsic Run to Aquia Run"
Joseph Herndon[910] (1827-1906)—"from Prince William Line to the Red House"
Alexander Hamilton Mountjoy[911] (1826-c.1902)—"from Red House to H. M. Jones old shop"
William T. Patton—"the road which Sanford Humphries was formerly surveyor"
Wesley Honey (1820-1909)—"the Road which William T. Masters[912] was formerly overseer of"
Gustavus Fritter[913] (1821-c.1900)— "the road which Charles Turner was formerly overseer of"
George K. Blackburn—"from Hartwood to Potomac Run"
Henry Payne (c.1837-1862)—"from Potomac Run to William Ball"
Robert C. Rogers[914] (c.1818-1888)—"from Richland Hill to D. S. Coakley's Store"
Dade Hooe[915] (c.1818-1881)—"from Stafford Court House to Accakeek run"
Alexander Reed (born 1792)—"from Potomac Run to the forks in the road near Catharine Master's"
Jefferson Heflin[916] (c.1811-1880)—"from signboard near Thomas Heflin's to Cooper Town"[917]
John Worrell—"from Stark's gate to Cooper Town"
George A. Bowling[918] (c.1817-after 1902)—"from Aquia road to Tackett's Mill"
James M. Hickerson (born c.1831)—"from Aquia run to Stafford Store"
James Pulaski Baker[919] (c.1825-c.1869)—"from signboard at E. Harding's to Dumfries road"
James H. Lowry[920] (c.1834-1868)—"from foot of Bellview Hill intersecting the White Oak road at the Post Oak near the old Blacksmith Shop"
James A. Daffan—"from Potomac run to Hopewell Meeting House"
Robert W. Taylor—"from Concord to Stark's gate"
John Henry Fritter (c.1824-1896)—"from the Telegraph road by Byram's store to branch near Barnet Fritter and Elijah Patterson"[921]

---

[909] Ludwell was the son of John Herndon (c.1794-1882) and Lucinda "Lucy" Combs (c.1796-c.1867). Around 1822 John and his family moved from Fauquier County to Stafford, settling near Stafford Store. Ludwell died as a result of a stroke suffered at the home of his son-in-law, Wallace Franklin (born c.1855) who lived at Coakley. In 1872 Ludwell was appointed one of the commissioners of the Free Bridge between Fredericksburg and Stafford County. At the time of his death, Ludwell was the oldest native of Stafford. He was for many years a member of Rock Hill Baptist Church.

[910] Joseph was the son of John Herndon (c.1794-1882) and lived near Stafford Store. He married Amanda Carter, the daughter of William Carter (1807-1874). During the War Between the States, Joseph served in the 9th Virginia Cavalry, Company A, Stafford Rangers. He was captured by a group from the 8th Illinois Cavalry near Poolesville, Maryland and was described as being about 5'11" tall with dark hair and eyes.

[911] Alexander served in the 9th Virginia Cavalry, Company A, Stafford Rangers.

[912] During the War Between the States, William T. Masters (1844-1914) served with Company I of the 47th Virginia Infantry and was captured at Manassas in August 1862. He took the oath in May 1863 and was sent to Washington. By profession William was a miller. He was the brother of James F. and John Masters.

[913] Gustavus was the son of Enoch Fritter (c.1765-c.1845) and ___ Grigsby (died c.1828). His first wife was Mary F. Cardine (c.1820-1874). He married secondly Caroline Wilson (c.1835-1881) and thirdly Mary Amelia Bettis (born c.1852).

[914] According to the 1860 Stafford census, Robert was born in Ireland.

[915] Dade was the son of Dade Hooe (c.1756-c.1837) and Nancy James (born c.1760) and was born in Prince William County. He died in Stafford unmarried.

[916] Jefferson was the son of William and Lydia Heflin and was a member of Rock Hill Baptist Church. In 1866 he served as clerk of that church and in 1874 was superintendent of the Sunday School.

[917] Cooper Town was an area roughly where Lake Arrowhead subdivision is now located.

[918] During the War Between the States, George A. Bowling served with Cooper's Battery and was wounded in the left knee.

[919] The son of Fielding Baker (1799-after 1870).

[920] James was the son of William and Susan Lowry and was a carpenter. In 1854 he married Lucinda Limerick (born c.1819), the daughter of John and Frances Limerick. He was born and died in King George County, though he lived part of his life in Stafford. He died of paralysis (stroke).

[921] Elijah T. Patterson (1808-1870) was the son of Perry and Winifred Patterson (c.1782-1850). During the War Between the States, he served in Company I of the 47th Virginia Infantry. On May 28, 1863 he was

Richard E. Monteith (born c.1837)—"from Robersons old Black Smith shop, until it intersects the White Oak near the Post Oak"

Capt. John Gray Pollock[922] (c.1831-1906)—"from Pollock's Mill to the Chatham Bridge"

Dr. Hugh Morson—"from the King George Line to Lacy's Mill"

James Pollard (born c.1800)—"from Berea Church to Falmouth"

William Embrey (born c.1825)—"from Richland Hill to Deep run"

James Cox—"on the Pudding Hill road from Black Swamp to Atwell Butlers"[923]

James Gollahorn (born c.1832)—"from Banks ford on Potomac run to the Warrenton road above Falmouth"

Samuel Gordon Wallace[924] (1831-1897)—"from Oders Shop on Banks road to the Warrenton road at Berea Church"

Surveyors—John M. Homes and William Barber

1866

Sheriff—Elias A. W. Hore
Coroner—Nathaniel W. Ford
Clerk—James E. Towson
Constables—William T. Patton, Richard Stark, Harris Hill, James W. Schooler[925]
Overseer of the Poor—William Armstrong
Surveyors of the Roads:

John E. Glascock (born c.1841)—"from the Aquia Road to St. Marysville"

___ Fleming—"from Harris Corn Houses to the white oak Road to George P. King's corner"

James Heflin[926]—"from the run at the foot of the Hill near G. B. Wallace on White Oak road to Scott's Ferry"

___ Walker—"between King's Farm and Boscobell from its intersection with the Road from Harris' Corn Houses to Hopewell and intersection to the White Oak road at Wallace's"

Thomas Johnston (born c.1835)—"from the ford on Potomac run near Stone's Mill to Banks road near Paul Hulls"

Robert F. Lunsford[927] (c.1832-1903)—"from the intersection of poplar road near James Lunsfords to the wood cutting road near William English's"

Raleigh Lewis Cooper (1832-1892)—"from Beaverdam run to the Fauquier line"

Armistead A. Armstrong (1816-1885)—"from Long Branch Ford to Mrs. Thomas Withers"

John Anthony (born c.1821)—"from the lower ford upon Potomac run to Claibourne run"

William Snellings—"from Potomac run to brick yard"

---

captured in Stafford and sent to Old Capitol Prison. He was later paroled and returned home to Stafford. Elijah was the father of Joseph S. and William P. Patterson (c.1838-1911).

[922] John was the son of William Pollock, Sr. (1797-1865) and Janet Gray. During the War Between the States, John enlisted with the Fredericksburg Artillery as a sergeant and was wounded at Chancellorsville. Shortly after the war, he married Estelle Lewis, the daughter of Fielding Lewis of King George. Around 1901 John moved from Stafford to King George. He died at his King George home, Hobson, and was buried in the Lewis cemetery at Marmion.

[923] Atwell Butler (c.1814-after 1870) married Lucy Ann Cox (c.1818-1853), the daughter of Samuel and Sarah Cox. Following the War Between the States, Atwell submitted a claim to the Southern Claims Commission asking to be reimbursed for $$7,901 worth of wood, fencing, and corn taken from him by the Union army. His claim was rejected.

[924] Samuel was the son of John Hooe Wallace (1793-1828) and Mary Nicholas Gordon (1800-1879), the daughter of Samuel Gordon (1759-1843) of Kenmore in Fredericksburg.

[925] According to the court minutes of Aug. 15, 1866, James failed to execute his bond as required by law. The justices ordered a new election at which time James was reelected and executed his bond.

[926] Probably James Edwin Heflin (1821-1901), the son of James Hefferlin (born 1786) and Mary Anna Walker (1790-1831). James E. Heflin married Susan T. Patterson (1824-1901), the daughter of Lucy Patterson of Fredericksburg. He was buried at Falmouth Baptist Church.

[927] Robert was the son of William (born c.1785) and Willie Lunsford (born c.1795). In 1861 he married Aphia F. Swetnam (born c.1844), the daughter of John A. (1792-1854) and Sarah Swetnam (born c.1811). Robert lived near Roseville.

William Gollahorn—"from corner of Ridgway farm intersection with telegraph road to Coakley's Store"
James L. Carter (born c.1834)—"from Waller's Fishery to the Telegraph road near Aquia"
Arthur A. Embrey (born c.1824)—"from St. George Branch to Garrisonville"
John Henry Bridwell[928] (c.1832-1891)—"from the Prince William Line and by Bellfair Mills to Garrison's Shop"
Dr. [Hawkins] Stone—"from the telegraph road by Garrisonville and Ebenezer to Aquia run"
Col. Thomas Conway Waller[929] (1832-1895)—"from Aquia run to Garrisonville"
Robert L. West—"from Stafford Courthouse to Aquia run"
George Herndon[930] (1821-1898)—"from Aquia Run to Stafford Store"
John M. Stewart (born c.1822)—"from the Woodcutting road near Elijah Patterson's to the Cole Landing"
Roy Herndon (1819-1898)—"from the Garrisonville and Stafford Store road to the woodcutting road passing by the Shelket's Mill"
James W. Watson[931] (born c.1819)—"from Andrew Chapel to intersection the Marlborough Road leading by Salem"
John H. Schooler—"from Long Branch to the Warrenton Road"
William Jones—"the road known as the Concord Road"
James Henry Eustace (born 1801)—"the road leading by his house"
John Fritter—"by Hugh Adie's to Mrs. Masters"
Thomas B. Hay[932] (c.1800-1868)—"from White Oak Meeting house to Pollock's Mill"
Henry Wood Moncure[933] (1836-1874)—"from Wamsley to Tusculum"
Thomas Griffis (c.1797-1886)—"from the Aquia Road near Gravelly Ridge to Telegraph Road"
Col. William H. Browne—"from Potomac run to Accakeek run via Snowden C. Hall's"
Gustavus B. Newton[934]—"from the stage road to King George line"
John Heflin—"commencing at Barnet Fritters branch and running to the fork adjoining Downman's Farm"
James W. Schooler—"from Coakley's old Store to Powers gate"
James Lowry (1817-1899)—"from Stafford Court House to Andrew Chapel"
John M. Luck[935] (1827-1888)—"from White Oak run to the run below G[ustavus] B. Wallace's"
Charles A. Tackett—"from Tackett's Mill to the intersection of the Aquia road in the place of George

---

[928] John was the son of Isaac Bridwell (c.1781-1866) and Mary Bradshaw (born c.1800). During the War Between the States, John served as a teamster with the 9th Virginia Cavalry. In 1872 he married Mary E. Gill (born c.1849).

[929] The son of Edward Waller (1805-1883) of Grafton near modern Anne E. Moncure Elementary School in Garrisonville. Thomas built and lived at Wayside which stood on the north side of Garrisonville Road (State Route 610) and is now the site of Stafford Marketplace. From October 1862-June 1863 he served as 3rd Major. Thomas was wounded at Brandy Station in Oct 1863. From June 1863-October 1864 he was 4th Lt. Colonel, and from October 1864-April 1865 4th Colonel. He returned to Stafford after the war.

[930] The son of John Herndon (c.1794-1882) and Lucinda "Lucy" Combs (c.1796-c.1862). George was born in Fauquier County and died in Laurel, Prince George's County, Maryland, but spent most of his life in Stafford on land adjoining that of his father. George died at the home of his daughter, Mrs. Virginia Ashby.

[931] James was the son of John and Nancy Watson. In 1868 he married Eliza Brooks (born 1845), the daughter of Thomas R. (born c.1801) and Elizabeth Brooks (born c.1797).

[932] Thomas was the son of William and Margaret Hay of Stafford. He married ___ Bruce and resided at Springfield, the old Bruce home.

[933] Henry was the son of Henry Wood Moncure (1800-1866) and Catherine Cary Ambler. In 1860 he married Julia Trent Warwick (1840-1906) and lived at Windsor Forest.

[934] It is not certain whether this was Gustavus, Jr. (born c.1845) or his father, Gustavus, Sr. (born c.1812). The latter was the son of Benjamin Newton (born 1769) and Nancy Butler. Gustavus, Sr. married first Matilda Cox, the daughter of Samuel Cox. He married secondly Eleanor Monteith, the daughter of Enos Monteith and Eleanor Thorn.

[935] John was born in Loudoun County, the son of Jordan B. and Adaline (Gatewood) Luck. He died in Stafford of a hemorrhage.

A. Bowling
- Strother Shackelford[936] (1840-1925)—"the road leading from the telegraph road"
- William Shepherd Cloe[937] (1832-1919)—"leading from Red House to Beaverdam run"
- James E. Schooler—"from Stafford Court House to Andrew Chapel"
- James Lowry—"from Andrew Chapel via Brooks Mill to Accakeek run"

Surveyor—John M. Homes

1867

Sheriff—Elias A. W. Hore
Constables:
- District 2—James W. Schooler, Charles A. Love[938] (born 1841)

Commonwealth's Attorney—John H. Suttle
Clerk—James E. Towson
Commissioner of the Revenue—Robert G. Hickerson
Superintendent of Schools—Edward Waller
School Commissioners—Arthur F. Clift, William T. Patton, Robert G. Hickerson, William Irvine, Fielding B. Stone, James Monteith, William H. Hansbrough
Overseer of the Poor—William Armstrong
Overseers of the Roads:
- Charles Seddon Heflin[939] (1829-1898)—"from Ficklen's bridge in Falmouth to Brickyard—Amos Rowley removed"
- Marshal Huffman (born c.1833)—"from Banks ford on Potomac run to its intersection with the Telegraph road near Daniel Embrey's"[940]
- John Anthony (born c.1819)—"from Potomac run to Accakeek run"
- Sydney Smith Lee[941] (1802-1869)—"from the Richland mill to its intersection with the Arkendale road"
- Thomas Ramey[942]—"from Spotted Tavern to the Fauquier line"
- John J. Leitch[943] (c.1822-1882)—"from A. K. Phillips' gate to Falmouth"
- Sidnor Powers[944] (born c.1838)—"from the Telegraph road through the Chappawamsic farm to its intersection with the river road"
- Armistead A. Armstrong—"from the Long Branch to Warrenton road"

---

[936] Strother married Anne Edwards.

[937] The son of Alexander (born c.1800) and Drucilla Cloe (born c.1800). During the War Between the States, William served in the 9th Virginia Cavalry, Company A, Stafford Rangers.

[938] Charles was born in Prince William County, the son of Henry and Eliza Love. In 1867 he married Ella M. Coakley (born c.1845), the daughter of David and Susan Coakley of Stafford.
   According to the court minutes of Jan. 19, 1867, the justices ordered an election in the Second District to elect a new constable to replace James W. Schooler who resigned. Charles A. Love was elected as his replacement.

[939] Charles was the son of William Hefflinger, Jr. (c.1777-1849) and Peggy Skinner. Charles married Nannie G. Latham (1829-1911) of Stafford and was buried at Union Church in Falmouth. He was a merchant.

[940] Following the War Between the States, Daniel submitted a claim to the Southern Claims Commission asking to be reimbursed for $1,984.75 worth of wood, corn, and fence rails taken from him by the Union army. His claim was rejected.

[941] Called Smith by his family, he was the son of Henry "Lighthorse Harry" Lee (1756-1818) and Ann Hill Carter (1773-1829) of Stratford Hall and was the brother of Robert E. Lee. Smith went to sea at the age of 15 and became the commander of the steamer *Princeton*. He joined Matthew Perry on his trip to Japan in 1853 and was later in charge of the Naval Academy at Annapolis. Prior to the outbreak of the War Between the States, Smith was in charge of the Philadelphia navy yard. He married Anna Maria Mason (1811-1898).

[942] This may have been Thomas Benton Reamy (1836-1910).

[943] John was the son of Ambrose and Lucy Leitch of Spotsylvania County. In 1854 he married Martha J. S. Russell (c.1826-1885), the daughter of Bartlett and Nancy Russell of Spotsylvania.

[944] Sidnor or Sidney was the son of Richard C. (born c.1805) and Catherine Powers (1812-1886). In 1867 he married Mary A. Thompson (born c.1845), the daughter of William A. and Mary A. Thompson.

James Cox—"from White Oak to the old stage road:

Zachariah Snellings (born c.1828)—"from the lower ford on Potomac Run to Claiborne Run in place of John Anthony removed from the neighborhood"

Charles Sterne (born c.1828)—"the road running by his farm and known as the Concord road"

Phillip S. Honey[945] (c.1835-1910)—"from P[atrick] England's gate to the intersection of the road leading from Falmouth to Warrenton"

John Green—"from Accakeek run to Arnold's Crossing at the Rail Road"

Abram Van Doran (born c.1828)—"from Accakeek run to the Court House:

Richard Stevens—"in the place of C[harles] W. Brewer resigned"

William Gollahorn—"from Potomac Run at E. A. W. Hores to intersect with the Aquia Road"

William A. Bryan[946] (1827-1871)—"from Coakley's Store to Peden's Hill"

William Armstrong (born c.1817)—"from Patterson Well to the Warrenton road at Yellow Chapel"

George B. Norman[947] (c.1846-before 1899)—"from the branch crossing the road at Whorton's gate to Simm's Point"

Gen. Fitzhugh Lee[948] (c.1835-c.1905)—"from the Richland Mill to intersection of Arkendale road"

James E. Berry[949] (c.1833-1913)—"from the lower ford on Potomac Run to Claiborns Run in place of John Anthony who has removed from the neighborhood"

Archie T. Roy[950] (died 1897)—"from the site of the old Hopewell meeting house to the point where the White oak Road to Fredericksburg crosses Claibourn's Run"

Richard Payne[951] (c.1832-1882)—"from Potomac run to Arnold's crossings in the place of A[lexander] M. Green who resigned"

John T. McCoy (1819-1905)—"from Beaver Dam Run to the Prince William Line"

Robert Mountjoy[952] (1828-1891)—"from Jones' shop to the Red House…in place of Alexander Mountjoy"

Alexander H. Mountjoy—"from Chappawamsic Road to the Stafford Store road"

William Skidmore (born c.1813)—"from Potomac Church to Crowsnest in the place of William H. Browne removed from the county"

Surveyor—John M. Homes

---

[945] In 1892 Phillip submitted a Confederate service pension application stating that he had served with the 9th Virginia Cavalry during which time a mule had fallen on him and that he was permanently disabled as a result.

[946] William was the son of Jesse Bryan and Eliza H. Grace. He was born in Cecil County, Maryland.

[947] George served in the 9th Virginia Cavalry, Company A, Stafford Rangers.

[948] The son of Sydney Smith Lee (1802-1869) and the nephew of Gen. Robert E. Lee. In 1852 he was appointed to the U. S. Military Academy and graduated in 1856. Upon graduation he was commissioned a second lieutenant in the cavalry and was severely wounded in a conflict with the Indians. In May 1860 he was appointed instructor of cavalry at West Point, but at the outset of the War Between the States, he resigned his commission and entered Confederate service as adjutant general of Gen. Richard S. Ewell's brigade. He served with the Army of Northern Virginia through all its campaigns. On July 25, 1862 he was made brigadier general and on Sept. 3, 1863 major general. Fitz was severely wounded at the Battle of Winchester. After the war, he resided at Richland in Wide Water. A proponent of peaceful co-existence between the North and South, in 1875 he delivered a speech promoting both sides working together to create a strong national life. He was one of the first leading men to do so and his opinion had a profound effect on the whole country. From 1886-1890 he served as the 39th governor of Virginia and in 1896 was sent by Grover Cleveland to be consul general to Havana.

In 1875 Fitzhugh Lee married Ellen Bernard Fowle.

[949] James was the son of Richard (c.1807-1867) and Sarah Berry (born c.1810). In 1860 he married served with the Fredericksburg Artillery throughout the War Between the States. He died at Leeland.

[950] Archie died of a stroke.

[951] Richard was the son of John and Cecy A. Payne.

[952] Robert married Mary Mildred Griffis.

1868

Sheriff—Elias A. W. Hore[953]

Constables—Richard Stark, William T. Patton, Charles Wesley Cloe[954] (1840-1901), Joseph Herndon, Harris Hill

Clerk—James E. Towson

Commissioner of the Revenue—Robert G. Hickerson

Surveyors of the Roads:

Lewis K. Knight[955] (c.1820-1893)—"of Coal Landing road in the place of John M. Stewart [born c.1822 removed from the County"

James Homes[956] (c.1812-after 1850)—From the Prince William line, until it intersects the road leading from the Bellfair Mill to the Stafford Store"

Edward McDowell[957]—"from Concord to St. George's branch"

Henry Levy Deshazo[958] (1816-1909)—"from Pollocks Mill to Scott's Bridge in the place of John G. Pollock resigned"

James M. Briggs—"from James H. Lunsfords shop to the Poplar road"

Joseph F. Swetnam[959] (born c.1838)—"from Pedens Gate to Falmouth in the place of Abram Van Doran removed from the County"

R. C. L. Moncure—"from Stafford Court House to the intersection of the road leading from Garrisonville to Aquia"

Henry Love[960] (c.1811-1873)—"from Coakley's Store to Peden's gate"

George P. King[961] (c.1812-1876)—"from the run east of Little Whim on the road from White Oak to the Chatham Bridge, in place of James Heflin"

Charles W. Limbrick—"between Kings farm and Boscobel (from its intersection with the Road from Harris Corn Houses) to old Hopewell and thence with the White Oak Road at Little Whim, in place of James Walker"

Charles F. Norman (born c.1834)—"by Ebenezer Church in the place of Hawkins Stone resigned"

William Bullock—"from the River Road near Pollock's Mill to White Oak"

Beverly W. Irvine[962] (c.1839-1922)—"surveyor of the Falmouth and Marsh road from Richard's Mill or Coakleys Store in place of Robert C. Rogers resigned"

Arba Randolph Packard—"from the Public Road near New Hope Church to the White Oak road along the lands of J. Stone, George P. King, A. R. Packard and others"

Nathaniel Ball[963] (1830-1906)—"from the Woodcutting road to the Coal Landing road through the land

---

[953] Elias resigned as sheriff at the October term of the court and was appointed crier of the court.

[954] During the War Between the States, Charles served with the 9th Virginia Cavalry.

[955] Lewis was the son of William Knight. During the War Between the States, he served with the 47th Virginia Infantry. He was buried off Embrey Mill Road (State Route 733) near the new Ebenezer Church.

[956] James married Mary Ratcliffe (1807-1867), the daughter of John Ratcliffe. James was born in Prince William County.

[957] This may be Edward Mason McDowell (1843-1878). He attended school in Fredericksburg and in April 1861 enlisted in Company A of the 30th Virginia Infantry. He was discharged almost immediately and enlisted in Company C. Edward was discharged in September 1861 because of a rheumatic heart.

[958] More commonly known as Levy Deshazo. He was the son of Catherine DeShazo (died 1872) and was born in Caroline County. In 1849 he married Ellen Elizabeth Taylor (died 1914) in Spotsylvania County. Levy came to Stafford c.1852 and lived near Capt. Simeon Peyton.

[959] Joseph served in the 9th Virginia Cavalry, Company A, Stafford Rangers.

[960] Henry was born in Maryland. During the War Between the States, he lived in Fredericksburg. After the war, he resided in Stafford.

[961] George was the son of Samuel King. He was born in Pennsylvania but lived much of his life in Stafford. In 1845 George married Susan Warren, the daughter of William Warren. He died of rheumatism.

[962] Beverly was the son of William Irvine (c.1781-1859), the Irish immigrant. The Irvines resided at Hartwood, the lovely brick home still standing on the southwest side of Warrenton Road (U. S. Route 17) near Hartwood Presbyterian Church. Beverly married Betty Lucas Bullard (1835-1891), the daughter of R. D. and A. Bullard.

of James E. Towson and others"[964]

Surveyor—John M. Homes

1869
Sheriff—Patrick B. Dunn
Constables—William Herndon[965] (1824-1904) Richard Stark, Charles W. Cloe,[966] Joseph Herndon
Jailer—James E. Schooler
Commonwealth's Attorney—George A. Kingston[967]
Commissioner of the Revenue—Robert G. Hickerson
Deputy Clerk—Charles Adams Bryan[968] (1849-1918)
Surveyors of the Roads:
    Samuel Fitzhugh[969] (1846-1923)—"from Pollocks Mill to Scotts Bridge in place of Levy Deshazo who has removed out of this County"
    Amos Jones[970] (c.1813-after 1870)—"from the woodcutting road to the Poplar Road"
    Absalom P. Rowe—"from Roys Corner on the Road from Potomac Church to the Telegraph road near the old Brick Kiln"
    James A. Anderson—"from Hardings Gate to Stafford Store Road in place of J[ames] P. Baker dec."
    Orlando Parsons Benson[971] (born c.1843)—"from Old Hopewell Meeting House to Claiborne's Run where the White Oak Road to Fredericksburg crosses it in place of A[rchie] T. Roy removed from the county"
    John A. Evans[972] (1832-1921)—"appointed Commr. of roads in account for the purpose of filling the vacancy occasioned by the resignation of A[sbury] W. Evans"
    Henry Garnet Chesley[973] (1843-1921)—"from the lower ford on the Potomac run, to Claiborne's run in place of James E. Berry who has removed from the neighborhood"
    William A. Heflin[974] (c.1839-after 1889)—"from Starke's lower gate to Fauquier County line in the place of John T. Worrel removed from the County"

---

[963] The son of William Ball (c.1799-after 1860). Nathaniel served in the 47th Virginia Infantry, Co. I. According to his obituary, he "served faithfully from Bull Run to Appomattox." Nathaniel married Jane Ball (1822-1909).

[964] This was the old road leading from Accokeek Iron Furnace (near Ramoth Baptist Church) to Coal Landing, part of which utilized Rocky Run as a road bed.

[965] William was the son of John Herndon (c.1794-1882) and Lucinda "Lucy" Combs (c.1796-c.1867). In 1856 he married Mrs. Isabella (Atchison) Berry (1832-1897), the daughter of Rodney and Cynthia Atchison.

[966] During the War Between the States, Charles served with the 9th Virginia Cavalry. He lived near Garrisonville.

[967] George Kingston married Emma L. Benson (1845-1882).

[968] Appointed deputy clerk in June 1869. Mr. Bryan was deputy clerk for 11 years and clerk of the court for 29 years. He also served as a commissioner of the court, commissioner of the revenue, was a member of the Methodist church, and was a staunch Republican. Charles was born in Cecil County, Maryland, but was a resident of Stafford for over 50 years. He died of heart failure.

[969] During the War Between the States, Samuel was a member of the Black Horse Cavalry of the 4th Virginia Regiment. He lived his later years in Fredericksburg.

[970] Amos resided on part of the old Carter farm, Ludlow, now Seven Lakes subdivision. According to the 1870 census, Thomas' parents were born in Pennsylvania.

[971] Orlando married Susan Carter Primmer (1850-1919), the daughter of Abraham Primmer (1811-1896).

[972] John served in the Confederate army under Col. Thomas Waller as a member of Company A, 9th Virginia Cavalry. During that service, he was held as a prisoner of war near Culpeper. John was found dead at his home in Garrisonville where he had fallen into a brush fire he was tending. In 1853 he married Maria Jane Homes. John was born in Maryland.

[973] The son of William S. Chesley and Mary Ann Ferneyhough (c.1818-1853). He lived at Willow Green, later known as Potomac Run Farm on Potomac Run Road (State Route 626). Henry married Mary Susan Ferneyhough (1845-1913).

[974] William served during the War Between the States and lost an eye at Spotsylvania.

Surveyor—John M. Homes

1870
Sheriff—Patrick B. Dunn
Jailer—James E. Schooler[975] and Henry J. Gifford (born c.1836)
Clerk—George Vowles Moncure
Deputy Clerk—Charles A. Bryan
Clerk of the Circuit Court—Richard Hughlett Bryan[976] (1821-1906)
Commonwealth's Attorney—George A. Kingston[977]
District Clerks:
    Aquia District—W. B. Lowry
    Falmouth District—Isaac Fines[978]
    Hartwood District—Richard T. Coakley (born c.1843)
Supervisors:
    Aquia—Edward Waller (1849-1919)
    Falmouth—John M. Luck
    Hartwood—Gustavus B. Wallace
Commissioner of the Revenue:
    Hartwood and Aquia districts—Ennever Lucas[979] (c.1842-1912)
    Falmouth—George P. King
Assessors:
    Aquia—George B. Norman[980]
    Falmouth—Thomas G. Moncure[981] (1837-1906)
    Hartwood—Ennever Lucas
Collectors:
    Aquia—Matthew Norman Towson[982] (born c.1846)
    Falmouth—James Oscar Lee (1847-1908)
    Hartwood—Beverly W. Irvine
Constables:

---

[975] At the March term, 1870 the justices "ordered that James E. Schooler turn over the jail keys and all other things pertaining thereby to P. B. Dunn Sheriff of this County, his office as jailor [sic] terminating with the qualifying of the said Dunn as Sheriff."

[976] The son of Joseph Bryan and Susan L. Mason of Bohemia Manor, Cecil County, Maryland. Following the War Between the States, Richard submitted a claim to the Southern Claims Commission asking to be reimbursed for $7,597 worth of produce and other commodities taken from him by the Union army. He was granted $1,814.50.

[977] At the April term, 1870 George Kingston presented his resignation. John H. Suttle was appointed in his stead.

[978] Probably the son of Isaac Fines (born c.1807).

[979] Ennever was the son of Albert G. (c.1806-1854) and Cornelia (Ennever) Lucas (1818-1884). He resided at Stanstead and, prior to the War Between the States, was a schoolteacher. During the war, he was an orderly sergeant in Capt. Charles Green's company of the 47th Virginia Regiment. For many years he was commissioner of the revenue for the First District in Stafford and at the time of his death was clerk of the Hartwood School Board and a notary public. Ennever never married. His funeral was conducted by the Rev. David Shopoff (1858-1934) of Hartwood Presbyterian Church and he was buried at Stanstead (*Free Lance*, Sept. 28, 1912).

[980] The son of Thomas (c.1790-1846) and Mildred Norman (born c.1805).

[981] Thomas was the son of the Hon. R. C. L. Moncure (1805-1882) and Mary Butler Washington Conway (1807-1895). During the War Between the States, Thomas served in the 9th Virginia Cavalry and was imprisoned at Point Lookout for several months. In 1866 he married Jean Charlotte Washington (born 1834). In 1872 Thomas was appointed one of the commissioners of the Free Bridge between Fredericksburg and Stafford County.

[982] The son of James E. Towson (1808-1888) and Agnes Ann Suttle (c.1811-1865).

Aquia—William T. Payne[983] (c.1846-after 1910), Thomas Lowry,[984] Charles W. Schooler, Sr.[985] (c.1840-1910)

Falmouth—C. E. W. Green, Charles Peyton William Limerick[986] (c.1841-1914), Mace Clements Purkins[987] (1840-1911)

Hartwood—Thomas H. Johnson, John H. Mills, William A. Embrey (born c.1825)

Registrars[988]—Harris Hill, Fielding B. Stone, John A. Ashby[989] (born c.1835), and ___ Conway

Commissioners of Elections:

Falmouth Precinct—Monroe Kelly (c.1818-1892), John M. Luck, Thomas H. Hewitt

White Oak Precinct—James Monteith, William H. Hansbrough, James A. Daffan

Hartwood Precinct—Thomas J. Skinker, William Irvine, James M. Briggs

Harwood Precinct—William Bryan, Gustavus B. Wallace, Flavius J. Ballard

Stafford Court House Precinct—Arthur F. Clift, James Lowry, Dade Hooe

James Griffith Store Precinct—Nathaniel W. Ford, William E. Moncure, Withers Waller

Stafford Store—Elias King[990] (1795-1876), James M. Hickerson, Benjamin C. Wamsley

Master's Precinct—Richard Jones, Edward McDowell, Ludwell Herndon

Overseers of the Poor:

Aquia—James E. Schooler

Falmouth—Ferdinand S. Pratt[991] (1826-1905)

Hartwood—George K. Blackburn

Commissioners of the Roads:

Aquia—Benjamin Ashley Bell[992] (1840-1905)

Falmouth—Littleton C. Fleming

Hartwood—John Peden

Surveyors of the Roads:

B. F. Nalls (born c.1837)—"from Stafford Court House to the road leading from Garrisonville to the

---

[983] During the War Between the States, William served with Company I of the 47th Virginia Infantry. He suffered a gunshot wound at Weldon Railroad in August 1864 while carrying the flag.

[984] At the April term, 1870 "Thomas Lowry, late Constable having inadvertently failed to give the bond required by law to have been given at the last term of this Court—It is recomended [sic] that the Governor of this State appoint him Constable there being no Constable at this term in the County."

[985] Charles was the son of John H. (1812-1875) and Laurinda Schooler (1815-1870). During the War Between the States, he served as a private in Capt. James D. Bruce's Company of the Stafford Guard, 47th Virginia Infantry. He was a color bearer and, according to his veteran's papers, "bore the colors with distinguished gallantry in every battle from Seven Pines to Chancellorsville where he was wounded through one of his legs or arms. From the time he was wounded there has been no regular color bearer to the Regt. and he a few days ago received a transfer to cavalry." In 1865 Charles married Jenny Watts.

[986] Charles died in Winchester, Virginia.

[987] Mace lived near Myrtleville Post Office in Stafford but was born in King George County. During the War Between the States, he served with the 34th Virginia Volunteers. He joined the Confederate service at West Point, Virginia in 1861 and served until the surrender at Appomattox. His commanding officer wrote of him, "He was a faithful soldier, fearless in the discharge of his duties, and an example of conscientious devotion to the principles for which he fought" (Auditor).

[988] This was the first year in which registrars were appointed "for each township and voting place."

[989] Possibly John A. Ashby, the son of Benjamin and Sarah Ashby of Prince William County. John married Martha W. Cole (1839-1864).

[990] The son of Basil King (born 1760) of Port Tobacco, Maryland. Basil moved to Prince William County where he was known for his exceptional cabinet making skills He also served his community as an undertaker. In 1819 Elias married Nancy H. Botts (1800-1868). He, too, was a fine cabinetmaker and was listed in the 1870 Stafford census as a wheelwright. Elias resided at Stafford Springs in the far northwest corner of the county. This property is now part of the Quantico Marine Corps reservation.

[991] During the War Between the States, Ferdinand served in Company K of the 30th Virginia Infantry. He was wounded near Richmond. He died and was buried in the family cemetery in King George County.

[992] Benjamin was the son of John H. and Jane Bell (born c.1801). In 1867 he married Frances Powers (1846-1918), the daughter of Richard Coleman Powers (born c.1805) and Catherine E. Powers (1812-1886). Benjamin served in the 9th Virginia Cavalry, Company A, Stafford Rangers.

telegraph road near Aquia run"
Robert McCormick of Little Falls—"from Pollock's Mill on the River Road to the Chatham Bridge in place of L[evy] Deshazo removed"
W. T. Franklin of Serena—"from the County line next to King George County to Pollock's Mill on the River Road in place of E. C. Walker removed from the County"
George T. Stern—"the road formerly worked by James E. Schooler leading from the Court House to Andrew Chapel"
John Truslow (born c.1820)—"supervisor of the Ridgeway Road in the place of William Gollahorn removed from the neighborhood"
Alexander E. Garrison (born c.1829)—" the road known as the river road to Hoes Fishing Shore"
Chancellor E. Nelson (born c.1834)—"from Aquia Run to Chappawamsic Run…Samuel H. Griffis released from serving as overseer of this road"
Benjamin Ashley Bell—"in the place of Samuel H. Griffis resigned…from Aquia Road to Chappawamsic Run"
Henry Clay O'Bannon (1843-1916)—"from Hartwood to Richard's ferry"

1871
Sheriff—Patrick B. Dunn
Clerk of the Court—Rev. John O. Tackett[993] (1848-1907)
Treasurer—Thomas Conway Waller (1832-1895)
Clerks:
    Aquia—Harrison B. Barnes
    Rock Hill—Benjamin F. Cooper (born c.1847)
Supervisors:
    Aquia—George M. Howard (born c.1830)
    Rock Hill—Thomas B. Reamy
Constables:
    Aquia—James Morton, Jr.[994] (1851-1902)
    Hartwood—Thomas H. Johnson and John H. Mills
    Rock Hill—Kendrick Ennis Herndon[995] (1839-1906)
Commissioners of the Revenue:
    Aquia—George B. Norman
    Falmouth—Thomas G. Moncure
    Hartwood—Ennever Lucas
Assessor:
    Aquia—Charles A. Bryan
Collector:
    Aquia—William M. Norman
Overseers of the Poor:
    Aquia—John Henry Fritter (c.1824-1896)

---

[993] The Rev. John Tackett was one of the four known children of Charles Addison Tackett (1814-1896). The first of this family to come to the New World was Lewis Tacquitt, a French Huguenot who settled on Cedar Run (now Fauquier County) just below Broad Run. In Stafford, the Tackett family owned and operated Tackett's Mill on the upper part of Aquia Run. For years, this local landmark provided a place to have grain milled, a store which carried many necessities, a lumber mill, post office, and a school. Tackett's Mill was long the center of life on upper Aquia Creek. This old building was dismantled, moved, and rebuilt in the shopping center at Lake Ridge in Prince William County.
John O. Tackett was buried in the Tackett-Burroughs family cemetery near Remington in Fauquier County.
[994] James also served as a justice of Stafford County in 1891. He was the son of James Morton (died 1859) who was a major county landowner and justice of the peace from 1835-1859.
[995] The son of John Herndon (c.1794-1882) and Lucinda "Lucy" Combs (c.1796-c.1867). In April 1861 Kendrick enlisted in the Confederate army in Col. Thomas Waller's Company, Stafford Rangers. He received the Southern Cross of Honor on Jan. 19, 1904. Kendrick married Mary Avarell Williams (1844-1932) and served as deputy sheriff under Hugh Adie from 1875-1889.

Rock Hill—John T. McCoy
Commissioners of the Roads:
> Aquia—John A. Evans
> Rock Hill—Francis Curtis[996] (1806-1891)

Superintendent of Schools—Addison Borst[997]
Surveyor—John M. Homes

1873
Clerk of the Court—Rev. John O. Tackett
District Clerks:
> Hartwood—Richard T. Coakley

Supervisors:
> Aquia—Albert Clift[998] (c.1808-1890)
> Falmouth—Henry Edwards
> Hartwood—Flavius J. Ballard
> Rock Hill—Lyman Kellogg

Commissioners of the Revenue:
> Aquia—Charles A. Bryan
> Falmouth—Thomas G. Moncure
> Rock Hill—Raleigh L. Cooper

Assessor:
> Hartwood—Basil Lucas (died 1909)

Collector:
> Hartwood—E. H. Love

Overseer of the Poor:
> Hartwood—George K. Blackburn

Commissioner of the Roads:
> Hartwood—John Peden

Superintendent of Schools—Raleigh L. Cooper
School Trustees:
> Aquia—William E. Moncure (Chairman), Edward Waller, Sr. (Secretary), Charles A. Tackett

Board of School Trustees:
> Aquia Township—William E. Moncure (chairman), Edward Waller, Sr. (secretary), Charles A. Tackett

1875
Sheriff—Hugh Adie[999] (1833-1918)

---

[996] Francis was the son of George Curtis, Jr. (c.1767-1844) and Jemima Payne (c.1774-c.1869) and he inherited his father's Ludlow estate. He was quite wealthy by Stafford standards, owning land in several counties. At one point, Francis owned nearly 1,000 acres in Stafford alone.
  Francis married first in 1829 in Fauquier Mary M. Stone (c.1809-1865), the daughter of William Stone. She died of typhoid fever on Mar. 23, 1865. He married secondly in 1869 Maria A. Duffy (born 1828). Francis was killed in a wagon accident and buried at Green Meadows, part of Ludlow.

[997] Addison married Bettie G., the daughter of James Garnett Taliaferro (c.1772-after 1850) of King George.

[998] An interesting cast concerning Albert Clift appeared in the court minutes of Sept. 22, 1885. According to these minutes, Albert was called to court "charged with a grave capital felony, we deem it but an act of justice to the accused—whose fame and happiness are deeply implicated in such a prosecution—to enter of record, not only the discharge of the accused from further trial, the charge being wholly unsustained, but that in our opinion nothing has been proved upon the trial of the cause which should impair the high standing of Mr. Clift, in the County of his Nativity and where he has always resided, as a citizen of great moral worth and integrity."

[999] Hugh was the son of Hugh Adie, Sr. and grandson of Benjamin Adie (1762-c.1825). He bought and lived at Woodford, the old Eustace home on Garrisonville Road (State Route 610) for many years. He served in the 9th Virginia Cavalry, Company A, Stafford Rangers. Hugh died unmarried.

Deputy Sheriff—Kendrick E. Herndon
Clerk of the Court—Charles Addison Tackett[1000] (1814-1896)
Treasurer—Thomas C. Waller

WAYSIDE: Home of Thomas C. Waller, county treasurer, 1875.

Commonwealth's Attorney—Jeremiah Bailey Jett[1001] (1832-1913)
Commissioners of the Revenue:
    Aquia—Charles A. Bryan
    Falmouth—Thomas G. Moncure
    Rock Hill—Raleigh L. Cooper
Supervisors:
    Aquia—Albert Clift
    Falmouth—Simeon C. Peyton
    Hartwood—Flavius Ballard
    Rock Hill—Lyman Kellogg
Superintendent of Schools—Raleigh L. Cooper
Surveyor—Dr. William Wardlow Eustace[1002] (1818-1886)

1877
Sheriff—Hugh Adie
Deputy Sheriff—Kendrick E. Herndon
Clerk of the Court—Charles A. Tackett
Supervisors:

[1000] The son of Charles Tackett, Sr. (1780-1834) who c.1800 built Tackett's Mill on Aquia Run. In 1817 Charles, Sr., along with his brother-in-law William Barber (1787-1881), started the "Mill Farm Seminary" school at Tackett's Mill. In 1836 the Mill Farm was sold to Charles' son-in-law, Peter Goolrick (1801-1868).
    The 1871 land tax records list Charles as owning 150 ½ acres near Tackett's Mill ($1,505 building assessment) and 214 ¼ acres (part of same with $1,071.25 building assessment). He served in the 9th Virginia Cavalry.
[1001] Judge J. B. Jett was the son of James and Ethelswitha Jett. He married Lucy I. Chinn (born 1832), the daughter of John LeRoy and Lucy E. Chinn. Judge Jett moved to St. Paul, Minnesota where he died.
[1002] Dr. Eustace was the son of John Henry Eustace (1791-1864) and Mary J. Wardlaw of Richmond. He graduated in 1844 with a medical degree from the Medical College of Virginia. In 1851 William married Martha Virginia Laub (1829-1872) of Philadelphia.

    Aquia—Albert Clift
    Falmouth—Simeon C. Peyton
    Hartwood—Flavius J. Ballard
    Rock Hill—Lyman Kellogg
Constable—Hartwood—Thomas H. Johnson
Treasurer—Thomas C. Waller
Commissioner of the Revenue—Thomas G. Moncure
Overseers of the Poor:
    Aquia—John A. Evans
    Falmouth—Richard E. Monteith
    Hartwood—George K. Blackburn
    Rock Hill—William Herndon
Superintendent of Schools—Raleigh L. Cooper
Surveyor—Dr. William W. Eustace

1879
Sheriff—Hugh Adie
Deputy Sheriff—Kendrick E. Herndon
Clerk—Charles A. Tackett
Treasurer—Thomas C. Waller
Commonwealth's Attorney—J. Bailey Jett

1880
Sheriff—Hugh Adie
Commissioner of the Revenue—Thomas G. Moncure
Supervisors:
    Aquia—Albert Clift
    Falmouth—Simeon C. Peyton
    Hartwood—Flavius J. Ballard
    Rock Hill—Lyman Kellogg
Constables:
    Aquia—Fielding P. Clift
    Falmouth—James H. Monteith (c.1845-1887)
    Hartwood—Thomas H. Johnson
    Rock Hill—Kendrick E. Herndon
Overseers of the Poor:
    Aquia—John A. Evans
    Falmouth—Richard E. Monteith
    Hartwood—George K. Blackburn
    Rock Hill—William Herndon
Superintendent of Schools—Raleigh L. Cooper
Surveyor—Dr. William W. Eustace

1881
Sheriff—Hugh Adie
Deputy Sheriff—Kendrick E. Herndon
Clerk of the Court—Charles A. Tackett
Deputy Clerk—Charles A. Bryan
Supervisors:
    Aquia—Albert Clift
    Falmouth—James O. Lee[1003] (1847-1908)

[1003] James was the son of William and Sarah H. Lee. A native of King George County, James was born at White Hall and moved when a child to Willow Dale in Stafford County. He was a supervisor of Stafford for 25 years and chairman of the board for 16. According to his obituary, James was an "active and influential member of the Old School Baptist Church." In 1873 he married Miss Lucy A. Luck (1854-

  Hartwood—Charles Lewis Kennedy[1004] (1846-1933)
  Rock Hill—Dr. Thaddeus Claybrook Montague[1005] (1838-1906)
Treasurer—Thomas C. Waller
Commissioner of the Revenue—Thomas G. Moncure
Constables:
  Aquia—Ajdlon C. Clift[1006] (1861-1887)
  Falmouth—Gouverneur T. Greenlaw[1007] (born c.1860)
  Hartwood—Thomas H. Johnson

1931), the daughter of John M. Luck (1827-1888) and Mary Anne Rowe (died 1902). An obituary written by his wife was published in the Baptist newspaper, *Gospel Messenger*. She stated that they had been baptized together at White Oak Church in April 1879 by Elder John Clark (1804-1882), formerly of Chappawamsic Baptist Church. James served as clerk of the church for the last 25 years of his life. On Sept. 28, 1908, a rainy morning, he went to harness his horse to go to the courthouse and fell from a ladder in the hay barn, breaking his back. He never recovered and died in his sleep on Oct. 11. He was buried in the family cemetery at Willow Dale (Littlejohn 49).

[1004] Charles was the son of Thomas A. Kennedy and was born in Westmoreland County. In 1871 he married Mary T. Schooler (born c.1837), the daughter of Thomas E. Schooler (born c.1787).

  The position of sheriff was far from being a "desk job." The residents of rural Stafford were active to say the least, some of which was reflected in a newspaper notice printed during Charles Kennedy's tenure as sheriff:

> The jail is now tenantless except Wm. H. Hunt, charged with the murder of Peter Schooler. It is a noticeable fact that there are less criminals in point of population and less jail birds from Stafford than any county in the State. We challenge comparison with any.
>
> There is a lively war going on between the fishermen of Aquia Creek and some non-resident fishermen, one of whom, Mr. James Arnold, of Maryland, has been arrested. The case comes up for trial here to-day before Justice Bryan, and a lively time is expected. R. H. L. Chichester, Esq., represents the Commonwealth and Hon. W. A. Little, Jr., Mr. Arnold.
>
> A lively row was started court day by several of the regular attendants of court imbibing too much cider. Some of those that were inclined to be comic were paying two negro men a quart of cider to kiss one another. Some of the party objected to the esculatory performance in public as a waste of material. A fight was started, knives were drawn and a general riot was imminent, when Sheriff Kennedy appeared upon the scene, and the party, seven or eight in number, were carried before Justice Bryan, some of whom were promptly fined, paid up and went on their way rejoicing.
> (*Free Lance*, Nov. 25, 1897)

  In 1928 Charles submitted a Confederate pension application stating that he had enlisted in the 15th Virginia Cavalry, Company D in 1862 and had served until the end of the war. He held the rank of private and had been a prisoner of war, being paroled in 1865. At the time of his pension application, he was suffering from high blood pressure and other infirmities of old age.

[1005] Thaddeus was the son of Edmund Healy Montague (died 1847) and Amanda Claybrook (died 1845) and was born in Middlesex, Virginia. His first wife was Celestine Louise Gordon (1841-1876) of Rosedale, the daughter of William Richards Gordon (1780-1855). Thaddeus married secondly Belle Ramey by whom he had five children. Dr. Montague graduated from the Medical College of Virginia in 1859 and entered Confederate service on May 14, 1861. He served with Generals Floyd and Albert Sidney Johnston in Kentucky and Tennessee during the campaigns of 1862. Following this he was made surgeon-in-charge of Emory and Henry Hospital where he treated soldiers from both sides of the war. Thaddeus was a Knight Templar Mason of Lodge 4, Fredericksburg. Prior to his death, he owned a drug store on Caroline Street in that town. From 1887-1889 he represented Stafford County in the Virginia House of Delegates but declined re-nomination. He was buried at Rosedale in Stafford.

[1006] In 1884 Adjlon married Bettie A. Griffis.

[1007] Also served as postmaster of Myrtleville 1890-1891.

Rock Hill—John W. Honey

Overseers of the Poor:
    Aquia—John A. Evans
    Falmouth—William Fleet Cox[1008] (1821-1905)
    Hartwood—George K. Blackburn
    Rock Hill—John McCoy
Overseers of the Road:
    Robert P. Blake (born c.1849)—"Warrenton road from Berea church to Falmouth"
    William P. Mahoney (born c.1839)—"road leading from Chappawamsic to Stone's Mill"
Superintendent of Schools—Strother Harding[1009]
Surveyor—Dr. William W. Eustace (1818-1886)

1883
Sheriff—Hugh Adie
Deputy Sheriff—Kendrick E. Herndon
Constable:
    Falmouth—Gouverneur T. Greenlaw
Clerk—Charles A. Tackett
Deputy Clerk—Charles A. Bryan
Treasurer—Thomas C. Waller
Commonwealth's Attorney—John Benjamin T. Suttle (c.1840-1884)
Commissioners of the Revenue:
    Aquia and Rock Hill—Kendrick B. Combs[1010] (c.1857-1912)
    Falmouth—Thomas G. Moncure
    Hartwood—Ennever Lucas
Supervisors:
    Aquia—Ajdlon C. Clift
    Falmouth—James O. Lee
    Hartwood—Charles L. Kennedy
    Rock Hill—Dr. Thaddeus C. Montague
Overseer of the Poor:
    Falmouth—Fleet Cox
Superintendent of Schools—Strother Harding
Surveyors—Dr. William W. Eustace and John M. Smith

1884
Commonwealth's Attorney—John B. T. Suttle, William Seymour White (1853-1897)[1011]

[1008] William was the son of Berryman Cox and Delila Payne. He married his cousin, Sarah Cox, the daughter of Samuel and Sarah Cox. Samuel was a brother of Charnock Cox, Jr. and lived across from Bethel Baptist Church on White Oak Road (State Route 218). He died at his home near White Oak and was buried at Bethel Church.

[1009] A brief newspaper notice states that Strother removed to the city of Washington (*Free Lance*, Feb. 27, 1891).

[1010] Kendrick was the son of Daniel Webster S. and C. W. Combs. In 1882 he married Delsey F. Briggs (1864-1941), the daughter of W. B. Briggs. Kendrick operated a sawmill. On Aug. 16, 1880 he conveyed to George M. Weedon, trustee, his "sawmill, carriages & fixtures," log carrier, oxen, and chains to secure a debt of $437.50 to the Cooper Manufacturing Company (Stafford Deed Book 1, p. 312). In 1910 he claimed a homestead exemption, listing 50 acres near Tackett's Mill, 2 horses, 1 colt, 3 cattle, 2 hogs, 15 barrels of corn, "fodder, blades, shucks, and hay," household and kitchen furniture (Stafford Deed Book 13, pp. 54, 71). He died at the age of 55 from an overdose of laudanum.

[1011] William was born in Fredericksburg, the only son of Capt. Chester B. and Fannie W. White. After graduating from college, he taught school for a few years before commencing the study of law in the office of his brother-in-law, Judge John Tackett Goolrick. He was admitted to the bar in 1875 and practiced with Judge Goolrick for several years. When Goolrick bought a local newspaper and renamed it *The Recorder*,

School Board—John Moncure Hull[1012] (1835-1908), Dr. Hawkins Stone, John M. Luck
Registrars:
    Stafford Courthouse—Luke Gallahan
    Brooke Station—Marion King Lowry[1013] (1854-1939)
    Griffis—Charles E. Gill (c.1818-1890)
    Rock Hill—Welford Montgomery Masters[1014] (1850-1929)
    Stafford Store—John W. Warren
    Falmouth—William Pierce Daffan[1015] (c.1860-1940)
    Hartwood—Robert P. Blake (born c.1849)
Judges of Elections:
    Stafford Courthouse—Joseph K. Bryan, Richard Henry Stevens, Richard M. Shelton[1016] (c.1819-1892)
    Brooke Station—Robert A. Lowry, John Paul Jones, James Morton, Jr.
    Griffis—Charles F. Norman, Asbury W. Evans[1017] (c.1836-1910), Frank Griffis
    Rock Hill—William Edward Heflin[1018] (1850-1921), James B. Garrison (born 1827), Richard A. Curtis[1019] (born c.1838)
    Stafford Store—John McCoy, John C. Cox[1020] (c.1825-1915), Seth Rousseau Combs[1021] (c.1828-c.1888)

---

he placed William in charge of the editorial department. At about this same time, Judge J. B. Jett left Virginia and the position of Commonwealth's attorney for Stafford became available. William was appointed to this position, took up residence near Stafford Courthouse, and won the subsequent election.

In 1891 he married Helen M. Stokes, the daughter of Gen. Henry H. Sibley, CSA. He moved back to Fredericksburg and renewed his activity at the newspapers, first with the *Free Lance* and then with the *Star*. He was part owner of the latter when he died.

William was one of the original members of the Battlefield Park Association and was chairman of the Battlefield Park Commission. In 1896 he was elected mayor of Fredericksburg and was president of the Virginia Press Association.

A newspaper notice stated, "Mr. W. S. White, who was appointed Commonwealth's Attorney of Stafford county to fill the vacancy occasioned by the death of the late Judge Suttle, and who, we learn will be a candidate for the position at the election in May, has removed from Fredericksburg to Stafford Court House" (*Fredericksburg Star*, Jan. 17, 1885).

[1012] John was the son of John Gascoigne Hull and Harriet Winston Shore. In 1861 he entered the Topographic Engineers of the Confederate Army and held the rank of adjutant of the corps. He remained in service until the end of the war. He married Anna Jane Moncure (born 1835), the daughter of R. C. L. Moncure of Glencairne. John was buried at Glencairne.

[1013] Marion was the son of James H. and Alice Lowry. In 1872 he was appointed one of the commissioners of the Free Bridge between Fredericksburg and Stafford County. Marion operated a gristmill in Brooke and in 1896 established a shingle mill there.

[1014] Welford was the brother of John W. Masters and died at his home in Washington, DC.

[1015] William was the son of James A. Daffan (c.1820-1890). He married Lizzie S. Pemberton (c.1862-c.1928) and moved to Fauquier County. He was buried at Goldvein Baptist Church.

[1016] Following the War Between the States, Richard submitted a claim to the Southern Claims Commission asking to be reimbursed for $500 worth of feed and cattle that had been taken from him by the Union army. He was granted $219. Richard died of consumption.

[1017] This man appears in the county court records as "Ashby W. Evans," but his obituary spelled his first name "Asbury." He lived near Onville and, during the War Between the States, served with the 9th Virginia Cavalry. He was deputy treasurer under Henry G. Chesley and was a member of Ebenezer Methodist Church in Onville. He was the brother of John A. Evans, the son of John R. Evans (c.1799-after 1873) and was born in Maryland.

[1018] William was the son of Jefferson W. Heflin (1811-1880) and Julia A. Templeman (1816-1892). He married Sally Udora McConchie (1852-1931), the daughter of William A. McConchie.

[1019] Richard was listed in the 1850 Stafford census as a part of the household of Francis Curtis (1806-1891) and Mary M. Curtis.

[1020] John lived at Onville and was the father of Walter S. Cox.

[1021] The son of Ennis Combs and Margaret Rousseau. Seth's first wife was Louisa L. Eskridge. He married secondly Elizabeth Edrington of Myrtle Grove.

Falmouth—"old judges reappointed"
White Oak—"old officers re-elected"
Hartwood—Robert N. Blake, Charles W. Brewer, George K. Blackburn

Overseers of Roads:
 John M. Gallahan—"from Stafford Courthouse to Accokee [sic], in place of H. Stevens, resigned"
 Everett Brown—"relieved as Overseer of the Road from Babcock's run to Scott's Bridge, and the same added to the portion of Amos K. Monteith[1022] from White Oak to Scott's Bridge"
 James Boutyard—"from Potomac Run to Accakeek, in place of John Green"
 Davis Jones—"from Dry Bridge to old railroad, or road leading to Thorny Point in place of John Green"

1885

Sheriff—Hugh Adie
Deputy Sheriff—Kendrick E. Herndon
Constables:
 Aquia—Ajdlon C. Clift
 Falmouth—William S. Monteith[1023] (1855-1903)
 Hartwood—John H. Stone[1024] (c.1838-1916)
 Rock Hill—John W. Honey
Commonwealth's Attorney—William S. White
Clerk of the Court—Charles A. Tackett
Deputy Clerks—Charles William Spindle[1025] (c.1837-1902) and Charles A. Bryan
Commissioners of the Revenue:
 Aquia and Rock Hill—Joseph K. Bryan
 Falmouth and Hartwood—Alexander M. Green
Land Assessor—John Moncure Ashby (1852-1918)
Supervisors:
 Aquia—Joseph K. Bryan
 Falmouth—James O. Lee
 Hartwood—Charles L. Kennedy

[1022] Amos K. Monteith (c.1839-after 1909) was the son of Thomas Monteith and Nancy Limerick. During the War Between the States, he served with the 9th Virginia Cavalry. In 1868 Amos married the widow Sarah Eliza (Rowe) Jones, the daughter of the Rev. John G. Rowe and Nancy McGuire.

 In 1889 Amos was arrested and charged with taking money from a letter. The newspaper article reported, "Upon information lodged yesterday through Commonwealth's Attorney W. S. White, of Stafford, Officer Robinson arrested Mr. Amiss Monteith, of Stafford, charted with abstracting $84.73 from a letter belonging to Mr. James Bloxton, of that county. When arrested the prisoner was at the R. F. & P. depot, on his way to Washington, and denied the charge. He was taken to the Mayor's Office, and telegrams sent to Stuart & Co. of Washington, who is claimed to have sent the money, but at the hour of going to press nothing had been heard, and the prisoner is still in Custody.

 Wm. A. Little, Jr., Esq., has been retained as counsel for the accused" (*Fredericksburg Star*, Apr. 17, 1889).

[1023] William lived near and was a member of Bethel Baptist Church. He was the brother of Amos K. Monteith and died of Bright's disease (kidney failure).

[1024] During the War Between the States, John served with the 47th Virginia Infantry. He was captured at Fredericksburg and Falling Waters and in 1904 received the Cross of Honor.

[1025] Charles was the son of Jefferson Spindle (c.1804-c.1868) and Maria Tackett (c.1810-1883). During the War Between the States, he served as a first sergeant in the 9th Virginia Cavalry, Company A, Stafford Rangers. He married his cousin, Nannie W. Tackett (died 1904).

 In his later years Charles lived at Brandy Station where he was a merchant and the senior partner of the mercantile firm of Spindle and Brother. He was accidentally killed one day while weighing some cattle on the siding. He stepped across the siding and onto the main track, not realizing that a train was coming. He was hit with such force that nearly every bone in his body was crushed. He was buried with Masonic honors at the Culpeper Confederate Cemetery.

Rock Hill—Edgar Smith Moore (1847-1899)
Overseers of the Poor:
    Aquia—Rolly Travis Shelton[1026] (1848-1935)
    Falmouth—Fleet Cox
    Hartwood—Madison F. Rollins[1027] (1828-1895)
    Rock Hill—William H. Heflin (1840-1911)
Electoral Board—Daniel Murray Lee[1028] (1843-1916), Powhatan Moncure, Charles M. Sterne[1029] (1827-1901)
Registrars:
    Aquia District, Brooke Precinct—Frank Clift
    Courthouse Precinct—Harrison B. Barnes
    Griffith's Precinct—James Bruce Gill[1030] (c.1845-1910)
    Falmouth District, Falmouth Precinct—John Walker Heflin[1031] (1851-1931)
    White Oak Precinct—John Farmer
    Hartwood District, Hartwood Precinct—Beverly W. Irvine
    Harwood Precinct—James W. Schooler
    Rock Hill District, Stafford Store Precinct—William Tolson (born c.1823)
    Master's Precinct—R. M. Jones
Judges of Elections:
    Aquia District, Brooke Precinct—Milton A. Ferneyhough[1032] (1846-1922)
        William W. Dix
        James L. Taliaferro[1033] (c.1814-1904)
    Courthouse Precinct—James Ashby[1034] (1854-1918)
        Charles W. Spindle
        Charles A. Bryan
    Griffith's Precinct—Benjamin Ashley Bell[1035] (1840-1905)
        Sidney Powers[1036] (1837-1895)

[1026] In 1871 Rolly married Jane Limerick (1851-1927) of Fredericksburg and was a member of Bethel Baptist Church.

[1027] Madison was the son of Thomas Rollins and Caroline E. Wallace.

[1028] Daniel was the son of Sydney Smith Lee (1802-1869) and Nannie Mason (1811-1898) and the nephew of Gen. Robert E. Lee. He was born and spent much of his youth in Alexandria. During the War Between the States, Daniel was a midshipman in the Confederate Navy and served until the end of the war. After the war, he settled in Stafford as a farmer and married Nannie Ficklen, the daughter of Joseph Burwell Ficklen (1800-1874) of Belmont. He died of heart failure at his residence, Highland Home.

[1029] Charles lived at Walnut Hill (later the Tolson farm) on Rock Hill Church Road (State Route 644) and he and his two wives are buried there. Charles married first Fanny Curtis Sterne (1842-1881) and secondly Mary Davis (1848-1923). Katie, the daughter of Charles and Mary, married Raymond Blake Tolson, Jr. (1912-1991) to whom Walnut Hill passed upon the death of Katie's parents.

[1030] When the 1850 Stafford census was compiled, James was included in the household of Charles E. (c.1818-1890) and Elizabeth V. Gill (born c.1824).

[1031] John was the son of Charles Seddon Heflin (1829-1850) and Nannie G. Latham (1829-1911). In 1875 he married Jonna C. Casey (1850-1936), the daughter of John Casey of Stafford County. John W. Heflin died in Los Angeles, California.

[1032] During the War Between the States, Milton served with Braxton's Battery. He was a member of Bellair Baptist Church near Leeland and died at his son's home in Fredericksburg.

[1033] James lived near Potomac Run. He was a Confederate veteran and was shot in the leg "which made him a cripple the remainder of his life" (Auditor).

[1034] James also served as superintendent of school from 1901-1918, dying in office. His obituary stated that for some years he served as superintendent of schools for Stafford and King George. His son, James Ashby, Jr. (1894-1950), served for many years as clerk of the court in Stafford.

[1035] Benjamin resided near Rectory Post Office in Wide Water. During the War Between the States, he was a scout with the 9th Virginia Cavalry.

[1036] In the 1850 Stafford census, this man was listed as "Sidnor" and was a member of the household of Richard C. Powers (born c.1805). He married Mary Ann Thompson (1845-1912). During the War Between the States, Sidney served in the Stafford Rangers, 9th Virginia Cavalry.

Falmouth District, Falmouth Precinct—Monroe Kelly
    James E. Berry (c.1833-1913)
    Abraham Primmer
White Oak Precinct—James M. Monteith
    Edward Taylor Rollins[1037] (1846-1921)
    Samuel Babcock[1038] (c.1806-1895)
Hartwood District, Hartwood Precinct—Edward M. Cropp[1039] (born c.1835)
    James M. Briggs (born c.1842)
    Robert C. Rogers (c.1818-1888)
Rock Hill District, Stafford Store Precinct—Seth R. Cooper[1040] (c.1837-after 1904)
    James B. Templeman (1822-1892)
    John C. Cox
Master's Precinct—Charles James French[1041] (1835-1920)
    William E. Heflin
    Nicholas Jones

Commissioners to Canvas Returns:
    Thomas Wallace[1042] (1852-1911), Charles W. Spindle, Ashby W. Evans, Charles French, James E. Berry[1043]

Overseers of the Roads:
    Madison F. Rollins—"of the Warrenton road from Hartwood to Christy's"
    W.H. Marshall—"leading from the Telegraph road through Chappawamsic farm to the river Road"
    George B. Griffis—"of the river road from Harris' shop to the culvert on the R.F. & P. R.R. at Waller's"

Superintendent of Schools—George Milton Weedon
Surveyor—Dr. William W. Eustace

1886

Overseer of the Road:
    John A. Maddox—"the road leading from R[andolph] C. Fitzhugh's corner, to the railroad, in Falmouth district"

1887

Sheriff—Charles L. Kennedy
Deputy Sheriff—Kendrick E. Herndon
Constables—Charles W. Schooler (Aquia)
    Rolly T. Shelton (Falmouth)
    John H. Stone
    G. W. Alexander, William H. Curtis (1857-1898) (Rock Hill)
Clerk—Charles A. Bryan
Deputy Clerks—Charles A. Bryan, J__ E. Herndon, Charles W. Spindle
Treasurer—Henry Garnett Chesley[1044] (1843-1921)

[1037] Edward was born in King George County. During the War Between the States, he served with the 9th Virginia Cavalry.

[1038] Samuel married Mariah D. Dewey (1818-1890) of New York.

[1039] Edward was included in the 1850 Stafford census as a part of the household of Robert Cropp (c.1800-1885).

[1040] Seth lived at Toluca and served four years with the 9th Virginia Cavalry.

[1041] Charles was the son of James French (1803-1865) and Sally A. Curtis (1812-1872) of Poplar Grove. He owned the old Downman tract, Windsor Forest, but lived at Poplar Grove (Eby, They 157) on Potomac Run.

[1042] Thomas died of a heart attack while walking across his field in Berea. He was the brother of Howson Wallace of Texas and married Harriet Eustace Moncure (1846-1911), the daughter of R. C. L. Moncure of Glencairne. He was a member of the Church of the Holy Spirit near Falmouth.

[1043] James was included in the 1850 Stafford census as part of the household of Richard Berry (c.1803-1867) and his wife, Sarah (born c.1810).

Commonwealth's Attorney—William S. White
Commissioners of the Revenue:
    Aquia and Rock Hill—Kendrick B. Combs
    Hartwood—Ennever Lucas
Supervisors:
    Aquia—James M. Jones (1844-1901)
    Falmouth—James O. Lee
    Hartwood—Robert A. Johnson
    Rock Hill—Dr. Thaddeus C. Montague
Overseers of the Poor:
    Aquia—Rolly T. Shelton
    Falmouth—Fleet Cox
    Hartwood—Madison F. Rollins
    Rock Hill—John T. McCoy
Superintendent of Schools—George M. Weedon
Surveyor—Edgar H. Randall[1045] (1853-1919)

1888

Constable—Robert A. Garrison[1046] (born c.1841)—Rock Hill
Jailer—Joseph K. Bryan
Deputy Treasurers—Asbury W. Evans, Rolly T. Shelton
Electoral Board—Daniel M. Lee, Powhatan Moncure, Edgar Moore
Overseers of the Roads:
    Isaac Boyer—"of Road district No. 1, Falmouth District" in place of William F. Hart
    William Skidmore—"Road district no. 11 and No. 12, Rock Hill district"
    John R. Smith[1047] (c.1832-1914)—"Road district #12, Hartwood district"
    Edward West[1048] (c.1846-1911)—"Road district #12, Aquia district"
    Henry L. Cooper[1049] (born c.1846)—"Road Nos. 9 and 10 in Rock Hill district"
    Mark Ricker[1050] (c.1849-1917)—"road leading from Berea church to Ellington's and from Swetnam's gate to Burgess' gate" in place of George W. Harding [born c.1843] removed from the county
    Nathaniel William Ford[1051] (1859-1894)—"from Aquia to Richland, and ordered with the means in his

---

[1044] Henry was born in Fredericksburg. At the outset of the War Between the States he joined the Fredericksburg Artillery, also known as Braxton's Battery. According to his obituary, "He enlisted at its origin, served in it throughout the bloody conflict, and was at Appomattox Courthouse at the surrender of Gen. Robert E. Lee...Mr. Chesley is credited with having fired that gun which history says killed General [John] Reynolds of the Union forces, when he came out with his staff to reconnoiter the position" (*Free Lance*, Oct. 18, 1921).
After the war, Henry returned to the area and settled in Stafford on Potomac Run. Around 1908 he moved back to Fredericksburg to live with his daughter, Mrs. Nelson C. Decker. While there he was associated with the firm of Chesley and Garner, wholesale grocers. He was a member of Fredericksburg Baptist Church and married Mary Susan Ferneyhough.

[1045] Edgar was the son of Aquilla Randall and was a carpenter as well as a surveyor. He also served as principal of Ebenezer School in Garrisonville (closed c.1890). Waller S. Gill (1871-1947) was his assistant at the school. As county surveyor, Edgar replaced Dr. William W. Eustace who died. Aquilla Randall moved to Stafford from Maryland.

[1046] Robert was the son of Rodney Garrison (born c.1807), wheelwright, and his wife, Jane (born c.1808).

[1047] John was the son of Lucinda Smith (born c.1804) and was listed in the 1850 Stafford census as a miner. In July 1861 he enlisted in Company C, 30th Virginia Infantry. John was paroled at Appomattox and was buried in the family burying ground in Stafford.

[1048] Edward was a merchant at Stafford Courthouse. He died of tuberculosis.

[1049] Henry was listed in the 1850 Stafford census as part of the household of Thornton (c.1810-after 1870) and Frances Cooper (born c.1817).

[1050] Marcus M. Ricker was originally from Acton, Maine. He came to the Fredericksburg area in 1865 and was employed by W. S. Embrey, Inc.

hands to repair the bridge where the Richland mill-race crosses that road"
Morris Truslow[1052] (c.1834-1907)—"Road district No. 14, Falmouth district" in place of Patrick Henry England, [1053] removed from the county
James Clift—"Road district #11, Falmouth district" in place of Charles William Peyton Limerick
Edgar S. Moore—"Road district #23, Rock Hill district" in place of Luther Bridwell

1889
Sheriff—Charles L. Kennedy
Deputy Sheriff—Joseph K. Bryan
Clerk—Charles A. Bryan
Deputy Clerks—Jackson P. Garrison (1853-1941), William W. Bryan (died 1938), Charles F. Norman
Treasurer—Henry G. Chesley
Commissioners of the Revenue:
    Aquia and Rock Hill—Kendrick B. Combs
    Falmouth—Ennever Lucas
Assessors:
    District No. 1—Charles J. Chartters[1054] (1853-1931)
        Deputy—John M. Hull
    District No. 2—Thomas B. Reamy
        Deputy—James Morton, Jr.
Supervisors:
    Aquia—James M. Jones
    Falmouth—James O. Lee
    Hartwood—Charles J. Henry
    Rock Hill—Edgar S. Moore

[1051] Nathaniel was the son of Nathaniel Waller Ford (1820-1880). A notice and resolution concerning young Nathaniel's death appeared in the Aquia Church vestry minutes and read:

> In chronicling the death of our friend and fellow member, Mr. N. W. Ford, who came to his end by the accidental discharge of a gun in his own hands, January the 5th, 1894; and in testimony of our high regard for him, we, the vestry of Overwharton Parish, in body assembled, pass the following resolutions.
>
> Whereas it has pleased Almighty God to take our friend and brother member from among us,
>
> Resolved, first That we extend heartfelt sympathy to the bereaved family.
>
> Second, That we miss his genial society, and his ready aid in all matters pertaining to the welfare of our church and other benevolent enterprises of our community.
>
> Resolved further, That the above resolutions be placed on the minutes of our Journal and a copy sent to his bereaved family, and also to the Southern Churchman for publication.
> Rev. J. H. Birkhead, Pres.
> Jas. Ashby, Secretary

[1052] Morris was the son of Benjamin Truslow (c.1792-1869) of Stafford County.
[1053] Patrick was the son of John England (1755-1851), a gunsmith at Rappahannock Forge, and Ann "Nancy" Musselman. The England home was called Seine Pocket Farm and was just west of the forge on the Rappahannock River. Patrick lived in Stafford all his life. He married first in 1836 Ann "Nancy" Truslow, the daughter of Benjamin Truslow and Nancy Dickens. He married secondly in 1849 Emily Emma Baker (died c.1909), the daughter of Moses Baker of Fauquier.
[1054] Charles was born in Spotsylvania County and later moved to Stafford. In 1892 he married Ella Morrison. Charles was a member of Wilderness Baptist Church when he lived in Spotsylvania, then joined Berea Baptist Church in Stafford.

Constables:
>Aquia—John A. Evans
>Falmouth—Rolly T. Shelton
>Hartwood—Robert Lee Dodd[1055] (c.1861-1921)
>Rock Hill—John R. Eustace

Overseers of the Poor:
>Aquia—Rolly T. Shelton
>Falmouth—Fleet Cox
>Hartwood—George E. Monroe[1056] (c.1857-1906)
>Rock Hill—John McCoy

Superintendent of Schools—George M. Weedon

Overseers of the Roads:
>Edward Robinson—"transferred from Road district No. 7 to No. 6, Aquia district"
>Charles Chartters—"Road district No. 1, Hartwood district" in place of A. D. Jett, resigned
>Peter S. Jett[1057] (born c.1836)—" Road district No. 3, Falmouth district" in place of John M. Luck, deceased
>Frederick Dent—"overseer of Coal Landing road"
>Thomas A. Clift—"of road from Telegraph road to Ramoth church"
>Thomas Waller and John Wickliffe Waller[1058] (1840-1921)—"transferred from Road district No. 17 to Road district No. 26, Aquia district"
>Robert S. Moncure[1059] (1857-1917)—"Road district #26, Aquia district, said district to begin at the end of Waller's land and to end at the old blacksmith's shop at Bloomington"
>Douglas Nelson Wigfield[1060] (1856-1898)—"Road district No 17, Hartwood district"
>Douglas N. Wigfield—"Road district Nos. 11 and 12, Rock Hill district" in place of E.B. Skidmore, resigned"
>John F. Clift[1061] (born c.1846)—"Road district No. 10, Aquia district, in place of S. C. Jett,[1062] resigned"
>Walter Carson—"Road district No. 2, Falmouth district" in place of Thomas Sollade, resigned
>Samuel Gallahan—"Road district No. 4, Aquia district" in place of Jack Gallahan, resigned
>James Musselman—"Road district No. 11, Aquia district" in place of Joseph Musselman, resigned
>Wilson B. Shackelford—"transferred from Road district No. 31, to Road district No. 14, Aquia district"
>Armistead Nelson—"transferred from Road district No. 13 to district No. 11, Aquia district"
>James Posey Bloxton[1063] (born c.1843)—"Road district #8, Aquia district" in place of E. C. Groves

---

[1055] According to his obituary, Mr. Dodd was a "prominent farmer, merchant, and miller of upper Stafford county [who] died at his home four miles above Hartwood Post Office" (*Free Lance*, Feb. 8, 1921). He married Ella Huffman and also served as a justice of the peace for Stafford. He was buried at Grove Church in Fauquier County.

[1056] George was the son of William and Frances Monroe. In 1877 he married Mary T. Downs (born c.1853), the daughter of Thomas and Amanda Downs. George lived near the gold mines between Warrenton Road (U. S. Route 17) and the Rappahannock River. He was buried at Cedar Hedge.

[1057] The son of Peter (born c.1802) and Catherine Jett (born c.1805).

[1058] John was known locally as "Johnny Reb" Waller and made his living selling horses and mules. He was the son of Thomas Conway Waller (1832-1895) and Sallie Medora Wickliffe (1857-1921). John was born at his father's Stafford home, Wayside, and later removed to Fauquier County. He married Elizabeth Clyde Gill (1877-1948).

[1059] Robert was the son of George V. Moncure (1826-1901) and Mary Conway Ashby (1830-1867). He was born at Chelsea on Wide Water Road (State Route 611). He died in his sleep (*Free Lance*, Dec. 4, 1917).

[1060] Douglas married Dora Lee Moore Parr (1861-1931). Both were born in Fauquier County.

[1061] John was the son of Albert (1808-1890) and Mary E. Clift (born c.1818).

[1062] Stapleton C. Jett (c.1837-after 1888) lived in Falmouth. During the War Between the States, he was wounded at Chancellorsville when a Minie ball passed through his right wrist. He was permanently disabled by the loss of the use of his right hand.

[1063] James was the son of Samuel B. Bloxton (born c.1799).

Other Overseers of the Roads:
    Hugh Wilson Daffan (born c.1865)   James Max   William H. Carter (c.1853-1928)
    Charles F. Norman   Nathaniel W. Ford   Henry L. Cooper
    Benjamin F. Jackson   John H. Clemmens   Wilson Decatur[1064] (c.1847-1935)
    William Woodward   Sebastian Graninger[1065] (1852-1901)
    Turner W. Herndon (1862-1939)
Surveyor—Edgar H. Randall

1890

Census Enumerator—Jaquelin Marshall Meredith[1066] (1833-1920)
Overseers of the Roads:
    Lemuel Segar[1067] (c.1870-1904)—"Road district No. 25, Aquia district...ordered to put his road in repair with the aid and material to be furnished by G. W. Middleton, Esq. at no charge or expense to the county, except the labor of the hands"
    William Thomas Wiggenton[1068] (1845-1921)—"Road districts No. 16 and 18, Hartwood district" in place of George K. Blackburn, deceased"
    Marius Sthreshley—"Road district No. 14, Falmouth district...ordered to blast certain rocks in his district at the lowest possible cost to the county"

1891

Sheriff—Charles L. Kennedy
Constables:
    Aquia—John A. Evans
    Falmouth—Rolly T. Shelton
    Hartwood—James Barber
    Rock Hill—Robert A. Garrison
Commonwealth's Attorney—William S. White
Clerk—Charles A. Bryan
Deputy Clerk—Charles F. Norman
Treasurer—Henry G. Chesley
Commissioners of the Revenue:
    Aquia and Rock Hill—Kendrick B. Combs
    Falmouth—Ennever Lucas
Supervisors:
    Aquia—Asbury W. Evans

[1064] Wilson was a farmer and merchant and a life-long resident of Wide Water.

[1065] Sebastian was born in Nierstein, Germany and came to the United States sometime prior to December 1848 when he married Mary Catherine Martin (1830-1897) in northern Illinois or southern Wisconsin. Mary was born in Alsace-Lorraine, France. A resident of Boone County, Illinois during the War Between the States, he was listed on the Illinois State Militia Roll, but didn't serve in the war. He was a naturalized citizen by the time he moved to Stafford in 1870. Sebastian was an asthmatic and the move might have been made for health reasons or because land was cheap in the South after the war. He bought 209 acres adjacent to the RF & P Railroad tracks at Leeland and very near Potomac Run. Old rails from the tracks were used as floor joists in the construction of the house. Sebastian farmed here and kept a vineyard and made wine in large vats in his basement. He died suddenly and was buried at his home at Leeland.

[1066] "Jack" Meredith lived at the Rectory in Wide Water. For many years following the War Between the States, he served as minister of Aquia Church. Because of the depressed post-war economy, the parishioners were able to pay him only a meager salary (and sometimes none at all). Consequently, he did various things to supplement his income. In addition to being a census enumerator, he also maintained a woodcutting business on Providence, another tract he owned in the northern end of the county.

[1067] Lemuel lived in Wide Water and died of tuberculosis at an early age.

[1068] William was a miller and operated the old Kellogg's Mill on what is now Abel Reservoir. He married Catherine Able (born c.1854).

        Falmouth—James O. Lee
        Hartwood—Charles J. Henry
        Rock Hill—John W. Honey
Overseers of the Poor:
        Aquia—John A. Decatur
        Falmouth—Fleet Cox
        Hartwood—George E. Monroe
        Rock Hill—John Wesley Cooper[1069] (1879-1947)
Superintendent of Schools—George M. Weedon
Surveyor—Edgar H. Randall

1892
Overseers of the Roads:
        Edgar S. Moore—"Road district No. 23" in place of Turner W. Herndon
        James E. Bowling—"Road district No. 8, Hartwood district," in place of Jesse R. Anderson[1070] (c.1843-1900), resigned
        George Gallahan—"Road district No. 23, Rock Hill," in place of Edgar S. Moore, resigned
        Richard A. Boutyard (1861-1932)—"Road district No. 13, Falmouth district," in place of W. J. Boutyard, deceased
        Patrick H. England—"from Crane's to Potomac Run"
        Charles Heflin—"Road district No. 16, Rock Hill district," in place of H. C. Clemens, resigned
Other Overseers of the Roads:
        Murray B. Embrey[1071] (born c.1841)   Marius Sthreshley

1893
Sheriff—Charles L. Kennedy
Constables:
        Aquia—John A. Evans
        Falmouth—Rolly T. Shelton
        Hartwood—Thomas H. Johnson
        Rock Hill—Robert A. Garrison
Clerk—Charles A. Bryan
Commissioners of the Revenue:
        Aquia and Rock Hill—Kendrick B. Combs
        Falmouth—Ennever Lucas
Supervisors:
        Aquia—James M. Jones
        Falmouth—James O. Lee
        Hartwood—Charles J. Henry
        Rock Hill—Dr. William Joseph Wallis[1072] (born c.1845)
Treasurer—Henry G. Chesley
Overseers of the Poor:
        Aquia—James Henry Decatur[1073] (c.1890-1940)
        Falmouth—Fleet Cox
        Hartwood—George E. Monroe

[1069] The son of James Cooper (1838-1917) and Malinda Musselman. John married Sallie Waller English (1879-1932), the daughter of Robert T. English and Sallie Margaret Withers.

[1070] Jesse was listed in the 1850 Stafford census as part of the household of John Anderson (born c.1812), stonemason, and his wife Philadelphia "Delphia" Curtis (c.1828-1898).

[1071] Murray was listed in the 1850 Stafford census as part of the household of Daniel Embrey (born c.1790).

[1072] William was the son of Alfred Wickliff Wallis (c.1813-c.1894) who came to Stafford c.1870 from Canada. The family settled on Windsor Forest, the old Downman farm on the southwest side of Garrisonville Road (State Route 610) between Joshua Road (State Route 643) and Rock Hill Church Road (State Route 644). Part of this farm is now a subdivision by the same name.

[1073] James was the son of Monroe Decatur. He lived at Onville and was buried at Ebenezer Church.

Rock Hill—William Henry Heflin[1074] (1840-1911)
Overseers of the Roads:
>Mr. Bubb—Road district #1, Falmouth, in place of Isaac Boyer removed from the county
>K. E. Bridwell—Road district #23, in place of Wilson Patton, resigned

Superintendent of Schools—George M. Weedon
Surveyor—Edgar H. Randall

1895
Sheriff—Charles L. Kennedy
Commonwealth's Attorney—Richard H. L. Chichester
Clerk—Charles A. Bryan
Deputy Clerk—John S. Martin
Supervisors:
>Aquia—Richard Ashby Moncure[1075] (1864-1923)
>Falmouth—James O. Lee
>Hartwood—Charles J. Henry
>Rock Hill—William J. Wallis

Treasurer—Henry G. Chesley
Commissioners of the Revenue:
>Aquia and Rock Hill—Kendrick B. Combs
>Falmouth—Ennever Lucas

Assessor:
>District 1—R. A. Jones
>>Richard Wirt Powers (1870-1934) (Assistant)
>
>Hartwood and Falmouth—Edward T. Rollins

Constables:
>Aquia—Thomas Shackelford
>Falmouth—Rolly T. Shelton
>Hartwood—Thomas H. Johnson
>Rock Hill—Walter Wamsley[1076] (1867-1923)

Coroner—Dr. William J. Wallis
Overseers of the Poor:
>Aquia—James H. Decatur
>Falmouth—Fleet Cox
>Hartwood—George E. Monroe
>Rock Hill—James T. Humphrey[1077] (1848-1926)

Superintendent of Schools—George M. Weedon

Overseers of the Roads:
>Amos K. Monteith—in Falmouth District, replacing E. S. Bubb removed from the county
>Sebastian Graninger—"the road from Leeland through A[braham] Primmer's estate and property of Sthreshley's heirs"

Surveyor—Edgar H. Randall

1897
Sheriff—Charles L. Kennedy
Constable:
>Falmouth—Welford Sullivan (died 1937)

[1074] The son of John E. Heflin (c.1816-after 1880). In 1866 William married Delia A. Armstrong (1845-1930), the daughter of Armistead A. Armstrong (1816-1885).
[1075] The son of George Vowells Moncure (1826-1901) and Mary Ashby (1830-1897).
[1076] The son of Benjamin C. Wamsley (c.1814-1886) and the twin brother of Warner Wamsley (1867-1950).
[1077] James was the son of Sanford Humphrey (born 1812) and Jane Primm. He married Sallie B. Fritter (1848-1921), the daughter of Gustavus B. Fritter (c.1824-after 1884) and Mary F. Cardine (c.1820-1874).

Clerk—Charles A. Bryan
Deputy Clerks—James Ashby (1854-1918), John S. Martin
Treasurer—Henry G. Chesley
Commissioners of the Revenue:
    Aquia and Rock Hill—Herbert Minor Tolson (1856-1936)
    Falmouth—Daniel W. Coakley[1078] (1850-1922)
Supervisors:
    Aquia—Robert Ambler Moncure (1864-1923)
    Falmouth—James O. Lee
    Hartwood—George E. Monroe
    Rock Hill—Thompson Smith Briggs[1079] (1860-1910)
Overseers of the Poor:
    Aquia—James H. Decatur
    Falmouth—Fleet Cox
    Hartwood—Robert L. Burton (1846-1923)
    Rock Hill—Lawrence A. Skinner[1080] (1855-1915)
Superintendent of Schools—George M. Weedon
Surveyor—Edgar H. Randall

1899
Sheriff—Walter Wamsley
Commonwealth's Attorney—Gustavus B. Wallace (1876-1955)
Clerk—Charles A. Bryan
Deputy Clerk—James Ashby
Treasurer—Henry G. Chesley
Commissioners of the Revenue:
    Aquia and Rock Hill—Wesley Knight (1846-1937)
    Falmouth—D. W. Coakley
Supervisors:
    Aquia—James M. Jones (term completed by Robert E. Lee Ford (1862-1943))
    Falmouth—James O. Lee
    Hartwood—Charles J. Henry
    Rock Hill—Robert F. Lunsford
Constables:
    Aquia—Frederick William Baber[1081] (1861-1937)
    Falmouth—Rolly T. Shelton
    Hartwood—Milton K. Courtney[1082] (1869-1932)
    Rock Hill—James Edward Armstrong (born 1857)
Overseers of the Poor:
    Aquia—James H. Decatur
    Falmouth—Fleet Cox
    Hartwood—Robert L. Burton (1846-1923)
    Rock Hill—Lawrence Ashton Skinner
Superintendent of Schools—George M. Weedon

[1078] Daniel was the son of John E. and V__ Coakley. In 1874 he married Mary J. Beal (born c.1856), the daughter of William L. and Hannah J. Beal.

[1079] Thompson was the son of James McDonald Briggs (1822-1900) and Louisa Ann Smith. He was a successful cattle farmer in Stafford.

[1080] The son of Harrison J. Skinner (c.1821-1862).

[1081] Fred was the son of William Baber (c.1834-1921) of Cleve, Yatton, England. Fred was born in England and became a naturalized U. S. citizen on Nov. 19, 1892. In 1886 he married Alice N. Riley (1861-1944), the daughter of Noah Riley (1813-after 1870) and Cleopatra O'Byrhim (born 1839). The Rileys and Babers resided on land in the north end of the county that is now part of the Marine Corps reservation.

[1082] Milton was the son of David Thomas Courtney (1839-1892) and Susan Jane Heflin (c.1844-1870).

Surveyor—Edgar H. Randall

1901
Sheriff—Walter Wamsley
Constables:
    Aquia—Thompson Shackelford
    Falmouth—Thomas E. Clark (1869-1935)
    Hartwood—James Barber
    Rock Hill—James E. Armstrong
Clerk—Charles A. Bryan
Deputy Clerk—John S. Martin
Treasurer—Henry G. Chesley
Commissioners of the Revenue:
    Aquia and Rock Hill—Wesley Knight[1083] (1846-1937)
    Falmouth—Daniel W. Coakley
Supervisors:
    Aquia—William T. Payne (c.1846-after 1910)
    Falmouth—James O. Lee
    Hartwood—Charles J. Henry
    Rock Hill—Robert F. Lunsford
Overseers of the Poor:
    Aquia—James H. Decatur
    Falmouth—Fleet Cox
    Hartwood—Robert L. Burton
    Rock Hill—Seth R. Cooper[1084] (c.1837-after 1904)
Superintendent of Schools—James Ashby
Surveyor—Edgar H. Randall

1903
Sheriff—Walter Wamsley
Deputy Sheriff—Thomas Jackson Moore
Constables:
    Aquia—William D. Riley (1846-1927)
    Falmouth--___ Payne
    Hartwood--___ Timmons
    Rock Hill--___ English
Clerk—Charles A. Bryan
Deputy Clerk—Edgar S. Moore (1879-1954)
Commonwealth's Attorney—Gustavus Brown Wallace (1876-1955)
Treasurer—Henry G. Chesley
Commissioners of the Revenue—Daniel W. Coakley and Wesley Knight
Supervisors:
    Aquia—William T. Payne
    Falmouth—James O. Lee
    Hartwood—Charles J. Henry
    Rock Hill—Cleveland Harding[1085] (1865-1928)

[1083] Wesley was a life-long resident of Stafford County and actively managed his many affairs until a few months before his death. His business career included successful ventures in lumber dealing, farming, and store keeping. Early on he acquired the title "Captain" as a result of his operating a sailing vessel used for carrying logs from Coal Landing to Washington and Baltimore. He had extensive land holdings which he farmed and kept a store at Coal Landing. For about 12 years he served as commissioner of the revenue for District 2, which was comprised of the Aquia and Rock Hill districts. He died at his home near Coal Landing and was buried in the family cemetery.

[1084] Seth lived at Toluca and served for four years in the 9th Virginia Cavalry.

[1085] Cleve was the son of Enoch (c.1806-1874) and Mary Eliza Harding 1826-1898).

Overseers of the Poor:
    Aquia—James H. Decatur
    Falmouth—Fleet Cox
    Hartwood—Robert L. Burton
    Rock Hill—Robert Lee Templeman (1860-1928)
Superintendent of Schools—James Ashby
Surveyor—Edgar H. Randall

1904

Deputy Sheriff—Harwood Simpson[1086] (1874-1955)
Constables:
    Aquia—Joseph K. Bryan
    Falmouth—Monroe S. Kelly and Crusie J. Jones (1880-1970)
Deputy Commissioner of the Revenue—William T. Green[1087] (1852-1926)
Deputy Treasurer—Asbury W. Evans
Registrar—Armistead Nelson[1088] (1855-1927)
School Trustees:
    Aquia—Robert S. Moncure, William A. Clift[1089] (c.1853-1923), Richard Arthur
        Cloe[1090] (c.1869-1953)
    Falmouth—Harry Clark, William Henry Rollins[1091] (c.1848-1932), Simeon C. Peyton
    Hartwood—Enneyer Lucas, Beverley W. Irvine[1092] (c.1839-1922), Thomas Wallace[1093] (1852-1914)
    Rock Hill—Richard M. Jones, Edward Lee Sterne[1094] (1864-1937), D. W. Patton (1852-1919)

1905

Clerk of the Court—Charles A. Bryan
Assessor—Thomas Wallace

1907

Sheriff—Richard C. L. Moncure
Constables:
    Falmouth—Luther D. Cox[1095] (c.1851-1919)

[1086] Harwood was the son of James Polk Simpson (born c.1845) and Louisa Bullock (born c.1851) and was educated in Stafford and Fredericksburg. During his early years, he worked for the Internal Revenue office in Richmond and afterward with the government oat Fort Eustis. He returned to Stafford in 1925 where he served as postmaster at Glendie until that office closed. He married Nettie G. Jett (died 1952) (*Free Lance-Star*, July 6, 1955).

[1087] William lived near Ruby. He died of a stroke (*Free Lance-Star*, Dec. 8, 1926).

[1088] Armistead was a life-long Stafford resident and lived near the courthouse (*Free Lance-Star*, Dec. 23, 1927).

[1089] William was a lifelong member of Ramoth Baptist Church and lived near Brooke. He never married, died of influenza, and was buried at Oak Hill Cemetery in Spotsylvania (*Free Lance*, Mar. 24, 1923).

[1090] The son of William S. Cloe (1832-1919) and Hannah Stark (1842-1884). He lived in the north end of the county until the government condemned his land in 1942. He then moved to Falmouth and served on the school board for 33 years and was a mail contractor for 12 years (*Free Lance-Star*, Mar. 14, 1953).

[1091] William was the son of James Taylor Rollins and Mary Pratt of King George. He married Florence Elkins of King George and was buried at the Glebe near the Stafford/King George line (*Free Lance-Star*, Sept. 2, 1932).

[1092] B. W. Irvine lived near Hemp Post Office. Following the War Between the States, he taught school for many years. He married Betty Benson (*Free Lance*, Sept. 2, 1922).

[1093] Thomas was the eldest son of Thomas Wallace (1796-1882) and Anne Coffman (1820-1889). He was born and resided at Woodview in Stafford and in 1880 married Harriet Eustace Moncure (1846-1928), the daughter of Judge R. C. L. Moncure. Thomas assisted in the erection of the Episcopal chapel called "Church of the Holy Spirit" in his neighborhood (*Free Lance*, July 11, 1914).

[1094] Edward lived at Roseville. He also served as a school trustee (*Free Lance-Star*, Jan. 21, 1937).

Hartwood--Edward Houghton
Rock Hill—James E. Armstrong
Clerk—Charles A. Bryan
Deputy Clerk—Edgar S. Moore
Commonwealth's Attorney—Gustavus B. Wallace
Commissioners of the Revenue—Thomas Wallace and Arthur Moore (1866-1952)
Deputy Treasurer—Charles Lafayette Chesley (1868-1952)
Supervisors:
    Aquia—William T. Payne
    Falmouth—James O. Lee
    Hartwood—Charles J. Henry
    Rock Hill—Cleve Harding
Overseers of the Poor:
    Aquia—William D. Riley
    Falmouth--___ Hudson
    Hartwood—Robert L. Burton
    Rock Hill—Seth R. Cooper
Superintendent of Schools—James Ashby
Surveyor—Edgar H. Randall

1909
Sheriff—Richard Cassius Lee Moncure, Jr. (1831-1917)
Clerk—Charles A. Bryan
Deputy Clerk—Edgar S. Moore
Treasurer—William Daingerfield Reamy[1096] (1852-1939)

[1095] The son of Austin Cox and Elizabeth Brown and the brother of James Cox (born c.1839). In 1875 Luther married Josephine Cox. Luther lived in White Oak.

[1096] The son of Joshua Reamy, Jr. (1792-1857) and Meriah Neale. William Reamy was born at Parke Farm. His brother, Thomas Benton Reamy (1836-1910), served as a justice of Stafford County.

    William was affectionately known as "Commodore." He served as treasurer of Stafford County from 1908-1932. At the time of his retirement, the *Free Lance-Star* newspaper printed an article about him stating "Commodore is beloved by thousands for his kindly and genial nature, is respected by all for his rugged honesty and unfailing loyalty to friends" (*Free Lance Star*, Sept. 4, 1939). His scrupulous honesty, meticulous management of the treasurer's office and ready wit endeared him to all in the county.
    Throughout his career as treasurer, he drove a horse and buggy from house to house, collecting taxes, Parts of the county were too distant from his farm for him to return in the evening, requiring him to spend nights in the homes of county residents. It was said that he knew all of the best cooks in the county and carefully planned his routes so that he finished his day at the home of an outstanding hostess.
    William was an immense man, very tall as well as heavy. Because it was difficult for him to get in and out of the buggy to open and close gates as he went from farm to farm, he usually employed a local lad to accompany him on his rounds, paying 25 to 50 cents for his day's efforts.
    Occasionally, "Commodore" would encounter a reluctant taxpayer as was the case in 1925 with a Romanian-born Stafford farmer in the Rock Hill District. The farmer owned the $1.50 capitation or "head" tax for his wife, which he refused to pay. When Mr. Reamy explained that he had to pay the tax, the farmer said in broken English, "I no pay, you take the woman in place." Mr. Reamy left with neither the tax nor the woman. The following year, Mr. Reamy returned to the Romanian farmer, again in quest of the $1.50 capitation tax. Again, the farmer refused to pay, offering instead his wife. This time Mr. Reamy agreed to take the wife, saying that he knew two bachelors in Fredericksburg who would gladly pay $1.50 for a wife. When the farmer asked the names of these men and was told that they were Judge Frederick W. Coleman and Attorney Gustavus B. Wallace, the Romanian quickly withdrew $1.50 from his pocket exclaiming, "Here, I pay. I don't want her to fall in them hands!" (*Free Lance-Star*, Nov. 13, 1926).
    In 1878 William Reamy married Sallie Combs (1860-1946) whose family had long been established on Chappawamsic Run. Sallie's father was opposed to the marriage "because he did not like the looks of the young man." At that time in Virginia, girls under the age of 21 had to have the consent of their parent or guardian before marrying. Knowing that was unlikely, the young couple eloped to

Deputy Treasurer—John William Payne[1097] (c.1858-1927)
Superintendent of Schools—George M. Weedon

1911
Sheriff—R. C. L. Moncure, Jr.
Constables:
    Aquia--___ Taliaferro
    Hartwood--___Schooler
    Rock Hill--___ Skinner
Clerk—George William Herring (1877-1966)
Commonwealth's Attorney—Gustavus B. Wallace
Treasurer—William D. Reamy
Deputy Treasurer—John W. Payne
Commissioners of the Revenue:
    Aquia and Rock Hill—Herbert Minor Tolson[1098] (1856-1936)
    Hartwood—Thomas Wallace
Supervisors:
    Aquia—William T. Payne
    Falmouth—William H. Rollins[1099] (born c.1838)
    Hartwood—Charles J. Henry
    Rock Hill—Cleve Harding
Overseers of the Poor:
    Aquia—William D. Riley
    Falmouth--___ Hudson
    Hartwood--___ Burton
    Rock Hill--___ Cooper
Superintendent of Schools—James Ashby
Surveyor—Edgar H. Randall

1915
Sheriff—Clarence Newman Knight[1100] (1878-1945)
Commonwealth's Attorney—Gustavus B. Wallace

Constables:
    Aquia—Frederick William Baber, Sr.[1101] (c.1850-1937)
    Falmouth—St. Clair Brooks (1883-1953)
    Hartwood—J. A. Nash
    Rock Hill—Stafford Tilden Heflin[1102] (1875-1938)
Clerk—George W. Herring
Deputy Clerk—Frank Peyton Moncure (1889-1969)

Baltimore where no such permission was required. There they were married, the newspaper notice stating, "As soon as word is received from the parents that the elopers will be forgiven, they will return to the Old Dominion" (*Virginia Star*, Apr. 27, 1878). Eventually, they returned home where they lived at Parke Farm, the old Carter plantation.

[1097] John lived near Brooke and was a member of Andrew Chapel Methodist Church. He married Susan Jane Winkler (1860-1935).

[1098] Herbert was the son of James E. Tolson (1795-1865) and Ann E. Hickerson (1827-1897). He lived near Stafford Store.

[1099] During the War Between the States, William served with the 30th Virginia Infantry and was wounded at Sharpsburg in September 1862. He deserted his unit in February 1865 and took the oath in Washington.

[1100] Clarence owned Knight Motor Company at the courthouse. He was also a member of Stafford's draft board and, at the time of his death, was a director of People's Bank of Stafford.

[1101] Fred was born in Bristol, England, but lived in Virginia for 56 years. He was a resident of Mount.

[1102] Tilden's first wife was Louisa Dora Beach. He married secondly Ocie Dye (1882-1971).

Commissioners of the Revenue:
    District #1—William T. Deacon (died c.1955)
    District #2—Herbert M. Tolson
Supervisors:
    Aquia—Welford Clinton Atchison[1103] (1848-1924)
    Falmouth—William H. Rollins
    Hartwood--___ Simpson
    Rock Hill—John Walter Maddox[1104] (1883-1949)
Overseers of the Poor:
    Aquia—William D. Riley
    Falmouth—Fielding B. Hudson
    Hartwood—John W. Cox
    Rock Hill—John H. Wilson (1887-1975)
Superintendent of Schools—James Ashby
Surveyor—Edgar H. Randall

1919

Sheriff—William E. Curtis[1105] (died c.1963)
Constables:
    Aquia—Fred W. Baber
    Falmouth—William E. Brooks (1854-1923)
    Hartwood—John B. Heflin (1878-1959)
    Rock Hill—Charles D. Taliaferro[1106] (1867-1949)
Clerk—James Ashby[1107] (1894-1950)
Treasurer—William D. Reamy
Deputy Treasurer—John W. Payne
Commonwealth's Attorney—Frank Peyton Moncure[1108] (1889-1969)
Commissioners of the Revenue—William T. Deacon (died c.1955) and Herbert M. Tolson
Supervisors:
    Aquia—George W. Herring
    Falmouth—William T. Peyton (1875-1955)
    Hartwood—Charles J. Henry
    Rock Hill—John W. Maddox
Overseers of the Poor:
    Aquia—William D. Riley
    Falmouth—Fielding B. Hudson (1873-1945)

[1103] Welford lived near Mount on what is now part of the Marine Corps reservation. He married Lydia C. Minnick (1852-1925).

[1104] John W. Maddox had a brother, Benjamin Maddox who owned a farm near present-day Lake Arrowhead. Benjamin owned a particularly hateful bull that was constantly escaping from his fenced pasture. Benjamin and the bull finally reached an understanding about these escapes. One day when the bull left his pasture to terrorize the neighborhood, Benjamin unloaded one barrel of his shotgun into the bull's side. His hide was thick enough that the bird shot didn't do him any permanent damage, but it stung enough that he remembered ever after having been shot. This didn't do anything to prevent the bull's escape, but Benjamin kept the shotgun on his porch and each time the bull left, Benjamin would take his shotgun and hike after him. As soon as the bull saw the man coming with the gun, he quit what he was doing, turned around, and lumbered slowly back to his pasture.

[1105] William was the founder of Lee-Curtis Insurance Company of Fredericksburg. He was also a carpenter.

[1106] Charles was the son of James Monroe Taliaferro (1809-1893) and Annie Coleman (1834-1892) of Loch Lomond and Springfield. In 1894 he married Ella M. Decatur (born 1875), the daughter of James D. and Sallie Decatur. Charles was buried at Aquia Church.

[1107] The son of James Ashby (1854-1918). He married Virginia Percifull (1896-1925).

[1108] Frank was the son of Dr. Walker Peyton Moncure (1842-1916) and Mary Joanna Hughes (1852-1939). He married Frances E. deLashmutt (1893-1966).

Hartwood—James W. Estes (1852-1929)
Rock Hill—John H. Wilson
Superintendent of Schools—Whitfield Dunaway Peyton[1109] (born 1870)
Surveyor—George Loyall Gordon, Sr.[1110] (1862-1952)

1923
Sheriff—William E. Curtis
Constable:
Falmouth—Claude W. Bourne
Clerk—James Ashby
Deputy Clerk—Virginia Carter[1111]
Treasurer—William D. Reamy
Deputy Treasurer—John W. Payne
Commonwealth's Attorney—Frank P. Moncure
Commissioners of the Revenue—Wade H. Simpson[1112] (born c.1876) and R. C. L. Moncure, Jr.
Supervisors:
Aquia—William Francis Powers (1875-1955)
Falmouth—Norman Nelson Berry[1113] (1885-1962)
Hartwood—Charles J. Henry
Rock Hill—J. W. Maddox
Superintendent of Schools—Whit D. Peyton
Surveyor—George L. Gordon, Sr.

1927
Sheriff—William E. Curtis
Constables:
Aquia—Powhatan Gallahan[1114] (1890-1935)
Rock Hill—Charles Julian Brewer (1880-1942)
Clerk—James Ashby
Deputy Clerk—Genevieve Leary
Treasurer—William D. Reamy

[1109] Whit finished the term of James Ashby who died in office. He was the son of Simeon C. Peyton (1829-1905) and for many years lived on his father's farm, Mt. Ringo, in Stafford. Whit was a traveling representative for the Sherwin-Williams Paint Company. In addition to serving as superintendent of schools from 1918-1924, he was also chairman of the Democratic Party of Stafford. Around 1928 he sold the farm and moved to Amelia County. Whit died in Richmond.

[1110] George was a civil engineer and was the last official surveyor of Stafford County. He was born in Albemarle County where his father was a doctor. George graduated from the University of Virginia, then was employed by the U. S. Geodetic Survey in West Virginia and other states. He also worked in the western states, including Oregon, surveying for the construction of new railroads. Prior to the building of the Panama Canal, he assisted with a survey in Colombia for a proposed alternate waterway.

In 1913 George married Sarah Travers Anderson (1874-1968) of Albemarle County and came to Stafford around 1920 to work as a surveyor. He continued surveying until he was past his 80th year. George was the father of the previous commissioner of the revenue, George L. Gordon, Jr. and was buried at Aquia Church.

[1111] Virginia was the first woman to hold this office in Stafford County.

[1112] Wade was the son of James P. Simpson (born c.1845) and Louisa Bullock (born c.1851). In 1900 Wade married Bessie Lunsford (born c.1878).

[1113] N. N. Berry was the son of Thomas Berry and Mary Watson. He was president of the People's Bank of Stafford, was a livestock dealer, and owned a grocery store in partnership with his son, Spencer B. Berry. For 50 years he was a deacon of Falmouth Baptist Church and taught Sunday School there for 61 years. He was also the church treasurer for 34 years. He married Mary Virginia Fritter (died 1946).

[1114] Powhatan was the son of Samuel Gallahan. A World War I veteran, he served in France where he was struck in the face with machine gun bullets. He lost most of his lower jaw and wore a metal jaw made for him by surgeons.

Commonwealth's Attorney—Lawrence Robert Rose Curtis[1115] (1890-1954)
Commissioner of the Revenue—R. C. L. Moncure, Jr.
Supervisors:
    Aquia—William F. Powers
    Falmouth—Nelson N. Berry
    Hartwood—Charles J. Henry
    Rock Hill—J. W. Maddox
Surveyor—George L. Gordon, Sr.

1928
Sheriff—William E. Curtis
Constable:
    Hartwood—Harry Selah Brown (c.1884-1967)
Clerk—James Ashby
Treasurer—William D. Reamy
Superintendent of Schools—Thomas Benton Gayle (died 1928)
Surveyor—George L. Gordon, Sr.

1929
Sheriff—William E. Curtis
Constable:
    Hartwood—William E. Weimer
Coroner—Dr. John Churchill Gordon[1116] (1871-1949)
Clerk—James Ashby
Treasurer—William D. Reamy
Superintendent of Schools—T. Benton Gayle
Surveyor—George L. Gordon, Sr.

1931
Sheriff—William E. Curtis
Constables:
    Aquia—Ivan D. Dent
    Falmouth—Paul Lightner
Clerk—James Ashby
Treasurer—Nelson N. Berry
Commonwealth's Attorney—Gustavus B. Wallace
Commissioner of the Revenue—R. C. L. Moncure, Jr.
Supervisors:
    Aquia—Clarence N. Knight
    Falmouth—Julian Vernon Brooks[1117] (1885-1956)
    Hartwood—Robert H. Estes
    Rock Hill—John W. Maddox
Superintendent of Schools—T. Benton Gayle
Surveyor—George L. Gordon, Sr.

[1115] Lawrence was a lawyer, civil engineer, and surveyor and lived at Chatham Heights. At the time of his death, Robert was serving as a substitute trial justice for Stafford and King George. He was a member of Ramoth Baptist Church.

[1116] The son of Dr. John Churchill Gordon (born 1831) of Albemarle County. John came to Stafford to fill a vacancy left by the death of a local physician. His brother, George Loyall Gordon (1862-1952), also settled in Stafford and became the county surveyor. John married Cornelia R. Borst (1880-1949).

[1117] Julian was the son of William Edwin Brooks (1854-1922) and Mary Osbourne England (1854-1925). He married Naomi Waller and lived near Brookwood Nursing Home.

1935
Sheriff—William E. Curtis

Constables:
    Aquia—Ivan D. Dent
    Aquia Upper District—John James Flippo (1869-1957)
    Falmouth—William Thomas Sullivan (1880-1962)
Clerk—James Ashby
Deputy Clerks—A. B. Gibson and Elizabeth M. Lambert
Treasurer—N. N. Berry
Commonwealth's Attorney—Gustavus B. Wallace
Commissioner of the Revenue—R. C. L. Moncure, Jr.
Supervisors:
    Aquia—Clarence N. Knight
    Falmouth—Julian V. Brooks
    Hartwood—Robert H. Estes
    Rock Hill—John W. Maddox
Superintendent of Schools—T. Benton Gayle
Surveyor—George L. Gordon, Sr.

1939
Sheriff—William E. Curtis
Constables:
    Falmouth—William T. Sullivan
    Rock Hill—Bailey Arrington
Clerk—James Ashby
Deputy Clerk—Elizabeth M. Lambert
Treasurer—N. N. Berry
Commonwealth's Attorney—Richard Henry Lee Chichester, Jr.[1118] (1904-1973)
Commissioner of the Revenue—R. C. L. Moncure, Jr.
Supervisors:
    Aquia—William Weedon Cloe[1119] (1898-1947)
    Falmouth—Julian V. Brooks
    Hartwood—Robert H. Estes
    Rock Hill—Robert L. Bridwell[1120] (1887-1972)
Superintendent of Schools—T. Benton Gayle
Surveyor—George L. Gordon, Sr.

1943
Sheriff—William E. Curtis
Clerk—James Ashby
Deputy Clerk—Elizabeth M. Lambert
Treasurer—N. N. Berry
Commonwealth's Attorney—R. H. L. Chichester
Commissioner of the Revenue—George Loyall Gordon, Jr.
Supervisors:
    Aquia—William W. Cloe

[1118] The son of Richard Henry Lee Chichester, Sr. (1870-1930) and Virginia Belle Wallace (1871-1961). He began practicing law in Stafford in 1928. He was appointed country trial justice in 1932 and held that position until being elected commonwealth's attorney (*Free Lance-Star*, July 17, 1973).

[1119] Until the expansion of the Quantico Marine Corps base in 1942, William lived at Laurel View. He was also a mail carrier in the Rock Hill District and a World War I veteran.

[1120] Mr. Bridwell ran a store on Garrisonville Road (State Route 610). He was well-like in the community because he was willing to extend credit to the local people during the Depression.

Falmouth—Julian V. Brooks
Hartwood—Ramah D. Coakley[1121] (1878-1956)
Rock Hill—Robert L. Bridwell
Surveyor—George L. Gordon, Sr.

1947
Sheriff—Alaric Ridout MacGregor[1122] (1906-1991)
Clerk—James Ashby
Deputy Clerk—Elizabeth M. Lambert
Treasurer—N. N. Berry
Commonwealth's Attorney—R. H. L. Chichester
Commissioner of the Revenue—George L. Gordon, Jr.
Supervisors:
    Aquia—McCarty Chichester "Mac" Moncure (1918-1993)
    Falmouth—Preston S. Snellings
    Hartwood—Wallace Hansford Abel (1909-1989)
    Rock Hill—Gordon M. Byram[1123]
Superintendent of Schools—T. Benton Gayle
Surveyor—George L. Gordon, Sr.

1951
Sheriff—Alaric R. MacGregor
Clerk—Samuel Lutz Alexander (1912-1972)
Deputy Clerk—Elizabeth M. Lambert
Treasurer—N. N. Berry
Deputy Treasurer—Ainsley Bennington Cloe[1124] (1896-1972)
Commonwealth's Attorney—R. H. L. Chichester
Commissioner of the Revenue—George L. Gordon, Jr.
Supervisors:
    Aquia—Harold T. Knight (1915-1978)
    Falmouth—Preston S. Snellings
    Hartwood—W. Hansford Abel
    Rock Hill—John W. McWhirt
Superintendent of Schools—T. Benton Gayle
Surveyor—George L. Gordon, Sr.

[1121] Ramah was the son of Douglas W. Coakley and Mary J. Beale. He married first Nora Bullock (died 1926) and secondly Maud Lunsford (died 1936). Ramah was a blacksmith by trade.

[1122] Alaric was the son of John Alaster MacGregor (1869-1953) and Bessie Knight (1879-1959). His first job was shoveling coal into the boiler of a steam shovel at the old George Washington Stone Corporation quarry at Mt. Pleasant on the north side of Aquia Creek. Stone from the quarry was carried by railroad down to a landing on the creek. There a huge wooden boom was used to pick up the blocks and load them onto waiting barges. On a dare, Alaric climbed the boom, nearly 100 feet tall, and stood on his head on the top of it. Alaric was paid a nickel a day for stoking the boiler, but quit after being promised a raise that was not forthcoming.

    Alaric was long known as one of the strongest men in Stafford County. Former commissioner of the revenue, George L. Gordon, remembers watching him repair an old truck. Alaric had removed the truck's engine and had placed it on the floor of his shop. Desiring to have the engine in a more convenient location, he reached down, picked up the engine in his arms, and carried it over to a workbench.

[1123] Mr. Byram ran Byram's Market, later Tyson's Store, at the intersection of Kellogg's Mill Road (State Route 651) and Mountain View Road (State Route 627).

[1124] The son of Richard Arthur Cloe and Mary Lee Weedon. In 1919 Ainsley married Gertrude Pittman. He not only served as deputy treasurer and treasurer of Stafford County, he was also a founder and member of the board of People's Bank of Stafford and served in World War I.

1955
Sheriff—Bobbie F. Burton
Clerk—Samuel L. Alexander
Treasurer—N. N. Berry
Deputy Treasurer—Ainsley B. Cloe
Commonwealth's Attorney—R. H. L. Chichester
Commissioner of the Revenue—George L. Gordon, Jr.
Supervisors:
    Aquia—Harold T. Knight
    Falmouth—Fitzhugh W. Heflin
    Hartwood—W. Hansford Abel
    Rock Hill—John W. McWhirt

1959
Sheriff—Alaric R. MacGregor
Clerk—Samuel L. Alexander
Treasurer—N. N. Berry
Deputy Treasurer—Ainsley B. Cloe
Commonwealth's Attorney—R. H. L. Chichester
Commissioner of the Revenue—George L. Gordon, Jr.
Supervisors:
    Aquia—Harold T. Knight
    Falmouth—Fitzhugh W. Heflin
    Hartwood—W. Hansford Abel
    Rock Hill—Gordon M. Byram
Superintendent of Schools—T. Benton Gayle

1960
Deputy Clerk—Helen B. Shackelford[1125] (1925-1982)
Superintendent of Schools—T. Benton Gayle

1963
Sheriff—Alaric R. MacGregor
Clerk—Samuel L. Alexander
Deputy Clerk—Helen B. Shackelford
Treasurer—Ainsley B. Cloe
Commonwealth's Attorney—R. H. L. Chichester
Commissioner of the Revenue—George L. Gordon, Jr.
Supervisors:
    Aquia—Ralph Metts
    Falmouth—James C. Crooks
    Hartwood—W. Hansford Abel
    Rock Hill—Gordon M. Byram
Superintendent of Schools—T. Benton Gayle

1967
Sheriff—Alaric R. MacGregor
Clerk—Samuel L. Alexander
Deputy Clerk—Helen B. Shackelford
Commonwealth's Attorney—R. H. L. Chichester
Commissioner of the Revenue—George L. Gordon, Jr.
Supervisors:
    Aquia—Harold T. Knight

[1125] This was Helen Butler who married Garland Davis Shackelford (1917-1992).

Falmouth—Fitzhugh W. Heflin
Hartwood—W. Hansford Abel
Rock Hill—George W. Embrey
Superintendent of Schools—Howard Sullins

1971
Sheriff—Richard L. Ashby
Clerk—Samuel L. Alexander
Deputy Clerk—Helen B. Shackelford
Treasurer—McCarty C. Moncure
Commonwealth's Attorney—Daniel McCarty Chichester
Commissioner of the Revenue—George L. Gordon, Jr.
Supervisors:
    Aquia—Ralph Metts
    Falmouth—Charles D. Nelms
    George Washington—Alvin Y. Bandy
    Griffis-Wide Water—Lindbergh A. Fritter
    Hartwood—W. Hansford Abel
    Rock Hill—George W. Embrey
Superintendent of Schools—Andrew G. Wright

1975
Sheriff—Richard L. Ashby
Clerk—Samuel L. Alexander
Treasurer—McCarty C. Moncure
Commonwealth's Attorney—Daniel M. Chichester
Commissioner of the Revenue—George L. Gordon, Jr.
Supervisors:
    Aquia—Ralph Metts
    Falmouth—Charles D. Nelms
    George Washington—Alvin Y. Bandy
    Griffis-Wide Water—Lindbergh A. Fritter
    Hartwood—W. Hansford Abel
    Rock Hill—George W. Embrey
    Tiebreaker—John A. Nere (1923-1997)

1977
Clerk—Samuel L. Alexander
Deputy Clerk—Helen B. Shackelford
Supervisors:
    Aquia—James Monroe Winkler (1878-1970)
    Falmouth—Charles "Togie" Payne
    Hartwood—W. Hansford Abel
Superintendent of Schools—Andrew G. Wright

1979
Sheriff—Richard L. Ashby
Clerk—Samuel L. Alexander[1126]
Deputy Clerk—Helen B. Shackelford
Treasurer—McCarty C. Moncure
Commonwealth's Attorney—Daniel M. Chichester
Commissioner of the Revenue—George L. Gordon, Jr.
Supervisors:
    George Washington—Alvin Y. Bandy

[1126] Lillian T. Knight completed un-expired term beginning 1980.

Griffis-Wide Water—Charles Wandrick
Rock Hill—George W. Embrey
Tiebreaker—John A. Nere
Superintendent of Schools—Andrew G. Wright

1981
Deputy Clerk—Helen B. Shackelford
Supervisors:
Aquia—Philip E. Hornung
Falmouth—Rebecca L. Reed
Hartwood—E. Lloyd Chittum
Superintendent of Schools—Andrew G. Wright

1983
Sheriff—Richard L. Ashby
Clerk—Lillian T. Knight
Treasurer—McCarty C. Moncure
Commonwealth's Attorney—Daniel M. Chichester
Commissioner of the Revenue—George L. Gordon, Jr.
Supervisors:
George Washington—Alvin Y. Bandy
Griffis-Wide Water—Lindbergh A. Fritter
Rock Hill—Ralph A. Marceron
Tiebreaker—Ferris M. Belman, Sr.
Superintendent of Schools—Andrew G. Wright

1985
Supervisors:
Aquia—Philip E. Hornung
Falmouth—Rebecca L. Reed
Hartwood—John M. Porter
At Large—Ferris M. Belman
Superintendent of Schools—Sidney Faucette

1987
Sheriff—Richard L. Ashby
Clerk—Lillian T. Knight
Treasurer—McCarty C. Moncure
Commonwealth's Attorney—Daniel M. Chichester
Commissioner of the Revenue—George L. Gordon, Jr.
Supervisors:
George Washington—Alvin Y. Bandy
Griffis-Wide Water—James F. Persinger
Rock Hill—Ralph A. Marceron
Superintendent of Schools—Sidney Faucette

1991
Sheriff—Ralph Williams
Clerk—Thomas M. Moncure
Treasurer—McCarty C. Moncure
Commonwealth's Attorney—Daniel M. Chichester
Commissioner of the Revenue—George L. Gordon, Jr.
Supervisors:
George Washington—Alvin Y. Bandy
Griffis-Wide Water—Lindbergh A. Fritter
Rock Hill—Robert C. Gibbons

Superintendent of Schools—Sidney Faucette

Sources:

Abercrombie, Janice L. and Slatten, Richard. *Virginia Revolutionary Publick Claims*. Athens, GA: Iberian Publishing Co., 1992.

Alcock, John P. *Five Generations of the Family of Burr Harrison of Virginia, 1650-1800*. Bowie, MD: Heritage Books, 1991.

Alexandria Gazette, July 9, 1862, obituary of William J. Green.

Anderson, Sarah T. *Lewises, Meriwethers, and Their Kin*. Richmond, VA: Dietz Press, Inc., 1938.

---. Personal notes for *Lewises, Meriwethers, and Their Kin*, c.1910, from the personal collection of George L. Gordon, Jr.

Auditor of Public Accounts, 1781-1787. Accession #APA 653. Richmond, VA: Library of Virginia.

Auditor of Public Accounts, 1776-1928. Accession #APA 254. Richmond, VA: Library of Virginia.

Barton, R. T., ed. *Virginia Colonial Decisions: the Reports of Sir John Randolph and by Edward Barradall of the Decisions of the General Court of Virginia, 1728-1741*. Boston, Mass.: Boston Book Co., 1909.

Bellomo, Barbara B. *The Continuing Genealogy of the Whitson Family and Others*. Denver, CO: self-published, 1994.

Benz, Katherine P. *The Tolson Family of Virginia and Missouri, Including Related Lines of Combs, Harrison, Bullitt, Ratcliffe, and Herndon*. Madison, Wisconsin, 1990.

Boddie, John B. *Virginia Historical Genealogies*. Baltimore, MD: Genealogical Publishing Co., 1990.

Bodine, Ronny O. *Thomas Owsley - a Virginia Gentleman*. Privately published.

Brent, Chester H. *Descendants of Coll. Giles Brent, Capt. George Brent and Robert Brent, Gent*. VT: Rutland Publishing Company, 1946.

"British Mercantile Claims, 1775-1803." *The Virginia Genealogist*, vol. 14, #1, (1970), pp. 169-177.

Brown, Alexander. *The Cabells and Their Kin*. Harrisonburg, VA: C. J. Carrier Co., 1978.

Brown, Stuart E. *Virginia Baron: The Story of Thomas 6th Lord Fairfax*. Berryville, VA: Chesapeake Book Co., 1965.

Bruce, Philip A. *Institutional History of Virginia in the 17th Century*. NY: B. P. Putnam and Sons, 1910.

Buckner, Mary Ann, ed. *Early Virginians*. Fredericksburg, VA, 1974.

Butler, Stuart Lee. *A Guide to Virginia Militia Units in the War of 1812*. Athens, GA: Iberian Publishing Co., 1988.

Chapman, Sigismunda M. *A History of the Chapman and Alexander Families*. Richmond, VA: Dietz Press, Inc., 1946.

Cloe, William W. Collection. *Free Lance*, (undated copy), "Sketch of Mr. G.M. Weedon's Life."

Copeland, Pamela C. and MacMaster, Richard K. *The Five George Masons: Patriots and Planters of Virginia and Maryland*. Charlottesville, VA; University Press of Virginia, 1975.

Coppage, A. Maxim and Tackitt, James W. *Stafford Co., Virginia, 1800-1850*. Concord, CA, 1982.

Crowe, Maude. *Descendants from First Families of Virginia and Maryland: a Family History and Genealogy Covering 350 Years, 1620-1970*. Self-published, 1978.

Des Cognets, Louis, Jr. *English Duplicates of Lost Virginia Records*. Baltimore, MD: Genealogical Publishing Co., 1981.

"Description of Virginia Commerce." *William and Mary College Quarterly Historical Magazine*, 1st series, vol. 14, (1905), pp. 87-93.

Deyo, William L. "The Monteith Family and the Potomac Indians." Fredericksburg, VA: self-published, 1996.

Dobson, David. *Scots on the Chesapeake, 1607-1830*. Baltimore, MD: Genealogical Publishing Co., 1992.

Dorman, John F. *Claiborne of Virginia: Descendants of Colonel William Claiborne, the First Eight Generations*. Baltimore, MD: Gateway Press, 1995.

Dowdey, Clifford. *The Virginia Dynasties*. NY: Bonanza Books, 1969.

"The Eustace Family." *William and Mary College Quarterly Historical Magazine*, vol. 11, (1902-1903), NY: Kraus Reprint Co., 1977, pp. 209-210.

Eby, Jerrilynn. *They Called Stafford Home: the Development of Stafford County, Virginia from 1600 Until 1865*. Bowie, MD: Heritage Books, 1997.

Field, Charles K. *A Genealogical and Biographical History of the Field Family of Massachusetts and Vermont and the French-Henry Families of Virginia and Texas*. Baltimore, MD: Gateway Press, Inc., 1985.

Fisher, Therese A. *Marriage Records of the City of Fredericksburg and of Orange, Spotsylvania, and Stafford Counties, Virginia, 1722-1850.* Bowie, MD: Heritage Books, 1990.

---. *Marriage Records of the City of Fredericksburg and the County of Stafford, Virginia, 1851-1900.* Bowie, MD: Heritage Books, 1994.

Fitzpatrick, John C., ed. *The Writings of George Washington, from the Original Manuscript Sources, 1745-1799.* Washington, DC: U. S. Government Printing Office, 1944.

Fleming, Lt. Col. Charles A., Austin, Capt. Robin L., Braley, Capt. Charles A. *Quantico: Crossroads of the Marine Corps.* Washington, DC: U. S. Government Printing Office, 1944.

Fleming, Edith C. *A History of Brooke.* Self-published, n.d.

Flournoy, H. W. *Calendar of Virginia State Papers and Manuscripts from January 1, 1808 to December 31, 1835.* NY: Kraus Reprint Corp., 1968.

Foote, A. Edward. *Chotankers: a Family History.* Florence, AL: Thornwood Book Publishers, 1982.

Ford, Worthington C. "The Will of Augustine Washington, Father of George Washington." *Wills of George Washington and his Immediate Ancestors.* Brooklyn, NY: Historical Printing Club, 1891.

Fredericksburg Circuit Court Records:
"Ficklen vs Tyler et al," SC/H/1809/98-18
"Cox vs Jett," CR/SC/H/1821/51-22
"Hewitt vs Samuel," CR/SC/H/1825/124-4
"Honey vs Harding," CI/H/1881/151-13
"McInteer vs McInteer," LC-H/1838/182-28
"Ficklen vs Tyler & als," CR/SC/H/1811?/98-18

The Fredericksburg Confederate Cemetery Register. Central Rappahannock Regional Library, Fredericksburg, VA.

Fredericksburg Daily Star, Oct. 4, 1906, obituary of James W. Beaty

Fredericksburg Ledger, Apr. 22, 1873, obituary of Landon J. Huffman

---, June 7, 1865, Charles C. Wellford beaten by Federal troops

Fredericksburg News, Mar. 26, 1850, marriage announcement of Harrison B. Barnes and Fanny L. P. Conway

---, July 24, 1856, obituary of Ezra Burr

---, Dec. 1, 1856, Simeon Peyton's advertisement for livery horses

---, Oct. 5, 1874, "Falmouth Then and Now"

Fredericksburg Star, Apr. 14, 1880, obituary of Nathaniel Waller Ford

---, May 24, 1884, "Registrars and Judges of Elections"

---, Mar. 25, 1885, Stafford Judges and Registrars

---, Sept. 6, 1884, suicide attempt of Silas Hailslip

---, Sept. 10, 1884, obituary of Silas Hailslip

---, Feb. 18, 1885, "The Roads"

---, Mar. 25, 1885, "Stafford Judges and Registrars"

---, July 27, 1886, "Stafford Roads"

---, Jan. 11, 1888, "Jottings from Stafford, Coakly, Va."

---, Apr. 17, 1889, arrest of Amos K. Monteith

---, June 28, 1890, report on the Stafford Board of Supervisors

---, July 1, 1891, "An Ancient Relic"

---, Feb. 17, 1892, obituary of James B. Templeman

---, Feb. 17, 1892, Mrs. James B. Templeman's home destroyed by fire

---, June 22, 1892, "Stafford News" (M. K. Lowry)

Free Lance, June 23, 1885, obituary of Duff Green, Jr.

---, Feb. 6, 1891, report of George J. Lightner and the Fredericksburg Free Bridge

---, Feb. 27, 1891, notice of the removal of Strother Harding

---, June 23, 1891, obituary of Alexander H. Mason

---, Mar. 4, 1892, obituary of Robert N. Blake

---, June 10, 1892, advertisement for Greenlaw's Celebrated Liniment

---, Aug. 9, 1892, obituary of Raleigh L. Cooper

---, Feb. 20, 1894, obituary of Dr. John H. Daniel

---, July 7, 1896, obituary of John H. Schooler

---, May 20, 1897, obituary of Samuel G. Wallace
---, Nov. 25, 1897, "Lively Row on Court Day—Trouble Between Fishermen"
---, Nov. 27, 1897, obituary of Wm S. White
---, Feb. 26, 1898, obituary of Robert G. Hickerson
---, Sept. 27, 1898, obituary of Robert L. Flatford
---, Dec. 8, 1898, obituary of Charles A. Sthreshley
---, Dec. 15, 1898, obituary of George J. Lightner
---, Jan. 21, 1899, obituary of John Randolph
---, Apr. 4, 1899, obituary of Henry W. Edwards
---, Aug. 29, 1901, obituary of Charles W. Cloe
---, Oct. 5, 1901, obituary of Noah Jones
---, Oct. 7, 1902, obituary of George M. Weedon
---, Oct. 28, 1902, obituary of Charles W. Spindle
---, Jan. 27, 1903, obituary of Dr. Hawkins Stone
---, Sept. 1, 1903, obituary of William S. Monteith
---, Jan. 21, 1904, obituary of Alexander M. Green
---, Mar. 19, 1904, obituary of James L. Taliaferro
---, Nov. 24, 1904, obituary of Francis T. Forbes
---, Jan. 30, 1906, obituary of J. Horace Lacy
---, Oct. 27, 1906, obituary of Nathaniel Ball
---, Dec. 25, 1906, obituary of Granville Embrey
---, Oct. 13, 1908, obituary of James O. Lee
---, Nov. 17, 1908, obituary of John M. Hull
---, June 9, 1910, obituary of Asbury W. Evans
---, Mar. 30, 1911, obituary of Mace C. Purkins
---, Apr. 15, 1911, obituary of Edward West
---, June 1, 1911, obituary of Whit D. Peyton
---, Sept. 28, 1912, obituary of Ennever Lucas
---, July 11, 1914, obituary of Thomas Wallace
---, Nov. 25, 1913, obituary of J. Bailey Jett
---, Nov. 4, 1915, obituary of John C. Cox
---, July 25, 1916, obituary of John H. Stone
---, Nov. 7, 1916, obituary of James W. Schooler
---, Dec. 19, 1916, obituary of Daniel M. Lee
---, Nov. 17, 1917, obituary of Marcus M. Ricker
---, Dec. 4, 1917, obituary of Robert S. Moncure
---, Feb. 26, 1918, obituary of Charles A. Bryan
---, Apr. 2, 1918, obituary of Hugh Adie
---, Nov. 26, 1918, obituary of James Ashby
---, Mar. 4, 1919, obituary of Maj. Edward S. Ruggles
---, Feb. 8, 1921, obituary of Robert L. Dodd
---, Oct. 18, 1921, obituary of Henry G. Chesley
---, May 23, 1922, obituary of Milton A. Ferneyhough
---, Sept. 2, 1922, obituary of Beverley W. Irvine
---, Mar. 15, 1923, obituary of Samuel Fitzhugh
---, Mar. 24, 1923, obituary of William A. Clift
Free Lance-Star, Nov. 13, 1926, retirement of William D. Reamy
---, Dec. 8, 1926, obituary of William T. Green
---, Dec. 23, 1927, obituary of Armistead Nelson
---, Dec. 4, 1929, obituary of Welford M. Masters
---, Dec. 11, 1931, obituary of Charles J. Chartters
---, Sept. 2, 1932, obituary of William H. Rollins
---, Feb. 23, 1933, obituary of Charles L. Kennedy
---, July 16, 1934, obituary of Whitfield D. Peyton
---, Mar. 20, 1935, obituary of Rolly T. Shelton
---, Oct. 16, 1935, obituary of Wilson Decatur

---, Nov. 29, 1935, obituary of Powhatan Gallahan
---, June 30, 1936, obituary of Herbert M. Tolson
---, Jan. 21, 1937, obituary of Edward L. Sterne
---, Mar. 16, 1937, obituary of Wesley Knight
---, Apr. 17. 1937, obituary of Frederick W. Baber
---, June 28, 1939, obituary of Marion K. Lowry
---, Sept. 4, 1939, obituary of William D. Reamy
---, Mar. 2, 1940, obituary of James H. Decatur
---, July 15, 1940, obituary of William P. Daffan
---, Sept. 4, 1945, obituary of Clarence N. Knight
---, Mar. 12, 1952, obituary of George L. Gordon, Sr.
---, Mar. 14, 1953, obituary of Richard A. Cloe
---, Oct. 28, 1954, obituary of Lawrence R. R. Curtis
---, July 6, 1955, obituary of Harwood Simpson
---, Nov. 15, 1956, obituary of Ramah D. Coakley
---, Dec. 17, 1962, obituary of N. N. Berry
---, July 17, 1973, obituary of Richard H. L. Chichester
French, David M. *The Brent Family.* Self-published, Alexandria, VA, 1977.
Gray, Gertrude E. *Virginia Northern Neck Land Grants.* Baltimore, MD: Genealogical Publishing Co., 1993.
Gucciardo, Dolores M. *Matheny-Gucciardo and Allied Families.* Self-published, June 1983.
Hagemann, James A. *The Heritage of Virginia.* Norfolk, VA: Donning Company Publishers, 1986.
Hall, Wilmer L., ed. *Executive Journals of the Council of Colonial Virginia.* Richmond, VA: Virginia State Library, 1967.
Harmon, Francis S. *Adam's Eves.* Self-published, 1964.
Harrison, Fairfax. *Landmarks of Old Prince William: a Study of Origins in Northern Virginia.* Baltimore, MD: Gateway Press, Inc., 1987.
"Harrison of Northern Virginia." *Genealogies of Virginia Families from The Virginia Magazine of History and Biography,* vol. 3, pp. 671-686.
Hayden, Horace E. *Virginia Genealogies: a Genealogy of the Glassell Family of Scotland and Virginia.* Baltimore, MD: Genealogical Publishing Co., 1979.
Heitman, Francis B. *Historical Register of Officers of the Continental Army During the War of the Revolution, April, 1775 to December, 1783.* Baltimore, MD: Clearfield Publishing Co., 1997.
Helligso, Martha S. *George Mason Including One Line of Descent and Related Lines of Demourvell, Fowke, French, Lee, Neale, Presly, Rodham, Spence, Sturman, Talbott, Thompson, Thoroughgood, and Youell.* Self-published, 1983.
Herndon, Dudley L., Jr. *The Herndons of the American Revolution, Part IV: #82, William Herndon of Prince William County, Virginia and his Descendants.* Baltimore, MD: Gateway Press, Inc., 1992.
Hodge, Robert A., ed. *Fredericksburg Cemetery Company Interment Register, 1844-1961.* Central Rappahannock Regional Library, Fredericksburg, VA, 1989.
Hopkins, Timothy. *The Kelloggs in the Old World and the New.* California: Sunset Press, 1903.
Hopkins, William L. *Some Wills from the Burned Counties of Virginia and Other Wills not Listed in Virginia Wills and Administration, 1632-1800.* Richmond, VA, 1987.
Hore, Elias A. W. "Account Book, 1843." MSS5: 3H 7817:1, Virginia Historical Society, Richmond, Virginia.
Houston, Lemuel W. *A Bank for Fredericksburg.* Fredericksburg, VA: National Bank of Fredericksburg, 1989.
Hudgins, Dennis R., ed. *Cavaliers and Pioneers: Abstracts of Virginia Land Patents and Grants,* vols. 4 and 5, Richmond, VA: Virginia Genealogical Society, 1994.
Jillson, Willard R. *Kentucky Land Grants.* Louisville: Standard Printing Co., 1925.
Johnson, John J. "Duff Green, Falmouth Industrialist." *Fredericksburg Times,* February 1996, pp. 9-14.

---. "The Falmouth Canal and its Mills: in Industrial History." *The Journal of Fredericksburg History,* vol. 2, Fredericksburg, VA: Historic Fredericksburg Foundation, Inc., 1997, pp. 25-43.
Johnston, Frederick *Memorials of Old Virginia Clerks.* Lynchburg, VA: J. P. Bell Co., 1888.

Joyner, Peggy S. *Northern Neck Warrants and Surveys, 1710-1780*. Self-published, 1986.
Kennedy, John P., ed. *Journal of the House of Burgesses of Virginia, 1770-1772*. Richmond, VA: Virginia State Library, 1906.
Kennedy, Mary S. *Seldens of Virginia and Allied Families*, vols. 1 and 2. NY: Frank Allaben Genealogical Co., 1911.
King, George H. S. "Memorial to Henry Fox, Gentleman, of 'Huntington,' King William County, Virginia." *Tyler's Quarterly Historical and Genealogical Magazine*, vol. 21, (1940), pp. 217-290.
---. "Notes of the Flourey Tract." Nov. 16, 1976. Central Rappahannock Regional Library, Fredericksburg, VA.
---. *The Register of Overwharton Parish, Stafford County, Virginia, 1723-1758*. SC: Southern Historical Press, 1986.
---. "Will of Major William Newton of Stafford County." *Tyler's Quarterly Historical and Genealogical Magazine*, vol. 23, (1941-42), pp. 222-236.
Krick, Robert K. *The Fredericksburg Artillery*. Lynchburg, VA: H. E. Howard, Inc., 1986.
---. *9th Virginia Cavalry*. Lynchburg, VA: H. E. Howard, Inc., 1982.
---. *30th Virginia Infantry*. Lynchburg, VA: H. E. Howard, Inc., 1983.
Lee, Edmond Jennings. *Lee of Virginia, 1642-1892: Biographical and Genealogical Sketches of the Descendants of Col. Richard Lee*. Baltimore, MD: Genealogical Publishing Co., 1983.
Lee, Ida J. "King William County Personal Property Tax Lists, 1782-1850." *William and Mary College Quarterly Historical Magazine*, series 2, vol. 7, (1927), pp. 114-122.
Leonard, Cynthia M. *The General Assembly of Virginia: July 30, 1619 - January 11, 1978: a Bicentennial Register of Members*. Richmond, VA: Virginia State Library, 1978.
Littlejohn, Janet D. "James O. Lee Obituary from the Gospel Messenger: Devoted to the Primitive Cause." *Magazine of Virginia Genealogy*, vol. 37, no. 1 (February 1999), pp. 49-50.
Lombus, William. *Latham: a Catalog of Virginia and Ohio Families*. Self-published, 1998.
Lowry, Noreta Weber. *The Lowry/Lowery Family, 1775-1987*. Arcadia, OH. 1987.
MacLean, Sir John. *Historical and Genealogical Memoir of the Family of Poyntz*. Baltimore, MD: Gateway Press, Inc., 1983.
Macrae, Emily. "The Wallace Family." *William and Mary Quarterly Historical Magazine*, vol. 13, (1905), pp. 177-182.
Mapp, Alf J., Jr. *The Virginia Experiment: the Old Dominion's Role in the Making of America (1607-1781)*. Richmond, VA: Dietz Press, Inc., 1957.
Mauzey, Armand J. "The Mauzey-Mauzy Family." *Genealogies of Virginia Families from The Virginia Magazine of History and Biography*, vol. 4, Baltimore, MD: Genealogical Publishing Co., 1981, pp. 308-315.
Maxwell, William, ed. "The Association in Westmoreland." *Virginia Historical Register*, vol. 2, Spartanburg, SC: The Reprint Co., 1973, pp. 14-18.
McIlwaine, H. R. *Minutes of the Council and General Court of Colonial Virginia*. Richmond, VA: Virginia State Library, 1924.
Meyer, Virginia M., and Dorman, John F., eds. *Adventurers in Purse and Person, 1607-1624/5*. Richmond, VA: Dietz Press, 1987.
Moncure, Thomas M. and Pynn, Molly A. *The Story of Aquia Church*. Fredericksburg, VA: Cardinal Press, Inc., 2000.
Morton, Richard L. *Colonial Virginia: the Tidewater Period, 1607-1710*, vol. 1, Spartanburg, SC: The Reprint, 1973.
---. *Colonial Virginia: Westward Expansion and Prelude to Revolution, 1710-1763*, vol. 2, Chapel Hill, NC: University of North Carolina Press, 1960.
Musselman, Carl P. and Mildred H. *Musselman-Powell and Bowling Families of Stafford and Spotsylvania Counties, Virginia*. Fredericksburg, VA: Bookcrafters, 1993.
Musselman, Homer D. *47th Virginia Infantry*. Lynchburg, VA: H. E. Howard, Inc., 1991.
---. *Veterans and Cemeteries of Stafford County, Virginia*. Fredericksburg, VA, 1996.

Nagel, Paul C. *The Lees of Virginia: Seven Generations of an American Family*. NY: Oxford University Press, 1990.

National Society of the DAR Centennial Administration. *DAR Patriot Index, Centennial Edition*. Washington, DC: NSDAR, 1994.
Nicklin, John B. "Benjamin Strother (c.1700-1765) and his Wives." *Tyler's Quarterly Historical and Genealogical Magazine*, vol. 19, (1938), pp. 224-227.
Norman, Jane T. *Thomas Norman of Virginia*. Self-published, 1976.
Nugent, Nell M. *Cavaliers and Pioneers: Abstracts of Virginia Land Patents and Grants*, vols. 1-3, Richmond, VA: Virginia State Library, 1979.
Owsley, Harry B. *Genealogical Facts of the Owsley Family in England and America, from the Time of the Restoration to the Present*. Chicago, IL, 1890.
Payne, Brooke. *The Paynes of Virginia*. Berryville, VA: Virginia Book Company, 1937.
Peyton Society of Virginia. *The Peytons of Virginia*. Baltimore, MD: Gateway Press, Inc., 2004.
"The Phillipses." *Weekly Maysville Eagle*, Mar. 29, 1876, Maysville Historical Society, Maysville, Kentucky.
Pierce, Alycon T. *Selected Final Pension Payment Vouchers, 1818-1864*. Athens, GA: Iberian Publishing Co., 1996.
Pippenger, Wesley E. *John Alexander: a Northern Neck Proprietor—His Family, Friends, and Kin*. Baltimore, MD: Gateway Press, 1990.
Political Arena, Oct. 16, 1827, notice of a meeting of Stafford citizens opposed to the election of Andrew Jackson
Porter, Albert O. *County Government in Virginia: a Legislative History, 1607-1904*. NY: Columbia University Press, 1947.
"Public Officers in Virginia, 1680." *The Virginia Magazine of History and Biography*, vol. 1, no. 3, (January 1894), pp. 225-252.
"Public Officers in Virginia, 1702, 1714." *Virginia Magazine of History and Biography*, vol. 2, no. 1, (July 1894), pp. 1-15.
Reamy, Morris R. *A History of the Reamy Family of Westmoreland and Stafford Counties in Virginia, 1655-1975*. Self-published.
Recum, Franz Y. *Withers—America or a Collection of Genealogical Data Concerning the History of the Male Line of James Withers (1680/1-1746) of Stafford County, Virginia*. NY, 1949.
Reese, Lee F. *The Ashby Book*. San Diego, CA, 1978.
Reps, John W. *Tidewater Towns: City Planning in Colonial Virginia and Maryland*. Williamsburg, VA: Colonial Williamsburg Foundation, 1972.
Rhodes, Howard J. *The Rhodes Family in Virginia: a Genealogy and History*. NY: Greenwich Publishers, 1986.
Robbins, Michael W. *The Principio Company, Iron Making in Colonial Maryland: 1720-1781*. NY: Garland Publishers, 1986.
Robertson, Haywood L. and Owsley, Laurel J. *The Owsley Family: a Partial Genealogical History*. Self-published, 1987.
Rose, Christine. *Ancestors and Descendants of Rev. Robert Rose and Rev. Charles Rose of Colonial Virginia and Wester Alves, Morayshire, Scotland*. San Jose, CA, 1985.
Rouse, Parke, Jr. *Virginia: the English Heritage in America*. NY: Hastings House Publishers, 1966.
Sandberg, Trudy J. and Gott, John K. *Valiant Virginian: the Story of Presley Neville O'Bannon (1776-1850)*. Bowie MD: Heritage Books, 1994.
Scott, Thomas C. "Ledger, 1817-1823." Accession #23327. Richmond, VA: Library of Virginia.
Scribner, Robert L., ed. *Revolutionary Virginia: the Road to Independence*, vol. 1. Charlottesville, VA: University Press of Virginia, 1973.
Selden, Jefferson S. *Samuel Selden the Immigrant and his Wife Rebecca Yeo Selden*. Self-published, 1981.
Shifflett, Crandall. "Unionism in Fredericksburg: the Case of Joseph B. Ficklen." Presentation at Wallace Library, Fredericksburg, VA, Sept. 25, 1994 (tape available from Belmont - Gary Melchers Museum, Stafford).
Southern Churchman, Aug. 4, 1848, obituary of John Gray, Esq., p. 115.
Sparacio, Ruth and Sam. *Stafford County, Virginia Deed and Will Abstracts, 1686-1689*. McLean, VA: The Antient Press, 1989.

Sparacio, Ruth and Sam. *Stafford County, Virginia Deed and Will Abstracts, 1699-1709.* McLean, VA: The Antient Press, 1987.
---. *Stafford County, Virginia Deed and Will Abstracts, 1722-1728, 1755-1765.* McLean, VA: The Antient Press, 1987.
---. *Stafford County, Virginia Wills, 1729-1748.* McLean, VA: The Antient Press, 1987.
---. *Stafford County, Virginia Deed and Will Abstracts, 1780-1786.* McLean, VA: The Antient Press, 1987.
---. *Stafford County, Virginia Deed and Will Abstracts, 1809-1810.* McLean, VA: The Antient Press, 1992.
---. *Stafford County, Virginia Deed and Will Abstracts, 1810-1813.* McLean, VA: The Antient Press, 1992.
---. *Stafford County, Virginia Deed and Will Abstracts, 1825-1826.* McLean, VA: The Antient Press, 1992.
---. *Stafford County, Virginia Order Book, 1664-1668/1689-1690.* McLean, VA: The Antient Press, 1987.
---. *Stafford County, Virginia Order Book, 1691-1692.* McLean, VA: The Antient Press, 1987.
---. *Stafford County, Virginia Order Book, 1692-1693.* McLean, VA: The Antient Press, 1987.
Stafford County Deeds and Wills:
  DB 26A-34—Nov. 7, 1865—inventory of Thomas N. Towson
Stafford County Land Tax Records, 1782-1861, 1870-1910, Stafford Courthouse, Virginia.
Stafford County Personal Property Tax Records, Stafford Courthouse, Virginia.
Stafford, George M. *General George Mason Graham of Tyrone Plantation and his People.* New Orleans: Pelican Publishers, 1947.
Stannard, William G. and Newton, Mary. *The Colonial Virginia Register.* Albany, NY: Joel Munsell's Sons, 1902.
Tarter, Brent, ed. "Stafford County Court." *Virginia, the Road to Independence,* vol. 7. Charlottesville, VA: University Press of Virginia, 1983, pp. 722-723.
Tayloe, W. Randolph. *The Tayloes of Virginia and Allied Families.* Self-published, Berryville, VA, 1963.
Templeman, Eleanor L. and Netherton, Nan. *Northern Virginia Heritage.* Middleburg, VA: Self-published, 1966.
Tucker, Norma. *Colonial Virginians and Their Maryland Relatives.* Baltimore, MD: Genealogical Publishing Co., 1915.
Tyler, Lyon G. *Encyclopedia of Virginia Biography.* NY: Lewis Historical Publishing Co., 1915.
"Virginia Council Journals, 1726-1753." *Virginia Magazine of History and Biography,* vol. 34, (1926), pp.345-357.
Virginia Herald, May 13, 1809, obituary of John Fitzhugh
---, Oct. 13, 1813, obituary of Dr. John M. Daniel
---, Mar. 2, 1816, marriage notice of Thornton Alexander and Frances A. Withers
---, Feb. 9, 1822, obituary of Jesse Hill
---, Jan. 17, 1827, advertisement for Gray's Mill
---, Jan. 21, 1829, obituary of Robert Lewis
---, May 6, 1829, obituary of John Wallace
---, Aug. 17, 1831, obituary of Thomas Seddon
---, Dec. 17, 1831, obituary of William Stringfellow
---, Apr. 17, 1833, Duff Green's report of the inspection of flour
---, June 13, 1835, William S. Sterne's advertisement for sale of Walnut Hill
---, Sept. 23, 1835, ad for the sale of the Flourey tract
---, Jan. 8, 1855, Harris Hill killed John Limerick
---, May 30, 1870, election results
---, May 29, 1871, election results
---, Mar. 4, 1872, commissioners of the Free Bridge
---, Apr. 29, 1872, notice of fire at Simeon Peyton's woodyard
---, May 26, 1873, election results
Virginia Star, May 14, 1873, Board of School Trustees for Aquia Township
---, Aug. 25, 1875, "Rain and Hail Storm in Stafford"
---, Feb. 21, 1877, announcement of the opening of E. A. W. Hore's new store
---, Apr. 27, 1878, marriage announcement of William D. Reamy and Sallie Combs
---, Jan. 31, 1887, notice regarding Arba R. Packard
"Virginia Troops in the French and Indian Wars." *The Virginia Magazine of History and Biography,* vol. 1, (1894), pp. 278-287.

Vogt, John and Kethley, T. William. *Stafford County, Virginia Tithables: Quit Rents, Personal Property Taxes and Related Lists & Petitions, 1723-1790*. GA: Iberian Publishing Co., 1990.

Washington, George. *The Diaries of George Washington, 1748-1799*. Cambridge, Mass: Riverside Press, 1925.

Watkins, C. Malcolm. *The Cultural History of Marlborough, Virginia*. Washington, DC: Smithsonian Institution Press, 1968.

Wayland, John W. *The Washingtons and their Homes*. Staunton, VA: McClure Printing Co., 1944.

Weekly Advertiser, May 9, 1857, obituary of George Kiger

White, James T. *Points of Interest in the Pohick Cemetery and Churchyard*. Lorton, VA, self-published, n.d.

Winston, Hugh J., Jr. *History of New Hope Methodist Church, Route 605 at 669*. Stafford, VA, self-published, 1962.

Wise, Erbon W. The Bridwell Family in America. Alexandria, Louisiana: Louisiana Offset Printers, 1978.

Withers, Robert E. *The Withers Family of the County Lancaster, England, and of Stafford County, Virginia, Establishing the Ancestry of Robert Edwin Withers, III*. Richmond, VA: Dietz Printing Co., 1947.

Wulfeck, Dorothy F. *Marriages of Some Virginia Residents, 1607-1800*. Baltimore, MD: Genealogical Publishing Co., 1986.

Chapter Four
Post Offices and Post Masters of Stafford

POSTAL SERVICE

We often take for granted daily mail delivery, giving little thought to this vital service unless a problem occurs. Yet daily delivery is a relatively modern convenience that evolved gradually over some 200 years. Colonial authorities recognized the need for a dependable postal system early on and on Mar. 2, 1693 the General Assembly passed a bill encouraging the creation of a postal system for the Virginia colony. As deputy postmaster, Thomas Neale was authorized to establish one or more post offices in each county and one at each of the chief ports and to fix rates for postage. In Stafford, the official port was at Marlborough though no documentation remains mentioning a post office there.

Lt. Gov. Francis Nicholson recognized the need for communication and cooperation between the colonies. In 1700 he arranged to hold a meeting in New York of the governors of that state, New Jersey, Pennsylvania, and Virginia to discuss several topics including the creation of a general postal system between the colonies, pirates, and the Wool Act of 1699. This meeting was successful and Nicholson planned a second meeting the following spring in Philadelphia but, for various reasons, this didn't materialize.

An attempt at an inter-colonial postal system between Maryland and Virginia was inaugurated in the fall of 1701 but was not successful. Several attempts to establish a continental postal system failed until Alexander Spotswood (1676-1740) became deputy postmaster general in 1732. Spotswood planned a route beginning at New Post (now Spotsylvania County) on the south side of the Rappahannock about three miles below Fredericksburg, south through Nansemond Courthouse to Norfolk and on to North Carolina. Mail was carried on these routes once per month, winter and summer.

Benjamin Franklin became deputy postmaster general in 1753 though the system was still under the control of the British government. Franklin improved the services but the rates remained very high. Consequently, most people avoided using the royal service and sent their mail by private, illegal carriers. As relations with England deteriorated throughout the mid-18th century, many colonists considered the postal fees simply yet another unfair tax.

One common method of mail delivery during this period was by way of the local ordinaries or taverns. Travelers checked with the tavern keeper when they were ready to continue on their journeys. If there were any letters headed in their general direction, they would hand carry them to the next ordinary, which was usually located about 15 miles farther on, the distance one could comfortably travel in a day. This system was slow and perhaps a bit uncertain, but it was free and, in general, worked quite well.

During the 19th and early 20th centuries, the postal service grew rapidly. From 1816 to 1847 prepayment of postage fees was optional. The sender could pay to mail the letter or could choose to let the recipient pay upon delivery. Rates were fixed at six cents per sheet for each 100 miles. The first official stamps were not issued until 1847. By 1863 the United States Post Office Department established three classes of mail and began to provide free delivery in many cities. Before the advent of this free urban delivery, there had been a delivery charge of two cents per letter paid by the recipient of the letter.

Not unexpectedly, improvements in transportation resulted in improvements in postal delivery. The first mail deliveries had been conducted by independent riders. By 1785 there were enough passable roads to engage stagecoaches in the mail delivery system. 1813 say the first use of steamships for mail delivery, a tremendous step forward in Virginia where there is an abundance of navigable water. In Stafford, the steamships regularly ran between Thorny Point or Aquia Landing on Aquia Creek to Alexandria, Washington, and Baltimore. This continued even after the RF&P Railroad was built north from Fredericksburg and the first postal contracts were granted to the railroads in 1835. Prior to the War Between the States, the tracks came north from Fredericksburg and turned east at Brooke following what is now Brooke Road (State Route 608). The long, straight stretch of this road was actually built on the old railroad bed which was abandoned after the war when the route was altered. The trains, then, only went as far north as Aquia Landing at the mouth of the creek. People, baggage, mail, and goods destined for northern locations departed the trains at Aquia Landing and boarded the steamships awaiting at the docks next to the railroad terminal.

1864 marked the birth of the railway post office which would continue to be standard in Virginia until the first quarter of the 20th century. Postal clerks sorted the mail while riding across the country on special railroad cars. As they passed through the station, they tossed sacks of mail for each town onto the railway platform from the moving train. Outgoing mail was hung in sacks from polls and was picked up from the poll as the train pulled out of the station. Compared to earlier attempts, this was truly modern, high-speed delivery and proved to be quite dependable. Before the era of home delivery, local residents stopped by their nearest railroad station to pick up their mail. For many people, their address consisted of merely their names and the name of the station closest to their homes. The stations in Stafford from north to south were Arkendale (also known as Richland), Aquia (on the south side of the creek), Brooke (also known as Accokeek), and Leeland.

Late 19th and early 20th century applications for new post offices filed with the U. S. Postal Service asked for distance and direction of the proposed post office from the nearest railroad station as that was where most of the incoming mail was delivered prior to making it to the actual post office. Some of the post offices of this period were in private homes, but many were in buildings such as stores and mills as that was where many people gathered on a regular basis. In Stafford, mail was sent to, picked up by individuals, and later delivered to homes from Bellfair Mills on Chappawamsic Creek, Tackett's Mill on Aquia Creek, Richland (previously Brent's Mill) in Wide Water, Thompson's Mill near the Fauquier/Stafford boundary, and Cropp's Mill, also near the Fauquier line.

What becomes obvious is that there were a great many more post offices during this period than there are now—nearly 50 in Stafford alone. While home delivery became a reality in the late 1920s, the roads were so poor that it was impossible to deliver mail to the entire county from one or two post offices. Consequently, the offices were usually five to ten miles apart and, during the first quarter of the 20th century, mail was delivered two, three, or occasionally, four times per week. As late as 1946, the only paved roads in Stafford were the Warrenton Road (U. S. Route 17) and Route 1. Not until after World War II was the Garrisonville Road (State Route 610) paved. The rural roads remained unpaved for another ten to twenty years.

The following is a listing of the 47 known post offices in Stafford, including a description of the location of each building. This information has been gleaned from post office records on file in the National Archives and includes a reference number that corresponds with the accompanying map.

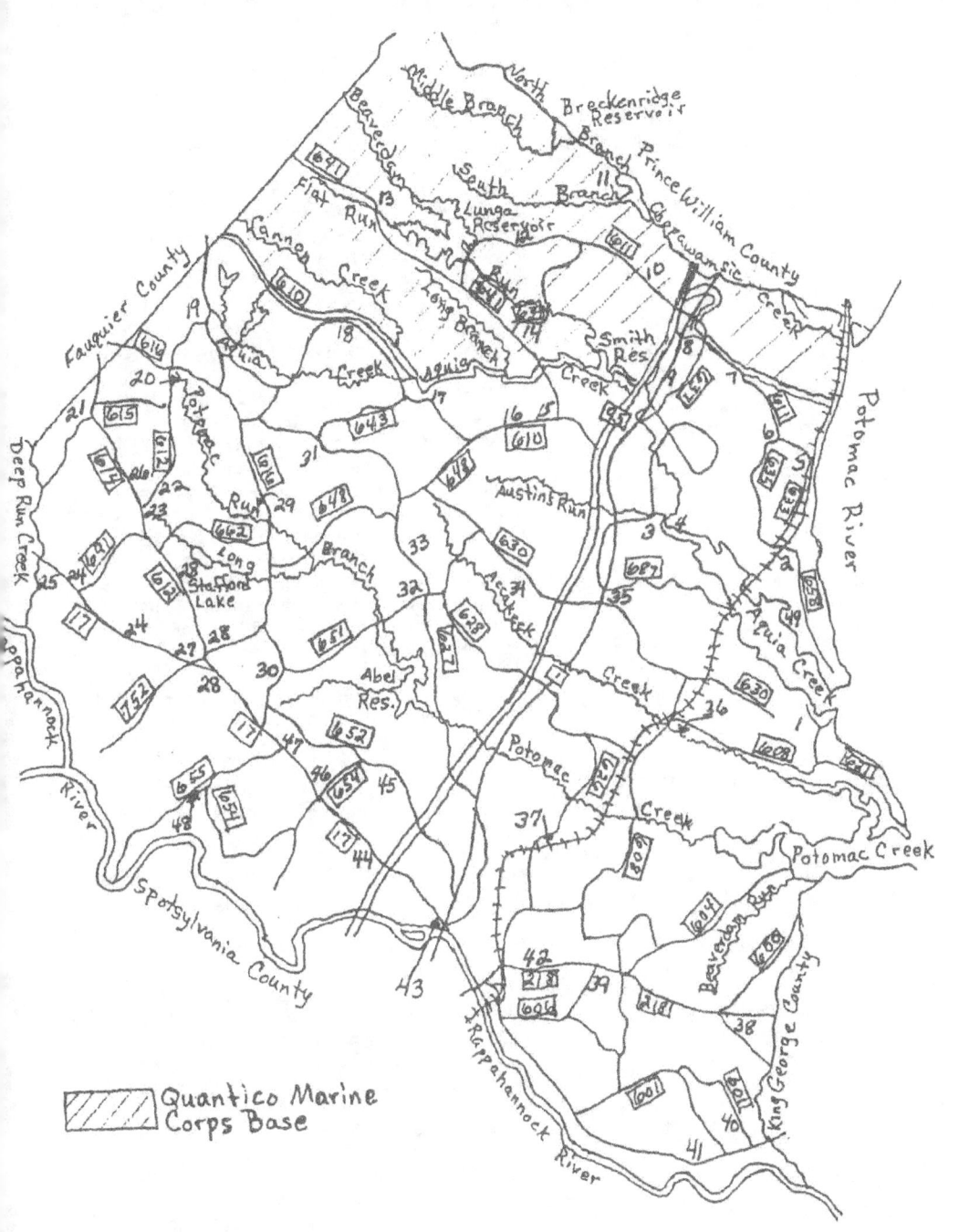

Stafford County Post Offices

Stafford County Post Offices

Map #	Name	Established or earliest known reference	Description
36	Accokeek	1857	Also known as Brook's Station or Brooke. On the route from Washington to Richmond. Request to relocate filed in 1949. The postmaster wished to move the building 50' north of the old site.
16	Adieville	1893	Probably near present-day Garrisonville Post Office as Hugh Adie resided just west of Garrisonville at Woodford.
4	Aquia	1799	On the route from Richmond to Washington. Nearest post offices were Brooke, 5m south; Alexandria, 40m north; Richland Mill, 5m northwest. Apparently, the RF&P Railroad built a new post office at Aquia in 1869 as a replacement for the office at Coal Landing. This was to be built on the south side of Aquia Creek and would serve about 40 families. This office was re-proposed in 1882 by George B. Griffis (born 1854) as being on the route from Blue Wing to Richland Mills. By 1882 the post offices nearest to Aquia were Garrisonville, 6m southwest, and Bellfair Mills, 12m northwest. This office was 4m northwest of the Blue Wing Station at Wide Water.
2	Arkendale	1912	60 feet east of the RF&P railroad. The nearest post offices were Wide Water, 2m north; Rectory, 4m northwest; Brooke, 4m south.
11	Bellfair Mills	1848	Located in the Rock Hill District. Nearest post offices were Shacklett's, 3.5m southwest; Joplin, 4m east; Kopp, 4m northwest.
46	Berea	1889	Originally called "Berear." Nearest post offices were Falmouth, 4m south; Hartwood, 4m north.
49	Blue Wing	1881	About ¾ mile south of Arkendale on Brent Point Road (State Route 658).
22	Burdis	1909	In western Hartwood at Huffman's Store. Deep Run was 1 mile west. Nearest post offices were Snellings, 3m north; Hartwood, 3m south; Storke, 4m west; Coakley, 3m east. On the route from Falmouth to Grove (Fauquier County).
11	Chappawamsic	1841	Probably at Bellfair Mills.
29	Coakley	1884	In Rock Hill District. Nearest post offices—Roseville, 6m northwest and Hartwood, 5m west. Population about 200. On the route from Stafford Courthouse to Mountain View. Proposed by Douglas W. Coakley in 1884. On the south side of U. S. Route 17.

3	Coal Landing	1868	On route from Washington to Richmond. Located on Aquia Creek and served about 40 families ("not yet a village"). The following year, proposal to replace office at Coal Landing with another to be called "Aquia Creek."
32	Crest	1891	On the route from Coakley to the courthouse. Nearest post offices were Mountain View, 1.5m north; Falmouth, 9m southeast; Musselman's, 2.25m northeast. Population about 200. Proposed by William M. Black in 1891.
21	Cropp	1909	1.5m from Deep Run and .25m from the county line. Nearest post offices were Heflin's, 3m northeast, and Goldvein (Fauquier County), 4m southeast.

Cropp Post Office

23	Dodd's	1890	In Hartwood District. 5m north of Deep Run. Nearest post offices were Storck, 2m west, and Hartwood, 2.25m northeast.
43	Falmouth	1794	Nearest post offices—Stafford, 9m north, and Fredericksburg, 1m south.
38	Fine's	1901	Also known as Hudsonville. Nearest post offices were Monteithville, 1.5m west and Passapatanzy, 4m east. Population about 100. Proposed by John A. Sullivan (1860-1947).
25	Fostersville	1884	In Hartwood District on the route from Falmouth to Bealton or Rockford. Nearest post offices were Thompson's Mill (Fauquier), 3.5m west; Richardsville (Fauquier), 8m southwest; Hartwood, 3.5m north. Population about 150 in 1891. Proposed by Robert A. Hughes in 1884.
1	Game Point	1851	On Aquia Creek at or near Thorny Point.
15	Garrisonville	1844	In Rock Hill District. Originally on the route from Brooke to

Stafford Store. Re-proposed in 1868 and a note in the margin of that paperwork reads, "There is no map at the Court House or in their possession, it having been carried off by the union army." Request in 1900 to move 744 yards west of the old site. By that time, this office was on the route from Stafford Store to Stafford (courthouse). Population in 1900 about 125. Another request to move filed in 1948, this time .5m west of the last old site. Nearest post offices were Stafford, 5m south; Ruby, 5m west; Toluca, 3.5m northwest; Onville, 3m north; Rectory, 4m east; Musselman's, 3m southwest.

30	Glendie	1922	In Hartwood District. Proposed in 1922 by Glendie Brook Young (1890-1952). Request filed in 1928 to move the office 1/5 mile southeast of its original location. Nearest post offices were Hemp, 3.5m west; Roseville, 7.5m northeast; Berea, 3.5m southeast. Located on the west side of Poplar Road 50' from the road.
28	Hartwood	1835	Nearest post offices were Falmouth, 9m southeast; Garrisonville, 10m east; Stafford Store, 15m northeast; Stafford Courthouse, 12m east; Storke, 2.5m west; Dodd's, 2.25m north. Site was moved c.1848 (distance of move unknown) and again c.1904 (1/4 mile north).

James Monroe's Store that housed one of the Hartwood post offices

20	Heflin	1909	In Rock Hill District. Nearest post offices were Cropp, 3m west; Burdis, 3.5m ___; Cromwell, 6m north. Located on the north side of the Warrenton Road 1 mile from the county line.
27	Hemp	1905	In Hartwood District on the route from Falmouth to Bealton (Fauquier County). Nearest post offices were Lance, 2m south; Hartwood, 2m north; Storke, 3.5m northwest. To serve a population of about 75-100. Proposed in 1905 by Frank Stewart (1864-1931).

Hemp Post Office and Frank Stewart's Store

48	Holly Corner	1926	In Hartwood District. Nearest post offices were Berea, 3.5m northwest; Burdis, 10m north; Glendie, 3.5m northeast. Proposed by David Alexander Monroe in 1926.
47	Lance	1887	Also known as "Free Lance." On the route from Falmouth to Bealton. Nearest post offices were Berea, 2m south; Hartwood, 4m north; Coakley, 7m northwest. To serve a population of about 100 families. Proposed by William G. Ballard.
37	Leeland	1882	On the route from Washington to Richmond and was 30 feet east of the Leeland railroad station. Nearest post offices were Brooke, 4.5m north, and Falmouth 3.5m southwest. To serve a population of over 100 families. Proposed in 1882 by Daniel M. Lee (1843-1916).
43	Little Whim	1872	On the route from Hampstead (King George County) to Fredericksburg. Nearest post offices were Fredericksburg, 2m west "with tall bridge intervening across Rappahannock," and Passapatanzy (King George County), 6m east. Proposed in 1872 by Samuel Babcock.
8	Midway Island	1943	Nearest post offices were Rectory, 2m east; Stafford, 8m south; Triangle (Prince William County), 3.5m north.
9	Millie's	1902	On the route from Wide Water to Mount. Nearest post offices were Wide Water, 3m east; Rectory, 3m northeast; Mount, 4m north. To serve a population of about 50. Proposed in 1902 by Waller Stone Gill (1871-1947).
39	Monteithville	1851	On the route from Hampstead to Fredericksburg on which mail was being carried three times weekly (in 1879). Nearest post offices were Passapatanzy, 5m east; Fredericksburg, 5m

			west; La Grange (King George County), 8m southeast. Proposed in 1879 by James Thomas Chinn (1851-1920).
10	Mount	1895	Nearest post offices were Rectory, 3m southeast; Bellfair Mills, 4m northwest; Garrisonville, 5m southeast. To serve a population of about 300. Proposed in 1895 by William Edward Mountjoy (1835-1898).
33	Mountain View	1870	Proposal by Silas L. Rose to move this office in 1887, "the office at Mountain View as now constituted 5 miles from Stafford courthouse discontinued this proposed office being more in the center of the population." On the route from Stafford Courthouse to Mountain View on which the mail was carried three times per week (in 1887). New office to be 1 mile north of the old office. Nearest post offices were Garrisonville, 6m northeast; Mussleman's, 3.5m southeast; Roseville, 4m northeast. To serve a population of about 100. By 1889 this was on the route from Coakley to Stafford. There was another proposal in 1890 to move this office 750 yards northeast of the existing site.
34	Musselman	1883	Nearest post offices were Crest, 2m southwest, and Stafford, 3.5m southeast.
40	Myrtleville	1889	On the route from Fredericksburg to King George Courthouse. Nearest post offices were La Grange, 6m east; Fredericksburg, 9m west; Monteithville, 5m north. To serve a population of about 50. Proposed by Gouverneur T. Greenlaw.
14	Onville	1886	Proposal to establish a post office at Oakland to be called Onville. On the route from Brooke to Stafford Store. Nearest post offices were Garrisonville, 4m southeast; Stafford Store, 4m northeast; Musselman's, 8m west. To serve a population of about 50.

Onville Post Office

7	Rectory	1895	Nearest post offices were Quantico, 5m northeast, and Garrisonville, 6m west. Proposed in 1895 by James B. Homes.
6	Richland Mill	1869	Located in the old Brent's Mill building one mile from Richland Station. Also known as Richland.
31	Roseville	1885	Proposed in 1885 by Silas L. Rose.

Roseville Post Office

18	Ruby	1903	To serve a population of about 118. Nearest post office was Toluca, 3m northwest. Proposed in 1903 by Mildred Narcissa Rose who considered changing the name to "Rosita."

Ruby Post Office

41	Serena	1869	Located 1 mile west of Muddy Creek on the route from Fredericksburg to Warsaw (Westmoreland County). This office was 8m west of Fredericksburg and served 36 families. Proposed in 1869 by Thomas W. Franklin (c.1844-1928).
12	Shacklett	1896	Proposal in 1896 to open a new post office 3m southeast of Bellfair Mills and 3m southwest of Chappawamsic Run. To serve a population of 50. Mail to be carried 6 times per week. On the route from Stafford Store to Brentsville (Prince William County). Proposed in 1898 by Nelson T. Shacklett (1856-1903).
45	Snellings	1885	Proposed by Charles A. Truslow (1860-1947).
26	Spottedville	1818	Established in August 1818. Probably at Spotted Tavern.
35	Stafford	1810	Operated for a time out of the old Garrard's Ordinary on the site of the present school board offices near the courthouse.
13	Stafford Store	1857	12m from Potomac River and 4m northwest of Aquia Run. Nearest post office was Landsdown (Prince William County), 6m north of Stafford Store.
24	Storke	1904	On the route from Falmouth to Bristow (Prince William County). Nearest post offices were Hartwood, 3m northeast, and Rockford, 2m northwest. To serve a population of about 100. Mail currently being delivered from Rockford post office. Notation on application, "I suggest 'Storke' in lieu of 'Frog Pond.' This was on U. S. Route 17, about 1.5 miles northwest of Richland Baptist Church. The post office was in a store, still standing but unused, on the north side of the road. Frog Pond School was on the opposite side of the road from the post office.
19	Tackett's Mill	1813	In Rock Hill District. The first known postmaster was Col. John Tackett (1788-1850). Two miles east of Toluca, 4m ___ of Cromwell, 9m northwest of Catlett.
17	Toluca	1893	3.5 miles west of Garrisonville on Garrisonville Road (State Route 610). On the route from Stafford Courthouse to Stafford Store. Population in 1893 was bout 150. In 1935 it was proposed to move this office 550 yards southwest of the existing site.
44	Tuan	1900	In Hartwood District on the route from Falmouth to Bealton. Nearest post offices were Berea, 2m west; Falmouth, 4m south; Lance, 4m north. To serve a population of 150. Proposed in 1900 by Wallace H. Snellings (1873-1943).
5	Wide Water		(Late Richland). 78 feet from the depot of the RF&P Railroad. Wide Water Road (State Route 611) continues straight on to the river. This lower end is rarely used but the Wide Water Station used to stand right against the tracks on the north side of the road. The post office was in a little frame building next to the station.

WIDE WATER RAILROAD STATION - From a photo dated 1959. This station stood on the west side of the tracks along the edge of the south lawn of Richland. Customers could send and receive telegraph messages at the station and the mail came and went from here by rail. Just to the south of the station was a store that served as the post office from the first few years of the 1900s until 1943 when that service was moved to Midway Island on Telegraph Road (State Route 637).

Notes on Individual Post Offices

Berea—The old Heflin's Store that housed this post office is still standing, though major renovations have drastically changed its appearance. Berea Post Office is now a plant nursery located at the intersection of Warrenton Road (U. S. Route 17) and Berea Church Road (State Route 654). Wilbur C. Heflin (1888-1965), who owned the store and operated the post office, was a Ford dealer. His car lot was directly across Route 654 from Berea Church. Fleet Drive (State Route 750), which parallels the north side of Route 17, is actually part of the old Warrenton Road. Heflin's Store originally fronted on this road and the old Ford dealership site is presently occupied by the Dominion Virginia Power parking lot.

Crest—This post office was in a pre-Civil War white frame house located at the intersection of Kellogg Mill Road (State Route 651) and Mountain View Road (State Route 627). During the early 20th century, the house was owned by Dr. William Wallace Gordon (died 1888) and his wife, Emma F. (Spraggins) Gordon. They purchased the house around the turn of the century and did extensive renovations, adding a long wing to the back and raising the roof.

This house had been built on the site of the old Guy's Tavern which burned or otherwise disappeared prior to the War Between the States. The old spring house used by the tavern is still standing very close to the road and a Guy family cemetery is located on the property.

When the Gordons bought the property, the house was in very poor condition. Union soldiers had used the home during the war and had carved graffiti into the windowsills. As part of the Gordons' renovations, the old small windows were replaced with larger windows and the inscribed window frames were stored in the attic.

Mrs. Gordon was a nurse by profession and gave up the post office in 1913 to return to nursing, taking a job helping a blind lady care for her two children.

The house burned around 1935.

Game Point—This post office acquired its unusual name from the Game Point Association, one of the many popular hunting clubs that existed after the War Between the States. The abundance of ducks on the waterways provided a major economic boost after the war when most people were living at merely a subsistence level. Other hunting clubs formed at Crow's Nest, Clifton, and Simms' or Brent's Point and were frequented by many Washington dignitaries, including presidents, who found Stafford a remote area well away from their busy lives in the city. A deed dated Mar. 14, 1888 provides a few details about the Game Point Association. On that date W. Miles Cary and his wife, Lillian B., J. L. Schoolcraft and his wife Ida C., W. Benjamin Palmer and his wife Ellen R., John W. Gill and his wife Louisa, Barton H. Grundy and his wife Mirriam Branch, John Cussins and his wife Susan Anne conveyed to the Game Point Association land "originally bought by the male parties of the first part for the use of themselves and their associates as a shooting box." They organized themselves and received a charter from the legislature of Virginia as the Game Point Association. The property they purchased was the old 300-acre Coal Trips tract that is now a Girl Scout camp. On Dec. 21, 1891 the Game Point Association took out a deed of trust with W. L. Boyd of Richmond for $300. Included in this instrument were boats, sink boxes, skiffs, and cast iron and wooden decoy ducks. The group sold the property on May 11, 1897 and seems to have dissolved the association. According to a map drawn during the War Between the States, Game Point was another name for Thorny Point and the post office may have been located there (Stafford Deed Book 3, p. 456).

Hartwood—Over the years this post office occupied at least five different locations, depending upon who was running it. When Robert C. Rogers (c.1818-1888) became postmaster in 1836, he handled the mail from his store which stood on the present site of the Bell Atlantic phone building. William Irvine, who lived at Hartwood (the large brick home on the south side of Warrenton Road (U. S. Route 17), became postmaster in 1842 and kept the post office in a small building on the front lawn of his home. There is some debate now among older members of the community as to whether that building was the little cottage/kitchen still located to the right of the house or whether the post office building was actually another structure nearer to the present highway and no longer standing.

An 1876 letter from William Irvine to Joseph Stewart states that Hartwood Post Office was "about a mile and quarter from our church [Hartwood Presbyterian Church]." At that time, the post office was run by Mary E. Shackelford (1849-1939) who lived on Shackelford's Well Road (State Route 754). This suggests the strong possibility that the post office was at that time located somewhere on that road, perhaps in her home. Mary was post mistress from 1870-1903.

When James Monroe was postmaster during the early days of the 20th century, he kept the post office in his store which was located on Hartwood Road (State Route 612) about 2.1 miles northwest of the intersection of routes 612 and 17. This little store is still standing and is located on the east side of Route 612 just before the turn into Curtis Park.

Just across from the Bell Atlantic building is a little house which was once Hemp Post Office. This building was built around 1890 by Frank Stewart[1127] (1864-1931) who lived in the lovely frame house still standing on the hill above. Mr. Stewart originally built this structure as a store, but began operating a post office there in 1903. Hemp and Hartwood operated simultaneously despite their close proximity. Post offices were often within a couple of miles of each other because, prior to home delivery, people had either to walk or ride horseback to get their mail. Mr. Stewart eventually gave up the post office but continued to run his store until he died in 1931. In 1945 Miss Margaret E. Monroe, the daughter of James R. Monroe, accepted the position of post mistress. For whatever reason, she didn't use her father's store as a post office, but settled instead in Frank Stewart's store. At this point, Hartwood Post Office took over what had been Hemp Post Office and continued as such until 1948.

The present Hartwood Post Office was built in 1964.

Monteithville—This post office was in a private home which used to stand on the south side of White Oak Road (State Route 218) across from White Oak School and across Caisson Road (State Route 603) from White Oak Primitive Baptist Church. A lovely white frame home presently stands on the site.

Stafford—Like most postal facilities, the Stafford Post Office moved from building to building though always remaining close to the courthouse. During and after the War Between the States, mail was handled by James E. Schooler (born c.1833) and his wife, Lucy E. (Hedgman) Schooler (born c.1834), who also operated the old Garrard's Ordinary. This building stood in the vicinity of what was the old Stafford Middle School and is presently used for the offices of the Stafford County School Board. By 1932, and probably earlier, mail was being handled at what is presently known as the Stafford Building, the newly renovated brick structure across Route 1 from the 7-11 store. Around 1950 the post office moved just south of the courthouse into a tiny brick building (still standing) very near the firehouse.

Home delivery in the county began in the late 1920s and until the 1960s would-be mail carriers placed bids for the job with the United States Postal Service. Bid winners faced the daunting task of delivering mail to remote, thinly populated areas accessed only by treacherous, muddy roads.

By the 1940s, mail destined for Stafford arrived by train at Brooke Station. From Brooke the sacks of mail were hauled by truck to the Stafford Post Office for delivery. County roads had been notoriously treacherous since the 17th century and as late as 1946 only routes 1 and 17 were paved. Heavy rain and snow or ice storms made mail delivery hazardous. A serious effort to pave the county's secondary roads was not undertaken until after World War II.

During the 1940s, the Stafford Post Office made home deliveries on two routes. One route led from the courthouse to Roseville and out to Poplar Road (State Route 616). The second route served the Garrisonville Road area. Wide Water had its own delivery and the Falmouth Post Office delivered mail from Eskimo's Hill (the intersection of routes 1 and 628) southward to Falmouth.

Storck—This post office was located about 1.5 miles north of Richlands Baptist Church at the intersection of Storck Road (State Route 691) and Warrenton Road (U. S. Route 17). The post office was in a country store on the northeast side of the road. Across the road from the store was Frog Pond School, one of the local public schools in the county.

Wide Water—It was common practice for millers and store keepers to act as postmasters. In the days before home delivery, most resident regularly visited their local mill or store, making these logical places to pick up or mail letters. Postmasters also occasionally used a corner of their homes as post offices.

Mail in the Wide Water area was handled from a variety of buildings that doubled as post offices. Old Brent's Mill served for many years as a post office and was also a store (Eby, They 50). Mail in this area was also delivered from the Rectory, Arkendale, and Blue Wing post offices. Arkendale, Wide Water,

---

[1127] Mr. Stewart was from York County, Pennsylvania.

and Rectory often operated concurrently, and the locations of the post offices changed with the installation of a new postmaster.

Brent's Mill burned c.1901 and the post office was moved to a store belonging to Alfred Joseph Pyke (1865-1938) of Richland and George William Herring (1877-1966). This was a large store that carried all manner of goods and was located on the north side of the end of Wide Water Road (State Route 611). George Herring became the official postmaster on Apr. 10, 1905 and handled the mail for many years. He was followed as postmaster by Richard Wirt Powers (1870-1934). The old store eventually deteriorated and a small cinderblock addition was built on the end wall. The remains of that addition are still visible adjacent to the railroad tracks. Across the road from the store was Samuel Decatur's blacksmith shop. The railroad station and a workman's cottage stood a few yards north of the store. Only the cottage survives and it is presently utilized as a home.

Shortly after the government's 1942 condemnation of land for the expansion of the Quantico Marine Corps base, Wide Water's mail service moved from the old store to Midway Island, a small military settlement on the west side of Telegraph Road (State Route 637). On June 30, 1959 the Wide Water mail was transferred to Stafford Post Office near the courthouse.

* * * * * * * * * * * *

POSTMASTERS OF STAFFORD COUNTY

Accokeek

John Mercer Brooke (1826-1906)	Dec. 11, 1857
Leonard P. Alexander (born c.1832)	July 2, 1858
Joseph Robinson (c.1818-after 1870)	Jan. 3, 1860
Discontinued June 22, 1866	
Reestablished Nov. 4, 1867	
Mrs. Annie C. Chewning	Nov. 6, 1867
Discontinued Jan. 17, 1868	
Reestablished Feb. 17, 1869	
John H. Schooler (1812-1875)	Feb. 17, 1869
Andrew D. Wroe (c.1818-after 1860)	Mar. 8, 1871
John Lowry (c.1808-after 1870)	June 27, 1871
Name changed to "Brooke's Station"	
John Lowry	Feb. 27, 1873
Samuel H. Jones[1128] (c.1833-1875)	Mar. 11, 1873
James Morton, Jr.[1129]	Mar. 29, 1876
Marion King Lowry[1130] (1854-1939)	Jan. 23, 1883
Name changed to "Brooke"	Mar. 12, 1884
James Morton	Aug. 28, 1885
Marion K. Lowry	July 10, 1889
Mrs. Alelia Pollard Lowry[1131]	Oct. 21, 1889
James Morton	Feb. 5, 1894
Charles Duff Green (1873-1957)	May 29, 1897
Edward W. Payne	Mar. 21, 1913
George Key Massie[1132] (1878-1951)	June 16, 1914

[1128] Samuel was born in Kentucky, the son of Garrison and Martha Jones. He was a merchant and died of consumption.

[1129] The son of James Morton, Sr. (died 1859) and Lucy Horton (c.1818-1898).

[1130] Served five terms in the Virginia House of Delegates. Marion was born at Brooke and was a member of Andrew Chapel Methodist Church. In 1905 he was appointed collector of internal revenue for the Second District of Virginia, a position he held until 1915 when he commenced a career in real estate.

[1131] Alelia was the wife of Marion King Lowry.

[1132] At the time of his death, George lived in Sylvania Heights, though he lived much of his life at Brooke. In addition to being postmaster he was a ticket agent for the RF&P Railroad.

John Paul Duncan (1898-1958)	Sept. 17, 1942
Frank A. Turner	July 1, 1948
Salkeld Stamper	May 16, 1949
John P. Duncan	Aug. 1, 1949
Frank A. Turner	Aug. 20, 1958

Adieville
Bronaugh Stone[1133] (1835-1899)	Oct. 31, 1893

Discontinued Dec. 27, 1894

Aquia[1134]
William Edwards	June 1799
Benjamin Williams	July 1806
Matthew Norman[1135] (c.1779-1814)	October 1808
Withers Waller[1136] (1785-1827)	December 1809
William Barton Stone (died 1845)	July 17, 1828
John H. Suttle (c.1807-1884)	Sept. 18, 1835
James W. Johnson[1137] (1821-1856)	Jan. 21, 1840

Discontinued—mail to Chappawamsick

John Marshall Homes (c.1818-1873)	Jan. 29, 1842
Leonard P. Alexander	Jan. 17, 1843
Willoughby Newton Carter[1138] (1800-1878)	Mar. 9, 1843
William F. Chapman	Apr. 2, 1844

Mail to Garrisonville July 30, 1844

Thomas H. Speake[1139]	Feb. 17, 1848

Aquia discontinued Dec. 21, 1848
Reestablished May 3, 1849

Elias A. W. Hore (1821-c.1891)	May 3, 1849

Discontinued
Aquia reestablished Jan. 21, 1851

George H. Cockrell	Jan. 21, 1851
Samuel D. Cockrell	June 1, 1852
George H. Cockrell	Aug. 8, 1853

Discontinued Mar. 25, 1854
Reestablished Mar. 5, 1855
Aquia changed to Chappawamsic

Aquia Run Mills[1140]
Col. John Tackett[1141] (1788-1850)	December 1813

[1133] The son of Thomas Stone and Hester Bronaugh.

[1134] John Catesby Edrington (1775-1820) and Hugh Adie provided surety.

[1135] Matthew was a veteran of the War of 1812.

[1136] Withers was the son of William Waller (1740-1817) of Concord and his third wife, Ursula Withers (1752-1815). Withers married Catherine Barret Conway (1746-1794).

[1137] James was the son of Joseph and Sally Johnson. He committed suicide.

[1138] Willoughby lived at Palace Green, a beautiful tract laying between Wide Water and Aquia Harbour subdivision. The Carters were long involved in quarrying along Aquia Creek. Willoughby married Harriet Milstead (1820-1900).

[1139] Possibly the Thomas H. Speake who enlisted in Company B of the Quantico Guards and died on June 30, 1862 from wounds received in the Seven Days Battles near Richmond.

[1140] This post office was established in December 1813 and was located at Tackett's Mill.

[1141] Col. John Tackett was probably born in Prince William County. His first wife was Enfield Mason (1796-1836), the daughter of Joel Mason (died 1817) and Sarah Bourne (c.1771-1835) of Stafford. John was the brother of Charles Tackett, Sr. (1780-1834). Both were sons of William Tackett, Jr. (c.1751-after 1830) and Frances Reno (c.1750-1796:99). John died in Shelby County, Illinois.

Discontinued January 1814

Arkendale
William Bankhead Lee[1142] (1882-1938)	May 27, 1912

Discontinued Feb. 3, 1920
Effective Feb. 14, 1920, mail to Wide Water
Reestablished Feb. 15, 1922

Mercer Ray Gooch[1143] (1887-1966)	Feb. 15, 1922
Mrs. Lelia May Sullivan	Apr. 3, 1925

Berear (late Snellings)
James Fenton Armstrong[1144] (born 1856)	Feb. 27, 1889

Name changed to "Berea" Nov. 19, 1898

William Dickerson	Nov. 19, 1898
Mildred C. Schooler[1145] (1848-1929)	Feb. 11, 1915
Clayton Simpson[1146] (c.1856-1927)	Mar. 16, 1916
Wilbur "Leroy" Coakley Heflin	Nov. 25, 1919
Edward E. Jones	July 7, 1927
Wilbur C. Heflin	Aug. 23, 1928

Discontinued Mar. 31, 1957

Blue Wing
George Edmonds
Mail to Richland Mar. 28, 1882

Burdis[1147]
Robert L. Huffman[1148] (1873-1946)
Discontinued Mar. 31, 1933—Mail to Hartwood

Chappawamsic
John Fendall Bell[1149]	Aug. 27, 1841

Discontinued Feb. 17, 1842

James A. Waller[1150] (born c.1831)	May 15, 1856

Discontinued Dec. 16, 1857

M.H. Alberger	Aug. 9, 1869
Thomas H. Bradley	Apr. 4, 1870

Discontinued July 29, 1870

George B. Griffis[1151] (born 1854)	Aug. 28, 1882

[1142] The son of Maj. John Mason Lee (1839-1924) and Nora Bankhead (1841-1915) and the grandson of Sydney Smith Lee (1802-1869) and Anna Maria Mason (1811-1898). He married Edith Balch.

[1143] Mercer was employed by the RF&P Railroad. He married Agnes Brooks (1895-1989).

[1144] The son of James and Ann E. Armstrong.

[1145] Mildred C. (Mills) Schooler was a native of Stafford and sister to John (born c. 1846) and Wyatt Mills. In 1875 she married Douglas W. Schooler (born c. 1848), the son of Charles C. Schooler (born c.1821).

[1146] Clayton was born in Prince William County but lived for many years in Berea. He was a partner in the Horton and Simpson automobile business in Fredericksburg and died in that town. He was buried at his family home in Gainesville.

[1147] This post office was near Dodd's Store in Hartwood.

[1148] Robert was the son of David W. Huffman and Sarah Monroe of Stafford.

[1149] The son of Ashley Bell (born 1770) and Susan Sutherland, both of Louisa County. John married Jane Adie.

[1150] The son of George Waller (1787-before 1856) and Harriett C. Alexander (born c.1803), the daughter of Lewis Alexander (died 1827).

[1151] The son of Samuel H. Griffis (born 1814). In 1884 George married Olivia D. McGhee (c.1862-after 1925) of Spotsylvania.

Discontinued Jan. 30, 1884—Mail to Richland

Coakley's[1152]

Douglas W. Coakley[1153] (born 1853)	Nov. 11, 1884
Frederick Euston Curtis[1154] (1860-1921)	Sept. 30, 1887

Name changed to "Coakley" Dec. 27, 1893

Ludwell Herndon[1155] (1823-1908)	Dec. 27, 1893
Wade H. Simpson	Apr. 8, 1903
Thomas E. Randall	Jan. 21, 1907
John L. Berry	June 9, 1910
William A. Franklin (1887-1970)	Oct. 26, 1912
Gordon W. Berry	Aug. 23, 1913

Discontinued June 29, 1918—Mail to Roseville

Coal Landing

M.H. Alberger	Dec. 2, 1868

Discontinued June 15, 1869

Crest

William Morgan Black[1156] (1848-1918)	July 24, 1891
William J. Lamb	Dec. 15, 1897
William M. Black	Apr. 16, 1898
Stapleton C. Jett[1157] (c. 1837-after 1888)	Dec. 17, 1898

[1152] In January 1888 an unidentified writer provided local newspaper subscribers with a delightful article about Coakley. Described as "a short geographical and historical sketch of Coakly," the article stated that the settlement of Coakley was founded in the year 1879. The writer described it as "peculiarly pleasant and fascinating; situated on the east bank of Potomac Run and west side of Poplar Road, leading from Latham's Fork to Christy's Store. According to the last census report, Coakly had but one inhabitant, but by marriage it has since increased to two." The author thought that by the next census the population of Coakley might increase to three or four. "Coakly, as a business centre, does an extensive business in butter, eggs, old hares, railroad ties, spoke-timber, tan-bark, &c. And, by the way, Coakly is to have a telephone. I have been credibly informed that Professor W[illiam] J. Wallis, of Toronto, Canada; C[harles] J. French of Pea Ridge; W[illiam] D. Reamy, of Parke, and John F. Curtis, of the 'sub-district," propose to form a body corporate for the purpose of establishing a telephone, beginning at Pea Ridge, the residence of Colonel French, by way of Coakly, Christy's Store to Falmouth. There will also be a branch office at the "Big White Oak," in the fork of the road near Berea church, for the benefit of your worthy correspondent J. W. S. We are deeply impressed with the idea of such an arrangement; it will be of incalculable service to the merchants of Coakly, especially at this season of the year, when the roads are bad they cannot get to market often; it will enable them to keep posted on the price for eggs, hare skins, and other market truck. The incorporators propose to name this line the Grape Vine Line, and have elected Mr. J[ohn] F. Curtis business manager. The write closed with a post script regarding the post office saying, "We forgot to mention that Coakly had a daily mail communication by way of Brooke's with the outside world" (*Fredericksburg Star*, Jan. 11, 1888).

[1153] Douglas was the son of John E. Coakley (c.1810-after 1870).

[1154] Frederick was the son of John Francis Curtis (1833-1908) and Sophronia Carter (1837-1911), the daughter of John Carter (1797-1861). Frederick married first Annie Rebecca Anderson (1858-1897), the daughter of John Anderson (c.1812-1868) and Philadelphia Curtis (c.1824-1894). He married secondly in 1900 Ethelina Malinda Jones, the daughter of Azariah and Jane Jones.

[1155] The son of John Herndon (c.1794-1882) and Lucinda "Lucy" Combs (c.1796-c.1867). Following the War Between the States, Ludwell submitted a claim to the Southern Claims Commission asking to be reimbursed for $455 in hogs, corn, and hay taken by the Union army. Unable to prove his allegiance to the Union, his claim was rejected. Ludwell died of a stroke at the home of his son-in-law, Wallace Franklin.

[1156] William was the son of James Black (c.1818-1850) and Delilia Bussell (1819-1896), the daughter of Randall Bussell and Frances Black.

Emma F. Gordon[1158] (died 1939)	Jan. 5, 1902
Abner O. Bryhim (1870-1942)	Dec. 19, 1902
Emma F. Gordon	June 24, 1903
Arthur R. Briggs	Mar. 22, 1913

Discontinued Oct. 15, 1915—Mail to Falmouth

Cropp

John Benjamin Heflin[1159] (1878-1959)	Mar. 16, 1909
Mrs. Mary Eliza Bowling Heflin[1160] (1878-1941)	Mar. 2, 1914
Miss Julia Marie Heflin[1161] (1907-2002)	Jan. 17, 1942

Discontinued Dec. 31, 1946—Mail to Hartwood

Dodd's[1162]

Robert Lee Dodd (c.1861-1921)	May 14, 1891
Cora E. Dodd	Aug. 6, 1907

Falmouth

William Wiggenton	March 1794
Seth B. Wiggenton	April 1799
Daniel Morgan[1163]	Oct. 1801
John M. Little	July 1803
William Richards (1765-after 1803)	April 1806
Thomas Seddon, Jr. (1779-1831)	July 1810
Edward Seddon (died 1812)	April 1812
Philip Alexander[1164]	December 1812
Murray Forbes (1782-1863)	Oct. 10, 1825
Joseph Burwell Ficklen, Jr.[1165] (1848-1905)	Jan. 3, 1866
Charles S. Heflin (1829-1890)	Jan. 16, 1866
George G. Lightner[1166] (1839-1898)	Mar. 30 1881

[1157] Stapleton was the born in Spotsylvania, the son of James Jett (c.1808-1878) and Catharine "Kitty" Suthard (born c.1812), the daughter of Allen Suthard and Mary Ledlow.

[1158] Emma was the wife of Dr. William Wallace Gordon of Richmond. Though she was born in Richmond, Emma lived for a number of years in the Mountain View area of Stafford. She died at the home of her daughter, Bessie M. Briggs.

[1159] John was a farmer. He was buried in Cedar Run Cemetery in Fauquier County.

[1160] Mary Eliza was the daughter of James E. Bowling and Julia Ann Embrey. She married John Benjamin Heflin (1878-1959), the son of Warren O. Heflin and Susan A. Harlow.

[1161] The daughter of John Benjamin Heflin (1878-1959) and the niece of Mary Eliza Bowling Heflin. Julia compiled most of Stafford County's WPA report in the 1930s.

[1162] The Dodds kept the post office in their store. Next to the store was Dodd's Cider Mill (still standing), quite a popular local attraction as they were noted for producing an especially fine apple brandy. C. N. Dodd had a small gas or steam-powered grist mill near the store where he ground meal for local farmers.

[1163] In 1799 Daniel was granted a merchant's license in Falmouth as Daniel Morgan and Brothers.

[1164] There were several Philip Alexanders living in the area at this time and it is uncertain which Philip this was. In 1815 one of the Philip Alexanders joined with Thomas Seddon (1779-1831) in the mercantile firm of Seddon and Alexander (*Virginia Herald*, Aug. 23, 1815).

[1165] The son of Joseph Burwell Ficklen, Sr. (1800-1874) and Anne Eliza Fitzhugh (born 1816). Joseph, Sr. was born at Belmont near Falmouth. He later moved to Fredericksburg where he died and was buried.

Joseph, Jr. was also born at Belmont and inherited his father's Bridgewater Flour Mills. He later became head of the Rappahannock Electric Light and Power Company of Fredericksburg. He married first Cary Gordon Hall and secondly in 1898 Ellen Caskie London (1866-1934). Joseph also owned Belmont Mill, one of the large commercial flour mills built on the Rappahannock.

[1166] George was a native of Falmouth and owned a store there. According to his obituary, Lightner "was a member of the original board of bridge, a commissioner of Stafford, and manager of the bridge and

Charles S. Heflin	May 22, 1885
George G. Lightner	June 27, 1889
Harry G. Lightner[1167] (born 1868)	Oct. 25, 1889
Francis L. Hill (1846-1913)	Feb. 3, 1894
Harry G. Lightner	Aug. 4, 1897
George Sebastian Graninger[1168] (1889-1942)	Nov. 30, 1914
Eddie O. Brooks[1169] (1880-1945) (acting)	Mar. 14, 1923
Miss Edith Ellen Payne[1170]	Jan. 16, 1928

Discontinued Feb. 28, 1963—Mail to Fredericksburg

Fines

John A. Sullivan (1860-1947)	Mar. 8, 1902
Minnie Hudson	Mar. 13, 1908

Discontinued Sept. 30, 1908—Mail to Passapatanzy

Fostersville

Robert A. Hughes	Apr. 16, 1884

Name changed to "Rockford" Nov. 16, 1891

Rockford

William D. Smith	Nov. 16, 1891
Minnie F. Embrey	Feb. 20, 1904

Discontinued June 24, 1904—Mail to Fauquier County

Game Point

William W. Dix	Dec. 1, 1851

Discontinued Mar. 30, 1853

Abel S. Lewellyn[1171] (c.1809-1857)	May 10, 1855
Edmund F. Southard	June 9, 1856

Discontinued Oct. 4, 1856

Garrisonville (late Aquia)

William Bayly	July 30, 1844
Robert Garrison	Jan. 20, 1846

Discontinued Jan. 14, 1848

Robert Garrison	Mar. 6, 1848
James Withers Stone (c.1805-1857)	July 9, 1852
James B. Garrison[1172] (born 1827)	Jan. 12, 1866
Mark Waters (c.1829-after 1870)	Jan. 29, 1866

---

afterwards both manager and treasurer…He took an active interest in politics and was for many years post master at Falmouth." He also served as a justice for Stafford in 1872.

[1167] Harry was the son of George J. Lightner. In 1890 he married Anne E. Jett.

[1168] Born in Berea, George was the son of Christian Frank Graninger (1861-1929) and Malinda Burgess (c.1863-1924), the daughter of James Burgess, also of Berea. He was educated at the Fredericksburg Normal School and, among his several jobs, taught school for several years. He and his first wife, Virginia Belle Brown (1891-1920), kept the post office in their grocery and dry goods store located to the immediate south of Lightner's Store in Falmouth. In later years, George traveled around the state selling supplies to service stations. He owned and resided on Spring Valley farm that is now a subdivision by the same name. He married secondly Emma Bettis Smith (died 1968) and, thirdly, c.1937 Mabel ___.

[1169] The son of William Edwin Brooks (1854-1922) and Mary Osbourne England (1854-1925). Eddie was known as an exceptional horseman and collected horse-drawn vehicles including two sleighs. He was the brother of Julian V. Brooks and resided in Falmouth.

[1170] Edith was the daughter of Gideon Cicero Payne (1861-1902) and Mary Long.

[1171] Abel was born in Norfolk County and kept an ordinary in Stafford.

[1172] James married Elizabeth Harriet Knight (1823-1901), the daughter of William Knight (before 1775-before 1830) and Glady Fritter (c.1780-c.1857).

James B. Garrison	July 29, 1867
William G. Nantes[1173] (born c.1840)	July 7, 1873
James B. Garrison	Mar. 1, 1876
Nannie Waller Blackburn[1174] (1848-1912)	Nov. 17, 1885
James B. Garrison[1175]	July 26, 1889
Nannie W. Blackburn	June 16, 1893
Jackson P. Garrison[1176] (1853-1941)	June 5, 1897
Lucy W. Garrison[1177] (1880-1920)	Feb. 26, 1914
Lenna L. Garrison[1178] (1890-1924)	Aug. 12, 1920
Robert Dallas Fritter[1179] (1876-1953)	Apr. 5, 1924
Mrs. Susie A. Riley	Aug. 1, 1946
Miss Dorothy C. Fritter[1180] (died 1973)	June 30, 1948

Glendie

Glendie Brook Young[1181] (1890-1952)	Aug. 15, 1922
Harwood Simpson[1182] (1874-1955)	May 24, 1928

Discontinued Jan. 31, 1936—Mail to Falmouth

Hartwood

James Cave	Feb. 23, 1835
Robert C. Rogers[1183] (c.1818-1888)	Nov. 30, 1836
Hugh Mercer Tennant[1184] (c.1845-after 1910)	Oct. 19, 1841
William Irvine (c.1781-1859)	July 7, 1842
John Peden (1820-1892)	May 11, 1866
Wilson Bunell Shackelford[1185] (1832-1915)	Apr. 16, 1867

[1173] According to the 1870 Stafford census, William was born on Prince Edward Island in Canada.

[1174] Nannie was the daughter of Edward Waller (1805-1883) of Grafton and his wife Susan Newton Conway (1814-1864). She married Charles F. Blackburn (1849-1899).

[1175] A newspaper article said of the Garrisonville Post Office, "The post office at Garrisonville will be removed to-day to the residence of J. B. Garrison, Esq., from Mr. C. F. Blackburn. Mr. G. has recently been appointed postmaster at that place" (*Fredericksburg Star*, Aug. 17, 1889).

[1176] The son of James B. Garrison (born c.1827) and Elizabeth Harriet Knight (1823-1901).

[1177] Lucy married Turner R. Garrison (1872-1919).

[1178] Lenna was the daughter of Robert L. Flatford (1852-1898) and Fannie Gill (1852-1936) and the wife of Ernest Valentine Garrison (1885-1958). She died from complications from childbirth.

[1179] The son of Enoch Fritter (1851-1926) and Lucy Ann Cooper (1853-1917), the daughter of Thornton B. and Frances (Watson) Cooper. Robert was a merchant and farmer. In 1908 he married Annis Alberta Halpenny (1876-1958), the daughter of Jacob Halpenny. At the time of his death, Robert was treasurer of Ebenezer Methodist Church.

[1180] Dorothy was the daughter of Robert Dallas Fritter (1876-1953) and Alberta Halpenny (1876-1958).

[1181] Glendie was the son of Samuel R. Young and Laura Gaylor of Berea. He was a World War I veteran and operated the store and post office in the little settlement named for him. He died at Kecoughtan Hospital and was buried at Berea Baptist Church.

[1182] Harwood was the son of James Polk Simpson and Louisa Bullock. As a young man he was employed in the IRS office in Richmond and, later, with the government at Fort Eustis. In 1925 he returned to Stafford, took up farming, and served as postmaster at Glendie. He was also co-chairman of the Republican Party in Stafford and was a delegate to the state GOP convention. In 1907 he married Nettie G. Jett.

[1183] Following the War Between the States, Robert submitted a claim to the Southern Claims Commission asking to be reimbursed for $1,918 worth of wood and corn taken by the Union army. His claim was rejected.

[1184] Hugh was the son of George and Anna S. Tennant. He was born in Caroline County but spent much of his adult life at Comorn, King George County. In 1842 Hugh married Eleanor A. S. Grymes in King George County. By 1850 he was a merchant in Caroline. In late 1864 Hugh was conscripted into Company K, 30th Virginia Infantry. He was paroled at Appomattox.

Mary E. Shackelford (1849-1939)	Mar. 19, 1870
William F. Graves[1186] (c.1835-1895)	July 8, 1879
Mrs. Mary E. Shackelford	July 29, 1879
Madison E. Rollins[1187] (c.1857-1903)	Jan. 13, 1890
William F. Graves	Aug. 22, 1890
Mary E. Shackelford	May 11, 1895
Milton K. Courtney (1869-1932)	Feb. 12, 1903
James R. Monroe	Aug. 25, 1904
Miss Margaret Elizabeth Monroe[1188] (c.1905-1959)	Mar. 16, 1945
Woodrow Fleming "Flip" Monroe[1189]	July 1, 1948
Beverly B. Gibbs	May 12, 1984

Heflin[1190]

Thaddeus Edward Courtney[1191] (1884-1960)	Mar. 16, 1909
Mrs. Laura Heflin[1192] (1868-1956)	Apr. 6, 1922

Discontinued Feb. 28, 1935—Mail to Hartwood

Hemp

Frank Stewart (1864-1931)	May 8, 1905

Discontinued Oct. 31, 1931

Holly Corner[1193]

David Alexander Monroe	Dec. 18, 1926

Discontinued Dec. 31, 1934—Mail to Berea

Lance

William G. Ballard	May 13, 1889
William J. Jacobs (c.1850-1926)	Mar. 13, 1891
Lucy Payne (1882-1946)	Jan. 25, 1912

Discontinued June 30, 1916—Mail to Berea

[1185] Wilson was the son of Uriah W. Shackelford and Diadema Hilman. In 1855 he married Mary Elizabeth Patton (born c.1835), the daughter of John Patton and Bathsheba McInteere. Wilson was a carpenter by profession and was buried in the Confederate Cemetery in Fredericksburg.

[1186] William was the son of Willis Graves (born c.1810) and made his living as a merchant in Hartwood. During the War Between the States, he was a member of Company C of the 30th Virginia Infantry. William died of pneumonia.

[1187] Madison moved from Stafford to Washington about 12 years before his death. There he was engaged in the mercantile business. He died, unmarried, of liver disease.

[1188] Margaret was the daughter of James R. Monroe and Annie Edwards and for 30 years was a teacher in Stafford and Culpeper counties. She was buried at Grove Baptist Church in Goldvein.

[1189] The son of James R. Monroe.

[1190] This post office was in a store popularly known as Wolfgang's Store.

[1191] Thaddeus was the son of John Courtney and Sally Price and was born in Fauquier County. From 1907 until he became ill in 1949, he kept stores in Hartwood and Washington. Thaddeus was buried at Grace Methodist Church in Stafford.

[1192] Laura was the daughter of William Henry and Delia Heflin and the wife of Welford Heflin (1897-1967). She was buried at Rock Hill Baptist Church.

[1193] The little settlement of Holly Corner was located in the heart of the gold mining region and at the intersections of routes 654 (Rocky Pen Road) and 655 (Holly Corner Road) and boasted a post office and a school.

Leeland[1194]

Daniel Murray Lee[1195] (1843-1916)	Aug. 25, 1882

Mail to Fredericksburg Oct. 5, 1882

William Bowler	Apr. 20, 1886
Charles A. Sthreshley[1196] (1872-1898)	Jan. 22, 1897
Charles W. Stone (1877-1951)	Nov. 17, 1899
Marius Sthreshley[1197] (1847-1931)	Oct. 11, 1900

Discontinued Jan. 3, 1901

Philip C. Payne	May 18, 1905
James H. Michael	Sept. 14, 1907
George Adam Bowler[1198] (c.1832-1920)	Apr. 25, 1908
Ada J. Berry[1199] (1892-1956)	May 2, 1914
Ada J. B. Jett	Aug. 27, 1915

Discontinued May 15, 1916—Mail to Fredericksburg

Little Whim

Samuel Babcock[1200] (c.1806-1895)	Dec. 6, 1872

Discontinued Aug. 6, 1875

Midway Island

Mrs. Lulu Lynn Griffis (died 1994)	Sept. 21, 1943

Discontinued Dec. 30, 1965—Mail to Quantico

[1194] In the early 1880s efforts were made to consolidate some of the many post offices, probably because of budget tightening. Staffordians were adamantly opposed to any cutbacks in service or convenience. In the fall of 1882 Leeland Post Office was closed and mail normally delivered there was sent to Fredericksburg. In 1885 a newspaper article regarding Leeland reported that Daniel Lee "without any Congressional assistance, has obtained from the acting assistant Postmaster General a promise that the post office at Leeland...on the R.F.&P. railroad, abolished by Gen. Mahone, should be restored. The railroad company has promised to make a station there."

[1195] Daniel was the fifth son of Sydney Smith Lee (1802-1869) and Anna Maria Mason (1811-1898) and a nephew of Robert E. Lee. In 1874 Daniel married Nannie E. Ficklen (1850-1933), the daughter of Joseph Burwell Ficklen (1800-1874) and Ann Eliza Fitzhugh. Daniel also served in the Confederate navy for four years. Around 1880 he built Highland Home on the west side of Deacon Road (State Route 607).

[1196] Charles was the son of Marius Sthreshley (1847-1931) and Fannie M. Clift. He died at his home of typhoid fever at the age of 27. According to his obituary, "for several years [he] had been the accommodating and faithful post master at Leeland." His wife, Lillie C. Jenkins, was taken ill at the same time but recovered. Charles and Lillie were buried at the family cemetery at Bellair.

[1197] Marius was the son of James Madison Sthreshley (1795-1869) and Mary Peyton Bolling Fitzhugh (born 1808). Marius' mother was the grand daughter of Henry Fitzhugh (1747-1815) of Bellair. He married Frances Marian Clift. After his wife's death, Marius moved in with his daughter in Washington, DC where he died.

[1198] According to his obituary, George was a sergeant in the Fredericksburg Artillery during the War Between the States.

[1199] Ada was the daughter of Oscar (1844-1913) and Lucy Berry of Leeland and the wife of Frank H. Jett of Richmond.

[1200] For many years, Samuel lived at Little Whim on White Oak Road (State Route 218). Towards the end of his life he moved in with his son-in-law, E. P. Holdridge of Mt. Vernon, New York where he died. Samuel was born in Massachusetts.

Millie's

Waller S. Gill[1201] (1871-1947)	Apr. 8, 1902
Wilson Decatur (1847-1935)	Mar. 9, 1904
Mary Decatur	Aug. 24, 1907
Benjamin H. Decatur	Oct. 7, 1909

Discontinued July 31, 1910—Mail to Wide Water

Monteithville

James Monteith	June 13, 1851
Col. Thomas Purkins[1202] (1791-1855)	Mar. 11, 1853
Col. Henry Carter Purkins[1203] (1828-1907)	July 17, 1855
Isaac Fines (born c.1807)	June 2, 1858

Discontinued Jan. 4, 1859

James Thomas Chinn[1204] (1851-1920)	Apr. 21, 1879

Discontinued Apr. 15, 1910—Mail to Passapatanzy

Mount

William Edward Mountjoy[1205] (1835-1898)	June 19, 1895
Rubin Edward Mountjoy[1206] (1869-1931)	Nov. 2, 1898
Clara Graves Mountjoy (1879-1961)	July 5, 1906
James E. Mountjoy[1207] (1879-1938)	Dec. 11, 1908
Mrs. Hazel L. Thomas	Aug. 13, 1938
Mrs. Esther A. Vida	Aug. 12, 1940
Michael Vida (1913-1990)	Sept. 26, 1940

Discontinued Nov. 14, 1942—Mail to Wide Water

[1201] Waller wore many professional hats. In addition to being postmaster, he also served as an assistant principal and teacher at Ebenezer School in Garrisonville (closed c.1890). He was also the lineman and technician for the Fredericksburg and Toluca Phone Company in the 1920s and 1930s. He was the son of Edward Gill (born c.1820).

[1202] Owned and resided at Hollywood (Eby, They 256). Like so many post offices, Monteithville seems to have moved from time to time. Thomas Purkins probably kept the office somewhere on or near his farm. Thomas was postmaster at Monteithville until his death in 1855, at which point his son, Henry C. Purkins, assumed the position.

[1203] Henry, the son of Thomas Purkins (1791-1855), was trained as a lawyer. In 1858 he moved to King George County, bought a farm there, and practiced law. The area around this farm is still known as Purkins' Corner. He married in King George Sally Carver, the daughter of Elzey Thornton Carver. During the difficult period of Reconstruction, Henry served as presiding justice in King George County. He was also supervisor of the poor and supervisor of the Rappahannock magisterial district as well as deputy clerk of the court.

[1204] James operated the Monteithville Post Office from his home at the intersection of Casson Road (State Route 603) and White Oak Road (State Route 218). This old home used to stand on the southeast corner of the intersection, diagonally across from White Oak School, now D. P. Newton's Civil War Museum. For many years James taught school in Stafford and the surrounding counties. He was a member of Bethel Baptist Church and died at White Oak.

[1205] William, also known as "Ned," was the son of Thornton Mountjoy (1794:7-1881). Around 1858 he married his cousin, Anna Elizabeth Mountjoy (1843-1913). In 1862 he enlisted in the 9th Virginia Cavalry as a private.

[1206] Rubin and Clara Mountjoy were husband and wife. Rubin was the son of William Edward Mountjoy (1835-1898) and Anne Elizabeth "Eliza" Mountjoy (1843-1913). For many years he was a merchant and postmaster at Mount. Following the 1942 condemnation, Rubin moved to Triangle. He was buried at Dumfries Cemetery.

[1207] James was the son of William Edward Mountjoy (1835-1898). He attended Valley View School near Richland in Wide Water. In 1903 he married Minnie Alice Roles (1880-1921), the daughter of Samuel and Pansy Roles of Prince William County. James lived at Mount where he and his brother, Richard E. Mountjoy (1884-1946), operated a general store. James was buried at Cedar Run Cemetery.

Mountain View

Myron Mansfield (born c.1826)	Sept. 22, 1870
James Morton, Jr.	Aug. 4, 1871
William M. Black	Sept. 16, 1872
Humphrey George[1208] (c.1818-after 1880)	Jan. 6, 1874
Discontinued Sept. 28, 1881	
Silas L. Rose[1209] (born c.1857)	Oct. 8, 1881
John E. Beale[1210] (1852-1936)	Nov. 19, 1884
Humphrey George	Mar. 22, 1886
Edgar William Armstrong[1211] (1855-1941)	Sept. 26, 1889
Annie May Wilson[1212] (1871-1959)	Aug. 28, 1895
James M. Bryant (1874-1898)	Feb. 2, 1897
Mary Elizabeth Wilson[1213] (born 1874)	Jan. 4, 1907
Dora Mason Guy[1214] (1885-1915)	Jan. 4, 1907
Discontinued Feb. 28, 1907—Mail to Crest	

Musselman[1215]

James Musselman	Oct. 9, 1883
Lillie Marshall Wilkerson[1216] (1886-1963)	May 29, 1907
Myrtie G. Wilkerson	Jan. 27, 1908
Minnie W. Byram[1217] (1872-1934)	May 7, 1908
Discontinued Sept. 14, 1918—Mail to Stafford	

Myrtleville[1218]

Gouverneur T. Greenlaw[1219]	Mar. 25, 1890
Mace Clements Purkins[1220] (1840-1911)	July 1, 1891

[1208] According to the 1860 census, Humphrey was a school teacher.

[1209] Silas was the son of James S. Rose (born c.1830). In 1885 Silas married Mary E. Heflin, the daughter of Wesley and Martha A. Heflin.

[1210] John resided at Glendie and was a member of Antioch Methodist Church.

[1211] Edgar was the son of George Henry Armstrong (1830-1863) and Elvira Fant Fritter (1834-after 1900), the daughter of Barnett Fritter (1792-1872) and Mary L. Fant. Edgar ran a sawmill and in 1893 married Susan "Snowie" Bryant (1874-1935), the daughter of Daniel T. Bryant and Mary Thomas Skinner. He lived at Chestnut Hill and was buried at Ramoth Church.

[1212] The daughter of William N. Wilson (1842-1917) and Mary Catharine Fritter (1836-1929). In 1899 Annie married Milton Mountjoy (1866-1943), the son of Alexander Hamilton Mountjoy (c.1827-c.1902) and Mary Mountjoy. Annie was a school teacher.

[1213] The daughter of William N. Wilson (1842-1917) and Mary Catharine Fritter (1836-1929). Mary married Robert Fallon of Baltimore.

[1214] Dora was the daughter of Robert E. Guy (1855-1905) and Susan Ellen Wine (1858-1922) of Mountain View. She died of tuberculosis.

[1215] This post office was located at the intersection of Courthouse Road (State Route 630) and Reids Road on the south side of Courthouse Road and the east side of Reids Road. Across the road from the post office was a store known locally as "the old brick store."

[1216] Lillian was the daughter of George Emmett Wilkerson (1857-1919) and Annie Mason Byram (1861-1897).

[1217] Minnie was the wife of George Byram of Mountain View.

[1218] Myrtleville and Monteithville post offices were both located on Hollywood Farm, though the exact location of Myrtleville is in question. Myrtleville didn't begin operating until after Monteithville had closed and the two seems to have been in different locations, though close, and they served the same neighborhood.

[1219] Gouverneur was living at Hollywood when it burned in 1890. He was also constable of Falmouth from 1881-1885 and a justice of the peace in 1891. A pharmacist by profession, Gouverneur moved his family from Stafford to Washington where he operated a drugstore and manufactured medicines.

Marion Wallace (Monteith) Purkins[1221] (died 1927)   July 13, 1910
Discontinued July 15, 1913—Mail to Fredericksburg

Onville[1222]
Edwin A. Evans	Aug. 17, 1886
Arthur Moore (1866-1952)	Mar. 14, 1888

Discontinued Feb. 28, 1889—Mail to Garrisonville

Mary E. Branch (or Bramel)	May 13, 1889
Theresa V. Fritter (born c.1848)	Apr. 6, 1892
Robert D. Fritter	Apr. 29, 1904
James H. Rohme	Sept. 21, 1908
Miss Hettie Evans (1876-1955)	May 10, 1910

Discontinued Oct. 24, 1942—Mail to Garrisonville ("Govt. taking land for maneuvers")

Rectory
Jennie B. Homes	Feb. 4, 1895
James L. Williams[1223] (1864-1935)	June 21, 1897
Mrs. Agnes L. Williams[1224] (1878-1956)	Nov. 8, 1935

Discontinued Oct. 31, 1950—Mail to Midway

Richland Mills[1225]
Charles N. Warren	May 6, 1869
Edward Rehil[1226] (c.1815-after 1870)	Mar. 28, 1870

Discontinued Jan. 5, 1882

George D. Edmonds	Jan. 26, 1882

Mail to Wide Water May 28, 1890

Roseville
Silas L. Rose	Jan. 28, 1885
James Marshall Rose[1227] (1886-1966)	Mar. 23, 1920
Mrs. Ida E. Rose	Dec. 5, 1956

[1220] Mace also served as constable of Falmouth in 1870 and from 1881-1885. He was a constable for Falmouth in 1870 and a justice of the peace in 1891. He was the brother of Col. Henry Carter Purkins and son of Col. Thomas Purkins (1791-1855).

[1221] The wife of Mace C. Purkins.

[1222] This tiny post office stood on the southeast corner of the intersection of Onville Road (State Route 641) and Camp Barrett Road (State Route 639). In later years, a small store was added to the side of the post office.

[1223] The son of James and Dicey Williams. In 1900 James married Agnes L. Riley (1878-1956), the daughter of Noah Riley (1813-after 1870) and Cleopatra O'Byrhim (born 1839). For many years, the Williams family operated Williams' Store within which was the Rectory Post Office. This old frame building, located on the south side of Wide Water Road (State Route 611) and across the road from Rectory farm, burned in the 1980s.

[1224] During Mrs. Williams' tenure as post mistress, there was a large parrot that resided in the store. He purportedly had an extensive vocabulary. Agnes was the widow of James L. Williams.

[1225] This post office was located in Brent's Mill across the road and very near the present Wide Water Fire Department.

[1226] The court minutes of Feb. 8, 1858 reveal that Edward was an Irish immigrant who applied for and received American citizenship. The minutes read, "Edward Rehil a native of that part of Great Britain called Ireland this day declared on oath that it is bona fide his intention to become a citizen of the United States, and renounces forever all allegiance and fidelity to any foreign Prince, Potentate, State or Sovereignty, whatever and particularly to Victoria Queen of Great Britain." He received his certificate of citizenship from the Stafford court on Apr. 17, 1861.

Edward was a miller by profession.

[1227] James was the son of Silas L. Rose.

Aleen F. Glenn (1925-1974) May 31, 1957
Discontinued Dec. 31, 1958—Mail to Stafford

Ruby
Mildred Narcissa Rose[1228] June 20, 1903
Mildred N. Fairfax July 27, 1907
Ashton A. Armstrong[1229] (1903-1959) Apr. 20, 1909
Charles W. Bridwell[1230] (1867-1953) Aug. 6, 1912
Harvey H. Mitchell (1877-1942) Aug. 11, 1913
Discontinued Sept. 30, 1914—Mail to Toluca
Bennett Heflin[1231] (1860-1954) May 8, 1924
Mrs. Hazel B. Heflin[1232] (1913-1997) Feb. 16, 1940
Mrs. Ruth H. Eustace Mar. 20, 1948
Discontinued May 31, 1948—Mail to Garrisonville
Mrs. Ruth H. Eustace[1233] (born 1920) Mar. 16, 1949

Serena
Thomas W. Franklin[1234] (c.1845-1928) Mar. 23, 1968
Discontinued Aug. 11, 1875

Shacklett
Nelson Tolson Shacklett[1235] (1856-1903) Feb. 23, 1898
James R. Shacklett Nov. 16, 1903
Charles W. Allegar[1236] (1882-1905) Oct. 2, 1905
Zephyr Abel (1875-1968) July 30, 1910
Discontinued Oct. 24, 1942—Mail to Quantico ("Govt. taking land for maneuvers")

[1228] In 1906 Mildred married Hannie F. Fairfax of Clifton, Virginia.

[1229] Ashton was the son of Ollie M. Armstrong. He sold cars at Skinker Motor Company.

[1230] The son of Charles W. (born c.1834) and Pauline Bridwell (born c.1837).

[1231] Carl Bennett Heflin was the son of Marshall Wesley Heflin (1820-1892) and Susan Frances Corbin. In 1890 he married Frances "Fannie" Lee Heflin, the daughter of Wesley Jefferson Heflin and Martha Ann Humphrey. Bennett kept the post office in his store which stood at the intersection of Garrisonville Road and Rock Hill Church Road (State Route 644), just east of Ruby fire house.

[1232] Hazel Jennie Brewer was the daughter of Charles Julian Brewer (1882-1942) and Jennie Alice Wigfield (born 1883). In 1932 she married Hosea Montgomery Heflin (born 1903), the son of Broaddus Romutain Heflin (1855-1941) and Rowena Alma Fritter (born 1868). Hazel was superintendent of the Sunday School at Rock Hill Baptist Church and worked for the Civil Service at the Basic School at Quantico. She was born in Washington and died in Charlottesville. Hosea Heflin constructed the little building that served as Ruby Post Office. This stood at the end of his driveway until Ruth Eustace became post mistress and it was moved down to her house. An addition was made to the building and it doubled as a convenience store.

[1233] Ruth Olga Heflin was the daughter of Clarence Joseph Heflin (1885-1947) and Olive Leone Heflin (1882-1967). In 1940 she married John Kelly Eustace.

[1234] Thomas was a native of Lancaster County, Pennsylvania, but lived in Virginia for over 50 years. He was a resident of Stafford for about 25 years.

[1235] Most of the Shackletts in Virginia descend from Benjamin Shacklett (1710-1784) and his two wives, Sarah Blancette and Catherine Tucker. Benjamin was the son of John Shacklet/ Shekerlie/Shakalit, who is believed to have been a French Huguenot born Jenade Jaquelot (1678-1718). Once the family arrived in America, the spelling of the name changed to Shacklett, spelled much as Jaquelot was pronounced.

Benjamin immigrated to the colonies around 1740 with his wife, Sarah Blancette. They had one son, John, who married Barbara Quick. Many of the Shacklett family settled in Kentucky. The branch of the family that established themselves in Stafford still have numerous descendants here today.

Nelson died suddenly after attending all-day services at church.

[1236] Charles was killed on the PD & W Railroad near Baltimore.

Snellings[1237]
Charles A. Truslow (1860-1947) — Aug. 16, 1887
Name changed to "Hull" Dec. 24, 1888
Discontinued Feb. 27, 1889—Mail to Berear

Spottedville
Postmaster	Date
Abner R. Alcock[1238] (died c.1831)	Aug. 1818
George G. Wheeler	Jan. 15, 1833
James M. Briggs[1239] (1787-1845) and John Smoot	Jan. 26, 1833
John Cason	Mar. 2, 1839
Edward Washington Latham[1240] (1811-1851)	Sept. 9, 1839
Edmond Fontaine Rose (1817-1893)	Apr. 18, 1857

Stafford Courthouse
Postmaster	Date
James W. Ford (1791-1865)	1810
Pichergru Woolfolk[1241] (c.1795-1862)	1815
Dr. Valentine Yelverton Conway (1803-1881)	1818
Samuel Adie	1826
Elijah Bell[1242]	1826
John B. Morton[1243]	1827
Moses W. Garrison	
John Moncure Conway (1779-1864)	1832
Eustace Conway (1820-1857)	May 7, 1836
Henry Rowzee Conway (1825-1863)	Nov. 4, 1844
Leonard P. Alexander	Nov. 9, 1853
William L. Morgan	Feb. 8, 1856
James E. Schooler	Dec. 19, 1860
Leonard P. Alexander	Jan. 12, 1866
Mrs. Lucy E. Schooler (born c.1834)	Apr. 17, 1866
Mrs. Mildred C. Lucas	July 16, 1867
Discontinued Aug. 27, 1868	
Miss Theresa E. Alexander	Oct. 1, 1868
Charles Adams Bryan (1849-1918)	Jan. 7, 1870
Thomas Lowry (c.1826-1911)	Dec. 20, 1870
Richard Hughlett Bryan (1820-1906)	Jan. 12, 1871
James Dent (born c.1848)	Dec. 20, 1872
Winfield Scott Bryan (1853-1893)	June 26, 1874
Charles A. Bryan	Dec. 12, 1879
Mary W. (Barnes) Rouse[1244] (c.1864-1918)	Aug. 31, 1885
Lucy (Barnes) Smith[1245] (died 1926)	Mar. 9, 1888

[1237] This post office was located in old Truslow's Store at the intersection of Truslow Road (State Route 652) and Enon Road (State Route 753). The store, now abandoned, is still standing.

[1238] Abner was the son of Thomas Alcock (1744-1834) who owned Spotted Tavern. At the time of his death, Abner owned 828 ½ acres, including Alcock's Mill that he acquired from his father c.1827. In 1816 Abner married Elizabeth Hazelgrove in Spotsylvania.

[1239] James lived at Stony Hill on Stony Hill Road (State Route 662). He was the son of David Briggs (1730-1813), a well-known lawyer who practiced in Stafford and Fredericksburg.

[1240] Edward was the son of Jesse Latham (died c.1826) and Betsy P. Horton. He died unmarried.

[1241] The son of Charles (1763-1803) and Frances Woolfolk (1760-1825) of Caroline County. In 1819 he married Angelina Frances Winston.

[1242] Probably a descendant of one of the six Bell brothers who were living in Stafford in the 1740s, namely John, James, George, Thomas, William, and Charles. They were most likely sons or grandsons of John Bell who died in Stafford c.1728.

[1243] John was the son of William Allen Morton of Washington.

[1244] Mary was burned to death in an accidental fire in Washington.

John M. Stevens	Sept. 6, 1889
William E. Stevens[1246] (1863-1925)	Nov. 16, 1890
Name changed to "Stafford" Feb. 2, 1895	
Alexander E. Bloxton (1846-1921)	Feb. 2, 1895
Lucy E. Bryan (1873-1945)	July 11, 1898
Richard C. L. Moncure[1247] (1831-1917)	Mar. 11, 1914
Edgar Smith Moore[1248] (1879-1954)	June 18, 1919
Miss Virginia W. Dent	Oct. 1, 1946
Earl C. Weir	Sept. 7, 1960
Gary H. Helms	Jan. 11, 1961
Myrtle V. MacGregor	Nov. 22, 1963
Mary S. Cloe	Nov. 25, 1972
Franklin D. Silver (officer in charge)	Nov. 19, 1976
Willie W. Roberts	June 18, 1977

Stafford Store

William Guy (born c.1814)	May 21, 1857
Discontinued Jan. 26, 1858	
Raleigh L. Cooper (1832-1892)	Apr. 26, 1860
James A. Anderson (c.1832-c.1869)	Apr. 12, 1866
Discontinued Oct. 4, 1867	
Reestablished Oct. 21, 1872	
Darwin Sunderlin[1249] (born c.1810)	July 25, 1873
Maggie D. Fritter (born c.1863)	May 23, 1900
Howard Hampton Shacklett (1880-1929)	Oct. 30, 1902
Marion Ratcliffe Tolson[1250] (1867-1952)	June 21, 1907
Mrs. Ora Genevieve (Sine) Tolson[1251] (c.1905-1959)	May 11, 1938
Discontinued Oct. 31, 1939	

Storck

George Storck[1252] (1850-1934)	May 20, 1904
Woodlie Storck[1253] (1859-1923)	Feb. 28, 1914
George Storck	Oct. 26, 1923
Mrs. Flossie L. Houghton[1254] (1883-1947)	Feb. 18, 1935
Discontinued Feb. 28, 1942—Mail to Hartwood	

[1245] Lucy died in Washington of pneumonia.

[1246] William married Lucy Bryant.

[1247] The son of R.C.L. Moncure (1805-1882) and Mary Butler Washington Conway (1807-1895). His first wife was Virginia Buchanan (1826-1881). He married secondly Harriet Mabel Taylor (1865-1895).

[1248] Edgar was the son of Edgar Smith Moore, Sr. (1847-1899). He married Clara Chewning and died at Pine Crest Nursing Home in Stafford.

[1249] Darwin was born in New York.

[1250] The son of James Alexander Tolson (c.1835-1896) and Mary Jane Ratcliffe (1837-1928). He was the grandson of Benjamin P. Tolson (c.1802-c.1870) and Prudence Payne (c.1811-1855). Marion was a farmer, postmaster, cabinet maker, and undertaker. In 1891 he married Emma Lee Davis (1873-1965).

[1251] Ora was born in Pennsylvania. She married Mitchell Tolson (1902-1992), the son of Marion R. Tolson (1866-1952). Ora and Mitchell moved to Prince William County following the government condemnation of their land in 1942 and lived on what is now Minnieville Road.

[1252] George was a native of Germany. Around 1875 he came to Stafford from New York to pursue gold mining and farming.

[1253] George and Woodlie Storck were husband and wife.

[1254] Flossie was the daughter of George Storck and the wife of Benjamin Houghton (1881-1957). She was buried at Richland Baptist Church

Tackett's Mill
Jefferson Spindle (c.1804-1861)	Feb. 15, 1841
Edward Templeman (born c.1821)	Jan. 28, 1846
Charles Addison Tackett (1814-1896)	May 2, 1857

Discontinued Oct. 4, 1866

Joseph W. Colbert[1255] (c.1839-1906)	Oct. 21, 1872
David Robinson	Jan. 21, 1876
Lawrence Ashton Skinner[1256] (1855-1915)	Dec. 16, 1880
Joseph Davis (1860-1932)	Aug. 15, 1884

Name changed to "Tackett Mills" Aug. 17, 1893

Talana[1257]
William Mountjoy[1258] (1866-1913)	Nov. 17, 1899

Discontinued Aug. 27, 1900

Toluca
William "Napoleon" Bailey Musselman[1259]	June 12, 1894
James Walter Shackelford (1876-1948)	Mar. 2, 1900
Albert Joseph Musselman[1260] (1863-1921)	July 30, 1903
Milton H. Homes[1261] (1871-1947)	Oct. 24, 1905
Walter Warren DeShields[1262] (1897-1952)	May 18, 1935
Mrs. Mae A. Kincheloe	Jan. 21, 1937

Discontinued Nov. 30, 1938—Mail to Garrisonville

Tuan
Wallace H. Snellings (1873-1943)	Oct. 4, 1900

Discontinued May 31, 1902—Mail to Falmouth

[1255] Joseph was born in Fauquier County. During the War Between the States, he was a member of the Black Horse Cavalry of Warrenton and served under Captain (later General) W. H. Payne. After the war, he kept a business on Commerce Street in Fredericksburg. He later moved to Portsmouth where he was struck by a streetcar and killed.

[1256] Lawrence owned and operated Tackett's Mills on Aquia Run. He married Sally Dodd (died 1933), the sister of Robert Lee Dodd (c.1861-1921) of Spotted Tavern. Lawrence was buried at Grove Methodist Church in Fauquier County.

[1257] The exact location of this office is unknown. It may have been near the Fauquier County line in the vicinity of Poplar Road (State Route 616), as this was where its only postmaster lived.

[1258] Known as "Willie" Mountjoy. He was the son of William E. Mountjoy (1835-1898), postmaster of Mount Post Office. In 1898 he married Gertrude A. Courtney (c.1880-1959) and lived near Rock Hill. He was buried at Mount but later moved to Cedar Run Cemetery.

[1259] Napoleon (1865-1921) was the son of Albert Joseph Musselman (1830-1906). His first career was in the lumber business in Fredericksburg, though he spent most of his life running a store in Toluca where he also kept a farm. In 1885 Napoleon married H. V. Holmes (born c.1864). In 1900 Napoleon gave up his store to his nephew, James W. Shackelford (1876-1948). The newspaper notice announcing this event described James as "young and energetic, and will build himself up as time progresses" (*Free Lance*, Jan. 23, 1900). Napoleon died of a heart attack at his home and was buried in the Holmes cemetery in Stafford.

[1260] The son of Albert Joseph Musselman, Sr. (1830-1906) and Frances Alice Knight (1830-1893). In 1887 he married Julia Lee Groves (1864-1943).

[1261] Milton was the son of Thomas Homes (c.1821-1886). In 1897 he married Agnes E. Shackelford (1877-1956), the daughter of Strother A. Shackelford (1840-1925) and Jane Eliza Mahoney (c.1843-1894). Milton lived in Garrisonville.

[1262] Walter was born in Falmouth and was a lifelong resident of Stafford County. A World War I veteran, he married Ethel Homes and owned a farm in Garrisonville.

Wide Water

Nannie Waller Moncure[1263] (1862-1903)	May 28, 1890
Richard C. L. Moncure[1264] (1831-1917)	Sept. 30, 1903
George William Herring (1877-1966)	Apr. 10, 1905
Richard Wirt Powers[1265] (1870-1934)	Apr. 8, 1912
Mrs. Lula Lynn Griffis (died 1994)	July 1, 1929
Mrs. Mae M. Moore (1898-1988)	Oct. 11, 1943

Woodcutting

Joseph C. Wine[1266] (c.1832-1090)	Apr. 30, 1858

Discontinued Sept. 8, 1858

[1263] Nannie Withers Waller was the daughter of Withers Waller (1825-1900) and Anne Eliza Stribling (1832-1903) of Clifton. She married Richard Cassius Lee Moncure (1856-1936).

[1264] Richard C. L. and Nannie Moncure were husband and wife.

[1265] Richard was the eldest son of Sidney Powers (1837-1895) and Mary Thompson (1845-1012) and lived in Stafford for most of his life. Prior to his death, he managed two stores in Triangle. For many years he was a member and treasurer of Aquia Church and at the time of his death was junior warden of the vestry. He married Temple Chewning (1879-1970) of Hanover County. Richard died of a stroke.

[1266] Joseph was a blacksmith. He married first Lucy Ann West (c.1832-1854) and secondly Catherine E. Wine (born c.1841).

Sources:

Axelson, Edith F. *Virginia Postmasters and Post Offices, 1789-1932*. Athens, GA: Iberian Publishing Co., 1991.
Duncan, Marion M. et al. *House of Moncure Genealogy*. Self-published, 1967.
Fredericksburg Star, Jan. 11, 1888, article about Coakley
---, Aug. 17, 1889, notice regarding the moving of the Garrisonville Post Office
Free Lance, Apr. 5, 1895, obituary of William F. Graves
---, Dec. 8, 1898, obituary of Charles A. Sthreshley
---, Dec. 15, 1898, obituary of George J. Lightner
---, Jan 23, 1900, notice of N. B. Musselman giving up his store
---, Sept. 22, 1903, obituary of Nelson T. Shacklett
---, Oct. 20, 1903, obituary of Madison E. Rollins
---, June 19, 1906, obituary of Joseph W. Colbert
---, Dec. 17, 1907, obituary of Henry C. Purkins
---, Mar 2, 1915, obituary of William S. Towson
---, June 8, 1915, obituary of Lawrence A. Skinner
---, June 22, 1915, obituary of Dora M. Guy
---, Mar. 28, 1918, obituary of Mary (Barnes) Rouse
---, July 10, 1920, obituary of James T. Chinn
---, Dec. 11, 1920, obituary of George A. Bowler
---, Nov. 8, 1921, obituary of Napoleon B. Musselman
---, Feb. 28, 1924, obituary of Lennie F. Garrison
---, Feb. 27, 1926, obituary of Lucy B. Smith
Free Lance-Star, Oct. 11, 1926, obituary of William J. Jacobs
---, Mar. 16, 1927, obituary of Clayton Simpson
---, May 17, 1928, obituary of Thomas W. Franklin
---, Dec. 16, 1929, obituary of Mildred C. Schooler
---, Aug. 11, 1931, obituary of Marius Sthreshley
---, July 7, 1934, obituary of Minnie W. Byram
---, Nov. 27, 1934, obituary of Richard W. Powers
---, Dec. 26, 1934, obituary of George Storck
---, Aug. 10, 1936, obituary of John E. Beale
---, Feb. 21, 1938, obituary of Alfred Joseph Pyke
---, July 30, 1938, obituary of William B. Lee
---, Feb. 1, 1939, obituary of Emma F. Gordon
---, Jan. 7, 1941, obituary of Edgar Armstrong
---, Aug. 24, 1942, obituary of George S. Graninger
---, Oct. 1, 1945, obituary of Eddie O. Brooks
---, Jan. 4, 1946, obituary of Robert L. Huffman
---, Mar. 3, 1947, obituary of Flossie L. Houghton
---, May 17, 1947, obituary of Milton H. Homes
---, Jan. 20, 1951, obituary of George K. Massie, Sr.
---, Mar. 4, 1952, obituary of Walter W. DeShields
---, May 7, 1952, obituary of Glendie B. Young
---, May 26, 1952, obituary of Marion R. Tolson
---, Oct. 30, 1953, obituary of Robert D. Fritter
---, June 2, 1954, obituary of Edgar S. Moore, Jr.
---, July 6, 1955, obituary of Harwood Simpson
---, Mar. 26, 1956, obituary of Laura Heflin
---, May 12, 1956, obituary of Ada B. Jett
---, May 23, 1959, obituary of Ashton A. Armstrong
---, Aug. 20, 1965, obituary of Wilbur C. Heflin
---, Nov. 29, 1966, obituary of Mercer R. Gooch

Hodge, Robert A., ed. *Fredericksburg Cemetery Company Interment Register, 1844-1989*. Central

Rappahannock Regional Library, Fredericksburg, VA.
Kinsey, Margaret B. *Mountjoy Omnibus*. Baltimore, MD: Gateway Press, 2001.
Krick, Robert K. *30th Virginia Infantry*. Lynchburg, VA: H. E. Howard, Inc., 1983.
Musselman, Carl P. and Mildred H. *Musselman-Powell and Bowling Families of Stafford and Spotsylvania Counties, Virginia*. Fredericksburg, VA: Bookcrafters, 1993.
Musselman, Homer. Veterans and Cemeteries of Stafford County, Virginia. Fredericksburg, VA: Bookcrafters, 1994.
National Archives Microfilm #841, Roll #135, "Postmasters of Stafford County, Virginia."
National Archives Microfilm #1126, Roll #625, "Post Offices of Stafford County, Virginia."
Rose, Christine. *Ancestors and Descendants of Rev. Robert Rose and Rev. Charles Rose of Colonial Virginia and Wester Alves, Morayshire, Scotland*. San Jose, CA, 1985.
Stafford County Deeds:
  DB 3-456—Oct. 4, 1888—deed—W. Miles Cary et al to Game Point Association
Sullivan, Audrey G. *Sebastian Groeninger: His European Ancestry and Descendants in Virginia, 1449-1969*. Self-published, Florida, 1970.
Virginia Herald, Aug. 23, 1815, co-partnership of Philip Alexander and Thomas Seddon

Contributors:
Mrs. Elizabeth Powers Armitage
William I. Bell
George L. Gordon
Marshall Heflin
Morgan Heflin
Dr. Stewart Jones
Mary Cary Kendall
Mrs. Myrtle MacGregor
Alaric R. MacGregor
Debra Miller
N. Richard Mountjoy
Mr. and Mrs. John Scott
Jane Cloe Sthreshley
Jim Tackitt

Chapter Five

Business Licenses

Ferries

1664—John Williams

1665—Col. Henry Meese[1267]   Mr. Fossaker[1268]
John Williams

1666—Col. Henry Meese   Mr. Fossaker
John Williams

1692—Capt. John Withers[1269] (1634-1699)

Retail Licenses[1270]

1790—Daniel Payne (1728-1796)   Lawson & Dunbar
Davenport & Triplett[1271]   Short & Richards
William Scandrett Stone[1272] (1764-1827)   Zachariah Vowles (died 1825)
David Allason[1273] (1736-after 1815)
Samuel (1759-1843) and Basil Gordon[1274] (1768-1847)

[1267] Col. Meese was granted a license to keep the ferry over Potomac Creek.

[1268] Probably Richard Fossaker (died 1676). He was licensed to keep the ferry over Aquia Creek (location unknown).

[1269] Capt. Withers was licensed "to keep the Ferry over Potomack Creek for the ensueing year for the sum of four thousand pounds of tobacco." Withers was unable to keep the ferry and John Waugh assumed the responsibility. It is unclear if this was the Rev. John Waugh or his son, John (1661-1716).

[1270] These licenses were granted annually by the county court in exchange for a fee.

[1271] A notation in the court records of June 14, 1790 states that an apprentice was to be bound to this company to learn nail making. This business was located in Falmouth. One of the partners may have been Burket Davenport (1730-1817).

[1272] William was the son of George Stone (1741-1771) and Mary Scandrett of Maryland. In 1787 he married Mildred "Milly" Richards, the daughter of John Richards (1734-1785) and Susannah Coleman (died 1778) of Ingleside in Falmouth. From 1800-1803 William owned the Mary Washington house on Charles Street in Fredericksburg. He was mayor of that town in 1801 and a member of the local Masonic Lodge. He was also a vestryman of St. George's Episcopal Church and lived in the Barton House, presently the site of the old Princess Anne Hotel.

[1273] The Allasons were Scots merchants. John Allason, formerly a resident of Glasgow, settled in Virginia before 1748. His son William (1712-1768) arrived with his father, kept a store in Falmouth, and died in Port Royal.

[1274] Samuel and Basil were sons of Samuel Gordon of Lochdougan, Scotland. They immigrated to Virginia in 1784 and maintained extensive mercantile stores in Falmouth. Samuel lived at Gordon Green Terrace on the south side of the Noble automobile dealership and Basil lived below him near the docks. In 1798 Samuel married Susannah Fitzhugh Knox (1775-1869). Basil married Anna Campbell Knox.

A newspaper article described the Scottish immigrant, "Basil Gordon, whose powdered hair, gold spectacles and scrupulously neat black suit is still remembered by the old residents…Mr. Gordon was a Scotchman, and settled in Falmouth more than half a century ago. By sterling integrity and extensive commercial transactions he accumulated and bequeathed to his heirs over two million dollars" (*Fredericksburg News*, Oct. 5, 1874).

1798—Alexander Morson
    Samuel & Basil Gordon
    John Adams
    David Allason
    William Oder
    George Richardson
    Seth Botts Wiggenton
    Dunbar & Vass
    Archibald McColley[1275]
    William P. Bayly[1276] & Co.
    John Browne

1799—William P. Bayley & Co.
    George Richardson
    Seth B. Wiggenton
    John Adams
    Dunbar & Vass & Co.
    William Edwards
    Alexander Morson
    Samuel & Basil Gordon
    Archibald McColley
    Daniel Morgan & Brothers[1277]

1800—William P. Bayley[1278]
    Lewis Edwards
    Morson & Roberts
    Seth B. Wiggington
    Samuel & Basil Gordon
    Daniel Morgan & Brothers
    David Allason
    William Edwards
    Elijah Nichols
    [Robert] Dunbar[1279] & Vass
    Archibald McColley
    John Adams
    Alexander Morson & Roberts

1801—Dunbar & Vass
    Archibald McColley
    Daniel Morgan
    John Adams
    Samuel & Basil Gordon
    Morson & Roberts

1802—Thomas B. Adams
    Joseph Davis
    Read & Enoch Browne
    Henry Woodrow
    John Browne
    Eli Nichols
    Moncure & Eustace

1803—Benjamin Weeks[1280] (died c.1824)
    Hazelwood Farish[1281] (born 1771)
    James Vass[1282] (c.1769-1837)
    John Slaughter
    Samuel Gordon
    Robert Dunbar

[1275] Possibly Archibald McCall (1734-1814), the son of Samuel McCall and Margaret Adams. Archibald, a Scots merchant, was a resident of Glasgow before coming to Tappahannock, Virginia in 1752. He married Catherine Flood and was a Loyalist. Several Essex County merchants owned lots in the town of Falmouth.

[1276] William Pierce Bayley (born 1773) was a merchant who, with partner Pierce Bayly, kept a store in Alexandria. They dissolved their partnership in 1800 and William formed a partnership with John Bayly and operated a store at Aquia (*Columbian Mirror and Alexandria Gazette*, Apr. 1, 1800).

[1277] A notation at the end of the 1799 personal property tax rolls stated, "Daniel Morgan & Brothers commenced business in September last year at which time he paid the Sheriff of Stafford for a retail license."

[1278] William was a veteran of the War of 1812. He married Mary L. Grymes and lived at Auburn on Aquia Run. William was a merchant in the town of Aquia.

[1279] Robert married Elizabeth Gregory Thornton (c.1767-1851), the daughter of Francis Thornton (died 1794) and Ann Thompson of Fall Hill. Robert was a Scots merchant who settled in Falmouth, made a great fortune, and then lost it.

[1280] Benjamin operated a dry goods store and grocery in Falmouth. He married Agnes Holliday.

[1281] Hazelwood was the son of Robert Farish (1735-c.1783) of Caroline County. He also kept a mercantile business in Fredericksburg.

[1282] James was a Scottish immigrant and former resident of Forres, Morayshire. He settled in Virginia c.1798 and married first Susanna Brooke. His second wife was Elizabeth B. Maury. James kept a store in Falmouth in which he sold groceries such as pineapples, cheese, kegs of herrings from Glasgow, and various types of teas. The newspapers contain several advertisements for his specialty wines and spirits.

David Allason
Eustace & Moncure & Co.
William Edwards

Eli Nichols
Henry Woodrow & Co.
Basil Gordon

1804—John Slaughter
Benjamin Weeks
Hazelwood Farish
Basil Gordon
Daniel Morgan
Eustace & Moncure & Co.
George Burroughs
William Edwards

Samuel Gordon
Thomas Seddon (1779-1831)
James Vass
Robert Dunbar
David Allason
Henry Woodrow
Eli Nichols
McRea & McMasters[1283]

1805—Matthew Norman (c.1779-1814)
George Burroughs
Samuel & Basil Gordon
Robert Dunbar
Thomas Seddon
John H. Suttle

Eustace & Moncure
Henry Woodrow
James Vass
George C. Ferguson[1284]
Benjamin Weekes

1806—Basil Gordon
William Richards[1285] (1765-after 1803)
Robert Dunbar
James Vass
Matthew Norman
George Burroughs
Eli Nichols

Samuel Gordon
Benjamin Weeks
Thomas Seddon
George C. Ferguson
Eustace & Moncure
Robert Swan (Richland Mill)
Andrew Leitch[1286]

1807—Robert Dunbar
Basil Gordon
Thomas W. Cowne
James Vass
George C. Ferguson
Brent & Cooke
Carter & Smith
Eustace & Moncure
John H. Suttle

Samuel Gordon
Benjamin Weeks
Spilman & Briggs
Murray Forbes
Thomas Seddon
Norman & Waller
Morton & Horton
George & Thomas Burroughs (died c.1815)

1808—Basil Gordon
Samuel Gordon
William Richards
George C. Ferguson

Robert Dunbar
Thomas Seddon & Company
James Vass
Benjamin Weeks

He also sold liver oil (by the barrel), spermaceti oil, plows, guns, tools, glass, rugs, kaleidoscopes, gunpowder, and linseed oil (*Virginia Herald* Mar. 20, 1816, Aug. 5, 1818). James also kept a store in Fredericksburg at what is now 309 William Street.

[1283] This business was operated by Robert McRea and Thomas McMasters.

[1284] George was the son of Samuel Ferguson and was a veteran of the War of 1812. He may be the same George C. Ferguson whose will was recorded in Augusta County, Virginia in October 1827. He was a resident of Petersburg when he sighed his will in 1819. This document mentioned his brother Samuel, nieces Louisa Ann and Caroline Mitchell Ferguson, and nephews Samuel Allen Ferguson and George Spottswood Ferguson.

[1285] William was the son of John Richards (1734-1785) and Susannah Coleman (died 1778) of Ingleside in Falmouth. He married Ann, the daughter of John and Ann Blackwell.

[1286] Andrew was the first pastor of White Oak Baptist Church when it was constituted in 1789.

1809—Thomas Burroughs[1287] (died c.1815)   John A. Ratliff
    Ficklen & Waller   Matthew Norman
    Norman & Waller   Brent & Cooke
    George Burroughs   John H. Suttle
    John Gray (1769-1848)   William Brent (1783-1848)
    William (1740-1817) & Withers Waller (c.1784-1827)

1810—Hansbrough & McInteer   John A. Ratliff
    Matthew Norman   William & Withers Waller
    Alexander Brawner   Robert Swan (at Forge Mills)
    Liggate & Mathews[1288]   Benjamin Weeks
    Samuel Gordon   Basil Gordon
    James Vass   George C. Ferguson
    Murray Forbes   Thomas Seddon
    Robert Dunbar   Thomas Briggs[1289]
    William Stringfellow (died 1831)   Ficklen & Waller
    Thomas Burroughs   William H. P. Tuckfield(?) & Co.

1811—Basil Gordon   Samuel Gordon
    Benjamin Weekes   James Vass
    Murray Forbes   Thomas Seddon
    Robert Dunbar   George F. Vowles & Brooke & Co.
    James Gallagher[1290] & Co.   Robert Swan
    Liggate & Mathews

1812—Aaron Holloway[1291] (died before 1820) Matthew Norman
    Bernard Harding   James Waller & Brothers

1813—Basil Gordon   Samuel Gordon
    James Vass   Murray Forbes
    Thomas Seddon   Elliott Fishback[1292] (1785-1814)
    William Brooke   Alexander Liggate
    William C. Beale   George F. Vowles
    Robert Swan   Bernard Harding
    Aaron Holloway   Matthew Norman
    James Waller & Brothers

1814—Charles & John Tackett   Matthew Norman
    James Waller & Brothers

[1287] In 1814 Thomas served in the militia as a substitute for the son of Thomas Larkin. He served under Capt. Alexander Howison.

[1288] This partnership operated in Falmouth.

[1289] Thomas operated a store in Falmouth in the building formerly occupied by Robert Dunbar. In 1809 he married Lucinda Short in Falmouth.

[1290] James had a store in Falmouth, but by 1813 was a merchant in Fredericksburg where he sold dry goods, hardware, and groceries (*Virginia Herald*, Sept. 30, 1815). In 1816 he married Frances Brundige, the daughter of Timothy Brundige of Dumfries, Virginia (*Virginia Herald*, June 22, 1816).

[1291] Aaron was the son of Asa Holloway (born 1744) and Abigail Wright. The Holloways were Quakers who had come to the Falmouth area during the mid-18th century to work at Hunter's Works, an iron furnace and manufacturing center built on the Rappahannock River about a mile above Falmouth.

[1292] Elliott was the son of Martin Fishback (born 1763) of Culpeper County and Lucy Amis. He kept a grocery store in Falmouth in which he sold items sugar as brown sugar, tea, herrings, fish oil, and dry goods (*Virginia Herald*, June 6, 1812). In 1813 Elliott served as a director of the Farmers Bank in Fredericksburg (*Virginia Herald*, Jan. 13, 1813).

1815—William Brooke, Jr.[1293]
    Murray Forbes
    Samuel Gordon
    Thomas Cropper Scott (1791-1857)
    James Vass
    William C. Beale
    Basil Gordon
    George M. Parsons[1294] & Company
    Thomas Seddon
    Hume V. Ross

1816—Cooke & Eustace
    Thomas Norman (c.1790-1846)
    Robert Horne
    Charles and John Tackett
    Withers and James Waller

Most of the men who were granted business licenses kept stores in Falmouth. A newspaper article in 1874 named "merchant princes [who] did business and resided within [Falmouth's] limits…Included were Basil Gordon, Joseph B. Ficklen (1800-1874), Duff Green (1792-1854), Murray Forbes (1782-1863), William C. Beale (died 1850), William Brooke, Thomas C. Scott (c.1789-1857), John M. O'Bannon (1800-1870), James Coon (c.1795-after 1860), George Latham (c.1780-c.1846), Mark Harding[1295] (c.1788-1873), and a host of 'small fry'" (*Fredericksburg News*, Oct. 5, 1874).

1817—Whitfield Brooke[1296]
    Jameson Corbin[1297] (born c.1790)
    Basil Gordon
    Robert Horne
    Thomas C. Scott
    Thomas Tutt[1298]
    George Frazier Vowles[1299]
    Tackett & Barber
    William Ford (1788-1834)
    William C. Beale
    Murray Forbes
    Samuel Gordon
    William Phillips
    Seddon & Alexander
    James Vass
    Cooke & Eustace
    Withers & James Waller

1818—William Ford
    John Starke
    Samuel Gordon
    William Phillips
    Jameson Corbin
    Robert Thomas
    James Vass
    George F. Vowles
    Duff Green (1792-1854)
    William Barber
    Withers & James Waller
    Basil Gordon
    William C. Beale
    Thomas Tutt
    Thomas Seddon
    Murray Forbes
    Thomas C. Scott

[1293] William kept a store in Falmouth in which he sold dry goods, groceries, hardware, cutlery, saddlery, etc. (*Virginia Herald*, July 8, 1815).

[1294] George Parsons kept one of the taverns in Falmouth. In 1815 he rented a house in Falmouth from Robert Dunbar. This building had previously been occupied by David Briggs as a law office (Dunbar).

[1295] Mark was the son of Mark Harding, Sr. and Nancy Young. He operated a grist mill at Loch Lomond on Potomac Run.

[1296] Whitfield kept a store in Falmouth in which he sold dry goods, hardware, and groceries (*Virginia Herald*, Apr. 13, 1816).

[1297] In 1817 Jameson opened a grocery and dry goods store in Falmouth. He sold items such as sugar, coffee, chocolate, gun powder, whiskey, rum, brandy, molasses, spices, soap and candles, papers, salt, leather, etc. (*Virginia Herald*, Mar. 12, 1817).

[1298] In 1816 Thomas married Margaret W. Garnett in Fredericksburg.

[1299] George was the son of Zachariah Vowles (died 1825) and Mary Frazier, the only child of George Frazier (died c.1765) of Fredericksburg.

1819—William Thomas
    William Ford
    James Heflin
    Withers & James Waller
    Robert Croughton[1303] (1791-1872)
    William Phillips
    James Vass
    George F. Vowles
    Murray Forbes
    Thomas C. Scott
    Samuel Gordon
    Senate Tackett (1770:80-1836)
    Valentine Potes[1300]
    Robert Taylor[1301]
    George Brent[1302]
    John Ryan[1304]
    William C. Beale
    Basil Gordon
    Duff Green
    Thomas Tutt
    Thomas Seddon
    Benjamin Corbin[1305] (born 1750)

1820—William Thomas
    William Barton Stone (died 1845)
    George M. Parsons
    James Vass
    William C. Beale
    George F. Vowles
    Lucy Stark
    William Ford
    Withers & James Waller
    Jameson Corbin
    Robert Croughton
    Benjamin R. H__zard
    Duff Green
    John Ellison

1821—John Good
    Withers Waller & Company
    William Ford
    John Potes
    Thomas C. Scott
    James Vass
    Basil Gordon
    George F. Vowles
    Rolly Latham[1306] (c.1795-1868)
    Duff Green
    Lucy Starke
    John Ellison
    William B. Stone
    William Thomas
    John Kenaday
    William Brooke
    Nathaniel Greaves (c.1769-after 1861)
    William C. Beale
    Thomas Seddon
    Murray Forbes
    John Oryan
    Jameson Corbin
    Samuel Gordon

1822—William B. Stone
    Withers & James Waller
    Elias Barber
    Nathaniel Greaves
    Samuel Gordon
    William Thomas
    William Ford
    John M. Barber
    Basil Gordon
    Jameson Corbin

[1300] The Potes family was not native to Stafford County. The 1782 King George land tax records list them with land in that county.

[1301] Probably Robert Taylor (1758-1851), the son of John Taylor (born 1725). Robert was born in Stafford.

[1302] In 1818 George Brent married Harriet Slater in Fredericksburg.

[1303] Robert was the son of Charles Croughton (c.1761-1819) and Elizabeth Hudson (died c.1791). Charles was probably born in England where his family was involved in the shipping and mercantile business. For several years Robert kept a grocery and dry goods store in Falmouth. He married his mother's first cousin, Thomas Reveley's widow, Elizabeth Stubberfield (died 1872) of Spotsylvania County. Around 1835 the couple moved to La Grange, Missouri and many of his descendants ended up in California.

[1304] John's last name appears in the records in several different forms, including Ryan, O'Ryan, Orion, etc. He was from Fauquier County. In 1822 John rented the corn mill in Falmouth where he also ground plaster, or lime, for agricultural use (*Virginia Herald*, Oct. 26, 1822).

[1305] Benjamin was the son of William Corbin (1720-1796) and Sarah Fant. In 1786 he married Nancy Ann Corbin (born 1767), the daughter of John Corbin and Frances Fant.

[1306] Raleigh Latham was the son of John Latham (c.1730-1834) and never married. He lived at Spotted Tavern.

        Murray Forbes
        James Vass
        William Brooke
        Thomas C. Scott
        Duff Green
        James Templeman

   William C. Beale
   John Oryan
   Lucy Stark
   Seddon & Alexander
   John Ellison

1823—William B. Stone
        William Thomas
        Elias Barber
        Newman Basil Starke (1799-1860)
        Basil Gordon
        William C. Beale
        Thomas Seddon
        Duff Green
        Murray Forbes

   Withers & James Waller
   William Ford
   James Bell
   Nathaniel Greaves
   Samuel Gordon
   James Vass
   William Brooke
   Thomas C. Scott
   Jameson Corbin

1825—John Kirk
        Nathaniel Greaves
        Benjamin Hall
        Jameson Corbin
        James Vass
        Philip Alexander
        Charles Tackett (c.1780-1834)
        William Thomas
        John H. Smoot

   Bales D. Johnston
   William & Samuel Gordon
   Basil Gordon
   Brooke & Ficklen
   Murray Forbes
   Duff Green
   William B. Stone
   Loyal Carter (died c.1847)

1826—Jameson Corbin
        Murray Forbes
        Nathaniel Greaves
        Basil Gordon
        James Vass
        John O'Ryan

   Brooke & Ficklen
   William C. Beale
   Duff Green
   Samuel Gordon, Jr.[1307] (1804-1890)
   Benjamin Hall

1827—Richard Stone (died before 1857)
        Enoch Harding (died c.1848)
        James Garrison
        Jameson Corbin
        John H. S. Potts
        Thomas C. Scott
        Brooke & Ficklen
        Benjamin Hall
        William C. Beale

   William Ford
   William B. Stone
   Loyal Carter
   William P. Cunningham[1308] (c.1795-after 1860)
   John Oryan
   Nathaniel Greaves
   Basil Gordon
   James Vass
   John Irwin

1828—William Ford
        John H. S. Potts
        William P. Cunningham
        John O'Ryan
        Nathaniel Greaves
        Jackson Rowles[1309] (c.1800-1882)

   Enoch Harding
   Jameson Corbin
   Thomas C. Scott
   Garnett Corbin
   John Irwin
   Edward Waller (1805-1883)

[1307] Samuel married Patsy Fitzhugh, the daughter of Battaile Fitzhugh of Santee, Caroline County.

[1308] William was a merchant and tailor. He kept a grocery and dry goods store adjoining his tailor shop in Falmouth. In his store he sold fabrics such as cashmere, flannel, silk, and cottons as well as domestic goods, hardware, hats, shores, etc. (*Virginia Herald*, July 13, 1825, Sept. 20, 1826). William married Elvira Norwood.

Murray Forbes
James Vass
Basil Gordon
Benjamin H. Hall
Robert Bronaugh
William Campbell

Duff Green
William C. Beale
Brooke & Ficklen
James Cave
William B. Stone

1829—John O'Ryan
Jameson Corbin
William P. Cunningham
Garnett Corbin
William C. Beale
William B. Billingsley[1310]
Benjamin Hall, Jr.
John M. O'Bannon
John Irwin
Richard & Thomas Stone
Strother Ficklen (died 1844)

Benjamin Hall
Thomas C. Scott
John H. S. Potts
Basil Gordon
Duff Green
Murray Forbes
James Cave
Mary Ellison
Richard Stone
Edward Waller
Edward Burrage[1311]

1833—Robert Garrison
Joseph D. Withers[1312] (born 1803)
Francis Cox
Joseph B. Ficklen
John F. Cox
Jameson Corbin
James Coones (c.1795-after 1860)
John M. O'Bannon
William P. Bowen & Company
Basil Gordon
William B. & Thomas Stone[1314]
Jeremiah Carter[1315] (c.1810-186_)
Charles Tackett

Thomas T. O'Dell
Duff Green
William C. Beale
John H. S. Potts
Hays & Baily
James Cave[1313]
Murray Forbes
Thomas C. Scott
John O'Rion
William Brooke, Jr.
John C. Crowley
Albion Robertson[1316]
Benjamin P. Tolson[1317] (c.1800-c.1879)

1834—William Brooke, Jr.
Duff Green
John M. O'Bannon
James Coones
John H. S. Potts
George Latham
Basil Gordon
Thomas C. Scott
James Cave

Joseph B. Ficklen
William C. Beale
William P. Bowen
Alfred C. Hays (born c.1795)
Murray Forbes
William Anderson
John F. Cox
Jameson Corbin
Carter & Smith[1318]

[1309] Jackson Rowles (or Roles) was the son of Jesse and Rosanna Roles. He never married and died in Stafford.

[1310] From 1823-1827 William was hired by Robert Dunbar of Falmouth to be toll collector on Dunbar's bridge over the Rappahannock. For this Billingsley was paid $200 per year and was provided with a house (Dunbar).

[1311] Edward owned and operated a tavern in the vicinity of Mountain View Fire Department.

[1312] Joseph's store was located in the "Woodcutting" in the central part of the county.

[1313] James kept a store "near Hartwood."

[1314] William and Thomas kept a store in the village of Woodstock.

[1315] Jeremiah's store was located at Stafford Courthouse.

[1316] Albion kept a store at Stafford Courthouse.

[1317] Benjamin's store was located "near Stafford Springs."

[1318] This store was located at Stafford Courthouse.

Friend Kellogg[1319] (1797-1839)
William B. & Thomas Stone
Joseph D. Withers
Joseph W. Honey[1323] (1810-1879)

Robertson & Suttle[1320]
Peyton & Hore[1321]
Robert Garrison[1322]

1835—Basil Gordon
    James Coones
    Alfred C. Hays
    Joseph B. Ficklen
    Duff Green
    Murray Forbes
    Jameson Corbin
    John M. O'Bannon
    John Millington[1324]
    Conway & Daniel[1326]
    James Cave

    William C. Beale
    Benjamin Hall, Jr.
    William Brooke, Jr.
    Scott & Baily
    Joseph W. Honey
    Edward & George Latham
    John H. S. Potts
    Friend Kellogg
    Sidney Stephens[1325]
    Hore & Peyton[1327]
    Jeremiah Carter[1328]

1836—William C. Beale
    John M. O'Bannon
    James Coones
    Duff Green
    Benjamin Hall, Jr.
    John Gollahorn[1329] (c.1795-after 1850)
    John H. S. Potts
    Sanford Cooper[1330]
    Hore & Peyton[1332]
    Daniel S. Coakley[1334] (c.1805-c.1866)
    James Cave
    Thomas Smith[1336] (born c.1814)

    Joseph B. Ficklen
    Basil Gordon
    Garrard Fugitt (c.1806-1841)
    William Brooke, Jr.
    Murray Forbes
    Scott & Baily
    Edward & George Latham
    John H. Suttle[1331] (c.1807-c.1885)
    Thomas H. Cushing Daniel[1333] (c.1811-1896)
    Friend Kellogg
    Zachariah Bradshaw[1335] (c.1785-before 1850)

[1319] Friend was the son of Ezekiel Kellogg (died 1828) and Luna Clark (born 1778) of Heartland, Connecticut. He was the brother of Lyman Kellogg who lived near modern Abel Reservoir on Potomac Run. Friend never married and died in Fauquier County. According to the notation in the tax records, Friend's store was located at "Stafford Springs."

[1320] This store was located in the village of Woodstock.

[1321] These men had stores at two locations—Tackett's Mill and Garrisonville.

[1322] Robert kept his store in Garrisonville very near the present post office.

[1323] Joseph Honey's store was located in Falmouth.

[1324] John's store was located at the Rappahannock Gold Mine near modern Richlands Baptist Church.

[1325] Sidney's store was located in Hartwood.

[1326] This store was located at Stafford Courthouse.

[1327] In 1835 these men kept two stores at Woodstock and Tackett's Mill.

[1328] Jeremiah's store was now located in Woodstock.

[1329] John married Penelope Ball (c.1789-1872), the daughter of William and Bettie Ball of Stafford.

[1330] Sanford's store was in Woodstock.

[1331] John's primary business was in Alexandria. He also kept a store in Woodstock.

[1332] In 1836 Hore & Peyton kept stores in Woodstock and at Tolson's Mill.

[1333] Thomas kept his store at Stafford Courthouse.

[1334] A notation in the tax records states that Daniel's store was located at or near "Jones' Shop."

[1335] This store was located at Hartwood.

[1336] Thomas' store was at the Rappahannock Gold Mine.

1837—Robert Rodgers[1337]
    Thornton Patton [1339] (1793-1869)
    Basil Gordon
    William Brooke, Jr.
    Garrard Fugitt
    Murray Forbes
    Edward & George Latham
    John M. O'Bannon
    Joseph W. Honey
    E. A. Janney
    Gilson Mauzy
    Thornton Patton
    Hore & Peyton
    Daniel S. Coakley
    Daniel Bradford[1338] (born 1815)
    Robert Garrison
    Joseph B. Ficklen
    Benjamin Hall, Jr.
    William C. Beale
    John H. S. Potts
    George Pickett's[1340] agent
    Duff Green
    Thomas C. Scott
    John H. Suttle
    Thomas Smith
    William & Benjamin Ashby
    Thomas H. C. Daniel

1838—William C. Beale
    Josiah F. Bayly
    Daniel S. Coakley
    Murray Forbes
    Robert Garrison
    Duff Green
    Joseph W. Honey
    Benjamin Hall, Jr.
    George H. Leitch
    Alexander H. Mason & Company
    John M. O'Bannon
    William W. Peyton & Company
    John H. Suttle
    Thomas Smith
    John C. Tolson
    William Brooke, Jr.
    James Coones
    Joseph B. Ficklen
    Garrard Fugitt
    Basil Gordon
    William Guy (born c.1814)
    Strother Harding
    James W. Johnson & Co.
    Charles Lawson
    George Pickett's agent
    Thomas J. Payne (c.1796-after 1850)
    Thornton Patton
    Thomas Stone
    Thomas C. Scott

1839—John H. S. Potts
    William C. Beale
    James Coones
    Joseph B. Ficklen
    Garrard Fugitt
    Basil Gordon
    Strother Harding
    James W. Johnson[1344]
    John M. O'Bannon
    Thomas J. Payne[1346]
    Thomas A. Withers[1341] (c.1814-c.1865)
    William Edwards[1342]
    Daniel S. Coakley[1343]
    Murray Forbes
    Robert Garrison
    Duff Green
    Benjamin Hall, Jr.
    George H. Leitch
    George Pickett's agent[1345]
    Thomas C. Scott

[1337] Robert kept a store in Hartwood.

[1338] Daniel was the son of Baldwin Bradford (c.1764-1848) of Culpeper and Betsy Foley (born 1776). He was born in Fredericksburg and kept a store in Falmouth. In 1837 Daniel married Mary E. Morriss in Fredericksburg.

[1339] Thornton was the son of George Patton (1757-1813) and Sarah Stringfellow (1766-1848) of Stafford. His store was located at Tackett's Mill.

[1340] George Pickett (c.1790-after 1850) was the son of Martin Pickett (died c.1804) of Fauquier County. By 1841 he operated a store in Fredericksburg.

[1341] Thomas' store was located "near Poplar Road."

[1342] William's store was located in Falmouth.

[1343] In 1839 Daniel's store was described as being near Potomac Run.

[1344] James kept a store in the village of Woodstock.

[1345] George's business was in Falmouth.

[1346] The 1839 tax records note that Thomas' store was located "near Falmouth."

James S. Petty[1347] (c.1806-1885)
Richard Burton[1349] (c.1821-c.1851)

Jefferson Spindle[1348] (c.1804-1861)

1840—Murray Forbes
John M. O'Bannon
Joseph B. Ficklen
Basil Gordon
Andrew B. Lunsford[1352] (born c.1822)
James W. Johnson
Thomas C. Scott
Benjamin Hall, Jr.
Thomas A. Withers
Peter Wiggenton[1356] (c.1813-1866)
Daniel S. Coakley[1358]
Jefferson Spindle
Richard Burton
Messrs. Bridwell & Whorton

James Coones
William C. Beale
William E. Brummet[1350] (born c.1809)
George Latham[1351]
Timothy Bridwell[1353] (c.1798-after 1860)
Messrs. Green & Lane[1354]
Strother Harding[1355]
Thomas B. Pickett & Company
Robert Garrison
Messrs. Stone & Petty[1357]
Thomas J. Payne[1359]
George H. Leitch
Elizabeth J. Grinnan[1360]

1841—Joseph W. Honey
Thomas T. Arrington[1362] & Son
George Latham
Arthur Fielding Clift (c.1815-1888)
Garrison & Harding
Strother Harding
Wiggenton & Kendall
Joseph B. Ficklen
William C. Beale
Susan Potts (1810-1895
Thomas C. Scott
James Coones
Richard Burton
Orpha Fugate

John F. Bell[1361]
James W. Johnson
Thomas J. Payne
William Guy
Daniel S. Coakley
Charles S. Petty[1363] (c.1818-after 1870)
Benjamin Hall, Jr.
Murray Forbes
Basil Gordon
Duff Green & John Green Lane (c.1814-1884)
Jefferson Spindle
John M. O'Bannon
Absalom Smith[1364] (died before 1850)

[1347] James died in Front Royal. He was a Methodist minister and lived for many years in Warrenton and in Falmouth where he was a tailor.
[1348] During this year Jefferson kept the store at Tackett's Mill.
[1349] Richard was running a store at Horsepen Gold Mine.
[1350] William's business was located at Stafford Store.
[1351] George's store was in Falmouth.
[1352] Andrew was the son of William Lunsford (born c.1785). His store was located in Hartwood.
[1353] Timothy's store was in Woodstock.
[1354] This store was located in Falmouth.
[1355] Strother's store was in Falmouth.
[1356] In 1840 Peter kept a store at Stafford Courthouse.
[1357] A notation in the tax records states that this business was located on Potomac Run.
[1358] This year Daniel's store was noted as being at "Bradshaw's."
[1359] Thomas' store was noted as being "near Salem."
[1360] Probably Elizabeth Jane Farish, the wife of John Grinnan. She kept a shop in Falmouth.
[1361] John Fendall(?) Bell was born in Fluvanna County. Around 1830 he married Jane Adie.
[1362] Thomas T. Arrington (c.1798-after 1860).
[1363] The 1860 census lists Charles as a tailor.
[1364] In 1830 Absalom operated what became known as the Eagle Gold Mine under the firm name of the Rappahannock Gold Mining Company.

1842—Hugh M. Tennant's[1365] agent
    Thomas J. Payne
    James Coones
    Murray Forbes
    George Latham, Jr.[1366] (born c.1802)
    Basil Gordon
    Benjamin Hall
    Chapman & Tolson
    George Pickett
    Joseph W. Honey
    Richard Burton
    Absalom Smith
    Jane Dowel
    Robert Beaty[1368] (c.1818-1855)
    James Jones
    Thomas Johnson (born c.1835)
    John F. Bell
    Thomas King
    Joseph B. Ficklen
    William C. Beale
    Green & Lane
    Thompson J. Sullivant
    Strother Harding
    Moore & Alexander
    Woffendal Kendall[1367] (born c.1811)
    John M. O'Bannon
    Daniel S. Coakley
    Jefferson Spindle
    James Taliaferro

1850—Thomas J. Payne
    Edward Templeman (born c.1821)
    Elias A. W. Hore
    William S. Chapman (born c.1822)
    James H. Cloe (born c.1823)
    Joseph W. Honey
    Thompson J. Sullivan
    Andrew J. Wickliff (born c.1830)
    Murray Forbes
    Harrison B. Barnes
    Alfred C. Hayes
    John M. O'Bannon
    William James Green (1825-1862)
    Daniel S. Coakley
    Lewis Smith (born c.1822)
    Robert Garrison
    Strother Harding
    Joel M. Kendall[1369] (born c.1827)
    Thomas H. Hewitt[1370] (c.1820-1872)
    John W. Rives (born c.1822)
    William W. Bowler (born c.1820)
    James B. Erwin (born c.1825)
    Frank T. Forbes[1371] (c.1825-1904)
    George B. Barnes (born c.1832)
    Richard W. Corbin (born c.1822)
    Robert Pitts (born c.1795)
    Duff Green
    Joseph B. Ficklen
    Richard Burton
    James W. Jerrol[1372] (born c.1831)

1859—Mountjoy & Herndon
    Daniel Coakley
    Joseph Roberson
    Edward Peipenbring
    George G. Lightner
    Mary E. Sullivan
    William L. Morgan & Co.
    William T. Masters (c.1823-1865)
    James W. Stone (1796-1869)
    J. B. Ficklen & Sons
    Charles A. Tackett
    Richard Burton
    Harrison J. Skinner
    Thomas H. Hewitt
    Murray Forbes
    William Guy
    Henry L. Coleman (died 1883)
    Orton & Older[1373]
    Leonard P. Alexander

[1365] Hugh Mercer Tennant (born c.1803) was a merchant and resident of Caroline County in 1850.
[1366] George was the son of George Latham (c.1780-c.1846) and inherited Spotted Tavern from his father.
[1367] The son of Barnett Kendall and Catherine Starke. In 1820 Moses Pilcher, Woffendal's step-father, was appointed his guardian. In 1782 Woffendal paid taxes on 245 acres in King George County (King George County Land Taxes).
[1368] Robert was the son of Robert and Charlotte Beaty. He was born in Stafford and died there, unmarried, at age 37.
[1369] Joel was the son of Robert Kendall (c.1787-1860).
[1370] Thomas owned several lots in Falmouth.
[1371] Frank was the son of Murray Forbes (1782-1863). In 1851 he married Ann Mercer Chew.
[1372] James was the son of James Jerrol (born c.1800).
[1373] Orton and Older were granted a license to operate a circus.

1860—Daniel S. Coakley
    Joseph B. Ficklen
    James Lane Green[1375] (1831-1902)
    Thomas H. Hewitt
    Jacob Stires (c.1831-after 1860)
    George W. Swetnam (born c.1830)
    Alexander Coones[1374] (born c.1838)
    Murray Forbes
    Dudley Herndon (1829-1909)
    James Withers Stone
    Mary Sullivan[1376]

1870—Thomas Ashby[1377] (born c.1839)
    Joseph B. Ficklen
    Silas Haislip[1379] (c.1822-1884)
    John N. Jones[1381] (born c.1821)
    William G. Nantes (born c.1840)
    Mathew N. Towson
    R. R. Bradshaw (c.1819-after 1870)
    Samuel Griffis[1378] (1814-c.1887)
    Charles S. Heflin[1380] (1829-1886)
    George G. Lightner
    Joseph F. Swetnam[1382] (born c.1838)

1880—Rawleigh L. Cooper[1383]
    Robert Flatford (c.1810-1892)
    William Herndon[1385] (1824-1904)
    George E. Monroe (c.1857-1906)
    John W. Christy[1388] (1836-1917)
    Fleet Cox[1390] (1821-1905)
    Charles Hewitt[1391] (born c.1852)
    Robert Lawrence Flatford[1384] (1852-1898)
    George Milton Weedon
    L. C. Skinner[1386] (born c.1856)
    George W. Evans[1387] (born c.1845)
    Landon S. Limbrick[1389] (c.1813-after 1880)
    Charles S. Heflin
    Fielding B. Burton[1392] (born c.1837)

[1374] Alexander was the son of James Coones (c.1795-after 1860) and Louisa Harwood (c.1806-1885).

[1375] James was the son of Duff Green (1792-1854) and Eliza Ann Payne (1806-1876). A newspaper notice regarding his political affiliations and the consequences thereof announced:

> We learn that Mr. James Lane Green, of Stafford county, who was one of Mahone's appointees as Mail Route Messenger between Fredericksburg and Baltimore via the Rappahannock river, has been removed, and it is rumored that a most excellent gentleman and staunch Democrat of this county whose name rhymes with Green, has been appointed his successor.
> (*Northern Neck News*, May 15, 1885)

[1376] The 1860 census listed Mary as a merchant and grocer.

[1377] In 1871 Thomas married Virginia G. Herndon (born c.1852). During the War Between the States, Thomas served with the 9th Virginia Cavalry.

[1378] Samuel was a grocer.

[1379] Silas was a millwright as well as a shop keeper.

[1380] Charles operated a "variety store" and sold groceries and dry goods.

[1381] John was a grocer.

[1382] John was a grocer.

[1383] Rawleigh was a dry goods merchant.

[1384] Robert Lawrence Flatford was the son of Robert Flatford (born c.1810), both of whom were dry goods merchants.

[1385] William sold dry goods and groceries.

[1386] Sold dry goods and groceries.

[1387] George was the son of T. J. and A. W. Evans. In 1874 he married R. P. Lunsford (born c.1853). George was born in Pennsylvania.

[1388] John was the son of John C. Christy and Elizabeth Gray Dudley (c.1798-after 1850). During the War Between the States, John enlisted in the 47th Virginia Infantry. He deserted from Richmond in June 1862, took the oath, and remained in Washington for some time before returning to Stafford. In 1882 he married Lucy V. Jones (born c.1833). John was a retail grocer and a cooper.

[1389] Landon was a grocer.

[1390] Fleet was a grocer. He was also a cooper.

Lemuel S. Limerick[1393] (c.1846-1904) William G. Nantes
George B. Griffis[1394] (born 1854) George Black (c.1800-after 1870)
Humphrey George[1395] (c.1816-after 1880) Benjamin Ashley Bell[1396] (1840-1905)
John Marshall Green[1397] (1849-1926) James Morton, Jr.[1398] (1851-1902)
James Edward Woody[1399] (c.1856-1928) Edward Waller[1400] (1849-1919)

1884—Hugh Adie & Company[1401]

1904—Jackson P. Garrison[1402]   Wallace & Moncure[1403]

1906—Charles Frank Towson[1404] (c.1852-1908)

1917—Mrs. Elijah C. Abel[1405]   George Lee Armstrong[1406] (1863-1952)
Jackson P. Garrison   Robert D. Fritter[1407]
Thomas Frank Boswell[1408] (died c.1933) Turner R. Garrison[1409] (1872-1919)
Eva E. Bell[1410] (1868-1948)   Sallie W. Gray[1411] (died c.1933)

[1391] Charles was the son of Thomas H. (c.1820-1872) and Jane E. Hewitt (born c.1824). In 1888 he married Evy L. Roberson (born c.1868).

[1392] Fielding sold groceries.

[1393] Lemuel was the son of Robert E. (born c.1825) and Elizabeth Limerick (born c.1815). In 1868 he married Ella Reeves (born 1857), the daughter of John H. and Jane Reeves. Lemuel sold groceries.

[1394] George was the son of Samuel H. Griffis (1814-c.1887).

[1395] Humphrey was born in England.

[1396] Benjamin sold groceries.

[1397] John was born near Stafford Courthouse, the son of John (born c.1821) and Mary A. Green (born c.1826). In 1920 he retired from the Bureau of Pensions in Washington where he worked for 38 years. John was a Mason, Past Noble Grand Master of the Independent Order of Odd Fellows, and a member of the Sons of the American Revolution. In 1874 he married Susan D. Crismond (born c.1842). He married secondly Inez MacGregor (1867-1941), both of whom are buried at Concord on Aquia Creek (*Free Lance*, Apr. 1, 1926).

[1398] James was a grocer.

[1399] James was a grocer and also kept a store in Fredericksburg (*Free Lance Star*, Dec. 20, 1928).

[1400] Edward was the son of Edward Waller (1805-1883) and operated a quarry on Aquia Creek.

[1401] Hugh paid the $5 fee "for the privilege of selling by retail Tobacco, Snuff and Cigars in his Store House at Coal Landing" (Moncure).

[1402] Granted a license to sell general merchandise in Garrisonville. As of 1917, Jackson had been in business for 20 years.

[1403] Granted a license to sell salt pickles in Falmouth. Their pickle factory was in Brooke, very near the present railroad station.

[1404] C. F. Towson was the son of James Edward Towson (1808-1888) and Agnes Ann Suttle (c.1811-1865). He sold dry goods, notions, and groceries in Falmouth. Charles married Lucy Randolph Nelson (1852-1937), the daughter of Dr. William Armistead Nelson (1817-1902) and Mary Robinson Moncure (1819-1883). He was a member of Falmouth Baptist Church.

[1405] Mrs. Abel's store was in Onville. She was Rosa H. Embrey (born c.1877), the daughter of Joseph C. W. and Miranda Embrey.

[1406] George was the son of George Henry Armstrong (1830-1863) and Elvira Fant Fritter (1834-after 1900). By occupation, George was a farmer and sawyer, but also operated a store. His first wife was Susan R. English (born c.1863). He married secondly Fannie L. Skidmore (1879-1967).

[1407] Robert's store was in Garrisonville. As of 1917 he had been in business for 44 years.

[1408] Kept a store at Williamsville, very near Dipple on Chappawamsic Creek and the Potomac River, probably at the fishery there. As of 1917 he had been in business for five years.

[1409] Turner's store was in Garrisonville. As of 1917 he had been in business for 20 years. He died of typhoid fever (*Free Lance*, Oct. 15, 1919).

[1410] As of 1917 Eva had operated a store at Oak Hill for three years.

[1411] As of 1917 S. W. Gray had operated a store in Stafford for 25 years.

Willie Bowin
Charles W. Bridwell[1413]
William Black[1415] (c.1848-1918)
John Hogan Benton[1417] (1882-1943)
Battle G. Bloxton[1419] (1874-1961)
W. Arthur Botts Brothers[1421]
Ashton C. Carter[1423] (died c.1934)
Margaret W. Cooper
Mrs. W. S. Castle[1426]
Thaddeus E. Courtney[1428] (1884-1960)
James Monroe Decatur[1430] (1866-1944)
Joseph Davis[1432] (1860-1932)
William Decatur[1434]
John Norton Dishman[1436] (1863-1951)

Milton H. Homes[1412] (1871-1947)
George W. Herring[1414]
Wesley Knight[1416] (1846-1937)
Elijah Alexander Groves[1418] (1853-1931)
John H. Leiber[1420] (born c.1858)
Massie & Winkler[1422]
Fannie Musselman[1424]
Nello Green Musselman[1425] (1892-1948)
Rubin E. Mountjoy[1427]
James Mountjoy & Brother[1429]
Ellis M. McClees[1431]
Wade Hampton Moore[1433] (1878-1952)
Thomas Porter[1435] (died c.1926)
Richard W. Powers

[1412] As of 1917 Milton had operated a store in Toluca for 11 years. He was the son of Thomas (c.1821-1886) and Martha E. Homes (1831-1908). In 1897 Milton married Agnes E. Shackelford (1877-1956), the daughter of Strother A. Shackelford (1840-1925) and Jane Eliza Mahoney (c.1843-1894).

[1413] As of 1917 Charles had operated a store at Shiloh (now part of Quantico) for five years.

[1414] As of 1917 George had been in business in Wide Water for 21 years.

[1415] As of 1917 William Black had operated a store at Crest (Mountain View) for 20 years.

[1416] As of 1917 Wesley had been in business at Coal Landing for 25 years.

[1417] John was born in Washington, DC and was the son of R. N. and Lillie Ida Benton. He was a sawyer by trade, but also operated a garage and service station at Crane's Corner (*Free Lance Star*, Mar. 3, 1943). He married Fannie D. Guy (1888-1951), the daughter of Robert E. Guy (1855-1905) and Susan Ellen Wine.

[1418] As of 1917 Elijah had operated a store at Brooke for 29 years.

[1419] As of 1917 Battle had kept a store at Mountain View for five years.

[1420] John kept a store at Dodson's Corner in what is now part of Quantico. He was the son of the Rev. Henry (born c.1823) and Jane R. Leiber of Locust Grove near Chappawamsic Run. In 1882 John married M. E. Shacklett (born c.1855), the daughter of Richard Davis Shacklett (1826-1896).

[1421] As of 1917 this store had been in operation at Stafford Store for 36 years.

[1422] This store opened near Brooke c.1914.

[1423] This store opened in Garrisonville c.1911. In 1918 Ashton married Gracie G. Raines at Ebenezer Methodist Church (*Fredericksburg Daily Star*, July 9, 1918).

[1424] Probably Frances Mary Musselman (1870-1936), the daughter of William Samuel Musselman and Elizabeth Musselman (1834-1924).

[1425] Nello operated a store in what is now part of the Quantico condemnation. He was the son of Albert Joseph Musselman (1863-1921) and Julia Lee Groves (1864-1943). He married Margaret Virginia Gallahan (1894-1981) and died at his home on Washington Avenue in Fredericksburg.

[1426] This was Beulah Roles Castle (1883-1968) who was buried in Cedar Run Cemetery. She operated a store at Shacklett, now part of Quantico.

[1427] As of 1917 Rubin had operated a store for 23 years. In 1917 his store was located at or near Bellfair Mills.

[1428] As of 1917 T. E. Courtney had operated a store at Heflin for ten years.

[1429] This store began operation c.1906. James Edward Mountjoy (1879-1938) was the son of William Edward Mountjoy (1835-1898) and Ann Eliza Mountjoy (1843-1913).

[1430] Monroe operated a general merchandise store at Onville for 40 years (*Free Lance Star*, Mar. 9, 1944). He was the son of James and Sarah Decatur. Monroe married Emma J. Shackelford (1868-1958), the daughter of Strother A. Shackelford (1840-1925) and Jane Eliza Mahoney (c.1843-1894).

[1431] In 1917 Ellis operated a store near Stafford Courthouse. He later joined with George W. Herring in a store in Wide Water.

[1432] As of 1917 Joseph had kept a store at Tackett's Mill for 32 years. He married Mamie Heflin (1866-1951).

[1433] This store opened c.1915 at English's Corner, now known as Moore's Corner.

[1434] Around 1907 William opened a store at or near Millie's Post Office.

[1435] As of 1917 Thomas had operated a store for 20 years. The location of this is uncertain.

Hattie A. English[1437] (1879-1935)
Powhatan English[1439] (1873-1950)
Shacklett & Co.[1441]
Charles D. Taliaferro[1443]
M.G. Smith[1445]
Marion R. Tolson
James L. Williams[1448]

Herbert C. Patton[1438] (1881-1956)
Silas L. Rose[1440]
George L. Stewart[1442] (c.1862-c.1931)
H. Wine[1444]
John A. Thompson[1446]
Walter Lee Watson[1447] (1876-1960)
W. H. Williams[1449]

1923—Mrs. M. G. Rose[1450]
Chester A. Zeller (1889-1945)
Wade H. Simpson[1452]
Wesley Knight[1453]

Walter L. Watson
Wilbur C. Heflin[1451]
Monroe Decatur

1924—Richard W. Powers
N. N. Berry[1454]

Wade H. Moore

1925—Joseph Davis
Herring & McClees[1455]

Richard Arthur Botts (1898-1981)
Lewis G. Stewart[1456] (1895-1963)

[1436] John was a lifelong resident of Brooke and was one of the first African American school teachers in Stafford. He was a member of Mt. Hope Baptist Church where he serves as clerk for 61 years and superintendent of the Sunday School for 63 years. After leaving teaching, he started the pickle factory at Brooke. He also managed the C. C. Lang Pickle Factory at Milford. John was buried at Mount Hope Baptist Church Cemetery near the Stafford County Landfill (*Free Lance Star*, May 31, 1951).

[1437] Hattie began operating a store at Toluca c.1916 or 1917. Her maiden name was Wilson and she was the wife of the Rev. John W. English (1880-1955).

[1438] Herbert operated a store at Mt. Airy, probably near Toluca.

[1439] The son of Robert T. English (1848-1906) and Sallie Margaret Withers (1851-1913), the daughter of John J. Withers (1819-1861) and Rosa E. Harding. A native of Mountain View, Powhatan kept a store at Ruby. He operated a lumber business in Stafford until 1921 when he moved away. Powhatan returned to Stafford in 1934 where he lived until becoming ill. In 1943 he moved to Alexandria. Before retirement, he worked for Cities Service Oil Company in Washington. Powhatan's first wife was Lillian Elma Heflin (born 1877). He married secondly Bessie Bolling of Stafford. Powhatan was also a veteran of the Spanish American War (*Free Lance Star*, Mar. 17, 1950).

[1440] As of 1917 Silas had been in business at Roseville for 25 years.

[1441] As of 1917 this company had been in business at Stafford Store for 25 years.

[1442] As of 1917 George had kept a store at the "Draw Bridge" (location unknown) for 18 years. His retail sales for that year totaled $8,878.00. In 1891 George married Mildred Pollard (born c.1867), the daughter of Henry and Eliza V. Pollard.

[1443] Charles kept a store at or near Bellfair Mills.

[1444] This individual kept a store at or near Musselman's Post Office.

[1445] Possibly Mary (Gray) Smith (1880-1967) who was buried at Regester Chapel.

[1446] John operated a store at or near Crow's Nest, probably catering to the men who were employed there cutting timber.

[1447] Granted a license to sell general merchandise in Brooke.

[1448] As of 1917 James had been in business at Rectory for 22 years.

[1449] Although the minutes of the Board of Supervisors meeting record that W. H. Williams kept a store at Williamsburg, this was probably a corruption of Williamsville.

[1450] Mrs. Rose was the executrix of Silas L. Rose, decd. She was granted a retail license to sell merchandise in Roseville. The heading on her bill read, "Cash is the Axle Grease of Business."

[1451] Granted a license to sell Ford automobile accessories and general merchandise.

[1452] Wade manufactured oak and pine lumber and railroad ties. His store was in Falmouth.

[1453] Wesley sold railroad ties, lumber, and general merchandise at Coal Landing.

[1454] N. N. Berry sold groceries, feed, and fresh meat.

[1455] Granted a license to sell general merchandise in Wide Water.

[1456] Lewis sold rubber, railroad ties, brass, raw furs, and pulp and cord wood.

1926—Lloyd Mason Byram[1457] (1894-1961)

1928—Ashton C. Carter[1458]

Ordinaries/Taverns

1665—John Mathews

1691—Capt. George Mason (1660-1716)

1768—Yelverton Peyton (1735-1794)

1780—Moses Phillips[1459] (c.1736-1811)

1785—Moses Phillips   William Dunnington
     Burdit Redish[1460]

1787—Michael Maze   Elizabeth Heath Peyton[1461] (born c.1740)

1789—Walter Greyham

1790—James Daw and Jeremiah Burns[1462] (died c.1791)
     John Bell   Henry Vowles (1752-c.1803)
     Thomas Peyton[1463] (died 1795)

[1457] Granted a license to sell general merchandise at Mountain View. Lloyd was the son of Daniel Strother Byram (1860-1927) and Lizzie M. Shelton (1860-1941).
[1458] Granted a license to sell general merchandise in Brooke.
[1459] Moses kept one of the two ordinaries adjacent to the courthouse, the other being operated by William Garrard (c.1715-c.1786). Moses' ordinary was on the south side of the courthouse on or very near the site of the Lewis Insurance Agency.
    By 1785 Moses Phillips had moved his family to eastern Mason County, Kentucky. With him were his wife and sons Edmund (c.1763-1839), John (born c.1773), Gabriel (born c.1769), Moses, Jr. (c.1775-1787), and Thomas and sons-in-law William and Peter Byram. They settled first near Lee's Station. In 1787 sons John, Moses, Jr., and Thomas were ambushed by Indians while working in their cornfield. Moses, Jr. and Thomas were killed and scalped. John was badly injured but recovered. By that time, Moses, Sr. had claimed 873 acres between present Orangeburg and Rectorville.
[1460] Burdit was listed in the 1783 and 1786 personal property taxes with several horses and cattle, but with no slaves. Family researchers have been unable to determine the relationship between Burdit and the rest of the Stafford Reddish family. By 1810 he was a resident of Madison County, Virginia.
[1461] Elizabeth was the wife of Yelverton Peyton and operated Peyton's Ordinary in the village of Aquia. This ordinary was licensed at least as early as 1768, though the loss of county records makes it impossible to determine if it was in operation earlier. Just prior to the Revolution, the ordinary was leased by Charles Tyler who placed a notice in the newspaper:

> to give notice that the RACES at Aquia, in Stafford county, on the second Thursday in September, are still continued. The first day's purse is for fifty pounds, and the second day's purse will be for twenty pounds. Those gentlemen who intend to start horses for either of the above purses are desired to enter them the day before the race with Charles Tyler, who keeps the tavern lately kept by Mr. Yelverton Peyton.

[1462] Daw and Burns were granted a license to keep an ordinary at the courthouse (location unknown).
[1463] Thomas was probably the fifth child of Yelverton Peyton. After the deaths of her husband and son, Elizabeth Peyton continued to operate the family's ordinary.

1791—James Dowdall[1464] (1758-1802) and George Fant (1745-1839)
    Anthony Marquis[1465] (1752-1821)   Jeremiah Burns
    Elizabeth Peyton   John Bell

"*Billiard Table*"—Henry Vowles

1792—William Young   David Jones
    Mary Burns   Jesse Hill[1466] (c.1745-1822)
    Ursula Morton (1771-1826)   John Bell
    William Broadhurst   James Dowdall
    George Fant

1793—Jesse Hill   Mary Burns
    Ursula Morton   John Curtis
    James Dowdall   George Fant
    Benjamin Turner

"*Billiard Table*"—Benjamin Turner

1794—James Mitchell (died 1822)   Ursula Morton
    George Fant   John Curtis
    Benjamin Turner

"*Billiard Table*"—Benjamin Turner

1795—James Mitchell   Ursula Morton
    Bennet Woodward[1467]   John Bell
    Michael Bowers   Benjamin Turner
    Harris Whitecotton[1468] (c.1768-1803)   William Young

"*Billiard Table*"—Benjamin Turner

1796—Newman B. Barnes[1469] (died 1853)   Michael Bowers
    John Crop   James Dowdall
    Jesse Hill   William Oder
    William Young   Ursula Morton
    James Mitchell   Daniel Peyton

[1464] James probably originated in Fauquier County where in 1788 he owned 586 acres. In 1782 he married Elizabeth Cropp (1765-1799), the daughter of James Cropp (died before 1780). Around 1785 he purchased and removed to Spotted Tavern on the western side of Stafford. James and Elizabeth later removed to Hardin County, Kentucky.

[1465] Anthony was the son of William Marquess (died c.1790). He married Elizabeth Winlock and was buried on his farm about ½ mile above the old Berea Post Office across Fleet Drive (State Route 750) from Berea Church.

[1466] Jesse's obituary stated that he died 'at his residence in Stafford county, on the 2d instant, after a short but severe illness…in the 77th year of his age" (*Virginia Herald*, Feb. 9, 1822).

[1467] Possibly the Bennett Woodward who married Eliza Scessall in 1778 in Prince George's County, Maryland.

[1468] Harris was the son of George Whitecotton, Jr. and Mary Harris and was born in Stafford County. In 1790 Harris married Margaret Shumate (1776-1819) in Fauquier County. Family history says that he died enroute to Augusta County in 1803.

[1469] Possibly the Newman B. Barnes who was a resident of Richmond County, Virginia in 1771. He owned lots in Falmouth.

"*Billiard Table*"—William Oder

1797—Ursula Morton   James Mitchell
   John Bell   John Crop
   George Fant   Jesse Hill
   William Oder   William Young

"*Billiard Table*"—William Oder

1798—Thomas Alcock[1470] (1744-1834)   Joseph Ashton[1471] (died 1809)
   John Bell   John Crop
   Jesse Hill   William Young
   Ursula Morton   Gustavus Scott (born c.1753)

1799—Thomas Holloway   Joseph Jordan
   James Mitchell   Ursula Morton
   William Oder   Benjamin Shacklett
   Thomas Alcock   Joseph Ashton
   John Bell   John Crop
   Jesse Hill   William Young

1800—Davis & Shacklett   Joseph Jordan
   Ursula Morton   James Mitchell
   William Oder   Richard Taylor
   Thomas Alcock   Joseph Ashton
   John Bell   John Crop
   Jesse Hill   James Templeman
   William Young

1801—John W. Porter   Richard Taylor
   Harris Whitecotton   Thomas Alcock
   John Bell   James Templeman
   William Young

1802—Lewis Edwards   Joseph Jordan
   James Mitchell   Richard Taylor
   Harris Whitecotton   Thomas Alcock
   John Bell   John Crop
   George Fant   James Templeman
   William Young

1803—Thomas Alcock   John Bell
   William Bell   John Crop
   James Templeman   William Young
   Ursula Morton   James Mitchell
   Moses Potes   Richard Taylor
   Harris Whitecotton

1804—Joseph Jordan   Eustace & Moncure & Co.
   Richard Taylor   Thomas Alcock

[1470] Thomas was the son of William Alcock (died 1768) of Caroline County. Prior to moving to Stafford, Thomas served as a tobacco inspector at Conway's and Roy's warehouses. In 1772 he married Fanny Hackett. He married secondly Anne Roane (c.1757-1836), also of Caroline. Thomas and Anne moved to Stafford c.1796 and purchased Spotted Tavern. They also operated a small grist mill near the tavern.
[1471] Joseph moved from Falmouth to Georgia where he died (*Virginia Herald*, Aug. 2, 1809).

William Bell
John Bell
Joel Ellington
William Young

Michael Bowers
John Crop
James Templeman

1805—Thomas Alcock
Edmond Morton
John Ashby[1472]
Eustace & Moncure
James Mitchell
Ursula Morton
William Bell
Archibald Rollow (1755-1829)

John Crop
George Fant
William Young
James Templeman
Michael Bowers
Joel Ellington
James Pilcher[1473] (born 1750)
Benjamin Weeks

1806—John Ashby
James Pilcher
William Young
William Bell
John Nash
Matthew Norman
James Mitchell

Christopher Blackburn (died c.1819)
William T. Reardon
John Crop
Richard Taylor
Benjamin Weeks
Ursula Morton

1810—William & Withers Waller
Matthew Norman
James Mitchell

John H. Suttle
Bloxton B. Kendall

1811—John W. Payne

1812—George W. Franklin

Bernard Harding

1813—John Peyton
Cossom Horton (died c.1820)
Lewis Dickinson
James Mitchell

James Hewitt
John W. Payne
Matthew Norman

1814—Joseph Reddish (1787-1873)
Cossom Horton
John Gollohon
James Mitchell
Bernard Harding

Barton Speake Stone
Matthew Norman
John W. Payne
Lewis Dickinson
James Waller & Brothers

1815—Thomas Alcock
John Bell
George Leitch
William Stringfellow[1475] (died 1831)

Christopher Blackburn
John Cropp, Sr.[1474] (died 1830)
Margaret Maddox
William Young

[1472] There were several John Ashbys living simultaneously in Stafford and it is unclear which John this was.
[1473] James was the son of Stephen Pilcher (born 1723) of Stafford and Lucy Clark. He married Nancy Murphy (born c.1748).
[1474] The son of James Crap/Cropp (died before 1780) and Joyce Hinson. John inherited land from his father and probably built a local landmark known as Cropp's Tavern. This served as a replacement for the old Spotted Tavern that was located nearby, but burned. John's first wife was Rosie Thomas, the daughter of William Thomas of Essex County. He married secondly Eliza Fallis (1798-c.1850), the daughter of Thomas Fallis and Polly James of Stafford.
[1475] The Stringfellows came to Stafford from Fauquier County, but it is not clear which William Stringfellow this was.

1816—Samuel Bloxton (died 1817)　　Thomas Alcock
　　　John Bell　　　　　　　　　　　Christopher Blackburn
　　　John Cropp, Sr.　　　　　　　　Mark Harding
　　　George Leitch　　　　　　　　　Margaret Maddox
　　　William Stringfellow　　　　　 Joel Rose
　　　William Primm　　　　　　　　　Robert Carroll
　　　John O'Ryan　　　　　　　　　　John W. Payne
　　　Thomas Norman　　　　　　　　　Withers and James Waller

"*Private Entertainment*"[1476]
　　　Dixon Browne

1817—Thomas Alcock　　　　　　　　Christopher Blackburn
　　　John Cropp　　　　　　　　　　 Mark Harding
　　　George Leitch　　　　　　　　　Margaret Maddox
　　　George M. Parsons.　　　　　　 John Ryan
　　　John Taylor　　　　　　　　　　Alexander Kendall
　　　George Latham　　　　　　　　　Mrs. B. Taylor
　　　John Butler　　　　　　　　　　William Young
　　　Lewis Dickenson　　　　　　　　John Starke
　　　George W. Franklin　　　　　　 Walter Maddox
　　　Charles Beach　　　　　　　　　Withers & James Waller
　　　Anderson D. White　　　　　　　James Hewitt
　　　William Ford　　　　　　　　　 Thomas Payne

1818—Benedicta Bloxton　　　　　　William Thomas
　　　Edward Burrage　　　　　　　　 William Ford
　　　Henry Flourey　　　　　　　　　Thornton Alexander (1790-1842)
　　　James Hewitt　　　　　　　　　 Daniel Lakeman
　　　Thomas Wilson　　　　　　　　　James Curtis
　　　John Bell　　　　　　　　　　　George M. Parsons
　　　Margaret Maddox　　　　　　　　Christopher Blackburn
　　　John C. Taylor　　　　　　　　 Mark Harding
　　　John O'Ryan

"*Private Entertainment*"
　　　Robert Taylor　　　　　　　　　George Burroughs
　　　Burdit Clifton[1477] (died 1821)

1819—Burdit Clifton　　　　　　　　Senate Tackett
　　　James Hewitt　　　　　　　　　 Robert Taylor
　　　Thornton Alexander[1478]　　　 William Thomas
　　　William Ford　　　　　　　　　 George Leitch
　　　John C. Taylor　　　　　　　　 George M. Parsons
　　　John Bell　　　　　　　　　　　Daniel Lakeman
　　　Christopher Blackburn　　　　　John Cropp, Sr.

[1476] During this period, county officials attempted to maintain some control over gambling and, no doubt, sought to enlarge the county coffers, by licensing gambling parlors as "private entertainment." Those granted a license were able to hose certain forms of gambling.
[1477] Burdit was the last of the Stafford County Clifton family. He was the son of Henry Clifton (born 1746) and Betty Hore (1751-1792) and the grandson of Burdit Clifton (1708-1761). In 1816 he married Hannah Waller, the daughter of William Waller (1740-1817) of Concord. Burdit was the only legatee of Capt. John Hore (died c.1809), brother of Elias Hore (1748-1852). Burdit and Hannah had no children.
[1478] Thornton took over Moses Phillips' old ordinary on the south side of the courthouse.

"House of Private Entertainment"
    Christopher Blackburn

1820—Benjamin Bronaugh
    Cossom Horton (died c.1820)
    Lewis Dickenson
    Edward Burrage
    Loyal Carter
    Thornton Alexander
    Robert Taylor

1821—George Leitch
    Cossom Horton
    John Bell
    William Bell
    Thornton Chilton
    Daniel Lakeman
    Benjamin Bronaugh
    John H. S. Potts
    James S. Cole
    Thornton Alexander
    Edward Burrage
    Thomas Harwood (1769-1845)
    Abner R. Alcock

1822—Robert Taylor
    Burkett G. Johnston
    Loyal Carter
    John Bell
    William Bell
    John C. Taylor & Company
    Thornton Chilton
    Edward Burrage
    John Latham
    John Latham[1479]
    William Rolls
    George Leitch
    Thornton Alexander
    Thomas Harwood
    James Templeman
    Elizabeth Bronaugh
    Lucy Starke

1823—Alexander Obyrhim
    Senate Tackett
    Loyal Carter
    William Brookes
    George Leitch
    Burkett G. Johnston
    Joseph H. Bell
    Thornton Alexander
    Lucy Halon
    Henry Rodgers
    Ezra Burr[1480] (c.1781-1853)
    Cossom Horton
    John Taylor & John H. S. Potts
    Thomas Harwood
    James Bell
    John Latham
    William Bell
    Abner R. Alcock

"Private Entertainment"
    Abram Howard[1481]
    William Brookes

1825—Elizabeth Bronaugh
    Julius Ackley
    Alexander Obyrhim
    Hugh Adie
    George Mason Cooke (1792-1866)
    Aden Fritter[1482] (c.1766-c.1826)
    Newman B. Barnes
    Robert Taylor
    William Thomas
    Thomas G. Moncure (1799-1836)

[1479] Possibly John Latham, Sr. (1730-1834). Around 1760 he married Margaret Hinson (died c.1780). John's second wife was Nancy Kendall (1755-1840) whom he married c.1783.

[1480] Ezra was born in Connecticut. In 1798 he married Abigail Burr in Fairfield, Connecticut. From 1816-1819 the local newspapers contain numerous small advertisements for Ezra's store in which his sold dry goods, hardware, and groceries. He was a member of the Yellow Chapel Temperance Society.

[1481] Abram was a blacksmith in Falmouth where he made and repaired items such as plows, axes, hoes, and other tools. Nearby he kept a "House of Private Entertainment: Where his neighbors or the weary traveler can at all times be refreshed, and that with the nicest fresh Oysters if desired" (*Virginia Herald*, Jan. 8, 1823). In 1825 Abram rented the Falls Mill from Robert Dunbar (Dunbar, Accounts).

[1482] Aden was the son of Richard Fritter and Elizabeth Horton (1726-1766).

      Allen Jones
      John H. S. Potts
      John Curtis
      Joseph H. Bell
      George Leitch
      Burkett G. Johnston

"*Private Entertainment*"
      Abram Howard

1827—Thornton Alexander
      James W. Stone (c.1796-1869)
      Robert Croughton
      George W. Billingsley[1486]
      James Garrison
      John Gollahorn
      George Leitch
      Jared Whitney
      John H. S. Potts
      Edward Burrage

"*Private Entertainment*"
      James Moxley

1828—Garnett Corbin
      Benjamin Heath
      Fielding Battaley
      Luke Masters
      Gustavus Ashby (born c.1800)
      James Garrison
      John Gollahorn
      Thomas G. Moncure
      Thomas Harwood
      John Cropp
      Thomas Alcock
      Thornton Alexander
      Edward Burrage

"*Private Entertainment*"
      Elizabeth Bronaugh

1829—Aaron Kendall
      John Jackson
      James Armstrong (c.1790-after 1850)
      Joseph M. Johnson

      Thornton Alexander
      William Bell
      Stephen P. Bowen[1483] (c.1813-1854)
      Ezra Burr
      John B. Taylor[1484]
      John Cropp

      William H. Browne

      Fielding Battaley[1485]
      Thomas Morton
      Priscy Chadwell (c.1770-after 1850)
      John E. Hewitt
      William Ford
      Thomas Alcock (1744-1834)
      John Curtis
      Thomas Harwood
      John Cropp
      Thornton Alexander

      James Cave
      Burkett G. Johnston
      Duff Green
      Henry Rodgers
      Stephen P. Bowen
      Jackson Rowles
      George M. Cooke
      John H. S. Potts
      George Leitch
      John Curtis
      Eliza Queen
      Priscy Chadwell

      Burkett G. Johnston
      Jameson Corbin
      George M. Cooke
      James Cave[1487]

[1483] Stephen was born in King George County and died there of heart disease.
[1484] The 1820 Stafford census listed John as a cabinet maker.
[1485] Fielding married Rebecca, one of the daughters of James Monteith of Stafford. By 1839 James and his wife were residents of Autauga County, Alabama.
[1486] In 1824 George took over the Falls Mills in Falmouth where he ground cornmeal (*Virginia Herald*, July 7, 1824).
[1487] James placed a notice in the local newspaper advertising his business. The notice read:

    FISH! FISH! FISH! The subscriber has rented a large FISHING ESTABLISHMENT, on the Maryland shore, and has made an arrangement with six others, to land fish at the

Thomas Morton
William Trussell
John H. S. Potts
George Leitch
Eliza Queen
Henry Rodgers
Luke Masters
Thomas Harwood

James Garrison
John Cropp
John Curtis
Thomas Alcock
Duff Green
Thornton Alexander
Edward Burrage

"*Private Entertainment*"
Gustavus Ashby

1830—William Barton Stone (died 1845)
Thomas Alcock[1488]
John H. S. Potts
Fielding Battaley
John Curtis
___ L. Rogers
Luke Masters
John Harwood

John R. Queen
George Leitch
Jameson Corbin[1489] (born c.1790)
James Cave
James Alexander
Thornton Alexander
Edward Burrage[1490]

"*Private Entertainment*"
John Cropp

William Irvine (c.1781-1859)

1831—James Masters
John Curtis
George Leitch
Abner Roane Alcock[1492] (died c.1831)
Jameson Corbin

William(?) Thomas[1491]
John H. S. Potts
Duff Green (1792-1854)
Thornton Alexander
Reubin Bowler[1493] (1800-1856)

Steam-Boat Landing (Bell-Plain) on the Potomac Creek, consequently, no disappointment or detention can exist; and will supply those who may think proper to encourage him with fish, on as good terms as they can be purchased anywhere. The subscriber has every convenience necessary—large quantity of hogs heads and salt. Salt will be furnished as low to customers as it can be purchased on the Potomac.—Distance from Fredericksburg or Falmouth, eight miles, and a good road. Persons getting out of horse food can be supplied on the spot on good terms.—Fishing season will commence on the 20th of this month and end on the 10th May.
James Cave   Stafford, March 20 (*Virginia Herald*, Mar. 17, 1832)

[1488] Thomas owned and operated Spotted Tavern on the western side of the county. According to the 1830 Stafford census, he owned 18 slaves. Thomas was the son of William Alcock (died 1768) of Caroline County and served in that county as a tobacco inspector at Conway's tobacco warehouse. His first wife was Fanny Hackett who predeceased him. He married secondly Anne Roane (c.1757-1836, also of Caroline). Thomas moved to Stafford c.1795.

[1489] Jameson lived much of his life in Culpeper County but kept an ordinary in the town of Falmouth. He married Mary Nelson Mason.

[1490] Edward Burrage rented property from John Holloway and attempted to operate a tavern there. This less-than-successful business was located on Kellogg's Mill Road (State Route 651) near the communication tower.

[1491] The innkeeper's first name was abbreviated and difficult to read. He was granted a license "to keep a tavern at Aquia."

[1492] Abner was the son of Thomas Alcock (1744-1834) and Anne Roane (c.1757-1836), owners of Spotted Tavern. He married Elizabeth (Seddon) Hazlegrove, the daughter of John Seddon, Sr. and widow of John Hazelgrove.

　　　　　Henry W.(?) Queen　　　　　　　　Charles Jones
　　　　　Baldwin Bradford[1494] (c.1764-1848)　Thomas Harwood[1495] (1769-1845)
　　　　　Henry Rodgers　　　　　　　　　　Peter Pollard

"*Private Entertainment*"
　　　　　William Irvine　　　　　　　　　　William Barton Stone (died 1845)

1832—James Morton (died 1859)　　　　　John H. S. Potts
　　　　　Frances A. Alexander[1496]　　　　　Baldwin Bradford
　　　　　John Curtis　　　　　　　　　　　John Cason[1497]
　　　　　John Smoot　　　　　　　　　　　Reubin Bowler[1498] (1800-1856)
　　　　　Jameson Corbin　　　　　　　　　James Cave
　　　　　John R. Queen　　　　　　　　　　Thomas Harwood
　　　　　Catherine Chadwell　　　　　　　　William Roles
　　　　　George Leitch

"*Private Entertainment*"
　　　　　William B. Stone

1833—James Beagle　　　　　　　　　　Gustavus Ashby (born c.1800)
　　　　　James Morton　　　　　　　　　　John M. Bronaugh (c.1733-1831)
　　　　　Baldwin Bradford　　　　　　　　Thomas Alcock
　　　　　Capt. William Barber (c.1789-1881)　Joseph D. Withers
　　　　　Peter King[1499] (died 1862)　　　　Thomas Bowler[1500] (1804-1887)
　　　　　A. M. Curtis (female)　　　　　　　Henry W. Queen
　　　　　James Cave[1501]

"*Private Entertainment*"
　　　　　William B. Stone　　　　　　　　　George Leitch

1834—Hore & Peyton[1502]　　　　　　　Baldwin Bradford
　　　　　Ann Alcock[1503] (died c.1839)　　　Fielding Battaley
　　　　　Joseph W. Honey[1504] (1810-1879)　Jameson Corbin
　　　　　William Barber　　　　　　　　　Fielding Peyton
　　　　　John Smoot　　　　　　　　　　　Roberson & Suttle[1505]

[1493] Reubin was the son of Charles Bowler. He was born in Caroline County and died in Stafford. Reubin married first c.1819 Mildred Jones (c.1802-c.1834) and secondly in 1835 Hannah Garner (born 1815), the daughter of John E. Garner (1775-after 1850) and Elizabeth Cole (died before 1850).
[1494] Baldwin was the son of Benjamin Bennett Bradford (born 1738) of Prince William and Fauquier and Ann Allen (born c.1730). In 1798 he married Betsy Foley (born 1776) of Fauquier. Baldwin died in Culpeper.
[1495] Probably the son of John Harwood (died c.1787) who lived near the intersection of Warrenton Road (U.S. Route 17) and Sanford Road (State Route 670).
[1496] Frances was the wife of Thornton Alexander who kept one of the two taverns at Stafford Courthouse.
[1497] John was the son of Thomas Cason. He died in Kentucky.
[1498] Around 1819 Reubin married Mildred Jones (c.1802-c.1834).
[1499] For many years Peter owned and resided at Coal Trips on the south side of Aquia Creek.
[1500] Thomas was born in Caroline County and died in Falmouth. He was the brother of Reubin Bowler (1800-1856) and married Anna M. Payne.
[1501] James kept an ordinary at Hartwood.
[1502] This ordinary was "on the fishing shore on the Potomac."
[1503] Ann (Roane) Alcock was the widow of Thomas Alcock. She was granted a license to keep an ordinary at Spotted Tavern.
[1504] In 1885 Joseph married Jane A. Harding (born c.1815), the daughter of Mark Harding (died c.1873).
[1505] Robinson and Suttle were authorized "to keep ordinaries at the fishing shores on the River Potomac."

Pierson King
Sidney Stephens

William Augustus Moncure[1506] (1803-1862)
Walker Smith[1507] (c.1806-1892)

"Private Entertainment"
George Leitch
Sidney Stephens

William B. Stone
Walker Smith

1835—John H. Suttle[1508]
Baldwin Bradford
William Barber
Friend Kellogg[1510] (1797-1839)
Thomas Smith

Hore & Peyton
Jameson Corbin
Edward and George Latham[1509] (c.1780-c.1846)
Joseph W. Honey
Fielder Peyton[1511]

"Private Entertainment"
Benjamin Smith[1512]
Ann Alcock

George Leitch

1839—William Guy, Sr.
Curtis M. Smith(?)
George Pickett
James W. Johnson
Richard M. Burchell
William H. Fitzhugh
Charles W. Jones[1514]

Henry L. Rodgers
Edward & George Latham
Stone & Petty
John H. S. Potts
Simon Watson[1513]
James Jones
Peter King[1515] (died 1862)

"Private Entertainment"
Wilford A. Smith[1516] (born 1795)

1840—Daniel S. Coakley[1517] (born c.1805)
William H. Fitzhugh[1518]

Andrew J. Bunnell
William H. Browne

[1506] The son of John Moncure (1772-1822) and Alice Peachy Gaskins (1774-1860).
[1507] Walker lived at Cedar Hedge, northwest of Falmouth on the Warrenton Road (U. S. Route 17). He and his family were involved in gold mining there.
[1508] John was licensed "to keep an ordinary at Aquia."
[1509] George was the son of Franklin Latham (1728-1823). In 1839 George bought Spotted Tavern in Stafford. He also owned several lots in Falmouth.
[1510] Friend was probably born in Heartland, Connecticut, the son of Ezekiel Kellogg (died 1828) and Luna Clark (born 1778). Friend Kellogg's name first appeared on the Stafford land tax records in 1834. He later removed to Fauquier County where he died unmarried. Friend was the brother of Lyman Kellogg (1813-1897) who lived near Abel Reservoir and was actively involved in county affairs.
[1511] Licensed to keep a tavern in his own house.
[1512] Probably the Benjamin Smith who married in 1832 Fenton Brooke.
[1513] According to a notation in the tax records, Simon kept an ordinary at one of the fishing shores in Stafford.
[1514] A notation in the tax records indicates that Charles had taverns in two (unspecified) locations.
[1515] Peter resided at Coal Trips on the north side of Courthouse Road and overlooking Aquia Creek. A notation in the tax records states that he maintained taverns in two (unspecified) locations.
[1516] Wilford was the son of Augustine Smith (died 1831) and Susannah Darnall. He married Mary Ann Elizabeth George.
[1517] Possibly Daniel Coakley (1801-1889), the son of William Coakley, Sr. (before 1765-1830) and Mildred Sullivan (1761-1812) whom he married in 1781. Daniel was a deacon of Hanover Baptist Church in King George County. He married first in 1821 Ann "Nancy" Massey; secondly in 1847 Elizabeth C. White (born 1816); and thirdly in 1858 Nancy Coakley.
[1518] William resided at Chappawamsic and a margin notation in the tax records stated that he maintained an ordinary at his "fishing shore."

Peter King
Charles W. Jones
George Latham
Jane Brooke
John Jones
George Pickett

James Jones
Charles S. Petty[1519] (c.1818-after 1870)
William Guy
Alexander Bowie
Timothy Bridwell

"*Private Entertainment*"
Jane Brooke

Wilfred A. Smith[1520] (born 1795)

1841—James Taliaferro
Peter King
Henry Moore (born c.1822)
William H. Browne
William Guy
Daniel S. Coakley

William H. Fitzhugh
James Homes (c.1812-after 1850)
Samuel Hasson
Alexander Bowie
George Latham
James L. and James M. Taliaferro

1850—Jeremiah Carter

1854—William T. Masters
Thompson J. Sullivan[1521] (born c.1820)
Elias A. W. Hore (1821-c.1891)

Daniel S. Coakley
George H. Cockrell

1855—William T. Masters
Abel S. Lewellyn[1522]
Thompson J. Sullivan

Elizabeth Latham
James Monteith
William L. Morgan[1523] (c.1806-1873)

Licenses rejected:
Thomas H. Hewitt

1856—Strother Byram[1524] (c.1820-c.1857)
Thompson J. Sullivan
James Monteith

Abel S. Lewellyn
Elizabeth R. Latham[1525] (born c.1811)
William L. Morgan

1857—Elizabeth Latham
Thompson J. Sullivan
James Monteith

William L. Morgan
Abel S. Lewellyn
Strother Byram

[1519] Charles was a tailor and lived in Hartwood.
[1520] Wilfred, or Wilford, was the son of Augustine Smith (died 1831) and Susannah Darnall. He married Mary Ann Elizabeth George.
[1521] Thompson was the son of Martin Sullivan, Jr. and E. Fugate.
[1522] Abel also served as postmaster at Game Point Post Office on Aquia Creek near Coal Trips.
[1523] William was born in King George County and employed himself there as a merchant. In the 1850s he moved to Stafford Courthouse where he owned the old Garrard's Ordinary to the northeast of the courthouse. Here he conducted business in partnership with Leonard P. Alexander. William married first Margaret Strother, the daughter of James Strother. Around 1855 he married secondly Jane, also the daughter of James Strother of King George County.
[1524] Strother was the son of Cuthbert Byram, Sr. (c.1797-1854) and Sarah H. Kendall (1785-1854). He was a merchant in Stafford and in 1856 married Sarah H. Patterson (born 1838), the daughter of Elijah (1808-after 1870) and Levenia Patterson. Sarah married secondly in 1861 Richard C. Embrey (born c.1837).
[1525] Elizabeth was the daughter of George Latham (c.1780-c.1846). Her brother, George Latham (born c.1802), inherited his father's Spotted Tavern.

1858—William L. Morgan[1526]   Leonard P. Alexander[1527] (born c.1832)
       Sarah W. Lewellyn

1859—Sarah W. Lewellyn   Henry L. Coleman[1528] (died 1883)
       Daniel S. Coakley   Leonard P. Alexander

1860—William T. Masters   Sarah W. Lewellyn
       Daniel S. Coakley   Joseph Roberson
       William L. Morgan

License Rejected:
       Edward Pipenbring[1529] (born c.1828)

1867—**License to keep a hotel**:
       William J. Lucas[1530] (c.1834-after 1870)   Fielding B. Burton[1531] (born c.1837)
       John W. Edwards[1532] (born c.1852)   Silas Haislip[1533] (died 1884)
       George G. Lightner[1534] (1839-1898)

1868—Silas Haislip   William J. Lucas[1535]
       Fielding B. Burton[1536]

1869—Schooler & Towson   William J. Lucas[1537]

1870—William J. Lucas

1878—Charles A. Bryan[1538]

1914—M. W. Cooper (House of Private Entertainment)

[1526] This year William was granted a license "to keep a house of Private entertainment."

[1527] Leonard was in business with William L. Morgan and operated the old Garrard's Ordinary just north of Stafford Courthouse. The 1860 Stafford census listed him as a "general agent."

[1528] Henry was the son of John W. Coleman (1788-1857) and Eliza Wigginton Templeman (died 1885) of Loch Lomond in Stafford. In 1851 Henry married Hannah A. Hedgman (born c.1831), the daughter of John T. Hedgman (c.1804-1857).

[1529] Edward was born in Germany and was a confectioner by trade.

[1530] William was born in Maryland.

[1531] Licensed "to keep a Hotel at his house in the town of Falmouth." Fielding married Virginia Webb (c.1844-1887) of Fauquier County. The 1860 census listed his occupation as cooper.

[1532] John was the son of John W. (born c.1819) and Virginia Edwards. In 1874 he married Maria Bolling (born c.1855), the daughter of Francis and Maria Bolling. John was licensed to keep a hotel "at his house in the town of Falmouth."

[1533] Granted a license "to keep a Hotel in the Town of Falmouth." The local newspaper carried two notices pertaining to Silas. The first stated, "An old and respected citizen, and a grocer on Commerce street, attempted suicide by shooting himself in the head with a pistol Thursday. The old gentleman has been in bad health for some time past, and it is supposed that his ailments and mental depression therefrom, were the cause of the rash act. Yesterday afternoon his condition was regarded as extremely critical. His recovery is not expected" (*Fredericksburg Star*, Sept. 6, 1884). A few days later, the newspaper reported his death (*Fredericksburg Star*, Sept. 10, 1884).

[1534] Licensed "to keep an Ordinary in the Town of Falmouth."

[1535] License granted "to keep a Hotel at his House."

[1536] License granted "to keep a Hotel at his house in the town of Falmouth."

[1537] According to the court minutes, "It is ordered by the Court that W. J. Lucas be permitted to put up a horse rack at his own expense upon the Court house lot next his own fence for the purpose of feeding the horses of the Public."

[1538] Charles was licensed to keep an ordinary and a house of private entertainment at the courthouse.

1917—Charles A. Bryan[1539]   M. W. Cooper[1540]

Liquor Licenses[1541]

1830—Jameson Corbin
    Edward Waller (1805-1883)
    Lewis Jones
    Basil Gordon
    John M. O'Bannon
    Duncan ___
    William B. Billingsley[1543]
    William W. B___
    Brooke & Ficklen
    Moses Garrison[1544] (born c.1776)
    Ficklen & Fant
    Daniel Jett[1546]
    Garnett Corbin
    Harberson Bradshaw
    Fielding Batterley[1547]
    Thomas Finnall[1548]
    John Orion[1549]
    James Coones[1550] (c.1795-after 1850)

    John T. Odell[1542]
    Richard Stone (died 1825)
    William Churchill Beale (died 1850)
    Duff Green
    John C. O'Bryan
    James W. Smith
    John H. S. Potts
    Murray Forbes
    Jeremiah Carter (c.1810-186_)
    Thomas J. Payne[1545] (born c.1796)
    Williams(?) & T. Stone(?)
    James Cave
    Joseph B. Ficklen
    Francis Cox
    Mary B. C___
    Duncan & Scott
    William Brooke (died 1842)

1832—Thomas J. Payne
    Duff Green
    John Francis Cox (c.1802-after 1850)

    Duncan & Scott
    Hays & Baily
    John Orion

[1539] Granted a license to keep a house of private entertainment near Stafford Courthouse.

[1540] Granted a license to keep a house of private entertainment (location not specified).

[1541] It was not uncommon for people to operate a tavern and sell liquor without a license. Periodically, these individuals were summoned to court and fined for their indiscretions. On June 14, 1790 the sheriff assembled a grand jury who bound over for the trial the following: "Ursla Morton, William Eaton, Calvert Porter, William Hollowday, Obediah McFarlin, Philemon Brummel and Michael Bowers (from his waggon)." Ursla Morton was actually Margaret Ursula Waller (1771-1826), the wife of Richard Morton (1771-1812). Ursula was the daughter of William Waller (1740-1817) of Concord and his second wife, Margaret Waller (1744-177_) of Spring Hill. Calvert Porter (born 1752) was the son of Calvert and Elizabeth (Cash) Porter. Obediah McFarlin was a native of Shenandoah County, Virginia where he worked as a teamster in the Shenandoah Valley. By 1803 he had returned to Shenandoah County and his name appears in that county's records through 1825. Obediah was in Stafford by May 24, 1779 when he signed the petition to move the courthouse to a new location. On June 7, 1798 he acquired 28 acres near the Rappahannock River adjoining the lands of James Hunter and Andrew Jackson.

[1542] "...who wished to sell by retail Rum Gin and other ardent spirits."

[1543] William was a veteran of the War of 1812.

[1544] Moses was a veteran of the War of 1812.

[1545] Thomas was listed in the 1850 Stafford census as a merchant.

[1546] Daniel was the son of Berryman Jett.

[1547] Fielding was a veteran of the War of 1812.

[1548] Thomas was the son of Robert Finnall. In 1830 he married Ann F. Ballard, the daughter of Judith Ballard.

[1549] John's last name sometimes appears in records as "O'Ryan." He operated one of the grist mills at old Rappahannock Forge.

[1550] James married Louisa Harwood (c.1806-1885), the daughter of Thomas Harwood (1769-1845) and Betsy Bussell.

James Coones
John H. S. Potts
William C. Beale
Whiting & Payne
Joseph B. Ficklen
Jeremiah Carter
James Cave
Alexander & Reid

Murray Forbes
Basil Gordon
John M. O'Bannon
Spotswood Pomfrey[1551]
Richard Stone
William B. Stone
Francis Cox
William Brooke

1833—William C. Beale
John H. S. Potts
James Coones
Joseph B. Ficklen
John M. O'Bannon
Basil Gordon
Jameson Corbin
Murray Forbes
John C. Crowley
Jeremiah Carter
James Cave
Charles Tackett (c.1780-1834)

Hays & Baily
William Brooke, Jr.
William B. Bowen[1552]
John Orion
John F. Cox
Francis Cox
Duff Green
William B. Stone
Albion Roberson
Benjamin Tolson[1553] (c.1763-1836)
Thomas C. Scott[1554]
Absalom W. Mills

1834—Daniel Coakley
Basil Gordon
John H. S. Potts
Carter & Smith
William B. & Thomas Stone
John M. O'Bannon
Duff Green
Duncan & Scott
William P. Bowen
Alfred C. Hayes
William Anderson
Friend Kellogg

William C. Beale
Murray Forbes
Hore & Peyton
Robertson & Suttle
Joseph B. Ficklen
Jameson Corbin
James Cave
William Brooke
James Coones
George Latham
John F. Cox

1835—Basil Gordon
John M. O'Bannon
Alfred C. Hayes
Murray Forbes
Joseph B. Ficklen
Scott & Bayly
James Coones
William Brooke, Jr.
Edward and George Latham[1555]
John Millington
James Cave

William C. Beale
Duff Green
John H. S. Potts
Jameson Corbin
Hore & Peyton
Daniel & Conway
Benjamin Hall, Jr.
Joseph W. Honey
Friend Kellogg
Sidney Stephens
Jeremiah Carter

1855—Licenses granted "to sell retail wine and ardent spirits":
William S. Chapman (born c.1822)
John Guy (born c.1816)
Murray Forbes
Thomas H. Hewitt

[1551] Spotswood married Mariah Porch (died 1855) and lived in Falmouth.
[1552] Probably William P. Bowen, the son of John Pratt Bowen (died c.1838) of the Glebe.
[1553] Benjamin lived near Stafford Store in the northern part of the county.
[1554] In 1815 Thomas married Mary L. Seddon in Fredericksburg.
[1555] George Latham served in the War of 1812.

George H. Cockrell
Richard Burton (died c.1859)
Daniel S. Coakley

Strother Byram
Lafayette Corbin[1556] (born 1824)

License rejected:
Daniel S. Coakley to sell retail spirits "at one of his storehouses" (at Jonesville)

1856—Richard Burton
William Guy (born c.1814)
Alexander & Schooler
John Guy
Strother Byram

Harrison J. Skinner (c.1821-1862)
Daniel S. Coakley
Thomas H. Hewitt
William T. Masters

1857—Richard Burton
Charles A. Tackett (1814-1896)
William Griffis
Henry F. Bryant (born c.1837)
James T. Abbot[1557] (died 1873)
William T. Masters

Moore & Waller
Luke Guy (1830-1858)
Harrison J. Skinner
Daniel S. Coakley
William Guy
Thompson J. Sullivan

1858—Elijah Patterson[1558] (1808-before Nov. 1870)

1859—Joseph Roberson
Dudley Herndon[1560] (1829-1909)

Robert Mountjoy[1559] (1828-1891)

1860—Licenses granted "to sell by retail spiritous liquors not to be drank where sold"
Edward Peipenbring
Jacob L. Stires (c.1831-c.1857)
Elijah Patterson
Obyrhim & Burton
Mary E. Sullivan (born c.1824)
Henry W. Grinnan (c.1806-after 1860)

Coones & Swetnam
Charles A. Tackett
Harrison J. Skinner
Dudley Herndon
Mrs. Eliza Guy (born c.1818)

[1556] Lafayette was born in Culpeper County, the son of Jameson Corbin and Mary Nelson Mason. He married Catherine Ramey (born c.1824).
[1557] Some time prior to his death, James had been a toll collector on Ficklen's bridge at Falmouth. He died in Manchester, Virginia.
[1558] Elijah was the son of Perry Patterson (1776-after 1850) and his wife Winifred (c.1782-1858). Following the War Between the States, Elijah submitted a claim to the Southern Claims Commissioner asking to be reimbursed for $921 worth of quartermaster stores. He was granted $414.50.
[1559] The son of Thornton Mountjoy (1794:97-1881). He enlisted in the 9th Virginia Cavalry at Stafford Courthouse. In April 1862 he was discharged after his third attack of pneumonia. In 1864 Robert married Mary Mildred Griffis (c.1844-1909), the daughter of Samuel H. Griffis (1814-c.1887).
[1560] The son of John Herndon (c.1794-1882) and Lucinda Combs (c.1796-before 1867). In 1859 he married Katherine A. Ennis (1839-1913). Dudley served as a private in both the 9th and 6th Virginia Cavalry and received the Southern Cross of Honor for his service. He died in Washington and buried in Triangle, Virginia.

1861—Paul Hoyer[1561] (c.1829-1885)   Harrison J. Skinner
     Robert E. Limbrick (born c.1825)   Elijah Patterson
     James Limbrick   George W. Lightner[1562]

1862—Licenses transferred:
     "The Comr. is ordered to transfer the unexpired term of Dudley Herndon to retail ardent spirits to James L. Carter [1825-1901]."
     "Leave is granted the Comr. of the Revenue to transfer the license of James Limbrick to retail liquor ardent spirits for his unexpired term to George Lightner."

1865—William J. Burton[1563] (c.1833-1896)   John W. Edwards[1564] (born c.1820)
     George Green (born c.1841)   Samuel H. Griffis (born 1814)
     James B. Garrison (born c.1827)   Silas Haislip
     Lightner & Burton   Charles A. Tackett
     Thomas Lowry (c.1826-1911)   James Griffis (c.1834-1872)

1866[1565]—William Knight[1566] (1815-1904)   Paul Hoyer
     Walker & Dent[1567]   Thomas Lowry
     Lightner & Burton   Silas Haislip[1568]
     Charles A. Tackett   Linn & Davis
     Samuel H. Griffis   Raleigh L. Cooper[1569] (1832-1892)

[1561] According to the 1870 census, Paul was born in Prussia. He settled in the area sometime prior to the War Between the States and in 1861 was granted a license "to retail and cut spirits not to be drank where sold in the neighborhood of the Eagle Gold Mine." Following the war, Paul submitted a claim to the Southern Claims Commission asking to be reimbursed for $2,071.70 worth of quartermaster stores. He was granted $687.25.

Paul also kept a store in Fredericksburg. A merchant's advertisement announced the opening of the store and informed readers that he would stock a full line of wall papers, window shades, paints, oils, etc. (*Virginia Star*, Mar. 24, 1877).

Paul's obituary described him as "an energetic, well known and highly esteemed citizen." He was a member of the Masonic Lodge and died in Fredericksburg.

[1562] George, a minister, was born in Maryland. In 1861 he "received a legal transfer of the license heretofore granted by the said Court to Coons and Swetnam at its May term 1860 to keep store as a merchant in the town of Falmouth and to retail spirits at his said store not to be drank where sold."

[1563] William, a cooper, was the son of William and Catherine Burton. In 1867 he married Drucilla Knight (born 1846), the daughter of Austin (born c.1822) and Elizabeth Knight. He lived near Lance.

[1564] The 1880 Stafford census states that John was a millwright in Falmouth.

[1565] The levies set in 1866 were as follow:
     $1.50 upon all white male tithables 21 years and older
     $50.00 upon every ferry running across the Rappahannock
     $5.00 "upon every merchant who is licensed to sell ardent Spirits, Wine etc by retail"
     $2.50 upon all other merchants
     .05 "upon every hundred dollars in value on land and buildings in said County"

[1566] William lived at Plumfield in the northern part of the county that is now part of the Marine Corps reservation. He died and was buried on his farm.

[1567] Licensed to sell retail ardent spirits at Helm's Fishery on Aquia Creek.

[1568] Silas was granted a license "to keep a Hotel and retail ardent spirits."

[1569] Samuel Griffis and Raleigh Cooper were granted licenses to sell retail ardent spirits "at their respective storehouses the Court being satisfied that the respective places are proper and convenient to the neighboring residents and that the said Griffis and Cooper are persons of sobriety and good character."

1867—William Walker (born c.1822)
    Withers Waller[1570] (1825-1900)
    William J. Lucas[1571]
    West & Ashby
    Fielding B. Burton[1572]
    James Griffis
    Henry Love[1575] (c.1811-1873)
    Gibson & Knight
    James L. Carter
    Paul Hoyer
    Charles A. Tackett
    Silas Hailsip[1573]
    Eilbeck Hunter Taliaferro[1574] (1844-1891)
    George G. Lightner

1868—John Newton Harper[1576] (1823-1907)
    Hickerson & Flatford[1578]
    Paul Hoyer
    Chewning & Lowry[1579]
    George J. Lightner[1580]
    Benjamin S. West[1581] (c.1829-1905)
    John N. Jones[1582]
    John W. Cooper & Co.[1577]
    Silas Haislip
    William J. Lucas
    Fielding B. Burton
    Samuel H. Griffis
    Taliaferro & Cooper

1869—Mathew Norman Towson[1583] (born c.1846)
    William J. Lucas[1584]
    Samuel H. Griffis
    John N. Jones

1870—Samuel H. Griffis
    William Ashby (born c.1814)
    Robert L. Flatford[1585] (1852-1898)

1878—Silas Haislip
    Lemuel S. Limerick[1586] (c.1846-1904)
    Fleet Cox
    William S. Towson[1587] (c.1853-1915)
    Fielding Burton
    Payne & Morton
    Charles A. Bryan
    Waller & Edmonds

[1570] Walker, Gibson, Knight, and Waller were granted licenses to sell retail ardent spirits "at their respective fishing shores."

[1571] Carter and Lucas were granted licenses to sell retail ardent spirits "at their respective storehouses."

[1572] West & Ashby, Tackett, and Burton were granted licenses to sell retail ardent spirits "at their respective storehouses."

[1573] Granted a liquor license to sell ardent spirits "at his Store House in the Town of Falmouth."

[1574] Eilbeck was the son of James Monroe Taliaferro (1809-1893) of Loch Lomond near modern Mount Olive Church in Stafford. On Apr. 21, 1861 Eilbeck enlisted with Company A of the 9th Virginia Cavalry as a musician. He was discovered to be underage and was discharged on Oct. 16, 1861. Eilbeck was a musician, painter, inventor, and merchant. By 1878 he was in Mississippi where he married Amanda Permelia Smith (1860-1918). It is believed that Eilbeck died in Georgia.

[1575] Griffis, Taliaferro, and Love were all granted licenses to sell liquor at their store houses.

[1576] The son of Dr. William Harper, Jr. (1787-1853) and Mary Thomas Newton (1789-1841) of Alexandria. He married Sarah Frances Andrews (1826-1911). From 1879 until her death, the couple operated the Mt. Pleasant Freestone Quarry on Aquia Creek.

[1577] License granted to sell Liquor "at their Store House."

[1578] License granted to sell Liquor "at their Store House."

[1579] License granted to sell Liquor "at their Store."

[1580] License granted to sell Liquor "at his Store House in the Town of Falmouth."

[1581] During the War Between the States, Benjamin served with the 9th Virginia Cavalry. He was held as a prisoner of war in Fredericksburg and was buried in Baltimore.

[1582] License granted to sell liquor "at Brooks Station or Accokeek."

[1583] Mathew was the son of James Edward Towson (1808-1888) and Agnes Ann Suttle (c.1811-1865).

[1584] License granted to sell liquor "at his place of business at Stafford Court House without fear of presentment provided he present to the Court at the next term thereof a certificate from the Comr. of the Revenue and takes our License regularly."

[1585] Robert owned the store at Coal Landing.

[1586] Lemuel lived in Falmouth. He died of cancer of the tongue (*Free Lance*, May 28, 1904).

Robert Flatford & Son

William Herndon[1588] (1824-1904)

1882—Josephine B. Newton

1888—Elijah Alexander Groves[1589] (1853-1931)
Richard C. Perry[1591] (c.1862-1908)
Joseph A. Armstrong (born c.1847)
D.W. Coakley

Joseph P. Black[1590] (c.1866-1908)
George G. Lightner
John M. Stevens
John Peyton Jones[1592] (born c.1842)

1889—Joseph W. Black
John M. Stevens[1593]
D. W. Coakley[1595]

Fielding B. Burton
Broaddus Herndon Chinn[1594] (1853-1922)
John H. Leiber[1596] (born c.1858)

1890—E. Alexander Groves

1892—John H. Leiber
Joseph A. Armstrong
E. Alexander Groves

George J. Lightner
Fielding B. Burton
Hume V. Ross

1895—Fielding B. Burton

John Armstrong

1898—Lindsay G. Roach & Company[1597]

[1587] For many years William operated a store at Coal Landing. He was a member of Ebenezer Methodist Church and died of "liver trouble" (*Free Lance*, Mar. 2, 1915).
[1588] William was licensed to sell liquor at Stafford Store.
[1589] Groves operated a store at Brooke for 40 years. He was the son of John T. Groves (c.1833-c.1899). The following notice appeared in a local newspaper:

> Mr. E. A. Groves, of Brooke, was here Thursday celebrating the 40th anniversary of his marriage. He said he was going home and set traps for his wild hogs in Marlborough, of which he catches and ships 50 to 100 each year (*Fredericksburg Daily Star*, Dec. 23, 1915).

[1590] Joseph was the son of John and Eliza Black. In 1889 he married Gabriella Boutchyard (born c.1872), the daughter of John and E. Boutchyard.
[1591] Richard was the son of John Robert Perry and Mary Elizabeth Murdock. In 1891 he married Sarah Frances "Fanny" Herndon (1870-1961). Richard died of stomach cancer. Shortly before his death, he purchased a lot on Commerce Street in Fredericksburg upon which he was having a large warehouse built.
[1592] The son of James and Susan Jones. In 1868 he married Marian L. Schooler (born c.1841), the daughter of John and Laurinda Schooler.
[1593] John was granted a license "to retail liquor and keep a bar at Stafford C. H."
[1594] Broaddus was the son of Robert Alexander Chinn and Sarah Jesse Rowe of Stafford. He lived much of his life in Stafford, but eventually moved to Sealston in King George County where he operated a store. He died unmarried of Bright's Disease and hear disease and was buried at White Oak Primitive Baptist Church.
[1595] Granted a license to sell spirits at Onville.
[1596] The son of the Rev. Henry Leiber (born c.1823). He was granted a license to sell spirits at Onville. John was born in Pennsylvania.
[1597] Lindsay Gordon Roach (c.1850-1939) was granted a license "to conduct said business near Roach's Mill." Roach's Mill was the old Chatham Mill and was located very near the Rappahannock River and below Woodmont Nursing Home.

Lindsay was the son of James Roach (born c.1834) and Jane Gordon Willis. He was born at Spring Hills in Orange County and came to Stafford with his parents around 1855. A highly successful businessman, Lindsay operated Roach's Grist Mill, organized the Coca-Cola Bottling Company in 1916,

1900 [1598]—E. W. Mills 　　　B. L. Payne	Fielding B. Burton John Potts Jones[1599] (1856-1914)
1903—W. F. Green[1600] 　　　Henry C. Vine (died c.1912)	Kendrick B. Combs (c.1857-1912)
1904—C. Howard Kennedy	Lindsay G. Roach & Company
1906—C. Howard Kennedy	Lindsay G. Roach

---

was a charter ember of the Elks Lodge, and from 1927-1931 served on the Fredericksburg City Council. He married Elizabeth Downes of Fredericksburg.

[1598] From time to time there was debate regarding the wisdom of permitting the sale of liquor. In 1900 the *Free Lance* carried the following report:

> STAFFORD COURT. At Stafford court Wednesday the day was spent in contesting the applications for granting liquor licenses. Judge Goolrick represented the applicants and Hon. T. Weldon Berrey the opponents. It was a trial full of interest. Among those who protested against the licenses were: Rev. Decatur Edwards, Rev. J. K. Gilbert, Messrs. E. W. Brooks, Payne, Sullivan, Jones and many others. They represented Falmouth as a place totally unsuitable for the sale of liquor on account of its being without legal protection; recited instances of church worship being disturbed by men under the influence of the liquid and fighting and rioting on Sunday. The other side said Falmouth was a model village, but they would like to have a magistrate and constable who would be a safeguard against any disorder. The opponents, without an exception, said if liquor was to be sold there they had no objection to the present dealers being grated license, but they were opposed to its being sold in Falmouth or anywhere else. Judge Chichester granted the licenses and gave protection by appointed Mr. Charles F. Towlson justice of the peace, and Mr. E. W. Brooks constable...A request was made to the court that the old court-house in the village be fitted up for a jail, which he will consider.
> (*Free Lance*, May 19, 1900)

[1599] John married Sarah West (1867-1935).

[1600] Green, Combs, and Vine were all granted licenses to distill fruit brandy.

Sources:

Columbian Mirror and Alexandria Gazette, Apr. 1, 1800, William P. Bayly's merchant advertisement
Dobson, David. *Scots on the Chesapeake: 1607-1830*. Baltimore, MD: Genealogical Publishing Co., 1992.
Dunbar, Robert. Accounts, 1821-1829. Papers. Accession #2004-039. Fredericksburg, VA: Central Rappahannock Heritage Center.
---. Papers. Agreements. Accession #2004-039. Fredericksburg, VA: Central Rappahannock Heritage Center.
Fisher, Therese A. *Marriage Records of the City of Fredericksburg and the County of Stafford, Virginia 1851-1900*. Bowie, MD: Heritage Books, 1994.
Fredericksburg Daily Star, Dec. 23, 1915, E. A. Groves celebrates 40th anniversary
---, July 9, 1918, marriage of Ashton C. Carter and Gracie G. Raines
Fredericksburg Ledger, Mar. 25, 1873, obituary of James T. Abbott
---, Apr. 22, 1873, obituary of Henry Love
Fredericksburg News, July 24, 1856, obituary of Ezra Burr
---, Dec. 1, 1856, advertisement of Simeon C. Peyton
---, Oct. 5, 1874, article about pre-Civil War Falmouth
Fredericksburg Star, Sept. 6, 1884, notice regarding Silas Haislip's attempted suicide
---, Sept. 10, 1884, obituary of Silas Haislip
Free Lance, Mar. 17, 1885, obituary of Paul Hoyer
---, Oct. 6, 1885, obituary of James S. Petty
---, Mar. 21, 1896, obituary of William J. Burton
---, May 19, 1900, objections to the sale of liquor in Falmouth
---, May 10, 1904, obituary of William Knight
---, May 28, 1904, obituary of Lemuel Limerick
---, May 19, 1908, obituary of Charles F. Towson
---, Dec. 17, 1908, obituary of Joseph P. Black
---, Sept. 28, 1912, obituary of Ennever Lucas
---, July 11, 1914, obituary of Thomas Wallace
---, Mar. 2, 1915, obituary of William S. Towson
---, Dec. 4, 1917, obituary of Robert S. Moncure
---, Apr. 2, 1918, obituary of William Black
---, May 22, 1919, obituary of D. W. Patton
---, Oct. 15, 1919, obituary of Turner R. Garrison
---, Sept. 2, 1922, obituary of Beverley W. Irvine
---, Mar. 24, 1923, obituary of William A. Clift
---, Apr. 1, 1926, obituary of John Marshall Green
Free Lance Star, Dec. 8, 1926, obituary of William F. Green
---, Dec. 23, 1927, obituary of Armistead Nelson
---, Dec. 20, 1928, obituary of James E. Woody
---, July 13, 1931, obituary of E. A. Groves
---, Sept. 2, 1932, obituary of William H. Rollins
---, July 11, 1935, obituary of Hattie A. English
---, Jan. 21, 1937, obituary of Edward L. Sterne
---, June 21, 1939, obituary of Lindsay G. Roach
---, Mar. 3, 1943, obituary of John H. Benton
---, Mar. 9, 1944, obituary of Monroe Decatur
---, May 17, 1947, obituary of Milton H. Homes
---, Mar. 17, 1950, obituary of Powhatan English
---, May 31, 1951, obituary of John N. Dishman
---, Mar. 14, 1953, obituary of Richard A. Cloe
Kinsey, Margaret B. *Mountjoy Omnibus*. Baltimore, MD: Gateway Press, Inc., 2001.
Krick, Robert K. *9th Virginia Cavalry*. Lynchburg, VA: H. E. Howard, Inc., 1982.
Lombus, William. *Latham: a Catalog of Virginia and Ohio Families*. Self-published, 1998.
Moncure Family Collection. Estate of Mrs. Louise Moncure, Stafford, Virginia.

Musselman, Carl P. and Mildred H. *Musselman-Powell and Bowling Families of Stafford and Spotsylvania Counties, Virginia*. Fredericksburg, VA: Bookcrafters, 1993.
Musselman, Homer D. *47th Virginia Infantry*. Lynchburg: H. E. Howard, Inc. 1991.
---. *Stafford County, Virginia Veterans and Cemeteries*. Fredericksburg, VA: Bookcrafters, 1994.
Northern Neck News, May 15, 1885, James Lane Green removed as Mail Route Messenger
Political Arena, Mar. 16, 1841, obituary of Gerrard Fugitt
Stafford County Land Tax Records
Stafford County Personal Property Tax Records
Virginia Herald, Aug. 2, 1809, obituary of Joseph Ashton
---, June 6, 1812, Elliott Fishback's merchant advertisement
---, Jan. 13, 1813, Elliott Fishback director of Farmers Bank
---, July 8, 1815, William Brooke, Jr.'s merchant advertisement
---, Sept. 30, 1815, James Gallagher's merchant advertisement
---, Nov. 11, 1815, Ezra Burr's merchant advertisement
---, Mar. 20, 1816, James Vass' merchant advertisement
---, Apr. 13, 1816, Whitfield Brooke's merchant advertisement
---, Apr. 13, 1816, Ezra Burr's merchant advertisement
---, June 22, 1816, James Gallagher married Frances Brundige
---, Mar. 12, 1817, Jameson Corbin's merchant advertisement
---, Aug. 5, 1818, James Vass' merchant advertisement
---, Dec. 2, 1820, Robert Croughton's merchant advertisement
---, Feb. 9, 1822, obituary of Jesse Hill
---, Oct. 16, 1822, John O'Ryan rented Falmouth corn mill
---, Jan. 8, 1823, Abram Howard's advertisement for blacksmith shop and house of private entertainment
---, July 27, 1824, George W. Billingsley manager of Falls Mills
---, July 13, 1825, William P. Cunningham's merchant advertisement
---, Sept. 20, 1826, William P. Cunningham's merchant advertisement
---, Mar. 17, 1832, notice of James Cave's fishing shore
Virginia Star, Mar. 24, 1877, advertisement for Paul Hoyer's store
von Staffenburg, Theodore F. *The Shumate Family*. Self-published, 1964.

Abbott, James T. (died 1873) 251
    John 158
    Mary 158
    Mary E. (Blackburn) (1824-c.1874) 158
Abel, Catherine (Wiggenton) (born c.1854) 193
    Elijah C. (1869-1913) 264
    Rosa C. (Embrey) (born c.1877) 264
    Wallace Hansford (1909-1989) 205-207
    Zephyr (1875-1968) 244
Abel Reservoir (Stafford County) 84, 148, 160, 193, 259
Abolitionist Movement 13
Ackley, Julius 272
Accokeek Bridge (Stafford County) 136, 161
Accokeek Creek/Run (Stafford County) 3, 6, 14, 43, 55, 56, 63, 137, 138, 151, 153, 161, 162, 167, 170, 171, 173-175, 187
Accokeek ford (Stafford County) 161
Accokeek Iron Furnace (Stafford County) 12, 49, 127, 139, 177
Accokeek plantation (Stafford County) 40
Accokeek Post Office (Stafford County) 222, 232
Accokeek Station (Stafford County) 220, 283
Accomac County, Virginia 88
Accotinct Run (Fairfax County) 45
Acton, Maine 190
Adams, John 252
    Margaret (McCall) 252
    Thomas B. 252
Adams County, Ohio 152
Adie, Ann Fisher (Tyler) (1756-1818) 131
    Ann (Waller) (1792-1870) 83
    Benjamin (1762-c.1825) 10, 131, 181
    Elizabeth (Parrender) (born 1729) 55
    Hugh 27
    Hugh (c.1783-after 1860) 181, 272
    Hugh (1833-1918) 114, 166, 173, 180-183, 222, 233, 264
    Jane (Bell) 234, 261
    Samuel 245
    Thomas B. (died 1836) 69
    William 55
    William (1729-1797) 55, 131
Adie, Hugh & Co. (business) 264
Adieville Post Office (Stafford County) 222, 233
Aetna Insurance Company 154
Albemarle County, Virginia 11, 15, 159, 164, 202, 203
Alberger, M. H. 234, 235
Albion (Stafford County) 91, 137
Alcock, Abner Roane (died c.1831) 148, 245, 272, 274
    Ann (Roane) (c.1757-1836) 269, 275, 276
    Elizabeth (Hazelgrove) 245
    Fanny (Hackett) 269
    Thomas (1744-1834) 148, 245, 269-272, 274, 275

    William (died 1768) 269
Alcock's Mill (Stafford County) 148, 269
Alexander, Capt. ___ 115
    Almira 147
    Anne Casson (Morson) (1781-1833) 60, 72, 145
    Anne (Fowke) (1690-1739) 45, 48
    Anne Fowke (Hooe) (1712-c.1776) 48, 55, 125
    Charles (1737-1806) 55, 56
    Elizabeth Ashton (Lee) (born 1760) 18
    Elizabeth (Dade) (1698-1736) 44
    Fielding (died 1847) 78
    Frances A. (Waller) 147, 275
    Frances (Fitzhugh) 41
    Frances (Stuart) (1728-after 1777) 51, 128
    G. W. 189
    Harriet C. (born c.1803) 234
    James 274
    John 152
    Capt. John (died 1677) 27, 37, 38, 41, 43, 44, 116
    John (1711-1763) 55, 58
    John (1735-1775) 6, 7, 56
    Julia Anton (Kale) (1833-1887) 84
    Leonard P. (born c.1832) 232, 233, 244, 262, 277
    Lewis (died 1827) 234
    Lucy (Brooke) (born c.1783) 84
    Lucy (Thornton) 6
    Marian M. (Clift) 78
    Minnie (Schooler) 78
    Parthenia (Dade) (Massey) (1709-1742) 49
    Philip 236, 257
    Capt. Philip (c.1664-1705) 43, 44, 47, 124
    Capt. Philip (1704-1753) 6, 10, 47-51, 124, 127
    Philip Thornton (1783-1817) 84
    Priscilla (Ashton) 41, 45
    Robert (c.1634-1704) 41-43, 45
    Maj. Robert (c.1688-1735) 45, 48
    Capt. Robert Brooke (c.1811-1878) 84
    Samuel Lutz (1912-1972) 205-207
    Sarah (Ashton) (Clifton) (born c.1675) 43, 44, 124
    Sarah Bruce (Casson) 58
    Sarah (Hooe) (c.1707-1758) 6, 47, 124
    Sigismunda Mary (Massey) (born 1745) 10
    Susan Pearson (Seddon) (died 1845) 13
    Susannah (Pearson) (born 1717) 58
    Theresa E. 244
    Col. Thornton (1790-1842) 146-149, 151, 271-275
    William (c.1736-1810) 133-138
    William A. (1744-1837) 10

William Pearson (1758-1804) 57-63
Alexander & Reid (business) 280
Alexander & Schooler (business) 281
Alexandria, Virginia 13, 14, 17, 19, 31, 38, 47,
    124, 188, 219, 222, 252, 259, 266, 283
Allason, David (1736-after 1815) 251-253
    John 251
    William (1712-1768) 151
Allegar, Charles W. (1882-1905) 244
Allen, Ann (Bradford) (born c.1730) 274
    Elizabeth (Waller) (1746-1768) 13, 131
    Hannah (Withers) (died 1801) 139
    Margaret 139
    William 139
Allerton, Elizabeth (Willoughby) (Overzee)
    (Colclough) 38
    Fear (Brewster) (died c.1635) 38
    Isaac (died 1659) 38
    Maj. Isaac (c.1627:30-1702) 38
Alsop, Albert B. (1820-1864) 161
    Elizabeth (Spindle) 77
Alta Vista (Spotsylvania County) 20
Alto (King George County) 15
Amaret Farm (Spotsylvania County) 154
Ambler, Catherine Cary (Moncure) 173
Amelia County, Virginia 202
American Revolution iv, 56, 58, 59, 60, 64, 65, 67, 73,
    107, 112, 128, 130, 137-139
Amherst County, Virginia 11, 134
Amis, Lucy (Fishback) 254
Anacostia (Washington, DC) 38
Anderson, Annie Rebecca (Curtis) (1858-1897) 92, 235
    David 116, 118
    Capt. George 5, 43, 44, 48, 119-121, 126
    James A. (c.1832-c.1869) 85, 165, 177, 246
    Jesse R. (c.1843-1900) 194
    John 43
    John (c.1812-1868) 235
    Luke 153
    Mary (Mathews) 43, 48
    Mary Miller (Scott) 164
    Philadelphia (Curtis) (c.1828-1898) 194, 235
    Rosanna (Doniphan) 126
    Sarah Travers Lewis (Gordon) (1874-1968)
    2, 202
    William 258, 280
Andrew, Marion (Morson) (Payne) (c.1724-1808)
    58, 60, 70
Andrew Chapel Methodist Church (Stafford County)
    91, 173, 174, 180, 200, 232
Andrews, George 118
    Sarah Frances (Harper) (1826-1911) 283
Annapolis, Maryland 8, 15, 174
Anne Arundel County, Maryland 8
Anne E. Moncure Elementary School (Stafford
    County) 173

Anthony, John (born c.1821) 159, 161, 172, 174
Antioch Methodist Church (Stafford County) 89,
    242
Apple Grove (Stafford County) 164, 165
Appleton, Frances (Gerrard) (Speake) (Peyton)
    (Washington) 3
    John (1640-1676) 3
Appomattox, Virginia 176, 179, 190, 238
Aqueduct Company of Fredericksburg 69
Aquia Church (Stafford County) 6, 10, 12, 14,
    15, 17, 49, 68, 105, 109, 123, 126, 140,
    164, 190, 193, 201, 202, 248
Aquia Creek/Run 3, 5, 10, 13, 16, 28, 39-41, 45, 47,
    49, 52, 59, 63, 66, 71-74, 76, 78, 80, 85,
    111, 116, 126, 127, 131, 147-149, 151, 154,
    164, 171, 173, 179, 180, 182, 184, 190,
    205, 219, 220, 222, 223, 228, 233, 247,
    251, 252, 264, 274, 277, 282, 283
Aquia Creek Ferry (Stafford County) 116, 251
Aquia District 113, 178-185, 188, 189, 192-208
Aquia Harbour Country Club 4, 61
Aquia Harbour subdivision 4, 5, 6, 61, 122, 127,
    139, 233
Aquia Landing (Stafford County) 219
Aquia Post Office (Stafford County) 222, 233, 237
Aquia Precinct 159, 187, 189
Aquia Road 71, 85, 114, 137, 139, 171-175, 180
Aquia Run Mills Post Office (Stafford County) 233
Aquia Station (Stafford County) 220
Aquia, Town 9, 42, 61, 62, 108, 136, 137, 147,
    151, 152, 156, 158-160, 172, 176, 252,
    258-261, 267, 274, 276
Aquia Town Center (shopping center) 62
Aquia Township (Stafford County) 115
Aquia Warehouse 108, 127, 129, 130, 134, 138,
    139, 141, 142
Arkendale Post Office (Stafford County) 222, 231,
    234
Arkendale Road (Stafford County) 174, 175
Arkendale Station (Stafford County) 220
Arkholme, England 39
Armstrong, ___ 92
    A. C. (Blackburn) (born c.1866) 93
    Ambrose 151
    Ann E. 234
    Armistead A. (c.1816-1885) 150, 172, 174,
    195
    Ashton A. (1903-1959) 244
    Catherine 150
    Delia Ann (Heflin) (1845-1930) 94, 195
    Edgar William (1855-1941) 242
    Elvira Fant (Fritter) (1834-after 1900) 242,
    264
    Fannie L. (Skidmore) (1879-1967) 264
    George Henry (1830-1863) 158, 242, 264
    George Lee (1863-1952) 264

James 150, 163, 234
James (c.1790-after 1850) 273
James Edward (born 1857) 196, 197, 199
James Fenton (born 1856) 234
James W. (born c.1839) 167
John 284
Joseph A. (born c.1847) 284
Mary Ann (Conyers) (born c.1789) 154, 158
Ollie M. 244
Susan R. (English) (born c.1863) 264
Susan "Snowie" (Bryant) (1874-1935) 242
Wellford B. (born c.1865) 93
William (born c.1817) 154, 159, 160, 162, 167, 170, 172, 174, 175
Armstrong's Arbor (Stafford County) 15
Army of Northern Virginia 175
Arnold, James, 184
    John 164
Arnold's Crossing (Stafford County) 167, 175
Arrington, Bailey 204
    Catherine (Bell) 153
    Thomas T. (c.1796-after 1860) 261
Arrington, Thomas T. & Son (business) 261
Ashby, Benjamin 179, 259
    Dorothea Farrer (Green) (1797-1865) 14, 166
    Dorothea "Dora" (Moncure) (1838-1911) 81
    Frances Vowles (Moncure) (1828-1910) 166
    Gustavus (born c.1800) 273-275
    James (1827-1861) 65, 166
    James (1854-1918) 188, 191, 196-201
    James (1894-1950) 188, 201-206
    John 270
    John A. 179
    John Moncure (1852-1918) 187
    Martha W. (Cole) (1839-1864) 179
    Mary Conway (Moncure) (1830-1897) 14, 89, 169, 192, 195
    Richard L. 207, 208
    Sarah 179
    Col. Turner (1789-1835) 14, 81, 166
    Gen. Turner (1828-1862) 14, 81, 166, 168
    Virginia G. (Herndon) (born c.1852) 173, 263
    Virginia (Percifull) (1896-1925) 201
    William 260
    William (born c.1814) 162, 167, 283
Ashby, William & Benjamin (business) 260
Ashland, Virginia 80
Ashmore, Charlotte (Keith) 83
Ashton, Gissie (Franklin) (born c.1848) 85
    Grace (Frizer) 43
    Dr. Horace D. (1821-1894) 85
    James 40
    James (died 1686) 38
    Capt. John (died 1677) 43, 44, 124
    Joseph (died 1809) 269
    M. T. 85

    Col. Peter 38
    Priscilla (Alexander) 41, 45
    Sarah (Alexander) (Clifton) (born c. 1675) 43, 44, 124
Atchison, Cynthia 177
    Isabella (Berry) (Herndon) (1832-1897) 90, 177
    Lydia C. (Minnick) (1852-1925) 93, 201
    Rodney 177
    Wellford Clinton (1848-1924) 93, 201
Atlanta, Battle of 15
Aubrey, Frances (Tanner) 46
    Francis (c.1685-1741) 46
    Henry (died c.1694) 46
    John (c.1623-c.1692) 46
Auburn (Stafford County) 80, 252
Augusta County, Virginia 253, 268
Austin Run (Stafford County) 39, 71, 85
Autauga County, Alabama 149, 273
Axton, John 115
Aylett, Anne (c.1736-1768) 18
    Mary (Lee) 10
Babcock, Maria D. (Dewey) (1818-1890) 189
    Samuel (c.1806-1895) 189, 225, 240
Babcock's Run (Stafford County) 187
Baber, Alice N. (Riley) (1863-1944) 195
    Frederick William, Sr. (1861-1937) 196, 200, 201
    William (c.1834-1921) 196
Bacon, Nathaniel 2
Bailey, Mary (Washington) 52, 129
Bainbridge, Fellow 15
Baker, Emily Emma (England) (died c.1909) 191
    Fielding (1799-after 1870) 146, 170
    James Pulaski (c.1825-c.1869) 170, 177
    John 156
    Moses 191
Balch, Edith (Lee) 234
Baldwin, Frances (Townsend) (Williams) 37
Ball, Bettie 259
    Hannah (Beale) (c.1674-before 1744) 45
    Hannah (Travers) (c.1683-1748) 48, 61, 127
    James H. (c.1831-1907) 160
    Jane (Ball) (1822-1909) 176
    Jane (Vernon) 138
    Col. Joseph (1649-1711) 48, 137
    Martha (Brumfield) 138
    Nathaniel (1830-1906) 176
    Penelope (Gollahorn) (c.1789-1872) 259
    Sarah (McCarty) (born 1705) 45, 123
    William 171, 259
    William (died 1782) 138
    William (1768-1815) 138
    William (c.1799-after 1860) 176
    Col. William (1674-1740) 45

Ballard, ___ 92
    Ann F. (Finnall) 279
    Aphia (Sanford) (c.1814-1846) 158
    Flavius Josephus (1808-1892) 158, 179, 181-183
    James (1763-1856) 162
    Judith 279
    William G. 225, 239
Balse, Oliver 115
Balthrop, Mary (Christian) 118
    William 118
Baltimore & Rappahannock Steam Packet Company 70
Baltimore County, Maryland 71, 87
Baltimore Iron Works (Maryland) 46
Baltimore, Maryland 149, 159, 197, 219, 242, 244, 263, 283
Bandy, Alvin Y. 207, 208
Bank of Quantico (Prince William County) 17
Bankhead, Dorothea (Minor) (1805-1868) 81
    Georgeanna Cary (Moncure) (1830-1890) 81
    Nora (Lee) (1841-1915) 234
    Dr. William (1795-1873) 81
Banks, Adam (died before 1690) 11
    Adam (1700-1755) 59, 133
    Frances (Bruce) (1735-1818) 11, 59, 62, 69, 133, 146
    George (1779-1837) 11, 72, 73, 146, 149
    Gerard (1725-1787) 11, 59, 60, 62, 69, 133, 134, 146
    Gerard (c.1759-1816) 62
    Gerard (1779-1837) 69
    Jemima Anne (Overton) (1789-1863) 11, 69
    Mary (Pettit) 136
    Rosanna (Bryan) (died after 1784) 59, 133
    Dr. William (died c.1687) 39
Banks' Ford (Stafford County) 114, 172, 174
Banks' Road (Stafford County) 172
Barber, ___ 88
    Ann (Tackett) 71, 77
    Edward 149, 154
    Elias (born c.1809) 256, 257
    James 193, 197
    John M. 256
    L. 149
    Sarah Roy (Mason) 154
    Thomas 106, 123
    Capt. William (1787-1881) 74-78, 149, 151, 154-156, 172, 182, 275, 276
Barker, Mary (Fristoe) (1735-1759) 64
Barnes, Frances L. B. (Peyton) (born c.1823) 161
    George B. (born c.1832) 262
    Harrison Brockenbrough (born c.1813) 29, 161, 180, 187, 262
    Lucy (Smith) (died 1926) 245
    Mary W. (Rouse) (c.1864-1918) 245

    Newman B. (died 1853) 268, 272
    Penelope (Manly) 55
    Richard 55
    Sarah (Hooe) (1742-1805) 55
Barnesville, Maryland, Battle of (1862) 164
Barnesville, Maryland 164
Barrow, Edward 121, 122
Barton House (Fredericksburg) 251
Basford, John 117
Basye, William 19
Baton Rouge, Battle of 15
Battaile, Sarah (Fitzhugh) 50
Battaley, Fielding 273-275, 279
    Rebecca (Monteith) 273
Battlefield Park Association 186
Battlefield Park Commission 186
Baxter, Eleanor (Taylor) 149
    Thornton 149
Bayl(e)y, Ambrose 27
    John 252
    Josiah F. 260
    Mary L. (Grymes) 252
    Pierce 252
    William 237
    William Pierce (born 1773) 252
Bayly, William P. & Co. (business) 252
Baylor, Frances 60
    Lucy (Morton) (born c.1726) 60
    Robert 60
Baynham, Alexander (died 1662) 2
Beach, Charles 271
    Louisa Dora (Heflin) 94, 200
    William 116
Beagle, James 148, 275
Beal(e), Hannah (Gordon) 69
    Hannah (Ball) (c.1674-before 1744) 45
    Hannah J. 89, 196
    Jane Briggs (Howison) (1815-1882) 69
    John 79
    John E. (1852-1936) 89, 242
    Mary J. (Coakley) (born c.1856) 196, 205
    N. A. (Lunsford) (born c.1851) 89
    Susan (Vowles) 69
    William 69
    William Churchill (1791-1850) 69-71, 149, 254-262, 280
    William L. 89, 196
    Winifred (Lee) (Brent) (1790-1833) 11, 65
Bealton Post Office (Fauquier County) 223-225, 228
Beaty, Charlotte 262
    James W. (died 1906) 159
    Mollie (Hart) 159
    Robert 145, 262
    Robert (c.1818-1855) 262
Beaverdam Run (Stafford County) 65, 77, 172,

174, 175
Bedford (King George County) 3-5, 50, 53
Bedfordshire, England 2
Belair (King George County) 19
Bel-Air (Spotsylvania County) 12, 159, 160, 164
Bell, Ashley (born 1770) 234
    Benjamin Ashley (1840-1905) 179, 180, 188, 264
    Catherine (Arrington) 153
    Charles 245
    Daniel 137
    Eleanor (Stark) (born c.1817) 153, 158
    Elijah 245
    Elizabeth (Ratliff) (1775-1847) 142
    Eva E. (1868-1948) 264
    Frances (Powers) (1846-1918) 179
    George 245
    James 245, 257
    Jane (born c.1801) 179
    Jane (Adie) 234, 261
    John 142, 267-272
    John (died c.1728) 245
    John Fendall 234, 261, 262
    John H. 179
    Joseph H. 272, 273
    Susan (Sutherland) 234
    Thomas 153, 245
    William 245, 270, 272, 273
    William (1771-1855) 142-150, 152
Bell Atlantic Building (Stafford County) 231
Bell View (Stafford County) 6, 10
Bellair (Stafford County) 52, 53, 85, 161, 240
Bellair Baptist Church (Stafford County) 188
Belle Grove (King George County) 16
Belle Plains (Stafford County) 6, 8, 27, 52, 80, 81, 158, 164, 273
Bellevue (Fauquier County) 169
Bellfair Mills (Stafford County) 65, 80, 86, 113, 114, 127, 145, 158, 159, 173, 176, 220, 228, 265, 266
Bellfair Mills Post Office (Stafford County) 222, 226
Bellmead (Stafford County) 161
Bell's Hill Road (State Route 631) 93
Bellview hill (Stafford County) 171
Belman, Ferris M., Sr. 208
Belmont (Fairfax County) 123
Belmont (Stafford County) 58, 70, 154, 188, 236
Belmont Mill (Stafford County) 236
Ben Franklin Store (Fredericksburg) 60
Bennett, Anna (Bland) 2
    Richard 2
Benson, Betty (Irvine) 198
    Dulcabella (Berry) 137 151
    Eleanor (Bullard) 75
    Emma L. (Kingston) (1845-1882) 177
    Enoch Berry 137, 138
    James (died 1812) 137
    James R. (1814-c.1890) 75, 77
    Orlando Parsons (born c.1843) 177
    Susan Carter (Primmer) (1850-1919) 177
    Susan R. 75
    William Willis Lewis (died 1815) 75
    Winifred Berry (Richards) 151
Benton, Fannie Daniel (Guy) (1888-1951) 265
    John Hogan (1882-1943) 265
    Lillie Ida 265
    R. N. 265
Berea (Stafford County) 189, 234, 237
Berea Baptist Church (Stafford County) 112, 168, 170, 172, 185, 190, 191, 230, 235, 268
Berea Church Road (State Route 654) 230
Berea Post Office (Stafford County) 137, 222, 225, 228, 230, 234, 239, 245, 268
Berkeley, Gov. William 2, 25
Berkeley Hundred (Charles City County) 2
Bermuda 3
Bernard, Behethland (Gilson) (Dade) (1635-1720) 38, 42
    Elizabeth (Hart) (Storke) 44, 52, 126
    Richard (1705-1753) 48, 49, 50, 51, 126
    Sallie (Lightfoot) 169
    Capt. Thomas (died c.1651) 42
    Mrs. William 33
Berry, Ada J. (Jett)
    Dulcabella (Bunbury) 128
    Dulcabella (Conway) 128
    Enoch (c.1700-1763) 128
    Gordon W. 235
    Harrison 95
    Isabella (Atchison) (Herndon) (1832-1897) 90, 177
    James Edward (c.1833-1913) 175, 177, 189
    John L. 235
    Lucy 240
    Mary A. (Payne) 93
    Mary Virginia (Fritter) (died 1946) 202
    Mary (Watson) 202
    Nelson Norman (1885-1962) 202-206, 266
    Oscar (1844-1913) 240
    Richard (c.1807-1867) 175, 189
    Sarah (born c.1810) 175, 189
    Spencer B. 202
    Thomas Weldon 15, 284
    Thomas 202
    William T. (c.1871-1942) 93
Berry Hill (Stafford County) 10
Bethel, Edward 133
    Mary (Mason) (died 1831) 137, 147
Bethel Baptist Church (Stafford County) 88, 94, 165, 185, 187, 188, 241
Bethel Church Road (State Route 600) 131, 153

Bethel Military Academy (Fauquier County) 15, 16
Bethlehem Cemetery (Alexandria, Virginia) 19
Bettis, Elizabeth (Embrey) (born c.1873) 93
    Georgeanna 93
    Mary Amelia (Fritter) (born c.1852) 171
    Thomas 93
Beverley, Ursula (Fitzhugh) 48
    Co. William 48
Bibb, William E. (c.1845-1910) 20
Billingsley, George W. 273
    Virginia Jane Lewis (Heflin) 16
    William B. 258, 279
Birkhead, Rev. J. H. 191
Black, Delilia (Bussell) (1819-1896) 235
    Eliza 283
    Frances (Bussell) 235
    Gabriella (Boutchyard) (born c.1872) 283
    George (c.1800-after 1870) 264
    James (c.1818-1850) 235
    John 283
    Joseph P. (c.1866-1908) 283
    Joseph W. 284
    William L. (c.1848-1918) 265
    William Morgan (1848-1918) 223, 235, 242
Black Horse Cavalry 177
Black Swamp (Stafford County) 172
Blackburn, A. C. (Armstrong) (born c.1866) 93
    Alexander W. (1817-1871) 159
    Ann (Conyers) (born c.1789) 154, 158
    Charles F. (1849-1899) 238
    Christopher (died c.1819) 154, 158, 269, 271, 272
    George K. (1824-1890) 158, 171, 179, 181, 185, 187, 183, 193
    Mary E. (Abbott) (1824-c.1874) 158
    Nannie (Waller) (1848-1912) 238
Blacksmith shop (Stafford County) 171
Blackwell, Ann 63, 253
    Ann (Richards) 63, 253
    John 63, 253
Blake, Kathleen (Scaggs) (born c.1873) 165
    Mary Ann (born c.1823) 165
    Robert Norman (c.1804-1892) 165, 168, 187
    Robert P. (born c.1849) 185, 186
    Samuel 168
    William Norman (c.1804-1892) 165
Blancette, Sarah (Shacklett) 244
Bland, Anna (Bennett) 2
    Edward (1613-1652) 2
    John (died 1632) 2
    Richard (1665-1720) 2, 118, 119
    Susanna (de Deblere) 2
    Theodorick (1629-1671) 2, 118, 119
    Theodorick (1662-1700) 2, 27, 118, 119
Bloomington (Stafford County) 55, 83, 131, 192
Bloxham, Thompson M. 152

    William 160
Bloxton, Alexander E. (1846-1921) 246
    Battle G. (1874-1961) 265
    Benedicta (Maddox) (Flourey) 271
    James 16, 187
    James Posey (born c.1843) 192
    Samuel (died 1817) 271
    Samuel B. (born c.1799) 192
    William 163, 164
Blue Wing Post Office (Stafford County) 222, 231, 234
Board of Supervisors, position of 113-114
Bohemia Manor (Maryland) 178
Bolling, Bessie (English) 266
    Maria (Edwards) (born c.1855) 278
Bonhomme Richard (ship) 64
Boone County, Illinois 193
Booth, Catherine (Fitzhugh) (died 1748) 51
    John Wilkes 15
Borst, Addison 181
    Bettie G. (Taliaferro) 181
    Cornelia R. (Gordon) (1880-1949) 203
Boscobel (Stafford County) 11, 12, 20, 51, 53, 59, 65, 67, 166, 172, 176
Boscobel Farms subdivision 51, 52
Boston, Massachusetts 13
Boswell, Thomas Frank (died c.1933) 264
Botetourt County, Virginia 149
Botts, Aaron (1746-1790) 141
    Albert Burnley (1841-1917) 33
    Catherine (Butler) 141
    Clinton Alexander (1861-1925) 93
    Cynthia Burton (Cooper) (c.1866-1957) 93
    Joseph (1748-1814) 141
    Nancy H. (King) (1800-1868) 179
    Richard Arthur (1898-1981) 93, 266
    Sabina (Bridwell) (c.1717-1785) 141
    Sarah (Browne) (1787-c.1826) 141
    Seth (1713-1776) 141
    W. Arthur 265
    William (1820-1868) 79
Botts, A. B. & Company (business) 33
Botts, W. Arthur & Brothers (business) 265
Bourbon County, Kentucky 131
Bourne, Claude W. 202
    George 64
    Sarah (Mason) (c.1771-1835) 64, 233
Boutchyard, E. 283
    Gabriella (Black) (born c.1872) 283
    James 187
    John 283
    Richard A. (1861-1932) 194
    William J. 194
Bowen, Burkett Pratt (c.1802-1852) 75-77, 156
    Elizabeth (Curtis) 75

John Pratt (died c.1838) 75, 280
    Rebecca (Jett) 132, 148
    Stephen (died 1749) 132
    Stephen P. (c.1813-1854) 273
    William B. 280
    William P. 258, 280
Bowen, William P. & Company (business) 258
Bowers, Michael 268, 270, 279
Bowie, Alexander 276
    Cora (Fitzhugh) 13
Bowin, Willie 265
Bowler, Anna M. (Payne) 275
    Charles 274
    George Adam (c.1832-1920) 240
    Hannah (Garner) (born 1815) 274
    Mildred (Jones) (c.1802-c.1834) 274, 275
    Reubin (1800-1856) 274, 275
    Thomas (1804-1887) 275
    William 240
    William W. (born c.1820) 262
Bowling, Francis 278
    George A. (c.1817-after 1902) 171, 173
    James E. 194, 236
    Julia Ann (Embrey) 236
    Maria 278
    Maria (Edwards) (born c.1855) 278
    Mary Eliza (Heflin) (1878-1941) 236
Boyd, W. L. 230
Boyer, Isaac 190, 195
Bradford, Ann Allen (born c.1730) 274
    Baldwin (c.1764-1848) 260, 274-276
    Benjamin Bennett (born 1738) 274
    Betsy (Foley) (born 1776) 260, 274
    Daniel (born 1815) 260
    Mary E. (Morriss) 260
Bradley, Thomas H. 234
Bradshaw, Harberson (c.1785-1843) 149, 279
    Jeremiah (c.1753-before 1803) 147
    Mary (Bridwell) (born c.1800) 173
    Nancy "Dicey" (Jeter) (died c.1823) 147
    R. R. (c.1819-after 1870) 263
    Zachariah (c.1785-before 1850) 147, 259
Bradshaw's (Stafford County) 261
Bramel, Mary E. 243
Branch, Mary E. 243
    Mirriam (Grundy) 230
Brandy Station (Culpeper County) 173, 187
Brandywine, Battle of (1777) 10, 131, 133
Brawner, Alexander 254
    Basil (c.1799-1893) 19
Braxton, Carter M. 77
    Elizabeth H. 77
    Sally Moore (Slaughter) (born c.1828) 77
Braxton's Battery 188, 189
Breezewood Farm (Spotsylvania County) 20
Brent, Capt. ___ 115

Anne (Carroll) (1733-1804) 9, 57, 138
Anne (Clifton) 43
Anne Fenton (Lee) (born 1754) 10, 11
Catherine (Trimmingham) (died 1751) 57
Daniel Carroll (1759-1814) 9-11, 59-64
Eleanor (Carroll) (born c.1737) 8, 10, 11
Elizabeth (Greene) (c.1655-1686) 3, 120
Euphan (Wallace) (Washington) (1765-1845) 9, 10
George 3, 256
Capt. George (1640-c.1700) 3, 4, 40, 111, 117-120
George (c.1703-1789) 46
George (1703-1778) 57
George (1760-1804) 9, 60-63, 138
Capt. Giles (1602-1671) 2, 4, 40
Giles (1652-1679) 47
Harriet (Slater) 256
Hugh (II) (1659-1716) 47, 122
Jane 8, 46
Jane (Mudd) 120
Margaret (c.1600-1671) 43
Marianna (Peyton) 3
Mary (Carter) 47, 122
Mary E. (Gill) (born c. 1849) 173
Mary Sewall (Chandler) (died 1694) 3
Molly (Fitzhugh) (Woodrow) 9, 61, 138
Nicholas (died 1711) 120, 121
Richard (c.1760-1814) 9
Robert (1730-1780) 9, 57, 137
Robert Carroll (died 1837) 61
Roxanna (Sommers) (1798-1882) 11, 65
Sarah (Gibbons) (c.1692-1733) 46
William (c.1677-1709) 46
Capt. William (1710-1742) 8, 46, 47, 53
Col. William (1733-1782) 7-11, 18, 53, 55-58,
William, Jr. (1783-1848) 11, 65-72, 77, 78, 254
Winifred Beale (Lee) (1790-1833) 11, 65
Brent & Cooke (business) 10, 253, 254
Brent Cemetery (Stafford County) 4, 61
Brent Point Road (State Route 658) 222
Brent's Mill (Stafford County) 10, 59, 151, 152, 155, 220, 227, 231, 232, 243
Brent's Mill Post Office (Stafford County) 231
Brent's Point (Stafford County) 40, 230
Brentown Road (Stafford County) 114, 148, 165
Brentsville, Virginia 228
Brewer, Alice "Jennie" (Wigfield) (1883-1971) 244
    Charles Julian (1880-1942) 202, 244
    Charles W. (1816-1892) 164, 170, 175, 187
    Hazel Jennie (Heflin) (1913-1997) 244
    John W. 166

Brewster, Fear (Allerton) (died c.1635) 38
Briarwood (Staffordshire, England) 2
Brick kiln (Stafford County) 158, 170, 177
Brick Store (Stafford County) 242
Brick yard (Stafford County) 172, 174
Bridges, (*see also Briggs*)
    Anthony 115
Bridgewater Flour Mill (Falmouth) 236
Bridwell, Ann (born c.1807) 166
    Benjamin 166
    Benjamin W. (c.1823-1856) 158
    Charles W. (born c.1834) 94, 244
    Charles W. (1867-1953) 94, 244
    Isaac (c.1781-1866) 173
    John Henry (c.1832-1891) 164, 173
    K. E. 195
    Lucy Ellen (Mountjoy) (c.1857-1935) 91
    Luther 191
    Margaret E. (Goodwin) (1842-after 1911) 166
    Mary (Bradshaw) (born c.1800) 173
    Mary E. (Gill) (born c.1849) 173
    Pauline (Herndon) (born c.1837) 94, 244
    Richard 147
    Robert L. (1887-1972) 93, 204, 205
    Sabina (Botts) (c.1717-1785) 141
    Timothy (c.1798-after 1860) 261, 276
    Virginia (Cooper) (born c.1870) 94
Bridwell & Whorton (business) 261
Brightwell, Ursula (Morton) 73
Briggs, Andrew (c.1861-1927) 92-94
    Arthur R. 236
    Bessie M. (Gordon) 236
    Charlotte Ashmore (Keith) (1782-1866) 83
    David (1730-1813) 72, 245, 255
    Delsey F. (Combs) (1864-1941) 185
    James (died 1843) 148
    James McDonald (c.1750-1810)
    James McDonald (1787-1845) 72-75, 83, 152-154, 245
    James McDonald (1822-1900) 83, 86, 159, 170, 176, 179, 189, 196
    Jean (McDonald) (c.1750-1810) 72
    Louisa Ann (Smith) 83, 196
    Lucinda (Short) 254
    Mary Frazier (Vowles) (1790-1852) 60
    Martha "Mattie" Ellen (Herndon) (born c.1862) 92
    Thomas 254
    Thompson Smith (1860-1910) 196
    W. B. 185
Briggs' Cemetery (Stafford County) 72
Briggs Station (Clarke County) 83
Bristol, England 44, 200
Bristow, Anne (Seal) 51
Bristow, Virginia 228
Bristow Post Office (Prince William County) 228

British Mercantile Claims 131
Brittingham, Betty (French) (Waugh) 47, 49
    Nathaniel 47, 49
Broad Run (Fauquier County) 45, 46, 180
Broadhurst, William 268
Broadwater, Charles (died 1733) 45
Bronaugh, Ann (Grayson) (born 176_) 71
    Benjamin 272
    Capt. David (1767-c.1853) 130
    Elizabeth 272, 273
    Hester (Stone) 233
    Col. Jeremiah (1702-1749) 52, 55, 125
    John (1743-1777) 55
    John M. (c.1733-1831) 148
    John M. 275
    John W. (c.1773-1834) 58
    Margaret (Grant) (c.1698-1756) 52, 53, 125
    Margaret (Murdock) 52
    Mary Anne (Carter) (born 1747) 55
    Mary (Doniphan) (Cooke) (1737-1781) 51, 52, 128
    Mary (Threlkeld) (Waugh) (died 1799) 59, 130
    Rebecca (Craine) 52
    Robert 258
    Simpha Rosa Enfield (Mason) (Dinwiddie) (1703-1762) 52, 55
    Col. William (1730-1800) 51-53, 55, 56
Brooke, Angelina (Edrington) (born c.1809) 13
    Ann Cary (Selden) 80
    Anne Mason Mercer (Selden) (1770-1812) 65
    Betty Lewis (Young) 168
    Clarissa T. (Robey) (died 1843) 89
    Elizabeth (Young) 71
    Fenton (Daniel) (born c.1828) 13, 74
    Fenton (Smith) 276
    Francis Taliaferro (c.1761-1851) 64, 65
    Henry Laurens (1808-1874) 80, 162, 163
    Jane 276
    John Mercer (1826-1906) 232
    John Taliaferro (1761-1821) 10, 64, 66, 71, 80, 141
    Julia Anton (Kale) (1833-1887) 84
    Dr. Lawrence (c.1758-1803) 64
    Lucy (Alexander) (born c.1783) 84
    Richard (died 1792) 64
    Robert 64
    Robert (1751-1799) 64
    St. George Tucker (1844-1914) 80
    Samuel Selden (1800-1861) 13, 71-76, 79, 148, 150-154, 156, 159, 162, 164, 166
    Samuel Selden, Jr. (1841-1918) 31, 168, 170

Sarah Virginia (Tucker) (born 1815) 80
Susanna (Vass) 252
Whitfield 255
William (died 1842) 138, 254, 256, 257, 272, 179, 180
William, Jr. 255, 258-260, 180
Brooke & Ficklen (business) 257, 258, 279
Brooke Post Office (Stafford County) 222, 225, 232, 235
Brooke Road (State Route 608) 37, 112, 219
Brooke Station (Stafford County) 89, 220, 231
Brooke Station Post Office (Stafford County) 232
Brooke Station Precinct 186, 188
Brooke, Virginia 16, 56, 91, 112, 126, 134, 163, 186, 198, 219, 223, 226, 264-267, 283
Brooke's Mill (Stafford County) 126, 134, 148, 174
Brooks, Agnes (1895-1989) 234
    E. W. 284
    Eddie O. (1880-1945) 237
    Eliza (Watson) (born 1845) 163, 173
    Elizabeth 163
    Elizabeth (born c.1797) 173
    George 65
    John M. (born c.1820) 163
    Julian Vernon (1885-1956) 203, 205, 237
    Mary Osbourne (England) (1854-1925) 203, 237
    Naomi (Waller) 203
    St. Clair (1883-1953) 200
    Thomas 163
    Thomas R. (born c.1801) 175
    William 272
    William Edwin (1854-1922) 201, 203, 237
Brookwood Nursing Home (Stafford County) 203
Brown(e), Ann (Scott) 146
    Belle (Garnett) (died 1936) 16
    Charity 153
    Delilah (Gaskins) (born c.1847) 153
    Dixon 150, 271
    Elizabeth (Cox) 199
    Elizabeth (Wallace) (born 1723) 9, 64, 136, 140
    Enoch 252
    Everett 187
    Hannah Ball (Daniel) (Hedgman (born 1780) 13, 68, 150
    Hannah (Cooke) 55
    Henry Selah (c.1884-1967) 94, 203
    Innis 141
    James 153
    Jane (Pope) (16_-1752) 121
    John 129, 252
    John (died c.1804) 55, 56, 58-60
    Joseph (died 1806) 146
    Judith (Lewis) (born c.1770) 64
    Letitia (Wishart) 75

    Margaret (Stone) 71
    Million (Waugh) (c.1763-1799) 59, 150
    Capt. Originall (1648-1697) 121
    Raleigh Travers (1753-1803) 59, 68, 131, 150
    Raleigh Travers, Jr. 13
    Raleigh Travers Cooke 150
    Sarah (Botts) (1787-c.1826) 141
    Virginia Belle (Graninger) (1891-1920) 237
    William 163
    William Hand (died 1852) 13, 75-81, 159, 162, 173, 175, 273, 276
Brown's Motel (Stafford County) 94
Bruce, ___ (Hay) 173
    Charles (c.1771-1845) 133, 139, 151
    Elizabeth (Pannell) 133
    Frances (Banks) (1735-1818) 11, 59, 62, 69, 132, 146
    Capt. James D. 179
    Robert 151
Brummet, William E. (born c.1809) 261
Brumfield, Martha (Ball) 138
Brummel, Philemon 279
Brundige, Frances (Gallagher) 254
    Timothy 254
Brunswick County, Virginia 52
Brunswick Parish (King George County) 72
Bryan, Justice ___ 184
    Annie L. (Bullock) 88
    Charles Adams (1849-1918) 177, 178, 180-182, 185, 187-189, 191, 193-199, 245, 278, 283
    Eliza (Cropper) (died 1890) 88
    Eliza H. (Grace) 175
    Jesse 175
    Joseph 88, 178
    Joseph K. (died 1948) 88, 186, 187, 190, 191, 198
    Lucy E. (1873-1945) 246
    Peter 267
    Richard Hughlett (1820-1908) 88-92, 178, 245
    Richard Hughlett, Jr. 88
    Rosanna (Banks) (died after 1784) 59, 133
    Susan 88
    Susan L. (Mason) 178
    Walter W. 88
    William 267
    William A. (1827-1871) 175, 179
    William W. (died 1938) 191
    Winfield Scott (1853-1893) 245
Bryan, Joseph & Son (business) 88
Bryant, Daniel T. 242
    Henry F. (born c.1837) 281
    James 151, 152

James M. (1874-1898) 242
Lucy (Stevens) 246
Martha Hewitt (Cowne) (died 1818) 66
Mary Thomas (Skinner) 242
Susan "Snowie" (Armstrong) (1874-1935) 242
Susan E. (Musselman) (1835-1890) 166
William 5
Bryhim, Abner O. (1870-1942) 236
Bubb, Mr. ___ 195
E. S. 195
Buchan, Rev. Robert (died 1804) 40
Buchanan, Andrew (died 1804) 9, 10, 66
James 59
John 46
Virginia A. (Moncure) (1881-1938) 16, 246
Buck, Penelope (Towson) (c.1753-1794) 71
Buckner, Elizabeth (Stith) 52
John 50
Philip (1639-1700) 41, 42
Maj. William (died 1716) 39, 40, 50, 52, 118, 119
Buckroe (Elizabeth City County) 52
Buenos Aires 11
Bull Run, Battle of (1862) 176
Bullard, A. 176
Betty Lucas (Irvine) (1835-1891) 176
Charles (1770:80-1850:60) 168
Charles Benson (1815-1873) 168
Eleanor (Benson) 75
Martha (Herndon) 168
R. D. 176
Sarah Ann (Chancellor) (1819-1915) 168
Bullitt, Ann (Carter) 129
Benjamin (1693-1766) 129
Diana Moore (Gwathmey) 129
Thomas (1730-c.1778) 129
Bullock, Annie L. (Bryan) 88
James (born c.1816) 163
John 93
Louisa (Simpson) (born c.1851) 198, 202, 238
Nora (Coakley) (died 1926) 205
William 176
Bunbury, Anne (Fowke) (born 1741) 56
Dulcabella (Berry) 128
Frances (Mason) (born 1688) 43
Sarah 56
Thomas 56
William (born c.1670) 42, 43, 117, 118
Bunnell, Andrew J. 276
Burchell, Richard M. 276
Burdett, Sarah (Fowke) 45, 47
Burdis Post Office (Stafford County) 222, 224, 225, 234
Bureau of Pensions (DC) 264
Burgess, Charles A. (c.1880-1951) 94
James 237
Malinda (Graninger) (c.1863-1924) 237

Burgess' gate (Stafford County) 190
Burns, Anthony (1834-1862) 13
Jeremiah (died c.1791) 267, 268
Mary 268
Burnside, Gen. Ambrose 30, 164
Burnt Ordinary (Stafford County) 147
Burr, Abigail 272
Edmund 147, 148
Ezra (c.1780-1853) 147, 272, 273
Burrage, Edward 258, 271-274
Burroughs, Basil 137
Elizabeth (Stone) (Tackett) (dead by 1833) 140, 147
Capt. George 134, 140-142, 253, 254, 271
John 153
Thomas (died c.1815) 253, 254
Burton, ___ 200
Bobbie F. 206
Catherine 282
Drucilla (Knight) (born 1846) 282
Fielding B. (born c.1837) 263, 278, 282-284
James B. (born c.1857) 90
M. W. (West) (born c.1858) 90
Marshall (born c.1817) 90
Richard (c.1821-c.1859) 261, 262, 280, 281
Robert L. (1846-1923) 196-199
Virginia (Webb) (c.1844-1887) 278
William 282
William J. (c.1833-1896) 282
Bushrod, Hannah (Washington) 18
Bussell, Betsy (Harwood) 179
Delilia (Black) (1819-1896) 235
Frances (Black) 235
Randall 235
Bute County, North Carolina 49
Butler, Ammorious (Herring) 17
Atwell (c.1814-after 1870) 172
Catherine (Botts) 141
Helen (Shackelford) (1925-1892) 206
John 271
Lucy Ann (Cox) (c.1818-1853) 172
Nancy (Newton) 173
Thomas A. 95
Butler Road (State Route 218) 61, 94
Byram, Annie Mason (Wilkerson) (1861-1897) 242
Cuthbert 168
Cuthbert (c.1797-1854) 277
Cuthbert (born c.1822) 168
Daniel Strother (1860-1927) 267
George 242
Gordon M. 205, 206
Jane (Musselman) (born c.1836) 168
Lizzie M. (Shelton) (1860-1941) 267

Lloyd Mason (1894-1961) 267
Lucy (Phillips) (c.1752-1836) 134
Minnie W. (1872-1934) 242
Peter (c.1760-c.1799) 134
Sarah (born c.1785) 168
Sarah (Gough) 134
Sarah H. (Kendall) (1785-1854) 277
Sarah H. (Patterson) (Embrey) (born 1838) 277
Strother (c.1820-c.1857) 277, 280, 281
Susan (Phillips) (1765-1834) 134
William, Sr. 134
William, Jr. (1764-1829) 134
Byram's Store (Stafford County) 171, 205
Byrd, Col. William 122
Byrd family 2
Byrne, George 127
Cabin Hill (Stafford County) 75
Cadiz, Spain 71
Caisson Road (State Route 603) 92, 231, 241
Caledon (King George County) 37
California 13, 256
Callender, Philip 136
Calwell, Mary Constance (Young) 33
Cambridge Street (Falmouth) 94
Camden, New Jersey 135
Camp Barrett Road (State Route 639) 243
Campbell, Alexander (died 1796) 18
    Rev. Archibald (born c.1754) 18
    Hannah (McCoy) 16
    John 18
    William 258
Campbell County, Kentucky 134
Canada 13, 84, 194, 138
Canning (King George County) 18
Cannon Run (Stafford County) 79, 154
Capitol Bank of Jackson (Mississippi) 159
Cardine, Mary F. (Fritter) (c.1820-1874) 171, 195
Carlisle, Pennsylvania 88
Carlton (Stafford County) 78, 85
Caroline County militia 62
Caroline County, Virginia 3, 21, 50, 61, 81, 85, 91, 127, 133, 143, 145, 147, 151, 176, 238, 245, 252, 257, 262, 269, 274, 275
Caroline District Minute Battalion 133
Caroline Street (Fredericksburg) 17, 60, 84, 184
Carroll, Anne (Brent) (1733-1804) 9, 57, 138
    Daniel 57
    Eleanor (Brent) (born c.1737) 8, 10, 11
    Robert 271
Carson, Walter 192
Carter, Amanda (Herndon) 171
    Ann (Bullitt) 129
    Ann Hill (Lee) (1773-1829) 174
    Ashton C. (died c.1934) 265, 267
    Betty Landon (Willis) (1684-1719) 123
    Catherine Griffin (Tayloe) (1761-1798) 19

Charles (1707-1764) 6, 56, 132
Charles of Ludlow (1738-1796) 6-9, 18, 56-60, 68, 132
Eliza Ludwell (Lee) 18
Eliza (Thornton) 18
Elizabeth 83
Elizabeth (Chiswell) (1737-1804) 6, 132
Elizabeth "Libby" A. (Primmer) (1824-1888) 161
Elizabeth M. (Tayloe) (died 1832) 19
Elizabeth (Wamsley) (c.1818-1886) 151
Frances A. (Tasker) (died 1787) 18
Frances (Lee) 11
Gracie G. (Raines) 265
Hannah (Neale) (died 1722) 122
Harriet Lucy (Maund) (born 1768) 18
Harriet (Milstead) 233
Henry (born 1755) 151
James (1684-1743) 47, 122, 123
James L. (born c.1834) 172
James L. (1825-1901) 282
Jeremiah 151
Jeremiah (c.1810-186_) 151, 258, 259, 277, 279, 280
Johnson (1797-1861) 161, 167
Joseph (1690-1764) 55, 151
Joseph (born 1759) 151
Katharine (Dale) 47
Landon (1751-1811) 10, 18
Landon (1757-1820) 19, 72, 79
Loyal (died c.1847) 83, 257, 272
Lucy (Fitzhugh) (1715-1763) 5, 8
Margaret E. (Shelton) (born c.1842) 83
Margaret (Mason) (died 1751) 56
Mary Anne (Bronaugh) (born 1747) 55
Mary (Brent) 47, 122
Mary (Stark) 160
Mary (Walker) (died 1742) 6, 132
Mildred Ann Byrd (Mercer) (1774-1837) 10
Priscilla (Churchill) (1705-1757) 123
Hon. Robert (1663-1732) 5, 6, 8, 44, 56, 123, 129
Robert, Esq. (1704-1732) 123, 124
Robert III (1728-1804) of Nomini 18
Robert Wormley (1792-1861) 19
St. Leger Landon (1785-1850) 18
Sophronia (Curtis) (1837-1911) 235
Susan B. (Moncure) 75
Thomas 47
Virginia 202
William 166
William (1807-1874) 80, 81, 152, 160, 163, 171
William E. (c.1825-after 1873) 83-86
William J. 163

William H. (c.1853-1928) 193
　　Willoughby Newton (1800-1878) 233
Carter & Smith (business) 253, 258
Carter family 200
Carver, Elzey Thornton 241
　　Sally (Purkins) 241
Cary, Edward 132
　　Lillian B. 230
　　Mary (Selden) (1704-1775) 52, 128
　　Richard (1621-after 1660) 40
　　W. Miles 230
Casey, John 188
　　Jonna C. (Heflin) (1850-1936) 188
Cash, Elizabeth (Porter) 279
Cason, John 245, 275
　　Thomas 275
Casson, Sarah Bruce (Alexander) 58
Castle, Beulah (Roles) (1883-1968) 265
　　W. S. 265
Catholic Cemetery (Stafford County) 61
Catholics 26
Catlett, Sarah Ann (Peyton) 161
Catlett, Virginia 228
Catoctin Creek 46
Cave, Elizabeth (Withers) 56
　　James 238, 258, 259, 273, 275, 279, 280
　　Jane Moore (Gray) (1811-1890) 166
Cave's Warehouses (Stafford County) 8, 27, 57, 127, 130, 131
Cecil County, Maryland 88, 175, 177, 178
Cedar Hedge (Stafford County) 192, 275
Cedar Hill (Westmoreland County) 59
Cedar Park (Anne Arundel County, Maryland) 8, 9
Cedar Run (Fauquier County) 129, 180
Cedar Run Cemetery (Fauquier County) 236, 241, 247, 265
Chadwell, Catherine 275
　　Elizabeth (Waller) 74
　　Lemuel 150, 153
　　Priscy (c.1770-after 1850) 273
Chambers, John 55
Chambersburg, Pennsylvania 159
Chancellor, Sarah Ann (Bullard) (1819-1915) 168
Chancellorsville, Battle of (1863) 168, 172, 179, 192
Chancellorsville, Virginia 77, 168
Chandler, Anne (Fowke) (Mason) (died after 1673) 2
　　Job (died c.1659) 2
　　Mary (Mason) 2
　　Mary Sewell (Brent) (died 1694) 3
Chapman, Constantia (Pearson) (1712-1788) 49
　　Jane (Taylor) 127
　　Jonathan (died before 1749) 49, 127
　　Louisa (Washington) (born 1743) 54
　　Margaret (Markham) 127
　　Nathaniel (1709-1760) 49, 127
　　Robert 153

　　Taylor (c.1715-1749) 127
　　Thomas (1769-1827) 127
　　William F. 233
　　William S. (born c.1822) 262, 280
Chapman & Tolson (business) 262
Chapman's Mill (Stafford County) 150
Chapman's Ordinary (Stafford County) 136, 139
Chappawamsic (Stafford County) 5, 6, 11, 39, 65, 86, 174, 185, 189, 276
Chappawamsic Baptist Church (Stafford County) 13, 64, 86, 165, 166, 184
Chappawamsic Creek/Run (Stafford County) 10, 12, 39, 41, 44, 46, 47, 64-66, 79, 80, 82, 85, 106, 114, 116, 127, 136, 137, 150, 152, 155, 171, 180, 199, 220, 228, 264, 265, 275
Chappawamsic Post Office (Stafford County) 222, 233
Chappawamsic Precinct 117, 118
Chappawamsic Road 114, 166, 175
Charles I, King of England 2
Charles City County, Virginia 118, 119
Charles County, Maryland 2, 45, 76, 127
Charles Street (Fredericksburg) 251
Charleston, South Carolina 9, 52
Charlottesville, Virginia 244
Chartters, Charles J. (1853-1931) 191, 192
　　Ella (Morrison) 191
Chartters' Place (Stafford County) 138
Chatham (Stafford County) 8, 29, 31, 57, 76, 161, 163, 166
Chatham Bridge (Stafford County) 166, 170, 172, 176, 179
Chatham Ferry (Stafford County) 161
Chatham Heights subdivision 203
Chatham Mill (Stafford County) 169, 284
Chatsworth (Henrico County) 8
Chelsea (Stafford County) 12, 14, 169
Chemung County, New York 161
Chesapeake Bay 3
Chesapeake City, Maryland 88
Chesley, Henry Garnett (1843-1921) 177, 186, 189, 191, 193-197, 199
　　Mary Ann (Ferneyhough) (c.1818-1853) 177
　　Mary Susan (Ferneyhough) (1845-1913) 177, 190
　　William S. 177
Chesley & Garner (business) 190
Chestnut Grove Cemetery (Herndon, Virginia) 93
Chestnut Hill (Stafford County) 242
Chew, Ann Mercer (Forbes) 160, 262
　　John James (1803-1870) 160
Chewning, Annie C. 232
　　Clara (Moore) 246
　　Dr. George H. 33

Temple (Powers) (1878-1970) 248
Chewning & Lowry (business) 283
Chichester, Daniel McCarty (1896-1986) 17
    Daniel McCarty 207, 208
    John H. 21
    Hon. Richard Henry Lee (1870-1930) 17, 184, 195, 204
    Richard Henry Lee, Jr. (1904-1973) 204-206
    Virginia Belle (Wallace) (1871-1961) 17, 204
Chichester-Graves Insurance Agency 17
Chickamauga, Battle of (1863) 15
Chilton, Thomas 152
    Thornton 272
Chimborazo Hospital 168
Chinn, Broaddus Herndon (1853-1922) 284
    Elizabeth (Griffin) (born 1773) 13, 18
    Elizabeth Griffin (Conway) 157
    James Thomas (1851-1920) 226, 241
    John LeRoy (1795-1854) 13, 76-78, 157, 182
    Joseph (1768-1803) 13, 18
    Joseph William (1798-1840) 18
    Lucy E. 182
    Lucy I. (Jett) (born 1832) 182
    Lucy (Leland) 13
    Mary 157
    Mary Ann (Smith) 19
    Robert Alexander 284
    Roxanna T. (Peyton) (1836-1898) 157
    Sarah Jesse (Rowe) 284
    William 157
Chiswell, Elizabeth (Carter) (1737-1804) 6, 132
    Elizabeth (Randolph) (1715-1776) 6, 132
    Col. John (c.1715-1766) 132
Chittum, E. Lloyd 208
Chotank (King George County) 45, 122, 125
Chotank Church (King George County) 52
Chotank Creek (King George County) 38, 42, 48
Chotank Parish (King George County) 115
Christ Church (Oxford, England) 44
Christian, Mary (Balthrop) 118
Christie(y), Elizabeth Gray (Dudley) (c.1798-after 1850) 263
    John C. 263
    John W. (1836-1917) 263
    Lucy V. (Jones) (born c.1833) 263
    Milton 139
Christy's (Stafford County) 189
Christie's Store (Stafford County) 235
Chunn, Susannah (Vowells) 60, 65
Church of England 109, 110
Church of the Holy Spirit (Falmouth) 189, 198
Church wardens, position of 110
Churchill, Elizabeth 123
    Lucy Harrison (Darby) 11
    Priscilla (Carter) (1705-1757) 123
Cities Service Oil Company (Washington, DC) 266

Claiborne, Ann (Fox) (1684-1733) 124
    Philadelphia (Fox) (died before 1765) 10
    Thomas (1681-1732) 124
    Thomas (1704-1735) 124, 125
Claiborne Run (Stafford County) 159, 172, 174, 177
Clare, Eliza Gibbs (Fitzhugh) 12, 13, 67
Clark(e), Benjamin 79
    Harry 198
    John 115, 116
    Rev. John (1804-1882) 80, 86, 184
    Lucy (Pilcher) 270
    Luna (Kellogg) (born 1778) 84, 160, 259
    Thomas E. (1869-1935) 197
    Virginia (Weedon) 86, 89
Clarke County, Virginia 12, 67, 83
Clay Street (Richmond) 165
Claybrook, Amanda (Montague) (died 1845) 184
Clearview (Stafford County) 9, 146
Clemens, H. C. 194
Clements, Edward 124
    Elizabeth (Fruye) 124
Clemmens, John H. 193
Clerk of the Court, position of 103-104
Clermont (Stafford County) 9, 10, 12, 39, 75, 147, 275
Cleve, England 196
Cleve (King George County) 6, 10, 18, 132
Cleveland, President Grover 175
Cleverly, William C. 95
Clift, Ajdlon C. (1861-1887) 184, 185, 187
    Albert (c.1808-1890) 31, 170, 181-183, 192
    Arthur Fielding (c.1815-1888) 78-82, 85, 86, 174, 179, 261
    Bettie A. (Griffis) 184
    Elizabeth "Sallie" (Elkins) 81
    Fielding (c.1774-1856) 81
    Fielding Lawrence (born c.1808) 81, 154
    Fielding P. 183
    Frances Marian (Sthreshley) 78, 140
    Frank 188
    James 191
    John F. (born c.1846) 192
    Marian M. (Alexander) (born c.1822) 78
    Mary E. (born c.1818) 192
    Thomas A. 192
    William A. (c.1853-1923) 198
Clifton, Anne (Brent) 53
    Betty (Hore) (1751-1792) 271
    Burdit (1708-1761) 271
    Burdit (died 1821) 271
    Hannah (Waller) 271
    Henry (born 1746) 271
    James (c.1640-1714) 39, 43
    Sarah (Ashton) (Alexander) (born c.1675)

124
    Capt. Thomas (born 1660) 43
Clifton family 271
Clifton (Stafford County) 43, 59 130, 148
Clifton Chapel (Stafford County) 15
Clifton, Virginia 244
Cloe, Ainsley Bennington (1896-1972) 205, 206
    Alexander (born c.1800) 158, 174
    Charles Wesley (1840-1901) 176, 177
    Drucilla (born c.1800) 158, 174
    Gertrude (Pittman) 205
    Hannah Kate (Stark) (1842-1884) 158, 198
    James H. (born c.1823) 262
    Mary Lee (Weedon) 205
    Mary S. 246
    Richard Arthur (c.1869-1953) 198, 205
    William Sheppherd (1832-1919) 158, 174, 198
    William Weedon (1898-1947) 204
Clover Hill (Stafford County) 10, 63, 64, 70, 71, 74, 154
Coakley, Ann "Nancy" (Massey)
    Daniel S. (c.1805-c.1866) 164, 170, 171, 259-263, 276, 277, 280, 281
    Daniel W. (1850-1922) 196, 197
    David 174
    Douglas W. (born 1853) 205, 222, 235, 284
    Elizabeth C. (White) (born 1816) 276
    Ella M. (Love) (born c.1845) 174
    Fielding Alexander (c.1836-after 1908) 170
    John (died 1874) 169
    John E. (c.1810-after 1881) 87, 88, 196, 235
    Mary J. (Beal) (born c.1856) 196, 205
    Mary L. (Lightner) (born c.1817) 87
    Maud (Lunsford) (died 1936) 205
    Mildred (Sullivan) (1761-1812) 276
    Nancy (Coakley) 276
    Nora (Bullock) (died 1926) 205
    Ramah D. (1878-1956) 205
    Richard T. (born c.1843) 178, 181
    Susan 174
    V. 196
    William, Sr. (before 1765-1830) 276
Coakley Post Office (Stafford County) 222, 223, 225, 226, 235
Coakley's Precinct 159
Coakley's Store (Stafford County) 170-172, 175, 176
Coal 81
Coal Landing (Stafford County) 5, 71, 111, 165, 173, 177, 197, 264, 266, 283
Coal Landing Post Office (Stafford County) 222, 223, 235
Coal Landing Road (Stafford County) 176, 192
Coal Trips (Stafford County) 10, 126, 230, 275, 277
Coalter, Mrs. 161
Cobb, Mary (Young) 33
Coca Cola Bottling Company (business) 284
Cocke, Catesby (born 1702) 123, 124

Cockrell, George H. 233, 277, 280
    Samuel D. 233
Coffman, Ann (Wallace) (1820-1889) 198
Colbert, Joseph W. (c.1839-1906) 247
Colclough, Elizabeth (Willoughby) (Overzee) (Allerton) 38
Cold Harbor, Battle of (1864) 163
Cole, Elizabeth (Garner) (died before 1850) 274
    James S. 272
    Martha W. (Ashby) (1839-1864) 179
Cole Hill (Prince William County) 86
Coleman, Anne E. (Taliaferro) (1834-1892) 19, 201
    Eliza Wigginton (Templeman) (died 1885) 277
    Frances (Crutcher) 65
    Frances (Gatewood) (c.1782-1853) 145
    Frederick W. 199
    Hannah A. (Hedgman) (born c.1831) 277
    Henry L. (died 1883) 262, 277
    John W. (1788-1857) 19, 277
    Richelieu 20
    Robert Spilsby (died 1761) 63
    S. Bernard (c.1902-1974) 20
    Susannah (Richards) (died 1778) 140, 251, 253
Coles County, Illinois 135
College of St. Omar (Netherlands) 57
Colonial Beach (Westmoreland County) 16
Colonial Forge High School (Stafford County) 168
Colston, Robert 42, 117, 118
Colt, Richard 43
Columbia 19, 202
Columbia, Missouri 64
Columbia University (Washington, DC) 15
Combs, Bolivar C. (1831-1862) 80
    C. W. 185
    Daniel Webster S. 185
    Delsey F. (Briggs) (1864-1941) 185
    Elizabeth (Edrington) 186
    Ennis 151, 186
    Joseph (c.1751-1810) 142
    Joseph Harrison 68
    Kendrick B. (c.1857-1912) 185, 190, 191, 193-195, 285
    Louisa L. (Eskridge) 186
    Lucinda (Herndon) (c.1796-c.1867) 171, 173, 177, 180, 235
    Margaret E. (Hore) (c.1784-1859) 154
    Margaret (Rousseau) (born c.1760) 142, 151, 186
    Mary E. (Hickerson) 80
    Mary (Williams) 68
    Polly (Williams) 138, 142
    Sallie (Reamy) (1860-1946) 199
    Sally (Wickliffe) 151
    Seth Rousseau (c.1828-1888) 186

William Rousseau (1784-1836) 151, 152
Commerce Street (Fredericksburg) 247, 278, 283
Commissioner of the Revenue, position of 112-113
Commissioners of the Customs 108
Committee on Revolutionary Pensions 18
Committees of Safety 48, 127
"Commonwealth vs Brown" 58
Commonwealth's Attorney, position of 114
Comorn (King George County) 90, 238
Compiler, The (newspaper) 11
Concord (Stafford County) 11, 13, 37, 49, 73, 74, 126, 127, 131, 159, 171, 176, 233, 264, 271, 279
Concord Road (Stafford County) 173, 174
Confederate army 157, 163, 166, 180
Confederate Cemetery (Fredericksburg) 87, 169, 239
Confederate navy 15, 188, 240
Confederate Soldiers' Home (Richmond) 169
Confederate States of America 13, 14
Confederate veterans 165
Congress Hall Hotel (Washington, DC) 90
Connecticut 84, 85, 272
Conner, Edgar R. (c.1878-1960) 17
Connor, John 136
Constable, Anne (Lee) (born 1622) 2, 38
Constable districts 105
Constable, position of 104-105, 114
Contest Mill (Falmouth) 58
Continental Army 57, 58
Continental Congress 8, 76
Continental Line 133, 138
Conway, ___ 179
    Agatha (Eustace) (1740-1826) 10, 58, 62
    Anne (Heath) (born 1721) 10
    Anne (Moncure) (born c.1750) 10, 140
    Catherine Barret (Waller) (1746-1794) 233
    Catherine Storke (Peyton) (1786-1865) 12, 75
    Christopher (born 1684) 128
    Dulcabella (Berry) 128
    Elizabeth Griffin (Chinn) 157
    Eustace (1820-1857) 245
    Eustace (1857-1887) 142
    George (born 1754) 10
    George Washington (1818-1879) 82, 156, 157, 158
    Henry R. 132, 144-147, 149, 150, 152-156
    Henry Rowzee (1825-1863) 157-160, 162, 164, 165, 167, 168, 245
    John Moncure (1779-1864) 12, 70, 75, 82, 142-147, 149, 150, 152-157, 245
    Margaret Eleanor (Daniel) (1807-1891) 12, 71
    Mary Butler Washington (Moncure) (1807-1895) 12, 16, 90, 157, 178, 246
    Mary Catherine Washington (Henry) (1806-1890) 75
    Sarah (Withers) 128
    Susan Newton (Waller) (1814-1864) 238

Dr. Valentine Yelverton (1803-1881) 75, 245
    Walker Peyton (1805-1884) 12, 28, 31, 71-81, 148, 151, 152, 154, 169
    Withers 128
Conway & Daniel (business) 259
Conway, Gordon & Co. (bank) 77
Conway, Gordon & Garnett National Bank 71, 77
Conway House (Falmouth) 69
Conway, Slaughter & Garnett (bank) 77
Conway's Warehouse (Caroline County) 269
Conyers, Ann (Blackburn) (born c.1789) 154, 158
    Benjamin 158
    Capt. Henry (16_-1733) 44, 123
    John (c.1754-1819) 77
    John (c.1789-c.1844) 154, 158
    Lethe (Shelton) (1780-c.1867) 84
    Mary Ann (Armstrong) (born c.1821) 154, 158
    Sinah "Sarah" Davis (Irvine) (c.1802-1841) 77
    Dr. William 44
Cooke, Elizabeth (Travers) 51
    Frances (Whiting) 44
    George Mason (1792-1866) 12, 70, 72, 73, 272, 273
    Hannah (Brown) 55
    John (died 1733) 51
    Col. John (1755-1819) 10, 12, 51, 58, 59, 71, 128, 141
    Mary (Doniphan) (Bronaugh) (1737-1781) 51, 52, 128
    Mary Thomson (Mason) (born 1762) 12, 51, 71
    Mordecai 5, 44, 122
    Sarah Mason (Selden) (Grayson) (1791-1861) 71
    Susanna (Fitzhugh) (1693-1749) 5, 44, 51, 53, 122
    Travers (1730-1759) 51, 128
Cooke & Brent (business) 10
Cooke & Eustace (business) 255
"Cooke vs Green" 10
Cook's Brigade 166
Coones, Alexander (born c.1838) 263
    James (c.1795-after 1860) 154, 255, 258-263, 279, 280
    Louisa (Harwood) (c.1807-1885) 154, 263, 279
Coones & Swetnam (business) 281
Cooper, ___ 200
    Benjamin F. (born c.1847) 180
    Betty 94
    Cynthia Burton (Botts) (c.1866-1957) 93
    Frances (born c.1817) 190
    Frances (Watson) 238

George R. (1832-1892) 94, 164
Henry L. (born c.1846) 190, 193
James (1838-1917) 194
John W. 89, 282
John Wesley (1879-1947) 194
Lucy Ann (Fritter) (1853-1917) 238
Malinda (Musselman) 194
Margaret W. 265, 278
Capt. Raleigh Lewis (1832-1892) 164, 172, 181-183, 246, 263, 282
Richard 136
Richard (1806-1892) 164
Sallie Waller (English) (1879-1932) 194
Sanford 259
Seth R. (c.1837-after 1904) 189, 197, 199
Thornton (c.1810-after 1870) 190
Thornton B. 238
Virginia (Bridwell) (born c.1870) 94
Cooper, John W. & Company (business) 282
Cooper Manufacturing Company 185
Cooper Town (Stafford County) 171
Cooper's Battery 164, 171
Copia County, Mississippi 69
Cople Parish (Westmoreland County) 45, 79, 123
Cople, England 2
Coppage, Eastham 152
    Marian (Curtis) (born 1808) 152
Corbin, Benjamin (born 1765) 256
    Catherine (Ramey) (born c.1824) 280
    Frances (Fant) 256
    Garnett 257, 258, 273, 279
    Harriet Ann (O'Bannon) (1813-1891) 78, 85
    Jameson (born c.1790) 78, 255-259, 273-276, 279, 280
    John 256
    Lafayette (born 1824) 280
    Mary Nelson (Mason) 274, 280
    Nancy Ann (Corbin) (born 1767) 256
    Richard W. (born c.1822) 262
    Sarah (Fant) 256
    Susan Frances (Heflin) 244
    William (1720-1796) 256
Cornwell, Richard 120
Coroner, position of 104-105
Corotoman (Lancaster County) 5, 8, 56
Cossom, Margaret (Field) (Hart) 123
Coton (Loudoun County) 11
Cotton mills 70, 77, 148
County Renfrew, Scotland 58
Courthouse Road (State Route 630) 71, 73, 76, 125, 168, 170, 242
Courthouses (Stafford County) 27-34
Courtney, David Thomas (1839-1892) 196
    Gertrude A. (Mountjoy) (c.1880-1959) 247
    John 239
    Milton K. (1869-1932) 196, 239

Sally (Price) 239
Susan Jane (Heflin) (c.1844-1870) 196
Thaddeus Edward (1884-1960) 239, 265
Cowne, Martha Hewitt (Buchanan) (died 1818) 66
    Susan (Latham) 66
    Thomas W. 66, 67, 253
Cowpens, Battle of (1781) 59
Cox, Mrs. ___ 166
    Ann "Nancy" (Newton) 167
    Austin 199
    Berryman 185
    Charnock, Jr. 160, 185
    Delia B. (born c.1800) 87
    Delila (Payne) 185
    Eliza T. (Lightner) (born c.1835) 87
    Elizabeth (Brown) 199
    Francis 149, 258, 279, 280
    Hugh 153
    James 172, 174
    James (born c.1816) 164, 167
    James (born c.1839) 199
    John C. (c.1825-1915) 186, 189
    John Francis (c.1802-after 1850) 149, 258, 279, 280
    John W. 201
    Josephine (Cox) 199
    Leah Owens (Monteith) (Owens) 160
    Lucy Ann (Butler) (c.1818-1853) 172
    Luther D. (c.1851-1919) 198
    Matilda (Newton) 173
    Presley 149
    Samuel 167, 172, 173, 185
    Sarah 167, 172, 185
    Sarah (Cox) 185
    Sarah (Jett) 149
    Walter M. (born c.1820) 157, 160-162
    Walter S. 186
    William Fleet (1821-1905) 163, 167, 170, 185, 188, 190, 192, 194-198, 263, 283
    Zachariah 145, 154
"Cox vs Jett" 132
Cox's Lane (Stafford County) 167
Craig, Adam 155
    Mary Bronaugh (Fox) (born c.1796) 155
    Mary (Mallory) 155
    William M. (born c.1792) 155
Craine, Rebecca (Bronaugh) 52
Crane's Corner (Stafford County) 194, 265
Crest (Stafford County) 88, 160, 163, 265
Crest Post Office (Stafford County) 223, 226, 230, 235, 242
Criglersville (Madison County) 15
Crismond, Susan D. (Green) (born c.1842) 264
Cromwell Post Office (Fauquier County) 224, 228
Crooks, James C. 206

Cropp, Edward M. (born c.1835) 189
    Eliza (Dowdall) (1765-1799) 268
    Eliza (Fallis) (born 1798) 138
    Elizabeth J. (Wharton) 81
    James 138
    James (died before 1780) 268, 270
    Dr. James Thomas (1829-1865) 81, 82
    James, Jr. (born 1755) 138
    James (died 1830) 138
    John 81, 268-270
    Joyce (Hinson) 138, 270
    Robert 138
    Robert (c.1800-1885) 189
    Rosie (Thomas) 81, 270
    Susan (Thomas) 138
    William P. 150
Cropp (Stafford County) 94
Cropp Post Office (Stafford County) 223, 224
Cropp's Mill (Stafford County) 147, 220
Cropp's Tavern (Stafford County) 147, 270
Cropper, Eliza (Bryan) (died 1890) 88
Crosby, George 43, 44, 47
    Mary (Mountjoy) (16_-1756) 43, 44
Cross of Honor 187
Croughton, Charles (c.1761-1819) 256
    Elizabeth (Hudson) (died c.1791) 256
    Elizabeth (Stubberfield) (Reveley) (died 1872) 256
    Robert (1791-1872) 256, 273
Crowe's (King George County) 52
Crowley, John C. 258, 280
Crow's Nest (Stafford County) 9, 12, 14, 44, 59, 71, 80, 163, 169, 175, 230, 266
Crucifix (Stafford County) 61
Crump, Susanna (Hewitt) (1723-1797) 134
Crutcher, Frances (Coleman) 65
    Hugh (died 1779) 65
    Robert (died 1829) 64-70, 140, 141
    Tarissa Hamble (Phillips) (born 1783) 65
    Thomas (1695-1786) 65
Cub Run (Fairfax County) 46
Culpeper Confederate Cemetery 187
Culpeper County, Virginia 11, 14, 46, 62, 65, 69, 70, 92, 154, 162, 177, 239, 254, 260, 274, 280
Cunningham, Elvira (Norwood) 257
    William 6
    William P. (c.1795-after 1860) 257, 258
Curtis, A. M. 275
    Anne C. (Leach) 87
    Annie Rebecca (Anderson) (1858-1897) 92, 235
    Elijah (c.1765-before Feb. 1829) 136
    Elizabeth (Bowen) 75
    Elizabeth (Jett) 148
    Elizabeth (Porch) 135
    Ethelina Malinda (Jones) 235
    Fielding (1793-1844) 87
    Francis (1806-1891) 87, 165, 181, 186
    Frederick Euston (1860-1921) 92, 235
    George, Sr. (1730-c.1806) 135, 148
    George, Jr. (1767-1844) 148, 150, 167
    Harriet A. (Payne) (born c.1822) 169
    Harriet "Hallie" Margaret (Reamy) (1840-1917) 87, 165
    James 271
    Jemima (Payne) (died c.1869) 167
    John 136, 268, 273-275
    John (c.1735-1813) 135
    John Francis (1833-1908) 235
    Lawrence Robert Rose (1890-1954) 203
    Louisa E. (Peden) (1829-1915) 87
    Mabel Clara (Graves) (Spicer) (died 1918) 92
    Maria A. (Duffy) (born 1828) 181
    Marian (Coppage) (born 1808) 152
    Mary (McIlhaney) 148
    Mary M. 186
    Mary M. (Stone) (c.1809-1865) 181
    Mildred (Newton) 167
    Philadelphia (Anderson) (c.1828-1898) 194, 235
    Richard (born c.1710) 135
    Richard (born before 1765) 152
    Richard A. (born c.1838) 186
    Sarah (Jones) 135
    Sarah "Sally" A. (French) (1812-1872) 86, 167, 189
    Sophronia (Carter) (1837-1911) 235
    Thornton 149
    William H. (1857-1898) 189
    William E. (died c.1963) 201-204
Curtis Park (Stafford County) 231
Cussins, John 230
    Susan Anne 230
Dade, Behethland (Bernard) (Gilson) (1635-1720) 38, 42
    Elizabeth (Alexander) (1698-1736) 44
    Elizabeth (Washington) (1734-after 1796) 56
    Frances (Townsend) (1667-1726) 44, 125
    Capt. Francis (1621-1663) 42
    Francis (c.1659-1698) 44
    Frances (Townsend) (Withers) (Hore) 39, 47, 48
    Mary (Massey) (1661-c.1794) 44
    Mary (Massey) (Hooe) 45, 48
    Mary (Washington) 51
    Parthenia (Alexander) (Massey) (c.1709-1742) 49
    Robert (1684-1714) 49
    Rose (Grigsby) (Newton) (Massey) (died 1785) 44, 120, 124

Susan (Fitzhugh) 123
    Townsend (c.1688-1761) 44, 45, 47, 123, 124
    Townsend (1707-1781) 49, 55, 56, 57, 59
Daffan, Hugh Wilson (born c.1865) 193
    James A. (c.1820-1890) 85, 161, 171, 179, 186
    Lizzie S. (Pemberton) (c.1862-c.1928) 186
    Luther Rice (c.1834-1906) 162
    Mary (Robertson) 162
    Nancy (born c.1795) 85, 161, 162
    Virginia Lula (Shelkett) (1833-1875) 161
    William (c.1777-1855) 85, 161, 162
    William Pierce (c.1860-1940) 186
Daffan family 53
Dale, Katharine (Carter) 47
Dale Academy (Madison County) 15
Daniel, Eliza (Mitchell) (died c.1835) 71
    Elizabeth (Lewis) 12, 67
    Emily Travers (Wallace) (c.1806-after 1860) 14, 20, 80
    Euphemia (Tolson) (1805-1844) 71
    Fenton (Brooke) (born c.1828) 13, 74
    Frances (Moncure) (born 1745) 9, 12, 64, 67
    Frances (Moncure) (1797-1871) 12
    Hannah Ball (Brown) (Hedgman) (born 1780) 13, 59, 68, 150
    Hannah Ball (Hedgman) (Foote) (Hardy) (1737-1829) 133
    James 48
    James (c.1680-1727) 61, 127
    Dr. John Henry Moncure (born 1813) 13, 14, 74, 75, 77, 78, 80, 159
    Dr. John Moncure (1769-1813) 12, 13, 64, 71, 74
    Dr. John Moncure (1800-c.1845) 71-74, 76, 80, 153
    Margaret Eleanor (Conway) (1809-1891) 12, 71
    Margaret Eleanor (Stone) (1771-1809) 71
    Margaret (Vivian) (died 1727) 48, 127
    Maria (Henderson) (born c.1837) 169
    Maria (Niven) (died 1792) 71
    Maria (Vowles) 71
    Mildred (Stone) (1772-1837) 9, 11, 12, 14, 80, 169
    Peter (1706-1777) 48-53, 55, 61, 127, 128, 133
    Peter Vivian (1784-1860) 11
    Samuel Greenhow (1810-1865) 169
    Samuel S. 151
    Sarah (Travers) (Pierson) (171_-1788) 48, 61, 127
    Thomas H. Cushing (c.1811-1896) 154, 259, 260
    Travers, Jr. (1763-1813) 9-12, 14, 61, 62, 80, 169
    Travers, Sr. (1741-1824) 9, 12, 13, 56, 64, 67, 68, 131-139, 141, 143

    Walter Raleigh (1783-1818) 12, 67-70
Daniel & Conway (business) 280
Danville, Virginia 162
Darby, Eliza Churchill (Fitzhugh) 11, 66, 86
    John 11
    Lucy Harrison (Churchill) 11
Darnall, Susannah (Smith) 276
Darrell, Ann (Fitzhugh) (Mason) 121
    Samson (1712-1777) 118
    William 121
Davenport, Burket (1730-1817) 251
Davenport & Triplett (business) 251
Davidson's Cotton Gins 148
Davis, Bayliss (c.1808-1857) 160, 162
    Emma Lee (Tolson) (1873-1965) 246
    Joseph 252
    Joseph (1860-1932) 247, 265, 266
    Joshua 124
    Joshua (died 1703) 45, 117
    Mamie (Heflin) (1866-1951) 265
    Mary (Sterne) (1848-1923) 188
    Thomas 161
Davis & Shacklett (business) 269
Daw, James 267
Day, John 138
de Deblere, Susanna (Bland) 2
de la Pryme, John (1715-1780) 64
    Margaret (Welch) (1709-1770) 64
Deacon, William T. (died c.1955) 201
Deacon Road (State Route 607) 161, 240
Decatur, Benjamin H. 241
    Ella M. (Taliaferro) (born 1875) 201
    Emma J. (Shackelford) (1868-1958) 265
    James 265
    James D. 201
    James H. 195-198
    James Henry (c.1890-1940) 194
    James Monroe (1866-1944) 265, 266
    John A. 194
    Mary 241
    Monroe 194
    Sallie 201
    Samuel 232
    Sarah 265
    William 265
    Wilson (1847-1935) 193, 241
Decatur Road (State Route 635) 40
Decatur's blacksmith shop (Stafford County) 232
Decker, Nelson C. 190
Declaration of Independence 6, 18, 76, 109
Deep Run (Stafford County) 154, 172, 222, 223
Degarnett, D. C. 30
DeLand, Florida 95
deLashmutt, Frances E. (Moncure) (1893-1966) 201
Democratic Reporter (newspaper) 84
Dennis, Helen 95

Dent, Frederick 192
    Ivan D. 203, 204
    James (born c.1848) 245
    Virginia W. 246
Derrick, Amy (Maddox) (16_-c.1740) 40
    Thomas 40
Deshazo, Catherine (died 1872) 176
    Ellen Elizabeth (Taylor) (died 1914) 176
    Henry Levy (1816-1909) 176, 177, 179
DeShields, Ethel (Homes) 247
    Walter Warren (1897-1952) 247
Devon, England 117
Dewey, Maria D. (Babcock) (1818-1890) 189
Dickens, Nancy (Truslow) 191
Dickenson College (Pennsylvania) 88
Dickerson, William 234
Dickinson, Edward 131, 132, 137
    Lewis 270-272
    Thomas 148
    William 152
Difficult Run (Fauquier County) 45
Dillon, Fred 95
Dinwiddie, Elizabeth (Fowke) (died 1781) 51
    Simpha Rosa Enfield (Mason) (Bronaugh) (1703-1762) 52, 55
Dipple (Stafford County) 10, 43, 59, 140, 155, 264
Disestablishment 109
Dishman, John Norton (1863-1951) 265
District Court for Eastern Virginia 11
Districts:
    Aquia 178-181, 183-185, 188, 190-208
    Coakley's 159
    Falmouth 149, 178-181, 183-185, 188, 190-206
    1st 114, 148, 161, 162, 165-167, 169, 170, 177, 191, 195
    4th 161, 162, 165, 167, 170
    George Washington 207, 208
    Griffis-Wide Water 207, 208
    Hartwood 183, 185, 188-208, 223-225, 228
    Rock Hill 180, 181, 183-185, 188, 189, 190-208, 222-224, 228
    2nd 114, 161, 162, 165, 167, 169, 170, 174, 191, 197
    3rd 161, 162, 165, 167, 170
Dix, Annie (Morton) (c.1842-1922) 73
    William W. 188, 237
Dixon, John (c.1740-1791) 58
Dixon's Warehouse (Falmouth) 132, 134, 136, 138, 142, 148, 149, 152, 154
Doc Stone Road (State Route 659) 76
Dodd, B. A. 88
    C. N. 236
    Columbia N. (Gray) (born c.1844) 88
    Cora E. 236
    Ella (Huffman) 192
    Humphrey (c.1815-1895) 88

    Robert Lee (c.1861-1921) 192, 236, 247
    Sarah Bell "Sallie" (Skinner) (died 1933) 247
    William Frank (c.1840-1909) 88, 90-92
Dodd's Cider Mill (Stafford County) 236
Dodd's Mill (Stafford County) 236
Dodd's Post Office (Stafford County) 223, 224, 236
Dodd's Store (Stafford County) 234, 236
Dodman, Col. John (born c.1613) 37, 38, 115, 116
Dodson's Corner (Stafford County) 265
Doggett, Dr. Andrew C. 33
Dogtown (Stafford County) 74
Dogue's Run (Fairfax County) 41
Dominnion Virginia Power 230
Doniphan, Alexander (1653-1717) 126
    Anderson 131
    Magdalin (Monteith) (Finnall) (born c.1740) 131
    Margaret (Mott) 48, 126
    Mary (Cooke) (Bronaugh) (1737-1781) 51, 128
    Mott (died c.1776) 48-53, 126, 128
    Rosanna (Anderson) 48, 126
    Thomas A. S. 152, 153
Dougherty, Capt. Edward P. 15
Douglas, Triplett (c.1811-1867) 149
Dovacke, Thomas 115
Dowdall, Elizabeth (Cropp) (1765-1799) 268
    James (1758-1802) 268
Dowding, Hugh 37
Dowell, Jane 262
Down(e)s, Amanda 192
    Elizabeth (Roach) 284
    Mary T. (Monroe) (born c.1853) 192
    Thomas 192
Downing, William 41
Downman's Farm (Stafford County) 173, 189, 194
Draw Bridge (Stafford County) 266
Drew Middle School (Stafford County) 94
Drewry's Bluff, Battle of (1864) 165
Drummond, Andrew 136
Drummond's old field 136
Drummond's Race Field (Stafford County) 76, 136
Dry Bridge (Stafford County) 187
Drysdale, England 58
Dublin, Ireland 50
Duck hunting 230
Dudley, Elizabeth Gray (Christy) (c.1798-after 1850) 263
Duffy, Maria A. (Curtis) (born 1828) 181
Dumfries Cemetery (Prince William County) 241
Dumfries Road 171
Dumfries, Virginia 6, 10, 15, 46, 49, 57-59, 68, 71, 159, 171, 254
Dunbar, Elizabeth Gregory (Thornton) (c.1767-1851) 252

Robert (c.1745-1831) 251-254, 258, 272
Dunbar & Vass (business) 252
Dunbar's Bridge (Falmouth) 258
Duncan, Deborah Thompson (Ford) (died 1813) 149, 159
 John Paul (1898-1958) 233
Duncan & Scott (business) 279, 280
Dunn, Patrick B. 177, 178, 180
Dunnington, William 267
Dye, Aldridge (born c.1828) 92
 Lizzie (Smith) (born c.1882) 92
 Mary 92
 Ocie Lephia "Letha" (Heflin) (1882-1971) 94, 200
Eagle Gold Mine (Stafford County) 261, 281
Eagle Mill (Falmouth) 69, 71
Eagle's Nest (King George County) 5, 8, 43, 57, 120
Eakin, Mary S. (Jameson) 149
Eastern View (Stafford County) 151
Eastwood (Stafford County) 91, 92
Eaton, William 279
Ebenezer Methodist Church (Stafford County) 77, 114, 153, 173, 176, 186, 194, 238, 265, 283
Ebenezer School (Stafford County) 190, 241
Edge Hill (Albemarle County) 15
Edge Hill (Stafford County) 71, 72
Edgefield (Stafford County) 151
Edmonds, George 234
 George D. 243
 Mary "Mamie" Catherine (c.1844-c.1927) 77
 Capt. William 58
Edmondson, Charles H. 89
Edmunds, Catherine (Hewitt) (1756-1823) 134, 136
 John (1732-1798) 134
Edrington, ___ (Tolson) 150
 Angelina (Brooke) (born c.1809) 13, 74
 Eleanor (Moncure) 85
 Elizabeth (Combs) 186
 Elizabeth Hawkins (Stone) (1810-1891) 147
 Elizabeth "Betty" (Helm) (c.1722-after 1797) 55
 Jemima Smith (Porter) (died 1816) 55
 John Catesby (1775-1820) 12, 68, 147
 John Catesby (1800-1879) 147, 151, 159, 166
 Sarah (Porter) (Stone) (1769-1816) 147
 William (c.1712-c.1796) 55
 William (c.1741-1794) 55, 130
Edwards, Andrew (1725-1788) 131
 Anne (Shackelford) 173
 Annie (Monroe) 239
 Rev. Decatur 284
 Elizabeth (Stark) 160
 Henry Washington (1829-1899) 166, 181
 John W. (born c.1819) 278, 282
 John W. (born c.1852) 278
 Lewis 252, 269

Maria (Bolling) (born c.1855) 278
Mary (Fleet) 57
Mary "Mollie" (Mountjoy) (1760-1839) 131
Mary (Stark) 153
Virginia 278
William 233, 252, 253, 260
Edrington's Company, 45th Virginia militia 12, 147
8th Illinois Cavalry 171
Eley's Ford (Culpeper County) 162
Elizabeth City County, Virginia 52, 117, 128
Elk Run (Stafford County) 114
Elkhorn, Battle of 15
Elkins, Frances/Florence (Rollins) 198
 Elizabeth "Sallie" (Clift) 81
Elk's Lodge 284
Ellerslie (Stafford County) 9, 14, 64, 80
Ellington, Joel 270
 Linwood H. 95
Ellington's (Stafford County) 190
Ellis, Lt. Charles (c.1650-1708) 41, 42, 43, 44, 120
 Elizabeth (Massey) (born c.1680) 44
 Thomas 118
Ellison, John 256, 257
 Mary 258
Ellwood (Spotsylvania County) 163
Elm Factory (Falmouth) 70
Elzey, Thomas 27
Embrey, Arthur A. (born c.1824) 173
 Daniel 174
 Daniel (born c.1790) 194
 Elizabeth (Bettis) (born c.1873) 93
 George W. 207, 208
 Granville (c.1828-1906) 166
 Henry A. (c.1805-after 1871) 85, 86
 Joseph C. W. 264
 Julia Ann (Bowling) 236
 Lina 93
 Mary E. (English) (c.1836-1865) 85
 Minnie F. 237
 Miranda 264
 Murray B. (born c.1841) 194
 Richard C. (born c.1837) 277
 Rosa H. (Abel) (born c.1877) 264
 Sarah H. (Patterson) (Byram) (born 1838) 277
 William 93
 William (born c.1825) 172
 William A. (born c.1825) 179
 William L. (born c.1870) 93
Embrey, W. S., Inc. (business) 190
Embrey Mill Road (State Route 733) 176
Emory and Henry Hospital 184
England 256, 264
England, Ann "Nancy" (Musselman) 191
 Ann "Nancy" (Truslow) 191

Emily Emma (Baker) (died c.1909) 191
John (1755-1851) 191
Mary Osbourne (Brooks) (1854-1925) 203, 236
Patrick Henry (1804-1882) 175, 191, 194
English, ___ 197
   Bessie (Bolling) 266
   Hattie A. (Wilson) (1879-1935) 266
   Rev. John W. (1880-1955) 266
   Lillian Elma (Heflin) (born 1877) 266
   Mary E. (Embrey) (c.1836-1865) 85
   Powhatan (1874-1950) 266
   Robert T. (1848-1906) 266
   Sallie Margaret (Withers) (1851-1913) 266
   Sallie Waller (Cooper) (1879-1932) 194
   Susan R. (Armstrong) (born c.1863) 264
   William 172
English's Corner (Stafford County) 265
Ennever, Cornelia (Lucas) (1818-1884) 178
Enon Road (State Route 753) 245
Episcopal Church 109
Erwin, James B. (born c.1825) 262
Escheator, position of 106
Eskimo's Hill (Stafford County) 231
Eskridge, Louisa L. (Combs) 186
Essex County, Virginia 5, 21, 46, 48, 49, 126, 127, 131, 252, 270
Estes, James W. (1852-1929) 202
   Robert H. 203, 204
Eustace, Agatha (Conway) (1740-1826) 10, 58, 62
   Ann (Gaskins) 58
   Capt. Hancock (1768-1829) 10, 11, 28, 62-64, 66, 67, 70, 140, 144
   Isaac (died 1795) 10, 58, 62
   James Henry (born 1801) 173
   James I. (born c.1826) 166
   John 166
   John Henry (1791-1864) 182
   John Kelly 244
   John R. 192
   Martha Virginia (Laub) (1829-1872) 182
   Mary J. (Wardlaw) 182
   Ruth Olga (Heflin) 244
   S. M. (Pritchett) (born c.1829) 166
   Tabitha (Henry) (died c.1840) 10, 62
   William 10
   Capt. William (1729-1801) 58
   Dr. William Wardlaw (1818-1886) 182, 183, 185, 189, 190
Eustace & Moncure & Company (business) 253, 269, 270
Evans, A. W. 263
   Asbury W. (c.1836-1910) 177, 186, 189, 190, 193, 198
   Edwin A. 243
   George W. (born c.1845) 263

Hettie (1876-1955) 243
John A. (1832-1921) 91, 177, 180, 183, 185, 186, 192-194
John R. (c.1799-1873) 82, 85, 86, 186
Maria Jane (Homes) 177
R. P. (Lunsford) (born c.1853) 263
T. J. 263
Ewall, England 61, 127
Ewell, Gen. Richard Stoddert (1817-1872) 175
   Bertrand (1715-1795) 129
   Capt. Charles (1713-after 1747) 129
Exon, England 117
Fair Haven (King George County) 51, 128
Fairfax, Hannie F. 244
   Mildred Narcissa (Rose) 244
   Thomas Lord 123
Fairfax County Resolves 7
Fairfax County, Virginia 4-6, 8, 9, 37, 41, 45, 47, 49, 56, 57, 74, 123, 125, 127
Fairfax Courthouse 86
Fairfield, Connecticut 272
Fairfield, South Carolina 55
Fall Hill (Spotsylvania County) 252
Falling Waters, Battle of (1863) 187
Fallis, Eliza (Cropp) (1798-c.1850) 138, 270
   Polly (James) 138, 270
   Thomas 138, 270
Fallon, Mary Elizabeth (Wilson) (born 1874) 242
   Robert 242
Falls Mill (Stafford County) 272, 273
Falmouth Baptist Church 172, 202, 264
Falmouth Bridge 87, 94, 105, 158, 236
Falmouth Cotton Factory 77
Falmouth District 149, 178, 179, 183-185, 188, 190-208
Falmouth/Hartwood District 113, 149
Falmouth Hotel (Stafford County) 70
Falmouth Masonic Lodge 147
Falmouth Post Office (Stafford County) 61, 222-225, 231, 236, 237, 247
Falmouth Precinct 159, 170, 179, 186-189
Falmouth Road 159
Falmouth Township 114
Falmouth, Virginia 7, 9, 11, 12, 15, 31, 58, 61, 63-66, 69, 70, 72, 74, 76, 77, 83-85, 87, 88, 112, 114, 136, 137, 139, 142, 145, 146, 148, 150, 153, 154, 158-161, 163, 164, 166, 170, 172, 174-176, 181, 185, 189, 192, 198, 223, 225, 228, 231, 235, 236, 242, 243, 247, 251, 252, 254, 255, 258-262, 264, 266, 268, 269, 272-276, 278, 279, 281, 284
Falmouth Warehouse (Stafford County) 127, 131, 132, 135, 137
Fant, Mrs. ___ 158
   Annie (Ficklen) (born 1774) 132

Betsy (1774-c.1826) 132, 151
Catherine (Stewart) 132, 135
Elizabeth Lewis (Sewell) 135
Fielding (1775-1824) 135
Frances (Corbin) 256
George (1745-1839) 135, 136, 268-270
George Stanfield (born 1778) 132
Hannah (Lewis) 132
James 136, 138
John Penn (born 1776) 132
Joseph (c.1738-1812) 132, 139
M. M. 135
Mary (Schooler) 149
Mary L. (Fritter) (1792-1861) 151
Nelson (born 1777) 135
Sarah (Corbin) 256
William (born c.1720) 132, 135
Farish, Elizabeth Jane (Grinnan) 261
Hazelwood (born 1771) 252, 253
Robert (1735-c.1783) 252
Farmer, Aphia (Sanford) (1784-1864) 158
John 188
Farmers & Merchants Bank (Fredericksburg) 21
Farmers Bank of Fredericksburg 64, 70, 254
Farmers Bank of Virginia 65, 69
Farmington, Battle of (1863) 15
Farrow, Abraham (c.1670-1731) 45
Abraham (died c.1743) 45
Faucette, Sidney 209
Fauquier, Gov. Francis (1703-1768) 54
Fauquier County, Virginia 5, 11, 14, 15, 49,
51, 58, 60, 66, 69-71, 81, 83, 84, 114,
127, 129, 134, 139, 146, 147, 150, 151,
154, 157, 160, 161, 163, 165, 166,
169, 171-174, 177, 180, 186, 191,
192, 220, 222, 223, 236, 237, 239,
247, 256, 259, 260, 268, 270, 274, 278
Fauquier White Sulphur Springs 11
Featherstone Farm (Prince William County) 17
Federal Hill (Fredericksburg) 64
Fenton, Grace (Mercer) 50
Ferguson, Caroline Mitchell 253
George C. 253, 254
George Spottswood 253
Louisa Ann 253
Samuel, Jr. 253
Samuel, Sr. 253
Samuel Allen 253
Ferneyhough, John 159
Mary Ann (Chesley) (c.1818-1853) 177, 190
Mary Susan (Chesley) (1845-1913) 177
Milton A. (1846-1922) 188
Ferrin, Susannah (1753-1783) 55
Ferry Road (State Route 606) 94
Fickett, Lewis P., Jr. 17
Ficklen, Anne Eliza (Fitzhugh) (born 1816) 236, 240

Annie (Fant) (born 1774) 132
Anthony Strother (died 1844) 11, 71, 146,
148, 258
Benjamin (1737-c.1806) 63-67
Benjamin (died 1821) 11, 69
Cary Gordon (Hall) 236
Charles (died c.1816) 71, 146
Ellen Caskie (London) (1866-1934) 236
Fielding (died 1809) 132
Joseph Burwell (1800-1874) 154, 188,
236, 240, 255, 258-263, 279, 280
Joseph Burwell, Jr. (1848-1905) 236
Margaret (Grant) 64
Mary (Strother?) 71, 146
Nannie (Lee) (1850-1933) 188, 240
Nannie (Mason) 188
Sarah 64
Susannah (Foushee) 11
William (c.1695-1756) 64
Ficklen & Fant (business) 279
Ficklen & Waller (business) 254
Ficklen, J. B. & Sons (business) 262
"Ficklen vs Tyler & als" 131
Ficklen's toll bridge (Falmouth) 170, 174, 281
Field, Margaret (Hart) (Cossom) 123
Mary (Hart) 44
15th Judicial Circuit Court 17
15th Virginia Cavalry 184
15th Virginia Regiment 9
5th Virginia Convention 7
Fines, Isaac 177
Isaac (born c.1807) 159, 178, 241
Mildred (born c.1787) 153
Fines' Post Office (Stafford County) 223, 237
Finnall, Ann F. (Ballard) 279
Jonathan (c.1727-c.1792) 131
Magdalin (Monteith) (Doniphan) (born c.1740) 131
Robert 279
Thomas 279
Finnall cemetery (Stafford County) 131
1st Continental Artillery 135
1st Virginia Convention 7
1st Virginia Regiment 52
Fishback, Elliott (1785-1814) 254
Lucy (Amis) 254
Martin (born 1763) 254
Fisher, Rev. Ernest E. (c.1880-1969) 93-95
Fisheries 147, 274-276, 282
Fitzhugh, Capt. ___ 12
Dr. Alexander (1786-1847) 12, 13, 67-69,
71-77, 152, 153
Alice (Thornton) 53
Ann (Frisby) (Rousby) (1727-1793) 6
Ann (Lee) (McCarty) (1683-1732) 5, 43,
120

Ann (Mason) (Darrell) 121
Ann (Randolph) (1747-1805) 57
Anna Barbara (McCarty) 45
Anne (Rose) (born 1763) 12, 59, 72
Anne Eliza (Ficklen) (born 1816) 236, 240
Battaile 257
Catherine (Booth) (died 1748) 51
Cora (Bowie) 13
Edmund C. (died 1883) 13
Eliza Churchill (Darby) 11, 66, 86
Eliza Gibbs (Clare) 12, 13, 67
Elizabeth (Stith) (born 1754) 52
Frances (Alexander) 41
Frances (Tabb) (1794-1868) 168
George (c.1690-1722) 5, 6, 49, 127
Hannah 48
Henry (1686-1758) 5, 44, 45, 47, 49, 51-53, 121-123, 128
Lt. Col. Henry of Eagle's Nest (1706-1742) 5, 8, 57, 126
Henry (1723-1783) 50, 52, 53, 55-57, 123, 136
Henry (1747-1815) 52, 240
Henry (born c.1820) 163
John (1727-1809) 53, 128
John (died 1733) 5, 44, 45, 123
John Bolling Stith (1778-1825) 168
John Rose (1795-after 1860) 12, 71-74, 76, 77, 156, 157
Lucy (Carter) (1715-1763) 5, 8, 57
Martha (Lee) (Turberville) (1716-1751) 6
Mary Ann "Nancy" (Randolph) (1747-1805) 8
Mary (Mason) (Strother) 5, 6, 49, 127
Mary Peyton Bolling (Sthreshley) (born 1808) 150, 168, 240
Mary (Stuart) 56
Molly (Brent) (Woodrow) 9, 61, 138
Nannie (Grayson) 13
Patsy (Gordon) 257
Randolph Coalter (1832-1902) 85, 87-91, 189
St. George Rose (1842-1925) 33, 87
Samuel (1846-1923) 177
Sarah (Battaile) 50
Sarah (Stuart) (1731-1783) 51, 59
Sarah (Thornton) 50
Sarah (Tucker) (1663-after 1701) 4, 5, 45
Susan (Dade) 123
Susanna (Cooke) (1693-1749) 5, 44, 51, 53, 122
Thomas (died 1719) 121, 122
Thomas (1725-1768) 51, 53, 55, 59, 61, 128
Thomas (1755-1819) 57
Thomas (1760-1820) 11, 12, 59, 60, 65, 67, 72, 134
Ursula (Beverley) 48
William 63
Col. William (1651-1701) 3, 4, 5, 38-40, 45, 118, 120-122
William (c.1678-1713) 4, 5, 43, 44, 120, 121
William (1721-1798) 6, 49, 51, 127
William of Marmion (1725-1791) 9, 48, 51, 53, 56, 126, 138
William of Chatham (1741-1809) 8, 9, 18, 28, 55, 57
William Henry (1788-1859) 11, 28, 65-71, 73, 75, 76, 86, 148-150, 152-154, 276
Fitzhugh's Mill (Stafford County) 151
Five Forks, Battle of (1865) 165
Flatford, Fannie Edmonia (Gill) (1852-1936) 165, 238
Lenna (Garrison) (c.1892-1924) 238
Robert (c.1810-1892) 263, 282
Robert Lawrence (1852-1898) 165, 238, 263, 283
Flatford, Robert & Son (business) 283
Fleet, John (1724-1792) 57
Mary (Edwards) 57
Sarah Ann (Jones) 57
William 57
Fleet's Bay (Northumberland County) 10
Fleet Drive (State Route 750) 230, 268
Fleming, ___ 172
Joyce (Washington) 122
Littleton C. (born c.1821) 163, 164, 179
Fling, George L. (born c.1843) 150
Flippo, John James (1869-1957) 204
Flood, Catherine (McCall) 252
Florida 133
Flour mills 64, 65, 69-71, 154, 236
Flourey, Benedicta (Maddox) (Bloxton) 271
Henry 271
Floury tract (Stafford County) 62
Floyd, Gen. John Buchanan (1806-1863) 184
Fluvanna County, Virginia 261
Foley, Betsy (Bradford) (born 1776) 260, 274
Fontaine, Ann (Morris) 11, 69
Sarah Rose (Rose) (1796-1863) 11, 69, 76
William 11, 69
Foote, Gilson (1736-1770) 133
Hannah Ball (Daniel) (Hedgman) (Hardy) (1737-1829) 133
Hester (Grant) 48
Hester (Hayward) (born 1640) 42
Katherine (Fossaker) 48, 125
Richard (1632-c.1697) 42
Richard (1666-1725) 42, 43, 48
Richard (1704-1774) 48, 49, 50, 125
Forbes, Ann Mercer (Chew) 160
Dr. David (1751-1789) 68
Delia (Smith) (1780-1841) 61
Francis "Frank" T. (c.1825-1904) 160, 262

Margaret (Sterling) (1754-1806) 68
Murray (1782-1863) 61, 68, 69, 146, 148, 149, 236, 253-263, 279, 280
Sallie (Innes) (Thornton) (1776-1807) 68
Ford, Deborah Thompson (Duncan) (died 1813) 149, 159
    Elizabeth Allen (Hore) (1791-1822) 12, 83, 149
    Elizabeth (Taylor) 12, 149
    James (died 1794) 12
    James (1768-1863) 149
    James Waller (1791-1865) 12, 143, 245
    John Taylor (died 1824) 135, 136, 142
    John William Duncan (c.1801-1876) 159
    Margaret Ursula (Waller) (1821-1901) 83
    Nathaniel Waller (1820-1880) 29, 31, 83-87, 114, 169, 172, 179, 190, 191
    Nathaniel William (1859-1894) 190, 193
    Patsy (Gregory) (c.1786-1858) 135
    Robert E. Lee (1862-1943) 196
    Capt. William (1788-1834) 12, 70, 83, 149, 150, 159, 255-257, 271, 273
Forge Mills (Stafford County) 254
Forres, Scotland 252
Forrest, Susannah (Waller) (1678-1748) 126
Fort Belvoir (Fairfax County) 4
Fort Eustis (Hampton Roads, Virginia) 198, 238
45th Virginia Regiment 12, 62, 64, 65, 142, 143, 147
Fossaker, John 41
    Katherine (Foote) 48, 125
    Mary (Fowke) (c.1700-1783) 47, 56, 125
    Mary (Withers) (Hathaway) 5, 42, 125
    Richard (1662-c.1735) 5, 41-43, 47, 120, 125
    Richard (died 1676) 5, 41, 116, 251
Foster, John 55
Fostersville Post Office (Stafford County) 223, 237
Four Mile Run (Fairfax County) 49
4th Virginia Convention 7
47th Virginia Infantry 148, 157, 160, 161, 163, 164, 168, 171, 176, 178, 179, 187, 263
4th Virginia Cavalry 166
4th Virginia Regiment 177, 178
Foushee, Susannah (Ficklen) 11
Fowke, Anne (Alexander) (1690-1739) 45, 48
    Ann (Bunbury) (born 1741) 56
    Anne (Chandler) (Mason) (died after 1673) 2
    Capt. Chandler (1692-1745) 47, 48, 51, 56, 125
    Elizabeth (Dinwiddie) (died 1781) 51
    Elizabeth Ann (Phillips) (died c.1830) 65, 153
    Col. Gerard (1618-1669) 2, 38
    Gerard (1662-1735) 45, 47, 122
    Gerard (c.1718-1781) 50, 51, 52
    Mary (Fossaker) (c.1700-1783) 47, 56, 125
    Mary (Mason) 2, 45, 122, 127
    Richard 2, 56
    Sarah (Burdett) (c.1665-1747) 45, 47
    Sarah (Roy) (1748-1821) 11
    Thomas (died c.1663) 2
Fowle, Ellen Bernard (Lee) 175
Fox, Ann (Claiborne) (1684-1733) 124
    Ann "Nancy" (Threlkeld) (1772-1828) 10, 137, 155
    Barbara (Wallace) (1766-1833) 64
    John (c.1770-1834) 10, 137-139, 155
    Mary Bronaugh (Craig) (born c.1796) 155
    Nathaniel (1748-1819) 10, 64, 131-134, 137, 144
    Philadelphia (Claiborne) (died before 1765) 10
    Sarah (Newton) 10
    Thomas (c.1710-1792) 10
Fox's Point (Stafford County) 151, 159
France 202
Franklin, Benjamin 219
    George W. 270, 271
    Gissie (Ashton) (born c.1848) 85
    S. M. 85
    Thomas (c.1789-c.1850) 147, 149, 152
    Thomas E. 85
    Thomas W. (c.1844-1928) 33, 85, 87-91, 228, 244
    W. T. 180
    Wallace (born c.1855) 171, 235
    William A. (1887-1970) 235
Franklin, Battle of (1864) 15
Franklin County, Kentucky 11
Franklin Road (Stafford County) 114
Frazier, Esther 60
    George (died c.1765) 60, 255
    Mary (Vowles) 60, 255
Fredericksburg and Falmouth Marine and Fire Insurance Company 12
Fredericksburg and Toluca Telephone Company 241
Fredericksburg Artillery 162, 166, 172, 175, 189, 240
Fredericksburg Baptist Church 190
Fredericksburg, Battle of (1862) 28, 30, 76, 167, 168, 187
Fredericksburg Cemetery 13
Fredericksburg City Council 19, 284
Fredericksburg Masonic Cemetery 9, 84, 168
Fredericksburg Masonic Lodge 147
Fredericksburg militia 70
Fredericksburg Normal School 237
Fredericksburg Post Office 223, 237, 240, 243
Fredericksburg Presbyterian Church 17
Fredericksburg Store 131
Fredericksburg Town Hall 64
Fredericksburg, Virginia 8, 9, 11-13, 15, 17-21, 31,

33, 60, 64, 65, 68-71, 76-79, 81, 83, 84, 87, 89, 90, 91, 94, 112, 135, 137, 149, 150, 154, 158-160, 162-164, 167, 169-171, 175-178, 184-186, 188-190, 198-201, 219, 225, 226, 228, 234, 236, 239, 245, 247, 251-256, 260, 263-265, 274, 280, 281, 283, 284
Free Bridge (Falmouth) 77, 81, 83, 84, 162, 164, 170, 171, 178, 186
Free Lance (newspaper) 186
Free Lance Post Office (Stafford County) 225
Freestone—*see Sandstone quarries*
French, Anna Guy (Isemonger) (born 1776) 167
    Betty (Brittingham) (Waugh) 47, 49
    Charles James (1835-1920) 86, 189, 235
    Hugh, Jr. (17_-1740) 47, 49
    James (1803-1865) 86, 167, 189
    John Isemonger (1847-1906) 87
    Mary (Mason) 37, 40
    Sarah "Sally" A. (Curtis) (1812-1872) 86, 167, 189
    William Lewis (born 1775) 167
French and Indian War 112, 113, 129
Friedland (King George County) 15
Frisby, Ann (Rousby) (Fitzhugh) (1727-1793) 6
    Peregrine (1688-1738) 6
Fristoe, Rev. Daniel (1739-1774) 64
    Lydia (Wells) (died 1830) 64
    Mary (Barker) (1735-1759) 64
    Thomas (1767-1815) 64, 66, 67, 142, 143
Fristoe's Mill (Stafford County) 80, 145
Fritter, ___ (Grigsby) (died c.1828) 171
    Aden (c.1766-c.1826) 272
    Anna E. (Litterel) (c.1804-1892) 154
    Annis Alberta (Halpenny) (1876-1958) 238
    Barnett (1792-1872) 151, 152, 171, 173, 242
    Betsy (Fant) (1774-c.1826) 151
    Caroline (Wilson) (c.1835-1881) 171
    Dorothy C. (died 1973) 238
    Elizabeth (Horton) 272
    Elvira Fant (Armstrong) (1834-after 1900) 242, 264
    Enoch (c.1765-c.1845) 171
    Enoch (1851-1926) 238
    Enos 154
    Glady (Knight) (c.1780-c.1857) 237
    Gustavus (1821-c.1900) 171
    Gustavus B. (c.1824-after 1884) 195
    John 173
    John (born 1752) 151
    John Henry (c.1824-1896) 171, 180
    Lindbergh A. 207, 208
    Lucy Ann (Cooper) (1853-1917) 238
    Maggie D. (Garrison) (born c.1863) 246
    Mary Amelia (Bettis) (born c.1852) 171
    Mary Catherine (Wilson) (1836-1929) 242
    Mary F. (Cardine) (c.1820-1874) 171, 195

    Mary L. (Fant) (1792-1861) 151, 242
    Mary Virginia (Berry) (died 1946) 202
    Reubin T. (c.1795-1874) 153, 154
    Richard 272
    Robert Dallas (1876-1953) 238, 243, 264
    Rowena Alma (Heflin) (born 1868) 244
    Sallie B. (Humphrey) (1848-1921) 195
    Theresa V. (born c.1848) 243
Frizer, Grace (Ashton) 43
Frog Pond Post Office (Stafford County) 228
Frog Pond School (Stafford County) 228, 231
Front Royal, Virginia 261
Fruye, Elizabeth (Clements) 124
Fugate (Fugitt), E. (Sullivan) 277
    Jarrett (Garrard) (c.1806-1841) 259, 260
    Orpha 261
Gaddis, Alexander (died c.1811) 139, 141, 142
    Alexander (c.1745-1786) 139
Gaines' Mill, Battle of (1862) 164
Gainesville, Virginia 234
Gallagher, Frances (Brundige) 254
Gallagher, James & Company (business) 254
Gallahan, Callie E. (Truslow) (born c.1860) 91
    George 194
    Jack 192
    John M. 187
    Luke (1853-1923) 186
    Margaret Virginia. (Musselman) (1894-1981) 265
    Powhatan (1890-1935) 94, 202
    Samuel (1855-1931) 192, 202
Galleher, Eliza Strother (Peyton) (1791-1822) 68
    John F. 21
Gallop, Phillis (Monteith) 131
Game Point Association 230
Game Point Post Office (Stafford County) 223, 230, 237, 277
Gant, William 138
Garland, Griffin 130
Garner, Elizabeth (Cole) (died before 1850) 274
    Hannah (Bowler) (born 1815) 274
    Henceford 170
    John E. (1775-after 1850) 274
    John Henceford (c.1811-1886) 170
Garnett, Belle (Brown) (died 1936) 16
    George W. (died 1876) 77
    Henry T. (c.1851-1933) 15
    Margaret W. (Tutt) 255
Garrard, James (1749-1822) 8, 56, 57, 59, 133, 135
    Mary Ann (Mountjoy) (1753-1823) 133
    Mary (Naughty) (born c.1721) 8, 133
    Col. William (c.1715-c.1786) 8, 9, 28, 56-58, 60, 130, 132-135, 267
    William, Jr. (c.1762-after 1833) 135

Garrard's Ordinary (Stafford County) 8, 28, 56, 130, 162, 167, 228, 231, 277
Garrison, Alexander E. (born c.1829) 180
    Elizabeth Harriet (Knight) (1823-1901) 237, 238
    Elzey 90
    Ernest Valentine (1885-1958) 238
    Henry T. (born c.1842) 92, 93
    Jackson P. (1853-1941) 191, 238, 264
    James B. (born 1827) 114, 163, 186, 237, 238, 282
    James H. 152, 155
    James Sanford (c.1820-1910) 164
    Jane (born c.1808) 190
    John L. (born c.1814) 167, 170
    John W. (born c.1852) 88, 90, 91
    Lenna L. (Flatford) (1890-1924) 238
    Lucy W. (1880-1920) 238
    Maggie D. (Fritter) (born c.1863) 246
    Mary (Garrison) (born c.1858) 90
    Moses, Sr. (born c.1776) 153, 279
    Moses W. 245
    Riddy 90
    Robert (c.1808-c.1852) 92, 150, 237, 258-262
    Robert A. (born c.1841) 190, 193, 194
    Rodney (born c.1804) 190
    Sarah 90
    Turner R. (1872-1919) 238, 264
    W. L. 90
Garrison & Harding (business) 261
Garrison's (Stafford County) 105
Garrison's Shop (Stafford County) 173
Garrisonville Post Office (Stafford County) 222-224, 226, 227, 237, 238, 243, 244, 247
Garrisonville Road (State Route 610) 71, 74, 76, 85, 164, 173, 194, 204, 220, 228, 231, 244
Garrisonville, Virginia 77, 113, 173, 176, 179, 190, 222, 228, 241, 247, 259, 264, 265
Gaskins, Alice Peachy (Moncure) (1774-1860) 12, 140, 275
    Ann (Eustace) 58
    Armistead 153
    Delilah (Brown) (born c.1847) 153
    Hannah (Hull) 12
    Henry (born c.1843) 153
    Henry Lee (1813-1846) 85
    Mary E. (Towson) (c.1818-c.1874) 85
    Col. Thomas 12
    Thomas T. (born c.1837) 85, 86
Gately, M. J. 33
Gatewood, Adaline (Luck) 173
    Eliza Elzira (Withers) (born c.1803) 145
    Frances (Coleman) (c.1782-1853) 145
    Capt. James 147
    John (c.1780-1846:51) 145
    Lucy Ann (Moncure) (1807-1895) 147, 275

Gatewood Cemetery (Washington, DC) 168
Gayle, Thomas Benton (died 1928) 203-206
Gaylor, Laura (Young) 238
Gee, Joseph C. (c.1836-c.1897) 166
GEICO Insurance Company 59, 146
General Court 26
Geneva, New York 68
Genius of Freedom (newspaper) 10
George, Rev. Cumberland 78
    Humphrey (c.1816-after 1880) 242, 264
    Mary Ann Elizabeth (Smith) 276
George II, King of England 32
George Street (Fredericksburg) 77
George Washington District 207, 208
George Washington Inn (Fredericksburg) 17
George Washington Stone Corporation 205
Georgetown University 16
Georgia 269, 282
Gerard, Anne Johnston (Heath) 55
Germany 277
Gerrard, Frances (Speake) (Peyton) (Appleton) (Washington) 3
    Rose (Tucker) (Newton) (born c.1629) 118
    Thomas 118
Gibbons, Jane (Stuart) (c.1700-1750) 51, 128
    Robert C. 208
    Sarah (Brent) (Scott) (c.1692-1733) 46
Gibbs, Beverly B. 239
Gibson, A. B. 204
    John 55
    Richard (died before June 1701) 45, 118
Gibson & Knight (business) 282
Gilbert, Rev. J. K. 284
Gifford, Henry J. (born c.1836) 178
Gilchrist, Charles Pierson (1891-1951) 94
    Ellen (Moncure) (1897-1971) 94
Gill, Charles Edward (c.1818-1890) 165, 186, 188
    Edward (born c.1820) 241
    Elizabeth Clyde (Waller) (1877-1948) 192
    Elizabeth V. (born c.1824) 188
    Fannie Edmonia (Flatford) (1852-1936) 165, 238
    James Bruce (c.1845-1910) 188
    John W. 230
    Louisa 230
    Mary E. (Bridwell) (born c.1849) 173
    Waller Stone (1871-1947) 190, 225, 241
Gilson, Maj. Andrew (1628-c.1698) 38, 42
    Behethland (Bernard) (Dade) (1635-1720) 38, 42
    Behethland (Storke) (died 1693) 123
    Elizabeth (Newton) (died 1763) 42
    Mary (Massey) 120
    Thomas (1665-1707) 42, 43
Gist, Col. Nathaniel 135
Glascock, Agatha Ann (Moncure) (born 1814) 85

George Garnett (1807-1879) 85
John E. (born c.1841) 172
Glasgow, Scotland 58, 71, 251, 252
Glebe (Stafford County) 75, 169, 198, 280
Glencairne (Stafford County) 12, 17, 90, 157, 161, 186, 189
Glendie (Stafford County) 89, 198
Glendie Post Office (Stafford County) 224, 225, 238, 242
Glenn, Alene F. (1925-1974) 244
Glooston, England 4
Gloucester County, Virginia 5, 41, 51, 79, 122, 127
Golatt, Joseph (c.1816-1879) 85
Gold mining 12, 170, 192, 275
Goldvein Baptist Church (Fauquier County) 186
Goldvein Post Office (Fauquier County) 223
Goldvein, Virginia 239
Gollahorn, George 167
    James (born c.1832) 172
    John 270, 273
    John (c.1795-after 1850) 259
    Penelope (Ball) (c.1789-1872) 259
    Thomas 158, 163, 167
    William (born c.1827) 170, 172, 175, 180
Gooch, Agnes (Brooks) (1895-1989) 234
    Mercer Ray (1887-1966) 234
Goochland County, Virginia 12
Good, John 256
Goodwin, John R. (c.1828-1911) 166
    Margaret E. (Bridwell) (1842-after 1911) 166
    Mary 166
    William 166
Goolrick, Charles O'Conor (c.1877-1960) 20
    Frances (White) 20
    John Tackett (born 1844) 20, 185
    Keating Nelson (1874-1921) 33
    Peter 20, 182
    Peter (1801-1868) 182
Goolrick Hall (University of Mary Washington) 20
Goose Creek (Loudoun County) 46
Gordon, Anna Campbell (Knox) 251
    Basil (1768-1847) 251-262, 279, 280
    Basil (1808-1891) 19
    Bessie M. (Briggs) 236
    Celestine Louise (Montague) (1841-1876) 184
    Cornelia R. (Borst) (1880-1949) 203
    Emma F. (Spraggins) (died 1939) 230, 236
    George Loyall, Jr. iii, 61, 202, 205-208
    George Loyall, Sr. (1862-1952) 106, 202-205
    Hannah (Beale) 69
    Dr. John Churchill (1871-1949) 203
    Lucy Woodford (Herndon) (born 1837) 19
    Lucy Penn (Taylor) (born c.1830) 19
    Mary A. M. 69
    Mary Nicholas (Wallace) (1800-1879) 172
    Patsy (Fitzhugh) 257
    Samuel 251-256
    Samuel (1759-1843) 19, 172, 251, 257
    Samuel, Jr. (1804-1890) 257
    Sarah Travers Lewis (Anderson) (1874-1968) 202
    Susanna Fitzhugh (Knox) (1775-1869) 19, 251
    William 257
    William K. (1799-1886) 77
    William Richards (1780-1855) 69, 184
    Dr. William Wallace (died 1888) 230, 236
Gordon Green Terrace (Stafford County) 251
Gospel Messenger (newspaper) 183
Gosse, Matthew 118
Gough, Sarah (Byram) 134
Gouldin, J. F. 91
    John L. (1859-1923) 91
    Julia Lane (Gray) (1871-1944) 91
    Victoria 91
Gourd's Fishery (Stafford County) 167
Grace, Eliza H. (Bryan) 175
Grace Methodist Church (Stafford County) 239
Grafton (Stafford County) 74, 173
Granger, Richard 38
Graham Cemetery (Orange County) 17
Graninger, Christian Frank (1861-1929) 237
    Emma Bettis (Smith) (died 1968) 237
    George Sebastian (1888-1942) 237
    Mabel 237
    Malinda (Burgess) (c.1863-1924) 237
    Mary Catherine (Martin) (1830-1897) 193
    Sebastian (1852-1901) 193, 195
    Virginia Belle (Brown) (1891-1920) 237
Grant, Andrew 55
    Hester (Foote) 48
    Capt. John (16_-1749) 48
    Capt. John (c.1704-1762) 52, 53, 125
    Margaret (Bronaugh) (c.1698-1756) 52, 53, 125
    Margaret (Ficklen) 64
    Margaret (Watts) (Strother) 48
    Mary (Mathews) 55
    Rosamond (Wright) (1733-1799) 52, 53
    William (c.1675-c.1734) 125
Gravelly Ridge (Stafford County) 173
Graves, Clara (Mountjoy) (1878-1961) 241
    Mabel Clara (Curtis) (Spicer) (died 1918) 92
    Thomas (born c.1832) 89
    Thomas F. 88
    William F. (c.1835-1895) 89
    Willis (born c.1810) 239
Gray, Adelaide Gettys (Hayman) (1830-1921) 91, 92
    Columbia N. (Dodd) (born c.1844) 88
    E. A. 88

Jane Moore (Cave) (1811-1890) 166
Jennett R. (Pollock) 150, 172
John (1769-1848) 148, 150, 254
John (1809-1848) 148, 150-154, 166
Julia Lane (Gouldin) (1871-1944) 91
M. G. 266
Mary (Smith) (1880-1967) 266
Robert Atchison (1830-1915) 91, 92, 166
Robert Hayman (1873-1938) 92-94
Sallie W. (died c.1933) 264
William 88
Gray's Mill (Stafford County) 148, 151
Grayson, Ann (Bronaugh) (born 176_) 71
    Benjamin (1763-1829) 71
    Catherine (Hedgman) (1760-1795) 13, 68, 148
    Nannie (Fitzhugh) 13
    Dr. Robert Osborne (1789-1841) 71-73
    Sarah Mason (Cooke) (Selden) (1791-1861) 71
    Susan Margaret (Peyton) (1787-1824) 71
    Col. William 135
Great Hunting Creek (Fairfax County) 38, 45, 124
Greaves, Nathaniel (c.1769-after 1861) 256, 257
Green, Alexander Morson (c.1828-1904) 162, 170, 175, 187
    Betsy (Jones) 11
    C. E. W. 179
    Capt. Charles 178
    Charles Duff (1873-1957) 232
    Capt. Charles Jones (born c.1840) 162, 164, 170, 177
    Dora Ashby (Wallace) (1854-1937) 20
    Dorothea Farrer (Ashby) (1797-1865) 14
    Duff (1792-1854) 15, 69, 70, 72-75, 83, 148-150, 153, 155, 162, 164, 170, 255-263, 273, 274, 279, 280
    Duff (c.1840-after 1902) 14, 154, 170
    Duff McDuff (c.1832-1885) 15, 83-85
    Eliza Ann (Payne) (1806-1876) 15, 70, 83, 170, 263
    Elizabeth (Brent) (c.1655-1686) 3, 120
    George (born c.1841) 282
    Hedgman (c.1800-1878) 167
    Inez (MacGregor) (1867-1941) 264
    Capt. James 11
    James Lane (1831-1902) 162, 170, 263
    John 161, 167, 175, 187
    John (born c.1821) 264
    John E. 158
    John Marshall (1849-1926) 264
    John W. 135
    Jones (1794-1858) 11
    Lettis (Smith) (Harrison) (died 1699) 41
    Mary A. (born c.1826) 264
    Parthenia (Newton) 158
    Robert 11
    Susan D. (Crismond) (born c.1842) 264

Susanna Elizabeth Margaret (Scott) (1800-1844) 11
W. F. 285
William 115, 116
Col. William James (1825-1862) 163, 262
William S. 158
William T. (1852-1926) 198
Green & Lane (business) 261, 262
Green County, Alabama 88
Green Hill (King George County) 48
Green Meadows (Stafford County) 148, 167
Greenbank (Stafford County) 11, 59, 62, 69, 133, 168
Greenbrier (White Sulphur Springs) 33
Greene, Elizabeth (Brent) (c.1655-1686) 3, 120
Greenlaw, Gouverneur Thomas (born c.1860) 89, 184, 185, 226, 242
    Sarah Virginia Braxton (Purkins) (1838-1903) 89
    William Price Underwood (1834-1869) 89
Greenlaw Medicine Company (business) 89
Greenock (Culpeper County) 11
Greenock, Scotland 58
Greenock Snow (ship) 58
Green's Tavern (Falmouth) 148
Gregg, James (died c.1724) 46
    Jane (Owsley) 46
    John (1706-c.1736) 46
    Lucy (Heabeard) (died c.1730) 38, 115
    Thomas (died 1699) 38, 40-43, 115, 116, 120
    Thomas, Jr. 120, 121
Gregory, Patsy (Ford) (c.1785-1857) 135
    Walter 135
Greyham, Walter 267
Griffin, Elizabeth (Chinn) (born 1773) 13, 18
Griffis, Bettie A. (Clift) 184
    Frank 186
    George B. (born 1854) 189, 222, 234, 264
    James (c.1834-1872) 282
    Lulu Lynn (died 1994) 240, 248
    Mary Mildred (Mountjoy) (c.1844-1909) 166, 175, 281
    Olivia D. (McGhee) c.1862-after 1925) 234
    Samuel H. (1814-c.1887) 158, 160, 166, 171, 180, 234, 263, 264, 281-283
    Thomas (c.1797-1886) 151, 173
    William 281
    William (c.1803-1857) 281
Griffis Precinct 186, 188
Griffis-Wide Water District 207, 208
Griffith, James 179
Griffith Store Precinct 179
Grigsby, ___ (Fritter) (died c.1828) 171
    Jane (died c.1756) 124

Jane (Prosser) 45
John 120
John (1624-1730) 45, 124
Rose (Newton) (Massey) (Dade) (c.1700-1785) 44, 45, 120, 124
Thomas (1680:95-1745) 45, 124
Grinnan, Elizabeth Jane (Farish) (born c.1816) 261
Henry W. (c.1806-after 1860) 281
John 261
Martha (Smith) (born c.1848) 92
Gristmills:
Alcock's 148, 269
Bellfair 66, 80, 86, 113, 114, 127, 145, 158, 159, 173, 176, 220, 228, 265, 266
Belmont 236
Brent's 10, 59, 151, 152, 155, 220 227, 232, 243, 253
Bridgewater 236
Brooke's 126, 134, 148, 174, 186
Chatham 169, 284
Contest 58
Dodd's 236
Eagle 69, 71
Fitzhugh's 151
Forge Mills 254
Fristoe's 80, 145
Gray's 148, 151
Harding's 149
Holloway's 149
Kellogg's 84, 160, 139, 149, 193
Lacy's 169, 172
Lewis' 149
Little Falls 151
Loch Lomond 62
Lowry's 16
Masters' 154
Mountjoy's 137
Newton's 137, 148
Pollock's 166, 170, 172, 173, 176, 177, 179, 180
Purcell's 166
Richards' 176
Richland 174, 175, 191, 253
Shelkett's 151, 173
Sterne's 152
Stone's 74, 76, 153, 172, 185
Tackett's 71, 77, 90, 160, 171, 173, 180, 182, 185, 220, 233, 259-261, 265
Thistle 69
Thompson's (Fauquier County) 220, 223
Tolson's 259
Grove Baptist Church (Fauquier County) 239
Grove Methodist Church (Fauquier County) 247
Grove Post Office (Fauquier County) 222
Groves, E. C. 192
Elijah Alexander (1853-1931) 265, 283, 284

John T. (c.1833-c.1899) 163, 283
Julia Lee (Musselman) (1864-1943) 247, 265
Grundy, Barton H. 230
Mirriam (Branch) 230
Grymes, Eleanor A. S. (Tennant) 238
Marion Landon (Taliaferro) (1815-1859) 19
Mary L. (Bayly) 252
Gunston Hall (Fairfax County) 2, 5, 6, 12, 20, 37, 51, 56, 71, 125
Gunston Hall (Staffordshire, England) 2, 47
Guy, Charles 163
Dora Mason (1885-1915) 242
Eliza (born c.1818) 281
Fannie Daniel (Benton) (1888-1951) 265
John (born c.1816) 280, 281
Luke (1830-1858) 281
Robert E. (1855-1905) 242, 265
Susan Ellen (Wine) (1858-1922) 242, 265
William (born c.1814) 246, 260-262, 281
Guy family cemetery (Stafford County) 230
Guy's Tavern (Stafford County) 230
Gwathmey, Diana Moore (Bullitt) 129
Robert R. 17
Hackett, Fanny (Alcock) 269
Hagley (King George County) 18
Hague (Westmoreland County) 21
Haislip, Silas (c.1822-1884) 263, 278, 282, 283
Hall, Benjamin 257-262, 280
Benjamin H. 258
Cary Gordon (Ficklen) 236
Robert 39
Snowden C. 173
Halley, Sarah (Harrison) 126
Halon, Lucy 272
Halpenny, Annis Alberta (Fritter) (1876-1958) 238
Jacob 238
Hammersley, Francis (c.1680-after 1720) 39, 40
Hammett, Lewis (c.1802-1892) 162, 164
Hammett farm (Stafford County) 170
Hampden-Sydney College 159
Hampstead (Stafford County) 8, 69, 76
Hampstead Post Office (King George County) 225
Hanover Baptist Church (King George County) 276
Hanover County, Virginia 11, 248
Hanover Street (Fredericksburg) 19
Hansbrough, Elijah 158
Frances Anne (Hooe) 14, 82
Maria L. Hansbrough (Hooe) 14
Peter (1796-1843) 14, 82
William Hooe (c.1803-1875) 31, 81-84, 169, 170, 174, 179
Hansbrough & McInteer (business) 254
Hardich, Lt. Col. William 37

Hardin County, Kentucky 268
Harding, Bernard 254, 270
    Byram 147
    Cleveland (1865-1928) 197, 199, 200
    Enoch 139
    Enoch (died c.1848) 257
    Enoch (c.1806-1874) 171, 197
    George W. (born c.1843) 190
    Jane A. (Honey) (born c.1815) 153, 275
    Mark 153, 255
    Mark (c.1788-1873) 255, 271, 275
    Mary Eliza (1826-1898) 197
    Mason 133
    Nancy (Young) 255
    Rosa E. (Withers) 266
    Strother 114, 260-262
    Strother (c.1808-1868) 80-84, 105
    Strother (c.1812-c.1853) 158
    Strother (born c.1853) 32, 88, 185
Harding's gate (Stafford County) 177
Harding's Mill (Stafford County) 149
Hardwich, Lydia (Walker) 49
Hardy, Hannah Ball (Daniel) (Hedgman) (Foote) (1737-1829) 133
    John (17_-1794) 133
Harewood (Jefferson County) 55
Harlow, Susan A. (Heflin) 236
Harper, John Newton (1823-1907) 283
    Mary Thomas (Newton) (1789-1841) 283
    Sarah Frances (Andrews) (1826-1911) 283
    Dr. William, Jr. (1787-1853) 283
Harris, Anne Frances (Hooe) 57
    Anne (Owsley) 4
    Mary (Whitecotton) 268
    William 116
Harris' corn houses (Stafford County) 164, 172, 176
Harris' shop (Stafford County) 189
Harrison, Benjamin (1726-1791) 139
    Burr (1637-1706) 41
    Burr (c.1668-c.1715) 44
    Burr A. 152
    Cuthbert 41
    Elizabeth (Peyton) (1771-1835) 62
    Isabella (Triplett) (Hore) (169_-1763) 47, 126, 127
    John Peyton (1750-1807) 62, 63
    John Rowzee 63
    Lettis (Green) (Smith) (died 1699) 41
    Mary (Mansbridge) 41
    Mary (Waller) 131
    Nathaniel (1713-1791) 27
    Philip 135
    Sarah (Halley) 126
    Tabitha (Hooe) 45
    Thomas (1665-1746) 44-47
    Capt. William 126
    William (died before 1757) 131
    William (1703-1745) 47-49, 126
    Gen. William Henry 19
Harrison family 74
Harrows, Charles A. 152
Hart, Edward (died 1703) 42-44, 123
    Elizabeth (Storke) (Bernard) 44, 52, 123, 126
    Margaret (Field) (Cossom) 123
    Mary (Field) 44
    Mollie (Beaty) 159
    Robert 159
    William F. 190
Hartwood (Stafford County) 58, 72, 77, 230, 258
Hartwood Baptist Meeting House (Stafford County) 58
Hartwood District 178, 179, 181, 183-185, 188-208, 223-225, 228
Hartwood Elementary School (Stafford County) 58
Hartwood Post Office (Stafford County) 89, 192, 222, 224, 225, 228, 230, 231, 234, 236, 238, 239, 246
Hartwood Precinct 159, 179, 186-189
Hartwood Presbyterian Church (Stafford County) 176, 178, 230
Hartwood Road (State Route 612) 145, 231
Hartwood School Board 178
Hartwood Township (Stafford County) 114
Hartwood, Virginia 162, 165, 170, 171, 176, 180, 189, 234, 239, 259-261, 275, 276
Harvard University 38
Harvey, John (died 1700) 41, 42, 118, 119
    Joseph 19
Harwood, Betsy (Bussell) 279
    John 274
    John (died c.1787) 150, 274
    Louisa (Coones) (c.1807-1885) 154, 263, 279
    Thomas (1769-1845) 272-275, 279
Harwood Precinct 179, 188
Hasson, Samuel 276
Hathaway, Mary (Waugh) (born 1679) 42
    Mary (Withers) (Fossaker) 5, 42, 125
    Thomas 5, 42
Havana, Cuba 175
Haxall, Mary Bell (Moncure) 12
Hay, ___ (Bruce) 173
    Margaret 173
    Thomas B. (c.1800-1868) 173
    William 173
Hayes, Alfred C. (born c.1795) 258, 259, 262, 280
Hayes & Baily (business) 258, 279, 280
Hayman, Adelaide Gettys (Gray) (1830-1921) 91, 92

Hays (King George County) 18
Hayward, Hester (Foote) (born 1640) 42
    Mildred (Thornton) 3
    Nicholas (died 1697) 38, 42
    Samuel (1640-1696) 3, 39, 40, 115-118
Hazel Hill Farm (Spotsylvania County) 77
Hazelgrove, Elizabeth (Alcock) 245
Heabeard, Lucy (Gregg) (died c.1730) 115
    John (died 1690) 38, 116
    Lucy (Thomason) (born 1656) 38, 39
    Margaret (Newton) (Travers) 116
    Richard 38, 116
    William (died c.1720) 11, 37, 38, 116
Head, William (born c.1812) 166
Hearse, James 117, 118
Heartland, Connecticut 84, 259
Heath, Anne (Conway) (born 1721) 10
    Anne Johnston (Gerard) 55
    Benjamin 273
    Elizabeth (Peyton) (born c.1740) 55, 267
    Samuel 55
Hedgman, Ann (Morton) 73
    Benjamin G. (born c.1836) 88
    Catherine (before 1687-after 1708) 6
    Catherine (Grayson) (1760-1795) 13, 148
    Elizabeth (Triplett) 46, 133
    George (1734-1760) 6, 73, 133
    George F. G. (born 1785) 73, 151
    Hannah A. (Coleman) (born c.1831) 277
    Hannah Ball (Daniel) (Brown) (born 1780) 13, 68, 150
    Hannah Ball (Daniel) (Hardy) (Foote) (1737-1829) 133
    John 73, 167
    John (1741-c.1764) 6
    John (1758-1796) 13, 68, 148
    John Grayson (1782-c.1845) 13, 68-76, 148-155
    John T. (c.1804-1857) 151, 152, 277
    Lucy E. (Schooler) (born c.1834) 167, 231
    Margaret (Mauzy) (1702-1754) 6, 44
    Mary 167
    Nathaniel (before 1682-1721) 6, 44, 133
    Nathaniel, Jr. (born 1729) 6, 46
    Peter (c.1700-1765) 5, 6, 44, 46-49, 128
    Peter Daniel Grayson (c.1800-after1885) 73, 88, 151, 161
Hefferlin, James (born 1786) 172
    Mary Anna (Walker) (1790-1831) 172
Hefflinger, Peggy (Skinner) 174
    William Jr. (c.1777-1849) 174
Heflin, Broaddus Romutain (1855-1941) 244
    Carl Bennett (1860-1954) 244
    Charles 194
    Charles Seddon (1829-1898) 174, 188, 236, 237, 263
    Clarence Joseph (1885-1947) 244
    Delia Ann (Armstrong) (1845-1930) 94, 195, 239
    Dora (Beach) 200
    Fitzhugh W. 206, 207
    Frances "Fannie" Lee (Heflin) 244
    Hazel Jennie (Brewer) (1913-1997) 244
    Hosea Montgomery (born 1903) 244
    James 166, 167, 172, 176
    James Edward (1821-1901) 172
    James L. (born c.1827) 163
    James Otto (c.1887-1969) 16
    Jefferson W. (1811-1880) 171, 186
    John B. (1878-1959) 201
    John Benjamin (1878-1941) 236
    John E. (c.1816-after 1880) 195
    John Walker (1851-1931) 188
    Jonna C. (Casey) (1850-1936) 188
    Julia A. (Templeman) (1816-1892) 186
    Julia Marie (1907-2002) 236
    Laura (1868-1956) 239
    Lillian Elma (English) (born 1877) 266
    Louisa Dora (Beach) 94
    Lydia 171
    Mamie (Davis) (1866-1951) 265
    Marshall Wesley (1820-1892) 244
    Martha Ann (Humphrey) 242, 244
    Mary E. (Rose) 242
    Mary Eliza (Bowling) (1878-1941) 236
    Nannie G. (Latham) (1829-1911) 174, 188
    Ocie Lephia "Letha" (Dye) (1882-1971) 94, 200
    Olive Leone (1882-1967) 244
    Rowena Alma (Fritter) (born 1808) 244
    Ruth Olga (Eustace) 244
    Sally Udora (McConchie) (1852-1931) 186
    Stafford Tilden (1875-1938) 94, 200
    Susan A. (Harlow) 236
    Susan Frances (Corbin) 244
    Susan Jane (Courtney) (c.1844-1870) 196
    Susan T. (Patterson) (1824-1901) 172
    Thomas 171
    Virginia Jane Lewis (Billingsley) 16
    Warren O. 236
    Welford (1897-1967) 239
    Wesley Jefferson 242, 244
    Wilbur "Leroy" Coakley (1888-1960) 230, 234, 266
    William 149, 152, 171
    William A. (c.1839-after 1889) 177
    William Edward (1850-1921) 186, 189
    William Henry (1840-1911) 94, 188, 194, 239
    William Nelson 16
Heflin (Stafford County) 265
Heflin's Post Office (Stafford County) 223, 224

Heflin's Store (Stafford County) 230
Helm, Elizabeth "Betty" (Edrington) (c.1722-after 1797) 55
Helms, Gary H. 246
Helm's Fishery (Stafford County) 282
Hemp Post Office (Stafford County) 198, 224, 225, 231
Henderson, Jannet (Wellford) 76
    John R., Jr. (1885-1948) 17
    Maria (Daniel) (born c.1837) 169
Henrico County, Virginia 8, 42, 57
Henry, Charles J. 191, 193-197, 199-203
    Edward Hugh 75
    Edward M. 84
    Elizabeth Washington (Peyton) 75
    James (1731-1804) 10
    Kate Kearney (Mason) 15
    Mary Catherine Washington (Conway) (1806-1890) 75
    Patrick 7, 18, 75
    Sarah Elizabeth (Moncure) 155
    Tabitha (Eustace) (died c.1840) 10, 62
Herndon, Amanda (Carter) 171
    Annie Frances (Weedon) (born 1867) 90
    Catherine A. (Keys) (1833-1906) 165
    Charles (1822-1883) 19, 30, 167
    Dudley (1829-1909) 263, 281, 282
    George (1821-1898) 163, 164, 173
    Isabella (Atchison) (Berry) (1832-1897) 90, 177
    J. E. 189
    John (c.1794-1882) 163, 165, 171, 173, 177, 180, 235
    Joseph (1827-1906) 171, 176, 177
    Kendrick Ennis (1839-1906) 180-183, 185, 187, 189
    Lee Roy (1819-1898) 157, 165, 173
    Lucinda (Combs) (c.1796-c.1867) 165, 171, 173, 177, 180, 235
    Lucy Woodford (Gordon) (born 1837) 19
    Ludwell (1823-1908) 92, 170, 179, 235
    Martha (Bullard) 168
    Martha "Mattie" Ellen (Briggs) (born c.1862) 92
    Mary Avarell (Williams) (1844-1932) 180
    Mary Frances (Mountjoy) (1826-1910) 87, 91
    Pauline (Bridwell) (born c.1837) 94, 244
    Rosanna Rebecca (c.1828-1903) 92
    Sarah Frances "Fanny" (Perry) (1870-1961) 283
    Turner William (1862-1939) 90, 193, 194
    Virginia G. (Ashby) (born c.1852) 173
    William (1824-1904) 90, 177, 183
Herndon, Virginia 93
Herring, Ammorious (Butler) 17
    Franklin Towles 17
    George William (1877-1966) 17, 200, 201, 232, 248, 265
    Pearl N. (Norvelle) (died 1953) 17
Herring & McClees (business) 266
Hewitt, Catherine (Edmunds) (1756-1823) 134, 136
    Charles (born c.1852) 263, 264
    Evy L. (Roberson) (born c.1868) 264
    Horace Broadman (1816-1882) 84-86
    J. H. 158
    James 270, 271
    James (died 1763) 134
    Jane E. (born c.1824) 264
    Jane (Smith) (1823-1871) 84
    John E. 273
    Jonas 84, 85
    Susanna (Crump) (1723-1797) 134
    Thomas H. (c.1820-1872) 179, 262-264, 277, 280, 281
    William (1740-1795) 57, 60, 62, 134-136
    William (died c.1850) 69, 71-75, 149, 151
    William (1824-1904) 263, 283
"Hewitt vs Samuel" 136
Hickerson, Anne E. (Tolson) (1827-1897) 71, 150, 159, 200
    Charles 151
    James M. (1831-1871) 165, 171, 179
    John H. (c.1818-c.1876) 159
    Mary E. (Combs) 80
    Mary Mason (Kendall) (born 1799) 151, 164, 165
    Mary Virginia (Massie) (Wamsley) (born 1853) 91, 164, 165
    Ransom M. (c.1794-1844) 151, 152, 159, 164, 165
    Robert G. (1829-1898) 32, 80-82, 87, 160, 164, 166, 168, 169, 174, 176, 177
Hickerson & Flatford (business) 283
Higgison, John 118
Highland Home (Stafford County) 188
Hill, Francis L. (1846-1913) 237
    Harris (c.1809-1908) 170, 172, 176, 179
    Jesse (c.1745-1822) 268, 269
    Leonard (died c.1814) 72, 145
    Mary A. (Latham) (c.1812-c.1860) 170
    Michael 115, 116
    Thomas (c.1781-c.1870) 72-78, 144-146, 153, 156, 157, 159, 162, 164
Hilman, Diadema (Shackelford) 239
Hilton, Wilson 135
Hinson, Joyce (Cropp) 138
    Margaret (Latham) (died c.1780) 272
Hitaffer, John 167
Hitt, William Snowden 33
Hobson (King George County) 172
Holdridge, E. P. 240
Holland, John 2

Holliday, Agnes (Weeks) 252
    William 138, 279
Holloway, Aaron (died before 1820) 254
    Abigail (Wright) 254
    Asa (born 1744) 254
    John (died c.1831) 139, 274
    Thomas 269
    Zachariah 152
Holloway's Mill (Stafford County) 149
Holly Corner (Stafford County) 239
Holly Corner Post Office (Stafford County) 225, 239
Holly Corner Road (State Route 655) 61, 162, 170, 239
Holly Hill (Caroline County) 143
Hollywood (Stafford County) 60, 72, 89, 145, 241, 242
Hollywood Cemetery (Richmond) 16, 161
Holmes, H. V. (Musselman) (born c.1864) 247
Holmes cemetery (Stafford County) 247
Home Depot (Stafford County) 76
Homes, Agnes E. (Shackelford) (1877-1956) 247
    Ethel (DeShields) 247
    James (c.1812-after 1850) 176, 276
    James B. 227
    Jennie B. 243
    John Marshall (c.1818-1873) 157, 159, 160-162, 164, 166, 168, 169, 172, 174, 175, 177, 181, 233
    Louisa (Templeman) (1830-1900) 161
    Maria Jane (Evans) 177
    Martha E. (1831-1908) 265
    Mary (Ratcliffe) (1807-1867) 176
    Milton H. (1871-1947) 247, 265
    Susan (Peters) 157
    Thomas (c.1821-1886) 247, 265
Honey, George 149
    Jane A. (Harding) (born c.1815) 153, 275
    John W. 184, 187, 194
    Joseph W. (1810-1879) 259-262, 275, 276, 280
    Philip S. (c.1835-1910) 175
    Wesley (1820-1909) 171
"Honey vs Harding" 153
Hooe, Alexander Seymour (1777-1835) 15
    Anne Fowke (Alexander) (1712-c.1776) 48, 55, 125
    Anne Frances (Harris) 57
    Anne (Peyton) (1754-1833) 68, 133
    Catherine (Taliaferro) (died 1731) 45
    Clarissa Bernard (Moncure) (1800-1829) 12
    Dade (c.1756-c.1837) 171
    Dade (c.1818-1881) 171, 179
    Elizabeth Mary Ann Barnes (Mason) (1785-1827) 55
    Elizabeth (Wallace) (c.1766-1850) 14, 80, 136, 139
    Frances Anne (Hansbrough) 14, 82
    Frances (Townsend) (Dade) (Withers) 39, 47, 48, 124, 125
    Gerrard (1733-1785) 55
    Harris (1736-1824) 57, 60
    Howson, Sr. (1696-1733) 48
    Howson (died 1777:81) 55
    Howson (died c.1796) 133, 139
    James 48
    Capt. John (1702-1766) 48, 49, 55, 125
    Maria L. Hansbrough (Hooe) 14
    Mary (Dade) 48
    Mary (Dade) (Massey) 45
    Nancy (James) (born c.1760) 171
    Col. Rice (1660-1726) 4, 39, 42-45, 47, 48, 120, 124, 125
    Rice, Jr. (born c.1692) 45
    Richardetta Barnes Mason (Ruggles) (c.1819-1902) 15
    Robert Howson (1748-1834) 63, 64, 66, 67, 69, 70, 72-75, 135, 136, 141, 146-150, 152, 153, 155
    Sarah (Alexander) (c.1707-1758) 6, 47, 124
    Sarah (Barnes) (1742-1805) 55
    Tabitha (Harrison) 45
    William (1743-c.1777) 14, 55-57, 82
Hooe's Ferry (King George County) 48
Hooe's Fishing Shore (Stafford County) 180
Hooker, Gen. Joseph (1814-1879) 30
Hooper, Thomas 117, 121, 122
Hope, Richard 116
Hope Creek (Stafford County) 148
Hope Patent (Stafford County) 5, 37
Hope Road (State Route 687) 8
Hopewell (Charles City County) 16
Hopewell (Spotsylvania County) 89
Hopewell Church (Stafford County) 158, 161, 162, 171, 172, 175-177
Hopkins, Samuel 50
Hopper, Thomas 44
Hord, Alan 61
    Jane (Miller) 61, 127
    John (1664-1747) 61, 127
    Kellis (c.1744-1815) 61-64, 66, 138, 139-141
    Mary "Molly" (Hord) (born 1744) 61
    Peter, Sr. (c.1715-c.1790) 61, 138
    Peter, Jr. 138
    Susanna (Shelton) (1742-1799) 84
    Thomas (1701-1766) 61
Hore, Betty (Clifton) (1751-1792) 271
    Catherine (Monroe) 127
    Capt. Elias (1700-1730) 45, 47, 126, 127
    Elias (1748-1832) 12, 83, 149, 151, 155, 271
    Elias A. W. (1821-c.1891) 31, 92, 155, 157, 164-169, 172, 174-176, 233, 262, 277

Elizabeth Allen (Ford) (1791-1822) 12, 83, 149
Isabella (Triplett) (Harrison) (169_-1763) 47, 126, 127
James 137
John 146, 149, 150
Capt. John (died c.1809) 271
Margaret E. (Combs?) (c.1784-1859) 155
Theodosia (Waller) (1753-1829) 12, 83, 149, 151, 155
Walter (1781-1858) 151, 155
Hore & Peyton (business) 259, 260, 275, 276, 280
Horne, Robert 255
Hornung, Philip E. 208
Horse racing 50, 267
Horsepen Gold Mine (Stafford County) 261
Horsepen Run (Stafford County) 14, 46
Horton, Betsy P. (Latham) 245
Cossom (died c.1820) 270, 272
Elizabeth (Fritter) 272
Lucy (Morton) (c.1818-1898) 73, 232
William 38, 116
Horton & Simpson (business) 234
Horton's gate (Stafford County) 159
Hot Springs, Virginia 129
Hotel Murphy (Richmond) 16
Houghton, Benjamin (1881-1957) 246
Edward 199
Flossie L. (Storck) (1883-1947) 246
Howard, A. Randolph 33
Abram 272, 273
Clarence R. 33
George M. (born c.1830) 180
Howard University 19
Howell, William J. 17
Howison, Capt. Alexander 254
Jane Briggs (Beale) (1815-1882) 69
Howson, Robert (died before 1697) 38
Hoyer, Paul (c.1829-1885) 281-283
Hudson, ____ 199, 200
Elizabeth (Croughton) (died c.1791) 256
Fielding B. (1873-1945) 201
Minnie 237
Hudsonville Post Office (Stafford County) 223
Huffman, David W. 234
Ella (Dodd) 192
Landon J. (c.1810-1873) 158
Marshall (born c.1833) 174
Robert L. (1873-1946) 234
Sarah (Monroe) 234
Huffman's Store (Stafford County) 222
Hughes, Robert A. 223, 237
Hugo, Capt. William H. 32
Huguenots 11, 244
Hull, Anna Jane (Moncure) (born 1835) 90, 186
Hannah (Gaskins) 12

Harriet Winston (Shore) 186
John Gascoigne 186
John Moncure (1835-1908) 90, 191
Paul (1809-1892) 85, 90, 163, 172
Sarah "Sally" Elizabeth (Moncure) (1809-1892) 86, 90
Hull Cottage (Stafford County) 86
Hull Post Office (Stafford County) 245
Hull's Memorial Chapel (Stafford County) 91
Hume, Patrick 117
Humphries, Bettie (Tankersley) (born c.1849) 85
Jane (Primm) 195
Julia J. 85
Sallie B. (Fritter) (1848-1921) 195
Sanford (born 1812) 171
Humphrey, James T. (1848-1926) 195
Jane (Primm) 195
Martha Ann (Heflin) 244
Sallie B. (Fritter) (1848-1921) 195
Sanford (born 1812) 195
Thomas 116
Hungerford, John Pratt (1761-1833) 18
Hunt, William H. 184
Hunter, Adam (1739-1798) 9
Frederick Campbell Stewart, Sr. (1837-1895) 14
Frederick Campbell Stewart, Jr. (c.1879-1929) 14
James (1721-1784) 9, 137, 167, 279
Rose (Turner) 14
Thomas Lomax (1875-1948) 16
Hunter's Iron Works (*see also Rappahannock Forge*) (Stafford County) 74, 138, 254
Hutt, Daniel 37
Hylton (King George County) 52, 129
Illinois 193
Illinois State Militia 193
Independence Mutual Fire Insurance Company of Alexandria 17
Independent Order of Odd Fellows 264
Indianapolis, Indiana 13
Ingleside (Stafford County) 63, 88, 251, 253
Ingleside subdivision 58
Innes, Sallie (Thornton) (Forbes) (1776-1807) 68
Interstate 95 45
Invernesshire, Scotland 69
Ireland 11, 147, 171, 243
Ireland, James 124
Isemonger, Anna Guy (French) (born 1776) 167
Irvine, Betty (Benson) 198
Betty Lucas (Bullard) (1835-1891) 176
Beverly R. W. (c.1839-1922) 176, 178, 188, 198
John (c.1794-1871) 29, 147, 156, 159
Sinah "Sarah" Davis (Conyers) (c.1798-1883) 77

William 230
William (c.1781-1859) 77, 78, 147, 174, 176, 179, 238, 274, 275
Irwin, John 257, 258
Jackson, Andrew 70
Benjamin F. 193
John 273
Gen. Thomas J. "Stonewall" 90
Jackson, Mississippi 70, 159
Jacobs, William J. (c.1850-1926) 239
James II, King of England 61
James, Anne (Strother) (born c.1710) 55
George (c.1702-1753) 55
John (c.1732-1794) 55-58
John, Jr. 136
Margaret (Morgan) (born c.1795) 162
Mary (Strother) 137
Mary (Wheeler) 55
Nancy (Hooe) (born c.1760) 171
Polly (Fallis) 138, 270
James City County, Virginia 2
James' Hill (Stafford County) 80
James' land (Stafford County) 162, 163
Jameson, David D. (1725:30-1794) 73
Enoch G. (born 1810) 149, 150, 152, 153
James (died 1736) 44, 122
Joel James (1801-after 1861) 147, 150, 152, 153
John (1763-1842) 73-75, 147, 149, 153, 154
Mary (Morton) 73
Mary S. (Eakin) 149
Jamestown, Virginia 1, 25, 26
Janney, E. A. 260
Japan 174
Jaquelot, Jenade (1678-1718) *see also Shacklett* 244
Jefferson County, West Virginia 55, 130
Jefferson Hotel (Richmond) 20
Jeffries, Sarah (Phillips) (born c.1740) 134
Jenkins, Lillie C. (Sthreshley) 240
Jerrol, James (born c.1800) 262
James W. (born c.1831) 262
Jeter, Nancy "Dicey" (Bradshaw) (died c.1823) 147
Jett, A. D. 192
Ada J. (Berry) (1892-1956) 240
Ann "Nancy" (Rollow) (1757-1830) 148
Anne E. (Lightner) 237
Barsheba (Porch) (c.1741-1817) 132
Berryman (born 1780) 279
Catherine (born c.1805) 192
Catherine "Kitty" (Suthard) (born c.1812) 236
Daniel 279
Elizabeth (Curtis) 148
Elizabeth Storke (Washington) 18
Ethelswitha 182
Francis (c.1735-1791) 132
Frank H. 240

Jeremiah Bailey (1832-1913) 182, 183
James 182
James (c.1808-1878) 236
Lucy I. (Chinn) (born c.1832) 182
Nettie G. (Simpson) (died 1952) 238
Peter (c.1717-1784) 132, 148
Peter (born c.1802) 192
Peter S. (born c.1836) 192
Rebecca (Bowen) 132, 148
Sarah (Cox) 149
Stapleton C. (c.1837-after 1888) 192, 235, 236
Susannah (Payne) 148
Thomas (died 1785) 18
William 135-137
Johns, Bishop ___ 15
Johnson, James W. (1821-1856) 233, 260, 261, 276
Joseph 233
Joseph M. 273
Robert A. 88, 190
Sally 233
Samuel 32
Thomas 262
Thomas H. (c.1820-1903) 159, 163, 179, 180, 183, 184, 194, 195
Johnson (James W.) & Company (business) 260
Johnston, Gen. Albert Sidney (1803-1862) 184
Bales D. 257
Burkett G. 272, 273
Joseph E. 19
Thomas (born c.1835) 172, 262
Johnston's Island 15
Jones, Bishop ___ 14
Allen 272
Amos (c.1813-after 1870) 177
Anne (Philpin) 135
Azariah 235
Bettie (Lacy) (born 1829) 163
Betsy (Green) 11
Brereton (1716-1795) 123
Cadwallader 4
Charles 274
Charles W. 276
Crusie J. (1880-1970) 198
David 268
Davis 187
Edward E. 234
Elizabeth Buckner (Sthreshley) 168
Elizabeth "Lettice" (Warner) (1720:25-1795) 123
Ethelina Malinda (Curtis) 235
Gabriel (1724-1806) 62
Garrison 232
George 135
H. M. 171
Henry 137, 149

James 150, 262, 276, 284
James M. 191, 194, 196
Jane 235
John 277
John N. (born c.1821) 263, 283
John Paul 19, 64, 186
John Peyton (born c.1842) 284
John Potts (1856-1914) 284
John W. (born c.1821) 159
Judith (Swan) (c.1680-1742) 47
Laurinda (Schooler) (1815-1870) 179
Lewis 279
Lewis, Jr. 146, 151
Lucy V. (Christy) (born c.1833) 263
M. C. 89
Marian L. (Schooler) (born c.1841) 284
Martha 232
Mattie H. (Morton) 89
Maurice (c.1659-c.1733) 47
Mildred (Bowler) (c.1802-c.1834) 274, 275
Nicholas 189
Noah (c.1821-1901) 163
R. A. 195
R. M. 188
Richard 179
Richard M. 198
S. H. 89
Samuel H. (c.1833-1875) 232
Sarah Ann (Fleet) 57
Sarah (Curtis) 135
Sarah Eliza (Rowe) (Monteith) 187
Sarah (West) (1867-1935) 285
Susan 284
Swan (1703-1736) 47
Thomas 147, 149, 151, 168
Thomas of Ludlow 151
W. B. 80
William 136
Jones' shop (Stafford County) 175, 259
Jonesville (Stafford County) 114, 115, 281
Joplin Post Office (Prince William County) 222
Jordan, Joseph 269
Joshua Road (State Route 643) 194
Julian, Charles (1774-1837) 11, 65
    Dr. John 68
    Jane (Moor) (1777-1851) 11, 65
    John (c.1738-c.1787) 11
    Margaret Isabelle (Lounds) 11
    Margaret Wilson (Skinker) (died 1863) 68, 78
Justices of the Peace (responsibilities) 25-28
"Justices vs Hunter &c" 9
Kale, Julia Anton (Alexander) (1833-1882) 84
Kecoughtan Hospital (Hampton, Virginia) 238
Keene, Elizabeth (Withers) (died 1769) 134
Keith, Charlotte (Ashmore) 83
    Charlotte Ashmore (Briggs) (1782-1866) 83

Isham 83
Kellogg, Ezekiel (died 1828) 84, 160, 259
    Frances A. (Waller) (1815-1887) 84, 160
    Friend (1797-1839) 259, 276, 280
    Luna (Clark) (born 1778) 84, 160
    Lyman (1813-1897) 16, 84-86, 160, 181-183, 259
Kellogg's Mill (Stafford County) 84, 139, 149, 160, 193
Kellogg's Mill Road (State Route 651) 149, 205, 230, 274
Kelly, Monroe (c.1818-1892) 83, 84, 179, 188
    Monroe S. 198
Kenaday, John 256
Kendall, Aaron 273
    Alexander 271
    Barnett 262
    Bloxton B. 270
    Catherine (Stark) (Pilcher) 262
    Eliza 166
    Elizabeth (Knight) (c.1794-c.1828) 87
    George 151
    Joel M. (born c.1827) 262
    Mary (Lee) 46
    Mary Mason (Hickerson) (born 1799) 151, 164, 165
    Mary (Stark) (1760-1858) 154
    Nancy (Latham) (1755-1840) 272
    Robert (c.1787-1860) 75-78, 150, 152, 153, 156, 159, 162, 164, 166
    S. M. (Pritchett) (Eustace) (born c.1829) 166
    Sarah H. (Byram) (1785-1854) 277
    William 151
    Woffendal (born c.1811) 262
Kenmore (Fredericksburg) 64, 159
Kennedy, Charles Lewis (1846-1933) 184, 185, 187, 189, 191, 193-195
    C. Howard 285
    Mary T. (Schooler) (1835-1904) 184
    Thomas A. 184
Kent, Samuel 119
Kentucky 8, 11, 56, 57, 130, 134, 135, 232, 244, 275
Kenyon, Elizabeth (Newton) 10, 65
    Sarah (Strother) 137
Keys, Catherine A. (Herndon) (1833-1906) 165
Kiger, George (c.1767-1857) 148-150, 154
Kimbrough, Maria Louise (Sims) 20
Kincheloe, Mae A. 247
King, Absalom (c.1791-1853) 148
    Basil (born 1760) 179
    Daniel 148
    Elias (1795-1876) 179
    George P. (c.1812-1876) 164, 172, 176, 178

Nancy H. (Botts) (1800-1868) 179
Peter (c.1806-1862) 275, 276
Pierson (died c.1841) 275
Samuel 176
Sarah 148
Susan (Warren) 176
Thomas 262
King and Queen County, Virginia 58
King George County, Virginia 4, 5, 8, 9, 11, 13-16, 18, 19, 21, 37, 38, 40, 42, 44, 45, 49-53, 56, 58, 60, 64, 82, 85, 114, 115, 125, 127-134, 137, 140, 153, 158, 162, 166, 169-173, 179, 180, 183, 188, 189, 198, 203, 225, 226, 238, 241, 256, 262, 273, 277, 284
King George Courthouse 17, 153, 160
King George Motor Company 14
King Street (Falmouth) 94
King William County, Virginia 10, 124
King's farm (Stafford County) 172, 176
Kings Highway (U.S. Route 3) 150
Kingsbury Iron Furnace (Maryland) 49
Kingston, Emma L. (Benson) (1845-1882) 177
George A. 177, 178
Kingston-Upon-Hull, England 118
Kirby Underwood, England 38
Kirk, John 257
Margaret (Schooler) 149
Knight, Austin (born c.1822) 282
Bailey (c.1787-1862) 87
Bessie (MacGregor) (1879-1959) 94, 205
Clarence Newman (1878-1945) 200, 203, 204
Daniel Webster S. (c.1824-1909) 87, 88, 91, 92
Drucilla (Burton) (born 1846) 282
Elizabeth 282
Elizabeth Harriet (Garrison) (1823-1901) 237, 238
Elizabeth (Kendall) (c.1794-c.1828) 87
Frances Alice (Musselman) (1830-1893) 247
Glady (Fritter) (c.1780-c.1857) 237
Harold T. (1915-1978) 205, 206
Capt. John Wesley (1846-1937) 94
Lewis K. (c.1820-1893) 176
Lillian T. 207, 208
Wesley (1846-1937) 196, 197, 265, 266
William (before 1775-before 1830) 237
William (1815-1904) 282
Knight Motor Company (Stafford County) 200
Knights of the Golden Horseshoe 64
Knox, Anna Campbell (Gordon) 251
John 6
Susanna Fitzhugh (Gordon) (1775-1869) 19, 251
Knoxville, J.V. (Milstead) 163
John J. (born c.1825) 163, 164
Lucy 163
M___ 151

Townley 163
Kopp Post Office (Prince William County) 222
Lacy, Bettie (Jones) (born 1829) 163
Maj. James Horace (1823-1906) 163, 166
Lacy House (Stafford County) 29, 31, 163
Lacy's Mill (Stafford County) 169, 172
Ladies' Confederate Memorial Association 163
LaGrange, Missouri 256
LaGrange Post Office (King George County) 226
Lake Arrowhead subdivision 201
Lake Ridge subdivision (Prince William County) 180
Lakeman, Daniel 271, 272
Lamb, William J. 235
Lambert, Elizabeth M. 204
Lancashire, England 39
Lancaster County, Pennsylvania 244
Lancaster County, Virginia 5, 6, 13, 18, 19, 21, 37, 38, 44, 47, 48, 56, 57, 117, 122, 157
Lance Post Office (Stafford County) 224, 225, 228, 239, 282
Landsdown Post Office (Prince William County) 228
Landstreet, Rev. ___ 85
Lane, Fountaine H. 150-152
George (died c.1823) 65-67
James 136
John Green (c.1814-1884) 261
Mary D. 65
Lang, C. C., Pickle Factory (Milford, Virginia) 266
Langhorne, Mary (Townshend) (died c.1694) 38
Larkin, Thomas 254
Latham, Betsy P. (Horton) 245
Edward 259, 260, 276
Edward Washington (1811-1851) 245
Elizabeth 277
Elizabeth R. (born c.1811) 277
Franklin (1728-1823) 276
George (c.1780-c.1846) 255, 258-262, 271, 276, 277, 280
George, Jr. (born c.1802) 262, 277
James 136
Jesse (died 1826) 154, 245
John 152, 272
John (c.1730-1834) 256, 272
Margaret (Hinson) (died c.1780) 272
Mary A. (Hill) (c.1812-c.1860) 170
Nancy (Kendall) (1755-1840) 272
Nannie G. (Heflin) (1829-1911) 174, 188
Noah H. (born 1814) 154
Raleigh "Rolly" (c.1795-1868) 114, 256
Susan (Cowne) 66
Thomas 155
Latham's Fork (Stafford County) 235
Laub, Martha Virginia (Eustace) (1829-1872) 182
Laurel, Maryland 163, 173

Laurel View (Stafford County) 204
Lawrenceburg, Kentucky 64
Lawson, Charles 260
    Henry 57
    James E., Jr. 156, 157
    Thomas (died 1793) 57
Lawson & Dunbar (business) 251
Leach—*see also Leitch*
    Anne C. (Curtis) 87
    James (died c.1823) 135, 139-144, 167
Leary, Genevieve 202
Ledlow, Mary (Suthard) 236
Lee, Ann (Fitzhugh) (McCarty) (1683-1732) 120
    Ann Hill (Carter) (1773-1829) 174
    Anna Maria (Mason) (1811-1898) 174, 234, 240
    Anne (Aylett) (c.1736-1768) 18
    Anne (Constable) (born 1622) 2, 38
    Anne Fenton (Brent) (born 1754) 10, 11
    Gen. Charles (1731-1782) 8
    Capt. Daniel Murray (1843-1916) 188, 190, 225, 240
    Edith (Balch) 234
    Ellen Bernard (Fowle) 175
    Eliza Ludwell (Carter) 18
    Elizabeth Ashton (Alexander) (born 1760) 18
    Gen. Fitzhugh (1835-1905) 86, 175
    Frances (Carter) 11
    Francis Lightfoot (1734-1797) 6, 18
    Capt. Hancock (1653-1709) 46
    Hannah (Ludwell) (1701-1750) 6, 18
    Henry "Lighthorse Harry" (1756-1818) 174
    James Oscar (1847-1908) 94, 178, 183, 185, 187, 190, 191, 193-197, 199
    James Oscar (c.1894-1952) 94
    John 46
    Capt. John (1643-1673) 2, 38
    Capt. John (c.1709-1789) 47, 49, 106, 127, 128
    John Hancock (1805-1873) 19
    Maj. John Mason (1839-1924) 234
    Julius L. (c.1822-after 1902) 165
    Lucy A. 94
    Lucy A. (Luck) (1854-1931) 183
    Martha (Fitzhugh) (Turberville) (1716-1751) 6
    Mary (Aylett) 10
    Mary (Kendall) 46
    Mildred (Washington) (born 1788) 18
    Nannie E. (Ficklen) (1850-1933) 188, 240
    Nannie (Mason) (1811-1898) 188
    Nora (Bankhead) (1841-1915) 234
    Philip Ludwell (1727-1775) 6
    Rebecca (Tayloe) (c.1748-1797) 18
    Col. Richard (1618-1664) 2, 38
    Hon. Richard (1647-1715) 5, 43, 120
    Richard Henry (1732-1794) 6, 18
    Gen. Robert E. 19, 163, 174, 175, 188, 190, 240
    Robert J.(?) 160
    Sarah H. 183
    Sydney Smith (1802-1869) 174, 175, 188, 234, 240
    Thomas 167
    Col. Thomas (1690-1750) 6, 18
    Thomas (1758-1805) 18
    Thomas Ludwell (1730-1778) 6, 7, 10, 18, 53, 55, 56
    Thomas Ludwell, Jr. (1751-1807) 11, 65, 139
    William 166, 183
    William Bankhead (1882-1938) 234
    Winifred Beale (Brent) (1790-1833) 11, 65
Lee-Curtis Insurance Agency (Fredericksburg) 201
Leechman, Elizabeth (Shelton) 152
Leedstown (Westmoreland County) 5, 18, 58, 59
Leedstown Resolutions 18, 126, 128, 133
Leeland (Stafford County) 175, 193, 195
Leeland District 113
Leeland Post Office (Stafford County) 225, 240
Leeland Station (Stafford County) 220, 225
Leeland Station subdivision (Stafford County) 161
Lee's Station, Kentucky 267
Leiber, Rev. Henry (born c.1823) 265, 284
    Jane R. 265
    John H. (born c.1858) 265, 284
    M. E. (Shacklett) (born c.1855) 265
Leicestershire, England 4
Leigh Street (Richmond) 77
Leitch, Ambrose 174
    Andrew 253
    Benjamin (died c.1812) 135
    George 270-276
    George H. 260, 261
    John J. (c.1822-1882) 158, 174
    Lucy 174
    Lucy (Rowe) 86
    Martha J. S. (Russell) (c.1826-1885) 158, 174
Leland, Lucy (Chinn) 13
Leon, James 89
Lewellyn, Abel S. (c.1809-1857) 237, 277
    Sarah W. (born c.1825) 277
Lewis, Betty (Washington) (1733-1797) 64
    Edward 46
    Elizabeth (Daniel) 12, 67
    Estelle (Pollock) 172
    Fielding (1725-1781) 64
    Fielding 172
    Hannah (Fant) 132
    Johanna (Linton) 46
    Judith (Lewis) (born c.1770) 64
    Lucinda (Smith) (born 1848) 20
    Dr. Magnus Muse (1864-1937) 33

Dr. Richmond (1774-1831) 12, 159
    Robert (1769-1829) 63, 66
    Sarah Travers (Scott) (1813-1891) 159, 164
    Col. Zachary (1731-1803) 67
Lewis cemetery (King George County) 172
Lewis Insurance Agency (Stafford County) 134, 267
Lewis' Mill (Stafford County) 149
Liberty Hall (Stafford County) 14, 20, 165
Liggate, Alexander 254
Liggate & Mathews (business) 254
Lightfoot, Philip 169
    Rosalie V. (Morson) (1819-1889) 169
    Sallie (Bernard) 169
Lightner, Anne E. (Jett) 237
    Eliza T. (Cox) (born c.1835) 87
    George G. (1839-1898) 87, 236, 237, 262, 263, 278, 283, 284
    Rev. George W. (c.1805-1886) 281, 282
    Harry G. (born 1868) 87, 237
    Mary L. (Coakley) (born c.1817) 87
    Paul 203
Lightner & Burton (business) 282
Lightner's Store (Falmouth, Virginia) 237
Limerick (Limbrick), Anne "Nancy" (Monteith) 153
    Charles Peyton William (c.1841-1914) 179, 191
    Charles W. 176
    Deliah A. (Moore) (born c.1847) 91
    Elizabeth (born c.1815) 264
    Ella (Reeves) (born 1857) 264
    Frances 171
    James 281, 282
    Jane (Shelton) (1851-1927) 188
    John 170, 171
    Landon (c.1813-after 1880) 91, 283
    Landon S. 263
    Lemuel S. (c.1846-1904) 264, 283
    Lucinda (Lowry) (born c.1819) 171
    Nancy (Monteith) 187
    Robert E. (born c.1825) 264, 281
Lincoln County, England 38
Lincoln County, Kentucky 136
Linden (Westmoreland County) 21
Linn & Davis (business) 282
Linton, Anthony 45
    Johanna (Lewis) 46
    John 45
    Mary (Page) 45
    Winifred (Presley) 45
    William 46
Literary Fund of Virginia 147
Litteral, Anna E. (Fritter) (c.1804-1892) 154
Little, John M. 236
    John P. 13
    Mary Alexander (Seddon) 13
    William Alexander (born c.1819) 20
    William Alexander, Jr. (c.1866-1944) 20, 184, 187
Little Falls (Stafford County) 42, 65, 137, 179
Little Falls Mill (Stafford County) 151
Little Hunting Creek (Fairfax County) 2, 4, 43
Little Whim (Stafford County) 76, 159, 164, 176, 240
Little Whim Post Office (Stafford County) 225, 240
Liverpool Point (Maryland) 32
Loch Lomond (Stafford County) 19, 62, 201, 255, 277, 282
Loch Lomond Mill (Stafford County) 62
Lochdougan, Scotland 251
Locust Grove (Stafford County) 134, 136, 265
Locust Hill (Stafford County) 8, 43, 56, 126
Locust Shade Park (Prince William County) 47
Lomax, John T. 135
    Martha (Roberts) 69
Lomax family 48
London, Ellen Caskie (Ficklen) 236
London, England 2, 41, 42, 44, 46
Long Branch (Stafford County) 167, 170, 173, 174
Long Branch ford (Stafford County) 172
Long, Gabriel 143, 155
    Mary (Payne) 237
Longwood (Westmoreland County) 18
Lord, John 37
Los Angeles, California 188
Loudon County, Tennessee 148
Loudoun County, Virginia 4, 11, 39, 46, 65, 167, 173
Louisa County, Virginia 19, 20, 234
Louisiana Legislature 157
Louisiana Supreme Court 157
Louisville, Kentucky 129
Lounds, Margaret Isabelle (Julian) 11
Love, Charles A. (born 1841) 174
    E. H. 181
    Eliza 174
    Ella M. (Coakley) (born c.1845) 174
    Henry (c.1811-1873) 174, 176, 282
    William 59, 130
Lowry, Alelia (Pollard) 232
    Alice 186
    James H. (c.1834-1868) 171, 186
    James L. (1817-1889) 85-87, 173, 174, 179
    John (c.1808-after 1870) 31, 83, 84, 232
    Lucinda (Limerick) (born c.1819) 171
    Marion King (1854-1939) 16, 186, 232
    Robert A. (died 1907) 186
    Susan 171
    Thomas (c.1826-1911) 178, 179, 245, 282
    W. B. 178
    William 171
Lowry's Mill (Stafford County) 16
Lucas, Albert G. (c.1806-1854) 178

Basil (died 1909) 181
Cornelia (Ennever) (1818-1884) 178
Ennever (c.1842-1912) 178, 180, 185, 193-195, 198
Fielding 148
Fielding (c.1840-1873) 148
Mildred C. 245
William J. (c.1834-after 1870) 278, 282, 283
Lucas' Tannery (Falmouth) 148
Luck, Adeline (Gatewood) 173
    John M. (1827-1888) 86, 87, 173, 178, 179, 186, 183, 192
    Jordan B. 173
    Lucy A. (Lee) (1854-1931) 183
    Mary Ann (Rowe) (1824-1902) 86, 183
Ludlow (Stafford County) 6, 132, 148, 177
Ludwell, Hannah (Lee) (1728-1782) 6, 18
Lund, Christopher (died 1674) 115, 116
    Elizabeth (Washington) 48
Lunn, Thomas 44
Lunsford, Andrew B. (born c.1822) 261
    Aphia F. (Swetnam) (born c.1844) 89, 172
    Bessie (Simpson) (born c.1878) 202
    James 172
    James H. 176
    James Leon 89
    Margaret 89
    Maud (Coakley) (died 1936) 205
    N. A. (Beale) (born c.1851) 89
    R. P. (Evans) (born c.1853) 263
    Robert F. (c.1832-1903) 88-91, 172, 196, 197
    William (born c.1785) 89, 172, 261
    Willie (born c.1795) 89, 172
Lunsford Hills (King George County) 39, 116
Lyon, James 138
Lyon's Farm, New Jersey 17
MacGregor, Alaric Ridout (1906-1991) 205, 206
    Alfred Henry (c.1898-1961) 95
    Bessie (Knight) (1879-1959) 94, 205
    Inez (Green) (1867-1941) 264
    John Alaster (1869-1953) 94, 205
    John Ridout (1829-1900) 94
    Mary Eliza (MacGregor) (born 1831) 94
    Myrtle V. 246
Machodoc (King George County) 2
Machodoc Creek (King George County) 38, 47, 125
Mackey, Catherine (Tankersley) 85
Maddox, Amy (Derrick) (16_-c.1740) 40
    Benedicta (Bloxton) (Flourey) 271
    Benjamin 201
    Dr. Edward (16_-1694) 40, 41
    John A. 189
    John Walter (1883-1949) 201-204
    Lazarus 58
    Margaret 270, 271
    Sarah (Peyton) 165

    Walter 271
Madison, James 64
Madison County, Virginia 15, 267
Mahoney, Gen. ___ 240
    Eliza Jane (Shackelford) (c.1843-1894) 247, 265
    William P. (born c.1839) 185
Mallory, Mary (Craig) 155
    William 155
Manassas Battlefield Park (Prince William County) 17
Manassas Nursing Home (Prince William County) 17
Manassas, Battle of (1862) 171
Manassas, Virginia 17, 171
Manchester, Virginia 281
Manly, Penelope (Barnes) 55
Manns, Paul W. 21
Mansbridge, Mary (Harrison) 41
    William (died 1697) 41, 118
Mansfield, Myron (born c.1826) 242
Marceron, Ralph A. 208
Markham, James (1786-c.1817) 47
    Margaret (Chapman) 127
Marlborough, Maryland 57
Marlborough (Stafford County) 4, 8, 10, 18, 39, 41, 42, 50, 52, 65, 119, 148, 151, 219, 283
Marlborough Point (Stafford County) 27, 37, 39, 50, 116, 161
Marlborough Point Road (State Route 621) 37
Marlborough Road (Stafford County) 159, 173
Marmion (King George County) 9, 48, 61, 138, 172
Marquis, Anthony (1752-1821) 137, 138, 149, 268
    Elizabeth (Winlock) 137, 268
    Samuel (c.1780-c.1850) 149
    William (died c.1790) 268
Marsh Road (Stafford County) 173
Marshall, John 18
    W. H. 189
    William Stannard 136
Martin, Dr. ___ 14
    John S. 195-197
    Lawrence 88
    Margaret (Morton) 73
    Mary Catherine (Graninger) (1830-1897) 193
    Patrick (c.1822-1895) 89
Mary Washington College 20
Mary Washington Hospital (Fredericksburg) 17, 87
Mary Washington House (Fredericksburg) 251
Mary Washington Monument (Fredericksburg) 70
Maryland 6, 13, 31, 32, 45-47, 49-53, 55, 71, 82, 87, 118, 120, 127, 128, 165, 176, 177, 186, 190, 219, 251, 273, 278, 281
Maryland-Virginia Dairymen's Association 17

Mason, Dr. Alexander Hamilton (1807-1858) 74-78, 146
    Ann (Darrell) (Fitzhugh) 121
    Ann (Thomson) (died 1762) 6
    Anna Maria (Lee) (1811-1898) 174, 234, 240
    Anna Maria (Murray) 12
    Anne (Chandler) (Fowke) (died after 1673) 2
    Bartlett 137
    Catherine (Mercer) (1707-1750) 50
    Charles 15
    Charles (1810-1888) 19
    Elizabeth (Westwood) (Wallace) (died 1824) 9
    Enfield (Tackett) (1796-1836) 147, 233
    Col. Enoch (c.1769-1828) 10, 19, 63, 64, 66-71, 74, 137, 139-142, 148, 150, 154
    Enoch, Jr. (c.1797-c.1835) 71, 72, 152, 153
    Frances (Bunbury) (born 1688) 43
    Frances (Matheny) 118
    French (1695-1748) 45, 122
    George (16_-c.1729) of Aquia 10, 63
    George I (1628-1686) 2, 3, 6, 37, 38, 40, 44, 63, 115-117
    Capt. George II (1660-1716) 2-5, 27, 40, 42-45, 49, 118-122, 127, 267
    George III (1690-1735) 5, 6, 39, 52, 54, 122, 123
    George IV (1725-1792) 2, 5, 6, 9, 12, 20, 37, 50, 71, 86
    James 137
    Jane 147
    Jane Allen (Smith) (died 1812) 74
    Joel (died 1813) 64, 66, 233
    John (1722-c.1796) 137
    John (1764-1824) 12
    John Enoch (1854-1910) 15
    John Thomson (1787-1850) 57
    Kate Kearney (Henry) 15
    Lewis (born 1757) 137, 147
    Lucy Wiley (Roy) (died c.1835) 11, 63, 70
    Margaret (Carter) (died 1751) 56
    Maria Jefferson Carr (Randolph) 15
    Mary (Bethel) (died 1831) 137, 147
    Mary Elizabeth (Mason) 71
    Mary (Fitzhugh) (Strother) 5, 6, 49, 127
    Mary (Fowke) 2, 45, 122, 127
    Mary (French) 37, 40
    Mary (Nelson) (172_-c.1801) 137
    Mary Nelson (Corbin) 274, 280
    Mary (Nicholson) 45, 122
    Mary/Lucy (Peyton) (1801-1838) 70, 148
    Mary Thomson (Cooke) (born 1762) 12, 51, 71
    Mary Thomson (Selden) (1731-1758) 52
    Nannie (Lee) (1811-1898) 188
    Nelson 137, 147, 149
    Nimrod 137
    Robert 147
    Sarah (Bourne) (c.1771-1835) 64, 233
    Sarah Roy (Barber) 154
    Simpha Rosa Enfield (Bronaugh) (Dinwiddie) (1703-1762) 52, 55
    Susan L. (Bryan) 178
    Thomson (1733-1785) 6, 9, 54, 56
    Wiley Roy 76
    William 140, 147
Mason, Alexander H. & Company (business) 260
Mason County, Kentucky 267
Masonic Cemetery (Fredericksburg) 9, 84, 168
Masonic Lodge 91, 251, 281
Masonic Lodge #4 (Fredericksburg) 17, 33, 164
Masonic Lodge #63 (Fredericksburg) 84
Mason's Mill (Fairfax County) 45, 122
Mason's Warehouse (Fairfax County) 122
Massachusetts 70, 164, 240
Massie(y), Alexander W. (died c.1839) 153
    Ann "Nancy" (Coakley) 276
    Betty (Washington) 52
    Dade (1679-1735) 44, 45, 120, 124, 125
    Elizabeth (Ellis) (born c.1680) 44
    George Key (1878-1951) 232
    John 116
    Mary (Dade) (1661-c.1694) 44
    Mary (Dade) (Hooe) 45
    Mary (Gilson) 120
    Mary Virginia (Hickerson) (Wamsley) (born 1833) 164, 165
    Mary (Washington) 45, 52, 125
    Parthenia (Dade) (Alexander) (1709-1742) 49
    Robert 47, 49
    Robert (1655-1689) 44, 120
    Rose (Newton) (Grigsby) (Dade) (c.1700-1785) 44, 120, 124
    Sigismunda Mary (Alexander) (born 1745) 10
    William 95
Massie & Winkler (business) 265
Massie's Store (Stafford County) 95
Masters, Mrs. ___ 114, 170, 173
    Catherine 171
    Gerrard 37
    James 274
    James F. 171
    John 171
    John W. 186
    John 171
    John W. 186
    Luke 146, 148, 149, 273, 274
    Welford Montgomery (1850-1929) 186
    William T. (c.1823-1865) 262, 277, 281
    William T. (1844-1914) 171, 172, 262, 277
Masters' Mill (Stafford County) 154
Masters' Store Precinct 159, 179, 188, 189

Mathena, Daniel (1638-1685) 118
    Sarah (Wentworth) (died 1700) 118
Matheny, Frances (Mason) 118
    William Wentworth (1664-1705) 118
Mathews, John 43, 116, 267
    Mary (Anderson) 43, 48
    Mary (Grant) 55
    Mary (Waller) 138
    Samuel (died 1659) 3
    Thomas 3
Mathis, John 115
Maund, Harriet Lucy (Carter) (born 1768) 18
    John James (died 1802) 18
Maury, Elizabeth B. (Vass) 252
Maury Camp #2 (Confederate Veterans) 165
Mauzy, Gilson 260
    John (c.1675-1718) 6, 44
    John (c.1696-1780) 127-129
    Margaret (Hedgman) (1702-1754) 6, 44
    Mary (Crosby) (Mountjoy) (16_-1756) 44
    Michael 44
Max, James 193
Maze, Michael 267
McBryde, Rev. R. J. 33
McCall, Archibald (1734-1814) 252
    Catherine (Flood) 252
    Margaret (Adams) 252
    Samuel 252
McCarty, Ann (Lee) (Fitzhugh) (1683-1732) 120
    Anna Barbara (Fitzhugh) 45
    Capt. Daniel (1679-1724) 45, 120
    Daniel (died 1743) 18, 123
    Daniel, Jr. (173_-1795) 18
    Maj. Dennis (1704-1742) 45
    Elizabeth (Pope) (Payne) (born 1667) 45
    Elizabeth (Smith) 18
    Mary (Mercer) (1740-1764) 18
    Sarah (Ball) (born 1705) 45, 123
McClees, Ellis M. 265
McColley, Archibald 252
McConchie, Sally Udora (Heflin) (1852-1931) 186
    William A. 186
McCormick, Robert 179
McCoy, Hannah (Campbell) 18
    John T. (1819-1905) 175, 180, 185, 186, 190, 192
McDaniel, Mrs. ___ 135, 136
McDonald, Ellen (Moor) 11
    Jean Briggs (c.1750-1810) 72
    Rev. Neal 72
McDowell, Gen. Irvin 30
    Edward Mason (1843-1878) 176, 179
McFarland, Margaret Elizabeth (Wallace) (died 1864) 88
McFarlin, Obediah 279
McGhee, Olivia D. (Griffis) (c.1862-after 1925) 234

McGuire, Nancy (Rowe) 187
McIlhaney, Mary (Curtis) 148
McInteer(e), Alexander (c.1730-1807) 146
    Bathsheba (Patton) 239
    Henry, Jr. 150
    Sarah (Patton) (died c.1844) 146
    Sarah (Sinclair) 146
"McInteer vs McInteer" 133
McKenzie, Lewis 84
McMasters, Thomas 253
McRea, Robert 253
McRea & McMasters (business) 253
McWhirt, John W. 205, 206
Meadow Branch (Stafford County) 155
Medical College of Virginia 182, 184
Meese, Col. Henry (died 1682) 3, 37, 38, 251
Melling, England 39
Memphis, Battle of 15
Mercer, Ann (Roy) (c.1729-1770) 8
    Catherine (Mason) (1707-1750) 50
    Grace (Fenton) 50
    John 50
    John (1704-1768) 8, 10, 18, 50-55, 65, 124, 128
    John Francis (1759-1821) 8, 9
    Mary (McCarty) (1740-1764) 18
    Mildred Ann Byrd (Carter) (1774-1837) 10
    Robert (1764-1799) 10
    Sarah Ann Mason (Selden) (born 1738) 52, 65
    Sophia (Sprigg) 9
Meredith, Rev. Jacquelin Marshall (1833-1920) 14, 193
Metts, Ralph 206, 207
Michael, James H. 240
Middleburg, Virginia 170
Middlesex County, Virginia 48, 61, 127, 168, 184
Middleton, G. W. 193
Midway Island Post Office (Stafford County) 225, 229, 240, 243
Midway Island, Virginia 232
Milford, Virginia 266
Mill dams 111
Mill Farm (Stafford County) 182
Mill Farm Seminary (Stafford County) 77, 182
Miller, Isabella (Triplett) 47
    Jane (Hord) 61, 127
Millie's Post Office (Stafford County) 225, 241, 265
Millington, John 259, 280
Mills, Absalom W. 280
    E. W. 284
    John (born c.1846) 234
    John H. (died 1928) 179, 180
    Mildred C. (Schooler) (c.1847-1929) 234
    Wyatt (1859-1929) 234

Millvale (Stafford County) 13, 64, 71, 74
Milstead, Harriet (Carter) 233
    J. V. (Knoxville) 163
    Samuel 163
Minnick, Lydia C. (Atchison) (1852-1925) 93, 201
Minnieville Road (Prince William County) 246
Minor, Dorothea (Bankhead) (1805-1868) 81
Mississippi 202
Mitchell, Eliza (Daniel) (died c.1835) 71
    Harvey H. (1877-1942) 244
    James (died 1822) 268-270
    William 71, 147, 151
Moncure, Agatha Ann (Glascock) (born 1814) 85
    Alice Peachy (Gaskins) (1774-1860) 12, 140, 275
    Anna Jane (Hull) (born 1835) 90, 186
    Anne (Conway) (born c.1750) 10, 140
    Anne Eliza (1895-1984) 173
    Catherine Cary (Ambler) 173
    Charles Prosser (born 1819) 77
    Clarissa Bernard (Hooe) (1800-1829) 12
    Dorothea "Dora" (Ashby) (1836-1911) 81
    Edwin Conway (178_-1816) 85
    Eleanor (Edrington) 85
    Ellen (Gilchrist) (1897-1971) 94
    Esther J. (Vowles) (1795-1833) 81
    Fanny Dulany (Tomlin) 157
    Frances (Daniel) (born 1745) 9, 12, 64
    Frances (Daniel) (1797-1871) 12
    Frances E. (deLashmutt) (1893-1966) 201
    Frances Vowles (Ashby) (1828-1910) 166
    Frank Peyton (1889-1969) 17, 200-202
    George Vowles (1826-1901) 14, 30, 89, 158, 160, 169, 178, 192, 195
    Georgianna Cary (Bankhead) (1830-1890) 81
    Harriet "Hallie" Eustace (Wallace) (1846-1928) 189, 198
    Harriet Mabel (Taylor) (1865-1895) 246
    Henry Wood (1800-1866) 173
    Henry Wood (1836-1874) 173
    Jean Charlotte (Washington) (1834-1916) 178
    Rev. John (1710-1764) 9, 51, 53
    John II (1747-1784) 10, 140
    John III (1772-1822) 10-12, 75, 63, 64, 66, 67, 140, 141, 144, 147, 275
    John IV (1793-1876) 12, 14, 68, 72, 81, 166, 167, 169
    John Conway (1827-1916) 157-160, 162, 164, 165, 167, 168
    Julia Trent (Warwick) (1840-1906) 173
    Lucy Ann (Gatewood) (1807-1895) 147, 275
    Mary Bell (Haxall) 12
    Mary Butler Washington (Conway) (1807-1895) 12, 16, 90, 157, 178, 246
    Mary Conway (Ashby) (1830-1867) 14, 89, 169, 192, 195
    Mary Joanna (Hughes) (1852-1939) 201
    Mary Robinson (Nelson) (1819-1883) 264
    McCarty Chichester (1918-1993) 205, 207, 208
    Nannie Withers (Waller) (1862-1903) 248
    Powhatan (1830-1908) 81-84, 188, 190
    Richard Ashby (1864-1923) 89, 90, 195
    Richard Cassius Lee, Sr. (1805-1882) 12, 13, 16, 29, 90, 157, 176, 178, 186, 189, 198, 246
    Richard Cassius Lee, Jr. (1831-1917) 16, 20, 198-200, 202, 204, 246, 248
    Richard Cassius Lee (1856-1936) 248
    Robert Ambler (1864-1923) 196
    Robert S. (1857-1917) 192, 198
    Sarah Elizabeth (Henry) 155
    Sarah "Sally" Elizabeth (Hull) (1809-1892) 86, 90
    Susan B. (Carter) 75
    Thomas Gaskins (1799-1836) 12, 68, 148, 272, 273
    Thomas Gaskins (1837-1906) 178, 180-185
    Thomas M., Jr. 17, 208
    Travers Daniel (1811-1886) 32, 75-78, 155-157, 159, 164-167
    Virginia A. (Buchanan) (1881-1938) 16
    Dr. Walker Peyton (1842-1916) 201
    William (1774-1832) 155
    William Augustus (1803-1862) 147, 149, 275
    William Edwin (1824-1888) 31, 81, 82, 170, 179, 181
Moncure & Eustace (business) 252
Moncure Elementary School (Stafford County) 173
Monk, Elizabeth (Walker) 49
Monmouth, Battle of (1778) 133
Monmouth, Duke of 61
Monroe, ___ 92
    Maj. Andrew (c.1630-c.1668) 43, 51
    Annie (Edwards) 239
    Catherine (Hore) 127
    David Alexander 225, 239
    Elizabeth (Mountjoy) 43
    Frances 192
    George E. (c.1857-1906) 192, 194-196, 263
    James 224
    James (c.1789-1867) 170
    James R. 231, 239
    Margaret Elizabeth (c.1905-1959) 231, 239
    Margaret (Storke) (Washington) 51
    Mary T. (Downs) (born c.1853) 192
    Sarah (Huffman) 234
    Thomas (died c.1777) 127
    William 192

Woodrow Fleming "Flip" 95, 239
Monroe's Creek (Westmoreland County) 43
Monroe's Store (Stafford County) 224, 231
Mont Anna (Stafford County) 157
Montague, Amanda (Claybrook) (died 1845) 184
    Belle (Ramey) 184
    Celestine Louise (Gordon) (1841-1876) 184
    Edmund Healy (died 1847) 184
    Dr. Thaddeus Constantine (1838-1898) 15, 184, 185, 190
Monteith, ___ 88
    Amos K. (c.1839-after 1909) 187, 195
    Anne "Nancy" (Limerick/Limbrick) 153
    Eleanor (Newton) 173
    Eleanor (Thom) 173
    Elizabeth (born c.1806) 168
    Enos 173
    Georgianna (Rowe) (born c.1834) 168
    James 168, 174, 179, 241, 273, 277
    James (c.1813-c.1859) 80-84, 153, 157, 159-162, 164, 166, 168
    James H. (c.1845-1887) 183
    James M. 189
    John S. (c.1829-after 1880) 162, 165, 167
    Leah (Owens) 160
    Magdalin (Doniphan) (Finnall) (born c.1740) 131
    Marion Wallace (Purkins) (died 1927) 243
    Mildred (Fines) (born c.1787) 153
    Nancy (Limerick) 187
    Phillis (Gallop) 131
    Rebecca (Battaley) 273
    Richard E. (born c.1834) 167, 171, 183
    Samuel Owens (born c.1787) 153
    Sarah Eliza (Rowe) (Jones) 187
    Sir Thomas (1694-1747) 131
    Thomas (1811-1858) 153, 187
    William (c.1822-1905) 168
    William S. (1855-1903) 187
Monteithville (Stafford County) 165
Monteithville Post Office (Stafford County) 160, 223, 225, 226, 231, 241, 242
Montgomery, Alabama 75, 142
Montgomery, Kentucky 141
Moor, Edward (died c.1806) 11, 59, 65, 130
    Ellen (McDonald) 11
    Jane (Julien) (1777-1851) 11, 65
Moore, Arthur (1866-1952) 199, 243
    Clara (Chewning) 246
    Deliah A. (Limerick) (born c.1847) 91
    Edgar S. 155
    Edgar Smith, Jr. (1879-1954) 197, 199, 246
    Edgar Smith, Sr. (1847-1899) 187, 190, 191, 194, 246
    George F. (born c.1847) 91-93
    Henry (born c.1822) 91, 159, 276
    Mae M. (1898-1988) 248
    Mary (Renno) 150
    Tabias 91
    Thomas Jackson 197
    Wade Hampton (1878-1952) 93, 265, 266
    William F. (c.1812-1864) 79, 80, 149, 150
Moore & Alexander (business) 262
Moore & Waller (business) 281
Moore's Corner (Stafford County) 93, 265
Morayshire, Scotland 252
Morgan, Daniel 236, 252, 253
    Jane (Strother) 277
    Margaret (James) (born c.1795) 162
    Margaret (Strother) 277
    William L. (c.1805-1873) 161, 164, 167, 245, 262, 277
Morgan, Daniel & Brothers (business) 236, 252
Morgan, William L. & Company (business) 262
Morris(s), Ann (Fontaine) 11, 69
    Frances (Reamy) 79
    Mary E. (Bradford) 260
Morrison, Ella (Chartters) 191
Morson, Alexander (1759-1822) 60, 61, 63, 64, 66, 72-74, 145, 169, 252
    Anne Casson (Alexander) (1781-1833) 60, 72, 145
    Arthur (1734-1798) 58, 60, 61, 72, 145
    Dr. Hugh (1811-1877) 169, 170, 172
    Marion (Andrew) (Payne) (c.1724-1808) 58, 60, 70
    Rosalie V. (Lightfoot) (1819-1889) 169
    William 153
Morson, Alexander & Roberts (business) 252
Mortimer, Mary Ann F. (Randolph) 149
Morton, Allen Waller 73
    Ann (Hedgman) 73
    Annie (Dix) (c.1842-1922) 73
    Edmond 270
    Elizabeth 73
    George 73
    George (1717-1765) 60
    James, Sr. (died 1859) 73-81, 89, 148, 180, 232, 275
    James, Jr. (1851-1902) 73, 89, 180, 186, 191, 232, 242, 264
    John 73
    John B. 245
    Lucy (Baylor) (born c.1726) 60
    Lucy (Horton) (c.1818-1898) 73, 232
    Margaret (Marton) 73
    Margaret Ursula (Waller) (1771-1821) 73, 268-270, 279
    Maria 73
    Mary 73
    Mary (Jameson) 73

       Mary (Mountjoy) (1769-1804) 60
       Mattie H. (Jones) 89
       Nancy 73
       Richard (1771-1812) 73, 279
       Robert Baylor (1761-1807) 60-62
       Thomas 73, 273, 274
       Thomas Mountjoy (1787-1859) 57
       Ursula (Brightwell) 73
       William 73
       William Allen 245
Morton & Horton (business) 253
Morton & Payne (business) 89
Mosley, John S. 17
       Robert 116
Mott, Margaret (Doniphan) 48, 126
Mottershed, Jonathan 117, 118
Mount (Stafford County) 93, 200, 225
Mount Airy (Richmond County) 19, 266
Mount Airy (Stafford County) 266
Mount Hope Baptist Church (Stafford County) 266
Mount Olive (Stafford County) 76, 136, 152
Mount Olive Baptist Church (Stafford County) 19, 282
Mount Pleasant (Stafford County) 10, 205
Mount Pleasant Freestone Quarry (Stafford County) 283
Mount Post Office (Stafford County) 226, 241, 247
Mount Ringo (Stafford County) 202
Mount Vernon (Fairfax County) 45
Mount Vernon, New York 240
Mountain Road (Stafford County) 148
Mountain View (Stafford County) 88, 222, 265-267
Mountain View Fire Department (Stafford County) 258
Mountain View Post Office (Stafford County) 223, 226, 242
Mountain View Road (State Route 627) 63, 69, 93, 113, 205, 230
Mountjoy, Alexander Hamilton (c.1826-c.1902) 87-89, 91, 158, 171, 175, 242
       Alvin (1745-1827) 131
       Anna Elizabeth (Mountjoy) (1843-1913) 241, 265
       Anne (Withers) (born 1748) 56
       Annie May (Wilson) (1871-1951) 242
       Aurelia (Reily) (died 1844) 151
       Clara (Graves) (1878-1961) 241
       Capt. Edward (c.1660-1712) 43, 44, 126
       Elizabeth (Monroe) 43
       Frederick Mason (1855-1924) 91-93
       Gertrude A. (Courtney) (c.1880-1959) 247
       James Edward (1879-1938) 241, 265
       John (1741-1825) 60, 133-135, 137
       John (c.1772-c.1844) 151
       Lucy Ellen (Bridwell) (c.1857-1935) 91
       Mary Ann (Garrard) (1753-1823) 133
       Mary (Crosby) (16_-1756) 43, 44
       Mary Frances (Herndon) (1826-1910) 87, 91, 242

       Mary "Molly" (Edwards) (1760-1839) 131
       Mary Mildred (Griffis) (c.1844-1909) 166, 175, 281
       Mary (Morton) (1769-1804) 60
       Mary (Payne) (1794-1856) 87
       Mary Mildred (Griffis) (c.1844-1909)
       Milton (1866-1943) 242
       Minnie Alice (Roles) (1880-1921) 241
       Phillis (Reilly) (1717-1771) 8, 56
       Richard E. (1884-1946) 241
       Robert (1828-1891) 166, 175, 281
       Rubin Edward (1869-1931) 241, 265
       Thomas (1739-c.1818) 56, 57, 60-64, 66, 130, 131, 133, 134
       Thomas (born 1740) 8
       Thornton (1794:7-c.1881) 87, 151, 166, 241, 281
       Capt. William (1711-1777) 8, 56, 126-128, 130, 131, 133
       William (1737-1820) 56, 135, 137, 138, 139
       William (1866-1913) 247
       William Edward (1835-1898) 226, 241, 247, 265
Mountjoy & Herndon (business) 262
Mountjoy, James & Brother (business) 265
Mountjoy's Mill (Stafford County) 137
Moxley, James 273
Mudd, Jane (Brent) (died 1711) 120
       Capt. Thomas 120
Muddy Creek (Stafford County) 40, 75, 169, 228
Mulberry Hill (Stafford County) 136, 167
Murdaugh, Dr. ___ 83
Murdock, Margaret (Bronaugh) 52
       Mary Eliza (Perry) 283
Murphy, Nancy (Pilcher) (born c.1748) 270
       W. Tayloe, Jr. 17
Murray, Anna Maria (Mason) 12
       Eliza (Peyton) (1791-1878) 68
       Henry William (1826-1881) 19
       James F. 150
       John 58
       Max M. (c.1890-1938) 94
Muse, Alexander A. 84
Musselman, Albert Joseph (1863-1921) 247
       Alice 166
       Ann Nancy (England) 191
       Delila (born c.1808) 168
       Elizabeth (1834-1924) 265
       Frances Alice (Knight) (1830-1893) 247
       Frances Mary (1870-1936) 265
       H. V. (Holmes) (born c.1858) 247
       James 192, 242
       Jane (Byram) (born c.1836) 168
       Jesse (born c.1794) 168
       Joseph 192

Joseph (1863-1921) 265
Julia Lee (Groves) (1864-1943) 247
Malinda (Cooper) 194
Margaret Virginia (Gallahan) (1894-1981) 265
Nello Green (1892-1948) 265
Susan E. (Bryant) (1835-1890) 166
Wesley A. (born c.1835) 166
William Napoleon Bailey (1865-1921) 247
William Samuel 265
Musselman's Post Office (Stafford County) 223, 224, 226, 242, 266
Mutual Assurance Society 69, 137
Myer, F. S. 79
Myrtle Grove (Stafford County) 147, 186
Myrtleville Post Office (Stafford County) 179, 184, 226, 242
Nalls, B. F. (born c.1837) 179
Nansemond County, Virginia 41
Nansemond Courthouse, Virginia 219
Nantes, William G. (born c. 1840) 238, 264
Nanticoke Indians 4
Nash, J. A. 200
    John 270
Natchez, Mississippi 147
National Archives and Records Administration 154
Naughty, Mary (Garrard) (born c.1721) 133
Neabsco Iron Furnace 57
Neale, Daniel 122
    Hannah (Carter) (died 1722) 122
    Meriah (Reamy) 79, 199
    Thomas 219
Nelms, Charles D. 207
Nelson, Armistead (1855-1927) 192, 198
    Chancellor E. (born c.1834) 180
    Henry (c.1700-c.1750) 137
    Lucy Randolph (Towson) (1852-1937) 264
    Mary (Mason) (172_-c.1801) 137
    Mary Robinson (Moncure) (1819-1883) 264
    Dr. William Armistead (1817-1902) 264
Nelson County, Virginia 11
Nere, John A. (1923-1997) 207
Netherlands 57
New Boscobel (Stafford County) 166
New Hope Church (Stafford County) 149, 164, 166, 176
New Hope Church Road (State Route 605) 164
New Jersey 17, 85, 219
New Jersey Campaign (1777) 133
New Market, Maryland 161
New Mexico 32, 133
New Orleans 19
New Post (Spotsylvania County) 219
New Salvington (Stafford County) 80
New York 11, 15, 18, 33, 65, 94, 189, 219, 246
Newburgh-Fishkill, New York 65
Newton, Ann "Nancy" (Cox) 167

    Benjamin (born 1769) 116, 173
    Blake Tyler (c.1890-1977) 21
    Charles Wesley (1897-1944) 93
    D. P. 241
    Eleanor (Monteith) 173
    Elizabeth (Gilson) (died 1763) 42
    Elizabeth (Kenyon) 10, 65
    Fanny Estelle (Rowe) 93
    Gerrard (c.1677-c.1706) 124
    Gustavus B. (born c.1812) 173
    Gustavus B. (born c.1845) 173
    Hugh (1785-1964) 93
    Isaac (c.1745-1838) 65, 66, 72, 73, 137, 141
    John 167
    John, Sr. 42, 137
    John (born c.1830) 162
    Joseph (c.1639-c.1697) 118
    Josephine B. 284
    Lucien 88
    Margaret (Heabeard) (Travers) 116
    Mary (Newton) (1878-1967) 93
    Mary Thomas (Harper) (1789-1841) 283
    Matilda (Cox) 173
    Mildred (Curtis) 167
    Nancy (Butler) 173
    Parthenia (Green) 158
    Peggy (Strother) 137
    Rose (Gerrard) (Tucker) (born c.1629) 118
    Rose (Grigsby) (Massey) (Dade) (c.1700-1785) 44, 120, 124
    Sarah (Fox) 10
    Thomas 118
    William (1705-1787) 137
    William (c.1712-1789) 65
    Maj. William (c.1686-c.1722) 65
Newton's Mill (Stafford County) 137, 148
Nicholas, John 63
Nichols, Elijah 136, 140, 252, 253
Nicholson, Lt. Gov. Francis 219
    Mary (Mason) 45, 122
Nierstein, Germany 193
19th Amendment 20
9th Virginia Cavalry 20, 28, 80, 83, 87, 89, 92, 158-162, 164, 166, 169, 171, 173-179, 182, 186-189, 197, 241, 263, 281-283
Niven, Maria (Daniel) (died 1792) 71
Nomini Hall (Westmoreland County) 18, 123
Norfolk County, Virginia 237
Norfolk, Virginia 58, 219
Normal School (Fredericksburg) 238
Norman, Charles F. (c.1834-c.1900) 88, 89, 176, 186, 191, 193
    Eleanor (Towson) (1782-1848) 71, 161
    George B. (c.1846-before 1899) 175, 178, 180

Matthew (c.1779-1814) 233, 253, 254, 270
Mildred (born c.1805) 178
Thomas (c.1790-1846) 72-74, 77, 155, 156, 178, 255, 271
William 147
William M. (c.1838-1918) 87, 88, 92, 180
Norman & Waller (business) 253, 254
Norman's gate (Stafford County) 151
North Anna, Battle of (1864) 168
North Carolina 49, 162, 219
North Stafford High School 165
Northampton County, Virginia 19
Northern Methodist Church 85
Northern Neck 6
Northern Neck Bar Association 21
Northern Neck Proprietary 122, 123
Northumberland County, Virginia 12, 21, 37, 43, 45-47, 61, 86, 106, 127
Norton, James 91
Norvelle, Pearl N. (Herring) (died 1953) 17
Norwood, Elvira (Cunningham) 257
Oak Grove (Stafford County) 72, 145
Oak Hill (Loudoun County) 167
Oak Hill (Stafford County) 264
Oak Hill Cemetery (Spotsylvania County) 198
Oakenwold (Stafford County) 81
Oakland (King George County) 19
Oakland (Stafford County) 65, 226
Oakley (Stafford County) 68, 78, 170
Oakwood (Stafford County) 75, 155
O'Bannon, Harriet Ann (Corbin) (1813-1891) 78, 85
Henry Clay (1843-1916) 78, 85-87, 180
John Maurice (1800-1870) 78-81, 85, 158, 255, 258-262, 279, 280
Pattie Ann (Payne) 85
Oberlin College 13
O'Brien, Valeria (Taliaferro) 19
O'Bryan, D. Wayne 17
John C. 279
N___ 144
Obyrhim, Alexander (c.1794-1854) 148, 272
Cleopatra (Riley) (born 1839) 196, 243
Obyrhim & Burton (business) 281
Occoquan (Prince William County) 133
Occoquan Iron Furnace 57
Odell, John T. 279
Thomas T. 279
Oder, William 252, 268, 269
Oder's Shop (Stafford County) 172
Ogle, Ann (Tayloe) (1772-1855) 19
Mary (Tayloe) (1807-1862) 19
Ohio River 129
Old Capitol Prison (Washington, DC) 167, 170, 172
Old School Baptist Church 183
Old Stage Road (U. S. Route 1) 16
Oliver, Matilda (Whitescarver) (Payne) 169

Onville (Stafford County) 77, 194, 264, 265, 284
Onville Post Office (Stafford County) 224, 226, 243
Onville Road (State Route 641) 52, 243
Orange County, Virginia 17, 20, 46, 60, 284
Orangeburg, Kentucky 267
Orchard Field (Stafford County) 167
Ordinance of Secession 13
Oregon 202
Orion, John 256-258, 271, 279, 280
Oronoco tobacco 106
Orton & Older (business) 262
Osborne, Robert 37
Overseers of the Poor, position of 109
Overseers of the Road, position of 110-112, 114
Overton, Jemima Anne (Banks) (1789-1863) 11, 69
Overwharton Parish (Stafford County) 3, 5, 37, 40, 47, 49, 81, 128, 191
Overzee, Elizabeth (Willoughby) (Colclough) (Allerton) 38
Owens, Leah Owens (Monteith) 160
Stanley A. 17
Thomas 160
Owsley, Anne (Harris) 4
Dorothea (Poyntz) (1631-1705) 4
Jane (Gregg) 46
Rev. John (1635-1687) 4
Capt. Thomas (1658-1700) 4, 41, 117, 119, 120
Oxford, England 2, 41, 44
Oxford University (England) 38
PD & W Railroad 244
Packard, Arba Randolph (1819-1902) 164, 176
Rebecca (1816-1887) 164
Page, Mary (Linton) 45
William (died 1716) 45
Paint Ridge (Stafford County) 162
Palace Green (Stafford County) 47, 122, 139, 151, 233
Palmer, Ellen R. 230
W. Benjamin 230
Panama Canal 202
Pannell, Elizabeth (Bruce) 133
Panorama (King George County) 48
Parke Farm (Stafford County) 19, 72, 79, 87, 145, 199, 200, 235
Parr, Dora Lee Moore (Wigfield) (1861-1931) 192
Parrender, Elizabeth (Adie) (born 1729) 55
Parry, Henry 121
Parsons, George M. 255, 256, 271
Parsons, George M. & Company (business) 255, 256
Pasker, Richard 119
Passapatanzy Creek (King George County) 11, 37, 38, 115-117, 125
Passapatanzy Post Office (King George County) 223, 225, 237, 241

Passapatanzy Precinct 118
Patrick, Gen. ___ 78
Patterson, Elijah T. (1808-1870) 171-173, 277, 281
    Joseph S. 172
    Levenia 277
    Lucy 172
    M. 147
    Perry (1776-after 1850) 171, 281
    Sarah H. (Byram) (Embrey) (born 1838) 277
    Susan T. (Heflin) (1824-1901) 172
    William P. (c.1838-1911) 172
    Winifred (c.1782-1858) 171, 281
Patterson's well (Stafford County) 175
Patton, Bathsheba (McInteere) 239
    D. W. (1852-1919) 198
    George (1757-1813) 146, 260
    Herbert C. (1881-1956) 266
    John 153, 239
    Mary Elizabeth (Shackelford) (born c.1835) 239
    Sarah A. (Perry) (born c.1822) 146
    Sarah (McInteer) (died c.1844) 146
    Sarah (Stringfellow) (1766-1848) 146, 260
    Thornton (1793-1869) 146, 149, 152, 260
    William T. (c.1822-1905) 30, 158, 160, 162, 165-172, 174, 176
    Wilson 195
Pawlett, Sir John 2
Payne, ___ 197
    Alexander 150
    Anna M. (Bowler) 275
    B. L. 285
    Cecy A. 175
    Charles "Togie" 207
    Daniel (1728-1796) 58, 251
    Delila (Cox) 185
    Edith Ellen 237
    Edward W. 232
    Eliza Ann (Green) (1806-1876) 15, 70, 83, 170, 263
    Elizabeth (McCarty) (Pope) (born 1667) 45
    Ezekiel 151
    Francis 148
    George (born c.1830) 162
    Gideon Cicero (1861-1902) 237
    Harriet A. (Curtis) (born c.1822) 169
    Henry (c.1837-1862) 160, 171
    J. A. 92
    Jemima (Curtis) (died c.1869) 148, 167
    Jesse 153
    John 164, 175
    John (c.1693-1750) 58
    John W. 270, 271
    John William (c.1858-1927) 91-93, 200-202
    Lucy (1882-1946) 239
    Marion (Andrew) (Morson) (c.1724-1808) 60, 58, 70
    Marshall 168
    Mary A. (Berry) 93
    Mary (Long) 237
    Mary (Mountjoy) (c.1794-1856) 87, 151, 166
    Matilda N. (Whitescarver) (Oliver) 169
    Pattie Ann (O'Bannon) 85
    Permelia (Rollow) 148
    Philip C. 240
    Prudence (Tolson) (c.1811-1855) 246
    Richard (c.1832-1882) 175
    Susan 151
    Susan Jane (Winkler) (1860-1935) 200
    Susannah (Jett) 148
    Thomas 271
    Thomas J. (c.1796-after 1850) 260-262, 279
    Gen. W. H. 247
    Capt. William (1755-1837) 70
    William T. (c.1846-after 1910) 178, 197, 199, 200
Payne & Morton (business) 283
Pea Fields (Stafford County) 139
Pea Ridge (Mason County, Kentucky) 134
Pea Ridge (Stafford County) 235
Peake, James B. 89
    John 119
    Louisa 89
    Mary H. (Robey) (died 1874) 89
Peale, Malachy (16_-1698) 39-41, 117, 118
Peale's Neck (Stafford County) 41
Pearson, Constantia (Chapman) (1712-1788) 49
    George B. 33
    Hannah (Ball) (Travers) (c.1683-1748) 48
    Lelwellington E. (born c.1823) 167
    Capt. Simon (died 1733) 49
    Susannah (Alexander) (born 1717) 58
Peden, Ann 87
    David 87
    John (1820-1892) 87, 88, 158, 165, 179, 181, 238
    Louisa E. (Curtis) (1829-1915) 87
Peden, W. H. Lumber Company (business) 92
Peden's gate (Stafford County) 170
Peden's Hill (Stafford County) 175
Peipenbring, Edward (born c.1828) 262, 277, 281
Pemberton, Lizzie S. (Daffan) (c.1862-c.1928) 186
Pender, Gen. William Dorsey (1834-1863) 164
Pendleton County, Kentucky 131, 133, 138
Penn, ___ (Phillips) 134
    William 134
Pennsylvania 89, 123, 176, 177, 219, 263, 284
Peoples' Bank of Stafford 200, 202, 205
Peoples' National Bank of Charlottesville 20
Peoples' National Bank of Manassas 17

Percifull, Virginia (Ashby) (1896-1925) 201
Perfitt, Roger 37
Perry, John Robert (born c.1822) 158, 160, 162, 283
    Mary Elizabeth (Murdock) 283
    Matthew 174
    Richard C. (c.1862-1908) 283
    Sarah A. (Patton) (born c.1822) 146
    Sarah Frances "Fanny" (Herndon) (1870-1961) 283
Persinger, James F. 208
Peters, Susan (Homes) 157
Petersburg, Virginia 253
Pettit, Benjamin (died 1800:05) 136
    Mary (Banks) 136
Petty, Charles S. (c.1818-after 1870) 261
    James S. (c.1806-1885) 261
Peyton, Ann (Samuel) (died 1842) 62
    Anne 5
    Anne (Hooe) (1754-1833) 68, 133
    Anne (Waye) (1731-1750) 5
    Catherine Storke (Conway) (1786-1865) 75
    Charles 152, 179
    Daniel 268
    Eliza (Murray) (1791-1878) 68
    Eliza Strother (Galleher) (1791-1822) 68
    Elizabeth (Harrison) (1771-1835) 62
    Elizabeth (Heath) (born c.1740) 6, 267, 268
    Elizabeth (Rowzee) (Waller) (Strother) (c.1715-1782) 5, 58, 127, 131, 133, 137
    Elizabeth Washington (Henry) 75
    Fielding 150, 152, 153, 275
    Frances (Garrard) (Speake) (Appleton) (Washington) 3
    Frances L. B. (Barnes) (born c.1823) 161
    Henry 5
    Henry (1744-1814) 108, 139-142
    John 270
    John (1691-1760) 5, 6, 48-53, 58, 126-128, 133, 137
    John Rowzee (1754-1798) 58, 60, 68
    Marianna (Brent) 3
    Mary Butler (Washington) (1760-1822) 70, 137, 148
    Mary/Lucy (Mason) (1801-1838) 148
    Robert T. (1823-1871) 161
    Roxanna T. (Chinn) (1836-1898) 157
    Rowzee (1789-1867) 28, 68, 69, 71, 72
    Samuel Heath (c.1770-1832) 62-64, 66, 68, 69, 71, 72, 139, 142-147
    Sarah 157, 161
    Sarah Ann (Catlett) 161
    Sarah (Maddox) 165
    Capt. Simeon Chancellor (1829-1905) 16, 80, 134, 157, 158, 164, 176, 182, 183, 198, 202
    Susan Margaret (Grayson) (1787-1824) 71
    Thomas (died 1795) 134, 138
    Thomas 157, 161
    Col. Valentine (1629-1665) 3, 37
    Dr. Valentine (1756-1815) 26, 70, 137, 138-141, 148
    Whitfield Dunaway (born 1870) 16, 201, 202
    William T. (1875-1955) 134, 201
    William Washington (1799-1847) 70-74, 148, 150-154, 260
    Yelverton (1735-1794) 6, 55-57, 62, 130, 139, 267
Peyton & Hore (business) 259
Peyton, William W. & Company (business) 260
Peyton's fence (Stafford County) 161
Peyton's Mill (Stafford County) 135, 136
Peyton's Ordinary (Stafford County) 6, 62, 267
Philadelphia Navy Yard 174
Philadelphia, Pennsylvania 8, 9, 20, 76, 88, 134, 182, 219
Phillips, ___ (Penn) 134
    Alexander Keene (1805-1892) 76, 136, 166, 167, 174
    Edmund (c.1763-1839) 267
    Elizabeth Anne (Fowke) (died c.1830) 65, 153
    Gabriel (born c.1769) 267
    John (born c.1773) 134, 267
    Lucy (Byram) (c.1752-1836) 134
    Moses, Sr. (c.1736-1811) 134, 267, 271
    Moses, Jr. (c.1775-1787) 134, 267
    Sarah (Jeffries) (born c.1740) 134
    Silem Frederick Gustavus (1790-c.1872) 153
    Susan (Byram) (1765-1834) 134
    Tarissa Hamble (Crutcher) (born 1783) 65
    Thomas 134, 267
    William 134, 255, 256
    Col. William (1744-1797) 58, 60, 62, 65, 133, 136, 137, 139, 153
    William R. 145
Phillips' house (Stafford County) 167
Phillips' Ordinary (Stafford County) 134, 267, 271
Philpin, Anne (Jones) 135
Philpot, John 46
Pickett, George (c.1790-after 1850) 260, 262
    Gen. George E. 13
    Martin (died c.1804) 260
    Thomas B. 261
Pickett, Thomas B. & Company (business) 261
Pickle Factory (Milford, Virginia) 266
Pickle Factory (Stafford County) 264, 266
Pierson, Capt. Christopher 127
    Hannah (Ball) (Travers) 61, 127
    S. W. (born c.1812) 61

Sarah (Travers) (Daniel) (died 1788) 127
Pilcher, Catherine (Stark) (Kendall) 262
    James (born 1750) 270
    Lucy (Clark) 270
    Mason (died c.1791) 131-133, 135, 137
    Moses 131, 262
    Nancy (Murphy) (born c.1748) 270
    Stephen (born 1723) 270
Pim, John 117
Pimmet's Run (Fairfax County) 45
Pine Crest Nursing Home (Stafford County) 246
Pine Grove (Stafford County) 159, 164
Pine Hill (King George County) 14
Piscataway Indians 4, 41
Pittman, Gertrude (Cloe) 205
Pitts, Benjamin T. (c.1889-1964) 20
    Carolinus 20
    Robert (born c.1795) 262
    Victoria 20
Platt, Edward 118
Pleasant Retreat (Stafford County) 62
Plumfield (Stafford County) 282
Plymouth, Massachusetts 38
Pohick Bay (Fairfax County) 4
Pohick Church (Fairfax County) 45, 123
Pohick Creek (Fairfax County) 45, 46, 122
Point Lookout (Maryland) 165, 178
Point Pleasant, Battle of (West Virginia) (1774) 133
Poles, William 136
Pollard, ___ 92
    Alelia (Lowry) 232
    Austin 164
    Eliza V. 266
    Henry 266
    James (born c.1800) 170, 172
    John 57, 58, 60
    Mildred (Stewart) (born c.1867) 266
    Peter 274
Pollard's (Stafford County) 153
Pollock, Atchison 150
    Estelle (Lewis) 172
    Jennett R. (Gray) 150, 172
    Capt. John Gray (c.1831-1906) 150, 172, 176
    Matthew 150
    William 31, 169
    William (1797-1865) 150, 172
    William G. (1829-1865) 161
Pollock's Mill (Stafford County) 166, 170, 172, 173, 176, 177, 179, 180
Pomphrey, Mariah (Porch) (died 1855) 279
    Spotswood 279
Poolesville, Maryland 171
Poor houses 109, 110, 113
Pope, Ann (Washington) 2
    Elizabeth (McCarty) (Payne) (born 1667) 45

Jane (Browne) (16_-1752) 121
Humphrey (died c.1684) 45
Nathaniel (1669-1719) 38, 42, 120, 121
Poplar Grove (Stafford County) 69, 86, 139, 167, 189
Poplar Road (State Route 616) 8, 68, 69, 84, 136, 139, 148, 167, 172, 176, 177, 224, 231, 235, 247, 260
Porch, Barsheba (Jett) (c.1738-1817) 132
    Elizabeth (Curtis) 135
    Mariah (Pomphrey) (died 1855) 279
    Mary 132
    Richard 132, 135
Port Conway (King George County) 16
Port Point (Stafford County) 39
Port Royal (Caroline County) 15, 61, 81, 169
Port Tobacco (Charles County, Maryland) 2, 179
Porter, Calvert 279
    Calvert (born 1752) 279
    Elizabeth (Cash) 279
    Jemima Smith (Edrington) (died 1816) 55
    John M. 208
    John W. 269
    Sarah (Stone) (Edrington) (1769-1816) 147
    Thomas (died c.1926) 265
Portsmouth, Virginia 247
Post Oak (Stafford County) 172
Post Offices:
    Accokeek 222, 232
    Adieville 222, 233
    Aquia 222, 233, 237
    Arkendale 222, 231, 234
    Bealton (Fauquier County) 223-225, 228
    Bellfair Mills 222, 226
    Berea 137, 222, 225, 228, 230, 234, 239, 245, 268
    Blue Wing 222, 231, 234
    Brent's Mill 231
    Brentsville (Prince William County) 228
    Bristow (Prince William County) 228
    Burdis 222, 224, 225, 234
    Chappawamsic 222, 233
    Coakley 222, 223, 225, 226, 235
    Coal Landing 222, 223, 235
    Crest 223, 226, 230, 235, 242
    Cromwell (Fauquier County) 224, 228
    Cropp 223, 224
    Dodd's 223, 224, 236
    Falmouth 61, 222-225, 231, 236, 237, 247
    Fine's 223, 237
    Fostersville 223, 237
    Fredericksburg 223, 237, 240, 243
    Free Lance 225
    Game Point 223, 230, 237, 277
    Garrisonville 222-224, 226, 227, 237, 238, 243, 244, 247

Glendie 224, 225, 238, 242
Goldvein (Fauquier County) 223
Grove (Fauquier County) 222
Hampstead (King George County) 225
Hartwood 89, 192, 222, 224, 225, 228, 230, 231, 234, 236, 238, 239, 246
Heflin's 223, 224
Hemp 198, 224, 225, 231
Holly Corner 225, 239
Hudsonville 223
Hull 245
Joplin (Prince William County) 222
Kopp (Prince William County) 222
La Grange (King George County) 226
Lance 224, 225, 228, 239, 282
Landsdown (Prince William County) 228
Leeland 225, 240
Little Whim 225, 240
Midway Island 225, 229, 240, 243
Millie's 225, 241, 265
Monteithville 160, 223, 225, 226, 231, 241, 242
Mount 226, 241, 247
Mountain View 223, 226, 242
Musselman 223, 224, 226, 242, 266
Myrtleville 179, 184, 226, 242
Onville 224, 226, 243
Passapatanzy (King George County) 223, 225, 237, 241
Rectory 188, 222, 224-227, 231, 243, 266
Richland Mills 222, 227, 228, 243
Rockford 223, 228, 237
Roseville 222, 224, 226, 227, 235, 243
Ruby 224, 227, 244
Serena 180, 228, 244
Shacklett 222, 228, 244, 265
Snelling's 222, 228, 245
Spottedville 228, 245
Stafford 223, 228, 231, 232, 242, 244-246
Stafford Store 224, 228, 246
Storck 222-224, 228, 231, 246
Tackett's Mill 77, 228, 233, 247
Toluca 224, 227, 228, 244, 247
Triangle (Prince William County) 225
Tuan 228, 247
Warsaw (Westmoreland County) 228
Wide Water 228, 231, 234, 241, 243, 248
Woodcutting 248
Potes, John 269
    Moses 269
    Valentine 256
Potomac Church (Stafford County) 27, 39, 62, 137, 138, 152, 153, 175, 177
Potomac Creek/Run (Stafford County) 4-6, 8, 9, 16, 27, 37, 39-41, 43, 44, 47, 50-52, 65, 73, 79, 80, 84, 86, 105, 111, 113-116, 124, 134, 137-139, 158, 159, 161, 162, 167, 170-175, 187-190, 193, 194, 235, 251, 255, 259-261, 273
Potomac Creek ferry 116, 119
Potomac Creek Precinct 117, 118
Potomac Ford (Stafford County) 112
Potomac Neck (Stafford County) 41
Potomac Parish 39
Potomac River 2, 3, 8, 10, 11, 43, 44, 50, 52, 53, 59, 106, 115, 149, 151, 152, 155, 160, 170, 228, 264, 275
Potomac Run Farm (Stafford County) 177
Potomac Run ford (Stafford County) 172, 175, 177
Potomac Run Road (State Route 626) 177
Potts, John H. S. (died c.1850) 148, 151, 257-260, 272-275, 279, 280
    Susan (1810-1895) 261
Powell, James Leavett (1834-1914) 19
Powers, Catherine E. (1812-1886) 174, 179
    Frances (Bell) (1846-1918) 179
    Mary Ann (Thompson) (1845-1912) 174, 188, 248
    Richard Coleman (born c.1805) 164, 174, 179, 188
    Richard Wirt (1870-1934) 195, 232, 248, 265, 266
    Sidney (Sidnor) (1837-1895) 174, 188, 248
    Temple (Chewning) (1879-1970) 248
    W. Dudley 33
    William Francis (1875-1955) 202
Powers' gate (Stafford County) 173
Powhatan (King George County) 19
Powhatan County, Virginia 77
Powlett, Mary (Sells) (Skinker) (c.1745-1798) 68
Poyntz, Dorothea (Owsley) (1631-1705) 4
Pratt, Ferdinand S. (1826-1905) 179
    Mary (Rollins) 198
Precincts:
    Aquia 159
    Brooke 188
    Coakley's 159
    Falmouth 159
    James Griffith's Store 188
    Hartwood 159
    Harwood 179, 188
    Masters' Store 159
    Stafford Store 159
    White Oak 159
Presley, Col. Peter 45
    Winifred (Linton) 45
Price, Sally (Courtney) 239
Primm, James (1754-1820) 63, 64, 133, 139-141
    Jane (Humphrey) 195
    John 133
    Margaret (Welch) (1709-1770) 64, 133
    William 271
Primmer, Abraham (1811-1896) 161, 167, 177, 189,

         195
    Elizabeth "Libby" A. (Carter) (1824-1888) 161
    Peter 161
    Pheoba 161
    Susan (Carter) (1850-1919) 177
Prince Edward Island, Canada 238
Prince George's County, Maryland 173, 268
Prince William Cavalry 86
Prince William County, Virginia 57, 65, 68, 71, 73,
    86, 89, 114, 115, 123, 124, 129, 139, 141,
    146, 148, 164, 166, 171, 173-176, 179, 225,
    228, 233, 234, 241, 246, 274
Prince William militia 139
Princess Anne Hotel (Fredericksburg) 251
Princess Anne Street (Fredericksburg) 158
Princeton (ship) 174
Princeton College 65
Principio Iron Company (Maryland) 49, 55
Pritchett, S. M. (Eustace) (born c.1829) 166
Privy Council of Virginia 11
Proprietors of the Northern Neck 112
Providence (Stafford County) 83, 193
Prussia 281
Pudding Hill (Stafford County) 153, 172
Purcell's Mill (Stafford County) 166
Purkins, Henry Carter (1828-1907) 241, 243
    Mace Clements (1840-1911) 179, 242, 243
    Marian Wallace (Monteith) (died 1927) 243
    Sally (Carver) 241
    Sarah Virginia Braxton (Greenlaw) (1838-1903)
        89
    Col. Thomas (1791-1855) 241, 243
Purkins' Corner (King George County) 241
Pyke, Alfred Joseph (1865-1938) 232
Quakers 139, 167
Quantico Creek/Run (Prince William County) 45, 46,
    124
Quantico Guards 233
Quantico Marine Corps reservation 43, 52, 65, 74-76,
    79, 81, 142, 147, 149, 151-154, 165, 179, 196,
    201, 204, 232, 233, 244, 265, 282
Quantico Mill (Prince William County) 45
Quantico Post Office (Prince William County) 227, 244
Queen, Eliza 273, 274
    Henry W. 274, 275
    John R. 152, 274, 275
Quick, Barbara (Shacklett) 244
Quisenberry, James S. 149
Quitman, Arkansas 148
R. F. & P. Railroad 187, 189, 193, 219, 222, 228, 232,
    234, 240
Railroad stations (Stafford County):
    Accokeek 220
    Aquia 220
    Arkendale 220
    Brooke 220

    Leeland 220
    Richland 220
Raines, Gracie G. (Carter) 265
Raleigh, Edward 131
Ralls, Edward (1725-1785) 139
    Kenaz (1763-after 1833) 139
    Mary (Rawleigh) 139
Ramey, Belle (Montague) 184
    Catherine (Corbin) (born c.1824) 280
    Thomas 174
Ramoth Baptist Church (Stafford County) 87, 177,
    192, 198, 203, 242
Randall, Aquilla (born c.1816) 190
    Edgar H. (1853-1919) 190, 194-201
    Thomas E. 235
    William 153
Randolph, Ann (Fitzhugh) (1747-1805) 57
    Charles Carter (1788-1863) 149, 152
    Elizabeth (Chiswell) (1715-1776) 132
    Maria Jefferson Carr (Mason) 15
    Mary Ann F. (Mortimer) 149
    Mary Anne "Nancy" (Fitzhugh) (1747-
        1805) 8
    Peter (1717-1767) 8
Ransdall, Wharton 51
Rappahannock County, Virginia 78, 117
Rappahannock Electric Light and Power Company
    236
Rappahannock Forge (Stafford County)—*see also
    Hunter's Iron Works* 77, 138, 139, 150,
    167, 191, 279
Rappahannock Gold Mine (Stafford County) 259,
    261
Rappahannock River 4, 11, 13, 14, 16, 38, 42, 44,
    46, 58, 61, 65, 69, 70, 78, 79, 87, 105, 106,
    114, 133, 135, 137, 146, 148, 167, 191,
    192, 219, 225, 254, 258, 263, 279, 284
Ratcliffe, John 176
    Mary (Homes) (1807-1867) 176
    Mary Jane (Tolson) (1837-1928) 246
Ratliff, John A. 254
    Elizabeth (Bell) (1775-1847) 142
Ravenswood (Stafford County) 81
Ravensworth (Fairfax County) 57
Rawleigh, Mary (Ralls) 139
Rawlings, George Chancellor, Jr. 17
Raymond, Battle of 15
Read & Enoch Browne (business) 252
Reamy, Berryman (c.1770-1850) 79
    Charlotte T. 79
    Frances (Morris) 79
    Harriet "Hallie" Margaret (Curtis) (1840-
        1917) 87, 165
    Jacob (c.1630-1721) 79
    Joshua (1747-1820) 79, 199
    Joshua (1792-1857) 78-80

Meriah (Neale) 79, 199
Sallie (Combs) (1860-1946) 199
Thomas Benton (1836-1910) 79, 87, 88, 165, 174, 180, 191, 199
William Daingerfield (1852-1939) 79, 91, 199-203, 235
Reardon, William T. 270
Reat, Eleanor (Thom) (1786-1869) 69
Reconstruction 241
Recorder, The (newspaper) 185
Rectorville, Kentucky 267
Rectory (Stafford County) 193, 243
Rectory Post Office (Stafford County) 188, 222, 224-227, 231, 243, 266
Rectory Road (Stafford) 55
Red House (Stafford County) 58, 136, 152, 171, 174, 175
Red House (Westmoreland County) 58
Red(d)ish, Burdit 267
Joseph (1787-1873) 270
Reddish family 267
Reed, Alexander (born 1792) 171
Rebecca L. 208
Reeves, Ella (Limerick) (born c.1857) 264
Jane 264
John H. 264
Regester Chapel (Stafford County) 266
Rehil, Edward (c.1815-after 1870) 243
Reid's Road (Stafford County) 242
Reil(l)y, Aurelia (Mountjoy) (died 1844) 151
Elizabeth 56
Phillis (Mountjoy) (1717-1771) 56
Thomas 56
Remington (Fauquier County) 180
Renfrew (County), Scotland 58
Ren(n)o, Col. Enoch (c.1740-1832) 150
Frances (Tackett) (c.1750-1796:99) 233
Mary (Moore) 150
Retirement (Stafford County) 40
Reveley, Elizabeth (Stubberfield) (Croughton) (died 1872) 256
Thomas 256
Reynolds, Gen. John 190
Richards, Ann (Blackwell) 63, 253
Benjamin Franklin (1806-after 1879) 151, 154
Elizabeth (Triplett) (1755-1826) 58, 140
Franklin 151
Capt. James 151
John (1734-1785) 58, 63, 140, 251, 252
Mildred "Milly" (Stone) 251
Susannah (Coleman) (died 1778) 63, 140, 251, 253
William (1765-after 1803) 63, 236, 253
William Brice 58
Winifred Berry (Benson) (1782-1856) 151

Richards' Ferry (Stafford County) 151, 180
Richards' Hill (Stafford County) 63
Richards' Mill (Stafford County) 176
Richardson, George 252
Richardsville Post Office (Fauquier County) 223
Richland (Stafford County) 175, 190, 229, 232, 241
Richland hill (Stafford County) 171, 172
Richland Mill (Stafford County) 174, 175, 191
Richland Mills Post Office (Stafford County) 222, 227, 228, 243
Richland Post Office (Stafford County) 228, 234, 235
Richland Station (Stafford County) 220, 227
Richlands (Stafford County) 135, 152
Richlands Baptist Church (Stafford County) 135, 228, 231, 246
Richmond College 16
Richmond Railway and Electric Company 165
Richmond County, Virginia 55, 117, 124, 125, 268
Richmond Railroad and Electric Company 165
Richmond, Virginia 66, 71, 77, 80, 94, 160, 161, 165, 169, 179, 182, 198, 202, 222, 223, 230, 233, 236, 240, 263
Ricker, Marcus M. (c.1849-1917) 190
Ridgeway (Stafford County) 70, 71, 172
Ridgeway Road (Stafford County) 180
Riley, Agnes L. (Williams) (1878-1956) 243
Alice N. (Baber) (1861-1944) 196
Ann H. 95
Cleopatra (O'Byrhim) (born 1839) 196, 243
Noah (1813-after 1870) 196, 243
Susie A. 238
William D. (1846-1927) 197, 199-201
River Road (Stafford County) 166, 174, 176, 179, 180, 189
Rives, John W. (born c.1822) 262
Roach, Elizabeth (Downes) 284
James (1834-1913) 284
Jane Gordon (Willis) 284
Lindsay Gordon (c.1850-1939) 284, 285
Roach, Lindsay G. & Company (business) 284, 285
Roach's Mill (Stafford County) 284
Roane, Ann (Alcock) (c.1757-1836) 269
Roanoke, Virginia 71, 168
Roberson, Charles H. (c.1823-1892) 167
Evy L. (Hewitt) (born c.1868) 264
Joseph 262, 277, 281
Roberson's blacksmith shop (Stafford County) 171
Roberts, Martha (Lomax) 69
William J. 69
Willie W. 246
Robertson, Albion 258, 280
Mary (Daffan) 162
Robertson & Suttle (business) 259, 275, 280

Robertson's Shop (Stafford County) 152, 161
Robey, Clarissa T. (Brooke) (died 1843) 89
    Henry Richard 89
    Mary H. (Peake) (died 1874) 89
    William Brooke (1839-1907) 89-92
Robinson, David 247
    Edward 192
    Joseph (c.1818-after 1870) 232
    Maj. William (1678-1742) 5
Rock Hill (Stafford County) 65, 247
Rock Hill Baptist Church (Stafford County) 161, 171, 239, 244
Rock Hill Church Road (State Route 644) 69, 152, 194, 244
Rock Hill District (Stafford County) 112, 113, 181, 183-185, 188-192, 194-208, 222-224, 228
Rock Hill Precinct 186, 189
Rock Hill Township 114, 115
Rock Rimmon (Stafford County) 74
Rockdale (Stafford County) 71, 150
Rockford Post Office (Stafford County) 223, 228, 237
Rocky Pen Road (State Route 654) 239
Rocky Run (Stafford County) 71, 111, 139, 177
Ro(d)gers, Henry 272-274
    Henry L. 276
    L. 274
    Robert 260
    Robert Campbell (c.1818-1888) 171, 176, 189, 230, 238
    William J. 15
Rohme, James H. 243
Roles, Beulah (Castle) (1883-1968) 265
    Jackson (c.1800-1882) 257, 258, 273
    Jesse 258
    Minnie Alice (Mountjoy) (1880-1921) 241
    Pansy 241
    Rosanna 258
    Samuel 241
    William 275
Rollins, Caroline E. (Wallace) 188
    Edward Taylor (1846-1921) 189, 195
    Florence/Frances (Elkins) 198
    James Taylor 198
    Madison F. (1828-1895) 188-190
    Madison E. (c.1857-1903) 239
    Mary (Pratt) 198
    Thomas 188
    William Henry (c.1848-1932) 198, 200, 201
Rollow, Ann "Nancy" (Jett) (1757-1830) 148
    Archibald (1755-1829) 132, 148, 270
    Permelia (Payne) 148
    Peter (1801-1873) 148
Rollow's (Stafford County) 153
Rolls, William 272
Rose, Capt. Alexander Fontaine (1780-1831) 69, 71, 76
    Anne (Fitzhugh) (born 1763) 59, 72
    Annie Brown (Skinker) (1848-1900) 170
    Edmund Fontaine (1817-1893) 81-84, 166, 168, 245
    Eliza S. (Wellford) (1827-1899) 76
    Ida E. 243
    James Marshall (1886-1966) 243
    James S. (born c.1830) 242
    Joel 271
    Col. John 59
    Dr. Lawrence Berry (1821-1877) 76-78
    M. G. 266
    Mary E. (Heflin) 242
    Mildred Narcissa (Fairfax) 227, 244
    Sarah Fontaine (1796-1863) 69, 76
    Silas L. (born c.1857) 226, 227, 242, 243
Rose Hill (Stafford County) 3, 44
Rosebank (Fauquier County) 14
Rosedale (Stafford County) 69, 184
Roseville, Virginia 92, 172, 198, 231
Roseville Plantation subdivision (Stafford County) 11
Roseville Post Office (Stafford County) 222, 224, 226, 227, 235, 243
Ross, Hume V. 255, 284
Rousby, Ann (Frisby) (Fitzhugh) (1727-1793) 6
Rouse, Mary W. (Barnes) (c.1864-1918) 245
Rousseau, Margaret (Combs) 186
    Mary (Combs) (born c.1760) 142, 151
Rowe, Absalom D. 177
    Fannie Estelle (Newton) 93
    Rev. George 86
    Georgianna (Monteith) (born c.1834) 168
    Rev. John G. 80, 168, 187
    Lucy (Leitch) 86
    Mary A. (Luck) (1824-1902) 86
    Nancy (McGuire) 187
    Sarah Elizabeth (Jones) (Monteith) 187
    Sarah Jesse (Chinn) 284
Rowland, Thomas 115
Rowles (*See Roles*)
Rowley, Amos 170, 174
Rowzee, Elizabeth (Strother) (Waller) (Peyton) (c.1715-1782) 58, 127, 131, 133, 137
Roy, Anne (Mercer) (c.1740-1770) 8
    Archibald T. (died 1897) 175, 177
    Lucy Wiley (Mason) (died c.1835) 63, 70
    Sarah (Fowke) (1748-1821) 11
Royal Ann (ship) 57
Roy's Corner (Stafford County) 177
Roy's fence (Stafford County) 161
Roy's Warehouse (Caroline County) 269
Ruby (Stafford County) 198, 266
Ruby Fire House (Stafford County) 244
Ruby Post Office (Stafford County) 224, 227, 244

Ruggles, Gen. Daniel (1810-1897) 15
    Edward Seymour (1843-1919) 15
    Mortimer (born c.1845) 15
    Richardetta Barnes Mason (Hooe) (c.1819-1902) 15
Rumford (Stafford County) 150
Russell, Bartlett 174
    Martha J. S. (Leitch) (c.1826-1885) 158, 174
    Nancy 174
Rustall, William 117
Ryan, John 256, 271
    John A. (c.1839-1918) 90-93
Sabine Hall (Richmond County) 19
St. George's Branch (Stafford County) 159, 173, 176
St. George's Episcopal Church (Fredericksburg) 33, 70, 251
St. George's Parish (Fredericksburg) 12
St. John's Church (Richmond, Virginia) 7
St. Joseph, Missouri 33
St. Mary's County, Maryland 60, 65
St. Marysville (Stafford County) 172
St. Paul, Minnesota 182
St. Paul's Churchyard 45
St. Paul's Parish (King George County) 56, 118, 128
Salem (Stafford County) 173, 261
Salisbury (King George County) 47
Salvington (Stafford County) 80, 164
Samuel, Ann (Peyton) (died 1842) 62
Samwaids, John 115
Sanders, Edward 116
Sandstone quarries 10, 11, 13, 28, 59, 65, 71, 72, 74, 137, 147, 156, 233, 283
Sanford, Aphia (Ballard) (c.1814-1846) 158
    Aphia (Farmer) (1784-1864) 158
    Lawrence (1778-1858) 158
    Sarah (Swetnam) (born c.1811) 89, 172
Sanford Road (State Route 670) 138, 274
Santee (Caroline County) 257
Savage, Alice (Thornton) (1653-1695) 123
    John (died c.1745) 122, 123
Sawmills 85, 87
Scaggs, George L. 165
    Georgiana 165
    Kathleen (Blake) (born c.1873) 165
Scandrett, Mary (Stone) 251
Scarlet, Martin (died 1695) 119
Scessall, Eliza (Woodward) 268
Schenectady, New York 18
Schoolcraft, Ida C. 230
    John L. 230
Schooler, ____ 200
    Abner (born 1775) 149
    Ann K. (Stone) (born c.1831) 80, 170
    Charles C. (born c.1821) 234
    Charles W., Sr. (1840-1910) 178, 189
    Douglas W. (born c.1847) 234
    James E. (born c.1833) 167, 170, 174, 177-180, 231, 245
    James W. (1824-1916) 165, 172, 174, 188
    John H. (1812-1875) 165, 167, 173, 179, 232, 284
    Laurinda (Jones) (1815-1870) 179, 284
    Lucy E. (Hedgman) (born c.1834) 167, 231, 245
    Margaret (Kirk) 149
    Marian L. (Jones) (born c.1841) 284
    Mary 170
    Mary (born c.1795) 80
    Mary (Fant) 149
    Mary T. (Kennedy) (born c.1837) 184
    Mildred C. (Mills) (1848-1928) 234
    Minnie (Alexander) 78
    Peter 184
    Thomas 149
    Thomas E. (born c.1787) 80, 165, 170, 184
    Virginia "Jenny" C. (Watts) (1848-1903) 179
Schooler & Towson (business) 278
Scotland 64, 72, 81, 151
Scott, Ann (Browne) 146
    Bradford Ripley Alden 164
    George B. (c.1821-1881) 71
    Gustavus (born c.1753) 269
    James 126
    Dr. James 159
    James McClure (1811-1893) 159, 164, 167
    Mary Lucinda (Seddon) 146, 280
    Mary Miller (Anderson) 164
    Mildred (Thomson) 159
    Sarah Travers (Lewis) (1813-1891) 159, 164
    Susanna Elizabeth Margaret (Green) (1800-1844) 11
    Thomas Cropper (1791-1857) 146, 148-150, 152, 154, 255-258, 260, 261, 280
Scott & Bayly (business) 259, 280
Scott family 155
Scott's Bridge (Stafford County) 176, 177, 187
Scott's Ferry (Stafford County) 172
Scott's Landing (Stafford County) 152
Scott's Run (Stafford County) 166
Seal, Capt. Anthony 51
Sealston (King George County) 284
2nd Virginia Regiment 63, 134
Seddon, Edward (died 1812) 236
    James Alexander (1815-1880) 79
    John 65
    John (1826-1863) 78, 80, 81
    Mary Alexander (Little) 13
    Mary Lucinda (Scott) 146
    Susan Pearson (Alexander) (died 1845) 13

Susan R. 65
Thomas (died 1810) 137
Thomas (1779-1831) 64, 66, 68, 69, 236, 253-257
Seddon & Alexander (business) 236, 255, 257
Seddon, Thomas & Company (business) 253
Segar, Lemuel (c.1870-1904) 193
Seine Pocket Farm (Stafford County) 191
Selden, Ann Cary (Brooke) 80
    Anne Mason Mercer (Brooke) (1770-1812) 65
    Cary (1783-1842) 28, 80
    Joseph (1680-1720) 128
    Mary (Cary) (1704-1775) 128
    Mary Thomson (Mason) (1731-1758) 52
    Col. Samuel (1725-1790) 55-58, 65, 128
    Sarah Ann Mason (Mercer) (born 1738) 65
    Sarah Mason (Cooke) (Grayson) (1791-1861) 71
Selden family 164
Sells, Mary (Powlett) (Skinker) (c.1745-1798) 68
Selwood (Stafford County) 163
Serapis (ship) 64
Serena Post Office (Stafford County) 180, 228, 244
Servicetown Truck Stop (Stafford County) 56, 150
Seven Days Battles 233
Seven Lakes subdivision 148, 177
Seven Pines, Battle of (1862) 160, 179
7th Virginia Regiment 60
70th New York Volunteers 32
Sewell, Elizabeth Lewis (Fant) 135
Shackelford, Agnes E. (Homes) (1877-1956) 247
    Anne (Edwards) 173
    Diadema (Hilman) 239
    Emma J. (Decatur) (1868-1958) 265
    Garland Davis (1917-1992) 206
    Helen (Butler) (1925-1982) 206, 207
    James Walter (1876-1948) 247
    Jane Eliza (Mahoney) (c.1843-1894) 247, 265
    Mary E. (1849-1939) 230, 231, 239
    Mary Elizabeth (Patton) (born c.1835) 239
    Strother A. (1840-1925) 173, 247, 265
    Thomas 195
    Thompson 197
    Uriah W. 239
    Wilson Bunell (1832-1915) 192, 238
Shackelford's Well Road (State Route 754) 58, 68, 230
Shacklett, Barbara (Quick) 244
    Benjamin 269
    Benjamin (1710-1784) 244
    Catherine (Tucker) 244
    Howard Hampton (1880-1929) 246
    James R. 244
    John 244
    M. E. (Leiber) (born c.1855) 265
    Nelson Tolson (1856-1903) 228, 244
    Richard Davis (1826-1896) 265
    Sarah (Blancette) 244
Shacklett & Company (business) 266
Shacklett Post Office (Stafford County) 222, 228, 244, 265
Shady Grove (Caroline County) 61
Sharpsburg, Battle of (1862) 200
Shelbourne (Stafford County) 74
Shelby County, Illinois 233
Shelby County, Kentucky 64
Shelkett, Eliza F. (Wamsley) (c.1827-1879) 79, 91
    John (1793-1857) 79, 151, 160, 162
    Lucy (Waller) 150
    Nancy (Stark) (1786-1834) 79, 151
    Rodham P. (1822-1899) 161
    Virginia Lula (Daffan) (1833-1875) 161
    William 150
Shelkett's Mill (Stafford County) 151, 173
Shelton, Eliza 83
    Elizabeth (Leechman) 152
    Elizabeth (Stark) (born 1777) 152
    Jane (Limerick) (1851-1927) 188
    John, Sr. (1740-1805) 84
    John, Jr. (1774-1818) 84
    John Conyers (c.1803-1883) 84, 169
    Lethe (Conyers) (1774-c.1867) 84
    Lizzie M. (Byram) (1860-1941) 267
    Margaret E. (Carter) (born c.1842) 83
    Richard Mason (c.1819-1892) 83, 186
    Rolly Travis (1848-1935) 188-190, 192-196
    Susanna (Hord) (1742-1799) 84
    Thomas (1776-1870) 152
    Thornton (1805-1851) 152
Shelton Shop Road (State Route 648) 93
Shenandoah County, Virginia 279
Shenandoah Valley (Virginia) 279
Sheriff, position of 101-103
Sherman Farm (Stafford County) 81
Sherwin-Williams Paint Company 202
Shiloh, Battle of (1862) 15
Shiloh (Stafford County) 265
Shingle mill (Stafford County) 186
Shopoff, Rev. David (1858-1934) 178
Shore, Harriet Winston (Hull) 186
Short, Lucinda (Briggs) 254
Short & Richards (business) 251
Short tract (Stafford County) 74
Shreveport, Louisiana 157
Shumate, Margaret (Whitecotton) (1776-1819) 268
Sibley, Gen. Henry Hopkins (1816-1886) 186
    Helen M. (Stokes) (White) 186
Sickles, Gen. Daniel E. 32
Silver, Franklin D. 246
    Isaac (c.1808-1901) 85
Silver City, New Mexico 32, 33
Simms' Point (Stafford County) 175, 230

Simpson, ____ 201
    Bessie (Lunsford) (born c.1878) 202
    Clayton (c.1856-1927) 234
    Harwood (1874-1955) 198, 238
    James Polk (born c.1845) 80, 198, 201, 238
    Louisa (Bullock) (born c.1851) 198, 201, 238
    Nettie G. (died 1952) (Jett) 198, 238
    Wade Hampton (born c.1876) 202, 235, 266
Sims, Dr. Frederick H. 20
    Frederick Wilmer (1862-1925) 20
    Lucy Payne (Winston) 20
    Maria Louise (Kimbrough) 20
Sinclair, Charles Armistead (c.1881-1974) 17
    Sarah (McInteer) 146
Sine, Ora Genevieve (Tolson) (c.1905-1959) 246
6th Virginia Regiment 131
Skidmore, E. B. 192
    Fannie L. (Armstrong) (1879-1967) 264
    William 190
    William (born c.1813) 175, 190
Skinker, Annie Brown (Rose) (1848-1900) 170
    John Howard (1814-1867) 68, 78-82, 162, 164, 166, 168
    Louisa Virginia Knox (died 1886) 68, 78
    Lucy E. Scott (1807-1896) 68, 78
    Margaret Wilson (Julien) (died 1863) 68, 78
    Mary (Sells) (Powlett) (c.1745-1798) 68
    Samuel Hampson (1785-1856) 67-69, 72-76, 78, 143, 144, 148, 169
    Thomas (born 1729) 68
    Thomas Julian (1819-1900) 169, 179
    William 68
Skinker Motor Company (business) 244
Skinner, ____ 200
    Harrison J. (c.1821-1862) 168, 196, 262, 281
    L. C. (born c.1856) 263
    Lawrence Ashton (1855-1915) 196, 247
    Mary Thomas (Bryant) 242
    Peggy (Hefflinger) 174
    Sarah Bell "Sallie" (Dodd) (died 1933) 247
Skyline Drive (State Route 615) 81, 145
Slater, Harriet (Brent) 256
Slaughter, Harriet 77
    John 252, 253
    John Warren (1820-1866) 71, 76-78
    Sally Moore (Braxton) (born c.1828) 77
    William 77, 78
"Slaughter vs Slaughter" 77
Sligo, Ireland 20
SMC Mulch Company (business) 65
Smith, Absalom (died before 1850) 261, 262
    Amanda Permelia (Taliaferro) (1860-1918) 282
    Augustine (died 1831) 276
    Augustine Jaquelin 74
    Benjamin (born c.1805) 276
    Curtis M. 276
    Delia (Forbes) (1780-1841) 61
    Edward 41
    Emma Bettis (Graninger) (died 1968) 237
    Fenton (Brooke) 276
    George Alexander (1775-1822) 61
    James M. 19
    James W. 279
    Jane Allen (Mason) (died 1812) 74
    Jane (Hewitt) 84
    John M. 185
    John R. (c.1832-1914) 190
    Joseph 60-62
    Joseph Blackwell (born c.1881) 92, 93
    Gen. Kirby 163
    Lettis (Green) (Harrison) (died 1699) 41
    Lewis (born c.1822) 262
    Lizzie (Dye) (born c.1882) 92
    Louisa Ann (Briggs) 83, 196
    Lucinda (born c.1804) 190
    Lucinda (Lewis) (born 1848) 20
    Lucy (Barnes) (died 1926) 245
    M. G. 266
    Martha (Grinnan) (born c.1848) 92
    Mary Ann (Chinn) 19
    Mary Ann Elizabeth (George) 276
    Mary Frances (Towson) 161
    Col. Nicholas (1666-1734) 18
    Sarah Jane (Spicer) (1846-1886) 92
    Slighton 150
    Susannah (Darnall) 276
    Thomas (born c.1814) 259, 260, 276
    W. Worth, Jr. (1887-1940) 20
    Walker (c.1806-1892) 275
    Wilfred A. (born 1795) 276
    William 62, 153
    William D. (born c.1848) 92, 237
    William Worth (died 1924) 20
Smith's Reservoir (Stafford County) 76
Smithsonia (Fredericksburg) 13
Smoot, John 245, 275
    John H. 257
Sneed, Warren Goodloe (1895-1961) 93
Snellings, Preston S. 205
    Wallace H. (1873-1943) 228, 247
    William 80, 167, 172
    William (born c.1821) 163, 170
    Zachariah (born c.1828) 174
Snellings' Post Office (Stafford County) 222, 228, 245
Snowden (Stafford County) 60, 78, 79, 145
Society Hill (King George County) 50
Society of the Cincinnati 64
Sollade, Thomas 192
Somerset (King George County) 57
Somerset (Stafford County) 81, 82
Somerset County, England 4

Sommers, Roxanna (Brent) (1798-1882) 11, 65
Sons of the American Revolution 264
Sophia Street (Fredericksburg) 60
South Carolina 94
Southard, Edmund F. 237
    Henry 137
Southern Claims Commission 84, 87, 154, 161, 163, 165, 170, 172, 174, 178, 186, 235, 238, 281
Southern Cross of Honor 86, 160
Southgate, John 69
    Wright 69
Southwick, Massachusetts 84
Southworth, Nancy 55
Spanish American War 94, 266
Speake, Thomas 3
    Thomas H. 233
Spencer, Col. Nicholas (1638-1689) 2, 38
    Nicholas 2
Spicer, Mabel Clara (Curtis) (Graves) (died 1918) 92
    Mallory Howard (1840-1906) 92
    Sarah Jane (Smith) (1846-1886) 92
Spilman & Briggs (business) 253
Spindle, Charles William (c.1837-1902) 187-189
    Elizabeth (Alsop) 77
    Jefferson (c.1804-1861) 77, 78, 154, 187, 247, 261, 262
    Maria A. (Tackett) (c.1810-1883) 77, 187
    William (1774-1836) 77
Spindle & Brother (business) 187
Spotswood, Alexander (1676-1740) 64, 219
    Mary (Voss) 64
    T. 64
Spotsylvania, Battle of (1863) 168, 177
Spotsylvania County, Virginia 89, 90, 94, 133, 134, 149, 154, 159, 163, 176, 191, 198, 219, 234, 236, 245, 256
Spotsylvania County Militia 56
Spotted Tavern (Stafford County) 147, 160, 170, 174, 228, 245, 247, 256, 262, 268-270, 275-277
Spottedville Post Office (Stafford County) 228, 245
Spraggins, Emma F. (Gordon) (died 1939) 230, 236
Sprigg, Sophia (Mercer) 9
Spring Grove (Caroline County) 81
Spring Hill (Orange County) 284
Spring Hill (Stafford County) 73, 125, 126, 279
Spring Valley (Stafford County) 237
Springfield (Stafford County) 151, 173, 201
Spy Hill (King George County) 16
Squire, John 118
Stacey, Symon 117
Stafford Building 231
Stafford County Courthouse 56, 71, 73, 85, 95, 105, 118, 136, 139, 151, 158, 162, 163, 166, 167, 170, 171, 173-176, 179, 180, 186, 187, 190, 198, 222-224, 226, 228, 258, 259, 261, 264, 265, 267, 271, 275, 277, 278, 281,
283, 284
Stafford County Juvenile and Domestic Relations Court 92
Stafford County Landfill 266
Stafford County militia 138
Stafford County School Board 56, 231
Stafford Courthouse Precinct 179, 186, 188
Stafford Guards 168, 179
Stafford Marketplace (shopping center) 173
Stafford Middle School 231
Stafford Post Office 223, 228, 231, 232, 242, 244-246
Stafford Rangers 83, 127, 159, 162, 169, 171, 174-176, 179, 180, 187, 188
Stafford Senior High School 70
Stafford Springs 105, 148, 179, 258, 259
Stafford Store 114, 164, 173, 176, 200, 226, 261, 265, 266, 283
Stafford Store Post Office 224, 228, 246
Stafford Store Precinct 159, 179, 186, 188, 189
Stafford Store Road 173, 175, 177
Staffordshire, England 2, 3, 37
Stage Road (Stafford County) 136, 149, 158, 159, 162-164, 166, 167, 170, 174
Stamp Act 127
Stamper, Salkeld 233
Stanard, Robert C. 135
Stanstead (Stafford County) 56, 132, 178
Staples, Waller R. 104
Star, The (newspaper) 186
Stark(e), Catherine (Kendall) (Pilcher) 262
    Eleanor (Bell) (born c.1817) 153, 158
    Elizabeth (Edwards) 160
    Elizabeth (Shelton) (born 1777) 152
    Hannah Kate (Cloe) (1842-1884) 158, 198
    James (c.1811-1860:70) 160
    John 255, 271
    John A. (c.1794-c.1865) 154
    Joseph (1771-1841) 153, 160
    Lucy 256, 257, 272
    Mary (Carter) 160
    Mary (Edwards) 153
    Mary (Kendall) (1760-1858) 154
    Nancy (Shelkett) (1786-1834) 151
    Newman Basil (1799-1860) 257
    Richard (c.1813-1877) 153, 158, 160, 162, 163, 165, 167-169 172, 177
    William (1754-1838) 154
Stark's gate (Stafford County) 171, 177
State Routes:
    218 (Butler Road) 61, 94
    218 (White Oak Road) 94, 131, 159, 171, 172, 175-177, 185, 231, 240
    600 (Bethel Church Road) 131, 153
    603 (Caisson Road) 92, 231, 241
    605 (New Hope Church Road) 164

606 (Ferry Road) 94
607 (Deacon Road) 161, 240
608 (Brooke Road) 37, 112, 219
610 (Garrisonville Road) 71, 74, 76, 85, 164,
    173, 194, 204, 220, 228, 244
611 (Wide Water Road) 40, 55, 169, 192,
    228, 232, 243
612 (Hartwood Road) 145, 231
615 (Skyline Drive) 81, 145
616 (Poplar Road) 8, 68, 69, 84, 136, 139,
    148, 167, 172, 176, 177, 224, 231,
    235, 247, 260
621 (Marlborough Point Road) 37
626 (Potomac Run Road) 177
627 (Mountain View Road) 63, 69, 93,
    113, 205, 230
630 (Courthouse Road) 71, 73, 76, 125,
    168, 170, 242
631 (Bell's Hill Road) 93
635 (Decatur Road) 40
637 (Telegraph Road) 4, 61, 229, 232
639 (Camp Barrett Road) 243
641 (Onville Road) 52, 77, 243
644 (Rock Hill Church Road) 69, 152, 194,
    244
648 (Shelton Shop Road) 93
648 (Stefaniga Road) 62, 148
651 (Kellogg's Mill Road) 149, 205, 230, 274
652 (Truslow Road) 245
654 (Berea Church Road) 230
654 (Rocky Pen Road) 239
655 (Holly Corner Road) 61, 162, 170, 239
658 (Brent Point Road) 222
659 (Doc Stone Road) 76
662 (Stony Hill Road) 72, 245
670 (Sanford Road) 138, 278
687 (Hope Road) 8
691 (Storck Road) 231
733 (Embrey Mill Road) 176
750 (Fleet Drive) 230, 268
753 (Enon Road) 245
754 (Shackelford's Well Road) 58, 68, 230
Steamboat Hotel (Natchez, Mississippi) 147
Stefaniga Road (State Route 648) 62, 148
Stephens, H. Samuel 91
    Sidney 259, 275, 280
Steptoe, Anne (1737-1777) 55
Sterling, Margaret (Forbes) (1754-1806) 68
Stern(e), Charles (1756-1818) 138
    Charles M. (1827-1901) 175, 188
    Edward Lee (1864-1937) 198
    Fanny Curtis (Sterne) (1842-1881) 188
    Francis (died 1804) 138
    George T. 180
    Katie (Tolson) (1884-1976) 188
    Mary (Davis) (1848-1923) 188

Susan (Waller) (1762-1834) 138
    William 151
    William S. (c.1789-after 1860) 152
Sterne's Mill (Stafford County) 152
Sterns, Edward 80
Stevens, H. 187
    John M. 246, 284
    Lucy (Bryant) 246
    Richard 175
    Richard Henry 170, 186
    William E. (1863-1925) 246
Stewart, Barnett (1814-1871) 150
    Catherine (Fant) 132, 135
    Frank (1864-1931) 224, 231, 239
    George L. (c.1862-c.1931) 266
    John 147
    John M. (born c.1822) 173, 176
    Joseph 230
    Lewis G. (1895-1963) 94, 266
    Mildred (Pollard) (born c.1827) 266
    Thomas 150
Stewart's Store (Stafford County) 225, 231
Sthreshley, Charles A. (1872-1898) 240
    Elizabeth Buckner (Jones) 168
    Frances Marian (Clift) 78, 240
    James Madison (1795-1869) 149, 168, 240
    Lillie C. (Jenkins) 240
    Marias (1847-1931) 78, 193, 194, 240
    Mary Peyton Bolling (Fitzhugh) (born
        1808) 150, 168, 240
    Capt. William 168
Stiff, Mary Katherine (Wellford) 79
Stires, Jacob L. (c.1831-after 1860) 263, 281
Stith, Lt. Col. Drury (born c.1695) 52
    Elizabeth (Buckner) 52
    Elizabeth (Fitzhugh) (1754-1786) 52
    John (1724-1773) 55
    Mary Townshend (Washington) 56
    Col. Robert 56
Stoke-Coursey, England 4
Stokes, Helen M. (Sibley) (White) 186
Stone, Ann (Schooler) (born c.1831) 80, 170
    Barton Speake 149, 150, 270
    Bronaugh (1835-1899) 233
    Charles W. (died 1842) 79, 158
    Charles W. (1877-1951) 240
    Elizabeth (Burroughs) (Tackett) (dead by
        1833) 140, 147
    Elizabeth Hawkins (Edrington) (1810-
        1891) 147
    Fielding Barton (born c.1827) 80-85, 88,
        90, 91, 170, 174, 179
    George (1741-1771) 251
    George W. (born c.1861) 74, 75
    Hannah 158
    Hannah Ann (Waller) (1823-1896) 76

Hannah (Withers) (c.1774-1857) 147, 152
Hawkins 147
Hawkins (1748-1810) 140
Dr. Hawkins (1816-1903) 76-78, 173, 176, 186
Hester (Bronaugh) 233
J. 176
James Withers (1796-1869) 158, 262, 263, 273
James Withers (c.1805-1857) 79, 80, 147,
     149, 150, 152, 153, 162, 237
John H. (c.1838- 1916) 187, 189
Lucy P. (Towson) (c.1806-c.1876) 71
Margaret (Brown) 71
Margaret Eleanor (Daniel) (1771-1809) 71
Mary M. (Curtis) (c.1809-1865) 181
Mary (Scandrett) 251
Mildred 170
Mildred (born c.1829) 80
Mildred (Daniel) (1772-1837) 80, 169
Mildred "Milly" (Richards) 251
Richard (died 1825) 147, 152
Richard (died before 1857) 158, 257, 258, 279
Sarah (Porter) (Edrington) (1769-1810) 147
T. 279
Thomas 149, 233, 258-260, 280
Hon. Thomas (1743-1787) 71, 76
William 181
William Barton (died 1845) 152, 153, 158,
     233, 256-259, 274, 275, 280
William Hawkins (c.1809-c.1851) 147,
     149, 150, 152, 170
William Scandrett (1764-1827) 251
Stone & Petty (business) 261
Stone Lick Creek(Kentucky) 134
Stone, Richard & Thomas (business) 258
Stone's Mill (Stafford County) 74, 76, 153, 172, 185
Stonewall Brigade 90
Stony Bridge (Stafford County) 138
Stony Hill (Aquia Creek) 58, 68, 126, 127, 133, 137
Stony Hill (Long Branch) 72, 83, 245
Stony Hill Road (State Route 662) 72, 245
Storck, Flossie L. (Houghton) (1883-1947) 246
     George (1850-1934) 246
     Woodlie (1859-1923) 246
Storck Post Office (Stafford County) 222-224, 228,
     231, 246
Storck Road (State Route 691) 231
Storke, Behethland (Gilson) (died 1693) 123
     Behethland (Strother) (1716-1753) 5
     Catherine (Washington) (born 1723) 59, 137
     Elizabeth (Hart) (Bernard) 123, 126
     Margaret (Washington) (Monroe) 51
     Nehemiah (died 1693) 123
     William (1690-1746) 123
Story, John 39
Strahan, Lt. David 41
Stratford Hall (Westmoreland County) 174

Street, Robert 115
Stribling, Anne Eliza (Waller) (1832-1903) 248
     Joell 41
Stringfellow, Sarah (Patton) (1766-1848) 146, 260
     Thomas 148
     William (died 1831) 146, 148, 254, 270,
          271
Strode, John (c.1735-c.1820) 125
Strother, Alice (Tyler) (c.1719-c.1792) 125
     Anne (James) (born c.1710) 55
     Anthony (1710-1765) 137
     B. H. 32
     Behethland (Storke) (1716-1753) 5
     Maj. Benjamin (c.1700-1789) 127-129
     Elizabeth (Rowzee) (Waller) (Peyton)
          (c.1715-1782) 58, 127, 131, 133,
          137
     George (died 1811) 137
     George W. (born c.1806) 163
     James 277
     Jane (Morgan) 277
     John 150
     Margaret (Morgan) 277
     Margaret (Thornton) 5, 49
     Margaret (Watts) (Grant) 125
     Mary (Ficklen) 71, 146
     Mary (James) 137
     Mary (Mason) (Fitzhugh) 127
     Sarah (Kenyon) 137
     Capt. William (c.1665-1726) 125
     William (c.1696-1733) 5, 49
Strother's Mill (Stafford County) 139
Stuart, Charles 54
     Rev. David (c.1692-1749) 128
     Frances (Alexander) (1728-after 1777) 128
     Frances (Washington) (born 1731) 54
     Jane (Gibbons) (c.1700-1750) 128
     John (1728-1787) 55, 56, 128, 129
     Mary (Fitzhugh) 56
     Sarah (Fitzhugh) (1731-1783) 59
     Dr. William Gibbons (1749-1796) 56
Stuart & Company (business) 187
Stubberfield, Elizabeth (Reveley) (Croughton) (died
     1872) 256
Suddath, Robert 125
     Sarah (Walker) 125
Sullins, Howard 207
Sullivan, Aubrey R. (died 1970) 94
     E. (Fugate) 277
     George (born c.1808) 161
     John A. (1860-1947) 233, 237
     Lelia May 234
     Martin, Jr. 277
     Mary E. 262, 263
     Mary E. (born c.1824) 281
     Mildred (Coakley) (1761-1812) 276

Thompson J. (born c.1820) 262, 277, 281
Welford (died 1937) 195
William 158
William Thomas (1880-1962) 204
Sullivant, Thompson J. 262
Sumner, John (1618-1670) 41
    Lt. Joseph (1641-1734) 41-44, 121
Sunderlin, Darwin (born c.1810) 246
Surry Light Artillery 170
Surveyor, position of 105-106
Suthard, Allen 236
    Catherine "Kitty" (Jett) (born c.1812) 236
    Mary (Ledlow) 236
Sutherland, Susan (Bell) 234
Suttle, Agnes Ann (Towson) (c.1811-1865) 178, 264, 283
    Catherine (Tolson) 150
    Charles Francis (born 1807) 153, 157
    John Benjamin T. (c.1840-1884) 185, 186
    John H. 253, 254, 270
    John H. (c.1807-1884) 150, 169, 174, 178, 233, 259, 260, 276
Swan, Robert 253, 254
Sweetzer, Houston K. (1881-1961) 33
Swetnam, Aphia F. (Lunsford) (born c.1844) 89, 172
    George W. (born c.1830) 163, 263
    John A. (1792-1854) 77, 78, 89, 156, 158, 172
    Joseph F. (born c.1838) 176, 263
    Sarah (Sanford) (born c.1811) 89, 172
Sylvania Heights (Spotsylvania County) 232
Tabb, Frances (Fitzhugh) (1794-1868) 168
Tackett, Ann (Barber) 71, 77
    Charles (1780-1834) 71, 72, 77, 152, 182, 233, 254, 255, 257, 258, 280
    Charles Addison (1814-1896) 146, 148, 150, 170, 173, 180-182, 185, 187, 247, 262, 281, 282
    Elizabeth (Burroughs) (Stone) (dead by 1833) 140, 147
    Enfield (Mason) (1796-1836) 233
    Frances (Reno) (c.1750-1796:99) 233
    Col. John (1788-1850) 228, 233, 255
    Rev. John O. (1848-1907) 180, 181
    Lewis (Tacquitt) 180
    Maria A. (Spindle) (c.1810-1883) 77, 187
    Senate (1770:80-1836) 256, 271, 272
    William, Jr. (c.1751-after 1830) 71, 233
Tackett & Barber (business) 255
Tackett-Burroughs Cemetery (Fauquier County) 180
Tackett's Mill (Stafford County) 71, 77, 90, 160, 171, 173, 180, 182, 185, 220, 233, 259-261, 265
Tackett's Mill Post Office (Stafford County) 77, 228, 233, 247
Tacquitt, Lewis 180
Talana Post Office (Stafford County) 247
Taliaferro, _____ 200

Amanda Permelia (Smith) (1860-1918) 282
Anne E. (Coleman) (1834-1892) 201
Bettie G. (Borst) 181
Charles D. (1867-1949) 201, 266
Catherine (Hooe) (died 1731) 45
Eilbeck Hunter (1844-1891) 282
Ella M. (Decatur) (born 1875) 201
James 262
James Garnett (c.1772-after 1850) 181
James L. (c.1814-1904) 188, 276
James Monroe (1809-1893) 201, 276, 282
John (1768-1852) 62
Richard (died c.1677) 45
Sarah 45
Taliaferro & Cooper (business) 283
Tandy, Ann (Waller) 127, 131
Tankersley, Bettie (Humphries) (born c.1849) 85
    Catherine (Mackey) 85
    Charles W. (born c.1840) 85
    Henry 85
Tanner, Frances (Aubrey) 46
Tappahannock, Virginia 252
Tasker, Benjamin (1690-1768) 46
    Frances A. (Carter) (died 1787) 18
Tayloe, Anne (Ogle) (1772-1855) 19
    Catherine Griffin (Carter) (1761-1798) 19
    Edward Thornton (1803-1875) 19
    Elizabeth M. (Carter) (died 1832) 19
    Ellen Elizabeth (Deshazo) (died 1914) 176
    John (III) (1772-1828) 19
    Lucy Penn (Gordon) (born c.1830) 19
    Mary (Ogle) (1807-1862) 19
    Rebecca (Lee) (c.1748-1797) 18
Taylor, Mrs. B. 271
    Eleanor (Baxter) 149
    Elizabeth (Ford) 12, 149
    Ellen Elizabeth (Deshazo) (died 1914) 176
    Harriet Mabel (Moncure) (1865-1895) 246
    Jane (Chapman) 127
    John 271, 272
    John (born 1725) 256
    John B. 273
    John C. 271, 272
    Richard 269, 270
    Robert (1758-1851) 256, 271, 272
    Robert W. 171
    Thornton 149
    William 61, 62
Taylor, John & Potts, John H. S. (business) 272
Taylor, John C. & Company (business) 272
Telegraph Road (Stafford County) 61, 112, 114, 171-173, 177, 189, 192
Telegraph Road (State Route 637) 4, 61, 229, 232
Templeman, Edward 161
    Edward (born c.1821) 160, 247, 262

Eliza Wigginton (Coleman) (died 1885) 277
James 257, 269, 270, 272
James B. (1822-1892) 161, 189
Julia A. (Heflin) (1816-1892) 186
Louisa (Holmes) (1830-1900) 161
Robert Lee (1860-1928) 93, 94, 198
Setha 161
Tennant, Anna S. 238
    Eleanor A. S. (Grymes) 238
    George 238
    Hugh Mercer (born c.1803) 238, 262
    Hugh Mercer (c.1845-after 1910) 238
Tennessee 163, 184
Texas 162, 170
Theinert, Edward W. 94
10th Virginia of Foot 133
3rd Virginia Convention 7
3rd Virginia Regiment 8, 9, 138
30th Virginia Infantry 165, 167, 168, 170, 176, 179, 190, 200, 238, 239
30th Virginia Regiment 89, 169
34th Virginia Volunteers 179
37th Virginia Regiment 81
Thistle Mill (Falmouth) 69
Thom, Alexander 69
    Eleanor (Reat) (1786-1869) 69
    Elizabeth (Triplett) 69
    Reuben Triplett (1782-1868) 69
Thomas, Hazel L. 241
    James 123-125
    Robert 255
    Rosie (Cropp) 81, 270
    Susan (Cropp) 138
    William 256, 257, 270-272
Thomason, Edward 39-41, 117
    Lucy (Heabeard) (born 1656) 39
Thomson, Ann (Mason) (died 1762) 6
    Mildred (Scott) 159
Thompson, Ann (Thornton) 252
    Henry 159
    Dr. Henry 159
    John A. 266
    John McKalaway 33
    Mary A. 174
    Mary Ann (Powers) (1845-1912) 174, 188
    Mathew 39-43
    Nathaniel 41
    William A. 174
Thompson's Mill (Fauquier County) 220, 223
Thomson, Ann (Mason) (died 1762) 6
    Mildred (Scott) 159
Thorn(e), Eleanor (Monteith) 173
    Thomas 121
Thornton, ___ 5
    Alice (Fitzhugh) 53

Alice (Savage) (1653-1695) 123
Ann (Thompson) 252
Anthony (1695-1757) 45, 47, 123
Catherine (Yates) (Wellford) (1760-1831) 79
Eliza (Carter) 18
Elizabeth Gregory (Dunbar) (c.1767-1851) 252
Francis (1651-1726) 45, 123
Col. Francis (died 1784) 50, 53, 55, 56
Francis (died 1794) 252
Col. Francis (1767-1836) 68
John (died 1777) 3
Lucy (Alexander) 6
Margaret (Strother) 5, 49
Mildred (Hayward) 3
Presley (1730-1812) 11
Rowland 53
Sallie (Innes) (Forbes) (1776-1807) 68
Sarah (Fitzhugh) 50
Capt. William E. 86
Thorny Point (Stafford County) 187, 219, 223
Three Tun Tavern (Falmouth, Virginia) 7
Threlkeld, Ann "Nancy" (Fox) (1772-1828) 10, 137, 155
    Christopher, Jr. (1698-1757) 130
    Col. Elijah (1744-1798) 10, 130, 132, 134, 137, 140
    Mary (Bronaugh) (Waugh) (died 1799) 130
    Susannah (Threlkeld) 129
Times-Dispatch (newspaper) 17
Timmons, ___ 197
    Thomas 151
Tobacco inspectors, position of 106-108
Tobacco warehouses:
    Aquia 127, 129, 130, 134, 138, 141, 142
    Cave's 127, 130, 131
    Dixon's 132, 134, 136, 138, 142, 148, 152, 154
    Falmouth 127, 131, 132, 135-137
Tolson, ___ (Edrington) 150, 159
    Amy A. (Weedon) (born 1849) 86
    Anne E. (Hickerson) (1827-1897) 71, 150, 159, 200
    Maj. Benjamin (c.1763-1836) 65, 66-68, 71-73, 145, 150, 153, 159, 280
    Benjamin P. (c.1802-c.1870) 246, 258
    Catherine (Suttle) 150
    Daniel 112
    Emma Lee (Davis) (1873-1965) 246
    Euphemia (Daniel) (1805-1844) 71
    George 150
    George (1726-1785) 65, 150
    Herbert Minor (1856-1936) 196, 200, 201
    James 31, 156, 164, 170

James Alexander (c.1835-1896) 246
James Edward (1795-1865) 71, 80, 86, 150, 159, 200
John C. 260
Katie (Sterne) (1884-1976) 188
Marion Ratcliffe (1867-1952) 246, 266
Mary Jane (Ratcliffe) (1837-1928) 246
Mitchell (1902-1992) 246
Ora Genevieve (Sine) (c.1905-1959) 246
Prudence (Payne) (c.1811-1855) 246
Raymond Blake, Jr. (1912-1991) 188
William (born c.1823) 159, 167, 188
Tolson family 127
Tolson's blacksmith shop (Stafford County) 164
Tolson's Mill (Stafford County) 259
Toluca (Stafford County) 90, 189, 197, 247, 266
Toluca Post Office (Stafford County) 224, 227, 228, 244, 247
Tomlin, Fanny Dulany (Moncure) 157
Topographic Engineers of the Confederate Army 186
Toronto, Canada 235
Townsend, Frances (Baldwin) (Williams) 37
Frances (Dade) (Withers) (1667-1726) 39, 44, 47, 48, 125
Frances (Hooe) (c.1667-1720) 124
Margaret (Washington) 122, 125
Mary (Langhorne) (died c.1694) 38
Mary (Washington) 42, 45, 48
Richard (born c.1606) 37, 38
Robert (1640-1675) 38, 116
Towson, Agnes Ann (Suttle) (c.1811-1865) 178, 264, 283
Charles Frank (c.1852-1908) 264, 284
Eleanor (Norman) (1782-1848) 71, 161
James Edward (1808-1888) 150, 156, 158-160, 169, 172, 174, 176, 178, 264, 283
John (c.1746-1832) 71
Lucy P. (Stone) (c.1806-c.1876) 71
Lucy Randolph (Nelson) (1852-1937) 264
Mary E. (Gaskins) (c.1818-c.1874) 85
Mary Frances (Smith) 161
Mathew Norman (born c.1846) 178, 263, 283
Penelope (Buck) (c.1753-1794) 71
Thomas (1780-1861) 71-73, 75, 77, 78, 85, 150, 154, 158, 161, 163
Thomas Norman (1822-1863) 161, 163
William S. (c.1853-1915) 283
Tramill, John 120
Tranquility (Stafford County) 80
Traveler's Rest (Aquia Run) 65, 153
Traveler's Rest (Rappahannock River) 92, 148, 161, 166
Travers, Elizabeth (Cooke) 51
Hannah (Ball) (c.1683-1748) 48, 61, 127
John 116
Margaret (Newton) (Heabeard) 116
Million (Waugh) (died 1748) 52

Rawleigh (16_-1722) 44, 48, 61, 127
Sarah (Daniel) (Pierson) (171_-1788) 48, 61, 127
Treasurer, position of 114
Triangle, Virginia 241, 248
Triangle Post Office (Prince William County) 225
Trice, Elizabeth (Walton) 20
Trimmingham, Catherine (Brent) (died 1751) 57
Triplett, Daniel (1753-1818) 58, 60, 62, 140
Daniel (1735-1799) 133, 137
Elizabeth (Hedgman) 46, 133
Elizabeth (Richards) (1755-1826) 58, 140
Elizabeth (Thom) 69
Francis (died c.1767) 140
Francis (1680-1772) 58
Isabella (Hore) (Harrison) (169_-1763) 47, 126, 127
Isabella (Miller) 47
William 46
Capt. William (1650-1725) 47, 58
William (died 1749) 45, 133
Trone, Julia (Weedon) 86
Trumbell, Elizabeth 41
Truro Parish (Fairfax County) 45
Truslow, Ann "Nancy" (England) 191
Benjamin (c.1792-1869) 191
Callie E. (Gallahan) (born c.1860) 91
Charles 91
Charles A. (1860-1947) 91, 228, 245
Frances 91
John (born c.1820) 180
Morris (c.1834-1907) 191
Nancy (Dickens) 191
Truslow Road (State Route 652) 245
Truslow's Store (Stafford County) 245
Trussell, William 274
Tuan Post Office (Stafford County) 228, 247
Tucker, Catherine (Shacklett) 244
Henry St. George (1780-1848) 80
John 4, 5, 118
Rose (Gerrard) (Newton) (born c.1629) 118
Sarah (Fitzhugh) (1663-after 1701) 4, 5, 45
Sarah Virginia (Brooke) (born 1815) 80
Tuckfield, William H. P. & Company (business) 254
Tump (Stafford County) 17
Turberville, Maj. George (1694-1742) 6, 52
Letitia (Waugh) 52
Martha (Lee) (Fitzhugh) (1716-1751) 6
Turner, Benjamin 268
Charles (born c.1825) 163, 171
Frank A. 233
Rose (Hunter) 14
Tusculum (Stafford County) 113, 114, 173
Tutt, Margaret W. (Garnett) 255

Thomas 255, 256
Twiford (Westmoreland County) 18
Tyler, Alice (Strother) (c.1719-c.1792) 125
    Ann Fisher (Adie) (1756-1818) 131
    Charles 267
    Francis (c.1688-after 1723) 125
    Capt. Henry (c.1710-1777) 104, 125-131
    Rebecca (born c.1695) 125
    Thomas Gowry Strother (c.1740-1816) 104, 131-134
Tyson's Store (Stafford County) 205
Union Church (Falmouth) 174
Union College (Schenectady, New York) 18
Union County, Kentucky 137
Union occupation 28-33, 76, 79, 80, 84, 87, 154, 161, 167
United Daughters of the Confederacy 86
United States Military Academy 175
United States Naval Academy 174
United States Navy 15
U.S. Route 1 (Jefferson Davis Highway) 8, 12, 16, 73, 81, 94, 112, 220, 231
U.S. Route 3 (King's Highway) 137, 150
U.S. Route 17 (Warrenton Road) 56, 59, 72, 74, 77, 87, 135, 139, 150, 162, 170, 176, 192, 220, 222, 228, 230, 231, 274, 275
United States Daughters of 1812 64
United States Geodetic Survey 202
United States Supreme Court 11
United States Telegraph Company 31
United States Treasury Department 18
University of Maryland 20
University of Pennsylvania 13, 74, 76
University of Virginia 15, 16, 20, 74, 202
Upper Machodoc Creek (King George County) 38, 41
Upper Marlborough, Maryland 8
Valey View School (Stafford County) 240
Van Buren, Martin 12
Van Doran, Abram (born c.1828) 175, 176
Vandegasteel, Giles (16_-1701) 5, 41, 118
    Martha (Waugh) 5, 49, 118
Vass, Elizabeth B. (Maury) 252
    James (c.1769-1837) 69, 252-258
    Susanna (Brooke) 252
Vaucluse Gold Mine (Orange County) 77
Vazquez, Irene 95
Vernon, Abner (died 1792) 138
    Jane 138
Vestavia Woods subdivision (Stafford County) 73, 125
Vestry, function of 101, 108-109
Vida, Esther A. 241
    Michael (1913-1990) 241
Viller's shop (Stafford County) 170
Vine, Henry C. (died c.1912) 284
Virginia Bank (Fredericksburg) 71, 77
Virginia Bar Association 20, 104

Virginia Court of Appeals 12
Virginia Declaration of Rights 5, 6, 37, 50
Virginia Home Guard 168
Virginia Line 9, 138
Virginia Military Institute 86, 157, 168
Virginia militia 64, 79, 83, 142, 147
Virginia Polytechnic Institute 17
Virginia Press Association 186
Virginia Society of the Cincinnati 65
Virginia State Dairymen's Association 17
Virginia Supreme Court of Appeals 17, 20, 64
Vivian, Margaret (Daniel) (died 1727) 48, 127
Voss, Mary (Spotswood) 64
    Nicholas 64
Vowles (Vowells), Alexander 62
    Esther J. (Moncure) (1795-1833) 81
    George Frazier 254-256
    Henry (1752-c.1803) 12, 60-63, 139, 140, 267, 268
    Maria (Daniel) 71
    Mary (Frazier) 60, 255
    Mary Frazier (Briggs) (1790-1852) 60
    Susan (Beale) 69
    Susannah (Chunn) 60, 65
    Thomas 60, 65
    Zachariah (died 1825) 65-69, 251, 255
Vowells' Tavern (Falmouth) 61
Vowles & Brooke & Company (business) 254
Wales 134
Walker, ___ 172
    Edwin C. (c.1828-1892) 170, 180
    Elizabeth 117
    Elizabeth (Monk) 49
    Endimion 117
    James 176
    Lydia Hardwick) 49
    Margery 117
    Mary Anna (Hefferlin) (1790-1831) 172
    Mary (Carter) (died 1742) 6, 132
    Sarah 49
    Sarah (Suddath) 125
    Thomas (died c.1726) 49
    William 148
    William (born 1710:25) 49
    William (died 1750) 49
    William (born c.1822) 283
Walker & Dent (business) 282
Walker's Battalion 160
Wall, Rev. Henry 14
Wallace, ___ 136
    Judge Alexander Wellington (1843-1927) 165
    Anne (Coffman) (1820-1889) 198
    Barbara (Fox) (1766-1833) 64
    Caroline E. (Rollins) 188
    Casper Wistar (1834-1907) 165

Dora Ashby (Green) (1854-1937) 20
Elizabeth (Brown) (born 1723) 9, 64, 139
Elizabeth (Hooe) (c.1766-1850) 14, 80, 136, 139
Elizabeth (Westwood) (Mason) (died 1824) 9, 10
Emily Travers (Daniel) (c.1806-after 1860) 14, 20, 80
Gustavus Brown 88
Gustavus Brown (1751-1802) 9
Gustavus Brown (1810-1882) 14, 20, 28, 31, 80-84, 114, 162, 164, 166, 168, 169, 172, 178, 179
Gustavus Brown (1876-1955) 17, 196, 197, 199, 200, 203, 204
Dr. Gustavus Michael (1849-1937) 14, 20
Harriet "Hallie" Eustace (Moncure) (1846-1928) 189, 198
Howson 189
James 9, 10
John (1761-1829) 14, 80, 136, 139
John Hooe (1793-1828) 172
Lee (c.1856-1935) 88-94
Margaret Elizabeth (McFarland) (died 1864) 88
Mary Nicholas (Gordon) (1800-1879) 172
Dr. Michael (1719-1767) 9, 64, 80, 136, 139
Samuel Gordon (1831-1897) 165, 172
Thomas (1796-1882) 198
Thomas (1852-1914) 189, 198-200
Virginia Belle (Chichester) (1871-1961) 204
Capt. William Brown (1757-1833) 64, 67, 134
Wallace & Herring Lumber Company (Alexandria, Virginia) 17
Wallace & Moncure (business) 264
Wallace's (Stafford County) 172
Waller, Mrs. ___ 166, 167
    Ann (born c.1798) 165
    Ann (Adie) (1792-1870) 83
    Ann (Tandy) 127, 131
    Anne Eliza (Stribling) (1832-1903) 248
    Betty Ann (Wickliff) (born c.1834) 165
    Catherine Barret (Conway) (1746-1794) 233
    Charles (1674-1724) 126, 127
    Charles (1702-1749) 5, 49, 126, 127, 131
    Edward (1706-1753) 49, 127, 131
    Edward (born c.1713) 126
    Edward (1768-1818) 74
    Edward (1805-1883) 13, 74-79, 81, 82, 86, 159, 162, 164, 166, 168, 174, 181, 238, 257, 264, 279
    Edward (1849-1919) 178, 264
    Elizabeth (Allen) (1746-1768) 13, 131
    Elizabeth (Chadwell) 74
    Elizabeth Clyde (Gill) (1877-1948) 192
    Elizabeth (Rowzee) (Peyton) (Strother) (c.1715-1782) 5, 127, 131, 133, 137
    Frances A. (Alexander) 147
    Frances A. (Kellogg) (1815-1887) 84, 160
    George (1703-1768) 125, 127, 128
    George (1787-before 1856) 11, 12, 234
    Hannah Ann (Stone) (1823-1896) 76
    Hannah (Clifton) 271
    Harriett C. (born c.1803) 234
    James 165, 254-257, 271
    James (17_-1824) 83
    James A. (born c.1831) 234
    James Ellen (c.1824-1862) 28, 165, 167
    John (1732-1753) 138
    John (died 1791) 130
    John Wickliffe (1840-1921) 192
    Lucy (Shelkett) 150
    Margaret Ursula (Morton) (1771-1821) 73, 268-270, 279
    Margaret Ursula (Ford) (1821-1901) 83
    Margaret (Waller) (1744-1777) 131, 279
    Mary (Harrison) 131
    Mary (Matthews) 138
    Nannie (Blackburn) (1848-1912) 238
    Nannie Withers (Moncure) (1862-1903) 248
    Naomi (Brooks) 203
    Sallie Medora (Wickliffe) (1857-1921) 192
    Susan (Withers) 139
    Susan Newton (Conway) (1814-1864) 238
    Susannah (Forrest) (1678-1748) 126
    Susannah (Stone) (1762-1834) 138
    Sylvanus 84, 150, 160
    Theodosia (Hore) (1753-1829) 12, 83, 149, 151, 155
    Col. Thomas Conway (1832-1895) 28, 158, 166, 173, 177, 180, 184, 185, 182, 192
    Ursula (Withers) (1752-1818) 131, 233
    William (1673-1703) 37
    William (1740-1817) 11, 13, 73, 131, 233, 254, 270, 271, 279
    Withers (1785-1827) 233, 254-257, 270, 271
    Col. Withers (1825-1900) 166, 179, 248, 282
Waller & Edmonds (business) 283
Waller, James & Brothers (business) 254, 270
Waller, William & Withers (business) 270
Waller, Withers & Company (business) 256
Waller, Withers & James (business) 255-257
Waller's Fishery (Stafford County) 158, 172, 189
Waller's land 192
Wallis, Alfred Wickliff (c.1813-c.1894) 194
    Dr. William Joseph (born c.1845) 194, 195, 235
Walnut Farm (Stafford County) 161
Walnut Hill (King George County) 18

Walnut Hill (Stafford County) 152, 188
Walton, Elizabeth (Trice) 20
　　　Herman H. (c.1876-1945) 20
Walton & Wood (business) 20
Walton Lumber Company (business) 20
Wamsley, Benjamin 151
　　　Benjamin C. (c.1814-1886) 79, 80, 88, 91,
　　　　　163, 179, 195
　　　Daniel 151
　　　Eliza F. (Shelkett) (c.1827-1879) 79, 91
　　　Elizabeth (Carter) (c.1818-1886) 151
　　　John W. (born c.1845) 91, 165
　　　Mary Virginia (Hickerson) (Massie) (born
　　　　　c.1853) 91, 164, 165
　　　Walter (1867-1923) 195-197
　　　Warner (1867-1950) 195
Wamsley (Stafford County) 173
Wandrick, Charles 208
War Between the States 14, 15, 19, 39, 52, 71,
　　　76-78, 80-87, 89, 92, 134, 148, 154,
　　　157, 158, 160-179, 186, 188, 189,
　　　192, 193, 198, 200, 219, 230, 231,
　　　235, 238-240, 247, 263, 281, 283
War of 1812 12, 13, 62, 64-69, 134, 138, 139,
　　　140-143, 145-152, 233, 252, 253, 279
Wardlaw, Mary J. (Eustace) 182
Warner, Elizabeth "Lettice" (Jones) (1720:25-1795) 123
　　　John (c.1680-1742) 123-126
　　　Margaret 123
Warren, Capt. ___ 139
　　　Charles N. 243
　　　John W. 186
　　　Susan (King) 176
　　　William 176
Warren's corner (Stafford County) 161
Warrenton Road (U.S. Route 17) 59, 72, 74, 77, 87, 109,
　　　114, 135, 139, 150, 159, 162, 170, 172-174,
　　　176, 185, 189, 192, 220, 224, 230, 231, 274,
　　　275
Warrenton, Virginia 78, 175, 247, 261
Warsaw Post Office (Westmoreland County) 228
Warwick, Julia Trent (Moncure) (1840-1906) 173
Washington, Ann (Pope) 2
　　　Anne (Steptoe) (1737-1777) 55
　　　Augustine (1694-1743) 42, 72
　　　Bailey, Jr. (1753-1814) 8-10, 59, 62, 134
　　　Bailey, Sr. (1731-1807) 5, 8, 9, 52, 55-57, 59,
　　　　　60, 62, 128, 136, 137
　　　Betty (Lewis) (1733-1797) 64
　　　Betty (Massey) 52
　　　Catherine (Storke) (born 1723) 5, 9, 137
　　　Catherine (Washington) 52
　　　Elizabeth (Dade) (1734-after 1796) 56
　　　Elizabeth (Lund) 48
　　　Elizabeth Storke (Jett) 18
　　　Euphan (Wallace) (Brent) (1765-1845) 9, 10

　　　Frances (Gerrard) (Speake) (Peyton)
　　　　　(Appleton) 3
　　　Frances (Stuart) (born 1731) 54
　　　George 2, 6, 42, 52, 64, 65, 130
　　　Hannah (Bushrod) 18
　　　Henry 59
　　　Henry (c.1720-1745) 18
　　　Henry (1694-1748) 47, 48, 52, 125, 129
　　　Jane Charlotte (Moncure) (1834-1916) 178
　　　John (1632-1677) 2, 3, 37, 40, 44, 125
　　　John (1663-1698) 47, 51, 125
　　　John (1668-1721) 45, 122, 125
　　　John (1671-1718:21) 41-44, 48
　　　John (c.1697-1742) 45, 52, 124, 125
　　　John (c.1716-c.1751) 51
　　　Col. John (1730-1782) 52, 53, 55, 56, 129
　　　John Augustine (1735-1787) 18
　　　Joyce (Fleming) 122
　　　Katherine 129
　　　Lawrence (1635-1676) 42, 122
　　　Lawrence (1728-c.1813) 55, 56
　　　Maj. Lawrence (c.1716-1752) 49
　　　Louisa (Chapman) (born 1743) 54
　　　Margaret (Storke) (Monroe) 51
　　　Mary (Bailey) 52, 129
　　　Mary Butler (Peyton) (1760-1822) 70, 137,
　　　　　148
　　　Mary (Dade) 51
　　　Mary (Massey) 45, 52, 125
　　　Mary (Townsend) 42, 45, 48
　　　Mary Townsend (Stith) 56, 122, 125
　　　Mildred (Lee) (born 1788) 18
　　　Nathaniel (c.1689-1718) 51
　　　Robert 55, 56, 59
　　　Samuel (1734-1781) 55, 56, 130
　　　Susannah (Ferrin) (1753-1783) 55
　　　Townsend (1705-1743) 48
　　　Col. William (1752-1810) 59, 131
Washington Asylum Hospital 20
Washington College (Lexington, Virginia) 163
Washington, DC 15, 16, 19, 20, 32, 78, 88, 90, 94,
　　　148, 158, 168, 171, 185-187, 197, 200, 222,
　　　223, 239, 240, 242, 244, 245, 263, 265, 266
Washington, Maryland 64
Washington Parish (Westmoreland County) 58
Washington Territory 13
Waters, Mark (c.1829-after 1870) 237
Watson, Eliza (Brooks) (born 1845) 163, 173
　　　Frances (Cooper) 238
　　　George (born c.1830) 166
　　　James W. (born c.1819) 163, 173
　　　John 163, 173
　　　Mary (Berry) 202
　　　Nancy 163, 173
　　　Simon 276
　　　Walter Lee (1876-1960) 266

Watts, Jenny (Schooler) 179
    Margaret (Strother) (Grant) 48, 125
Waugh, Alexander (166_1722) 118
    Betty (Brittingham) (French) 47, 49
    David (168_-1753) 118
    Gowry (1734-1783) 52, 53, 55, 58
    Capt. James (c.1705-1750) 5, 49, 50, 125, 126
    John 48
    Rev. John (1630-1706) 4, 5, 37, 39, 40, 44, 49, 52, 118, 251
    John, Jr. (1661-1716) 5, 42-44, 49, 118-121, 251
    Joseph (c.1736-1763) 59
    Joseph (died 1747) 52, 118
    Letitia (Turberville) 52
    Martha (Vandegasteel) 5, 49, 118
    Mary (Bronaugh) (Threlkeld) (died 1799) 59, 130
    Mary (Hathaway) (born 1679) 42
    Million (Brown) (c.1763-1799) 59, 150
    Million (Travers) (died 1748) 52
Waugh Point (King George County) 3, 5, 37, 39
Waverly (King George County) 17
Waye, Anne (Peyton) (1731-1750) 5
Waynesboro, Battle of (1864) 86
Wayside (Stafford County) 173, 182, 192
Webb, Virginia (Burton) (c.1844-1887) 278
Weedon, Amy A. (Tolson) (born 1849) 86
    Annie Frances (Herndon) (born 1867) 90
    George 86
    George Milton (1840-1902) 86-88, 90, 189, 190, 192, 194-196, 200, 263
    Julia (Trone) 86
    Marshall B. 86
    Mary Lee (Cloe) 205
    Virginia (Clark) 86, 90
Weeks, Agnes (Holliday) 252
    Benjamin (born c.1824) 252-254
Weimer, William E. 203
Weir, Earl C. 246
Welch, Margaret (Primm) (1709-1770) 64, 133
Weldon Railroad, Battle of (1864) 178
Wellford, Catherine (Yates) (Thornton) (1760-1831) 79
    Charles Carter (1802-1872) 79
    Eliza S. (Rose) (1827-1899) 76
    Jannet (Henderson) 76
    John Spotswood (1825-1911) 76
    Mary Katherine (Stiff) 79
    Dr. Robert (1753-1823) 79
    Thomas 79
Wells, Carty, Sr. (17_-1781) 64
    Charles 55
    Lydia (Fristoe) (died 1830) 64
West, A. 90
    Benjamin S. (c.1829-1905) 31, 83, 84, 86, 87, 283
    Edward (c.1846-1911) 190
    James 90
    James (born c.1810) 163
    John 3, 41-44, 121
    Lucy Ann (Wine) (c.1832-1854) 248
    M. W. (Burton) (born c.1858) 90
    Robert L. 173
    Sarah (Jones) (1867-1935) 284
West & Ashby (business) 282
West Farm (Stafford County) 10, 12, 59, 128
West Grove (Fairfax County) 74
West Point Military Academy 19, 175
West Point, Virginia 179
West River (Anne Arundel County, Maryland) 8
West Virginia 202
Westebbe, Barbara 61
    Richard 61
Westfall, Capt. Abell 135
Westminster School (Bristol, England) 44
Westmoreland County, Virginia 3-6, 8, 18, 21, 37-39, 42, 45, 47, 49, 52, 58, 79, 115-118, 120, 121, 123, 125, 184, 228
Westover (Charles City County) 2, 118, 119
West's Road (Stafford County) 139
Westwood, Elizabeth (Wallace) (Mason) (died 1824) 9, 10
Whaling, Posey 152
Wharton, Elizabeth J. (Cropp) 81
    John 81
Wheeler, George G. 245
    John (1684-1746) 55, 126
    Mary (James) 55
Wheeling Conventions 14
Whiston, John 37
White, Anderson D. 271
    Capt. Chester B. 185
    Elizabeth C. (Coakley) (born 1816) 276
    Fannie W. 185
    Frances (Goolrick) 20
    Helen M. (Stokes) (Sibley) 186
    William Seymour (1853-1897) 185, 187, 190
White Hall (King George County) 183
White Oak (Stafford County) 88, 132, 149, 151, 165, 175, 176, 185, 187, 199, 241
White Oak Meeting House (Stafford County) 151, 153, 161, 173, 253, 284
White Oak Precinct 159, 179, 187-189
White Oak Road (State Route 218) 94, 131, 159, 171, 172, 175-177, 185, 231, 240
White Oak Run (Stafford County) 134, 170, 173
White Oak School (Stafford County) 231, 241
White Sulphur Springs 33
Whitecotton, George, Jr. 268
    Harris (c.1769-1803) 268, 269
    Margaret (Shumate) (1776-1819) 268

Mary (Harris) 268
Whitescarver, Matilda N. (Oliver) (Payne) 169
Whiting, Frances (Cooke) 44
    John 55
Whiting & Payne (business) 279
Whitney, Jared 273
Whorton's gate (Stafford County) 175
Wichita, Texas 15
Wickham, Gen. Williams Carter (1820-1888) 86
Wickliff(e), Andrew J. (born c.1830) 262
    Betty Ann (Waller) (born c.1834) 165
    Davie 165
    Emilie 165
    Sallie (Combs) 151
    Sallie Medora (Waller) (1857-1921) 192
Wicomico (Northumberland County) 10
Wicomico Creek (Northumberland County) 41
Wide Water Fire Department (Stafford County) 243
Wide Water Post Office (Stafford County) 228, 231, 234, 241, 243, 248
Wide Water Road (State Route 611) 40, 55, 169, 192, 228, 232, 243
Wide Water Station (Stafford County) 228, 229
Wide Water, Virginia 12, 14, 17, 40, 53, 59, 81, 139, 155, 169, 175, 188, 193, 220, 222, 225, 233, 241, 265, 266
Wigfall, Gen. Louis Trezevant (1816-1874) 86
Wigfield, Alice "Jennie" (Brewer) (1883-1971) 244
    Dora Lee Moore (Parr) (1861-1931) 192
    Douglas Nelson (1856-1898) 192
Wiggenton, Catherine (Abel) (born c.1854) 193
    Peter (c.1813-1866) 154, 261
    Seth Botts 236, 252
    William 236
    William Thomas (1845-1921) 193
Wiggenton & Kendall (business) 261
Wilderness Baptist Church (Spotsylvania County) 191
Wilderness, Battle of (1864) 168
Wilkerson, Annie Mason (Byram) (1861-1897) 242
    George Emmett (1857-1919) 242
    Lillie Marshall (1886-1963) 242
    Myrtie G. 242
Wilkinson's patent 136
Willford, William 118
William and Mary, College of 6, 8, 16, 21, 76, 105, 133, 147
William Street (Fredericksburg) 60, 253
Williams, ___ 138, 279
    Agnes L. (Riley) (1878-1956) 243
    Alexander P. (died c.1839) 72, 145-147, 149-154, 156
    Benjamin 149, 233
    Cassius (c.1840-1862) 164, 167
    Charles 138
    Dicey 243
    Frances (Baldwin) (Townsend) 37

    Hannah B. 138, 142
    James 243
    James L. (1864-1935) 243, 266
    John 251
    John P. (born c.1800) 142
    John Pope (1739-1809) 138
    Mary Avarell (Herndon) (1844-1932) 180
    Mary (Combs) 68
    Nathaniel Pope 68, 69, 71, 138, 142-144
    Pearson (c.1743-c.1824) 68, 142
    Polly (Combs) 142
    Ralph 208
    Lt. Col. Robert 37
    W. H. 266
    W. S. 153
    Walter 138, 142
    William 41, 42
Williams' Store (Stafford County) 243
Williamsburg, Virginia 2, 7, 8, 25, 26, 45, 49, 111, 118
Williamsville (Stafford County) 264, 266
Willis, Betty Landon (Carter) (1684-1719) 123
    Jane Gordon (Roach) 284
Willoughby, Elizabeth (Overzee) (Colclough) (Allerton) 38
Willow Dale (Stafford County) 183
Willow Green (Stafford County) 177
Wilmington, Delaware 88
Wilna (Richmond County) 19
Wilson, Annie May (Mountjoy) (1871-1959) 242
    Caroline (Fritter) (c.1835-1881) 171
    Hattie A. (English) (1879-1935) 266
    John H. (1887-1975) 201, 202
    Mary Catherine (Fritter) (1836-1929) 242
    Mary Elizabeth (Fallon) (born 1874) 242
    Thomas 271
    William N. (1842-1917) 242
Winchester, Battle of 175
Winchester, Virginia 179
Windmill Point (Stafford County) 50
Windsor (King George County) 56
Windsor (Stafford County) 59
Windsor Forest (Stafford County) 5, 8, 9, 52, 77, 128, 155, 173
Windsor Forest (Wallis home) (Stafford County) 194
Windsor Forest subdivision (Stafford County) 194
Wine, Catherine E. (born c.1841) 248
    H. 266
    Joseph C. (c.1832-1909) 87, 88, 163, 170
    Lucy Ann (West) (c.1832-1854) 248
    Susan Ellen (Guy) (1858-1922) 242, 265
Winkler, James Monroe (1878-1970) 207
    Susan Jane (Payne) (1860-1935) 91, 200
Winlock, Elizabeth (Marquis) 137, 268
    William 136

Winston, Angelina Frances (Woolfolk) 143, 245
    Lucy P. 20
    Lucy Payne (Sims) 20
    William A. 20
Wisconsin 193
Wiser, John 116
Wishart, Letitia (Browne) 75
    Wilhelmina (Taliaferro) (born 1772) 19
Withers, Ann 39
    Ann (Mountjoy) (born 1748) 56
    Charles (c.1761-1818) 138
    Eliza Elzira (Gatewood) (born c.1803) 145
    Eliza J. 78
    Elizabeth (Cave) 56
    Elizabeth (Keene) (died 1769) 134
    Frances (Townsend) (Dade) 39, 47, 48
    Hannah (Allen) (died 1801) 139
    Hannah (Stone) (c.1774-1857) 136, 147, 152
    James 60
    James (1680-1746) 126, 134, 135
    James (1736-c.1818) 138
    James (died 1791) 134, 136
    Capt. John (1634-1699) 4, 5, 39, 40-42, 116, 118, 119, 251
    John (1713-1794) 139
    John J. (1819-1861) 78-81, 166
    Joseph (1757-after 1798) 134
    Joseph D. (born 1803) 145, 146, 258, 259, 275
    Keene (1728-1756) 56
    Mary (Hathaway) (Fossaker) 5, 42, 125
    Rosa E. (Harding) 266
    Sallie Margaret (English) (1851-1913) 194, 266
    Sarah (Conway) 128
    Susan (died before 1810) 138
    Susan (Waller) 155
    Thomas (1724-1784) 134
    Thomas A. (c.1814-c.1865) 157, 160, 162, 165, 167, 172, 260, 261
    Ursula (Waller) (1752-1818) 131, 233
    William (probably died 1684) 39
    William (c.1636-1698) 39, 116
Withers' Mill (Stafford County) 136
Wolf Trap Branch (Fairfax County) 45
Wolfgang's Store (Stafford County) 239
Wolfmarsh (Clarke County, Virginia) 169
Wood, James 47
    Jeffrey 117
Wood(w)ard, Andrew Jackson (1878-1959) 93
    Bennet 268
    Eliza (Scessall) 268
    William 193
Woodbourne (Stafford County) 14, 166, 169
Woodbridge, Benjamin, Jr. 17
Woodbridge, Virginia 17
Woodcutting (Stafford County) 87, 258
Woodcutting Post Office (Stafford County) 248

Woodcutting Road (Stafford County) 114, 172, 173, 176, 177
Wooderd (Stafford County) 168
Woodford, William 60
Woodford (Stafford County) 10, 12, 222
Woodmont Nursing Home (Stafford County) 284
Woodrow, Henry 58, 138
    Molly (Fitzhugh) (Brent) 138
Woodstock (Stafford County) 4, 9, 57, 61, 74, 83, 138
Woodstock, town of (Stafford County) 258-261
Woodview (Stafford County) 198
Woody, James Edward (c.1856-1928) 264
Wool Act (1699) 219
Woolfolk, Angelina Frances (Winston) 143, 245
    Charles (c.1763-1803) 143, 245
    Frances (1760-1825) 143, 245
    Pichergru (c.1795-1862) 143, 144, 245
Worchestershire, England 3
World War I 17, 94, 202, 204, 205, 238, 247
Worrel, John T. 171, 177
Wright, Abigail (Holloway) 254
    Andrew G. 207, 208
    John (1735-1791) 52, 53
    Rosamond (Grant) (1733-1799) 52, 53
    William (c.1700-1789) 52, 53
Wroe, Andrew D. (c.1818-after 1860) 232
Wye, Samuel 117
Wyoming (Stafford County) 74, 149, 154
Yates, Catherine (Thornton) (Wellford) (1760-1831) 79
    Charles (1728-1809) 59
    Rev. Robert 79
Yatton, England 196
Yeardley, Gov. George 25
Yellow Chapel (Stafford County) 151, 175
Yellow Chapel Temperance Society 272
Yeocomico Church (Westmoreland County) 120
York County, Pennsylvania 231
York County, Virginia 38, 39, 125
Yorkshire, England 5, 118
Yorktown, Battle of (1781) 9, 138
Yorktown, Virginia 9, 39, 138
Young, ___ 92
    B. C. 33
    Betty Lewis (Brooke) 168
    Edgar M. 32, 33
    Edgar M., Jr. 33
    Elizabeth (Brooke) 71
    Glendie Brooke (1890-1952) 224, 238
    John James 33
    Laura (Gaylor) 238
    Mary (Cobb) 33
    Mary Constance (Calwell) 33
    Mattie 33
    Nancy (Harding) 255

      Original (born c.1740) 129
      Samuel R. (1868-1944) 238
      Vincent 115, 116, 118
      William 268-271
Zeller, Chester A. (1889-1945) 266
Zion Baptist Church (Canada) 13
Zion Tabernacle Church (Stafford County) 85